Do not mark or damage this item
Charges may apply    Y0-BKH-228

✓ EH 9/18/13

**THE OPERAS OF
LEONARDO VINCI,
*NAPOLETANO***

*Portrait of LEONARDO VINCI in the Biblioteca del Conservatoro di Musica S. Pietro a Majella in Naples*

# THE OPERAS OF
# LEONARDO VINCI, *NAPOLETANO*

*Kurt Markstrom*

University of Manitoba

OPERA SERIES No. 2

PENDRAGON PRESS
HILLSDALE, N.Y.

**Other Titles in OPERA series:**

No.1    Daniel Heartz *From Garrick to Gluck: Essays on Opera in the Age of Enlightenment,* edited by John A. Rice

Library of Congress Cataloging-in-Publication Data

Markstrom, Kurt, 1954-
The operas of Leonardo Vinci, Napoletano / Kurt Markstrom.
   p. cm. -- (Opera series; no. 2)
Originally presented as the author's dissertation (doctoral)
University of Toronto, 1993.
Includes bibliographical references (p.350) and index
ISBN 978-1-57647-094-7 (alk. paper)
1. Vinci, Leonardo, d. 1730. Operas. 2. Opera--Italy--18th century. I. Title.
   ML410.V7778M37 2006b
   782.1092--dc22
Copyright 2007 Pendragon Press

*"DIO! LA VITA! E NELLA VITTA!"*
Ivo La Croce, poeta Strongolana

*to Emma Birgitta and Victoria Lovisa Markstrom*

# TABLE OF CONTENTS

| | |
|---|---:|
| LIST OF PLATES | *viii* |
| PREFACE | *xi* |
| INTRODUCTION | *xvi* |
| LIBRARY SIGLA | *xviii* |

### 1. THE EARLY YEARS

| | |
|---|---:|
| Establishing a Date and Place of Birth | 1 |
| Strongoli and its Princes | 3 |
| Vinci and the Conservatorio dei Poveri di Gesù Cristo | 6 |
| A Student at the Conservatory | 9 |
| Leaving the Conservatory and the Sansevero Appointment | 13 |
| The Cantatas | 16 |

### 2. VINCI AND THE *COMMEDIA PER MUSICA*

| | |
|---|---:|
| Initial Success | 19 |
| The Neapolitan *Commedia per Musica* | 24 |
| The First Surviving *Commedia per Musica* | 27 |
| *Li zite 'ngalera* and its Opera Buffa Anticipations | 31 |
| The *Commedia per Musica* Abandoned | 38 |

### 3. TRANSFER TO THE HEROIC THEATRE

| | |
|---|---:|
| The Rosary Oratorio | 45 |
| First Essay in the *Dramma per Musica* | 46 |
| The Last Palace Première | 49 |
| *Silla Dittatore*: Act I and Alternate Arias | 52 |
| The Intermezzo *Albino e Plautilla* | 57 |
| Vinci and the Roman Carnival | 61 |
| Lucchini's *Farnace* | 67 |
| *Farnace*: Variety with a Vengeance | 70 |
| Extended Stay in Rome | 77 |

### 4. STAMPIGLIA'S HEROIC COMEDIES

| | |
|---|---:|
| Papal Celebrations and the Final *Commedia* | 82 |
| Collaboration with Old Stampiglia | 84 |

|   |   |
|---|---|
| *Eraclea* and the Spirit of Terpsichore | 88 |
| First Venetian Commissions | 97 |
| *La Rosmira fedele* and Faustina | 103 |
| *Partenope* and Vinci's Debt to Sarro | 107 |
| *Elpidia* and the English Connection | 114 |
| Parma and the Return to Naples | 116 |
| The Court Appointment | 119 |

## 5. THE FIRST COLLABORATIONS WITH METASTASIO

|   |   |
|---|---|
| Salvi's *Astianatte* and Racine's *Andromaque* | 123 |
| *Astianatte*: the Opening Scenes | 128 |
| Vinci and Metastasio's Roman Triumph | 135 |
| *Didone abbandonata*: Dominance of the Title Role | 145 |
| Handel Caught "Stealing" | 154 |
| Mad Dash to Venice | 155 |
| *Siroe re di Persia* and the Accolades of Quantz | 162 |
| *Miserere* and Farewell to Venice | 169 |

## 6. GOTHICK HISTORIES, POLITICAL ALLEGORIES AND ASSORTED SCANDALS

|   |   |
|---|---|
| *Ernelinda* and *La fede tradita* | 172 |
| Ernelinda's Maddening Dilemma | 178 |
| The Molière Intermezzo | 184 |
| A "Polish" Opera for a Runaway Polish Princess | 188 |
| *Gismondo re di Polonia*: the Lead Roles | 193 |

## 7. STAMPIGLIA, METASTASIO AND THE ROMAN REPUBLIC

|   |   |
|---|---|
| A Scantily Revised *La caduta de' Decemviri* | 201 |
| *La caduta de' Decemviri*: a Study in Contrasts | 205 |
| *Flacco/Servilia*: Comic Scenes and Intermezzo | 211 |
| An Opera for Giovanni Battista Pinacci | 213 |
| And He Chose a Subject "to Please the Romans" | 216 |
| *Catone in Utica*: the Tragic Hero and his Daughter | 220 |
| *Catone* Revisions and Revivals | 230 |

## 8. THE WEDDING AT PARMA

|   |   |
|---|---|
| *Fratello* Leonardo | 232 |
| Congregazione del Rosario | 233 |
| Frugoni's Wedding Opera | 236 |
| *Medo*: Baggage Arias, Entrance Arias, and Ringhini's Sets | 245 |

| | |
|---|---|
| The Gala Equestrian Ballet | 254 |
| An Opera for the New Viceroy | 256 |
| Metastasio's Roman/Venetian Premières | 259 |
| *Semiramide riconosciuta*: Act II Confrontation and Aftermath | 265 |
| New Impresarios at the delle dame | 273 |
| A Second *Farnace* | 274 |

**9. THE TRIPLE COLLABORATION WITH METASTASIO**

| | |
|---|---|
| The Dauphin's Birthday Cantata | 278 |
| Two Operas for the Price of One | 287 |
| Alessandro and the Quarrelling Lovers | 293 |
| Berenstadt's Snuff Caper | 302 |
| *Artaserse*: Grétry's Critique Expanded | 310 |
| The *Artaserse* Revivals | 320 |

**10. DEATH AND POSTHUMOUS FAME**

| | |
|---|---|
| Vinci, Hasse and Metastasio | 327 |
| Sorting Through the Death Records | 328 |
| Vinci "Il Giocatore" | 333 |
| A Love Vendetta? | 336 |
| Vinci's "*Grosso Frego*" and the Siren's Sword-Wielding *"Protettore"* | 338 |
| Poison | 342 |
| Vinci in Memoria | 344 |

| | |
|---|---|
| BIBLIOGRAPHY | 349 |
| INDEX | 375 |
| INDEX OF VINCI'S WORKS | 391 |

# LIST OF PLATES

**Cover and Frontispiece.** Portrait of Leonardo Vinci     *ii*

**Plate 1.** View of the town of Strongoli built on the ruins of the ancient town of Petelia in Brutium: designed by Després and engraved by Ghendt, 1781.     4

**Plate 2.** View of the Piazza and Palazzo Real of the Kingdom of Naples: designed by Renard Architecte and engraved by Pellier, 1781.     48

**Plate 3.** Floor Plan of the Teatro Alibert from Dumont's *Parallèle de Plans des Plus Belles Salles de Spectacles D' Italie et de France,* c. 1774.     63

**Plate 4.** Caricature of Carlo Broschi "Farinello" as Berenice in Vinci's *Farnace*, by Pier Leone Ghezzi, Rome 1724.     65

**Plate 5.** Caricature of Domenico Gizzi, probably as Araspe in Albinoni's *Didone*, Venice, 1725, attributed to Marco Ricci.     67

**Plate 6.** Caricature of Leonardo Vinci by Pier Leone Ghezzi, Rome, March 1724.     81

**Plate 7.** Caricature of Faustina Bordoni in her Roman debut, by Pier Leone Ghezzi, March 1722.     100

**Plate 8 & 9**. Caricatures of Antonio Barbieri and Giovanni Giovanni Ossi in their roles as Flaviano and Antioco from Orlandini's *Berenice*, Venice, 1725, attributed to Marco Ricci.     105

**Plates 10 & 11.** Caricatures of Carlo Scalzi and Carlo Bernardi, in their roles as Oreste and Pilade in Vinci's *Ifigenia in Tauride,* Venice, 1725, attributed to Marco Ricci.     105

LIST OF PLATES            xi

**Plate 12**. Caricature of Vittoria Tesi, attributed to Marco Ricci. 126

**Plate 13**. Caricature of Giacinto Fontana "Farfallino" by Pier Leone Ghezzi, Rome, July 1728. 138

**Plate 14**. Caricatures of Leonardo Leo and the tenors Giovanni Antonio Reina and Gaetano Valetta by Pier Leone Ghezzi, Rome, July 1726. 142

**Plate 15**. Caricature of Marianna Benti Bulgarelli "La Romanina" by Pier Leone Ghezzi, Rome, July 1728. 146

**Plate 16**. Caricature of Nicola Grimaldi in an oriental role, probably in the title role of Vinci's *Siroe*, Venice, 1726, attributed to Marco Ricci. 157

**Plates 17 & 18**. Caricatures of Giovanni Paita and Giovanni Carestini in oriental roles, probably as Cosroe and Medarse in Vinci's *Siroe*, Venice, 1726, attributed to Marco Ricci. 158

**Plate 19**. Engraving of Nicola Porpora by C.Bondi, 1819. 172

**Plates 20 & 21**. Caricatures of Giovanni Battista Pinacci and Giovanni Battista Minelli, the latter in the role of a Roman General,, attributed to Marco Ricci. 215

**Plate 22**. Pietro Righini, Stage Design for *Medo*, Act I/i. 238

**Plate 23**. Pietro Righini, Stage Design for *Medo*, Act I/ix. 238

**Plate 24**. Pietro Righini, Stage Design for *Medo*, Act II/i. 239

**Plate 25**. Pietro Righini, Stage Design for *Medo*, Act II/ix. 239

**Plate 26**. Pietro Righini, Stage Design for *Medo*, Act III/i. 240

**Plate 27**. Pietro Righini, Stage Design for *Medo*, Act III/v: 240

**Plate 28**. Pietro Righini, Stage Design for *Medo*, Act III/xi. 241

**Plate 29**. Pietro Righini, Stage Design for *Medo*, Act III/ scena ultima. 241

**Plate 30**. Salvatore Colonnelli: Courtyard of the Palazzo Altemps, residence of the most Emminent and Reverend Cardinal Melchoir di Polignac, Minister to the Most Christian King in Rome, Magnificently ornamented to the design of Cavalier Pietro Leone Ghezzi. 284

**Plate 31**.  Caricature of Leonardo Vinci by Pier Leone Ghezzi, Rome, c.1730. 286

**Plate 32**. Portrait of Don Francesco Vici *maestro di cappella* in Fano by Carlo Magini, dated 1776. 332

**Plate 33**. View of the city of Naples, taken from the suburb of the Chiaia by Berteaux after a painting by Vernet, engraved by Nicollet. 333

**Plate 34**. The Impresario Giuseppe Polvini Faliconti playing cards with the publisher Filippo de' Rosi, by Pier Leone Ghezzi, Rome, 1730. 336

**Plate 35**.  Engraving of Leonardo Vinci by C. Biondi, 1819. 341

**Plate 37**. Filippo Juvarra. "Monumento a L. Vinci" in *Memorie sepolcrale,* Turin: 1735. 347

# PREFACE

This book is based on my doctoral dissertation on the operas of Leonardo Vinci (University of Toronto, 1993). After undertaking a post-doctoral study of the operas of Vinci's rival Nicola Porpora in 1995-97 and becoming involved in Don Neville's Metastasio project, I revised the text of the dissertation, incorporating new information from my Porpora and Metastasio studies as well as recent research from a new generation of Italian scholars. I submitted the manuscript for publication in 1999. In the time between the submission and its publication, what I predicted in my original covering letter has actually come to pass: in the same way that Vivaldi came to notice on the coattails of Bach's intense popularity during the mid-20th century, Vinci has ridden Vivaldi's coattails at the end of that same century. In the process Vinci has been transformed from an arcane academic subject that required explanations about who he was (i.e. not the painter) and why I was studying his music, to a fashionable and marketable composer in the *settecento* music revival business. Part of this new recognition is due to Christophe Galland's very successful production of *Li zite 'n galera* in Bari in 1999 with Antonio Florio and the Cappella della Pietà dei Turchini and the subsequent award-winning recording on Opus 111. As a result of this newly-awakened interest, Gaetano Pitaresi organized a conference at the Conservatorio di musica in Reggio Calabria in 2002 to which I was invited. After the conference, I made a *pellegrinaggio* to Vinci's hometown of Strongoli, where I met Luigi La Croce, the Figaro of Strongoli who, in turn introduced me to Gianfranco Russo and Sergio Iritale of the Festival dell'Aurora in the provincial capital of Crotone. I made a proposal to President Iritale to bring together plans for inaugurating a new collected edition of Vinci's works with performances of these works at the Festival dell'Aurora and the founding of a Centro di Studi Leonardo Vinci. The scores from these productions would, in turn, provide the raw material for the beginnings of the complete edition. The "Progetto Leonardo Vinci" was inaugurated in his hometown of Strongoli hosted by President Iritale, followed by a performance of the intermezzo *Erighetta e Don Chilone* at the Festival dell'Aurora in Crotone. This prodigious collaboration continued in 2004 and 2006 with the modern premières of *La Rosmira* and *Eraclea*, the former in an edition by Dinko Fabris and the latter in an edition I prepared. All three performances were outstanding, featuring some of the best young musicians in Italy today. To one who began this study with a couple of Garland facsimiles and an assortment of contradictory dictionary entries, this development has been rather bewildering, but absolutely wonderful. I am thankful to have played a role in some of these events and especially hankful to Sergio Iritale and Gianfranco Russo for mnaking them possible.

As in all long-term academic undertakings, there are many people to thank, first and foremost being my thesis supervisor Carl Morey and co-supervisor Mary-Ann Parker of the University of Toronto. They were instrumental in obtaining, for me, research fellowships frpm the Social Sciences and Humanities Research Council of Canada (SSHRC) in 1987/88 and 1988/89 and an Ontario Graduate Scholarship in 1989/90, which allowed me to do the original research in Italy, Germany and England, as well as the SSHRC Postdoctoral fellowship in 1995-97 for my Porpora studies. Carl Morey was also crucial in helping me secure my current position at the University of Manitoba where I have been able to complete the transformation of the thesis into a book. In this process, I would especially like to acknowledge the encouragement of the current director at the School of Music at the University of Manitoba, Dale Lonis, who gave me generous support for my return to Italy during the spring/summer of 2002 and 2003,which not only produced an abundance of new material for the book, but allowed me the opportunity to make these important new connections.

I am grateful to the many librarians whom I have pestered off and on over the years of my Vinci study: in particular Francesco Melisi of the Biblioteca at the Conservatorio di Musica S. Pietro a Maiella in Naples and Dom Gregorio di Francesca at the Biblioteca dell' Abbazia in Montecassino. I would also like to thank Hugh Cobbe of the Department of Manuscripts at the British Library, Reference Division, Gottfried Minkenberg of the Bischöfliches Preisterseminar in Münster, Paul Raspé of the Bibliothèque of the Conservatoire Royal de Musique in Brussels, Pam Thompson of the Library of the Royal College of Music in London, Katherine Hogg of the Library of the Royal Academy of Music in London, and Helmut Hell of the Stadtsbibliothek in Berlin.Special thanks go to my Neapolitan colleagues Francesco Cotticelli and Paologiovanni Maione for showing me how to get at the court records in the Archivio di Stato di Napoli and for introducing me to the Archivio Storico of the Banco di Napoli. I must also thank Nelia Del Mercato of the Banco di Napoli for teaching me how to use the rather complex indices to the payment records of the Archivio Storico, and Don Antonio Illibato of the Curia Arcivescovile di Napoli for allowing me access to the records of the Conservatorio dei Poveri di Gesù Cristo; his assistance in finding the phantom death record of Vinci was invaluable. I should also thank the librarians at the University of Toronto: Kathleen McMorrow and

*PREFACE*

Suzanne Meyers Sawa at the Music Library, Richard Landon at the Thomas Fischer Library, and at the University of Manitoba Library, Vladimir Simosko. I must, of course, acknowledge Rheinhard Strohm for bibliographic groundwork on which everyone in this field is dependent, as is evident in the abundance of "Strohmnotes" throughout the text.

Unless otherwise stated, I have made all the translations from Italian, Neapolitan, French, German, and Spanish sources myself. As a principal, when referring to characters in mythology or history, I have used the standard English name (i.e. Julius Caesar and Jason), whereas in specific reference to the characters in Vinci operas, the Italian name is used (i.e. Giulio Cesare and Giasone).

Finally I would like to thank Nicola Schaefer for helping me proofread the first three agonizing rounds of page proof, Rachel Hinton for supplying most of the dates in the index, and my editor, Claire Brook, for putting up with and accommodating my continual changes with each round of proofs. The book is surely the better for it.

Kurt Markstrom
Winnipeg, August 27, 2005

# INTRODUCTION

The emergence of the "new style" or "*galant*," or "pre-classical," or "rococo," or my preferred term, "early classical style,' is one of the most important musical developments of the first half of the eighteenth century, the period that is known within the conventional periodization of music history as the late Baroque—the age of Bach and Handel. Although these masters are regarded as the epitome of the late Baroque style, it was the emergence of this "new style" that was such a disruptive factor in their lives, and, in retrospect, has come to be regarded as responsible for the end of the period they are considered to exemplify. I first encountered this phenomenon when writing my Master's thesis on the operas of Handel and was perplexed by the develpment that transformed my hero from a fashionable composer on the leading edge of the latest developments to an old-fashioned "learned" master within some half-dozen years, contributing to a series of operatic failures that would eventually compel him to abandon opera and forge a new career in oratorio. Of the culprits in this development, Pergolesi was well-known, and Hasse, somewhat less. There was, however, a composer who had supposedly developed this style even before Pergolesi and Hasse, a composer who had to be distinguished from his famous fifteenth-century Florentine namesake.

The mysterious figure of Leonardo Vinci, Napoletano, who has been represented to posterity by two jovial caricatures, produced a string of successful operas during a brief career of little more than a decade, died amid rumors of poison, and was hailed by connoisseurs of the later eighteenth century as one of the originators of the modern (i.e.Classical) style. According to Charles Burney:

> Vinci seems to have been the first opera composer who... without degrading his art, rendered it the friend, though not the slave, to poetry by simplifying and polishing melody and calling the attention of the audience chiefly to the voice-part, by disentangling it from fugue, complication, and laboured contrivance.
>
> Charles Burney, *A General History of Music*, 1789)

Burney's emphatic statement was the decisive factor in my choice of the music of Vinci as the subject of my doctoral dissertation. I set out to determine which elements create the simple polished melodies and uncomplicated accompaniments that so impressed Burney and to pinpoint the time when those elements began to emerge in Vinci's works. My research on Vinci began as a statistical analysis of the text setting, periodic structure, harmonic rhythm, and texture/orchestration in the 450 *da capo* arias in his fifteen surviving *opere seria*. The results of my research indicate that there is a close connection between the careful setting of an aria text and the standardization of periodic structure (Burney's polished melody that is the friend of poetry) and the slow rate of harmonic change and the simple transparent textures (Burney's uncomplicated accompaniments that call attention chiefly to the voice part). Thus the Classical style, with its emphasis on simple periodic melodies, slow-moving diatonic harmonies, syncopated rhythms, and transparent textures, originated in Italy during the 1720s with Vinci's operas at the very forefront of this monumental stylistic change. This change, already hinted at in his early comic operas, emerges in the mid-1720s with his settings of two heroic comedies by Silvio Stampiglia, coming to full bloom during the years 1726-30 in his collaboration with the ultimate poet of the *dramma per musica*, Pietro Metastasio, with whom he produced his greatest works: *Didone abbandonata, Siroe re di Persia, Catone in Utica, Semiramide riconosciuta, Alessandro nell'Indie*, and *Artaserse*.

In the midst of my statistics-gathering, I came to see a need for a comprehensive survey of all of Vinci's surviving operas that would allow each work to be appreciated as a musical/dramatic entity rather than a source to be mined for data on stylistic development. The dissertation, therefore, was expanded into a two-volume work, the first a chronological survey of Vinci's operas, and the second a stylistic study of the recitatives and the *da capo* arias with a single list of sources created for both volumes. The survey of the operas eventually became the dissertation, with a summary of two sections from the stylistic study to serve as the conclusion. The latter was published as the article "Burney's Assessment of Leonardo Vinci" in *Acta Musicologica* (Vol. 68/2, 1995: 142-63). Although the original statistical study of the music was eventually completed, it is still sitting on the shelf in manuscript waiting its turn. Its absence accounts for two peculiarities in the present work: first a rather abrupt ending and second, the continued references to the stylistic change that takes place in Vinci's music. It is the detailed investigation into the elements of this stylistic change as seen in the context of the all-important *da capo* arias that provides the proper conclusion to this volume and will, one hopes, find its way to publication in the future.

# LIBRARY SIGLA

| | |
|---|---|
| A-WGM | Wien, Gesellschaft der Musikfreunde |
| A-Wn | Wien, Osterreichische Nationalbibliothek Musiksammlung |
| B-Bc | Bruxelles, Conservatoire Royale de Musique, Bibliothèque |
| B-Br | Bruxelles, Bibliothèque Royale Albert 1$^{re}$ |
| C-Tu (Th.Fischer) | Toronto, University oofg Toronto, Thomas Fischer Library |
| CS-PU | Praha, Universitni knihovna |
| D-B | Berlin, Staatsbibliothek, Preussischer Kulturbesitz, Musikabteilung |
| D-Bds | Berlin, Deutsche Staatsbibliothek |
| D-Bfb | Burgsteinfurt, Fürstlich Bentheimische Bibliothek |
| D-Dl | Dillingen an der Donau, Kreis- und Studienbibliothek |
| D-Dlb | Dresden, Sächsische Landesbibliothek |
| D-DO | Donaueschingen, Fürstlich Fürstenbergische Hofbibliothek |
| D-FRu | Freiburg, Albert-Ludwigs-Universität, Universitätsbibliothek |
| D-Hs | Hamburg, Staats- und Universitätsbibliothek, Musikabteilung |
| D-HAmi | Halle, Universitäts und Landesbibliothek Sachsen-Anhalt |
| D-HVl | Hanover, Niedersächsische Landesbiblohek |
| D-Kl | Kassel, Murhard'sche Bibliothek und Landesbibliothek |
| D-KA | Karlsruhe, Badische Landesbibliothek, Musikabteilung |
| D-LEm | Leipzig, Musikbibliothek der Stadt Leipzig |
| D-Mbs | München, Bayerische Staatsbibliothek, Musikabteilung |
| D-MElr | Meiningen, Staatliche Museen mit Reger-Archiv |
| D-MUs | Münster, Bibliothek der Bischöflichen Priesterseminars: Santini-Sammlung |
| D-ROu | Rostock, Universitätsbibliothek |
| D-SHs | Sondershausen, Stadt- und Kreisbibliothek |
| D-Sl | Stuttgart, Würtenbergische Landesbibliothek |
| D-SWl | Schwerin, Mecklenburgische Landesbibliothek |
| D-W | Wolfenbüttel, Herzog-August-Bibliothek, Musikabteilung |
| F-Pc | Paris, Bibliothèque du Conservatoire national de musique |
| F-Pn | Paris, Biblothèque natonal |
| GB-Cfm | Cambridge, Fitzwilliam Museum |
| GB-Ckc | Cambridge, Rowe Music Library, King's College |
| GB-CDp | Cardiff, Public Libraries, Central Library |
| GB-Lam | London, Royal Academy of Music |
| GB-Lbm | London, British Library |

# LIBRARY SIGLA

| | |
|---|---|
| GB-Lcm | London, Royal College of Music |
| GB-Lgc | London, Gresham College (Guildhall Library) |
| GB-Lk | London, King's Music Library (British Library) |
| GB-Ob | Oxford, Bodleian Library |
| GB-T | Tenbury, St. Michael's College Library |
| I-Ac | Assisi, Biblioteca comunale |
| I-Bc | Bologna, Civico Museo Bibliografico-Musicale (Conservatorio Statale di Musica G. B. Martini Biblioteca) |
| I-Bu | Bologna, Biblioteca Universitaria |
| I-Fc | Firenze, Biblioteca del Conservatorio di Musica L. Cherubini |
| I-Fm | Firenze, Biblioteca Marucelliana |
| I-Fn | Firenze, Biblioteca Nazionale Centrale, Dipartimento Musica |
| I-FAN | Fano, Biblioteca Comunale Federiciana |
| I-FE Walker | Ferrara, the Walker Private Collection |
| I-Gi | Genova, Biblioteca dell'Istituto Musicale (Conservatorio di Musica N. Paganini) |
| I-G, Ivaldi | Genova, the Ivaldi Private Collection |
| I-Ma | Milano, Biblioteca Ambrosiana |
| I-Mb | Milano, Biblioteca Nazionale Braidense |
| I-Mc | Milano, Biblioteca del Conservatorio di Musica G. Verdi |
| I-MAC | Macerata, Biblioteca Comunale Mozzi-Borgetti |
| I-MC | Montecassino, Biblioteca del' Abbazio |
| I-MOe | Modena, Biblioteca Estense |
| I-Nc | Napoli, Biblioteca del Conservatorio di Musica S. Pietro a Majella |
| I-Nf | Napoli, Biblioteca Oratoriana dei Filippini |
| I-Nlp | Napoli, Biblioteca Lucchese-Palli (Biblioteca nazionale) |
| I-Nn | Napoli, Biblioteca nazionale |
| I-P, Museo Civico | Padova, Biblioteca del Museo Civico |
| I-Pi | Padova, Biblioteca dell' Istituto Musicale (Conservatorio di Musica Cesare Pollini) |
| I-PAc | Parma, Biblioteca del Conservatorio, Sezione Musicale della Biblioteca Palatina |
| I-PEc | Perugia, Biblioteca Comunale Augusta |
| I-PL, Pagana | Palermo, Roberto Pagano, private collection |
| I-Rc | Roma, Biblioteca Casanatense |
| I-R, Istit. Germanico | Roma, Biblioteca dell'Istituto Storico Germanico (Sezione Storia della Musica) |
| I-Rn | Roma, Biblioteca Nazionale Centrale Vittorio Emanuele II |
| I-Rsc | Roma, Biblioteca del Conservatorio di Musica Santa Cecilia |
| I-Rvat | Roma, Biblioteca Apostolica Vaticana |
| I-REm | Reggio nell'Emilia, Biblioteca Municipale Panizzi |
| I-Tn | Torino, Biblioteca nazionale universitaria |
| I-Vc | Venezia, Biblioteca del Conservatorio di Musica B. Marcello |
| I-Vcg | Venezia, Casa di Goldoni, Biblioteca |

| | |
|---|---|
| I-Vgc | Venezia, Fondazione Georgio Cini, Istitute de lettere, musica e teatro |
| I-Vnm | Venezia, Biblioteca nazionale Marciana |
| P-C | Combra, Portugal, Biblioteca General da Universidade |
| Pl-Kc | Krakow, Biblotka Czartoryskich |
| SL-LS | Ljubljana, Franciskanski Samostan, Knijiznica, Glavni Knijizni Fond |
| US-AAu | Ann Arbor, University of Michigan, Music Library |
| US-AUS | Austin, University of Texas at Austin, Music Library |
| US-BE | Berkeley, University of California, Music Library |
| US-LAu | Los Angeles, University of California, Music Library |
| US-U | Urbana, University of Illinois, Music Library |
| US-Wc | Washington, Library of Congress, Music Division |

# 1

# THE EARLY YEARS

## Establishing a Date and Place of Birth

Since the eighteenth century Leonardo Vinci's birth and death dates have been open to speculation. For example, at the end of the discussion of Vinci in *A General History of Music* Charles Burney speculates:

> I have been able to find no more of his works after this period [the 1730s]; so that he must either have begun late, or been cut off early in life, as his great and durable renown seems to have been acquired in the short space of six years of his existence.[1]

There are two different versions of Vinci's beginnings. The first, that he was born in Naples in 1705, can be traced back to the first edition of Gerber's dictionary of composers from 1790-92.[2] Although this information was not repeated in the revised edition from 1812-14, where it was simply omitted, it was repeated by several later writers, including the entries in the dictionaries of Choron and Fayolle from 1811 and Bertini from 1814.[3] The entry on Vinci in the *Biografia degli uomini illustri del Regno di Napoli* from 1819 places the date of birth back fifteen years to 1690 and this is repeated in the *Dictionary of Musicians* from 1825.[4] Cnfirming the 1690 date, the entry in the Marchese di Villarosa's *Memorie*

---

[1] Charles Burney, *A General History of Music: from the Earliest Ages to the Present Period (1789)*, with critical and historical notes by Frank Mercer (New York, Dover, 1957; first published London: 1776-89), II, 917.

[2] Ernst Ludwig Gerber, *Historisch-Biographisches Lexikon der Tonkünstler (1790-1792)*, ed. Othmar Wessely (Leipzig: Breitkopf, 1790; repr. ed. Graz: Akademische Druck-u.Verlagsanstalt, 1977).

[3] Alexandre Étienne Choron and François Joseph Fayolle, *Dictionnaire historique des musiciens: artistes et amateurs, morts ou vivans* (Paris: Valade, 1811) & Giuseppe Bertini, *Dizionario storico-critica degli scrittori di musica* (Palermo: Tipographia Reale di guerra, 1814-15).

[4] G. B. G. Grossi, "Leonardo Vinci: Celebre Maestro di Cappella, Nacque in Napoli nel 1690, Ove mori nel 1732" in *Biografia degli uomini illustri del Regno di Napoli: Ornata de loro rispettivi ritratti*, ed. Martuscelli, Vol. VI (Naples: Niccola Gervasi Gigante, 1819) & *Dictionary of Musicians, from the Earliest Ages to the Present Time* (London: Sainsbury, 1825).

*dei compositori di musica del regno di Napoli* from 1840 establishes a new birthplace for Vinci "born circa the year 1690 in Strongoli, a city in Calabria." This has been repeated by most subsequent entries on Vinci, including those in François- Joseph Fétis' *Universelle des musiciens* and Francesco Florimo's *La Scuola Musicali di Napoli,* both of whom omit Villarosa's "circa" delimiter.[6] Villarosa, in turn, based his entry directly, at times word for word, on the extended entry on Vinci in Tome III of the unpublished *Apoteosi dell'Arte Musicale*, Giuseppe Sigismondo's magnum opus, completed in 1820, though much of the research dating from the previous century. In the entry on Vinci, Sigismondo states that the composer was "born circa 1690, in Calabria, vassal of Prince Strongoli."[7] There are no parish registers in Strongoli before the nineteenth century because of the fires that plagued the city, the last one being set by the French in 1806/07.[8] Thus, there is no record of birth or baptism for Leonardo Vinci.

Edward Dent was the first to question Villarosa's c.1690 birth date because it made Vinci's stage debut in 1719, at the supposed age of twenty-nine, rather late for an Italian opera composer of this period.[9] Although Dent's suggestion of a later birth date, c. 1695, was given support by Prota-Giurleo's "discovery" of a second death record and has been taken up by most subsequent writers on Vinci, including the present author in his entries on the composer in the *New Grove Dictionary of Opera* and the revised *New Grove Dictionary of Music and Musicians,* this record is highly suspect and must now be rejected (see Chapter 10). Therefore the Villarosa/ Sigismondo c.1690 date, which coordinates with the date inferred in the actual death record, should stand as the date of birth of Leonardo Vinci.

---

[5] Marchese di Villarosa, Memorie dei compositori di musica del regno di Napoli (Naples: Stamperia Reale, 1840), 223: "Nacque circa l'anno 1690 in Strongoli città della Calabria."

[6] François-Joseph Fétis, *Biographie Universelle des musiciens: et bibliographie générale de la musique*, 2nd ed. (Paris: Firmin-Didot, 1884), 356 and Francesco Florimo, *La Scuoula Musicale di Napoli e i suoi conservatori*, 4 vols. (Naples: 1880-82; repr. Bologna: Forni, 1969), III, 186.

[7] Giuseppe Sigismondo, *Apoteosi dell'Arte Musicale* (Naples: 1820; unpublished ms. in Berlin catalogued as "Materialien zu einer Geschichte der Musik der Neapolitaner Schule"), Vol. III, 102; "nacque circa il 1690, in Calabria vassali del Principe di Strongoli. . ."

[8] Salvatore Gallo, *Vecchio Campanile: La Chiesa di Strongoli nella storia della città dall'alto medio evo alla soppressione del Vescovato* (Cosenza: Fasano Editore, 19??), 191.

[9] Edward J. Dent, "Notes on Leonardo Vinci," *The Musical Antiquary* IV (1912/13), 193; this view was seconded by Alberto Cametti, "Leonardi Vinci e i suoi drammi in musica al Teatro della Dame (1724-30)" in *Musica d'oggi* VI/10 (1924), 297.

## Strongoli and its Princes

The town of Strongoli is fully described in Abbé de Saint Non's *Voyage Pittoresque ou description des Royaumes de Naples et de Sicile* because of its ancient origins as Petelia of Magna Grecia, fitting in with the numerous descriptions of towns set amid the picturesque ruins of Anti-quity. Strongoli during the eighteenth century, according to the Abbé, showed:

> vestiges of the riches and the magnificence of Ancient Petelia; all its surroundings are still strewn with fragments and pieces of fluted columns with Dorian capitals in the style of those at Paestum.[10]

The comparison to the great temples at Paestum would have been the highest compliment at that time. Saint Non then describes how earthquakes have carved out "hills, valleys and cliffs" making it "very difficult to actually judge the grandeur and the form of the ancient city:"

> The shocks have been so powerful that the debris of the antique walls which one finds remains rather complete, although perched on the rock, fifteen feet thick, absolutely inclined, and completely out of balance.[11]

His description of the picturesque ruins coordinates with the lovely print of the town by Déspres that is included along with many others in this sumptuous travelogue (see Plate 1 on p. 4). Although the city has expanded over the years, the outlines of the Déspres print can still be observed in Strongoli today: the *cappellina* on the far left with the Ionian Sea and the Crotonese coast in the distance, the old castle on the far right and at the center, the Cathedral of S. Maria del Capo and behind it the Capuchin monastery.[12] Saint Non then describes the wealth and prosperity of the princes:

> the principality of Strongoli, we learned, is worth fifty thousand livres in rents, and would be susceptible to greater worth if they exploited the mines of sulphur, lead, mercury, gold and silver which exist in the mountains; they are all there in Calabria and in abundance; it is perhaps the richest and most fertile land in the Universe in all types of productions.

---

[10] [Jean Claude Richard] Abbé de Saint Non, *Voyage Pittoresque ou description des Royaumes de Naples et de Sicile* (Paris, 1781), Vol. III, 101.

[11] Ibid., 102.

[12] With the Baroque architecture of the old town, with its narrow winding streets and spectacular vistas, a certain amount of careful restoration could make this city an attraction, complementing the picturesque neighboring town of San Severina. Moreover the surrounding region, with its tranquil olive groves and vineyards, makes Saint Non's claim that this "is the richest and most fertile land in the Universe" seem not unreasonable, the perfect foil for the rustic beauty of the Silla Massive to the west.

*Figure 1. View of the town of Strongoli built on the ruins of the ancient town of Petelia in Brutium: designed by Després and engraved by Ghendt, 1781.* [13]

> One is really astonished with all these advantages, to find in the midst of these treasures of nature, only villages in ruins, only poor inhabitants, without clothes, or those in misery, with weak or savage appearance. [14]

The Abbé is obviously exaggerating to make a political statement, contrasting a very wealthy prince in a land of abundance inhabited by poor wretches "without clothes" or "in misery." During the eighteenth century, the Kingdom of Naples was infamous for its unequal distribution of wealth and according to the good Abbé, Strongoli exemplified that shameful characteristic. This then was the world in which Leonardo Vinci spent his early years.[15] Fortunately for the young Vinci, he became attached, in some manner, to one of the wealthy Strongoli princes.

The prince in question was Girolamo Pignatelli, "Principe di Strongoli e Conte di Melissa, e Grandi delle Spagne della prima classe."[16]

---

[13] Saint Non, Op. cit., III, Plate 56, 101.

[14] Ibid., 103.

[15] Vinci's first local biographer, Pelaggi (*L. Vinci* from 1894) speculates on the music of Vinci's youth, perhaps taking his inspiration from the youth of Haydn, by describing "how many nights spent in ecstatic vigil to the sounds of a guitar or rustic bagpipe; how many times he wept for a sad Calabrese song or to the grave accents from a church" (quoted in Gallo, *Vecchio Campanile*, 191). Considering the strong folk elements in certain arias in Vinci's comic operas, most notably the opening aria of *Li Zite 'n galera*, it is possible that Vinci may have taken an interest in the folk music of Calabria in the same way that Haydn did some thiry years later in the folk music of Burgenland.

[16] Fondo Pignatelli, b. 1, Archivio di Stato, Naples.

The Pignatelli family at that time was one of the most powerful and influential families in the Regno, having come to prominence in the fourteenth century through their support for Charles of Anjou.[17] Among the more powerful members of this family were Antonio Pignatelli who, as Innocent XII (1691-1700), was the Pope during Vinci's youth, and Francesco Pignatelli, who would become archbishop in Naples in 1703 and patron of the Conservatorio dei Poveri di Gesù Cristo during Vinci's early years in Naples. When Prince Girolamo married Maria Caracciolo in 1695, it was with the personal blessing of his "zio" Pope Innocent XII.

Presumably Vinci showed musical promise early in his life, perhaps as a choirboy and/or organist at the Cathedral in Strongoli, and that his family or a local patron could afford to send him to school in Naples. Considering Sigismondo's feudal reference, one could assume that it was his liege lord Girolamo Pignatelli, Prince of Strongoli, who footed the bill. Unfortunately there are no references to Vinci in the Pignatelli Archives in the Archivio di Stato in Naples, which consist only of important documents relating directly to the family: marriage contracts, wills, feudal deeds, military citations, and letters from notable persons, such as Prince Eugene and Metastasio.[18]

Nothing is known of Vinci's parents. In a recent booklet on Vinci produced by the Comunale di Strongoli, the author, Francesco De Siena describes how Vinci's parents:

> must have undertaken a journey lasting several days and nights, in the retinue of the court of Prince Pignatelli who moved periodically to his noble residence in the Chiaia, a small fishing village in the immediate vicinity of the capital of the Kingdom of the Two Sicilies.[19]

There is no record of this journey or any other reference to the Vinci family, though the record of burial in S. Caterina a Formiello in Naples refers to "eredi" which suggests the presence of some family in Naples at the time of his death. Nor is there any support for De Siena's supposition that the Vinci family was part of the Pignatelli household, though this is certainly a possibility. The only element of De Siena's scenario that can be substantiated is that the Strongoli Pignatelli family moved to Naples about the time of Vinci's entrance into the Conservatory; in the

---

[17] Gallo, *Vecchio Companile*, 189.

[18] Fondo Pignatelli, b. 1 & B. 2, Archivio di Stato, Naples.

[19] Francesco de Siena, *Leonardo Vinci: vita ed opera del compositore calabrese detto "Lo Strongoli"* Opera Patroncinata dall'Amministrazione Comunale di Strongoli (Crotone: Futura, 1997), 14. The Chiaia was actually a fashionable and rather sprawling suburb of Naples at the time.

Pignatelli Archive there are three letters written by Cardinal de la Tremoille from 1706/1707 addressed to "I principi di Strongoli/Napoli."[20]

## Vinci and the Conservatorio dei Poveri di Gesù Cristo

Sigismondo's crucial phrase concerning Vinci's origins, connects him with the Conservatory where he studied during his youth: "vassal of Prince Strongoli, he studied music in Naples at the Conservatorio dei Poveri di Gesù Cristo under the school of Gaetano Greco."[21] Founded in 1591 by Marcello Fossataro, the Conservatorio dei Poveri di Gesù Cristo was one of the four great Neapolitan conservatories.[22] In contrast to the other three conservatories which were under the control of the Viceroy, the Poveri di Gesù Cristo was controlled by the Archibishop of Naples, who at this time was Francesco Pignatelli.[23] Located in the Spaccanapoli on the Via Tribunale in a little piazza across from the church of Gerolomini, the site of the Conservatory is today distinguished primarily by the facade of its former Chapel, S. Maria della Colonna, which is still clearly visible, though blocked off from the crowded street by an iron railing.[24] Although originating as humble orphanages, the Neapolitan conservatories came to specialize in musical instruction. These institutions were not regarded as purely music schools but music was regarded as a means of supporting the charitable work of the orphanages.[25] In order to cultivate this specialization and bring in additional income, the conservatories began to accept gifted children as paying boarders in addition to the orphans. It should be emphasized, however, that neither

---

[20] Fondo Pignatelli, b. 1, Archivio di Stato, Naples.

[21] Sigismondo, *Apoteosi dell'Arte Musicale*. One of the entrance requirements of *convittore* at the Conservatorio S. Maria di Loreto, was that he have a guarantor or *persona idonea* living in Naples or its environs. (Michael F. Robinson, "The Governor's Minutes of the Conservatory S. Maria di Loreto, Naples" *Royal Musical Association Research Chronicle*, no. 10 (1972), 54-55.

[22] On the Neapolitan conservatories, see Florimo, *La scuola musicale di Napoli*, Vol. II and Salvatore Di Giacomo, *I quattro antichi conservatorii di musica di Napoli* (Milan: Remo Sandron, 1928).

[23] The *Constitutiones et Ordinationes Consertvatoris Pauperum Derelictorum* of the Poveri di Gesù Cristo is transcribed in Giacomo, *I Quattro antichi conservatoriidi musica di Napoli*, II, 39-51.

[24] Both the chapel and the church of the Girolomini on the other side of this little piazza are at present abandoned and in a state of great disrepair, the sense of ruin aggravated by the large garbage dumpsters that are located in the middle of the square. However, part of the old Conservatory buildings is used by the "suore missonarie della carità di Madre Teressa di Calcutta." Carlo Raso, *Guido Musicale del Centro Antico di Napoli* (Naples: Colonnese Editore, 1999): 107-112.

[25] Robinson, "The Governor's Minutes of the Conservatory S. Maria di Loreto," 84-85; in a similar fashion the Neapolitan banks, originally, charitable institutions providing interest-free pawn loans for the poor, came to use their revenue-generating services

all the boarders nor all the orphans were musicians.[26] Because of the money that boarders or the *convittore* brought in to the Conservatory and their connection with a local guarantor, they received better treatment than the orphans. At the Conservatorio di S. Maria di Loreto, for example, each *convittore* (or *educando* as they were called at this institution), received a loaf of bread and a carafe of wine every day and could come and go from the Conservatory at their leisure.[27]

Prota-Giurleo, in his landmark article on Vinci, states that the composer entered the Conservatorio dei Poveri di Gesù Cristo as one of these boarders or *convittori* on November 14, 1708, paying an annual fee of thirty-six ducats.[28] Rosa Cafiero, however, in her research of the Conservatory records at the Archivio Storico Diocesano in Naples could not find this important record.[29] After searching through the records for the years 1706 through 1716, the author found the following at the end of the 1706 volume: "I have received from Leonardo Vencia on January 12, 1707 an entrance fee of six ducats."[30]

"Vencia" was one of a large group of students who entered the Conservatory at the beginning of 1707, swelling the list of *convittori* to forty-seven,. He was assigned an annual fee of twenty ducats: "Leonardo Vencia to pay twenty ducats for the year beginning from the twelfth of January, 1707."[31] The annual fee varied considerably from student to student, according to their usefulness in the musical performances and perhaps also to their financial circumstances.[32] Also true of the mature

---

(such as interest-bearing loans) as a means of supporting their charitable work, hence the sacred names of both the conservatories and banks of Naples. Even as the money-making specializations came to dominate these institutions, the ideals of their charitable origins remained intact, creating continued tensions throughout the eighteenth century. *The Historical Archive of Banco di Napoli* (Naples: Banco di Napoli, 1988), 51-61.

[26] Helmut Hucke, "Verfassung und Entwicklung der alten napolitischen Konservatorien," *Festschrift Helmuth Osthoff sum 65. Geburtstage* (Tutzing: Hans Schneider, 1961), 51-61.

[27] Robinson, "The Governor's Minutes of the Conservatory S. Maria di Loreto," 52-53.

[28] Ulisse Prota-Giurleo, "Leonardo Vinci," *Convegno musicale* II (1965): 3. This major source on Vinci is flawed because of its complete lack of documentation, making it difficult to distinguish Prota-Giurleo's original research from paraphrases from other sources and from free invention.

[29] Rosa Cafiero, "Il 'venerabile conservatorio di S. Maria della Colonna, detto de' Poveri di Gesù Cristo' negli anni di Leonardo Vinci:" paper presented at the conference *Leonardo Vinci: architetture sonore nella Napoli del viceregno austrico: convegno internazionale di studi*, Conservatorio di Musica Francesco Cilea, Reggio Calabria, 10-12 June 2002.

[30] *Libro di tutte le Spese chi si l'anno per Servitio del Conservatorio de P overi di Giesù Christo dal R. D. Bartolomeo Vigilante. . .P.mo di Gennaro 1706 avanti...*

[31] Ibid.

[32] Hucke, Op. cit., 147-48.

Leonardo Vinci, young Vencia had problems paying his fees. According to a note scribbled by the Controller below the entry he would pay ten ducats now and ten at the end of the semester, with the new sum of ten ducats written over the original twenty: "I have received ten ducats and he promises the rest to us at the end of the semester."[33] Apparently Vencia was late with the other ten ducats and was temporarily expelled until full payment was made: "The said Lonardo Vencia is reinstated with this payment on the 14th of November; I have received the ten ducats on the 14th of November 1707."[34] As the mature Leonardo Vinci, Vencia also used the Neapolitan form of his first name, "Lonardo."

Although a large number of his class did not make it into the second year, they still dominate the *convittori* roster of 1708. Among those who made it was Vencia, whose name appears in a new transformation in two almost identical payments:

>From Lonardo Vezzia the 8th of November 1708   7-2-10
>From Lonardo Vezzia the 30th of November 1708   7-2-10[35]

The close proximity of the two identical payments suggests that the first is a late payment. The reduced rate from ten ducats to seven ducats, two tari and ten grana[36] suggests that Vencia/Vezzia must have been making himself useful in musical performances, to justify the reduction (see below).

If the Leonardo/Lonardo Vencia/Vezzia is the same person as the Leonardo Vinci who turns up at the Teatro Fiorentini as the composer of the opera *Lo Cecato fauzo* in 1719, which seems likely, then he would have been seventeen or eighteen years old, using the approximate birth date of 1690 derived from Sigismondo and the death record. This would mean he would have been older than his fellow students, who would have entered at the normal age, between eight and ten years old. This late start should not be regarded as a problem any more than an opera debut in the late twenties rather than late teens. Niccolò Piccinni explained to Burney that "the boys are admitted from eight or ten to twenty years of age; that when they are taken in young they are bound for eight years; but, when more advanced, their admission is difficult."[37] However, as shall be seen with regards to his entrance into the Real Cappella, Vinci did not always follow the normal course.

---

[33] *Libro di tutte le Spese chi si l'anno per Servitio del Conservatorio de Poveri di Giesù Christo.*

[34] Ibid.,10.

[35] *Conto de R.do D. Bartolomeo Vigilante Proc.re. del Cons.io di Pov.i Giesù Xsto della sua Amministr.e di Anno del P. mo Gennaro 1708 E per tutta Xbre.* 7-2-10

[36] Like old pounds, shillings and pence, the ducat was worth five tari, and the tari, twenty grana; *The Historical Archive of Banco di Napoli*, 19.

[37] Charles Burney, *The Present State of Music in France and Italy*, 311.

## A Student at the Conservatory

According to Burney, who published a valuable account of the conservatories in *The Present State of Music in France and Italy* from 1773, life at the conservatories was not particularly pleasurable:

> The only vacation in these schools, in the whole year, is in autumn, and that for a few days only: during the winter, the boys rise two hours before it is light, from which time they continue their exercise, an hour and a half at dinner excepted, till eight o'clock at night.[38]

After attending Mass, most of the morning was spent in musical instruction from the teachers, who were professional musicians. Piccinni reported to Burney that the musical staff generally consisted of:

> two principal *Maestri di Cappella*, the first of whom superintends and corrects the compositions of the students; the second the singing and gives lessons. That there are assistants, who are called *Maestri Secolari*; one for the violin, one for the violoncello, one for the harpsichord...and so for other instruments.[39]

Although Piccinni's account suggests an entourage of *Maestri secolari* assigned to specific instruments as in a modern conservatory or faculty of music, the reality suggests that the norm was somewhat less lavish—that often there were only two or three of these instrumental instructors; for example, there was only one teacher for stringed instruments and one for winds at both the Conservatories of Gli Poveri dei Gesù Cristo and S. Maria di Loreto for much of the eighteenth century.[40]

The afternoon was devoted to the liberal arts, albeit interrupted by dinner from three to four. The subjects, which were taught by the clerics on staff, included Grammar, Latin, Mathematics, History, Geography, Literature and Poetry, depending upon the day of the week and the year of the student.[41] The juxtaposition between the liberal arts education of the original orphanages and the specialized career-orientated musical instruction of the conservatories sometimes created problems; for example the students at the S. Maria di Loreto complained to the Board of Governors in June of 1707 about the "humanities class because it is not

---

[38] Ibid., 338.
[39] Ibid., 311.
[40] Hucke, Op. cit, 144 and Robinson, Op. cit., 49-50. It was only in the 1770s that the violin position at the Loreto was divided to include a specific *maestro* for cello.
[41] Florimo, *La scuola musicale di Napoli*, II, 76; information based on a pamphlet by Emmaunele Imbimbo and the *mutuo insegnamento* rules form the archives of the Conservatorio San Pietro a Majella (see also chart on pp.156-57).

necessary and is even a notable impediment to the study of music which is their principal object and will be their prime means of livelihood."[42]

Typical of Naples, then as now, was the problem of overcrowding. Much of the day was spent in the common rooms "where the boys practice, sleep, and eat."[43] Burney describes one of these common rooms in a visit to the Conservatorio di S. Onofrio in 1770:

> In the common practising room there was a *Dutch concert*, consisting of seven or eight harpsichords, more than as many violins, and several voices, all performing different things, and in different keys: other boys were writing in the same room;
> ...
>
> The beds, which are in the same room, serve for seats to the harpsichords and other instruments. Out of thirty or forty boys who were practising, I could discover but two that were playing the same piece.[44]

Although Burney admits that such communal practising "may teach the boys to attend to their own parts with firmness, whatever else may be going forward at the same time," he believed it was also responsible for "the slovenly coarseness so remarkable in their public exhibitions; and the total want of taste, neatness, and expression...till they have acquired them elsewhere."[45]

One of the principal reasons for musical instruction becoming the specialization of the conservatories, is that they provided music for the myriad of churches, chapels, convents, and confraternities throughout the city and its environs. During the course of the seventeenth century there was an increasing demand for more music and better performances and the conservatories were happy to supply this demand. The account books of the Conservatorio dei Poveri di Gesù Cristo are dominated by entries, listing the numerous performances of masses, vespers, processions, and especially the *flotte*. These performances in and around Naples netted hundreds of ducats for the Conservatory coffers. Table I on p. 18 reproduces the entries of the "Music and Processions" for the first six months of 1708 to give an idea of some of the performances that young Vencia/Vezzia was involved in during his second year as *convittore* at

---

[42] Quoted in Michael F. Robinson, "The Governor's Minutes. . . ," 36. On this occasion, the board decided to "suspend the humanities class" leaving the option that the class could be restored "should necessity arise or the present reasons for its suspension cease to apply."

[43] Burney, *The Present State of Music in France and Italy,* 336.

[44] Ibid., 336-37. Presumably "Dutch Concert" was a chauvinistic euphemism for cacophony.

[45] Ibid., 337.

the Conservatorio dei Poveri di Gesù Cristo. The sub-total of 468-1-18 calculated towards the end of June, rising to 806-2-13 ducats by the end of the year, indicates how lucrative these performances were for the Conservatory, covering a substantial part of the operating costs of the institution.[46]

The "Musiche, e processione incerte" for the first six months of 1708, like other such lists, is dominated by the *flotte* which were a speciality of Naples, partaking of the same distinctive religious tradition that produced the elaborate nativity scenes. The *flotte* were connected directly with the "devotion to the sacred sacrament" and involved "the young orphans" from the conservatories; according to a petition to the King by Board of Governors of the Conservatorio S. Maria di Loreto, it became the custom that whenever the sacrament was "carried around the houses of the sick, to accompany it with the sweet and devout melody of their instruments and of the hymns and canticles they sing."[47] The direct connection between the *flotte* and the devotion to the sacrament accounts for the plethora of entries within the month of June under its separate heading of "Giugno Corpo Domini" and the sending out the sacrament to the "houses of the sick" accounts for the numerous *flotte* sent out to the hospital of S. Giovanni Maggiore. The Neapolitan tradition of the *flotte* became quite celebrated, the Loreto Board of Governors boasting that "in all Catholic Europe there is no place where (the sacred host) comes out of the churches with more pomp and decorum" than in Naples.[48] Although the *flotte* dominate the account books of performances at the conservatories, they were the domain of the orphans and at S. Maria di Loreto the *convittore* were not required to take part in them.[49]

However, most of musical performances, including the *flotte*, were usually carried out by a small squad of boys, sometimes referred to as a *paranza*, under the direction of a student master or *capoparanza*.[50] These musical performances not only augmented the coffers of the conservatories and gave the boys a practical outlet for their studies, but also encouraged independence and authority on the part of the senior students who supervised them.[51] Di Giacomo reproduces the payment records

---

[46] According to Hucke (Op. cit.), the *musiche incerte* accounted for more than half of the total income of the Poveri di Gesù Cristo, 149.

[47] Quoted in Robinson, Op. cit., 63.

[48] Ibid., 63.

[49] Ibid., 52-53.

[50] The terminology is confusing, with "paranza" used interchangeably with "flotta" (as in the April entry for Battiuli in the Appendix), whilst other times it refers to an ensemble of violins (as in the following entries on Pergolesi). In contrast to Hucke who equates "flotta" with "paranza" (Hucke, Op. cit., 150), "flotta" here refers to a specific musical/devotional activity and "paranza" to a more generic ensemble led by a "capoparanza".

[51] Robinson, *Naples and Neapolitan Opera* (Oxford: Clarendon Press, 1972), 15.

for the violin *capoparanze* from the Conservatory accounts of 1729/30, among which was a certain "Jesi" who is identified as the young Pergolesi from the town of Jesi.[52] In his discussion with Burney, Piccinni mentions that some of these student leaders, "after having served their time out, are retained to teach the rest."[53]

In his *General History of Music* Burney provides additional information about Vinci's student years at the Conservatory that is as problematic as it is intriguing:

> [he] is said to have run away from the conservatorio of *Gli poveri in Giesu Cristo*, at Naples, where he was the scholar of Gaetano Greco, on account of a quarrel with Porpora, a student of the same school.[54]

This anecdote seems plausible considering the rivalry between the two composers in later life and would seem to support the Sigismondo/Villarosa c.1690 birth date, making the two rivals near-contemporaries, Porpora having been born in 1686. Moreover, "Vencia" had already been expelled during his first year as *convittori* for late payment of his annual fees. According to Di Giacomo, unauthorized leave from the Conservatory was punishable by incarceration[55] and, if Burney's account is true, Vinci would have been severely punished for this serious misconduct. The problem with this anecdote is that there are no references to Porpora in the books of the Conservatory during these years [56] and by the time Vinci enrolled at the Conservatory in November of 1708, he had already made his debut as an opera composer with *Agrippina*. However, the absence of a reference does not rule out the possibility that young Porpora continued his association with his school up to, or even after his opera debut—the Conservatory records provide regular lists of *convittori* and faculty, but not a regular listing of the student teachers.

---

[52] Di Giacomo, *I quattro antichi conservatorii di musica di Napoli*, 109-111. De Siena puts his own spin on Prota-Giurleo's supposed entrance record for Vinci by stating that the "pensionante" who entered the Conservatory in 1708 was known "by a nickname that he carried all his life: 'Lo Strongoli'" (*Leonardo Vinci: vita ed opera*, 14)—obviously basing it on Pergolesi's nickname "Jesi," derived from his home-town. While it is possible that the student Vinci may have been nicknamed "Lo Strongoli," in later life he does not appear to have a nickname other than the generic "Napoletano," which was sometimes used to identify the composer when he was working outside of Naples, hence the title of the present work.

[53] Burney, *The Present State of Music in France and Italy*, 312.

[54] Burney, *A General History of Music*, II, 916.

[55] Di Giacomo, *I quattro antichi conservatorii*, II, 89.

[56] Although "Aniello Porpora" regularly appears during these years in the "entrate dell'heredita di Laia," (list of donors) Aniello is not the same person as Nicola Antonio, and it is unlikely that a young composer's name would appear on a list of donors.

Although Sigismondo and Burney name Gaetano Greco as Vinci's teacher, he cannot have been his first teacher. During Vinci's years as *convittore*, Nicola Ceva, is listed as *maestro di cappella*. It is not known why Greco left his position in May of 1706.[58] It may be related to the confused succession of *maestri di cappella* at court during this same period that resulted from the War of Spanish Succession (see Chapter 4). Perhaps Greco, like Scarlatti, decided to pursue his career away from Naples during these years of crisis, allowing the vice-maestro to take over his position. However, just as Mancini was demoted when Scarlatti returned to Naples, so was Ceva, when Greco returned to his position in April of 1709.[59]

Instruction in composition at the Conservatory consisted of lectures and assignments. The latter were written on the *cartelle*, heavy pieces of varnished linen which could be re-used like a blackboard.[60] These assignments were corrected by the maestro in front of the other students, with comments and explanations. A lecture then followed based on issues that arose in the correcting of the assignments. At the end of the year, exams were conducted before both staff and students in assembly.[61]

## Leaving the Conservatory and the Sansevero Appointment

The next reference to Vencia/Vezzia occurs in the list of *convittori* from 1709, even though this particular record refers to a payment that was made at the end of the previous year, actually in between the last two payments:

From Lonardo Vencì finished the 14th of November 1708  2-2-10[62]

The term "saldo" indicates Vencì has finished paying.[63] But finished paying what? According to Prota-Giurleo, after three years of residence

---

[57] *Conto de R. Do D. Bartolomeo Vigilante Proc.re. del Cons.io di Pov.i Giesù Xsto...*

[58] Di Giacomo, Op. cit., II, 89.

[59] Ibid. 163-64. Because of Greco's influential position as teacher of Porpora, Vinci, and Domenico Scarlatti, he has attracted some scholarly attention, notably a study by Friedrich Lippmann, "Sulle composizioni per cembalo di Gaetano Greco" in *La Musica a Napoli durante il Seicento: atti del convegno internazionale di studi: Napoli, 1985*, ed. Domenico Antonio D'Alessandro and Agostino Zino (Rome: Edizione Torre d'Orfeo, 1987) 285-306. The article contains numerous examples of Greco's keyboard music which rather surpisingly anticipates the sonatas of Domenico Scarlatti.

[60] Given the complete absence of sketches or composing scores, one wonders whether much of Vinci's actual composing in later life was done on the *cartelle*.

[61] Di Giacomo, Op. cit., II, 89-90.

[62] *Conto del R. do D.Lorenzo Balbi Rettore e Procuratore del Conservatorio de Poveri di Giesù Christo. Da Gennaro 1709 à 4 Xbre.*

[63] Ironically, this is the same date as Prota-Giurleo's entrance record for Vinci.

at the Conservatory (i.e. 1711) Vinci was exempted from his *convittori* fee because he was now making himself useful in some manner.[64] This same progression had occurred several years earlier for Nicola Porpora who entered the Conservatory as a *convittore* in September 1696 and in 1699 was exempted from the payment.[65] Certainly one can imagine Vinci, like Porpora and Pergolesi, staying on at the Conservatory after his final *convittore* payments as a *capoparenza* and then later perhaps being retained as a student teacher or *maestrocello* after graduation. Moreover, it would have been during these senior years that he would have had the opportunity to study composition under Gaetano Greco, hence the student/teacher relationship between Vinci and Greco described by both Sigismondo and Burney.

The one problem in assuming that Vinci stayed on at the Conservatory, progressing from *capoparanze* to *mastrocello*, is that this is the last reference to Vencia/Vezzia/Vencì in the records of the Conservatorio dei Poveri di Gesù Cristo.[66] Although Piccinci described the standard course of study at the conservatories as eight years, the studies of the *convittore* could sometimes be rather brief, as the Board of the Governors at the S. Maria di Loreto complained in 1750:

> experience has shown, as soon as they have learnt some first rudiments of whatever sciences are taught to them, they leave at once, or else pretend they need pay fees no longer, or reduced fees at least.[67]

While it is possible that Vencia/Vezzia/Vencì, after having his fees reduced at the end his first year, had his fees waived completely at the end of his second, the lack of subsequent references suggests that he may have taken the other route described by the Loreto Board of Governors, namely, that after having his fees reduced at the end of his first year, he

---

[64] Prota-Giurleo, "Leonardo Vinci," 3.

[65] Frank Walker, "A Chronology of the Life and Works of Nicola Porpora," in *Italian Studies 4* (1951), 30, quotes these two key records as follows: "Nicola Porpora pays 18 ducats a year commencing from September 29, 1696" and (1699) "Nicola Porpora no longer pays."

[66] The reference to "Dal Vinc. Ed altri Acampare 30__" from 1711 looks like a payment to Vinci, but the super-scripted circle above the period indicates that this is an abbreviation of the name Vincenzo and undoubtedly refers to the student Vincenzo Carafa who entered the school the same year. Another possible referencce occurs in one of the two entries under *Spese diverse* "Per lettera di Roma a Calabria," the second with a name scribbled in small letters, with the price scrawled on top. Although the abbreviated name looks like "L. Vinci" to one searching for the name, the curvature of the two capital letters suggest an "A" and "O" in eighteenth-century script, rather than an L and V.

[67] Quoted in Robinson, "The Governor's Minutes of the Conservatory S. Maria di Loreto, Naples," 53. Hucke also mentions that the course of study could be considerably longer, as much as twelve to fourteen years, for the precious castrati (Op. cit., 149).

left the Conservatory at the end of the second. In fact the strange final payment for 2-2-10 appears to round off his final payment to his original bi-annual fee of ten ducats, suggesting that his departure came before the end of the second year, with this final payment making up for not fulfilling his duties because of his premature departure. In an entry on Vinci in the English *Dictionary of Musicians* published by Sainsbury in 1825, there is a statement about the composer's early career which the author originally ignored because it contradicted the standard view of Vinci's conservatory years. Seen from this new perspective, however, it could be regarded as a concise summary of the composer's youth: "This composer announced at an early age the rarest ability, and although he devoted but few years to his studies, they were not less complete."[68]

Regardless of whether Vinci left the Conservatory towards the end of 1708 or stayed on as a *capoparanze/mastrocello*, one is still confronted with strange anomaly of not having a single reference to the composer until the libretto and performance notice of Vinci's first opera, *Lo cecato fauzo* from April of 1719. One way to account for this lacuna would be to develop an alternate scenario, namely that Vinci returned home to Strongoli after his studies at the Conservatory to become the organist and choir director at the Cathedral, perfecting his craft, before going back to Naples where he obtained the patronage of Prince Sansevero and his first opera commission. Such a career progression would not have been uncommon. This return to Strongoli could have been as early as the "saldo" of November of 1708 or may have been some years after 1709, allowing for Vinci's alleged studies with Gaetano Greco. The records of this Strongoli career, like his baptismal records, would have been lost in the fires of 1806/07. Although this scenario has no more basis in fact than Prota-Giurleo's, it does tie in better with the surviving references to Vencia/Vezzia/Vencì at the Conservatory and accounts for the complete lack of reference to Vinci in the decade between 1709-1719.

The performance notice of Vinci's first opera, *Lo cecato fauzo* from April of 1719, describes the composer as "Maestro di Cappella della Casa del Principe di S. Seviero."[69] According to Prota-Giurleo, upon leaving the Conservatory after the usual ten years of study, Vinci was appointed *maestro di cappella* for Don Paulo di Sangro, Prince of Sansevero, one of the most powerful and prestigious of the old Neapolitan aristocracy. Prota-Giurleo then goes on to describe how Vinci's main duty for the Prince was to teach music to his young protegé, nephew and

---

[68] *Dictionary of Musicians, from the Earliest Ages to the Present Time.*

[69] *Avvisi du Napoli,* April 25, 1719 (No. 19); unless otherwise indicated, all quotations from the *Avvisi* are taken from handwritten copies made by Carl Morey.

heir, Raimondo, who during his lifetime was to achieve fame as "the most illustrious there has ever been in literature in this Kingdom."[70] Since Prota-Giurleo makes no references to documents relating to Vinci's duties for the prince (i.e. salary, contracts, commissions), one can assume that he came to this conclusion by combining the reference to "della Casa del Principe di S. Seviero" from the performance notice to *Lo cecato fauzo*, with the presence of the young Raimondo in this house. Moreover, he claims that Vinci's tenure as *maestro di cappella* for the Prince came to an end after two years with Raimondo's departure for Rome to study at the Jesuit Seminary.[71] There is no mention of when Raimondo departed for Rome. This would have to have been during the summer of 1719 in order to coincide with Vinci ceasing to use the Sansevero title with his second opera *Le ddoie lettere* from July of 1719 (i.e. four months later).[72] Unless documents are discovered, Prota-Giurleo's description of Vinci's Sansevero appointment can only be regarded as a possible scenario.[73]

## The Cantatas

Although Vinci is not known to have written any music specifically for the Sansevero, it is possible that most of the solo cantatas were written for the entertainment of the Prince, in the same way that most of Handel's cantatas were written for the Sunday evening *conversazione* of Prince Ruspoli in Rome during the previous decade.[74] It is known that this type of refined entertainment was also cultivated by certain Neapolitan princes. Vinci's colleague Bonifacio Pecorone describes how his main duty in the service of Prince Carlo Sanseverini was to sing cantatas twice weekly for the entertainment of the Prince and his court.[75]

[70] Proto-Giurlea, "Leonardo Vinci," 3.

[71] Ibid., 3-4.

[72] The only information the author could find on Raimondo's departure was that he was "presque enfant" when he began his studies in Rome, which he would have been in 1719 at age 10. *Biographie universale: Ancienne et modene*, ed. Joseph François Michaud (Paris: Michaud, 1811-12), "Sansevero Raimondo."

[73] In contrast to the Pignatelli family, there do not appear to be any Sansevero archives at the Archivio di Stato in Naples nor in the standard inventory of private archives in Italy. One might search the Archives of the Banco di Napoli for payments issued by the Prince during the years 1716-19. However, a search of the indexes or *pandette* at four of the eight Neapolitan banks, the Spirito Sancto, Pietà, San Giacomo, and Santa Maria del Popolo for the second half of 1718 and the first half of 1719 turned up only a few entires for the Prince Sansevero at the San Giacomo, but the account books or *libri maggiore* (1718/II, 74 & 1719/I, 72) contained no references to Lonardo Vinci.

[74] On Vinci's cantatas. see Teresa Maria Gialdroni, "Vinci 'operista' autore di cantate," in *Studi in onore di Giulio Cattin* (Rome: 1990), 307-29.

[75] Stephen Shearon, "Musical Activity in Early Eighteenth-Century Naples: the Memoirs of Bonifacio Pecorone." Paper given at the Conference: *Music in Eighteenth-Century Italy,* Cardiff University, 12-15 July 1998.

There are also preserved in Zaragoza five Spanish cantatas attributed to Vinci, along with another three attributed to Porpora.[76] These Spanish cantatas are bi-textual and, with one exception, are provided with a sacred text or *tonos divinos* and a secular text or *tonos humanos*. The one exception is Vinci's most celebrated cantata, "Mesto o dio," with its original Italian text and a Spanish translation. While "Mesto o dio" is written on Italian paper, the four Spanish cantatas appear to be written on mid-eighteenth-century Spanish paper.[77] Although the paper seems to be Spanish, the works may not be Spanish originals but, rather, parodies of Italian cantatas.[78] The substituted Spanish *tonos divinos* texts allowed the works to be performed in Zaragoza cathedral as sacred *villanciccos*, while the *tonos humanos* texts were added later, perhaps when it was no longer considered necessary to mask this repertoire in a sacred guise.[79] Therefore, with the exception of the "Mesto o dio" which exists in numerous copies, the four other works may preserve in Spanish guise four lost Italian cantatas by Vinci, augmenting the composer's small output of cantatas.[80] The other possibility is that these are actual sacred *villanciccos* by Vinci, composed at a time when the genre was coming more under the sway of the Italian cantata.[81] Vestiges of the Spanish regime in Naples remained after the Austrian conquest, with the old Neapolitan aristocracy continuing to use their old Spanish titles and court documents continuing to be written in both official languages, Italian and Spanish. Whether original Spanish *villanciccos* or Spanish parodies of lost Italian cantatas, these works were probably written during Vinci's early years in Naples.

---

[76] Giulia Anna Romana Veneziano, "Un *Corpus* de cantatas Napolitanas del siglo XVIII en Zaragoza: Problemas de difusión del repertorio italiano en España" in *Artigrama: Revista del Departamento de Historia del arte* 12 (1996-97) 277-91.

[77] Ibid., 279.

[78] Ibid., 280.

[79] Ibid., 280-81.

[80] Ibid., 283. According to Giulia Anna Romana Veneziano, only ten of the fifteen cantatas listed by Gialdroni can be securely attributed to Vinci (Gialdroni, "Vinci 'operista'autore di cantate").

[81] Veneziano, "Dal 'tono humano' al 'divino:' cantate di Vinci in Spagna." Paper presented at the conference *Leonardo Vinci: architetture sonore nella Napoli del viceregno austriaco: convegno internazionale di studi*, Conservatorio di Musica Francesco Cilea, Reggio Calabria, June10-12, 2002.

## Table 1. Music and Processions in *Certe* 1708[82]

**January:**
| | |
|---|---|
| For three services at Gesù delle Monache | 12___ |
| For music and a Procession at the Congregation del Bambini | 4-2-10 |
| For a *Flotta* to S. Giovanni Maggiore to the hospital | _3-1 |
| For a *Flotta* at the *Porto sallu* on the first and 6th of January | 5___ |
| For two *Flotte* at S. Petido | 8___ |
| For another *Flotta* at S. Dionise *à draj.e* to the hospital | _3-10 |
| For a *Cambio di cornetto* at the Consolatione | _2-10 |
| For two *Flotte* at S. Sebastiano | 2-2-10 |
| For a *Flotta* to Capua on the day of S. Sebastiano | 9___ |
| For three services at S. Francesco di Sales | 9___ |
| For another *Flotta* at S. Giovanni Mag. to the hospital | _3-10 |

**February:**
| | |
|---|---|
| For a mass and procession to Cardito at *S. Biaso* | 8___ |
| For a mass at Concezione de Spagnoli | 2___ |
| For two *Flotte* to S. Sebastiano with angels and S. Biaso | 2-2_ |
| For a *Flotta* to S.Alvina and S. Agata | 3___ |
| For two *Flotte* to the statue of *S. Biaso* | 4___ |
| For a *Flotta* of the little boys to *S. Biaso alla Giud.* | _2-10 |
| For a mass for the dead to S. Agata L'Orefici | 1-2-10 |
| For music at the Castell à Mare | 10___ |
| For music at S. Antonio | 7___ |
| For a *Flotta* to S. Giovanni Maggiore to the hospital | _3-10 |

**March:**
| | |
|---|---|
| For two *Flotte* to S. Marcellino and S. Felicite | 6___ |
| For two *Flotte* to the Statue of S. Tommaso d'Aquino | 3___ |
| For a mass at S. Anna dei Lombardi and at S. Giudo | 1-2-10 |
| For another mass in the parish church of the Archbishop for S. Gioachino | 1-2-10 |
| For three services at S. Petito for S. Benedetto | 9___ |
| For three services at S. Gaudosio *d.o .G* | 9___ |
| For three services at S. Otrudua *d.o G* | 12___ |
| For two *Flotte* at the Schareillino *d.o G* | 6___ |
| For the Fridays in March at S. Domenico Soriano | 4___ |
| For the Fridays in March at the S. Maria Avvocata | 7-2-10 |
| For the Fridays in March at the *Misericoriello* | 3___ |
| For a *Flotta* at S. Girolamini on the last Friday | 2___ |
| For a voice and a maestro di cappella at S. Giovanni maggiore for eight days of excercises | 3___ |

**April:**
| | |
|---|---|
| For four services at S. Anna dei Lombardi during Holy Week | 6___ |
| For three services at Giesù Vecchio in Holy Week | 9___ |
| For two masses at the Recitanti on Holy Thursday and Saturday | 2-2-10 |
| For two instrumentalists and an organist at S. Agata L'orefici | _2-10 |
| For a mass at Giesù delle Monache for Easter | 4___ |
| For a *Flotta* to the hospital at S. Giovanni Maggiore | _3-10 |
| For a *Flotta* to the hospital at the *Pietra* | 4___ |
| For two instrumentalists at the Incurabili | 2___ |
| For a *Flotta* in black every Friday [in April] | 7___ |
| For a *Flotta* every day [in April] | 8___ |
| For four *paranze* in the procession *di Battiul.i* with twenty angels | 24___ |
| For a mass at S. Francesco delle Monache | 3___ |
| For three services at *Ducentola* and S. Guido | |
| For a *Flotta* in black at S. Giovanni Maggiore | _3-10 |

| | |
|---|---|
| For a *Flotta* at the statue of S. Severo | 4-2-10 |
| For two *Flotte* at the statue of S. Pietro Martire *it assist.no* | 11___ |

**May:**
| | |
|---|---|
| For a mass and procession at the Fratte | 9___ |
| For two voices, four instrumentalists and *mrd* & *Cap.o* to Caserta | 7-2-10 |
| For a *Flotta* to the *Infermi*, of S. Giovanni Maggiore | _3-10 |
| For a mass and vespers at Sacramento & S. Chiara *Mad.rio* | 6___ |
| For four voices and four instruments at S. Esremo S. Luoui | 1-2-10 |
| For a *Flotta* to Giugliaro & S. Crescendia | 6___ |

**June:**
| | |
|---|---|
| For three services in black at Trinità delle Monache | 12___ |
| For two *Flotte* to the statue of S. Filippo Neri | 3___ |
| For two *Flotte* to S. Marcellino | 6___ |
| For a *Flotta* to the hospital at S. Maria della Rotonda | 2-10 |
| For another *Flotta* at *S. Elitania* | 1-2-10 |
| For a mass for the dead at S. Agata l'orefici | 2-1_ |
| For two *Flotte* to the statue of S. Antonio di Padua | 4___ |
| For two *Flotte* to S. Sebast.o & SS. Pietro e Paulo | 2-2-10 |

**Corpo Domini**
| | |
|---|---|
| For a mass and procession to Cardito | 10___ |
| For a mass and procession to Donnaregina | 9___ |
| For a *Flotta* to S. Giovanni Maggiore | 8___ |
| For three services at Sacramento | 9___ |
| For a mass and a *Flotta* to Carvisino | 10___ |
| For a mass and a *Flotta* to Gontivello | 10___ |
| For a mass and a *Flotta* to Posilippo | 10___ |
| For a *Flotta* to Carmiro | 2___ |
| For a *Flotta* to S. Angelo l'Arena | 9___ |
| For a trumpet sent *to* Frassio | 4___ |
| For three *Flotte* and a vespers to S. Giorgio Maggiore | 10___ |
| For two *Flotte* to S. Angelo a Syrio | 8___ |
| For a *Flotta* to *S. Teresa Ognibene* | 6___ |
| For a mass at S. Girolamo | 4___ |
| For three masses and a procession at Aversa | 9___ |
| For a *Flotta* to *Vita* | 3___ |
| For a *Flotta* to the *scalsi & di Ag.no* | 3___ |
| For a *Flotta* to *l'Angelo à Hirio* | 1-1_ |
| For two *Flotte* and a mass at Gennaro all'Olmo | 6___ |
| For a *Flotta* to S. Eliggio Maggiore | 7___ |
| For a *Flotta* to S. Ligorio | 2-2-10 |
| For a *Flotta* to S. Girolamo | 2-2-10 |
| For a *Flotta* to *di Fren.o* | 3___ |
| For a mass and procession to *Quinderi* | 5___ |
| | 468-1-18 |
| For three services at S. Francesco di Salej | 5___ |
| Two *Flotte* to S. Francesco delle Monache and S. Silvano | 5___ |
| For a music to Raito | 14___ |
| For three services at Sacramento and S. Maria del Carmine | 9___ |
| For two services at S. Maria Antesaecula by day | 6___ |
| For three services at S. Marrgherita by day | 5___ |
| For a mass at the Misericordia | 1___ |
| For a vespers at Vita | 1.2.10 |
| For a *Flotta* to the hopsital at S. Giovanni Maggiore | _3-10 |
| For a verspers at the *Veregini* | 1-2-10 |

---

[82] *Conto del R.do D. Bartol.o Vigilante Proca.di Poveri di Giesù Xsto...dal Gennaro 1709.* The author has not been able to make out all the abbreviations in these assignments and the ones that are too difficult have been left as is in the translation in italics.

# 2

# VINCI AND THE *COMMEDIA PER MUSICA*

## Initial Success

Vinci made his operatic debut on April 19, 1719 at the Teatro Fiorentini in Naples, setting to music Aniello Piscopo's *commedia per musica*, *Lo cecato fauzo*.[1] His contribution is singled out in a performance notice in the court newsletter *Avvisi di Napoli*:

> Sunday night their excellencies the viceregents went to the Teatro dei Fiorentini to listen to the *opera in musica* in Neapolitan dialect which succeeded marvellously, for the distinguished dramatic personae who acted in it, as for the music, composed by the virtuoso Leonardo Vinci, *Maestro di Cappella* in the house of Prince S. Seviero, which contributed each night to the nobility of this [entertainment].[2]

A collection of arias from this opera survives which provides a glimpse of Vinci's style at the beginning of his career.[3] The arias display certain traditional aspects, such as the prevalence of the minor mode and dotted rhythms, which give the music a resemblance to the music of Alessandro Scarlatti. There are two *siciliano* arias "Amor achisto core" and "Sò le ssorva," the former notated in 3/8 and the latter with a rustic gigue lilt (see Example 2.1 on p.20). "So le ssorva" employs a motto beginning which is as rare as the *siciliano* in Vinci's later works.[4] Sometimes the

---

[1] Copies of the libretto found in I-Bu, -Nc, -Nn (Lucchesi Palli), -RA, -Rsc; Claudio Sartori, *I libretto italiani a stampa dalle origini al 1800* (Cuneo: Bertòla e Locatelli Editori, 1990), No. 5349; synopsis of the comedy with excerpts in Michele Scherillo, *L'opera buffa napoletana durante il Settecento: Storia letteraria*, 2nd ed. (Milan: Remo Sandron, 1916), 126-33.

[2] *Avvisi di Napoli*, April 25, 1719, No. 19; unless otherwise indicated, all quotations from the *Avvisi* are taken from manuscript copies by Carl Morey, which are in his private possession.

[3] The collection (A 615) in the Biblioteca del Conservatorio di Musica S. Pietro a Majella contains eleven arias and two duets.

[4] "So le ssorva e le nespol'amare" has been recorded, along with the duets "Che bella 'nzalatella" and "Maremene, haggio visto 'na cosa" from *Le Cecato fauzo*, by Antonio Florio and the Capella De'Turchini on *Vinci/Leo L'opera Buffa Napoletana* (Opus 111 OPS 30-184).

Example 2.1 "Sò le ssorva" *Lo cecato fauzo*, additional aria

melodies have a gestic quality that seems to call out for action on the part of the singer. For example, in "Cechimma fauza mo crepa," the ascending repetitions of "schiatta" (to kill) followed by fermatas would have been accompanied by some type of threatening gesture:

Example 2.2 "Cechimma fauza mo crepa" *Lo cecato fauzo* III/v

The duet "Che bella nzalatella" features the juxtaposition of high and low sonorities, the soprano accompanied by violins and violas and the tenor accompanied by basso continuo, with the full orchestra playing only in duet passages and ritornellos.[5]

A second opera appeared in July, *Le ddoie lettere*, on a libretto by one Agniolo Birini. This sequel could be another indication of the success of Vinci's first opera, or, if the two operas were commissioned to-

---

[5] It is surprising to come across Handelian echoes in these early comic arias: the opening theme of "Che bella 'nzalatella" is similar to that in the organ concerto Op.4, no. 2; the use of the "schiatta" repetitions of "Cechimma fauza mo crepa" similar to the repetitions in "Tutto può donna" from *Giulio Cesare*; and "Amor achisto core" anticipates "How beautiful are the feet" from *Messiah*. Although it is known that Handel was familiar with Vinci's heroic operas, these echoes suggest that he may also have been familiar with some of the music from the comic operas.

gether, an indication of the initial confidence that the impresario had in the young composer. Vinci is designated in the libretto to *Le ddoie lettere* but without his title.[6] This omission implies that he left the service of Prince Sansevero some time between the productions of *Lo cecato fauzo* in April and *Le ddoie lettere* in July of 1719. A notice in the *Avvisi di Napoli* indicates that *Le ddoie lettere* was given an additional performance at the request of the viceregal couple:

> Sunday night his excellency the Viceroy with the Viceregent went to the Teatro dei Fiorentini to listen to the *opera in musica* in Neapolitan dialect, repeated especially for their excellencies the viceregents who were greatly pleased, being joined there by a vast number of ladies and gentlemen.[7]

Although only three months separate Vinci's first two operas, the viceregal couple for whom he conducted was different on each occasion. *Lo cecato fauzo* was dedicated to Countess Barbara Erbestein, wife of the Viceroy Marshall Wirech Daun. Daun had served as Viceroy in Naples since 1713, a powerful position for him since he was the general who conquered the Kingdom for the Habsburgs in 1707.[8] Emperor Charles VI, however, concerned about the corruption of his government, recalled the general to Vienna, replacing him with Graf Johann Wenzel Gallas, the Imperial ambassador in Rome.[9] Graf Gallas arrived in Naples on July 2 and the performance of *Le ddoie lettere* on July 9 was probably intended to celebrate the arrival of the new viceregal couple. When the opera was revived during the autumn of that same year, the libretto was dedicated to yet another viceroy. Shortly after his arrival in July, Graf Gallas developed a fever and died within the month. Gallas was succeeded by his recent successor in Rome, Cardinal Wolfgang Schrattenbach, Prince Bishop of Olmutz.[10]

That *Lo cecato fauzo* and *Le ddoie lettere* owed their success more to Vinci's music than to the libretti is suggested by the fact that he col-

---

[6] Libretto in I-Nc: Claudio Sartori, *I libretti italiani*, No. 7226.

[7] *Avvisi di Napoli*, July 11, 1719; quoted in Ulisse Prota-Giurleo, "Leonardo Vinci" *Convegno musicale* II (1965), 4. The fact that this notice only appears in Prota-Giurleo and not in the other sources makes this record a little suspect.

[8] Heinrich Benedikt, *Das Königreich Neapel unter Kaiser Karl VI: Eine Darstellung auf Grund bisher unbekannter Dokumente aus den Österreichischen Archiven* (Vienna: Manz Verlag, 1927), 42-62.

[9] Ibid., 207-208.

[10] This sequence of première in July and revival in the fall is based on the performance notice quoted in Prota-Giurleo above and the fact that the only known libretto of *Le ddoie lettere* (B-Bc) is dedicated to Cardinal Schrattenbach, who did not arrive in Naples until August 29, 1719 (Sartori, *I libretti italiani*, No. 7226). This revival of *Le ddoie lettere* may be the unnamed "opera in lingua Napoletana" referred to in the *Avvisi di Napoli* on October 31, 1719 (No. 45).

laborated with two different poets, Piscopo and Birini. Another factor that would have played a role in Vinci's success was the debut of four new singers in *Lo cecato fauzo*: the sopranos Giacomina Ferraro, Ippolita Costa, and Rosa Cerillo and the bass Giovanni Romanielli. Rosa Cerillo was not named in the cast list of either opera; the reason, according to Benedetto Croce, was that she was Piscopo's mistress.[11] Piscopo was a controversial figure who was the subject of a satiric anthology, *La Violejeda*, consisting of over a hundred satiric poems by several writers, foremost among them being Francesco Oliva from whose name the title derives.[12]

Vinci continued to compose at least two operas a year for the next three years for the Teatro dei Fiorentini, employing the same core group of singers. In 1720 Vinci produced *Lo scassone*, described as a "crapiccio pe mmuseca" [*sic*], and *Lo scagno*, described as "fantasia marenaresca." The anonymous libretti to *Lo scassone* and *Lo scagno* were dedicated to Cardinal Schrattenbach by the impresario Berardino Bottone.[13] In the dedication, Bottone describes how "the Teatro Fiorentine has need of some assistance because of the mad excesses of Fortune" and that only by carrying the name of the Cardinal on the title page will the opera "attract less criticism and everyone will listen with a little more taste."[14] From the preface to *Lo scagno*, one learns that the text is by the same author as *Lo scassone* (which is attributed to Bottone in a note by Sigismondo on the title page), and that the former appeared after the latter. From this one can infer that *Lo scassone* was produced during Carnival of 1720, and that *Lo scagno* appeared either during the spring or summer, the assumption based on the appearance of a third opera in the fall. *Lo castiello saccheato* was premièred on October 26 and according to the *Avvisi di Napoli* was a great success:

> Last Saturday the opera in Neapolitan dialect entitled *Lo castiello saccheato* was produced for the first time at the Teatro de' Fiorentini, which succeeded wonderfully well and to the utmost taste of the nobility and the others who have heard it, due to the good graces of the impresario Berardino Bottone, no shortcuts were taken.[15]

---

[11] Benedetto Croce, *I teatri di Napoli: secoli XV-XVIII* (Naples: Luigi Pierro, 1891), 243-44.

[12] Vittorio Viviani, storia del teatro napoletano (Naples: Guida Editori, 1969), 274. In the satire Piscopo is described as Rosa Cerillo's lover.

[13] Libretto for *Lo scassone* is in I-Nc and *Lo scagno* is in I-Bc -Mc -Rsc & US-NYp; (Sartori, *I libretti italiani*, Nos. 21098 & 21070). The aria "Songo le femmene" from *Lo scassone* can be found in Biblioteca del Conservatorio di Musica S. Pietro a Majella in Naples (34-5-26); Reinhard Strohm, *Italienische Opernarien des frühen Settecento (1720-1730)*, 16/II of *Analecta Musicologica* (Cologne: Arno Volk, 1976), 216.

[14] *Lo scassone: crapiccio pe mmuseca: da rappresentarese a lo Tiatro de li Sciorentine de la città de Napole nchist' anno 1720* (Naples: Francesco Ricciardo, 1720).

[15] *Avvisi di Napoli*, October 29, 1720 (No. 44)

*Lo castiello saccheato* was on a libretto by Francesco Oliva, who was the rival of Piscopo and the principal author of the satire *La Violejeda*.[16] Although the first two operas that year were by Vinci, this third opera was a collaboration between Vinci and Michele de Falco. Falco, a graduate of the Conservatorio di Sant' Onofrio, initiated his career in 1712 with one of the early comic operas, *Lo Masiello*, written in collaboration with his teacher Nicola Fago.[17] Falco was not a regular composer at the Teatro dei Fiorentini, his most recent work being with Piscopo on *Lo mbruoglio d'ammore* in 1717. The libretto to *Lo castiello saccheato* states that "all of the third act and the arias designated by this % are by Signor Leonardo Vinci, *maestro di cappella* napoletano."[18]

The production of *Lo barone de Trocchia* from Carnival 1721 was distinguished for its ballets, which were a novelty in Naples, particularly on the comic stage:

> At the Teatro dei Fiorentini was performed for the first time, the fourth opera in Neapolitan dialect, entitled *Lo barone de Trocchia*, that has attained the satisfaction of the public, as much for the composition of the music as for the varied and curious incidents [of the plot] and the famous ballets that are seen in it.[19]

As with *Lo scassone* and *Lo scagno* from the previous year, the anonymous libretto to *Lo barone de Trocchia* is dedicated to Cardinal Schrattenbach by the impresario Bottone.[20] The libretto of Vinci's next opera *Don Ciccio*, produced at the Teatro Fiorentini on September 6, 1721, is by Bernardo Saddumene.[21] According to the *Avvisi di Napoli* the new collaboration produced fine results: "On Saturday the *commedia in musica* in the Neapolitan dialect *Don Ciccio* went into production for the first time at the Teatro dei Fiorentini, and has succeeded beyond all

---

[16] See Francesco Oliva, *Opere Napoletane*, ed. by Carla Chiara Petrone (Rome: Bulzoni Editore, 1977).

[17] Salvatore Di Giacomo, *I quattro antichi conservatorii di musica di Napoli* (Milan: Remo Sandron, 1928) II, 80-86 contains a miniature biography of Falco, or Farco as he was known in Neapolitan.

[18] Libretto in I-Fn and B-Bc; Sartori, *I libretti italiani* ( No. 5195). Synopsis of the plot in Scherillo, *L'opera buffa napoletana*, 177-180.

[19] *Avvisi di Napoli*, January 28, 1721 (No.5).

[20] Libretto in I-Nc (Sartori, *I libretti italiani* [No. 3778]). Manferrari lists another *commmedia per musica* in three acts, *Le feste napoletane*, supposedly composed by Vinci in 1721 for the Teatro dei Fiorentini (Umberto Manferrari, *Dizionario universale delle opere melodrammatiche* [Florence: Sansoni Antiquariato,1955], 381). Although it is possible that such a work could have appeared in the spring or summer of 1721 between *Lo Baròne* and *Don Ciccio*, the lack of a libretto and similarity of its title with *La festa de Bacco* from 1722 makes this work suspect—probably another variant of this flexible title.

[21] Libretto in GB-Lbl; Sartori, *I libretti italiani* ( No. 8147).

possibilities."[22] The success of this production led to several subsequent collaborations between Vinci and Saddumene.

Vinci had become virtual house composer at the Teatro dei Fiorentini, having eclipsed Antonio Orefice, the composer who had originated the *commedia per musica*. Not until the coming of Piccinni at mid-century would another composer dominate the stage of the Fiorentini to the same extent.[23] Vinci's initial success contrasted with that of his colleagues and rivals such as Porpora who, after the successful production of *Agrippina* in 1708, had to wait more than two years for a second commission and Leo who had to wait almost four yours after his debut with *Il Pisistrato* in 1714. It must be admitted, however, that part of Vinci's success had to do with timing—Porpora and Leo began their careers with the return of Scarlatti to Naples, whereas Vinci began his with Scarlatti's retirement. Moreover, several years later, Hasse would in turn match the brilliance of Vinci's initial success and in the process, provide him with a formidable rival (see Chapter 6).

## The Neapolitan *Commedia per Musica*

The Neapolitan *commedia per musica*, the operatic genre that Vinci cultivated during his early years as an opera composer, is a full-length comic opera that makes extensive use of the Neapolitan dialect. In its length and language, therefore, it differs from the contemporary comic intermezzo, which is a short series of comic scenes sung in standard literary Tuscan, originally intended to be performed within a full-length *dramma per musica*.[24] Although the *commedia per musica* was originally sung throughout in Neapolitan, the dialect gradually gave way to the introduction of more and more Tuscan.

The origins of the *commedia per musica* can be traced to the private performance of *La Cilla* in 1707 by Francesco Antonio Tullio and Michel'Agnolo Faggioli at the palace of Prince Chiusano.[25] The success of *La Cilla* was such that the impresarios of the Teatro dei Fiorentini decided to present a pair of these new Neapolitan comedies during the

---

[22] *Avvisi di Napoli,* September 9, 1721(No. 37).

[23] See listing of Fiorentini productions in Francesco Florimo, *La scuola musicale di Napoli*, IV, 35-.

[24] See Charles E. Troy, *The Comic Intermezzo* (Ann Arbor: UMI Press, 1979) and Graham Hood Hardie, "Leonardo Leo (1694-1744) and his Comic Operas *Amor vuol sofferenze* and *Alidoro*," Ph.D. Dissertation, Cornell University, 1973.

[25] Although the music of this landmark opera is lost, some of the music has been preserved, according to Dinko Fabris, in several cantatas attributed to Faggioli in the Conservatory Library in Naples. One of them has been recorded: *L'Amante Impazzito: Cantate Napoletane Barocche,* III, Pino de Vittorio, Cappella della Pietà de' Turchini, Antonio Florio (Symphonia SY 96147).

Carnival season of 1709: *Patrò Calienno de la Costa* by Antonio Orefice and Agasippo Mercotellis and *La Spellecchia* by Tomaso di Mauro and Carlo di Petris.[26] Although the Teatro Fiorentini opened as an opera theatre in 1706 to rival the productions of *dramma per musica* at the Teatro San Bartolomeo, the success of the new comic operas soon caused the management to phase out the serious operas. The theatre was destroyed by fire in 1711 and when it reopened in 1713 a series of heroic operas by Sarro, Porpora, and Fago was presented.[27] This second attempt to rival the San Bartolomeo could not have been very successful; after Carnival 1714 the Teatro dei Fiorentini abandoned the *dramma per musica* to become the first comic opera theatre. Therefore the establishment of comic opera in Naples, like the establishment of public opera in Venice in the previous century, appears to be directly connected with the marketing strategy of a particular theatre.

Not only did the Teatro dei Fiorentini establish the new genre, but it cultivated its own singers, librettists, and composers. The comic genre and the Neapolitan dialect, in part, required this specialization. As for the theatre, Napoli Signorelli described it in 1779 as "disproportionately more long than wide, and the remaining stairs, entrances, corridors, and back-rooms, all indicating an overall shabbiness."[28] Presumably in 1719, when the theatre had been recently renovated, there would have been less cause for complaint. The orchestra was relatively small, consisting of 12 violins, 2 violas, 2 cellos, 2 basses, 2 oboes, 2 trumpets and 1 harpsichord.[29]

While the comic scenes of *seicento* opera, the source of the intermezzo, were undoubtedly an influence, the direct precedents for the Neapolitan *commedia per musica* can be found in the full-length comic opera that was cultivated as an alternative genre during the second half of the seventeenth century, the musical equivalent of the classical Latin comedy. The principal center for this alternate genre was Florence, where the poet Giovanni Maria Moniglia and the composer Jacopo Melani produced a series of comic operas for the Teatro Pergola.[30] Like the Nea-

---

[26] Scherillo suggested that Agasippo Mercotellis is a *nom de plume* for Giaseppo Martoscelli (*L'opera buffa napoletana*, 62). Croce thinks the author was Nicolo Corvo because of the similarities with his prose comedy *La Perna* (*I teatri di Napoli*, 234-35), while Robinson believes *La Perna* may be derived from the opera (*Naples and Neapolitan Opera*, 188-89).
[27] *Enciclopedia della spettacolo* (Rome: Le Maschere, 1954-62) "Napoli" by Chiara Serino. See listing of Fiorentini poroductions in Florimo, *La scuola musicale di Napoli*, IV, 35-39.
[28] Pietro Napoli-Signorelli, *Storia critica de' teatri antichi e moderni* (Naples: Vincenzo Orsino, 1790), VI, 248.
[29] Andrea Della Corte, *Piccinni: Settecento italiano* (Bari: Giuseppe Laterza, 1928), 7; neither source nor date is given, but if these figures date from the time of Piccinni, then the orchestra presumably would have been smaller in Vinci's day.
[30] See Robert Lamar Weaver, "Florentine Comic Operas of the Seventeenth Century,"

politan *commedia per musica*, these are full-length works with comic plots in contemporary settings with characters drawn from the lower ranks of society. Although these *seicento* works provide precedents for full-length comic opera, they are written in standard literary Tuscan. Regional dialects are sometimes employed, though introduced as special effects into the Tuscan dialogue in the same way in which foreign languages, such as Spanish, German and Latin were introduced.[31] The precedent for the Neapolitan dialect comes from the spoken theatre.[32] The play *La deana o lo lavenaro* by Nicola Maresca, performed and published the year before *La cilla,* is written in Neapolitan throughout. There are also a set of scenarios for improvised *commedie dell'arte* plays in Neapolitan dating from the 1690s that call for substantial musical inserts.[33]

During the fall of 1718 and winter of 1719 the Teatro dei Fiorentini tried another experiment by producing full-length comic operas in Tuscan, all three on libretti by Francesco Tullio: *Il Gemino amore* by Antonio Orefice, *Il Trionfo dell'onore* by Alessandro Scarlatti, and *La Forza della virtù* by Francesco Feo. The introduction of literary Tuscan was accompanied by the introduction of serious characters and subjects as exemplified by the key words of the titles, "amore," "onore," "virtù," which together read like an old aristocratic motto. It would appear that this experiment was not a complete success, because the Neapolitan dialect returned in the spring of 1719 with Piscopo and Vinci's *Lo cecato fauzo*. The experimental season, however, allowed for the gradual introduction of serious characters and subjects into the *commedia per musica* of the 1720s and 1730s. In the preface to the libretto *La noce de Beneviento* from April of 1722, Bernardo Saddumene alludes to this expansion of the genre:

> In writing this comedy, I have had to obey the person giving the orders and not let my fancy direct me. Therefore I have not created the usual sort of work with low-class persons only, but have also included civilised people in it, just as if it were

---

Ph.D. Dissertation, University of North Carolina, 1959. Only a handful of *seicento* comic operas survive with music, including Moniglia and Melani's *Il poltestà di Colognole* (Florence, 1657), Alessandro Stradella's *Trespolo tutore* (Genoa, 1678), and Bernardo Pasquini's *Idalma* (Rome, 1680), the latter published in facsimile in the Garland Opera Series, 11.

[31] Ibid, 112.

[32] Reinhard Strohm, *Die italienische Opera im 18. Jahrhundert* (Wilhelmshaven: Heinrichshofens Verlag, 1979), 147, suggest that the *commedia per musica* may have been cultivated privately by the Neapolitan nobility prior to the first performance of *La Cilla*, though there does not appear to be any evidence for this practice.

[33] Francesco Cotticelli, "L'approdo alla scena. Ancora sulla nascita dell'opera comica." Paper presented at the conference *Leonardo Vinci: architetture sonore nella Napoli del viceregno austriaco: convegno internazionale di studi,* Conservatorio di Musica Francesco Cilea, Reggio Calabria, 10-12 Giugno 2002.

a "cloak and dagger" comedy (as the expression is). The object is to make a new work, not so much for the sake of the changes of situation as for the Neapolitan speech which is of two types, the one civilized and the other coarse, to suit the characters concerned, and in order not to make our language too difficult for certain foreigners in the cast.[34]

Saddumene's words indicate that these innovations originated from the management and not the librettist or composer. Moreover, the introduction of a more refine type of Neapolitan speech, as well as literary Tuscan, was used to depict these "civilized people" and to accommodate the difficulties that certain non-Neapolitan singers in the cast experienced in singing the "language." The reference to "cloak and dagger" comedy indicates that the use of literary Tuscan also involved a greater emphasis on romantic intrigue. The Spanish *commedia de capa y espada* was an important influence on seventeenth-century opera, and this Tuscanization process links the Neapolitan *commedia per musica* more closely to the rich heritage of seventeenth-century opera.[35]

## The First Surviving *Commedia per Musica*

Vinci's *Li zite 'ngalera* is the first Neapolitan *commedia per musica* to survive complete with music.[36] It also has the distinction of being the first surviving opera by Leonardo Vinci and therefore is of pivotal importance in both the study of comic opera and the music of Vinci. Because of its unique position, *Li zite 'ngalera* became the first opera by Vinci to be revived, first at the Maggio Musicale in Florence in 1979

---

[34] Quoted in Robinson, *Naples and Neapolitan Opera*, 194.

[35] Ibid., 195-96. On the other hand, Robinson also sees this Spanish influence as an anticipation of certain operatic developments in the late eighteenth and early nineteenth centuries.

[36] There is a single score of *Li zite 'ngalera* in the library of the Conservatorio San Pietro a Majella in Naples (Rari I-6-Id). This important manuscript has been published, along with its libretto, in facsimile as Leonardo Vinci, *Li zite 'ngalera*, Vol. [25] of *Italian Opera 1640-1770*, ed. Howard Mayer Brown (New York, 1979). It is one of the two known autograph scores by Vinci and is signed and dated on the first page: November 20, 1721. The score begins with Ciccariello's canzonetta, suggesting that originally there was no sinfonia, although one could have been added prior to performance. For some unknown reason, the final pages of Act I and II are missing, and the final inscription in Act III has been vigorously crossed out. Because the score contains numerous revisions and is almost illegible in places, it is described by Mayer Brown in the Preface to the facsimile as "evidently a composing score." If one looks closely at the revisions, however, one sees that the majority occur in the recitatives (14 out of 19 of the revisions) and those that occur in the arias usually involve cuts and cosmetic modifications rather than important compositional changes, suggesting that this is a final draft and not a composing score. The manuscript is written on two types of paper, one with the rearing horse watermark and the other with a fleur de lys, the two standard types of watermarks that can be found in contemporary Neapolitan scores of Vinci's operas.

under the direction of Roberto De Simone and then in Bari under the direction of Christophe Galland. From the latter derives the award winning recording by the Antonio Florio and the Cappella de'Turchini.[37]

*Li zite 'ngalera* was first performed during Carnival 1722 at the Teatro dei Fiorentini. The composer is not mentioned in the printed libretto, but a notice in the *Avvisi* singles out the Vinci's contribution to the success of the production:

> On Saturday the *opera in musica* in Neapolitan dialect entitled *Li zite 'ngalera* was put on stage for the first time at the Teatro Fiorentini, attaining the summit of satisfaction of the most excellent Viceregents who went there to listen to it with almost all the nobility....The music, composed by the celebrated maestro di cappella, Leonardo Vinci, contributed not a little to the excellence that was attained.[38]

*Li zite 'ngalera* was dedicated to Maria Livia Spinola, wife of the new viceroy Marc' Antonio Borghese, Prince of Sulmona who replaced Cardinal Schrattenbach in 1721, because of the Cardinal's involvement in the long contentious papal conclave that followed the death of Clement XI in 1719.[39] Vinci's growing reputation is suggested by the adjective "celebre" in the performance notice, while the reference to "almost all the nobility" belies the common notion that comic opera was cultivated primarily by a bourgeois audience. When it was revived at the Teatro della Pace in November of 1724, the impresario justified the revival by stating that *Li zite 'ngalera* "made Naples crazy when it was done at the Fiorentini."[40]

The libretto of the 1722 production provides an incomplete list of the original cast—the presence of un-named singers perhaps indicative of the less-than-prestigious status of the comic theatre:[41]

---

[37] Leonardo Vinci, *Li zite 'ngalera*, Cappella de' Turchini, dir. Antonio Florio (Opus 111 OPS 30-212/213). Typical of many recordings of eighteenth-century operas, this one contains numerous cuts, allowing a full-length three-act opera to fit on two CDs. Although most of the twelve cuts involve recitative, there are five arias cut (one each for Carlo, Rapisto, Ciccariello, Maneca, and Col' Agnolo) as well as an arietta (Maneca). There is also a very large section of recitative cut in the middle of Act II that includes the only accompanied recitative (by chance, three of these omitted items are represented by examples in the following discussion: Examples 2.4, 2.5, and 2.7). An extended passage of recitative has been discreetly re-composed by Antonio Florio in Act I to make up for an entire page missing in the autograph in scene 12, as well as the addition of a Turkish dance that is identified as an anonymous "Danza dei Turchi" published in Nuremberg 1716. The accompanying notes by Giulia Anna Romana Veneziano, are a shortened version of the notes accompanying the libretto for the Bari production.

[38] *Avvisi di Napoli*, January 6, 1722, No. 2.

[39] Benedikt, *Das Königreich Neapol unter Kaiser Karl VI*, 213-14.

[40] Libretto in I-N, Soc. Storia Patria; Sartori, *I libretti italiani* ( No. 25413). Quoted in Scherillo, *L'opera buffa napoletana durante il Settecento*, 151. (See also Chapter 3.)

[41] Bernardo Saddumene, *Li zite 'ngalera: Commeddeja* (Naples: Lebraria de Ricciardo, 1722), *Italian Opera Librettos, 1649-1770,* 60 (New York: Garland, 1979).

| | | | |
|---|---|---|---|
| Carlo: | Giacomina Ferrara | Federico Mariano: | n.n. |
| Belluccia: | Poleta Costi | Col'Agnolo: | n.n. |
| Ciomma: | Rosa Cerillo | Meneca: | Semmuono de Farco |
| Titta: | Filippo Calantro | Rapisto: | Giovanne Romaniello |
| Assan: | n.n. | Ciccariello: | n.n. |
| | | Schiavottella: | Lavora Monti |

Simone de Falco, who was probably related to Vinci's former collaborator Michele de Falco, was a regular tenor at the Teatro dei Fiorentini from 1717 until 1731, achieving a considerable reputation playing transvestite *vecchia* roles. As previously mentioned, the bass Giovanni Romaniello and the sopranos Giacomina Ferrara, Ippolita Costi, and Rosa Cerillo first appeared at the Teatro Fiorentini in *Lo cecato fauzo*, and were closely associated with Vinci. Filippo Calantro may have been a younger sibling of the violinist Giacobbe Calandro who, according to Sigismondo, was a fellow student and friend of Vinci at the Conservatory.[42] These singers provide the core of the Teatro Fiorentini casts until 1724 when the opening of a second comic opera house, the Teatro della Pace, provided another outlet for their specialized talents.

*Li zite 'ngalera'* libretto was written by Bernardo Saddumene and is one of the "second generation" comedies which reaffirmed the importance of the Neapolitan dialect, characters, and setting, but retained elements of the Tuscanization experiment, such as the occasional use of serious characters and situations, "capa y espada" intrigue and Tuscan speech.[43]

> **Synopsis**: the plot concerns two couples, Belluccia and Carlo and Ciomma and Titta. Twelve years previous, Carlo Clemeno deserted Belluccia in Sorrento. He now lives in Vietri where he has fallen in love with a local beauty, Ciomma, who is also loved by Titta and by the barber Col'Agnolo. Having learned of Carlo's residence in Vietri, Bellucia disguises herself as a man named Peppariello in hopes of winning back Carlo. Her disguise is so successful that the much-loved Ciomma and her old aunt Meneca fall in love with him/her. The plot centers around the complex process of redirecting the wayward passions of Carlo and Ciomma which are the source of everyone's problems. The complications intensify in Act III with the preparations for a play wherein Belluccia/Peppariello

---

[42] Giuseppe Sigismondo, *Apoteosi dell'Arte Musicale* (Naples, 1820); unpublished manuscript in Berlin, catalogued as "Materialien zu einer Geschichte der Musik der Neapolitaner Schule), III, 105.

[43] For these reasons, Benedetto Croce condemns Saddumene for betraying the true substantial nature of the *commedia per musica* "which is the exact reproduction of Neapolitan low life" for the cultivation of a curious and confused type of romantic comedy (*I teatri di Napoli*, 240).

appears in a counter-disguise as a woman. Comedy is supplied not only by the two *vecchi*, Meneca and Col'Agnolo, who appear ridiculous because they try to interfere with the young lovers, but also by Meneca's old servant Rapisto and Col'Agnolo's young servant Ciccariello. The Tuscan element comes to the fore with the appearance of Capitano Federico Mariano, Belluccia's father, who threatens to kill Carlo for betraying his daughter. However, Bellucia and the other characters intercede on behalf of Carlo. After Carlo offers to pay for his crimes with his life and Belluccia in turn offers to die with Carlo, Mariano relents, forgives Carlo and blesses their betrothal, and together they sail back to Sorrento on the galley, hence the name of the opera, which translates literally as the "The Fiancées on the Galley."

The complexities of plot are balanced by the simple, direct language of poetry which may have influenced the poetic style of Pietro Metastasio. The young Roman poet was familiar with the *Li zite 'ngalera* and referred to it in several of his later *drammi per musica*,[44] most notably in *L'Olympiade*.

The vocal casting tends to enhance the symmetrical arrangement of the characters. The four young lovers are sung by high voices (three sopranos for Belluccia, Ciomma, and Carlo and an alto for Titta), while the three *vecchi* are sung by low voices (two tenors for Meneca and Col'Agnolo and bass for Mariano). Of the servants, the young Ciccariello is sung by a soprano while the old servant Rapisto is sung by a bass. This equivalence between high voices and young lovers and low voices and older people is achieved by using three transvestite roles: Carlo and Ciccariello are "trouser" roles while Maneca is a "drag" role. Because eighteenth-century comic opera rarely employed castrati, the alto role of Titta is thought to have been sung by Filippo Calantro, falsetto. However, considering the number of castrati that were being turned out by the conservatories in Naples, it seems more likely that Titta and other "falsettist" roles in the *commedia per musica* were probably sung by castrati who specialized in comic roles.[45] The transvestite roles combined with the disguises create the same type of complex intrigue and sexual ambiguity that was beloved by Venetian audiences in the seventeenth century.[46] The roles of Meneca, the old amorous woman sung by a tenor, and Ciccariello, the young amorous boy sung by a soprano, are

---

[44] Piero Weiss, "Ancora sulle origini dell'opera comica: il linguaggio: *Pergolesi Studies/Studi Pergolesiani,* Vol. I, ed. Francesco Degrada (Stuyvesant, N.Y., Pendragon Press, 1986), 129-34

[45] As in Rome and the Papal State where the ban on women appearing on the stage would have resulted in the regular use of castrati in females roles in comic opera.

[46] Nina Treadwell presents a fascinating exegesis on the implications of sexual ambiguity in *Li Zite 'ngalera* in "Female Operatic Cross-Dressing: Bernardo Saddumene's Li-

the eighteenth-century descendants of the comic characters of Venetian opera, such as Arnalta and Valletto in Monteverdi's *L'Incoronazione di Poppea* and Aristea and Tibrino in Cesti's *Orontea*.

## *Li zite 'ngalera* and its Opera Buffa Anticipations

Perhaps the most remarkable music in the opera occurs in the opening pages, in Ciccariello's arietta "Vorria reventare sorecillo." This piece has been quoted as an example of the influence of Neapolitan folksong on the music of the *commedia per musica*.[47] Not only does it have the 12/8 meter, minor mode, and flattened supertonic associated with Neapolitan folk-song, but its phrasing, which fits uneasily into standard rhythmic patterns of 12/8, suggests that this may actually be a Neapolitan street-song:

Example 2.3 "Vorria reventare sorecillo" *Li zite 'ngalera* I/i

The arietta is basically a monophonic song with the string orchestra playing brief unison interludes between the vocal phrases in the style of the *colascione*, the guitar-like instrument of the Neapolitan streets.[48] In this opening scene the young servant sits alone outside his master's shop in the early hours of the morning with *colascione* in hand, singing his complaint on the loneliness of bachelorhood. The use of a popular canzonetta at the beginning of the opera was a convention that dates back to the origins of the genre in *La Cilla*, and is employed for its symbolic value

---

bretto for Leonardo Vinci's 'Li zite'n Galera' (1722)" *Cambridge Opera Journal* (July 1998): 131-56

[47] Transcribed in part in Nicola D'Arienzo, "Origini dell'opera comica" *Rivista musicale italiana*, VI (1899), 473-74, and in full in Robinson, *Naples and Neapolitan Opera*, 222-24.

[48] Strohm, *Die italienische Oper im 18. Jahrhundert*, 151.

as if to announce to the audience that "voi entrate nel mondo d'ogni giorno."[49] The opening scene of *Lo Scassone* is equally evocative, suggesting a rustic *veduta* from an old Neapolitan painting; the hero Peruonto sings a dance song "Songo le Forentane" accompanying himself on a *colascione,* while the ladies dance with tambourine and castanets.[50]

Anyone expecting to find more of these sorts of earthy Neapolitan flavors in the rest of the work will be disappointed. The score consists for the most part of a regular alternation of simple recitative and da capo aria. Some of the arias are somewhat reminiscent of J.S. Bach, such as Carlo's "Si ll'arme desperate," Titta's "Oh Dio pecche pecche," and Col'Agnolo's "Come quanno è notte scura:"

Example 2.4 "Come quanno è notte scura" *Li zite 'ngalera* III/xi

Although one might be tempted to regard these pieces as a manifestation of the "gusto austriarco" that was prevalent in Naples following the Austrian conquest, they result musically from the combination of the minor mode and a more contrapuntal and instrumental approach to melody and harmony, elements that are rare in Vinci's later music. Many of the aria melodies tend to be tuneful and dance-like, such as Carlo's elegant minuet "Mme senta allegrolillo" (see Example 2.5). Sometimes Vinci strives for a more simple and declamatory style of melody, of the type that would become common in his later operas. Ciomma's "Và dille, che'è no sgrato" has been singled out for its declamatory concision and dramatic insight, anticipating Vinci's later style[51] (see Example 2.6).

---

[50] *Lo Scassone*, Act I/i. Somewhat more refined and conventional descendants of this same convention can be found in Polidoro's serenade "Mentre l'erbetta" and Vanella's "Passo ninno da ccà," which initiate Pergolesi's *Il Flaminio* and *Lo frate 'nnamorato* respectively.

[51] D'Arienzo, "Origini dell'Opera comica," VI (1899), 481-82; Strohm, *Die italienische Oper im 18. Juhrhundert*, 149; and Weiss, "Ancora sulle origini dell'opera comica," 130-33. Claude Palisca has selected Bellucia's arietta "T'aggio mmideja" (Act I/xi) to exemplify the new "short, tuneful phrases" of comic opera in the 5th

Example 2.5 "Mme senta allegrolillo" *Li zite 'ngalera* I/iv

Example 2.6 "Và dille, che'è no sgrato" *Li zite 'nglera* I/i

edition of Donald Jay Grout and Claude V. Palisca, *A History of Western Music* (New York; Norton, 1996), 452-53. The difficulties in proof-reading Neapolitan are exemplified by the fact that the aria title appears differently in the text and the example and both versions are incorrect; although the inconsistency was weeded out in the 6th and 7th editions, the "j" (which is actually important in coordinating the end rhyme of the arietta and following recitative) is still missing.

The peculiar ritornello, with its thrice repeated motives in the bass accompanied by choral strokes in the upper strings was probably intended to accompany some type of prodding or dismissive gesture from Ciomma who wants Col'Agnolo to deliver her amorous message to Peppariello/Bellucia.

The arias of *Li zite 'ngalera* differ from those in Vinci's heroic operas in their modest scoring and absence of coloratura, resulting in simpler, less ornate melodies and smaller formal dimensions. The orchestra is expanded and coloratura introduced on one occasion, Capitano Mariano's only aria "Or più non mi fa guerra." It is no coincidence that this aria, scored for two trumpets, two oboes, strings and continuo, is allotted to the only heroic character of the cast, the only character to use the Tuscan dialect. The combination of Tuscan poetry, the trumpets and oboes, and the coloratura are specifically exploited for their heroic connotations.[52] Only in the march, which introduces this scene, and perhaps in the lost overture, are the the trumpets and oboes used again.

With the exception of Carlo's final recitative/arioso "Si date me la morte," Bellucia's "Qual doppo lunga e faticosa caccia" is the only other accompanied recitative in the opera. This is a setting from the seventh canto of Tasso's *Gerusalemme liberata*, which Belluccia reads, after Col'Agnolo has comically mutilated a passage of Tasso from the chapter in order to show him how this poetry should be read. The strings here function almost as aural quotation marks or italics. Although this passage of recitative is accompanied by string orchestra, it is rather different from the accompanied recitatives in Vinci's heroic operas for which he was to attain a certain renown. Instead of free recitative verse, this is a setting of two stanzas of narrative poetry (the second strophe beginning at m.8), with each stanza set to similar music, creating a closed form (a-a') in F major, replete with a key signature. The repetitive formulaic nature of the musical setting suggests that Vinci was approximating or even adopting one of the formulas that contemporary bards employed for reciting Tasso: accompanying themselves on a stringed instrument.[53] The rather archaic quality of "Qual doppo lunga," derived from the ancient reciting formulas, may be the reason why Dent described the voice part as remniscent of Jacopo Peri's monodic recitative, which also derives from this tradition. [54]

---

[52] The ritornello and first vocal period are transcribed in Weiss, "Ancora sulle origini dell'opera comica," 145-46.

[53] Burney describes just such a recital during his visit to Rome in 1770 when one Mazzanti sang "the poem of Tasso to the same melody as the Baccarolli do at Venice, with infinite taste, accompanying himself with the violin;" Charles Burney, *Music, Men and Manners in France and Italy: 1770*, ed. H. Edmond Poole (London: Folio Society, 1969), 139.

[54] Edward J. Dent, "Notes on Leonardo Vinci," *The Musical Antiquary* IV (1912/13), 196.

Example 2.7 "Qual doppo lunga" *Li zite 'ngalera* II/ix

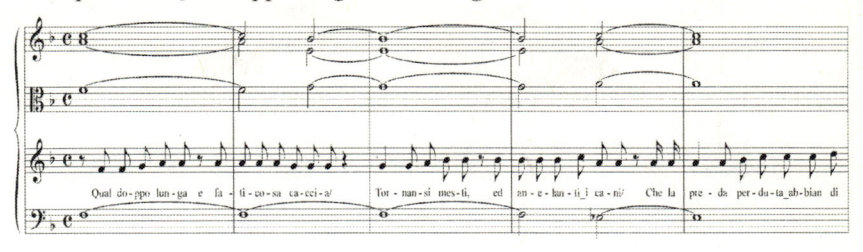

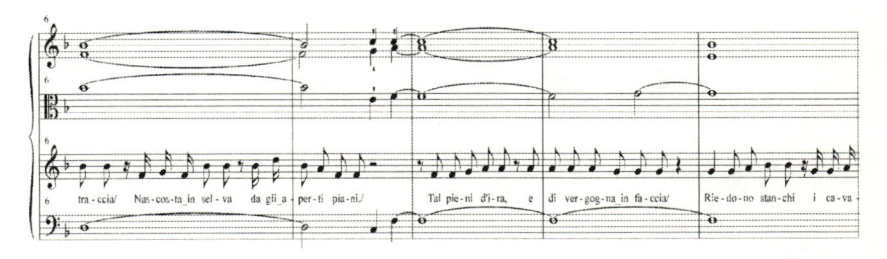

The other pieces in the opera that stand out are the ensembles, which consist of two duets, a trio, a quartet, and a quintet, plus the miniature final *coro*. Two of these, the duet "Che buò che spera" and the trio "Fortura, cana, o Dio!" are treated essentially as exit *da capo* arias for two and three voices; the characters each have their own text which has been set as a single melody shared between the soloists in a dialogue, with the voices coming together only at the cadences. The comic duet "Core, mio carillo" in Act III is based on a double disguise. The servant boy Ciccariello, portrayed by a woman, is disguised as a girl and is requested by Ciomma to act out a love scene with the old servant Rapisto.[55] They sing a mock love duet in A major, complete with written-out cadenzas. The final ritornello is interrupted as they burst out in laughter and then, in recitative, decide to act out a lovers quarrel. The two servants enter into an duel of insults sung as a patter song in Presto 12/8 meter. The conrasted bipartite form would become a popular aria form in late eighteenth-century comic opera.

The quartet and quintet at the end of Acts I and II have been singled out as predecessors of the *opera buffa* finale. In contrast to the finales in late eighteenth-century comic opera, these are in a single section with no changes of texture, meter, and situation, the Act I finale only seventeen measures long, and the Act II finale only twenty-two measures. Although the former is incomplete, it appears that only the final page is missing; the text has been sung once and, without a modulation to the dominant,

---

[55] Excerpts from both duets, "Che buò che spera" and "Core, mio carillo," are transcribed in D'Arienzo, "Origini dell'Opera comica," 482-86.

one does not expect a binary form; without a second strophe of text, one does not expect *da capo* form. In spite of their brevity, they have the basic ingredients of the *opera buffa* finale. The librettist has brought all his comic characters on stage and involved them in some conflict (the commotion over Ciccariello shaving Rapisto in Act I and Col'Angolo stuck in a window in Act II), the finale occurring at the moment of greatest tension when the insults begin to fly. In the Act I finale, Saddumene has even included one of the romantic characters, Ciomma, to produce a quintet.[56] The busy accompaniment of unison violins and continuo, especially of the Act II quartet, provides a continuous framework upon which the insults of the comedians are superimposed. This is a very early example of a fecund technique that would transform ensemble writing through the infusion of newly developed idioms and techniques of eighteenth-century music.[57]

Example 2.8 "Vi che masto" *Li zite 'ngalera* II/xviii

[56] The first half of the quartet in Act I is transcribed in D'Arienzo, "Origini dell'Opera comica," 486-88.
[57] Dent, from a Mozartian perspective, regards Vinci's ensembles as closely related to the style of Scarlatti, with treatment of the violins "decidely old-fashoned;" Edward J.

As the century progressed, the librettists gradually began the verses for the finale further away from the end of the Act. By 1760, Carlo Goldoni would begin the verses for the finale to Act I and Act II of *La buona figliuola* two or three pages before the end of the act (sixty-three and eighty-four verses as opposed to ten and thirteen verses in Saddumene's finales). These extended finale verses, combined with the new symphonic techniques of the mid-century, allowed Piccinni to compose finales 360 and 280 measures long, finales which can be termed Mozartian both in form and style.[58] Because of the backward extension of the comic finale, the finales in *Li zite 'ngalera* should be compared only with the final *imbroglio* section of the classic comic finale rather than the entire piece.[59] Therefore, the main difference between the finales of the Neapolitan *commedia per musica* and the Classical *opera buffa* is that the lead-up to the *imbroglio* was intended to be set as recitative in the former and as a series of connecting ensembles in the latter. In *Lo Scassone*, something of this backward extension is suggested by the use of two consecutive quartets connected at the end of Act II by recitative (of fourteen and sixteen lines respectively) accommodating the entrance and exit of a two characters.

Vinci would not have attended all of the performances of *Li zite 'n galera*. By the tenth of February he was in Rome, his presence attested to by a caricature of the composer that is now in the Pushkin Museum in Moscow: "L. Vinci Napolitana famoscisima compositor di Musica & Teatri/ fatto da Mei Cav. Ghezzi 10 Febbraio 1722."[60] According to Ghezzi, by 1722 Vinci was already regarded as "famoscisma" outside of Naples. Cultural links between Rome and Naples during the Habsburg regime were strong and numerous and were intensified when Marc Antonio Borghese, Prince of Sulmona, was appointed viceroy of Naples inApril of 1721.[61] Although the reason for Vinci's trip is not known, while in Rome he probably made connections with the Teatro Alibert, which would furnish him with his first commission for an opera outside Naples. Ghezzi's caricature of Vinci will in turn be used as a sketch for the oft-reproduced full-length caricature of the composer (see Chapter 9).

Dent, "Ensembles and Finales in 18th century Italian Opera," *Internationale Musik-gesell-schaft, Sammelbände* 12 (1910-11), 115.
[58] Niccolò Piccinni, *La Cecchina, ossia La buona figliuola*, Vol. [80] *Italian Opera 1640-1770*.
[59] Reinhard Strohm, *Die italienische Oper im 18. Jahrhundert*, 157-58.
[60] Giancarlo Rostirolla, "Nuovi documenti sulla presenza di Leonardo Vinci a Roma" Paper presented at the conference *Leonardo Vinci: architetture sonore nella Napoli del viceregno austriaco*, 10-12 June 2002. Reproduced in Giancarlo Rostirolla, *Il "Mondo Novo" musicale di Pier Leone Ghezzi*, with essays by Stefano La Via and Anna Lo Bianco (Rome: Accadema Nazionale d Santa Cecila & Milan: Skira, 2001), 244.
[61] Benedikt, *Das Königreich Neapol unter Kaiser Karl VI*, 214-25.

## The *Commedia per Musica* Abandoned

Vinci's activities over the next year can be traced in some detail because of the author's discovery of payment records or *fede di credito* in the Archivio Storico del Banco di Napoli, which document payments made to him by the impresario at the Teatro Fiorentini, Berardino Bottone. These payment records are traceable through Bottone's accounts; Vinci, like most musicians of the time, probably would not have had a bank account. The reason that these payment records are so informative is that each contains a detailed description of the goods or services that were being paid for so that the banks could "verify that the payment conditions had been fully met before paying a *fede di credito*."[62] Besides the new information these records shed on the life of Vinci, they also show the inner workings of an Italian opera theatre during the first half of the eighteenth century.

On July 17, 1722 the first of a series of payments was made by Bottone for twenty ducats "to Lonardo Vinci on account of the opera that he must do at the Teatro Fiorentino in the month of September of 1722;" this payment, however, was not for Vinci but was to be given "by him to Aniello Barba."[63] No mention is made of why he has to pass on these twenty ducats, presumably a debt of some sort. This type of deflected payment, known as *bancali*, was very common at the time and can be traced back to the beginnings of the banking system in Naples in the late sixteenth century.[64] The next two payments, both issued on July 27 for ten ducats each, were for Vinci, with one of the payments specifying that the composer is to present these "to the cashier Genaro Russo;" this record also mentions that it brings the composer's payment to forty ducats with "the others he has received from our bank and are on account of the composition in music that Vinci is now making for the forthcoming opera at the Teatro Fiorentino according to their agreement."[65] By August 19 the score of the opera, which now had a title, was presumably complete, with two payments for five and twenty-five ducats made to Vinci for "the composition of the music he has been writing for the opera entitled *La festa di Bacco* for the Teatro dei Fiorentini."[66]

---

[62] *The Historical Archive of Banco di Napoli* (Naples: Banco di Napoli, 1988) 20.
[63] Archivio Storico dell'Istituto Banco di Napoli—Fondazione: Banco di Spirito Santo, *Libro Maggiore del 1722* (I Semestre, fol. 2729) conto intestato a Bernardino Bottone: Giornale copiopolizze di casse del 1722, matricola 1097, partite estinte il 17 Luglio, 558.
[64] *The Historical Archive of Banco di Napoli*, 18-22. The oldest surviving *fede di credito* in the Banco di Napoli from 1590 is one of these *Bancali* that functioned somewhat like paper money, which was not common in Italy until the late 19th century.
[65] Archivio Storico dell'Istituto Banco di Napoli—Fondazione: Banco di Spirito Santo, *Libro maggiore del 1722* (I Semestre, fol. 2729), conto intestato a Berardino Bottone: Giornale copiopolizze di casse del 1722, matricola 1097, partite estine il 27 Luglio, 574.
[66] Ibid., (II semestre, fol. 1216), Giornali copiopolizze di casse del 1722 (mat. 1104) Partite estinte il 19 Agosto, folio 1216, 48.

The librettist with whom Vinci collaborated on *La festa di Bacco* was Francesco Tullio, one of the originators of the *commedia per musica* and the Tuscan experiment of 1718.[67] When the opera was premièred on August 29, the notice in the *Avvisi di Napoli* presents another title:

> Saturday evening of last week was the first performance of the *opera in musica* in Neapolitan dialect, entitled *Il Trionfo di Bacco*, at the Teatro dei Fiorentini, which for the composition of the words and for that of the music has merited universal applause.[68]

*La festa di Bacco*, as the title appears in the libretto, was dedicated to yet another new viceroy, Cardinal Michael Friedrich Althann, Bishop of Waitzen. The prince of Sulmona, who fell out of favor with the Emperor over a family dispute concerning his son's marriage, was replaced by one of the Emperor's most trusted diplomats. Cardinal Althann had engineered the papal conclave of 1720/21, which resulted in the election of a pope sympathetic to Habsburg concerns.[69] In contrast to the previous spate of viceroys, Cardinal Althann's regime was to last until 1728 and many of Vinci's subsequent operas for Naples were dedicated to him.

After the première on August 29, 1722, three additional payments for ten ducats each were made on September 2 and 11 "for the composition of the *opera in musica* that Lonardo has made entitled *La Festa di Bacco* that has actualy been performed at the Teatro dei Fiorentini and for the other tasks he has done and is doing."[70] In all Vinci received one hundred ducats for the composition of the opera, paid in installments. The first was an advance of twenty ducats paid on July 17 upon beginning the composition of his opera, the second, another advance of twenty ducats on July 27 while composing the score, and then thirty for the completion of the score on August 19. Another thirty in three ten ducat payments followed after the première for overseeing the rehearsals and conducting the traditional first three performances.[71] A running total of Vinci's hundred ducats is included in most of the payment records. The use of the Neapolitan form of his name in his payment records suggests that he regularly went by the name "Lonardo," reserving the more formal "Leonardo" for his dealings with the court and abroad.

---

[67] Libretto in I-Nc and US-NYp; Sartori, *I libretti italiani* (No. 10060). Synopsis in Scherillo, *L'opera buffa napoletana,* 116-17. In the libretto Tullio is identified by his pet name, Col'Antonio Feralintisco.

[68] *Avvisi di Napoli,* September 1, 1722 (No. 367).

[69] Benedikt, *Das Konigreich Neapol unter Kaiser Karl VI,* 213.

[70] Archivio Storico dell'Istituto Banco di Napoli—Fondazione: Banco di Spirito Santo, *Libro Maggiore del 1722* (II Semestre) *Giornali copiapolizze di cassa* 1722 (mat. 1006) Partite estinte il 11 Settembre, folio 1216, 110.1216).

[71] This system with advances is still used today in the construction industry of Naples.

Later that year, in October, there was a revival of *La festa di Bacco* or *Trionfo di Bacco* in the town of Vasto to celebrate the induction of the Marchese d'Avalos into the Order of the Golden Fleece.[72] While Vinci may have been involved in this production, he would have been extremely busy at this time with the première of his first *dramma per musica* at the Teatro S. Bartolomeo and the revival of *Il castiello sacchiato* at the Fiorentine. The latter had originally been a collaborative effort between Vinci and Michele de Falco. Because the original composer designation to de Falco was omitted for this revival, Prota-Giurleo was of the opinion that Vinci replaced the music that de Falco had written for the original production of 1720.[73] This, however, is contradicted by a statement in the libretto which simply reverses the order of the attributions note in the original (see above):

> All the recitative and the unmarked arias in the first and second act are by Signore Michele de Falco....All the arias, however, designated with the sign % are by Leonardo Vinci, maestro di cappella Napoletano, who has set the entire third act both the recitatives as well as the arias.[74]

Although Vinci was involved in this revival, it would not have been a high priority, the composer's attention being focussed on the production of his first *dramma per musica* (see Chapter 3).

The next payment to Vinci, made on October 12th, was neither for this revival nor the *dramma per musica*, but "on account of the opera he must set in music as *maestro di cappella* of the Teatro dei Fiorentini in the future Carnival."[75] Vinci's carnival opera for 1723 was *Lo Labborinto*, described as a "Commedeja del lo segnore Bernardo Saddumene"— the librettist of *Li Zite 'n galera*.[76] The payment of five ducats mentions that "the contract negotiated between them is in the hands of the notary Giovanni Tufarelli of Naples" indicating that opera commissions were

---

[72] Ausilia Magaudda & Danilo Constantini, "Le corrispondenze dall'Abruzzo nella *Gazzetta di Napoli*: un contributo per la riconstruzione dei rapporti musicale fra la capitale e le province" in *Archivo Storico per la Province Napoletane* (Naples: Società Napoletana di Storia Patria, 2000), 397-400. The *commedia per musica* was part of a series of celebrations that included three plays "in prosa" as well as a solemn Te Deum "da due cori di musici" with the usual canon rounds and illuminations. Although there is no indication of the singers who took part in this revival, the opera was performed three times and accompanied by ballets danced by "six pages of the marchessa."

[73] Ulisse Prota-Giurleo, "Leonardo Vinci" *Convegno musicale* II (1965), 5.

[74] Libretto in B-Bc, GB-Lbm, and US-NYp; Claudio Sartori, *I libretti italiani* (No. 5196).

[75] Archivio Storico dell'Istituto Banco di Napoli—Fondazione: Banco di Spirito Santo, *Libro Maggiore del 1722* (II Semestre), conto intestato di Berardino Bottone: *Giornali copiopolizze di cassa* 1722 ( mat.1107) Partite estinte il 12 Ottobre, folio 1568, 146.

[76] Libretto in I-Ra, B-Bc, and US-NYp; Sartori, *I libretti italiani*, No. 14080.

legal contracts between impresario and composer requiring the necessary documentation. The contract is referred to in the next payment of January 30, 1723 for twenty-one ducats for "the opera that must be performed in the Carnival of the current year 1723 which this Lonardo is at present composing in music in conformity with the past contract."[77] With the next payment of ten ducats on March 1st the legal documentation for this commission had become more than just a formality; the ten ducats were paid:

> by virtue of the royal mandate of the auditor general Don Muzio di Majò sent on the fifth of the previous month in documents of the Chancellor and are faithful to that sum determined on the first of last month, by which he was ordered to pay them to Lonardo Vinci.[78]

It would seem that at the beginning of February of 1723 Vinci took Bottone to court for failing to fulfill the commitments of his contract. The events of this court case are difficult to trace, taking place in the brief time between Vinci's last payment on January 30 and the Auditor General's mandated payment on February 5. What Vinci's cause for complaint would have been is not clear, other than the usual problem of the impressario being short on cash and late on payments. Opera has always been an expensive art form and when produced as a commercial venture, made for narrow profit margins, with the impresario often on the verge of ruin.[79] Perhaps, the only thing unusual thing about this type of small-claims case is that there were not more of them in opera, especially in Naples where the lawsuit was something of a speciality.[80]

Part of the problem may have been that the advance on *Lo Labborinto* was a little meagre and makeshift, with Vinci receiving only five ducats when he began the composition. The payment of

---

[77] Archivio Storico dell'Istituto Banco di Napoli—Fondazione: Banco di Spirito Santo, *Libro Maggiore del 1723* (I Semestre), *Giornale copiopolizze di cassa* 1723, (mat. 1111) Partite estinte il 30 Gennaro, folio 1716, 115.

[78] Ibid., (mat. 1115) Partite estinte il 1 Marzo, folio 1716, 180.

[79] See John Rosselli, *The Opera Industry n Italy from Cimarosa to Verdi: The Role of the Impresario* (Cambridge: Cambridge University Press, 1984).

[80] According to Joseph Addison, " when a Neapolitan Cavalier has nothing else to do, he gravely shuts himself up in his closet, and falls a tumbling over his Papers to see if he can start a Law suit, and plague any of his Neighbours" (*Remarks on Several Parts of Italy & ct. in the Years 1701, 1702, 1703,* 207-208). In opera there may have been an unwritten law about settling these matters out of court, hence Metatasio's anger with Porpora when he took the impresario Francesco Cavanna to court over the premiere of *Issipile* in 1732 (Kurt Markstrom "The Eventual Premiere of *Issipile*: Porpora and the Palchetti War." Paper at the conference *Music in Eighteenth-Century Italy*, Cardiff, June 1998).

twenty-one ducats for the second part of the advance on January 30, refers to "the other nine ducats he has received from Bottone," so somewhere along the line Vinci received another four ducats, bringing his advance to thirty ducats rather than the forty he received for *La Festa di Bacco*. However, the next payment, on March 4 of ten ducats, states emphatically that it was "to fulfil the 100 ducats for the final opera to be produced by him at the Teatro dei Fiorentini during carnival 1723."[81] Thus there is an obvious interruption of fifty ducats in Vinci's payments, though these (as well as the stray four ducats) could have been paid out in cash or in a deflected, *bancali* payment. An additional payment follows on March 24 of thirty ducats, which does not belong to the missing payments for *Lo Laborinto*, but is:

> an honorarium for his efforts made in the revival of the opera entitled *Il castiello sacchiato* done several years ago at the Teatro dei Fiorentini, and repeated in the month of November 1722 at the same theatre.[82]

It is possible that this long-delayed payment for the revival of *Il castiello sacchiato*, was what initially compelled Vinci to resort to the courts. In accepting payment Vinci agreed that "remaining satisfied with this payment, he cannot seek anything more in this regard."[83] Not surprisingly this court case brought about the end of the collaboration between Vinci and Bottone, as well as his position as virtual house composer or, as the initial payment for *Lo Laborinto* refers to him, "come maestro di Cappella nel Teatro dei Fiorentini."

Arias from both *Lo labborinto* and *La festa di Bacco* survive in an anthology in the Santini Collection in Münster.[83] Some of these arias show a considerable change in style compared with those in *Lo cecato fauzo* and *Li zite 'ngalera*. For example the following ritornellos could easily serve as preludes to heroic arias from Vinci's Metastasian operas: the ritornello to "Voglio vedere mprimmo" would be appropriate to a gently syncopated *cantabile* aria, that to "Sento nò speretillo" would be appropriate to an heroic *alla breve*, and that to "Comm'à cerva feruta" would anticipate the agitated *aria parlante*:

---

[81] Archivio Storico dell'Istituto Banco di Napoli—Fondazione: Banco di Spirito Santo, *Libro Maggiore del 1723* (I Semestre) *Giornale copiopolizze di casse* 1723 (mat. 1113) Partite estinte il 4 Marzo, folio 1934, 89.

[82] Ibid., (mat. 1115) Partite estinte il 24 Marzo, folio 1934, 259.

[83] Anthology 4239 in the Santini-Sammlung in the Bibliothek des Bischöflichen Priesterseminars contains nine arias from *La festa de Bacco* in 1 Teil and three arias from *Lo labborinto* in 2 Teil.

THE COMMEDIA PER MUSICA

Example 2.9a "Voglio vedere mprimmo" *La festa di Bacco*

Excample 2.9b "Sento nò speretillo" *La festa di Bacco*

Example 2.9c "Com'à cerva feruta" *Lo labborinto*

The aria "O chisto, o la morte" from *La festa di Bacco* anticipates Vinci's later formal experiments by introducing largo recitative passages at the beginning of each vocal period.[85]

 *Lo labborinto* was to be the last of the series of comic operas that Vinci produced at the Teatro dei Fiorentini. The reason for the abrupt end to his successful comic career probably has as much to do with the new opportunities that came his way at the Palazzo Real and the Teatro Bartolomeo during the fall of 1722 (see Chapter 3) as it does with the falling out between Vinci and Bottone during the winter of 1723. Vinci began his career as an exclusive composer of the *commedia per musica* and ended his career as an exclusive composer of the *dramma per musica*, with little overlap. This contrasts with the careers of composers such as Leo and Pergolesi, who composed for either the comic or heroic theatre, depending upon the commission. In fact, this development appears to have resulted in the two Leonardos, Vinci and Leo, in effect, trading places. Leo began his career as a composer of the *dramma per musica* and, after a tentative start, produced a regular series of works for the Teatro San Bartolomeo and the Real Palazzo. With Vinci's move into the heroic genre, Leo's commissions from the court all but disappeared and, as if to compensate for the lack of work, he produced a series of comic operas, first at the Teatro Fiorentini and then at the Teatro Nuovo. These events suggest that Vinci used the *commedia per musica* as a vehicle for establishing a local reputation. The Neapolitan dialect, however, restricted these works to the Regno; to establish a European reputation, it was necessary to cultivate the cosmopolitan genres, the oratorio, the intermezzo and above all the *dramma per musica* or *opera seria*. Thus, once Vinci had established a name for himself as a composer of the *opera seria*, he abandoned the *commedia per musica*.

---

[85] In a detailed discussion of "Simbé so'nzemprecella" from *La festa di Bacco*, Reinhard Strohm contrasts its concise classic text setting with that in "Vi par che siate robba" from Scarlatti's *Trionfo dell'onore* (Reinhard Strohm, *Italienische Opernarien*, I, 22-28).

# 3

# TRANSFER TO THE HEROIC THEATER

## The Rosary Oratorio

Vinci was busy during the fall of 1722 and winter of 1723. He composed the oratorio *Le Gloria del S.S. Rosario* for the Congregation of the Rosary in the Royal convent of S. Caterina a Formiello to celebrate the Festival of the Rosary on the first Sunday in October.[1] The Congregation was a lay confraternity, one of many similar institutions in Naples and throughout the Kingdom, that went under various names (congregazione, confraternità, arciconfraternità, oratorio, ritiro, etc.), with more than three thousand societies documented within the Regno di Napoli during the period 1588-1800.[2] Although involved in charitable work and alms, they were primarily self-serving institutions concerned with the spiritual practices of their members and with the *culto dei morti*, the burial service and the administering of benefices. As an extension of the latter, they were also involved in the payment and administration of dowries, usually intended for the daughters and nieces of their constituency. The confraternities also had an important role in the artistic life of the kingdom, producing elaborate oratories, chapels, altars, statues, and paintings as well as services, processions and concerts to celebrate their associated feasts and political events of the kingdom. Because of the prominence of music within the confraternities, several were devoted to musicians, such as the S. Cecilia in the church of Montesanto, and the Monte dei musici in the church of S. Giorgio, which functioned somewhere between confraternity and professional musicians union.[3] During the first half of the eighteenth century, the Confraternity of the Holy Rosary at S. Caterina a Formiello featured some of the more important musical

---

[1] Although not listed in Sartori's *I libretti italiani*, there is a copy of the libretto in the National Library in Naples: *Le Glorie del SS. Rosario: Oratorio in musica da recitarsi nella Congregatione di Santa Caterina à Formello di questa Città per la Festività della Vergine del Rosario Nostra Signora in questo presento Anno 1722*, Musica del Signor Lonardo Vinci (Naples: per il Monaca, 1722).

[2] Danilo Costantini and Ausilia Maguadda, "Attività musicali promosse dalle confraternite laiche nel Regno di Napoli (1677-1763)" in *Fonti d'archivio per la storia della musica e dello spettacolo a Napoli tra XVI e XVIII secolo*, ed. Paologiovanni Maione (Naples: Editoriale Scientifica, 2001), 79.

[3] Ibid., 98-101 and 119-22

performances.[4] The Congregazione del S.S. Rosario consisted of a series of fraternities under the direction of the Dominican order, which promoted the practice of the Rosary and a more uniform system of its recitation.[5]

Records at S. Caterina a Formiello refer to Vinci's "ufficio di maestro di cappella" (see Chapter 10).[6] Although it is not known when this appointment was made or, if indeed this was an actual position, the composer's association with this institution may go back to the beginning of his career.   Sigismondo lists an oratorio, *La Protezione del Rosario,* from 1719 and, though there is neither a score, libretto nor performance notice, his statement carries a certain authority since he was a member of the confraternity and had access to their records.[7] The libretto to *Le Glorie del S.S. Rosario* unfortunately does not match up with either of the two surviving oratorio scores by Vinci: *Maria Dolorata* and the "Prime Parte" of an untitled oratorio for four voices, Maria, Angelo, Alba, Selim, both in the Conservatory library in Naples.  While it is possible that *Le Glorie del S.S. Rosario* and *La Protezione del Rosario* are one and the same work, like *La festa di Bacco* and *Trionfo di Bacco,* it seems more likely that these are two different rosary oratorios—two different lost oratorios by Vinci.

## First Essay in the *Dramma per Musica*

*Publio Cornelio Scipione* was premièred at the Teatro San Bartolomeo on November 4, 1722 in celebration of the nameday of Emperor Charles. Most of Vinci's Neapolitan operas were produced for the birthday or nameday of the Emperor or Empress, hence the dates October 1, and November 4, August 28, and July 8 feature prominently in the chronicles of Neapolitan opera during the Austrian regime.  St. Charles day, November 4, was particularly important for Naples since it was also the nameday of the last Spanish Habsburg and the first Spanish Bourbon. Although the birthday or nameday began solemnly with a festal Mass,

---

[4] Ibid., 131-36.

[5] Herbert Thurston, "Confraternity of the Holy Rosary" in *The Catholic Encyclopedia: An International Work of Reference on the Constitution, Doctrine, Discipline, and History of the Catholic Church,* ed. Charles G. Herbermann, Edward A. Pace, Condé B. Pallen, et al. (New York: Robert Appleton, 1912).

[6] Quoted in Salvatore Di Giacomo, *I quattro antichi conservatorii di musica di Napoli,* (Milan: Remo Sandron, 1928), II , 84.

[7] Giuseppe Sigismondo, *Apoteosi dell'Arte Musicale* (Naples, 1820; unpublished manuscript in Berlin catalogued as "Materialien zu einer Geschichte der Musik der Neapolitaner Schule"), III, 110. It is possible that Vinci's devotion to the rosary may go back to his youth; the Pignatelli family, to whom he was bound as "vassal," founded the lovely Chapel of Santa Maria del Rosario in the Cathedral of Strongoli in 1687. Salvatore Gallo, *Vecchio Campanile: La Chiesa di Strongoli nella storia della città dll'alto medio evo alla soppressione del Vescovato* (Cosenza: Fasano Editore), 189.

the main event was the *cuccagna*, a strange combination of Classical allegory, Baroque theatrical architecture, and base popular spectacle. The *cuccagna* was an elaborately designed float based on a classical subject in honour of the monarch, set up in the Piazza Real Palazzo (see Plate 2 on p. 48). The float was made up primarily of ham, sausage and cheese, and once the formal ceremony was complete, it was unceremoniously sacked by the hungry crowd.[8] After watching this bizarre spectacle from the palace balconies, the Viceroy and his court would proceed to an ornately decorated theatre for the première of a new opera. The juxtaposition of the *cuccagna* and the opera seems to have been rather maliciously designed to emphasize the difference between the brutish commoners and the cultured aristocracy that was quite in keeping with a kingdom infamous for its unequal distribution of wealth. Therefore the gala productions of Vinci's Neapolitan operas should be perceived against the bizarre background of the *cuccagna*.

The extended notice in the *Avvisi di Napoli* suggests that Vinci's first essay in the heroic genre was a great success:

> Wednesday...was produced at the Teatro San Bartolomeo, the new opera entitled *Publio Cornelio Scipione*, which attained universal applause for the music, being by the celebrated Maestro di Cappella Leonardo Vinci; as well as for the acknowledged good taste of the impresario...; for the performers, among those who distinguished themselves, the virtuoso Giovanni Battista Pacini who created the principal role of *Scipione*, the well-known virtuosa Faustina Bordoni who created the part of *Analgilda*, and the important virtuosa Antonia Mereghi who with sublime spirit performed the part of *Lucejo*, as also the Virtuoso Annibale Pio Fabri who played the role of *Indibile*; the other singers, being among the best on the contemporary Italian stage, also did themselves honor.[9]

Of the principals, Antonia Mereghi was singled out for her "sublime spirit" in spite of the presence of the great Faustina.[10] The opera remained on stage until the beginning of December. Another indication of the success of *Publio Cornelio Scipione* is found in a copy of the libretto which con-

---

[8] Heinrich Benedikt, *Das Königreich Neapel unter Kaiser Karl VI*, 619-20.

[9] *Avvisi di Napoli*, November 10, 1722 (no. 46).

[10] Faustina caught the fancy of Bonfacio Pecorone, a bass from the Cappella Real. In his memoirs, he tells an amusing story about how he sang the role of Neptune in the celebratory serenata at the palace, before the première of Vinci's opera and, wanting to hear Faustina, went directly to the theater in costume. At the end of the opera, he was compelled to walk home, still dressed as Neptune, causing considerable consternation among the palace guards. Stephen Shearon, "Musical Activity in the Early Eighteenth-Century Naples: The Memoirs of Bonifacio Pecorone," paper given at the conference: *Music in Eighteenth-Century Italy*, 12-15 July, Cardiff University, 1998.

**Plate 2.** *View of the Piazza and Palazzo Real of the Kingdom of Naples: designed by Renard, Architecte and engraved by Pellier, 1781.*[11]

tains a note in a contemporary hand: "with the music of this opera, the impresarios made great profits, thereby replacing the [orginal] expense, every night that it was performed."[12] The impresarios referred to are Nicolo Gaultieri and Aurelio del Po who had taken over the management of the Teatro San Bartolomeo after Nicola Serino's death.[13] Serino's domination of the Neapolitan theatrical scene, like that of Scarlatti, dated back to the late seventeenth century. It is likely that this change in theatre management was responsible for introducing the operas of younger composers, such as Porpora, Vinci, and Hasse, to the Neapolitan public.

*Publio Cornelio Scipione* is based on a libretto by Agostino Piovene, originally written in Venice in 1712 for Carlo Francesco Pollarolo.[14] The story of Publius Cornelius Scipio's conquest of Spain was popular during the early eighteenth century, particularly in Habsburg lands where it provided an illustrious antique parallel for the Emperor's campaigns in Spain during the War of Spanish Succession.[15] The libretto was revised

---

[11] [Jean Claude Richard] Abbé de Saint Non, *Voyage Pittoresque ou description des Royaumes de Naples et de Sicile* (Paris: 1781), I, Plate 94, opposite 78.

[12] *Publio Cornelia Scipione: Drama per musica: Da rappresentarsi nel Teatro di S. Bartolomeo il dì 4. Novembre di quest'Anno 1722.* (Naples: Presso Francesco Ricciardo, 1772); copy in I-Nc; Rari 10.7.5 (2).

[13] Benedetto Croce, *I teatro di Napoli: secolo XV-XVIII*, 252. Aurelio del Po is familiar in Handelian biography as the rogue who married Anna Strada because he could not afford to pay her salary.

[14] Strohm, *Italienische Opernarien* II, 227; citation to Pollarolo's opera in Taddeo Wiel, *I teatri musicale veneziani del settecento: catalogo delle opere in musica rappresentate nel secolo XVIII in Venezia* (Venice: Fratelli Visentoini, 1897), 31.

[15] Besides Piovene, Scipio provided the subject for libretti by Zeno and Salvi, the

for the Neapolitan production by Bernardo Saddumene, whose principal task was to rewrite and replace aria texts to accommodate the singers and composer, and to provide a comic intermezzo to be performed between the acts of the opera proper.[16] The Neapolitan love for comedy was such that the city could support two comic opera theatres and still insist that every heroic opera be fitted with these comic intermezzi. For *Publio Cornelio Scipione* Saddumene provided the intermezzo *Ermosilla/Bacocco,* which was performed by the comic duo Santa Marchesina and Gioacchino Corrado. The scores for both the opera and intermezzo have been lost, and only a handful of arias survive in anthologies.[17]

After the triumph of his first *dramma per musica* Vinci still had to complete what was to be his last commission for the Teatro dei Fiorentini, Saddumene's comedy *Lo labborinto,* which would, in turn, lead to a court case (see Chapter 2). Vinci also wrote the cantata *Parto ma non qual core* for his *prima donna* Faustina Bordoni upon her departure from Naples. A copy of this cantata for soprano and basso continuo now in Montecassino is dated 1723, and contains the inscription "La partenza dell Faustina."[18] With her next engagement in Florence for the summer, Faustina would have left Naples after the Carnival production of Sarro's *Partenope,* and therefore the cantata would have been written some time in the spring of 1723.

## The Last Palace Première

*Silla Dittatore,* Vinci's second *dramma per musica* and the first to survive complete, is the most traditional of his fifteen extant operas. With regards to its libretto, music, and production, *Silla* is the opera by Vinci that is most closely linked to the works of his predecessors in Naples: Scarlatti, Mancini, and Sarro. *Silla Dittatore* was premièred on October 1, 1723 in celebration of Emperor Charles's birthday, at the Real Palazzo in Naples. The notice in the *Avvisi di Napoli* reports that:

> in the evening they [the court] proceeded to the grand hall called "de' Svizzeri," where they listened to the *Opera in*

---

latter rearranged by Paolo Rolli in 1726 as *Scipione* and set to music by Handel. Winton Dean and John Merrill Knapp, *Handel's Operas 1704-1726,* 607.

[16] *Publio Cornelio Scipione: Drama per musica.*

[17] The arias "Col laccio al piede," "Perchè no vuoi ch'io parli" and "Quando rimbomba il tuono" can be found in an anthology (X.111) at the Bibliothèque du Conservatoire national de musique in Paris and the aria "Benchè scoglio alle tempeste" in an anthology (22-1-2) in Biblioteca del Conservatorio di Musica S. Pietro a Majella in Naples. Strohm, *Italienische Opernarien* II, 228.

[18] Ms. 6-B-20/8 (formerly 126 E 18); listed as Cantata no. 11 in Teresa Maria Gialdroni, "Vinci operista autore di cantate," *Studi in onore di Giulio Cattin* (Rome, Edizione Torre d'Orfeo, 1990), 321.

> *Musica*, entitled *Silla Dittatore*; it was preceded by a Prologue, alluding to the coronation of his Imperial and Catholic Majesty as King of Bohemia, [consisting] of two beautiful scenes, the first, representing the Valley of the Hegra with the rebellious giants and the other a celestial palace with the coronation of His Imperial Catholic Majesty.[19]

Neither the text nor the music of the Prologue has survived. Vinci probably composed the music to the Prologue; in his application to the Real Cappella in 1725, he makes mention of the "operas and prologues" that he composed for the Viceroy, "Monsignore d'Althann"[20] (see Chapter 4).

Later that month *Silla Dittatore* was produced for the public at the Teatro San Bartolomeo. The sequence of an official palace première followed by a commercial run at the San Bartolomeo reflects a venerable Neapolitan tradition. Many of Scarlatti's Neapolitan operas, commissioned for official birthdays or name days, had their premières at the Real Palazzo before beginning their commercial run at the Teatro San Bartolomeo.[21] The palace première of *Silla Dittatore*, like its prologue, gives this work a link with the old tradition of opera as court spectacle. It was the last of a long series of palace premières that date back to the origins of opera in Naples.[22] This break with tradition after *Silla* may be due to major renovations to the San Bartolomeo, which are mentioned in the performance notice concerning *Silla Dittatore* in the *Avvisi di Napoli*:

> Sunday evening [was] the first performance of the new *Opera in Musica* entitled *Silla Dittatore* at the Teatro di S. Bartolomeo which, accommodated with a new order of stalls and beautifully painted overall, produced a most noble view.[23]

These renovations made the San Bartolomeo a superior venue to the Sala de' Svizzeri for gala opera performances; subsequent palace galas were relegated to the occasional serenata. Cardinal Althann, perhaps used to the more luxurious Teatro Alibert in Rome, requested the renovations to the San Bartolomeo in order to bring it up to the standards of the Alibert which had been newly renovated by Francesco Galli Bibiena in 1719 (see below). The cast of *Silla Dittatore* consisted of:

| | | | |
|---|---|---|---|
| Silla: | Nicola Grimaldi | Emilia: | Marianna Benti Bulgarelli |
| Valeria: | Benedetta Sorosini | Pompeo: | Antonia Merighi |

---

[19] *Avvisi di Napoli*, October 5, 1723 (No. 41).

[20] Archivio di Stato di Napoli, Italia: Segreteria dei Viceré, fascio 1707, documenti pervenuti il 25/X/1725.

[21] *The New Grove Dictionary of Music and Musicians*, "Scarlatti, Alessandro: Worklist by Malcolm Boyd.

[22] See Ulisse Prota-Giurleo, *I teatri di Napoli nel '600: La commedia e le maschere* (Naples: Fasto Fiorentino, 1962).

[23]*Avvisi di Napoli*, October 19, 1723 (No. 43).

Domizio: Annibale Pio Fabbri   Plautilla: Santa Marchesina
Cloro:   Caterina Levi        Albino:    Gioacchino Corrado
        Stage architect: Giovanni Battista Olivero

With Nicola Grimaldi "Nicolino" and Marianna Benti Bulgarelli "La Romanina" in the lead roles and Gioacchino Corrado and Santa Marchesina in the comic roles, the cast is rather similar to those in Scarlatti's last Neapolitan operas.[24]

The libretto for *Silla Dittatore* is based on Vincenzo Cassiani's *Il tiranno eroe*, first set to music by Tomaso Albinoni for Venice in 1711.[25] The preface to the libretto mentions that "many arias throughout the opera have been altered in favor of the music," standard procedure when adapting old libretti. In addition, the scrupulous adaptor has admitted that several of these altered aria texts "have come from very renowned pens [and] in order not to defraud [them] of their deserved applause, will be distinguished with a star.*"[26] The story of *Silla Dittatore*, like that of Gamarra and Mozart's *Lucio Silla*, is an elaborated account of the enigmatic abdication of the Roman dictator Sulla in 79 BC:

> **Synopsis**: After the defeat of Mario and the republican conspirators, Silla captures Valeria, daughter of one of the republican leaders, Domizio. Although Silla loves Valeria, he swears vengeance against her and her father, Domizio, who is actually present in disguise as Valeria's servant. As her servant Silla enlists Domizio as go-between in his suit of Valeria. Domizio has meanwhile enlisted Silla's general, Albino, to his cause, to bring down the tyrant. In order to shore up his power, Silla has allied himself with the Nubian prince Cloro, intending to seal the alliance with marriage to his daughter Emilia. The daughter disapproves because she is in love with the patrician Pompeo who intends to ask Silla for her hand in marriage. Silla frees Valeria and declares his love. She responds that she could never love her father's enemy. Silla tells Emilia that he has accepted the request for her hand from a true hero which she interprets as Pompeo. At the beginning of Act II, Silla pursues his seduction of Valeria with the disguised Domizio compelled to play along. Emilia is shocked to find out that the suitor her father has accepted as her husband is Cloro. She scornfully rejects him and in anger he challenges his rival Pompeo to a duel.

---

[24] See cast lists for Scarlatti's late operas in Francesco Florimo, *La scuola musicale di Napoli e I suoi conservatori*, IV, 7-19.

[25] Strohm, *Italienische Opernarien*, II, 228; citation to Albinoni's opera in Wiel, *I teatri musicale veneziani del Settecento*, 26.

[26] [Vincenzo Cassiani] arr., *Silla Dittatore: dramma per musica* (Naples: Francesco Ricciardo, 1723), Preface; libretto in I-Mb & -Nc; Sartori, *I libretti italiani* (No. 22023).

Domizio and Valeria resolve that the tyrant must fall, but are caught by Silla in their farewell embrace, forcing him to reveal his true identity. As Domizio is led away to prison, Silla tells Valeria that if she now gives in to his desires, he will go easy on her father. To stall for time Valeria flatters Silla with hope. The insidious dictator then gives in to Emilia's wish to marry Pompeo, only to have her fiancée arrested on charges of treason, telling Emilia that the only way to save his life is to marry Cloro. As Pompeo is about to be executed, Albino releases both Pompeo and Domizio and together they lead a *coup d'état* against Silla. To arrive at a happy ending, the librettist introduces a counter-coup led by Valeria, who decides she is in love with her captor and will protect him against her father. Silla forgives the conspirators and abdicates, allowing for his union with Valeria and Emilia's with Pompeo.

The libretto of *Silla Dittatore* contains elements that look back to the turn of the century. In contrast to the heroes of the *dramma per musica*, Silla is indeed tyrannical and violent. For example, he is ready to kill his daughter for not approving his choice for her husband and is not afraid of using blackmail in order to win Valeria. Not only does Silla attain the love of Valeria but she turns against her father in order to defend Silla, while his daughter Emilia sides with the conspirators in order to save Pompeo from execution. This type of filial disobedience contrasts with the usual long-suffering heroines of the *dramma per musica*. Moreover, the cynical "all's fair in love and war" type of morality is closer to Minato than Metastasio. In addition, the republican overtones of the finale in which Silla abdicates in favor of the republican conspirators, while appropriate to Venice, appear rather incongruous in the Regno. Such an ending may have been interpreted as a subtle warning to their Austrian Habsburg overlords; several of Vinci's subsequent operas for Naples contain a similar object lesson: that rebellion is the price of tyranny. The description of Silla's voluntary abdication of the dictatorship as "the most beautiful of his actions" that can serve as a "mirror of the most beautiful virtue that shines in the heroic soul of Your Eminence" suggests that the criticism of the regime may have extended to the dedications addressed directly to the Viceroy. [27]

## *Silla Dittatore*: Act I and Alternate Arias

The traditional aspects of the libretto and the production are reflected to a certain extent in the music of *Silla Dittatore*.[28] Edward Dent described the music as being "very much under the style of Scarlatti, with several

---

[27] Ibid.
[28] Two scores of *Silla Dittatore* survive. According to Strohm, the one in the Biblioteca

arias that one could call rather Handelian."[29] Dent's overall assessment of the opera as a conservative work written under the influence of the old master is valid. One might question, however, whether the influence of Alessandro Scarlatti was more of an indirect rather than a direct one. Although Vinci would have been familiar with some of the music of Scarlatti, who was at that time living in retirement in Naples in the five-year period prior to the composition of *Silla*, only one Scarlatti opera had been performed in Naples, *Cambise,* in 1719.[30] If popularity can be attested by the number of operas produced, then the most popular composer at this time was undoubtedly Domenico Sarro, who had seven operas produced during the five years prior to the première of *Silla*.[31] Therefore Sarro was probably the more important musical influence that Vinci would have contended with when he began his career as a composer of the *dramma per musica*. In Naples, Sarro, along with Mancini, represent a generation between that of Scarlatti and Vinci, cultivating a style that has many elements in common with their near contemporary Handel and thus the influence of Sarro and Mancini could also account for the "rather Handelian" flavor to many of the arias in *Silla* detected by Dent. Vinci was probably familiar with some of Handel's music; *Agrippina* and *Rinaldo* were produced at the Teatro San Bartolomeo

---

Estense in Modena (F. 1231) is an incomplete copy of the one in Naples (*Italienische Opernarien* II, 228). The Neapolitan manuscript (Rari 32-4-13) was probably proof-read and modified by the composer, hence the changes and corrections in the recitative in Act III, scenes ix and x. Francesca Sabrina Donato gives a detailed analysis of these changes, which occur on folios 145-48 of this score, in her paper "Sull'edizione critica di Albino e Plautilla" (See fn.35 below). These changes and corrections, plus the absence of the prologue and the presence of the intermezzo and the additional and replacement arias, seem to indicate that the Neapolitan manuscript represents the second production of *Silla Dittatore* that took place at the Teatro S. Bartolomeo. Each act of the Neapolitan score ends with the pious inscription L.D.M.S.V., which is characteristic of Vinci's Neapolitan copyist(s). In addition to the two scores in Naples and Modena, there are a number of arias in several anthologies in the Santini Collection in Münster. The Neapolitan score, from which the excerpts below are taken, consists of the following musical numbers:

*Silla Dittatore:*

| 27 *da capo* arias (+ 1 Alternative aria) | 1 *da capo* duet |
|---|---|
| 1 accompanied recitative    1 Sinfonia | 1 *coro* |

*Plautilla/Albino:*

| 4 *da capo* arias | 1 *da capo* duet |
|---|---|
| 1 accompanied recitative | 1 through-composed duet |

Totals: 40 set pieces (34 *da capo*)

[29] Edward J. Dent, "Notes on Leonardo Vinci," *The Musical Antiquary* IV (1912/13),196

[30] See performance list in Strohm, *Italienische Opernarien* II, 302-308; on the late operas of Scarlatti, see Carl Morey, "The Late Operas of Alessandro Scarlatti," Ph.D. Dissertation: Indiana University, 1965 (Ann Arbor: UMI, 1974).

[31] Sarro's *Arsace* from December 1718 is reproduced in facsimile in *Italian Opera 1640-1770,* 22.

in 1713 and 1718 respectively (there were in fact as many productions of Handel as there were of Scarlatti in Naples during Vinci's youth).

Although *Silla Dittatore* is only Vinci's second *dramma per musica*, the music, particularly of Acts I and III, is of a high quality and is often well coordinated with the drama. In *Silla* Vinci proved that he had mastered the traditional musical style of his older colleagues. The opening scenes are dominated by Silla, who vows to wreak vengeance upon Valeria, daughter of one of the principal conspirators, Domizio. Silla's aria "Non pensi quel'altera" is basically an *aria all'unisono* in which the unison vocal phases alternate with brief martial ritornellos for violins in parallel thirds (see Example 3.1). These ritornellos, like the modest dimensions of the opening vocal period, give the aria a turn-of-the-century sound.

Example 3.1 "Non pensi quel Altera" *Silla Dittatore*, Act I/ii

As in the operas of Sarro, there is an abundance of dance-inspired arias.[32] Valeria responds to Silla's threats in her opening aria, "Innocente prigioniera," a gavotte in A major, in which she tells him that she goes to her chains an innocent prisoner. Silla's daughter Emilia and Pompeo reaffirm their love for each other. "Bella tu vuoi ch'io spero" is an F-major sarabande, in which Pompeo celebrates Emilia as "la mia speranza." In the next scene her father's ally, the Nubian prince Cloro, declares his love for Emilia. In "Dal tuo più bel sembiante" Emilia praises Cloro's virtues, but then dismisses him with a repeated "non mi piace." The aria is set as a rather melancholic *allemanda* in G minor, in which Vinci contrasts Emilia's praise and dismissal through a juxtaposition of minor and major tonality, which could be very effective with the appropriate stage action:

Example 3.2 "Del tuo più bel sembiante" *Silla Dittatore*, ActI/iv

Three of the remaining five arias in Act I are minuets. The first, "Fiumicel che hà piccol'onde," was soon to be incorporated, both words and music, into *Farnace* (Act I/xvi). The second, "Vedrai negli' occhi," contains an ingenious example of musical irony. In this scene, Silla tells Emilia that he has chosen a husband for her. Emilia fools herself into thinking that the intended is her true love Pompeo when, in fact, it is

---

[32] Almost half of the arias in Sarro's *Arsace* are dance, or dance-inspired, arias, as can be gleaned from the abundance of arias in 3/8, 2/4, and 3/4 meters.

Cloro. Silla's words are set to a solemn minor-mode melody, which in turn is juxtaposed with an irreverent major-mode ritornello, with its quirky repeated notes not only depicting the "Fiamma d'amor" of the suitor, but perhaps also laughing at Emilia for mixing up the suitors:

Example 3.3 "Vedrai negl'occhi" *Silla Dittatore*, Act I/ix

The other two arias are interesting from the perspective of Vinci's stylistic development. Valeria's "Amati, non poss'io" is one of the more conservative pieces in the opera; if played instrumentally it would not be out of place as a prelude to a Corelli sonata. In the score preserved at the Conservatory in Naples this aria has been provided with an alternative, "No hà quell' augelleto," sewn into the score on a separate folio. This alternative aria is in a different style; with its ascending triadic theme above a descending scale of repeated notes in the bass, the piece has the characeristics of an heroic aia from Vinci's later works:

Example 3.4 "No hà quell' augelleto" *Silla Ditttore* I/vii

The theme is repeated, with the second phrase extended via a coloratura passage with its distinctive scotch snaps balancing the previous dotted rhythms. Pompeo's "Quel traditore tiranno amore" is also a later addition, having been sewn into the score in a similar fashion; in the libretto this scene ended in recitative. This interpolated piece anticipates the *alla breve* aria, with its pseudo-imitative opening theme leading to the second period, which modulates to the dominant, features a lilting syncopated melody with prominent appoggiaturas, supported by *Trommelbass*, that provides a "galant" contrast to its initial "learnedness:"

Example 3.5 "Quel traditore tiranno amore" *Silla Dittatore* I/xi

Because the opera does not appear to have been revived, these two additional arias undoubtedly originated from the public performances at the San Bartolomeo. These arias, which anticipate Vinci's mature style, continue the innovations that were observed in several of the surviving arias from *La festa de Bacco* and *Lo labborinto* (see Examples 2.9a-c). That these fashionable arias appear to be thrown in for good measure as additional arias to Act I suggests that Vinci conceived the arias of his first *dramma per musica* in a more traditional style and that he introduced these innovations somewhat tentatively by the back door.

## The Intermezzo *Albino e Plautilla*

The libretto of *Silla Dittatore* was revised for Vinci. Cassiani's original *dramma per musica*, following the reforming ideals of the Arcadians, contains only serious scenes and characters. The preface to the libretto explains that "to give it a somewhat joyful character, scenes (which they call 'Buffo,' added to the end of the act) have been appended by the person responsible for adapting the opera for this theatre."[33] This reference, combined with the reference to the missing prologue, suggests that, in the process of moving the production to the S. Bartolomeo, not only were new arias added but the prologue was omitted and a new intermezzo inserted between the acts. The person responsible was probably Bernardo Saddumene, the author of *Li Zite 'ngalera*, who had revised *Publio Cornelio Scipione* for Vinci the previous year. Because most of Vinci's operas for the S. Bartolomeo are based on Venetian *seria* libretti, they had to be revised to accommodate the current craze for comedy in Naples by including intermezzi. Typical of Neapolitan practice, the comic characters also take part in the drama, usually as servants/confidantes to the main characters. In Vinci's *Silla Dittatore*, the buffo role is assigned to one of the conspirators in Cassiani's drama, Albino. Although in the comic transformation Albino loses his alto range and noble status, he still takes part in the crucial *coup d'état* at the end of the drama. Albino's buffa counterpart, Plautilla, has been added to the drama as a confidante to Emilia. According to contemporary practice, Albina and Plautilla appear together in three comic scenes, providing the finales to Acts I and II and the penultimate scene in Act III.

In the first intermezzo, Albino and Plautilla discuss how he should dress when he goes to the Senate. The scene consists simply of a recitative dialogue and concluding duet, the latter through-composed rather than *da capo*. In the second intermezzo Plautilla appears disguised as a scholar to teach Albino lessons in philosophy and language. In contrast to the Intermezzo in Act I, the recitative dialogue in this intermezzo is interrupted by arias for each of the characters before culminating in the duet.[34] Plautilla's aria, sung during the philosophy lesson, contains pompous Latin phrases set in broad sustained phrases that in turn are juxtaposed with short fragmented phrases tossed between voice and *basso continuo*. In Albino's "AEIOU bella cosa," which is sung during the language lesson, the vowels are set as a scale in half-notes surrounded by reiterated string accompaniment, like a comic *cantus firmus* or a mock singing exercise:

---

[33] *Silla Dittatore: dramma per musica; Da rappresentarsi nel Real Palazzo di questa Città Festeggiandosi il feliccismo giorno natalizio della Sac. Ces. Catt. Real Maestà Carlo VI Imperador Regnante* (Naples: Ricciardo Stampatore, 1723), Preface.

[34] This highlights the difference in scene structure between the intermezzo and the *dramma per musica*, the latter consisting of a continous recitative dialogue or monologue culminating in an exit aria for one of the characters or occasionally a duet, while the former often consists of a recitative dialogue culminating in a duet but with the recitative dialogue frequently interrupted by interpolated arias for one or both of the characters sung at each other without exit.

Example 3.6 "A E I O U bella cosa" *Silla Dittatore* II/xii

The concluding duet, like the one in the previous act, is a through-composed ensemble. In the final intermezzo the pedant reveals herself as Plautilla and asks Albino to dance. Albino sings a dance song that has a flavor of folksong, something of a rustic forlana. However, Albino gets carried away and offends Plautilla who then in an *accompagnato buffo* calls upon the devils to punish him for trying to kiss her and touch her. It is rather unusual that of the two accompanied recitatives in *Silla Dittatore*, the most extended, seventy-one as opposed to thirteen measures, is used in the intermezzo (a similar anomaly can also be found in Scarlatti's *Tigrane* and its intermezzo *Orcone e Dorilla*). When the squabble is resolved Plautilla and Albino decide to marry, allowing for the traditional buffo love duet. Vinci highlights the comedy by juxtaposing extended "churchly" cadences with the silly hocket exchanges on "Bicche/Bacche"(see Example 3.7 on Page 60). *Plautilla e Albino* is one of only two intermezzos to survive from Vinci's Neapolitan operas (three including the comic scenes in *La caduta dei Decemviri*).[35]

---

[35] This intermezzo is being prepared in a critical edition by Francesca Sabrina Donato; "Sull'edizione critica di Albino e Plautilla" paper given at the Giornata di Studi "Leonardo Vinci e gli Intermezzi comici napoletani nella prima metà del Settecento" Crotone/Strongole, May 28, 2003.

Example 3.7 "Mia sposa/Mio Sposo" *Silla Dittatore* III/x

After the production of *Silla Dittatore*, Vinci provided music for solemnities in honor of the patron saint at S. Caterina a Formiello. According to the *Avvisi di Napoli*:

> Last Thursday, the 25 of November, the day dedicated to the glory of S. Catherine virgin and martyr, the Dominican fathers of the province of Lombardy celebrated with magnificent pomp the festival of the saint in the Royal Church of S. Caterina a Formiello,...with select music *a più Cori* by the virtuoso Leonardo Vinci.[36]

The Royal Convent S. Caterina a Formiello was under the administration of the Dominican order. The term "a più Cori" suggests music for double choir and orchestra, along the lines of Vivaldi's *Dixit Dominus* (RV 594) and Pergolesi's *Missa Romana*. Of the handful of sacred pieces that are attributed to Vinci, the one work that can be securely identified with the composer, the Missa Brevis for eight-part choir and orchestra in the Santini Collection in Münster may well have originated as this music "a più Cori."[37]

## Vinci and the Roman Carnival

The *dramma per musica, Farnace,* Vinci's first opera produced outside Naples, was premièred on January 8th, 1724 at the Teatro Alibert in

---

[36] *Avvisi di Napoli*, November 30, 1723 (No. 49).

[37] The Missa Brevis received its first modern performance at the Convegno Leonardo Vinci in Reggo Calabria on June 11, 2002 by the Coro e Orchestra del Conservatorio di musica F. Cilea directed by Antonino Sorgonà in an edition by Gaetano Pitarresi.

Rome.[38] The *Avvisi di Napoli*, which occasionally described cultural events in other cities such as Rome, Vienna, and Venice, mentions this important production:

> Rome, 21 January / On Saturday evening at the Teatro D'Alibert the *Opera in Musica* entitled *Farnace* [appeared] for the first time on stage and carried general applause for the music composed by Signor Vinci, Napoletano.[39]

A typical scenario for the production of a Carnival opera in eighteenth-century Italy is described in *Lettre sur le méchanisme de l'opéra italien* (1756), attributed to Jossé de Villeneuve, finance minister to Charles de Lorraine in Tuscany:[40]

> An individual or company undertakes to produce an opera for carnival season. They [the directors] send for singers and dancers from various Italian cities, who, arriving from different directions, find themselves united in a cast without ever having seen or met each other. They call from Naples or Bologna, where the best musical schools are, a *maestro di cappella*. He arrives about a month prior to December 26 when the spectacle is to begin. They designate the drama that has been chosen for him; he composes twenty-five or twenty-six arias with orchestral accompaniment and the opera is complete, since the recitative costs too much trouble to notate. He gives the arias one by one, as soon as they are written to the singers, who learn them with ease, since most are great musicians. As for the recitatives, they [the singers] do not take the trouble to study them, a fleeting glance suffices; they are content to repeat only what the prompter reads loudly to them, and the harpsichord keeps them in the tonality. They hold five or six rehearsals and in less than a month the opera appears on stage.[41]

---

[38] Florino (*La scuola musicale di Napoli* III, 186) refers to a production of *Semiramide* in Rome in 1723, a reference repeated in several subsequent sources including Eitner, Manferrari, *MGG*, and the first edition of *The New Grove*. During the 1720s the Teatro delle Dame usually produced only two operas per season and in 1723 these were Pollarolo's *Cosroe* and Porpora's *Adelaide*. This mis-attribution perhaps stems from a mix-up with Porpora's *Semiramide regina dell'Assiria* produced at the San Bartolomeo during the spring of 1724.

[39] *Avvisi di Napoli*, January 25, 1724 (No. 5).

[40] This important essay is attributed to Calzabigi by Daniel Heartz in *Haydn, Mozart, and the Viennese School, 1740-1780* (New York: Norton, 1995): 158-64.

[41] *Lettre sur le méchanisme de l'opéra italien* (Naples [Paris], Duchesne & Lambert, 1756); German ed., "Jossé deVileneuves Brief über den Machanismus der italienischen Oper von 1756," trans. Robert Hass, *Zeitschrift für Musikwissenschaft* 7/2 (Dec.,1924), 129-63; although the original edition is not readily available, key passages in the original French are quoted in Henri Bédarida, "L'opéra Italien jugé par un amateur Français en 1756, *Mélanges de Musioclogie: offerts à M. Lionel de la Laurencie* (Paris: Société Française de Musicologie, 1933), 191.

Although this scenario dates from the mid-century, it is applicable to Rome of the 1720s. One can imagine Vinci arriving in Rome at the beginning of December (after conducting the St. Catherine's Day music), spending the month composing the arias in conjunction with the singers, with the rehearsals beginning some time before Christmas, and delays postponing the première until the eighth of January.[42]

*Farnace* was the first of a successful series of operas that Vinci was to produce at the Teatro Alibert in Rome. In a letter written in Rome in March of 1731 Baron de Pollnitz gives a detailed, if somewhat critical description of this theatre:

> Of all these Theatres there is but one that's good for anything, and that's the Ladies Theatre, commonly call'd the Theatre of Aliberti, because 'twas built by order of one Count Aliberti. The Room is excessively large, so that the voices are lost in it; it has seven Rows of Boxes, so low and little, that it makes the Room look like a Hen roost; the Pit will hold 900 Persons with Ease; The Stage is spacious, very high, and finely decorated... The Habits of the three principal Actors are magnificent, but those of the rest are horrible. Their Voices are good, and so are their instruments for the most part.[43]

The ground plan of the theatre was reproduced in Dumont's *Parallèle de Plans des Plus Belles Salles de Spectacles D'Italie* where it can be compared with other theatres in Rome as well as other cities (see Plate 3 on facing page). The Teatro Alibert was one of the largest theatres of the eighteenth century, with a stage that measured about seventy feet wide by ninety feet deep. An account from about the same period by another German tourist in Rome describes the appearance on stage of "the most magnificent chariot...drawn by six beautiful horses" during an opera performance at the delle Dame as an indication of "the vastness of the theatre."[44] The amphitheatre, which measured fifty feet wide by fifty-five feet deep, represented something of a turning away from the crescent and horseshoe plans and a return to the old-fashioned rectangular hall.[45]

---

[42] One wonders whether there may be some connection between Villeneuve's surprising description of the improvisation of the recitative and the fact that many operas from the early eighteenth century do not survive; for example, the only opera produced at the Teatro Alibert to survive complete with recitative prior to *Farnace* is Porpora's *Adelaide* from 1723.

[43] [Karl Ludwig Freiherr von Pollnitz], *The Memoirs of Charles-Lewis, Baron de Pollnitz* (London: D. Browne, 1737), Letter XXXI, Rome, March 10, 1731, 65.

[44] Johann Wilhelm Hertel's *Sammlung Musikalischer Schriften* (1757). Quoted in the preface of the German translation of *Lettre sur le méchanisme de l'opéra italien*: "Villeneuve's Brief über den Mechanismus der italienischen Oper," 131.

[45] Alberto De Angelis, *Il teatro Alibert o delle dame: 1717-1863* (Tivoli: Arti Grafiche A. Chicca, 1951), 15.

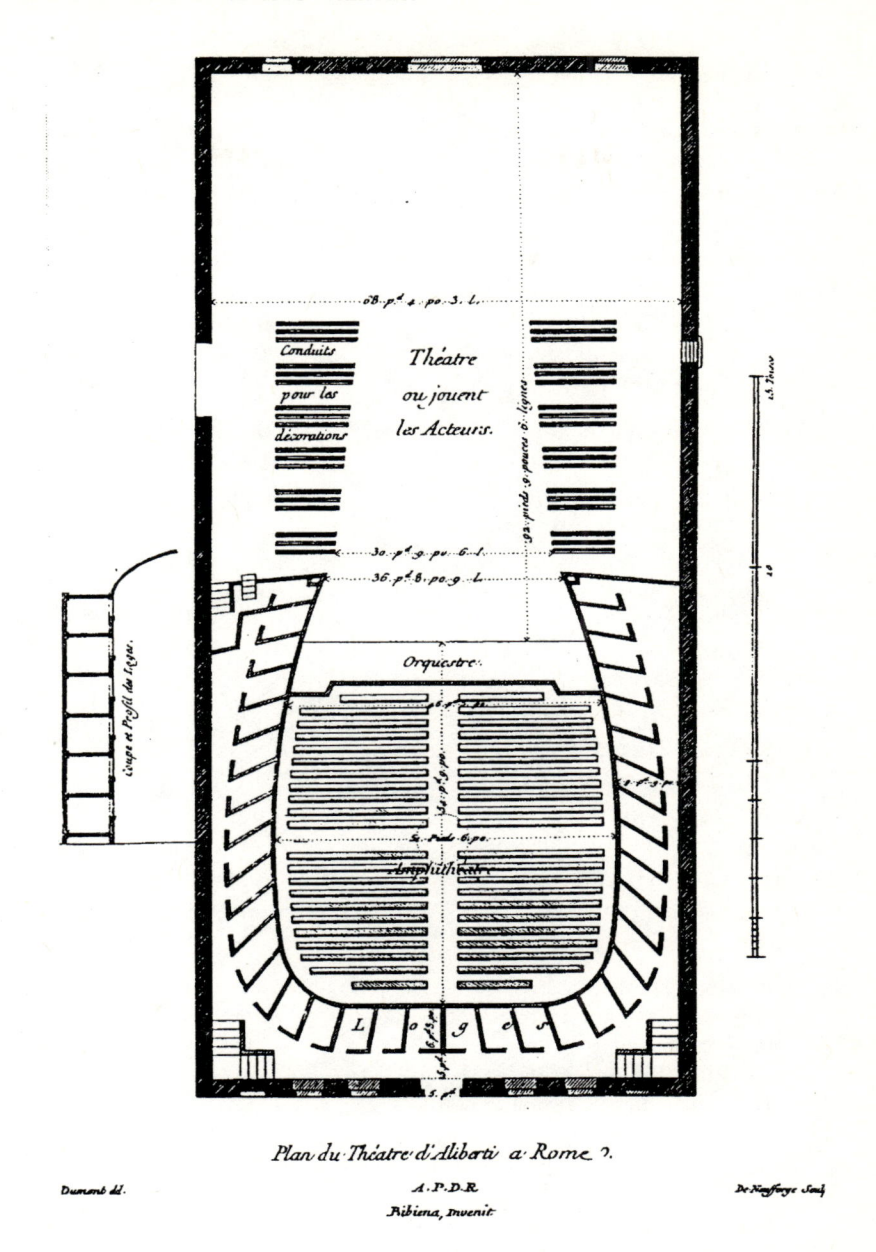

**Plate 3.** *Floor plan of the Teatro Alibert from Dumont's* Parallèle de Plans des Plus Belles Salles de Spectacles D'Italie et de France, *c. 1774.* [46]

[46] Gabriel Pierre Marin Dumont, *Parallèle de Plans des plus Belles Salles de Spectacles d'Italie et de France avec des détails de Machines Théatrales* (Paris: Mia au Tour, c. 1774; reprint ed. New York: Benjamin Blom, 1968), Pl. 10.

This, combined with seven tiers, each with thirty-six boxes, was probably responsible for the effect of a hen roost for Pollnitz. The theatre was located around the corner from the Piazza di Spagna where Francesco De Sanctis had just completed the facade of SS. Trinità de' Pellegrini and was currently working on his famous staircase.[47] When completed in 1726, this became the most fashionable area in Rome; according to Pollnitz "to hear a Roman speak of the Square of Spain, one would think it the finest place in the World."[48] Traditionally the foreigners' quarter during the eighteenth century, this part of the city was known as the "English Ghetto" because of the large number of English visitors as well as residents, among the latter being the Old Pretender James Edward Stuart, the principal patron of the Teatro Alibert.

What bothered Pollnitz most about the productions at the Teatro Alibert and other Roman theatres was the absence of women on stage:

> out of a ridiculous Scruple, if I may venture to call it so, which they have here, that Women should not be seen at the Theatres. This is the Reason that the Operas of Rome are vastly inferior to the other Operas of Italy. There is not perhaps a more ridiculous Sight than to see these creatures who are but half Men, play the parts of Women; yet, thò they have neither Air nor Gracefulness, they are applauded here as much as the best Actresses are elsewhere.[49]

The "ridiculous Scruple" Pollnitz refers to is the decree of Sixtus V from 1588 which banned women from the stage. It was enforced with great strictness, except for a brief period in the 1670s under the protection of Queen Christina.[50] Because of this ban, the casts of Roman opera consisted primarily of castrati for both male and female characters. The cast in *Farnace*, for example consisted of one tenor and seven castrati, three of them in female roles:

| | |
|---|---|
| Pompeo: Domenico Federici | Berenice: Carlo Broschi |
| Farnace: Domenico Gizzi | Tamiri: Filippo Finazzi |
| Gilade: Luca Mengoni | Selinda: Domenico Rumi |
| Aquilio: Raffaeli Baldi | La Pace: Guiliano Felli |
| Choreographer: Sebastiano Scio | Battle director: Giuseppe Ciocchetti |

The great Carlo Broschi "Farinello," who began his career in Rome singing female roles, sang his last transvestite role as Berenice in Vinci's

---

[47] Rudolf Wittkower, *Art and Archtecture in Italy 1600-1750*, 3rd ed. The Pelican History of Art, ed. Nikolaus Pevsner & Judy Nairn (Harmondsworth, Middlesex: Penguin Books, 1973), 377-79.

[48] *The Memoirs of Charles-Lewis, Baron de Pollnitz* I, 4.

[49] Ibid., Letter XXI, Rome, March 10, 1731, 65.

[50] De Angelis, *Il teatro Alibert o della dame*, 47-55.

*Farnace.* At the end of the season he was depicted in costume in a caricature by the Roman artist Pier Leone Ghezzi (see Plate 4 below).

**Plate 4.** *Caricature of Carlo Broschi "Farinello," as Berenice in Vinci's* Farnace, *by Pier Leone Ghezzi, Rome 1724.* [51]

---

[51] Pier Leone Ghezzi, "The Famous Castrato: Il Farinelli" from The Pierpont Morgan Library, Department of Drawings and Prints, Add. JS 1984-1986; Ghezzi's inscription reads: "Farinello Napolitano/ famoso cantoro di soprano che/ canta nel Teatro d'Aliberti nell'anno 1724./ fatto di me Cav. Ghezzi di 2 Marzo 1724."

Domenico Gizzi, who sang the title role, was singled out along with Farinello in a review at the end of the season (see below). Although Gizzi was a soprano in the Cappella Real in Naples, he cultivated his stage career exclusively outside of Naples.[52] Later that year he was depicted in a caricature, probably as Araspe in Albinoni's *Didone* from 1725 (see Plate 5 on facing page).

*Farnace* represents part of a trend that saw the ascendency of a new generation of Neapolitan composers in Rome. During the first years of its operation, from 1718 to 1720, the Teatro Alibert featured the operas of Francesco Gasparini.[53] These were produced to rival those of Alessandro Scarlatti at the Teatro Capranica. Gasparini's operas were replaced by those of Nicola Porpora between the years 1721 to 1723. Porpora's star pupil, Farinello, who performed during the 1722 and 1723 seasons, undoubtedly contributed to Porpora's success. In response to these productions at the Alibert, the Teatro Capranica imported Antonio Vivaldi for two seasons. The Teatro Alibert countered this Venetian challenge by bringing in Antonio Pollarolo, who produced his *Cosroe* alongside Porpora's *Adelaide* during the 1723 season.[54] Venetian opera, however, did not become an integral part of the Roman opera repertoire. Moreover, the regular productions of Scarlatti and Gasparini in Rome, which almost constitute a Roman school, were put into the shadows after the Roman debuts of Porpora and Vinci. Within a few short seasons, Scarlatti and Gasparini found themselves relegated to the sidelines as "learned" composers. Just as Porpora's debut with *Eumene* symbolically triumphed over Scarlatti's swan song *La Griselda* in 1721,[55] Vinci's debut with *Farnace* would have overshadowed Gasparini's final opera, *Tigrena*, produced privately at the Palazzo de Mello de Castro during this same Carnival season.

The libretto to *Farnace* mentions Sebastiano Scio as "Direttore dei Balli." In Rome ballet was used in the same way as the comic intermezzo in Naples to provide musical interludes between the acts of a

---

[52] A decree by the Archibishop of Naples prevented church musicians from singing on the stage and thus it seems Gizzi was content to restrict his stage career to foreign cities in order to cultivate a church career within Naples.

[53] Emilia Zanetti, "La presenza du Francesco Gasparini in Roma gli ultima anni 1716-27," *Francesco Gasparini: 1661-1727: Atti del primo convegno internazionale*, Camaiore, 1978, ed. Fabrizio Della Seta and Franco Piperno (Florence: Leo S. Olschki, 1981), 275-76.

[54] While in Rome, Pollarolo was caricatured by Ghezzi (*Il Nuovo Mondo*, I, f.55, Ottob. lat 3112). Upon returning to Venice he would succeed his father as vice-maestro at S. Marco in Venice; *The New Grove Dictionary of Opera*, "Pollarolo (Giovanni) Antonio" by Olga Termini.

[55] According to the *Avvisi di Napoli* for February 18, 1721 (No. 8) Porpora's *Eumene* was judged "superior" to Scarlatti's *La Griselda*.

***Plate 5.*** *Caricature of Domencio Gizzi, probably as Araspe in Albinoni's* Didone, *Venice 1725, attributed to Marco Ricci.*[56]

*dramma per musica.* While ecclesiastical propriety may have considered ballet a less frivolous divertissement than comedy, the papal ban resulted in male ballerinas, who were considered by certain Northerners, such as Pollnitz, as the epitome of bad taste: "their dancers are too bad to behold, and you can't imagine any thing more hideous."[57] Like the comic intermezzi, these ballets had little or no connection with the drama. According to Francesco Algarotti, ballet "never was a constituent part of the drama, is always foreign to the business and very often repugnant to it."[58] In contrast to the comic intermezzi, however, the ballet music was provided by the ballet master rather than the composer, hence the libretto to *Farnace* and all of Vinci's subsequent Roman operas refer to ballet, but no ballet music survives. Although some of the

---

[56] Reproduced from Edward Croft-Murray, *An Album of Eighteenth-Century Venetian Operatic Caricatures: formerly in the Collection of Count Algarotti* (Toronto: Art Gallery of Ontario, 1990), 36.

[57] *The Memoirs of Charles-Lewis, Baron de Pollnitz,* Letter XXXI, Rome, March 10, 1731, 65.

[58] Francesco Algaroti, *Saggio sopra l'opera in musica* (Livorno: Coltellini, 1763); English ed: *An Essay on the Opera* (Glasgow, 1768), 68.

ballet music was newly composed, according to the *Lettre sur le méchanisme de l'opéra italien* most of it was adapted from French sources:

> the *Maestro di cappella* does not take the trouble to compose the "airs de ballet" since the ballet has no earnings and has no link with the piece. [Because] the ballet is only an hor-d'oeuvre or danced interlude, they make a rhapsody of different "symphonies," mostly of French origin, and these are always the most applauded [within the ballet].[59]

Therefore ballet music in Italian opera stands in complete contrast to the divertissements in French opera, which were integral to the drama, conceived from the outset to provide the musical highlights of the score.

## Lucchini's *Farnace*

In contrast to the libretti of *Publio Cornelio Scipione* and *Silla Dittatore*, which were revisions of earlier Venetian dramas, the libretto of *Farnace* was written specifically for Vinci by the Venetian librettist Antonio Maria Lucchini.[60] Vivaldi, who was in Rome at that time for the production of his *Giustino* at the rival Teatro Capranica, had worked previously with Lucchini on *Tieteberga* for the Teatro San Moisè in 1717 and would later set his own version of *Farnace* in 1727 for the Teatro Sant' Angelo in Venice.[61]

For his drama Lucchini chose as his subject Pharnaces II, King of Pontus (63-47 BC). The drama centers on Pharnaces' attempts to establish a kingdom on the Bosporus after the death of his father Mitridate Eupator. His Kingdom was confirmed by Pompey, which provides the drama with its *lieto fine*. Lucchini probably derived Farnace's fanatical fear of the Roman triumph, which supplies the motivation behind his actions, from the fact that during the civil war Pharnaces tried to extend his Kingdom but was defeated by Julius Caesar at Zela and subsequently led captive through Rome in Caesar's triumph (it was in this triumph that Caesar first used the motto "Veni, vedi, vinci").

---

[59] *Lettre sur le méchanisme de l'opéra italien*, quoted in Henri Bédarida, "L'opéra Italien jugé par un amateur Français en 1756," 197.
[60] Copies of the libretto in I-Bc, I-MAC, I-Rsc, I-Vgc, D-FRu, F-Pc, and P-C; Sartori, *I libretti italiani*, No. 9732.
[61] In the critical edition of *Giustino* Strohm proposes that it was Lucchini who arranged Pariati's 1711 reworking of Beregan's libretto for Vivaldi; see Reinhold Strohm, "The Critical Edition of Vivaldi's 'Giustino' (1724)," *Nuovi studi vivaldiani: edizione e cronologia critica delle opere*, ed. Antonio Fanna and Giovanni Morelli, Studi di musica Veneta quaderni Vivaldiani 2 (Florence: Leo S. Olschki, 1988), 412-13. *Giustino* has been recorded by Alan Curtis and the Complesso Barocco (Virgin 7243 5 45518 2 6).

**Synopsis**: Berenice Queen of Campodocia, in alliance with the Roman Pro-consul Pompeo, makes war against King Farnace of Ponto. Berenice intends to retrieve by force her daughter Tamiri, who was abducted by Farnace. Prior to the battle, Farnace has Tamiri swear that in the event of his defeat, she will kill herself and their son to prevent them from being led captive through the streets of Rome. The battle takes place and Farnace is defeated. Tamiri, unable to kill her son, hides him in the royal mausoleum, and is about to kill herself when she is captured by her mother Berenice. A subplot is interwoven with the main plot, involving Farnace's sister Selinda, who, as captive, soon captivates the hearts of both Berenice's captain Gilade and Pompeo's captain Aquilio. When Berenice is about to destroy the Royal mausoleum, Tamiri rushes in to stop her, revealing the hiding place of her son, who is quickly snatched up by Berenice as bait to assist her in capturing Farnace. Although defeated, the wily Farnace has eluded capture by hiding in the royal mausoleum. Having witnessed this event, he comes out of hiding and disowns his wife for not having carried out the promised murder/suicide. Farnace then enlists Selinda in his plot against the victors. Selinda in turn manages to seduce both Gilade and Aquilio to their cause. However, Farnace's assassination attempt on Pompeo is foiled and he is arrested. Before a military tribunal, Farnace is condemned and is about to be executed when a *coup d'état* breaks out led by Gilade and Selinda. To avoid capture by her enemies, Berenice takes Tamiri hostage, compelling Farnace to surrender. Tamiri intercedes on behalf of her husband. Berenice relents and the moment she forgives Farnace, the goddess Pace descends and proclaims peace. Farnace and Tamiri and Gilade and Selinda are united.

Even by eighteenth-century standards the plot of *Farnace* seems overly complex, particularly the finale in which Lucchini has strung together a series of incongruous events to create a bizarre climax: an attempted assassination (comically bungled because both Farnace and Gilade make the attempt at the same time), a secret military tribunal, a firing squad of bows and arrows, a *coup d'état*, a double hostage-taking incident, a double last-minute conversion, and finally a superfluous baroque *deus ex macchina*.[62] During the *coup d'état*, Pompeo, who would have repre-

---

[62] The entry on Vinci in the *Enciclopedia dello spettacolo* reproduces an engraving of a "Macchina con la reggia di Marte" identified as a stage setting from Vinci's *Farnace* (Hellmut Hucke, "Vinci, Leonardo," Plate CLXXIX) by G. B. Bernabò and P, Pilaia, based on a set by one "F.G." who is Francesco Galli-Bibiena. However, there is no scene in Vinci's *Farnace* where it could have been used because the machine in the final scene is for Pace not Marte. Moreover, the libretto to *Farnace* lists Giuseppe Ciocchetti as the stage designer with no mention of F. G. The set probably originates

sented to the audience the august power of Rome, even loses his *"virtù"* and threatens the execution of Farnace's son to save Berenice's life. In addition, the sub-plot concerning the rivalry between Gilade and Aquilio for the love of the cunning Selinda is definitely *mezzo carattere* and shows a strong link with the comic scenes of *seicento* Venice. Lucchini apparently had a reputation for being something of a scribbler, and unfortunately *Farnace* does nothing to contradict that reputation. [63]

Like many of the productions at the Teatro Alibert during the 1720s, *Farnace* was dedicated by the director to "Giacomo III Re d'Inghilterra" the Stuart Pretender to the English throne. The story of the proud Farnace's rash attempts of to regain his crown from his foreign conquerors Berenice and Pompeo was probably intended as a flattering representation of the Old Pretender's continued attempts to regain the English throne. The *deus ex macchina* role of Pace, which brings about the happy ending, probably represented the Mother Church, whose benevolent mediating role would bring about a just and peaceful resolution of this conflict.

### *Farnace*: Variety with a Vengeance

Like the libretto, the voluminous score of *Farnace* appears to be rather sprawling and haphazard.[64] No score by Vinci exhibits such variety,

---

from the 1720 season when Francesco Galli, having just renovated the theatre for Count Alibert, designed the stage sets for three operas by Gasparini.

[63] "Lucchini, Antonio Maria" by Michael Talbot in *The New Grove Dictionary of Opera*. The revisions Lucchini made for Vivaldi the following year would eliminate some of these complications, without removing the overall cobbled effect of the drama.

[64] There is a single surviving score of Vinci's *Farnace* in the Santini Collection in Münster (4543 in 3 vols., 16 x 22 cm.) initialled and dated "Agosto 1729 G.F.C." at the end of Act III by Francesco Cantoni, the Roman copyist. The manuscript is not through-copied; it consists of a series of thirty-one separate aria fascicles on a variety of paper in several hands, each titled "Del Vinci/ in Alibert 1724." These fascicles have been connected by the recitative and the remaining sixteen arias, which have been through-copied by Cantoni. While the through-copied parts date from 1729, the fascicles presumbably date from the 1724 production. This connection with the performance is reinforced by the appearance of the two additional arias:"Non trova mai" at the end of Act III and "Offendo il tuo amore' inserted as an alternatre aria to "Parli di madre amante" in Act I—probably two of the "six new arias" Vinci wrote for the unexpected revival. These independent aria fascicles were produced as part of a practice of selling copies of individual arias to the audiences as souvenirs of a production. Two collections of arias from *Farnace* can be found at the Bibliothèque du Conservatoire in Paris (D. 124741 & D. 14259). The Santini score, from which the excerpts below are taken, consists of the following musical numbers:

| | | |
|---|---|---|
| 37 *da capo* arias | 1 arietta | 2 alternative *da capo* arias |
| 1 accompanied recitative | 2 Sinfonias | 1 *da capo* quartet |
| | Totals: | 40 *da capo* + <u>5 non *da-capo*</u> = |
| | | 45 set pieces |

such diversity, almost as if the young composer was trying to display everything he knew in order to ensure the success of his first commission from outside Naples. This all-inclusive approach makes *Farnace* an interesting work but not one of Vinci's most aesthetically satisfying. The most obvious feature that sets *Farnace* apart from Vinci's other operas is its length. While later works, beginning with *La Rosmira fedele*, contain between twenty-five to thirty arias (which is much closer to the number mentioned in the mid-century *Lettre*), *Farnace* contains thirty-seven *da capo* arias plus two additional arias. With these numbers, the score resembles those of early eighteenth-century masters such as Scarlatti (for example *Tigrane* with forty-three *da capo* arias and *Griselda* with forty-one).[65]

As in *Silla Dittatore,* Vinci adopted a more traditional style for the majority of the arias in *Farnace*. Some of the arias such as "Cara destra" and "Lasciar di sospirar" seem to look back to the turn of the eighteenth century, with their lack of a regular ritornello and binary structure and unusual modulations in the first section. In "Bei labri io penserò" the lack of binary structure and the miniature dimensions of this tuneful dance air (i.e. the second vocal period begins in m.11) seem to suggest the popular turn-of-the-century style of Giovanni Bononcini's *Camilla*:

Example 3.8 "Bei labri io penserò" *Farnace* I/xvii

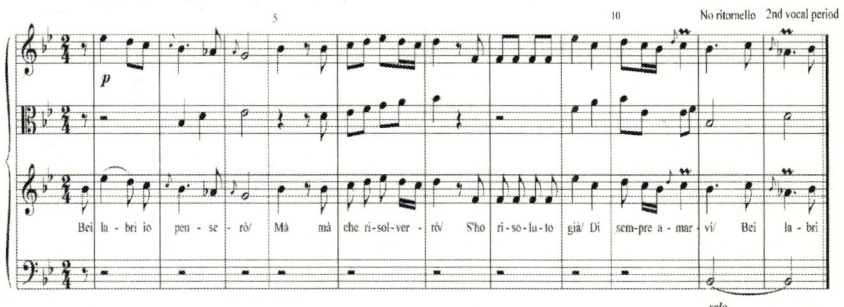

This turn-of-the-century simplicity is also apparent in Pompeo's arietta "Tu campioni, tu guerrieri" which, though scored for full orchestra of trumpet, horns, oboes and strings, is really nothing more than an elaborate twenty-five measure fanfare with a superimposed vocal line. The influence of Alessandro Scarlatti can be detected in certain arias, such as "Un caro e dolce sguardo," a minor-mode love song with Neapolitan-sixth harmony and imitative writing:

---

[65] Strohm noticed a similar expansiveness in Vivaldi's *Giustino*, with forty-four arias, and comes to the conclusion that the numerous small cuts throughout the autograph score are part of an overall trimming down of the work: Strohm, "The Critical Edition of Vivaldi's 'Giustino' (1724)," 411.

Example 3.9. "Un caro e dolce sguardo" *Farnace*, Act I/x

Other arias are remniscent of Vivaldi, such as "Forte eroe" and "Anche a Giove," concerto-style arias, the first with contrasted strings and oboe, the second with a unison theme followed by tremolo sequential passages. Berenice's "Lascierò d'esser spietato" is reminiscent of Vivaldi and features an unusual obbligato solo for *saltiero*, a type of psaltery:

Example 3.10 "Lascierò d'esser spietato" *Farnace*, Act II/xv

Vivaldi's *Giustino*, produced at the Teatro Capranica during the same season, also contains an aria for *saltiero*.[66] *Giustino* was the second opera performed at the Teatro Capranica during Carnival, which suggests that Vivaldi borrowed the idea of this "Vivaldian" *saltiero obbligato* from Vinci. This indicates that there was a certain mutual influence between the two composers (see below).

[66] Antonio Vivaldi, *Giustino: Dramma per music di Nicolò Beregan*, ed. Reinhard Strohm (Milan : Ricordi, 1991), 313-20. The aria in question, "Ho nel petto un cor

In contrast to many of Vinci's later operas, *Farnace* contains several arias in the lamenting or pathetic manner. According to Francesco Tosi's *Opinioni de'cantori antichi e moderni*, which had been published the previous year, the pathetic "is what is most delicious to the Ear, what most sweetly affects the Soul, and is the strongest Basis of Harmony."[67] One of the finest of these pathetic arias is Pompeo's "Mi piace m'inamora," a brooding sarabande in D minor, distinguished by its short disjunct melodic phrases, dotted rhythms, appoggiaturas, trills, and echo effects:

Example 3.11 "Mi piace m'inamora" *Farnace* I/xv

Although the aria may have the characteristics of a lament, it is set to an amorous rather than a grieving text in which Pompeo expresses his infatuation for Tamiri. A similar anomaly arises in Tamiri's "Forse o caro," a melancholic minuet in C minor scored for flutes and strings *senza cembalo*, which she sings when she has finally been reconciled with the bellicose Farnace. From similar examples in his later works one can infer that Vinci associated dance-inspired arias in the minor mode not with sorrow but with passion. The melancholic effect of Tamiri's aria is emphasized in the final ritornello by the omission of the flutes, leaving the strings to complete the ritornello an octave lower.

---

si forte" has been recorded by Cecilia Bartoli on her *Vivaldi Album* (Decca 466 569-2) as well as on the recording of *Giustino* by Alan Curtis and Il Complesso Barocco (Virgin Veritas 7243 5 45518 2 6).

[67] Pier Francesco Tosi, *Observations on the Florid Song: or Sentiments on the Ancient and Modern Singers,* trans. Mr. Galliard (London: J. Wilcox, 1743; reprint ed., London: William Reeves, 1967), 107.

In spite of the numerous traditonal elements, there are notable examples of the new style that was becoming the speciality of Vinci and his Neapolitan colleagues. "Da qual ferro" contains the gentle syncopations, rhythmic enchainments, and ornate coloratura that would soon become an essential part of the new or "galant" style:

Example 3.12 "Da quel ferro" *Farnace* I/iii

The new style also manifests itself in some of the minuet arias. Tamiri's "Sbigottisce il pastorello" represents a blending of the minuet and heroic coloratura aria, producing music that would not be out of place as the third movement in a classical symphony:

Example 3.13 "Sbigottisce il pastorello" *Farnace* III/x

The virtuoso leaps and cascades in the first violins and the wave-like passages in the violas and basses are used to depict the storm imagery of the text.

As in *Silla Dittatore*, the new style is employed in the two additional arias, "Offendo il tuo amore" and "Non trova mai riposo," written for Domenico Gizzi and Farinello—presumably two of six new arias that Vinci wrote for the unexpected revival of *Farnace* later that same season (see below). "Offendo il tuo amore" contains the same lilting syncopations as "Da quel ferro," while "Non trova mai riposo" employs an ornamented periodic melody above *Trommelbass*:

Examples 3.14. "Non trova mai riposo" *Farnace*, Additional Aria

The feint into the minor mode at the beginning of the main theme, depicting Berenice's grief, was to become an important expressive device of the modern "galant" style dominated by the major mode. This characteristic of the new Italian style was described by the French traveller Charles De Brosses:

> They hardly ever compose in the minor mode, almost all of their airs are written in the major; but they mix in with them, without one being aware of it, some phrases in the minor, which surprise and seize the ear to the point of affecting the heart.[68]

It would seem that Vinci's new style made an impact on Vivaldi's music. This is evidenced in several arias in *Giustino*, notably "Mio dolce

---

[68] Charles De Brosses, *Lettres familières écrites d'italie a quelques amis en 1739 et 1740* (Paris: Poulet-Malassis et de Broise, 1858), I, 251.

amato sposo" and "Il piacere della vendetta," which are as modern as anything in Vinci's *Farnace*. Along with the *saltiero* aria "Ho nel petto un cor," Vivaldi highlights these Vinci-inspired arias by placing them as the finales to Acts I and II sung by the heroine and hero and as the opening of Act III sung by the villain. It is the presence of pieces in the Vinci vein such as "Mio dolce amato sposo" that is one of the main distinguishing features between Vivaldi's early and late works, as exemplified in the differences between the concertos of Op. 3/4 and Op. 8/9. In this divide, the opera *Giustino*, the work that Vivaldi wrote immediately after his contact with Vinci, is crucial.[69]

*Farnace* also contains Vinci's first exended accompanied reciative, "O Figlio, o troppo tardi," in which the distraught Queen says farewell to her son then hides him in the royal mausoleum. This extended accompanied recitative can easily stand comparison with the more celebrated examples in *Didone abandonata* (see below), demonstrating that Vinci came to master this declamatory dramatic style early in his career. Particularly impressive is the passage in which Tamari leads her son into the mausoleum, the brief orchestral ritornello depicting the boy's reluctance to enter:

Example 3.15 "O Figlio, o troppo tardi" *Farnace* I/xi

---

[69] In describing this new influence in the music of Vivaldi, one should be careful not to overestimate the influence of Vinci. There was another Neapolitan composer who would have made a major impact on Vivaldi the previous season, when his *Ercole su'l Termodonte* came up against Porpora's *Adelaide*. Conceived to showcase the talents of his pupil Farinelli, Adelaide became one of Porpora's most successful and influential works and its success undoubtedly would have made an impact on Vivaldi when he was composing his next Roman opera, *Giustino*.

[Musical notation excerpt with lyrics: "vi-vi tem-po for-se ver-rà, che tu ri-pi-gli L'in-do-le ge-ne-ro-sa e che-ri-tol-ga a la lu-pa ti-ran-nà L'usur-pa-todo-"]

Handel included an orchestral passage very similar to this in Jephtha's accompanied recitative "Deeper and deeper still"—two-and-a-half measures, beginning on the second half of the third beat, with pounding dotted rhythms in contrary motion, rising in the upper strings and descending in the basses—to highlight the hero's realization that "Heav'n heard my thoughts, and wrote them down." In his extensive use of accompanied recitative, Vinci may have been following the lead of Nicola Porpora, who included extended and impassioned accompanied recitatives in his serenatas *Angelica* and *Gli orti esperidi* from 1720/21.[69]

## Extended Stay in Rome

According to a notice in the *Avvisi di Napoli*, *Farnace* was revived at the end of the season because of the failure of the second opera, Luccio Antonio Predieri's *Scipione*:

> the dramma entitled *Scipione*, recently on stage at the Teatro Alibert, displeased this public, not for the music composed by Signor Predieri Bolognese, but for the poor composition of the libretto [that was] without incident; for this reason the opera entitled *Farnace* was performed again in this theatre and carried the same applause as at the première, especially for the music by Signor Vinci Napoletano, for the addition of six new arias that were left out of the libretto, and for the quality of the performers, particularly Signori Farinello and Gizzi.[70]

This lack of *accidenti* in Zeno's *Scipione nelle Spagne* refers not only to the lack of incidents but also the lack of complications, which allowed the *accidenti*-laden *Farnace* to dominate the 1724 season at the Teatro Alibert. The additional exposure of the music undoubtedly contributed

---

[69] *Gli orti esperidi* contains six examples, accounting for 156 measures, including an early example of an accompanied dialogue. While *Angelica* contains only three accompanied recitatives, two of these are employed in conjunction with two ariettas to create an extended *scena* of 123 measures depicting Orlando's madness.

[70] *Avvisi di Napoli*, February 29, 1724 (No. 10).

further to the success of Vinci's first Roman opera. According to Charles Burney: "So great was the success of this drama, that he was called upon to furnish at least one opera every year till 1730, when he composed two."[71] Although the entry on Vinci in the *Dictionary of Musicians* from 1825 identifies the composer's first Roman opera as *Semeramide*, the description of the reactions of audience and composer are most interesting, suggesting that the author may have had access to a unique, albeit unreliable, source of information on Vinci:

> The applause of the Romans, who are not more difficult to satisfy than any of the Italians, flattered the self-love of the young artist; he was animated with fresh ardour, and continued to receive the reward of his zeal. The Romans were struck with the melody of his airs, the science of his accompaniments and the brilliancy of his style, which was the purest and finest of his time, then so fertile in great masters.[72]

The description of the Roman reaction to Vinci's musical style has a definite *settecentesco* feel to it, while the portrait of the young artist experiencing the first flush of success, inspiring him, in turn, to further success, ties in with Metastasio's reference to his colleague chasing after a fame that continually eluded him (see chapter 10). Although one could dismiss the latter as simply an elaboration upon Metastasio's comment, the purport of the entire passage seems to ring true.

Vinci's opera was not the only success of the 1724 season. The flautist Johann Joachim Quantz, who visited the city later that year, refers to:

> the so-called Lombardic style, heretofore unknown to me, which had previously been introduced in Rome by Vivaldi through one of his operas, and which made such an impression on the inhabitants that they wanted to hear almost nothing that did not resemble this style.[73]

Vivaldi's whereabouts between the première of *Giustino* in Rome and that of the serenata composed for the Venetian embassy in celebration of the wedding of Louis XV in September of 1725, are a mystery. Considering Quantz's remark, it seems likely that he remained in Rome after

---

[71] Charles Burney, *A General History of Music*, II, 916.

[72] *Dictionary of Musicians, from the Earliest Ages to the Present Time*. In this entry the author challenges the above-mentioned generalization about the Roman audience being the most critical in all Italy.

[73] Johann Joachim Quantz, "The Life of Herr Johann Joachim Quantz, as Sketched by Himself," trans. Paul Mueller, *Forgotten Musicians*, ed. Paul Nettl (New York: Philosophical Library, 1951), 299; originally appeared as "Lebensläuffe" in Friedrich Wilhelm Marpurg, *Historisch-kritische Beyträge zur Aufnahme der Musik* (Berlin: Verlag Joh. Jacob Schüzens, 1754; reprint. ed., Hildesheim: Georg Olms Verlag, 1970), 223.

Carnival where he created this vogue for the Lombard style.[74] The exact nature of the Lombard style is difficult to determine. It does not appear to be merely the extensive use of Lombard rhythms, which are sparingly used in *Giustino* and in Vivaldi's next major work, the celebrated concertos of Op. 8, published by Roger/Le Cène in December. Perhaps the Lombard style refers to the new rhythmic variety that was to become a hallmark for the new style, with its free mix of Lombards, Scotch snaps, dotted rhythms, triplets, duplets, sextuplets, all enlivened with ornaments and appoggiaturas. Perhaps it is also related to the new lilting eighth-quarter-eighth-note pattern that recreates the Lombard rhythm at a higher rhythmic level.

*Farnace* was produced at the Teatro Pergola in Florence during Carnival 1726. Although no composer is listed in the libretto, references in two letters by the impresario Lucca Casimiro degli Albizzi indicate that this production was based on Vinci's opera.[75] The Florentine *Farnace* was revived again in 1733, according to the impresario because "the requests of the many people who would like to see it again, even though it was performed here only a few years ago."[76] Vivaldi composed his own setting of *Farnace* for Venice the following year; it achieved considerable success, becoming something of a repertory piece.[77] Even though Vivaldi's *Giustino* may have been just as successful as Vinci's *Farnace* and Vivaldi's *Farnace* would replace Vinci's on the Italian opera circuit, *Giustino* was Vivaldi's last Roman opera commission and it was Vinci who "was called upon to furnish at least one opera every year" for Rome.

After the production of *Farnace*, Vinci was again caricatured by the Roman artist Pier Leone Ghezzi. Beside his talents as an artist, Ghezzi was also an amateur musician and, at his home in the Via Giulia, he held concerts on Wednesday evenings at which he presided at the *violone*.[78] Musicians feature prominently in his caricatures, including numerous

---

[74] See Michael Talbot, "Antonio Vivaldi" in *The New Grove Italian Baroque Masters* (New York: Norton, 1984), 281; Michael Talbot, *Vivaldi*, 2nd ed. The Dent Master Musicians (London: Dent, 1993) 53-55; Reinhold Strohm, "Vivaldi's Career as an Opera Producer," *Essays on Handel and Italian Opera* (Cambridge: Cambridge University Press, 1985), 152-55; Reinhard Strohm, *Giustino by Antonio Vivaldi: Introduction, Critical Notes, and Critical Commentary* (Milan: Ricordi, 1991), 7-8.

[75] William C. Holmes, *Opera Observed: Views of a Florentine Impresario in the Early Eighteenth Century* (Chicago: University of Chicago Press, 1993), 204.

[76] Quoted in Ibid.

[77] Vivaldi's *Farnace* was revived at the Teatro de la Zarzuela in Madrid in October of 2001 from which a fine recording was made by the Concert des Nations, dir. Jordi Savali (Alia Vox AV 9822 A/C).

[78] Lucia Guerrini, *Marmi antichi nei disegni di Pier Leone Ghezzi, Biblioteca Vaticana documenti e riproduzione* 1 (Vatican: Biblioteca apostolica, 1971), 9.

singers (see the caricatures of Faustina, Farfallino, and La Romanina in Chapters 4 and 5) and composers.[79] Among the latter is the oft-reproduced caricature of Vivaldi from Carnival 1723, as well as those of Vinci. Ghezzi made two caricatures of Vinci during this stay in Rome, a side profile sketch, which is now in the British Library Collection of Prints and Drawings, and a full-length caricature that derives its profile of the face directly from the sketch.[80] The full-length caricature (see Plate 6) is titled and dated: "Signor Vinci, Neapolitan composer of music, the same who composed the comedy for Alibert in the year 1724, made by me cavalier Ghezzi on March 30 of this year." Although the reference to "la comedia" may be appropriate to the *mezzo carattere* aspects of Lucchini's libretto, Ghezzi is using the term according to contemporary usage as a synonym for opera. The date of March 30 indicates that Vinci stayed on in Rome after the production of *Farnace*, perhaps to enjoy his recent success and to make connections for future commissions. Setting aside the comic distortion inherent in the genre, the composer appears as a well-dressed gentleman wearing a three quarter-length coat with large cuffs and buttons, a lace shirt, square-toed shoes and a shoulder-length wig tied with ribbons. With sword at his side, the tip jutting out at the back of his coat, and tricorn hat in his left hand, he extends his right-hand, almost as if he has just made a reverence to a lady or person of quality.[81] Such a man probably would have made a good impression in Roman aristocratic society. Although one might be reading too much into this caricature, it should be remembered that one of the goals of this new genre was to capture spontaneously something of the subject's personality, in contrast to the formal portraiture of the time. There is another caricature of Vinci by Ghezzi which though undated, appears to have originated in the late 1720s (see Chapter 9).

---

[79] Some 384 prints have been published, with copious annotations and analysis by Giancarlo Rostirolla. *Il "Mondo novo" musicale di Pier Leone Ghezzi*, with essays by Stefano La Via and Anna Lo Bianco (Rome: Accademia Nazionale di Santa Cecilia & Milan: Skira, 2001).

[80] The sketch was discovered by Giancarlo Rostirolla, "Nuovi documenti sulla presenza di Leonardo Vinci a Roma" paper presented at the conference: *Leonardo Vinci: architetture sonore nella Napoli del viceregno austriaco: convegno internazionale di studi*, Conservatorio di Musica Francesco Cilea, Reggio Calabria, 10-12 Giugno 2002. This side profile sketch and full-length caricature must have been standard procedure for Ghezzi, for *Il nuovo Mondo* contains many of them bound together; for example for Faustina (Ottob.lat 3113 f.69 & 70) and La Romanina (Ottob.lat 3116 f.144-145).

[81] In another context, Rostirolla describes this dress as "abito di gala"(*Il "Mondo novo,"* 299).

**Plate 6.** *Caricature of Leonardo Vinci by Pier Leone Ghezzi, Rome, March 1724.*
© Biblioteca Apostolica Vaticana (Vatican)[82]

---

[82] Pier Leone Ghezzi, *Il nuovo Mondo*, IV, f. 135; unpublished manuscript in the Bibliioteca Apostolica Vaticana, Ottob.lat 3115.

# 4

# STAMPIGLIA'S HEROIC COMEDIES
## Papal Celebrations and the Final *Commedia*

After the première and subsequent revival of *Farnace* and a rather extended stay in Rome, Vinci would have returned to Naples some time in April of 1724. According to the *Avvisi di Napoli* he produced music for the Confraternity of the Rosary at S. Caterina a Formiello on May 5 in honor of Pope Pius V:

> Friday of the past week at the Royal church of S. Caterina...was solemnized the feast of the glorious Pope Saint Pius V with lavish display and choice music, made by the celebrated Maestro di Cappella Leonardo Vinci.[1]

The Confraternity honored this ascetic sixteenth-century pope (canonized in 1712) because he established the commemoration of the Rosary in 1571 in celebration of the great naval victory of Lepanto.[2] As was the case with the St. Catherine's Day celebrations from the previous year, it is not known what music was performed. One possibility is that the *Missa Brevis* was performed on this occasion, scaled down from *a più cori* for double choir and orchestra to the *Missa à otto voce* that is now in the Santini Collection in Münster.[3] In June, according to the *Avvisi*, more music was commissioned by the Confraternity: "a solemn Te Deum à Più Cori of choice music by the celebrated virtuoso Leonardo Vinci."[4] Following the death of Innocent XIII on March 7th 1724, a protracted Papal conclave was held, with a decision not reached until the end of

---

[1] *Avvisi di Napoli*, May 9, 1724 (No. 20).

[2] *The Catholic Encyclopedia*, s.v. "Rosary, Feast of the Holy Rosary." The connection between the rosary and great military victories over the "infidel" was further strengthened in 1711 when Clement XI promoted the commemoration to a full Feast after Prince Eugene's victory over the Turks at Peterwardein. Since both were great Habsburg victories and S. Caterina was a "Real Chiesa" there may well have been political overtones to the feast.

[3] Another possible candidate would be the Mass in A major that exists in two sets of parts in the Biblioteca del Conservatorio di Musica S. Pietro a Majella in Naples, attributed to Porpora in one manuscript (Rel.3363) and to Vinci in the other (Rel. 3364). However, this library contains a large collection of sacred music by Porpora in parts, making the Porpora attribution more likely.

[4] *Avvisi di Napoli*, June 20, 1724 (No. 26).

May because of the competing Bourbon and Habsburg factions.[5] The Te Deum conducted by Vinci was to celebrate the elevation of Pietro Francesco Orsini as Pope Benedict XIII. There is a Te Deum attributed to Vinci in Berlin and it would be tempting to assign it to this occasion. However, the Te Deum is not *a più cori* and Strohm has questioned the authenticity of the attribution.[6] Although it is tempting to assign these works to these documented performances, it should be emphasized that there is a definite problem in linking up the contemporary references to Vinci's sacred music, to the handful of sacred works by Vinci that survive.[7]

Also in May of 1724, *La mogliere fedele,* a new *commedia per musica,* was premièred. The reason for this return to comedy was the inauguration of a new theatre, the Teatro della Pace. It originated in 1718 as a private theatre for dialect comedies in the home of Prince Chiusano Caraffa, but was later established as a public venue for *commedia per musica.* Savero Donati writing in 1749, described the theatre as narrow and small with only three rows of stalls, specializing in "burlesque comedy in Neapolitan dialect [sung] by singers of mediocre ability...for the satisfaction of less cultivated people."[8] Vinci, however, considered the inauguration of the theatre important enough to interrupt his new career as a composer of the *dramma per musica*. As was the case with the regular audience at the Teatro Fiorentine, the crowd for the inauguration, according to the *Avvisi di Napoli*, was primarily aristocratic:

> Last Sunday evening was [produced], at the Teatro della Pace, the first *Opera in musica* in Neapolitan dialect entitled *La mogliere fedele*, which attained the satisfaction of all the nobility, by its words as well as by the music composed by the celebrated virtuoso, Maestro di Cappella Leonardo Vinci.[9]

The only hint that the Teatro della Pace was not in the same league as the other two theatres was the absence of the Viceroy, with the dedication going to the Viceroy's nephew, Carl Emanuel Althann. This opera may have been composed at the request of the latter. The reference to "the

---

[5] J. N. D. Kelly, *The Oxford Dictionary of Popes* (Oxford: Oxford University Press, 1986), 294.

[6] The Te Deum attributed to Vinci in the Amalienbibliothek is considered by Strohm to be a forgery because certain pieces in this collection are misattributed to Vinci (but see below). Reinhard Strohm, *Italienische Opernarien* , Vol. II, 244.

[7] In the descriptions of music in the churches in Naples and Rome from this period, the number of references to the performances of Music "à più cori" and of Te Deums, suggests that the libraries and churches in these cities should contain collections of Te Deums and music for double choir. Either much of this material has been lost or there is a significant repertoire of eighteenth-century sacred music waiting to be discovered.

[8] Quoted in Benedetto Croce, *I teatri di Napoli: secoli XV-XVIII* , 258.

[9] *Avvisi di Napoli*, May 16, 1724: (No. 21).

service rendered to Conte Emanuel," the *nipote* to Cardinal Althann, in Vinci's application for a position in the Real Cappella (see below) probably refers to this work and perhaps other services. That the performance standards at the première may have left something to be desired is suggested by the preface to the libretto for the revival of *La mogliere fedele* at the Teatro Nuovo in 1731. After obliquely praising the music which is "by one who was the *ne plus ultra* among *maestri di cappella* and is called Vinci," the impresario promises that the opera "will now succeed even better because the [musicians] are more virtuoso."[10] According to Viviani's *Storia del teatro napoletano*, Nicola Corvo was the author of the libretto, a stormy tale of deception and revenge that "directly anticipates the romantic drama."[11] The score, sharing the fate of most early Neapolitan *commedie per musica*, has not survived.

## Collaboration with Old Stampiglia

Vinci's *Eraclea* was premièred on October 1st 1724 in celebration of Emperor Charles's birthday. The *Avvisi di Napoli* reported that:

> in the evening his eminence the Viceroy went to hear the opera that was performed for the first time at the Teatro di S. Bartolomeo, entitled *L'Eraclea*, which attained complete satisfaction of the eminent prince, as of all the nobility and other classes of people who went to hear it, through the excellent composition of the words, which were by the renowned Imperial poet Silvio Stampiglia, and also of the music, that is by the celebrated Maestro di Cappella Leonardo Vinci.[12]

Although commissioned for the Emperor's birthday, *Eraclea* was premièred at the Teatro S. Bartolomeo rather than the Real Palazzo. As mentioned previously, *Silla Dittatore* was the last in a long series of palace premières. Recent renovations made the Teatro San Bartolomeo the preferred venue for command performances.

With the exception of a single singer, the cast of *Eraclea* was different from *Silla*, consisting of:

Marcello: Francesco Giucciardi   Eraclea: Vittoria Tesi
Damiro: Carlo Broschi   Flavia: Anna Maria Strada
Decio: Diana Vico   Irene: Anna Guglielmini
Ilisso: Caterina Levi
    Stage design: Giovanni Battista Olivieri
    Ballet: Sebastiano Scio

---

[10] *La mogliere fedele: commeddea pe mmuseca,* da rappresentarese a lo Teatro Nuovo ncoppa Monte Cravaneo nchist'autunno dell' anno corrente 1731 (Naples, 1731).

[11] Vittorio Viviani, *Storia del teatro Napoletano*, 287-88.

[12] *Avvisi di Napoli*, October 3, 1724 (No. 40).

One of the reasons for this change is that half the cast from the previous year had been engaged by the Teatro San Cassiano in Venice.[13] It would seem that someone connected with the San Cassiano had attended the première of Domenico Sarro and Pietro Metastasio's *Didone abbandonata* earlier that year and was so impressed by the drama and its accompanying intermezzo that they hired not only the poet but also the principals, La Romanina and Nicolino, and the comic duo, Corrado and Santa Marchesina for the Venetian premières of *Didone abbandonata* and *Impresario delle isole Canarie*. In Naples, Nicolino and La Romanina were replaced by Farinello and Vittoria Tesi. Farinello had made his Neapolitan debut the previous spring in Porpora's *Amare per regnare*. Although Farinello was the *primo uomo*, the lead male part was sung by Diana Vico, a Venetian contralto who specialized in trouser roles (having created Dardano in Handel's *Amadigi* in 1715). Most Neapolitan operas of this period contain at least one trouser role and in the case of Decio, such a role was particularly advantageous since the hero is disguised as a woman throughout the opera. The title role was also sung by a contralto, Vittoria Tesi, who was celebrated for both her singing and acting talents, while the *prima donna* role was sung by Anna Maria Strada who was later to make her reputation in London as Handel's faithful soprano during the 1730s.

Silvio Stampiglia's *Eraclea* was originally written for Alessandro Scarlatti in 1700 and performed at the same theatre.[14] The *dramma per musica* is based on two unrelated events of the Punic Wars as recounted by Livy.[15] The slaughter of Heraclia and her daughters, after the assassination of her father, the Tyrant of Syracuse, provides the opening scene for the opera. In Livy's account a messenger arrives too late to stay the execution whereas in the opera, the messenger, Damiro, arrives in time to prevent the slaughter and the opera then proceeds on its fictitious course. The hero, on the other hand, is based on Decius Magius of Capua, who remained loyal to Rome amidst the conquest of the city by Hannibal.[16] In Livy, Decius escapes to Alexandria in Egypt where Stampiglia has him become friends with Eraclea's husband Sossipo, who is also in exile in that city. After the death of Sossipo, Decio makes his

---

[13] See cast lists in Taddeo Wiel, *I teatri musicali veneziani del Settecento: catalogo delle opere in musica rappresentate nel secolo XVIII in Venezia*, 71-75.
[14] Alessandro Scarlatti, *Eraclea*, ed. Donald Jay Grout, Vol. I: *The Operas of Alessandro Scarlatti*, general ed. Donald Jay Grout (Cambridge, Mass.: Harvard University Press, 1974), Preface, 3-4.
[15] Livy, *The war with Hannibal: Books XXI-XXX of The History of Rome from its Foundation*, tr. Aubrey de Sélincourt, ed. Betty Radice. (Harmonsworth: Penguin Books, c. 1965) Bk. XXIV, Ch. 7 and 26.
[16] Ibid., Bk. XXIII, Ch. 7-10.

way to Syracuse to protect the widow amidst the Roman coup d'état, thereby bringing together the hero and heroine of his tale, which is set against the siege and conquest of Syracuse by Marcus Claudius Marcellus.[17] Joined to this historical fiction is a romantic comedy between the daughters of Eraclea and two Syracusian cavaliers and a bizarre farce between Eraclea's tutor and Decio's servant disguised as a girl.

The drama was revised for Vinci by the aging poet ("da lui rinovato") who in 1724 was living in Naples in semi-retirement.[18] Because of the changes that had taken place in opera since the turn of the century, the drama had to be extensively revised. In Vinci's version of the libretto, the romantic comedy between the daughters and their suitors has been revised in order to simplify the romantic intrigue and ennoble the minxish character of the daughters, while the farce, with its strong ties to early Venetian opera, has been completely omitted. The latter is rather surprising when one considers the usual practice of adding comic intermezzi at the end of acts for subsidiary characters (i.e. for Albino and Plautilla in *Silla Dittatore*).

> **Synopsis**: After the Roman order to exterminate the royal house of Syracuse, Eraclea and her daughters Flavia and Irene are saved from assassins by Decio, who is disguised as a woman named Aldimira in order to protect the princesses. Having fallen in love with Eraclea from the descriptions of her late husband, Decio reveals his true identity to Eraclea and declares his love. The grieving queen requests that he will "love, serve and be silent" without asking for any reward. Decio decides that for the time being, the best way to serve Eraclea is to retain his disguise with the approach of the Roman army. The Roman Council Marcello arrives at the head of the army to establish Roman rule, and immediately falls in love with Eraclea. Owing her life and the lives of her daughters to the magnanimity of the conqueror, Eraclea cannot reject Marcello's love. His courtship of Eraclea is particularly frustrating to Decio because as a loyal Roman, Marcello is his leader. Decio is continually on the verge of revealing his identity and challenging Marcello, as in the ballroom scene where he appears in a counter-disguise as a man, only to be revealed as his original cover Aldimira. Marcello ironically enlists Decio's aid in his courtship of Eraclea, egotistically interpreting Decio's reluctance as a sign that she/he is in love with him. When asked about this reluctance, Aldimira/Decio replies that a friend, "il cavalier amator" secretly loves Eraclea.

---

[17] Ibid., Bk. XXIV, Ch. 33-36 and Bk.XXV, Ch. 23-31.
[18] Libretto in I-Nc and I-Bc; Claudio Sartori, *I libretti italiani* (No 9019).

When Marcello asks who is this rival, she/he replies that they will soon meet. Decio decides that it is his duty as a Roman to cede his claims on Eraclea to his leader Marcello. When Decio reveals his true identity and abandons his suit of Eraclea, Marcello, not to be outdone, cedes his claims, thereby allowing Eraclea and Decio to be united. The romantic comedy involving Eraclea's daughters operates almost independently of the main plot and generates almost as much dialogue. In this quasi-independent comedy, the flighty Flavia wants to love only for pleasure, while the stoic Irene scorns love. In loving Damiro for her pleasure, Flavia experiences only pain and jealousy because of his unreliable character. To scorn love, Irene pretends to love Iliso but in playing the game, actually falls in love and goes through all the languishing and torments. After experiencing the pains of love, they reject their lovers in Act III before being reconciled and united in the final scene.

In *Eraclea*, Stampiglia exploits the traditions of disguise and sexual ambiguity of seventeenth-century Italian opera, at a time, ironically, when his Arcadian colleagues were attempting to rid opera of these conceits. This exploitation reaches a climax in the Ballroom scene in Act II, where his male lead (disguised as a woman and sung by a woman) appears in counter-disguise as a man at a court ball, only to be "unmasked" as a woman —or rather, as a woman disguised as a man who is actually a man disguised as a woman disguised as a man, but sung by a woman. Having achieved this dizzying degree of sexual ambiguity, Stampiglia freezes the situation with Eraclea's abrupt order: "Until you hear otherwise, you will serve me in this dress"— an order that the audience "gets" but the other characters would perceive as the princess wanting her maid to serve her dressed like a man (which in the original libretto may have been a reference to Queen Christina and her sexual preferences). This ambiguous situation is maintained until the *scena ultima* and the final unmasking, which ironically is not an unmasking at all, but rather the undeceiving of the rest of the cast. Although one could explain the absence of comic intermezzi in *Eraclea* by the lightweight nature of both the principal drama and the romantic comedy, neither of which needs comic relief, there is a specific reason for this break with Neapolitan tradition. In *Eraclea* the comic intermezzi were replaced by ballets. The absence of the regular buffo singers, Gioacchino Corrado and Santa Marchesina, during the fall of 1724 and Carnival 1725, compelled the directors of the Teatro San Bartolomeo to look for an entr'acte replacement. It was decided to engage a ballet master rather than another pair of comedians. Vinci may have had something to do with this, since he was in charge of the first two operas that season and had experimented successfully with ballet at the Teatro Fiorentini in his *La festa di Bacco* in 1722. Moreover, the ballet master, Sebastiano Scio, had provided the ballets for his *Farnace* during the previous Carnival and, with the closure of the theatres during the Holy Year of 1725, Scio and his troupe were not needed in Rome. Although performances of comic intermezzi in Naples resumed with the return of Corrado in the spring of 1725, *Eraclea* anticipates operatic productions of the Bourbon era. In 1736 King Charles III banished the intermezzi from the *dramma per musica* in Naples, replacing them with ballets according to the current practice in operatic centers such as Rome and Venice.[19]

## *Eraclea* and the Spirit of Terpsichore

Indicative of the changes in eighteenth-century Italian music, Stampiglia's libretto from 1700 could be revived for performance a quarter century later, whereas Scarlatti's music could not— in spite of the fact that both were living in Naples at the time. Not only was Scarlatti's music not revived, but Vinci's score shows few parallels, composing his *Eraclea* as if Scarlatti's had never existed.[20]

The one aspect that Vinci and Scarlatti's scores have in common is the abundance of ensembles. Vinci's *Eraclea* contains a duet, a trio, two quartets, and two choruses. With one exception these can be found in Stampiglia's original libretto for Scarlatti, which contained an even larger number of ensembles: ten duets, two choruses, a quartet and a septet.[21]

---

[19] Michael F. Robinson, *Naples and Neapolitan Opera*, 162.

[20] There is a single surviving score of Vinci's *Eraclea*, now housed in the Biblioteca dell'Abbazia in Montecassino 6-C-4/6 in 3 vols., 21 x 28 cm. (formerly 126 E 24-26). Like most of the Vinci scores in this collection, it formerly belonged to Don Vincenzo Bovio (1809-1860), abbot at Montecassino, a member of the powerful Bovio family in Naples. The inclusion of the incomplete ballet music, and the numerous minute corrections, either in pen or by some very neat cutting and pasting, suggests that the score was copied under the composer's direction, and then perhaps proofread by the composer. Therefore, this manuscript may have been the official theatre score from which the performance parts were copied. Like the score to *Silla*, each act ends with the pious inscription L.D.M.S.V. The Montecassino score of *Eraclea*, from which the excerpts below are taken, consists of the following musical numbers:

| | |
|---|---|
| 2 sinfonias | 5 dances |
| 30 *da capo* arias | 3 *da capo* ensembles |
| 1 aria with coro | 1 through-composed ensemble |
| 2 ariettas | 2 accompanied recitatives |
| 1 coro | Totals: 47 set pieces (33 in *da capo* form) |

*Eraclea* received an outstanding modern première at the Festival dell'Aurora in May, 2005 in an edition prepared by the author and conducted by Roberto Zarpellon. The cast consisted of Barbara Di Castri, Krisztina Jonas, Alessandra Vavasori, Barbara Vignadelli, Paola Quagliata, Monica Tonietto, and Kim Sung Woo and was accompanied by the Orchestra del Festival dell'Aurora, made up primarily of members of Venice Baroque.

[21] Facsimile of libretto in Scarlatti, *Eraclea*, ed. Grout.

Vinci's trio "Che maestà, che brio" is sung with the arrival of Marcello, who sets the plot in motion by falling in love with Eraclea. In brief asides he expresses his love for her, while Decio fumes with jealousy and Eraclea reminds him of his promise. Originally "Che maestà" was a septet, but the roles for the young lovers were omitted because of changes in the subplot, which does not begin until after the trio.[22] Although the characters exit at the end of the trio, it is a relatively modest through-composed piece (twenty measures including ritornellos) rather than an exit *da capo*. The duet and quartets, on the other hand, are conceived as large-scale *da capo* forms taking the place of the exit arias. The quartet "Mi tormento/è mia pena" is modelled on the quartet in *Farnace*; both are in F minor, quadruple meter, moderate tempo, in pathetic style with similar dimensions, including the absence of opening ritornellos. The derivative nature of the *Eraclea* quartet and its absence in the original libretto, suggests that it owed its genesis to the composer who wished to replicate the quartet in *Farnace*. Tutti passages, though infrequent, are somewhat more extended and dynamic than those in the *Farnace* quartet. The first vocal period begins with solos, progresses to duets, and culminates in a quartet passage—the final cadence, introduced by a pause and sung by all the voices *sotto voce*. After the intermediate ritornello, the second vocal period begins with an unexpected recitative-like passage for Eraclea and Decio before the lyricism returns.

Reinhard Strohm has described *Eraclea* as a *mezzo carattere* dance opera.[23] It is the only Vinci opera for which ballet music survives. Seven dances are bound at the beginning and end of Act II in the Montecassino score. These unnamed dances are modest binary pieces, in triple or simple duple meter, with only one in compound meter. Rather surprisingly, only the bass line is given, suggesting that they were intended as sketches to be completed by the *maestro di ballo*, Sebastiano Scio. These sketches were probably included because they are by Vinci. Although ballet musc in eighteenth-century Italian opera was traditonally the domain of the ballet-master (see Chapter 3), Vinci may have provided these dance sketches because he and his *maestro di ballo* were trying to connect the ballets with the opera as was the practice in France. The ballet at the end of Act II ties in with the final scene as a fleet of ships arrive in the port of Syracuse from Libya, sent by the Roman Senate to deliver "numerous sacks of grain" to the starving "victors and vanquished" of the besieged city.[23] The *ballo* rep-

---

[22] The original was the septet to which Dent took exception because the vocal parts were arranged on a single stave in the manuscript; *Alessandro Scarlatti, his Life and Works*, 55-58.

[23] *Eraclea: Drama per musica di Silvio Stampigla...Da Lui Rinovato, da rappresentarsi nel Teatro di S. Bartolomeo nell'Autunno del 1724* (Naples: Francesco Ricciardo, 1724): Act II/xii & vii, 41 & 37.

resents African and Moorish slaves from the ships unloading the sacks of grain. While this is a clever way to introduce a typical "ballet di mori," the ballet at the end of Act I is more inventive. In contrast to the violence of the opening scenes of Act I, the final scenes are set against preparations for a "gran danze Real" to celebrate the Roman victory. Towards the end of Act I, Irene announces that the "hour of the ball is at hand;" the ballet at the end of the act then is a masked ball, the ballet set in the "Sala del Festino" that provides the backdrop for the Ballroom scene at the beginning of Act II.[24]

Through Vinci's and Scio's clever intersection, the *ballo* intermission moves smoothly into the drama proper, as tension builds between Eraclea's Roman suitors. Decio, who appears at the masked ball in counter-disguise as a man, is compelled to challenge Marcello in his suit of Eraclea. Just as the incident is about to become violent, Decio is revealed as his cover Aldimira. The action is accomplished in recitative that is spliced up by two composed minuets, the first scored for full orchestra with trumpets and oboes and the fragmentary second for generic two-part orchestra, separated by recitative dialogue that lead to Decio's challenge. After defusing the sitauton, Eraclea leads her guests in a dance-song, "Son Nemici e sempre insieme," which is labelled a "contradanza" in the score. Typical of dance music there is much repetition, as each section of this binary dances is stated by the orchestra before being taken up by the singers: first by Eraclea, then by Decio, and finally by the entire cast in chorus,. In this experiment in connencting the conventional Italian ballet interlude with the opera, Vinci and Scio have anticipated the reforms of Handel and Marie Salle in *Alcina* and *Ariodante* in London ten years later, and Jommelli and Noverre at the court of Stuttgart some thirty years later.

The influence of Terpsichore, however, extends beyond this ballroom scene. The score to *Eraclea* contains a large number of arias based on dance rhythms—over a third of the thirty-four arias and ensembles. Dance-inspired arias are perhaps suggestive of the influence of Domenico Sarro (whose *Arsace* contains about the same proportion of dance-like arias).[25] The most common dance type is the minuet. Marcello's "M'accese vibrato" begins with a theme similar to that in "Qual nave smarrito" from Handel's *Radamisto,* which is also in the same key. While Handel developed this theme into a grand Baroque sarabande of great nobility, Vinci created a most elegant minuet:

---

[24] Ibid. Act I/vii, xiii, & xxi, 20, 23, & 27.
[25] Sarro's *Arsace* from December 1718 is reproduced in facsimile in Vol. 22 of *Italian Opera 1740-1770.*

Example 4.1. "M'accese vibrato" *Eraclea* I/ix

The rhythmic acceleration within the second phrase, from eighths to sixteenths to triplet sixteenths, contributes to the elegant effect. The theme of Irene's "Sento già che và nascondo," on the other hand, derives from the duet "Se fedel, cor mio" in Porpora's *Gli orti esperidi* from 1721. Vinci shifted the motives around with an ingenuity worthy of Handel, employing the theme as heard in Porpora's ritornello but tying it on to the end of one of Porpora's vocal phrases, the beginning of which Vinci employed to begin his second phrase (mm.11-13):

Example 4.2. "Sento già che và nascondo" *Eraclea* I/xiv

Handel also borrowed this theme, using it for Cleopatra's great seduction aria "V'adoro pupile" from *Giulio Cesare*.

Although the minuet is the standard dance type, others can be found such as the passepied in Irene's "Non scherzi con amor," the gavotte in Flavia's "Non sà che sia," and the bourrée in Damiro's "L'ape ingegnosa:"

Example 4.3a. "Non scherzi con amor" *Eraclea* III/ii

Example 4.3b "Non sà che sia" *Eraclea* II/iii

Example 4.3c "L'ape ingegnosa" *Eraclea* II/ii

[Musical notation with syllables: "ro - sa/ Vo - lan - do và/ vo - lan 6 - 6 - 6" and "do vo lan -6 - do và./" marked "tutti"]

In these and several other dance arias, Vinci employs a simple thematic structure consisting of a repeated initial phrase, followed by a florid sequential phrase that sets up the modulation to the dominant. The florid sequential phrase in the simile aria "L'ape ingegnosa" expands the bourrée into a coloratura aria via sextuplet coloratura flourishes depicting the flight of the bee.

In certain arias Vinci appears to have picked up where he left off with regards to stylistic development in the additional arias in *Silla* and *Farnace* (see Chapter 3). That these additions were well received in Naples is suggested by the fact that they have their counterparts in *Eraclea*. Flavia's "Il ruscelletto amante dell'erbe" is based on Valeria's substitute aria "No hà quell Augelletto" (compare Example 4.4a on p. 94 with Example 3.4 on p. 56). Both are simile arias set to *settenario* verse, sung by the heroine at the end of Act I, based on ascending triadic themes above a descending-scale bass in repreated notes, with the phrase twice repeated.[26] The presence of the recorder and the pizzicato strings in the *Eraclea* aria, however, create a sweeter, more delicate effect appropriate to the "ruscelletto" imagery and the character of Flavia. Decio's "Son tormentato di una tiranna" shows affinities with Pompeo's addi-

---

[26] *Settenario:* a standard verse type consisting of seven syllables (minus or plus one depending upon the verse ending) that became standard in writing aria texts; other verse types include the *senario* (six syllable), *quinario* (five syllable) and *ottonario* (eight syllable); see Antonio Scoppa, *Traité de la poésie italienne, rapportée a la poésie française* (Versailles: L'imprimerie de Jacob, 1803).

Example 4.4a. "Il ruscelletto amante dell'erbe" *Eraclea* I/xv

Example 4.4b "Son tormentato di una tiranna" *Eraclea* I/xi

tional aria "Quel traditore tiranno amore" (compare Example 4.4b with Example 3.5 on p. 57). Both are complaints in *quinario* verse, sung by the hero at the end of Act I in *alla breve* style, and though one is in the major and one in the minor mode, the second themes of both arias are similar. The minor mode in "Son tormentato," combined with the driving syncopated rhythms and melody that tend to splinter into three-note fragments, creates a tempestuous effect when taken at a fast tempo, transforming this simple *alla breve* aria into a clear anticipation of the *aria agitata* of Vinci's final opera.

The new style is also manifest in the musical/dramatic climax of the opera, Eraclea's *scena* at the beginning of Act III. When Decio tells Eraclea of his decison to "cede her" to his rival and superior Marcello, Eraclea, in a brief arietta, calls for revenge. After Decio explains that he must renounce her to preserve his glory, Eraclea declares that she will die to preserve her honor. Her threatening vow is expressed in an accompanied recitative leading to an *ombre* aria in which she swears that her ghost will haunt him. This unusual *unisono* aria in C minor is dominated by its driving dotted rhythm broken by pungeant chromatic appoggiaturas that Pergolesi would later recall in "Fac, ut partem Christe mortem" from his *Stabat Mater*.

Example 4.5a "Son l'ombre d'Eraclea" *Eraclea* III/i

Contrasts are introduced in the second section as the dotted rhythms are accompanied by rich chromatic chordal harmonies, creating the effect of a Chopinesque funeral march:

Example 4.5b "Son l'ombre d'Eraclea" *Eraclea* III/i

The unisons, on the other hand, are augmented to sharply articulated half-notes, the latter then fragmenting the vocal line with syncopating rests, simulating Eraclea's dying gasps. The new style is also evident in Farinello's final aria, "Stando Amore," a massive coloratura aria with obbligato trumpet. With its competitive solos for trumpet and voice that could easily be extended via extempore improvisation, "Stando Amore" may have been modelled on the aria in which the celebrated duel took place between Farinello and a Roman trumpet virtuoso.[27]

Although more traditional arias can be found, particularly in Act III, such as Eraclea's Handelian cantilena "Queste pupille almeno" or Decio's Vivaldian *tempesta di mare* "In questa mia tempesta," much of the score of *Eraclea* is pervaded by a new spirit and a new style. This new style may in part be related to Vinci's contact with Stampiglia. The pronounced *mezzo carattere* nature of both the main plot and the sub-plot, with their seventeenth-century intrigue perhaps suggested to Vinci

---

[27] According to Farinello's first biographer Sacchi, this took place during his Roman debut during Carnival 1722, presumably in Porpora's *Flavio Anicio Olibrio*; Giovanale Sacchi, *Vita del cavaliere don Carlo Broschi detto il Farinell*, ed. Alessandro Abbate with a preface by Vittorio Paliotto (Naples: Flavio Pagano, 1994; originally published in Venice: Coleti, 1784), 35.

a freer use of the new style he had developed in his comic operas. Moreover Stampiglia's libretti contained one element that Vinci appears to have found most congenial: idealized sentimental romance.

## First Venetian Commissions

*Eraclea* was followed in December 1724 by a pasticcio on Stampiglia's *Turno Aricino* arranged by Vinci and Leo. The ailing poet was then severely ill and delegated the job of adapting his 1702 libretto to his son. Vinci set the recitatives in Act I, as well as a quartet and four arias, and Leo set the remaining recitatives, a duet and seven arias, four of the latter being the only surviving music from this pasticcio; according to the libretto:

> the performers have been permitted to place in this opera diverse arias to their satisfaction...; many of these have had the words changed, while others have been left because they can pass for the subject.[28]

These interpolated arias represent a cross-section of the contemporary operatic scene, including arias by Porpora, Scarlatti, Lotti, Porta, Capelli, Vivaldi and others. Although Vinci appears to have displaced Leo at the Teatro San Bartolomeo, this collaboration suggests that Leo was not averse to working with his successful rival. The pasticcio was probably Vinci's commission, but other commitments compelled him to delegate some of the work to Leo. Vinci was not even in Naples for the première. Alongside the review of *Turno Aricino* in the *Avvisi di Napoli* for December 5, there is a notice concerning the revival of *Li Zite 'ngalera* at the Teatro della Pace that provides information on the composer's whereabouts:

> Wednesday of last week the opera in Neapolitan dialect *Li Zite 'ngalera* went on stage for the first time at the Teatro della Pace, set to music by Maestro di cappella Leonardo Vinci, who today finds himself in Venice, his music having carried there great approval.[29]

By early December Vinci had left for Venice to prepare for the première of his first Venetian opera, *Ifigenia in Tauride* which initiated the Carnival season at the Teatro San Giovanni Grisostomo, a season that was to include the première of *La Rosmira fedele*. It is possible that Vinci travelled with Metastasio and La Romanina, who would have been going to Venice at this time to join their colleagues Gizzi, Corrado, and Santa Marchesina for the Venetian première of *Didone abbandonata*.[30]

---

[28] Strohm, *Italienische Opernarien* II, 284.
[29] *Avvisi di Napoli*, December 5, 1724 (No. 50).
[30] Gizzi, Corrado, and Santa Marchesina already appeared at the San Cassiano in the autumn production of Orlandini's *Antigona*; Taddeo Wiel, *I teatri musicali veneziani del settecento*, 70-71.

In his Venetian commissions, Vinci was following the lead of Leo who had produced *Timocrate* at the Teatro Sant' Angelo during the Carnival of 1723. While *Timocrate* set the precedent for Venetian commissions going to Neapolitan composers, Vinci's *Ifigenia in Tauride* and *La Rosmira fedele* initiate a period of pronounced Neapolitan influence in Venice with the principal commissions going to visiting Neapolitan composers such as Vinci, Porpora, Leo, Sarro, and Hasse rather than to local composers such as Vivaldi and Porta.[31] This trend is exemplified in Burney's *A General History of Music*, where not only is the chapter on eighteenth-century Venetian opera dwarfed by the following chapter on Neapolitan opera, but the former is dominated by references to works by Neapolitan masters. According to Burney 1725 was the year "the Venetian theatre first heard the natural, clear, and dramatic strains of Leonardo Vinci, in his two operas of *Ifigenia in Aulide* and *La Rosmira Fidele*."[32] Vinci's commissions for the Carnival of 1725 were doubly precious because this was a jubilee year when the theatres in Rome were closed, making commissions in Venice all the more competitive; Vivaldi, for example, did not produce an opera this season. Although the Neapolitan influence never reached the hegemony it did in Rome, because of the multiplicity of theatres and the great Venetian operatic tradition, it was not until the advent of Galuppi that a native Venetian could challenge the popularity and prestige of the Neapolitan masters. Not only did Vinci obtain two Venetian commissions during this competitive season, but these were from the Teatro San Giovanni Grisostomo, the greatest and most magnificent of the many Venetian opera theatres. According to the chronicle of Carlo Bonlini "with the spaciousness of its superb size...and with the magnificence of its more than regal dramatic representations, it has henceforth acquired the applause and the esteem of all the world."[33]

The reference in the *Avvisi di Napoli* to "his music having carried there great approval" suggests that Vinci's music was already known in Venice prior to the première of *Ifigenia in Tauride*, through arias from his latest operas and through cantatas. In *Il teatro alla moda*, Marcello refers satirically to the managers of the theatre restaurants ingratiating themselves with the great singers by providing free drinks and "frequently presenting, to the *prima donnas*, cantatas from Naples."[34] The person

---

[31] Compare the lists before and after Vinci's *Ifigenia* in Weil, *I teatri musicali*, 76.
[32] Charles Burney, *A General History of Music*, Vol. II, 908; perhaps with Gluck's recent masterpieces in mind, Burney mixed up his *Ifigenias in Aulide* and *Tauride*.
[33] Carlo Bonlini, *Le glorie della poesia e della musica* (Venice: c.1730; reprint ed., Bologna: Arnaldo Forni Editore, 1979), 27.
[34] [Benedetto Marcello], *Il teatro alla moda: o sia metodo sicuro, e facile per ben comporre, & esequire l'Opere Italiane in Musica all'uso moderno* (Venice: "Aldaviva Licante," [c.1720]; reprint ed., Venice: Tipografia dell'Ancora, 1887), 12

responsible for introducing Vinci to Venice was undoubtedly Marcello's protege, Faustina Bordoni. She was familiar with Vinci's talents through her role in *Publio Cornelio Scipione* and probably carried away at least one sample of Vinci's work when she left Naples in the spring of 1723: the cantata nicknamed "La partenza del Faustina." With Faustina featured in all three operas produced at the San Giovanni Grisostomo during Carnival 1725, the impresario obviously planned the entire season around the young star. Pier Leone Ghezzi, who heard Faustina's Roman debut in March of 1722 at the Palazzo di Colonna, captured the event in a caricature (see Plate 7 on p. 100) and in an accompanying note stated that: "the woman sang to perfection with complete vocal agility and as much polish, without any affectation.[35] It seems likely that Vinci's association with Faustina goes back to her debut; he was sketched by Ghezzi the previous month and would probably have been in Rome for the event. A strange unidentified figure appears prominently in the foreground in Ghezzi's caricature of Faustina, which by coincidence looks a lot like Vinci.[36] He has the same build, is wearing the same coat, the same wig and the same shoes, and is carrying the same hat and sword (with the sword jutting through the flap of his coat) as in his full-length caricature of Vinci from 1724. It is like the Vinci caricature from the back (compare Plate 7 with Plate 6 on p.81). If this figure is Vinci seen from the back, why is he being portrayed in this caricature of Faustina? Perhaps because he was making his debut in Rome this same season? Perhaps because there was some special relationship between the two, that would be manifest in their subsequent collaborations in Naples and Venice.

According to the *Avvisi di Napoli* Vinci and Faustina carried the day over their rivals at the S. Angelo, S. Cassiano and S. Moisè theatres:

> Venice December 30: the evening of S. Stefano performances of opera and comedy are resumed, as well as the opening of the grand cassino. The new offering at the S. Giovanni Crisostomo is entitled *Ifigenia* which carried there all the applause, with music by the Neapolitan maestro di cappella Leonardo Vinci, specifically summoned for this opera; that at the S. Angelo is *Seleuco*; that at the S. Cassiano is *Didone abbandonata*; and the other at the S. Moisè is *Agide Re di Sparta*.[37]

---

[35] Pier Leone Ghezzi, *Il Nuovo Mondo*, II, f. 69; unpublished manuscript in the Biblioteca Apostolica Vaticana, Ottob.lat 3113.

[36] Although there is no mention of the person in the foreground in Ghezzi's note, Rostirolla states that " to underline her petite stature, Ghezzi has drawn beside her a male figure in gala dress with sword and scabbard, probably a *cameriere* or a *maestro di camera* or master of arms in the Colonna household;" Giancarlo Rostirolla, *Il "Mondo novo" musicale di Pier Leone Ghezzi*, essays by Stefano La Via and Anna Lo Bianco (Rome: Accademia Nazionale di Santa Cecilia & Milan: Skira, 2001), 299.

[37] *Avvisi di Napoli*, January 9, 1725 (No. 3).

**Plate 7** *Caricature of Faustina Bordoni in her Roman debut, by Pier Leone Ghezzi, March 1722.* c Biblioteca Apostolica Vaticana (Vatican)[38]

[38] Pier Leone Ghezzi, *Il Nuovo Mondo*, II, f.69.

Not only are the composers of the other operas not listed (Giovanni Zuccari for *Seleuco*, Tomaso Albinoni for *Didone*, and Giovanni Porta for *Agide*) but no mention is made of the prominent Neapolitan contingent in *Didone*. In spite of Metastasio's Venetian debut with *Didone*, the report confirms Burney's statement that 1725 was the year the Venetians discovered "the natural, clear, and dramatic strains of Leonardo Vinci."

The libretto of *Ifigenia in Tauride* is by Benedetto Pasqualigo, a Venetian nobleman, and treats the same subject as Gluck's *Iphigenie en Tauride*. It is the only five-act libretto set by Vinci. The five-act *tragedia per musica* is a relatively rare phenomenon, resulting from a concern, on the part of several reformers, to make the opera libretto conform more closely to spoken tragedy (notable examples being Roberti's *Il Mitridate Eupatore* written for Scarlatti's Venetian debut in 1707 as well as Piovene's original *Publio Cornelio Scipione* that served as the basis for Vinci's first *opera seria*). An indication of Pasqualigo's classicist tendencies is evidenced by his selection of a classical tragedy as the source for his drama. The frontispiece features an engraving, presumably of Ifigenia surrounded by symbols of the arts which includes scrolls representing the tragedies of Sophocles and Euripides.[39] A more recent source for Pasqualigo's libretto would have been Pier Jacopo Martello's *L'Ifigenia in Tauris* from 1709, one of the most popular as well as controversial plays on the spoken stage.[40] Like Martello, Pasqualigo includes the same elegy by Ovid in his Preface, but replaces the original Latin with a verse translation in Italian.

Vinci's libretto was the second version of Pasqualigo's drama, the original having been set to music by Giuseppe Maria Orlandini for the same theatre in 1719, with Faustina in the title role.[41] Orlandini happened to be working at the S. Giovanni Grisostomo that season. Indicative of the eighteenth-century love of novelty, he produced a new opera, *Berenice*, rather than revise his *Ifigenia*, thereby allowing Vinci to compose a new setting of this drama. Since Pasqualigo was the librettist for *Berenice*, one can assume that he was also responsible for revising his *Ifigenia* "for the purpose of singing the second time."[42]

---

[39] Libretto in I-Bc, I-Mb, I-MOe, I-P, Museo Civico, I-R, Istit.Gemanico, I-Rse, I-Vgc, I-Vnm, F-Pn, US-LAu, and US-W(Schatz 10750). Sartori, *I libretti italiani* (No. 12749).

[40] Pier Jacopo Martello, *Teatro*, ed. Hannibal S. Noce (Rome: Laterza, 1981), II; *L'Ifigenia in Tauris* was a favorite of the great director and actor Luigi Riccoboni "Lelio," who often performed it and edited the Venetian edition of 1711 (Ibid., 798-800).

[41] Sartori, *I libretti italiani* (No. 3957).

[42] *Ifigenia in Tauride: tragedia di Merindo Fesanio past, arc, Variata ad uso di Cantarsi le Second Volta* (Venice: Marino Rosetti, 1725).

In several biographical entries on Vinci, *Ifigenia in Tauride* is described as the composer's first opera. This mistake dates back to the first edition of Gerber's *Lexikon der Tonkünstler*; in the entry on Vinci, Gerber describes how the success of his first opera in Venice was such that "most of the great Italian cities wanted him as composer."[43] Although this faulty information was omitted in the second edition of Gerber, it was repeated in several standard sources from the early nineteenth century: Bertini, Choron & Fayolle and the *Biografia degli uomini illustri*. *Ifigenia in Tauride* has also been described as Vinci's masterpiece. This judgment originates with the entry on Vinci in *Biografia degli uomini illustri del Regno di Napoli* which describes the work as the "frutto della ispirazione e del genio, " which was then transformed by Fétis into the standardized "son chef-d'oeuvre" and translated by Florimo into "Il suo capolavoro," a description repeated by numerous subsequent writers.[44]

Although there is no known full score of this important work, a complete collection of arias in keyboard score survives in the Biblioteca Marciana in Venice.[45] The first impression that one receives from this collection is that the influence of Vivaldi, already encountered in *Farnace*, is even more apparent in Vinci's first Venetian opera.[46] According to Quantz, Vivaldi's operas in Rome made a favorable impression (see Chapter 3). That this impression was shared by Vinci is suggested by his apparent adoption of Vivaldi's style in several arias in *Farnace*. When Vinci obtained his commission from the Teatro San Giovanni Grisostomo, he probably set out to adapt his music to the tastes of the Venetian public. Since the most important contact Vinci had with Venetian opera was the production of Vivaldi's *Giustino* at the Teatro Capranica in 1724, it seems likely that when adjusting his music to Venetian taste, the style of Vivaldi would have been uppermost in his mind.[47]

---

[43] Gerber, *Historisches-Biographisches Lexikon der Tonkünstler* (1790-1792), I, c. 731.

[44] *Biografia degli uomini illustri del Regno di Napoli: Ornata de loro rispettivi ritratti*, Vol. VI; François-Joseph Fétis, *Biographie Universelle des musiciens*, 2nd ed. ; and Francesco Florimo, *La Scuola Musicali di Napoli e i suoi conservatori*, III, 186.

[45] Cod.t.IV 477: four of these arias ("L'onde chiara," "Dolce orror," "Dea triforme," and "Rondinella, che dal nido") can also be found in full score in the Santini-Sammlung in Münster (4266).

[46] With the proviso that not all of the characteristics associated with Vivaldi music are unique to the composer, that some of the Vivaldisms would have been common coin of early eighteenth-century Venetian music.

[47] Vivaldi's whereabouts during Carnival 1725—in fact the entire period between the première of *Giustino* in Rome during Carnival 1724 and that of the serenata composed for the Venetian embassy in celebration the wedding of Louis XV in September of 1725—are a mystery; see Michael Talbot "Antonio Vivaldi" in *The New Grove Italian Baroque Masters*, 281; Michael Talbot *Vivaldi*, 2nd ed., The Dent Master Musicians,

## *La Rosmira fedele* and Faustina

*La Rosmira fedele* was the second opera by Vinci premièred at the Teatro San Giovanni Grisostomo during Carnival season of 1725,[48] appearing at the end of the season after *Ifigenia in Tauride* and Orlandini's *Berenice*. The cast of *La Rosmira fedele*, identical to the casts in *Ifigenia* and *Berenice*, consisted of:

> Rosmira: Faustina Bordoni     Arsace: Carlo Scalzi
> Partenope: Antonia Merighi     Armindo: Antonio Barbieri
> Ormonte: Giovanni Ossi     Emilio: Carlo Bernardi
>     Ballet: Francesco Aquilante
>     Stage design: Gioseppe & Domenico Valeriani[49]

This was the first time that Vinci worked with the Lombard castrato, Carlo Scalzi, who had begun his career in this theatre during the years 1719-21 singing cadet roles alongside Faustina.[50] Faustina and Antonia Merighi had appeared together during the 1722/23 season in Naples in Vinci's *Publio Cornelio Scipione*, as well as in Sarro's setting of this same drama, *Partenope*. In the latter, Faustina also played Rosmira, while Merighi played Arsace as a trouser role.[51] Owen Swiney, the Royal Academy agent in Venice, noted sarcastically that Faustina was very pleased with the role that Vinci created for her, a role which he thought was completely inappropriate:

> I know the Faustina is in love with herselfe in this opera but if she'l take my advice, she shou'd never attempt it— she is, in it, a little part coquette, and neither she herselfe, nor no body else can tell what she wou'd be at.[52]

---

according to Strohm, he was probably in Rome, "the very fact that 'Anno Santo' was so lavishly celebrated could have attracted Vivaldi who may have hoped to produce concertos and sacred music" (Iamong the latter, the *due cori* settings of the Dixit Dominus and Beatus vir)' Reinhard Strohm, *Giustino by Antonio Vivaldi*, 8.

[48] The collection in the Marciana that contains the arias from *Ifigenia in Tauride* (Cod.t.IV 477) also contains arias from the other operas performed that season: *Ifigenia* is listed as Opera 2ª, Orlandini's *Berenice* as Opera 3ª, *La Rosmira* as Opera 4, with Francesco Brusa's *Il Trionfo della virtù*, produced during the Autumn 1724, as Opera 1º.

[49] Libretto in I-Bc -Mb -R,Istit.Germanico -RVl -Vgc -Vnm, US-BE -LCu -Wc, YU-Ls; Sartori, *I libretti Italiani* (No. 20203); Sartori lists another version of this same libretto (No. 20204 in I-Rn -Vnm); the author has not seen this version, but from the entry in Sartori, it appears to differ from the original in that its dedication is signed by Donarello Giuni.

[50] See cast lists in Wiel, *I teatri musicali veneziani del settecento*, 53, 56, & 59.

[51] She would continue her tour of the cast by creating the role of Rosmira in Handel's *Partenope* from 1730.

[52] Quoted in Elizabeth Gibson, *The Royal Academy of Music 1719-1728: the Institution and its Directors* (New York: Garland Publishing, 1989), 369.

Referring disparagingly to both Merighi and the role of Partenope, Swiney stated that they deserved each other: "the part of Partenope...is only fit for Merighi or the Diana Vico or some He-She-Thing or other."[53] From his remarks, it would appear that the sexual ambiguity of the female characters and certain female singers was considered offensive by Swiney. During this season the male cast members were depicted in caricatures attributed to Marco Ricci: Barbieri and Ossi in Greco/Roman dress, probably in their roles as Flaviano and Antioco from Orlandini's *Berenice,* and Scalzi and Bernardi in their roles as Oreste and Pilade in *Ifigenia in Tauride,* who appear in their opening scene "vestiti ad uso de Sciti" (see Plates 8-11 on p. 105). Carlo Bernardi was the brother of the famous Francesco Bernardi "Senesino" as the caricature specifies, although, according to Swiney, he did not share his brothers talent: "his Singing 'tis D\_\_\_."[54] His poor singing may account for an anomaly in the casting. The powerful tenor voice of Antonio Barbieri (to judge from the music both Vinci and Vivaldi wrote for him) is given the shy languishing role of Armindo, while the cadet role of the barbarian Emilio is given to the castrato Bernardi—an exact reversal of a more typical *settecento* casting, for example, Handel's *Partenope.*

Vinci's *La Rosmira fedele* is a setting of Silvio Stampiglia's *Partenope* which had originally been produced in Naples in 1699 with music that has subsequently been attributed to Luigi Mancia.[55] The libretto is particularly attractive, exemplifying Stampiglia's elegance and wit:

> **Synopsis**: Queen Partenope of Naples is at war with the neighboring city of Cuma. Rosmira, princess of Cyprus comes to her court disguised as a man named Euremene in search of her former lover Arsace Prince of Corinth. As one of Partenope's courtiers, Arsace has fallen in love with Partenope, who returns his love. Another courtier, Armindo Prince of Rhodes, is secretly in love with Partenope, and confides his secret to Euremene/Rosmira, who promises to help him attain his goal. When Euremene/Rosmira is confronted by Arsace, she reveals that she is indeed Rosmira. Arsace begs for forgiveness, but Rosmira tells him that she requires only one promise, to which he consents, namely that he will not reveal her true identity regardless of what happens. Rosmira then sets out to humiliate Arsace before the eyes of Partenope and the entire court. In order to justify her game of one-upmanship

---

[53] Ibid.

[54] Ibid., 371. The "D" is undoubtedly a polite abbreviation for deuce or damned.

[55] The libretto is the subject of an article by Robert Freeman, "The Travels of Partenope," *Studies in Music History: Essays for Oliver Strunk*, ed. Harold Powers (Princeton, New Jersey: Princeton University Press, 1968): 356-85.

Antonio Barbieri

Giovanni Ossi

***Plates 8 & 9*** *Caricatures of Antonio Barbieri and Giovanni Ossi probably in their roles as Flaviano and Antioco from Orlandini's* Berenice, *Venice, 1725, attributed to Marco Ricci.* [56] *(Algarotti-Gellman Album, Nos. 2 & 34)*

Carlo Scalzi

Carlo Bernardi

***Plates 10 & 11*** *Caricatures of Carlo Scalzi and Carlo Bernardi probably in their roles as Oreste and Pilade in Vinci's* Ifigenia in Tauride, *Venice, 1725, attributed to Marco Ricci.*[57] *(Algarotti-Gellman Album, Nos 26 & 31)*

---

[56] Reproduced from Edward Croft-Murray, *An Album of Eighteenth-Century Venetian Operatic Caricatures: formerly in the Collection of Count Algarotti* (Toronto: Art Gallery of Ontario, 1990), 32 & 64.

[57] Ibid., 61 & 56.

with Arsace as that between two rivals, she feigns love for
Partenope. This feigned suitor is joined by yet another suitor
when Emilio, the general of the Cumean forces, comes with
an offer of peace and marriage, an offer scornfully rejected
by Partenope. In the forthcoming battle, the Cumean forces
are defeated and Emilio is taken prisoner. Although Emilio
is captured by Arsace, Euremene/Rosmira claims him as his/
her prisoner, and continually challenges Arsace, insulting him
for not taking up the challenge. The confused Arsace, torn
between his oath and his honor, his former love for Rosmira
and present love for Partenope, passively allows Rosmira
complete freedom in her abuse, much to the amazement of
Partenope and her court. The determined Rosmira/Euremene
eventually goads the reluctant Arsace into a duel and the
reluctant Armindo into confessing his love to Partenope.
Euremene/Rosmira reveals Arsace as a traitor, allowing
Partenope to transfer her passion to the faithful Armindo.
Arsace's humorous unmasking of Rosmira, insisting that they
fight the duel bare-chested, brings about an end of his
penitential humiliation, allowing Rosmira to forgive him.

As in *Eraclea*, the story of *Partenope/La Rosmira* centers on the wooing of a Queen by several suitors. Stampiglia wrote *Partenope* and *Eraclea* in 1699 and 1700 just prior to the War of Spanish Succession when the courts of Europe were caught up in a flurry of complex negotiations concerning the succession to the Spanish Empire, of which the Kingdom of Naples was second only to Spain, in prestige if not in importance. Both Partenope, Queen of Naples, and Eraclea, Princess of Syracuse in Sicily, were intended to represent the Kingdom of Naples or, as it was sometimes known, the Two Sicilies, and the suitors, the rival Habsburg, Bourbon and Wittelsbach candidates to the Spanish Empire. The death of the Wittelsbach candidate shortly after the production of *Partenope* resulted in the reduction of the suitors to two in *Eraclea*, the sequel of *Partenope*. In Sarro's resetting for Naples in 1722, and even more so with Vinci's for Venice in 1725, the details of the political allegory would have been lost, but the basic outlines would have remained intact because the dispute between the Habsburgs and Bourbons over the Kingdom of Partenope was to dominate Italian politics for the next half century, hence the numerous settings of this drama.

This is the only Vinci opera that is known under two different titles: in the libretto as *La Rosmira fedele* and in the autograph score as *Partenope*. The opera was probably renamed before the libretto went to press, in honor of the *prima donna* Faustina; she was the star and the other two Carnival operas were already named after her roles. The new title would also distinguish it from Domenico Sarro's setting premièred in Naples in 1722. Sarro's setting of *Partenope* had been revised for him by Stampiglia, and it is this revised version that Vinci used for his *La Rosmira*.[58] In Stampiglia's revised version the majority of the aria texts were replaced by new ones, fourteen of which reappear in Vinci's opera.[59] The new intermezzo which Stampiglia had added for Sarro to replace the old comic subplot was omitted, its place being taken the ballets of Francesco Aquilante.

## *Partenope* and Vinci's Debt to Sarro

It would appear that Vinci did not use Sarro's libretto but, rather, Sarro's score of *Partenope* as the basis for his setting. According to Robert Freeman, the choruses, the Act II sinfonia, and almost all of the recitative have been lifted directly from Sarro's *Partenope*.[60] The unusual structure of the autograph score of Vinci's *La Rosmira fedele* in the British Museum, one of only two known Vinci autographs, confirms Freeman's fortuitous discovery that the work is based on pre-existing material.[61] For a composer whose self-borrowings are relatively infrequent, this

---

[58] Although the worklists in the entries on Vinci by Robert Meikle in the old *The New Grove* and Helmut Hucke in the old *MGG* attribute this Neapolitan production to Vinci, with the proviso that some of the music may be by Sarro, the libretto of the 1722 *Partenope* states that Sarro is the composer; Conservatorio di Musica S. Pietro a Majella di Napoli, Biblioteca, *Catalogo dei libretti d'opera in musica dei secoli XVII e XVIII*, ed. Francesco Melisi (Naples: Anno Europeo della Musica, 1985), No. 1108.

[59] Freeman, "The Travels of Partenope," 384.

[60] Ibid.

[61] The autograph in the British Library (R.M.20.6.11; additional 14232) consists of independently numbered fascicles, each beginning with a recitative and ending with an aria. Recitatives and internal pieces (such as the occasional arietta, coro or sinfonia) were copied at the beginning of each fascicle from Sarro's score and then the aias were added later to the fascicle as they were composed by Vinci. When the newly-composed arias were added, the shorter pieces resulted in blank pages, while the larger pieces required a second fascicle, hence the numerous blank pages throughout the manuscript. Frequently the endings of Sarro's recitative had to be adjusted to accommodate Vinci's arias, albeit the restricted key possibilities and the flexible key relationships between recitative cadence and aria, did not require the recitative cadence to be replaced in every instance. There are two exceptions to the procedure described above: in Act I fascicles 10-13 have been copied as a single unit and at the end of Act III, the trio spills into a second fascicle. The reason for the latter is that blank pages have been left, for no apparent reason, between the altered recitative cadence and the trio, followed directly by the *scena ultima*, suggesting that it was copied only after the trio was complete. The majority of the music was probably composed in Venice; the autograph is written on a different type of manuscript paper from that used by Vinci in *Li Zite 'ngalera* and in the contemporary manuscript sources of his Neapolitan and Roman operas, with a triple crescent watermark, typical of several types of contemporary Venetian papers. This same triple crescent watermark also appears in the aria collection in the Biblioteca Marciana (Cod.it.IV.477) mentioned above, which contains arias from the four operas produced at the Teatro San Giovanni Grisostomo in 1725. These arias are in short score for voice and

substantial bit of piracy is rather surprising, especially so since in a typical pasticcio it was the arias that were borrowed and the recitative newly composed, such as in the pasticcio *Elpidia* based on Vinci's arias from *La Rosmira* (see below). Why Vinci chose to borrow the recitative, the most expendable part of a *settecento* opera, in *La Rosmira* is unknown: perhaps it was to save time, perhaps because it spared Faustina the trouble of learning a new set of recitatives. Such a scenario would require Vinci to have access to Sarro's score in Venice, perhaps his own copy or, more than likely, through Faustina, who as the original Partenope, may have received a copy of the score "in partenza." This work demonstrates both the proximity of pasticcio and composition and the hegemony of the aria in eighteenth-century Italian opera, since it is Vinci's set of new arias that transforms Sarro's *Partenope* into Vinci's *La Rosmira fedele*.[62]

The influence of Vivaldi and the Venetians, encountered in *Ifigenia in Tauride*, is also evident in *La Rosmira fedele*, beginning with the opening aria. In "Spiegati, e di che l'ami," in which Rosmira urges Armindo to declare his love for Partenope, the long sequential theme is reminiscent of Vivaldi (for example the aria "Mi fa da piangere" from *Tito Manlio*):

Example 4.6. "Spiegati, e di che l'ami" *La Rosmira fedele* I/iv

continuo, with opening ritornellos omitted and subsequent ritornellos abbreviated. An aria collection in the Santini Sammlung in Münster contains arias from *La Rosmira fedele* and *Ifigenia in Tauride* (4266) and there is also a manuscript copy of the autograph score from an early twentieth-century manuscript in the Library of Congress (M1500.V64.P4). The autograph score of *La Rosmira fedele*, from which the examples below are taken, consists of the following musical numbers:

| 23 *da capo* arias | 2 *da capo* ensembles |
|---|---|
| 3 ariettas | 2 accompanied recitatives |
| 3 sinfonias | 3 choruses |

Total: 36 musical numbers (25 in *da capo* form)

*La Rosmira* was given an outstanding modern premiere at the Festival dell'Aurora in June of 2004 in an edition by Dinko Fabris with Sonia Prina, Maria Ercolano, and Maria Grazia Schiavo as the principals, accompanied by the Cappella della Pietà Dei Turchini conducted by Antonio Florio.

[62] In comparing Vinci and Sarro's settings of Armindo's "Al mio tesoro," Strohm singles out Vinci's for its ingenious integraton of text setting, motivic development, and rhythmic organization, contrasting it with Sarro's more conventional setting from 1722. Strohm, *Italienische Oper-narien des frühen Settecento*, I, 45-47. All of Vinci's aria and part of Sarro's are transcribed in II, 78-82.

The scenes associated with the battle in Act I produce a series of Vivaldian arias "Quest'anima accesa" and "A far straggi" are written in concerto-like style with unison opening themes and final cadences separated by long sequential passages with tremolo string accompaniments.[63] Emilio's "Forti schieri," sung as the Cumean general leads his troops into battle, is based on a triadic Vivaldian theme (similar to that in "Lo spietato, e crudo amore" from *L'Incoronazione di Dario,*) and contains fanfare passages in which pairs of sixteenths are superimposed against triplet sixteenths. During Partenope's triumphal entrance into Naples at the beginning of Act II, she sings the aria "Care mura." Originally an entrance arietta (and as such it was set by Handel), it has been changed into a full da capo aria while remaining at the beginning of the Act. The extended orchestrally-conceived opening ritornello creates the impression of an introductory sinfonia with vocal obbligato. The unusual scoring—for strings, oboes and timpani (although the latter stave has been left blank)— and the idiomatic writing, which juxtaposes the parallel thirds of the oboes with rapid scales and dotted unisons of the violins, seems to be more in keeping with a Vivaldi sinfonia than a Vinci aria. Vinci also re-used one of the more Vivaldian arias from *Eraclea*, "In vanno s'affana," which is distinguished by its strident unison theme and extended sequential passages. These sequential passages include the subsidiary material from the ritornello, with its lazy bass producing dissonant seconds. Vinci straightened out the syncopations in the violins from the original, with repeated sixteenths, as if to make Partenope's version of the aria a bit more Vivaldian.

Example 4.7 "In vano s'affanna" *La Rosmira fedele* II/v

---

[63] In contrast to the other arias in the opera, these have been copied together with their recitatives as a single unit in fascicles 10-13 of the autograph.

Consecutive use of sequences, employing more than three repetitions, in this aria, as well as in the theme to "Spiegati, e di che l'ami" above, while frequently encountered in the music of Vivaldi, are not that common in the music of Vinci where sequence is generally used with more restraint.

Although some of the arias in *La Rosmira* are clearly derivative of Vivaldi and the Venetians, other arias continue the stylistic innovations of *Eraclea*. The aria "Sento che và comprendo" begins as a Vivaldian "Tempesta di mare" with the orchestra rattling away on the tonic until the introduction of a dissonant second. At this point, where one would expect Vivaldi to start piling on more seconds, Vinci resolves the second, slows down the rhythm in the bass and introduces a new phrase more reminiscent of Mozart:

Example 4.8. "Sento che và comprendo" *La Rosmira fedele* II/iv

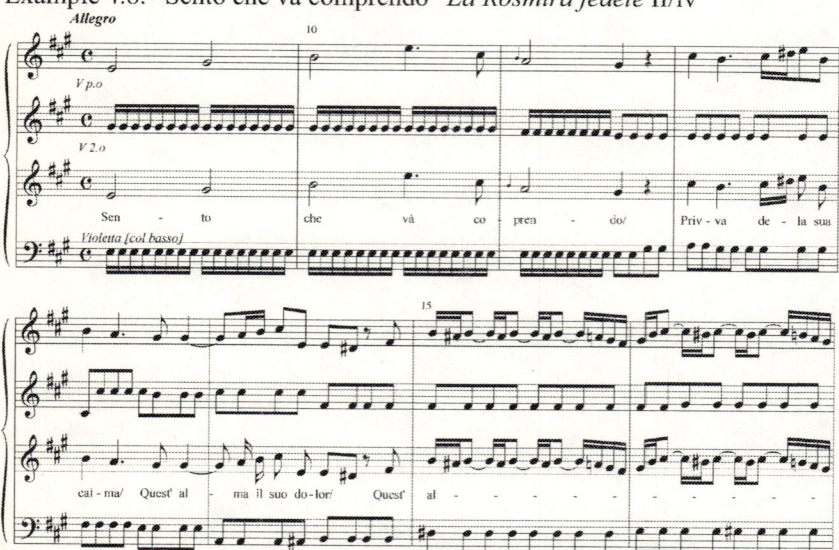

Chromaticism is introduced later in conjunction with syncopation on a melisma to depict the phrase "quest' alma il suo dolor/ this sorrow of the soul." In "Tormentosa crudel gelosia," these same elements, syncopations, chromaticism, and *Trommelbass,* are employed in a very different manner, in the minor mode to create the agitated sentimental effect that was later employed by North German composers in the *Emfindsamer* style. In this aria the main theme, with its repeated notes and descending harmonic minor scale, is syncopated above a walking bass, while *Trommelbass* is introduced for the subsidiary material which is also based on a repeated-note motive.[64]

Example 4.9. "Tormentosa crudel gelosia" *La Rosmira fedele* II/iii

The syncopated rhythm of the main theme became a standard formula for Vinci and many subsequent composers, particularly in pathetic or sentimental arias in duple meter. The reluctance to employ the minor mode is manifest not only in it being one of only two minor mode *da capo* arias in the opera, but also in the instability of the minor mode.[65]

---

[64] Although *Trommelbass* was to become a hallmark of the new Neapolitan style of Vinci and Porpora, it appears to be a Venetian technique. Marcello refers to it as "ten thousand low Es in the basso continuo above which complete and original operas will be composed...all this a present from several modern composers" (*Il teatro alla moda,* 102). Vivaldi, to whom Marcello frequently alludes in his satire, appears to be a key figure in its cultivation. His first opera *Ottone in Villa* from 1713 contains several examples. Although Vinci used the *Trommelbass* sparingly in his comic operas (3/29 or 10% of arias in *Li Zite 'ngalera*), it is used with greater frequency in his first two surviving heroic operas (33/70 or 47% of arias in *Silla Dittatore* and *Farnace*)—perhaps its slow changing harmonies suggestive of heroic stance. Beginning this season, there is a further increase in the use of this accompanimental technique, which then remains constant for the rest of his career (in 278/380 or 73% of arias in the operas *Eraclea* and *La Rosmira* to *Alessandro* and *Artaserse*). This increased use of *Trommelbass* was perhaps inspired by his first-hand acquaintance with the music of Vivaldi and the Venetians during the years 1724/25.

[65] The trend away from the minor moder can be observed in the operas of the previous decade. For example, in the late operas of Alessandro Scarlatti, the major mode out-

No sooner is the tonic established in the first vocal phrase than it moves abruptly into the relative major where it remains until the end of the second vocal period.

In Arsace's "Amante che incostante" Vinci employs the same sextuplet coloratura that he had used in Damiro's "L'ape ingegnosa" (see Example 4.3c above); however, in this instance decorated with appogiaturas above two interconnected sequences, the first resolving upon the second:

Example 4.10 "Amante che incostante" *La Rosmira fedele* II/xi

This type of coloratura was described by Marcello in *Il Teatro alla moda* as "a certain new semi-quaver passage bound as three by three"— complaining that it was being introduced "in all the arias, presto, pathetic, allegro," regardless of the context.[66] In "Amante che incostante" however, it is used specifically to depict the flightiness of Amor, in the same way that it was employed to depict the flight of the bee in "L'ape ingegnosa." Nevertheless, the fleeting garlands of syncopated sextuplet coloratura make the music seem rather lightweight for this moment of psychological perception as the wayward, self-indulgent Arsace comes to the realization that the inconstant lover always loses in the end and is abandoned and condemned by all. Vinci, however, reserved his most intense music for Arsace's final aria "Barbara mi schernisci," a Baroque lament in C minor, wherein the despairing hero complains to Rosmira that

---

numbers the minor mode by a ratio of almost three to one. This trend continues in the early operas of Vinci, where major-mode arias outnumber minor-mode arias by about five to one (of the 103 *da capo* arias and ensembles in *Silla, Franace,* and *Eraclea*, eighty-two are in the major mode and twenty-one in the minor mode.) Beginning with *La Rosmira fedele*, the number of minor-mode arias drops off considerably, from about seven per opera to two or three. In the remaining operas from *La Rosmira* to *Artaserse*, the ratio of major to minor increases to more than ten to one (of the 347 *da capo* arias in Vinci's later operas, a mere thirty-one are in the minor mode). This major/minor ratio of ten to one is more in keeping with the late eighteenth century (for example, only eleven of Haydn's 104 symphonies are in the minor mode).

[66] [Marcello], *Il teatro alla moda*, 92.

she has taken her desire for vengeance too far. Besides the minor mode and slow tempo, the aria is distinguished by its dotted rhythms, dissonant harmonies, and short fragmented phrases. The latter culminate in an unusually rapid text declamation, made up of repeated text fragments, at the end of the vocal periods (mm.8/9) that creates a sense of impassioned urgency:

Example 4.11 "Barbara mi schernisci" *La Rosmira fedele* III/iii

The aria may have been the model for "Cieca notte" from Handel's *Ariodante*, which features a similar increase in the velocity of the text declamation at the end of the vocal periods. It is known that Handel was familiar with this aria, which was incorporated into his pasticcio *Elpidia* (see below).

Music and drama are well coordinated in the trio at the end of Act III. In this scene Arsace, having already been exposed as a traitor before Partenope and her court by Rosmira, is submitted to further humiliation by the two ladies. This humiliation culminates in a trio in which Rosmira and Partenope call out for vengeance against Arsace, who protests meekly in asides. The trio is more of an *aria à tre* than an ensemble (hence the single vocal line in the example below), with the voices coming together only for three measures. The tripartite structure (a-b-a) of the exposition depicts the pairing-off of Rosmira and Partenope against Arsace, whose pathetic asides are set off further by the minor mode and chromaticism (see Example 4.12 on p. 114). Although Handel's setting of *Partenope* from 1730 evidences a much closer coordination between drama and music, in the setting of this trio, Vinci's shows greater dramatic subtlety and finesse than Handel's simple minor-mode minuet setting of this text.

Example 4.12 "Un core infedele" *La Rosmira fedele* III/vii

## *Elpidia* and the English Connection

Handel's setting of *Partenope* is often cited as being one of his more serious flirtations with the new style developed by Vinci and his colleagues.[67] Considering his penchant for borrowing, the absence of parallels between Handel's and Vinci's settings of *Partenope* suggest that Handel was not familiar with Vinci's opera when composing his version of this drama in 1730.[68] He was, however, familiar with at least six arias from *La Rosmira*, which appeared in the pasticcio *Elpidia*, performed by Handel at the Royal Academy of Music in May of 1725. Although designated as "Opera de Leonardo Vinci à Londra 11 Mai 1725" in the manuscript in the British Library,[69] *Elpidia* is now regarded as one of Handel's pasticci, based on arias from Vinci's *La Rosmira* and *Ifigenia* and Orlandini's *Berenice*.[70] From the correspondence of Owen Swiney, however, *Elpidia* appears to be more his creation than Handel's, the ac-

---

[67] Richard A. Streatfeld, *Handel* (London: Methuen, 1910; reprint ed., with introduction by J. Merrill Knapp, New York: Da Capo, 1964), 244; and Winton Dean, *Handel and the Opera Seria* (Berkeley: University of California Press, 1969), 31-32.
[68] According to Strohm, Handel used the text to Caldara's setting for Mantua from 1708; Reinhard Strohm, "Handel and his Italian Opera Texts" *Essays on Handel and the Italian Opera*, 61.
[69] *L'Elpidia, overo li Rivali Generosi: Drama per Musica*, Mss. Additional 31606.
[70] Reinhard Strohm, "Handel's pasticci," *Essays on Handel and Italian Opera*, 167-69 and 200-201.

tual idea for the pasticcio coming from his attendance at the Teatro S. Giovanni Grisostomo during Carnival season of 1725, when the three contributing works were produced. In a letter dated January 23, 1726 he refers to a payment of fifty pounds for "the opera of Elpidia" and of this sum, forty went "for copying the Score, and Vinci's regalo."[71] Besides making all the arrangements in this, Swiney's role probably involved the selection of the drama, the selection of the arias, and the placing of the arias within the drama:

> —as for the selection of the drama, Swiney was much concerned about the libretti chosen for performance at the Royal Academy; in the case of Vinci's *La Rosmira*, a pasticcio allowed the music to be re-used in a more "elevated" setting
> —as for the selection of arias, Swiney was in a better position than Handel to judge which were the best arias of the 1725 season in Venice, since for Handel to do this, he would have had to have access to the scores of all three Carnival operas in London shortly before their premières
>
> —as for the placing of the arias, Swiney refer to this activity in the context of another pasticcio, in a letter from March of 1726, having been informed that one of the arias "I placed in the opera of *Vinceslao*" had already been performed by Cuzzoni in Elpidia.[72]

Thus it would seem that Swiney, after attending the operas at the S. Giovanni Grisostomo decided to create his own opera by selecting a drama to his liking, Zeno's *I rivali generosi*, selecting his favorite arias from the three operas, having these arias copied, and then placing them in the context of the new drama. Handel's role in *Elpidia* would have been limited to composing the recitative and rehearsing and conducting the new opera.[73] From Swiney's selection of arias, it would appear that he was much taken with Vinci's music; he borrowed seven arias and a quartet from *Ifigenia* and six arias from *La Rosmira*, while only taking three arias from Orlandini's *Berenice*[74] and none from the first opera of the season, Brusa's *Il Trionfo della virtù*.[75] This dominance of Vinci's

---

[71] Quoted in Gibson, *The Royal Academy of Music*, 372.

[72] Ibid., 363.

[73] In a letter from October 4, 1726 Swiney refers to another pasticcio "wherein the Faustina & Cuzzoni are to have two very equal and very good parts...as for the recitative...I'll leave 'em to be composed by Padre Attilio [Ariosti], or any other Master Messrs. de L'academie think fit to employ." Quoted in Gibson, *The Royal Academy of Music*, 370.

[74] Reinhard Strohm, "Handel's pasticci," *Essays on Handel and Italian Opera*, 167-69 and 200-201.

[75] According to Swiney, Brusa's music was "intollerable" (Gibson, *The Royal Academy of Music*, 355).

arias was undoubtedly the reason for the honorarium paid to Vinci, who was still in Venice when Swiney was concocting *Elpidia*. Swiney, therefore, may have been responsible for introducing Handel to the music of Vinci. That the Saxon was impressed by this is proven by the preponderance of Vinci's arias in Handel's pasticci, most of which were his own creations and not Swiney's.[76] To judge from the twelve performances in 1725 and another six in 1726, as well the three collections of arias and overtures that were published by Walsh,[77] *Elpidia* achieved considerable success, in the process establishing in London a taste for Vinci and the new Neapolitan style.

Towards mid-century John Walsh published a collection entitled "Twelve Solos For a German Flute or Violin with Thorough Bass for the Harpsichord or Violoncello Compos'd by Sig$^r$ Leonardo Vinci and other Italian Authors."[78] Although Sonatas 3-12 can be found in a collection published in Augsburg as "Sonate da camera a due...di Santo Lapis...Opera Prima,"[79] it is possible that the first two sonatas are by Vinci. Publishers such as Walsh often dealt in half truths rather than bold lies. If Sonatas Nos. 1 & 2 are by Vinci, then the title page attribution "by Sig$^r$ Leonardo Vinci and other Italian Authors" is indeed correct, though rather misleading. During the eighteenth century, the flute was not an instrument much cultivated in Italy, as opposed to Northern Europe. When Italian composers wrote for the instrument it was often wit a Northern patron or performer in mind (for example, Scarlatti' set of sonatas for flute and strings, written for Quantz in 1725). Therefore it is possible that Vinci composed two flute sonatas for Quantz during thius season when both were in Venice. The sonatas made their way to England with Quantz in 1727 and were later published by Walsh, with the sonatas by Santo Lapis used to bulk up the Vinci sonatas to a full set of twelve.

## Parma and the Return to Naples

*La Rosmira fedele* must have made a favorable impression on Francesco Farnese, Duke of Parma, since he brought the composer and most of the cast to Parma to produce another Stampiglia drama, *Il trionfo di Camilla* in the spring of 1725 (only the tenor and the cadet roles were different). Similarly, Duke Rinaldo of Modena, must have been impressed by

---

[76] See lists of contents in Strohm, "Handel's pasticci," 200-211.
[77] Strohm, "Handel's pasticci," 167 and William C. Smith and Charles Humphries, *A Bibliography of the Musical Works Published by the Firm of John Walsh: During the Years 1721-1766* (London: The Bibliographical Society, 1968), Nos. 1508-1511.
[78] *A Bibliography of the Musical Works Published by the Firm of John Walsh*, No.1513.
[79] Strohm, *Italienische Opernarien* II, 246.

Metastasio's *Didone abbandonata* at the Teatro S. Cassiano since that spring he brought Metastasio and three of the principals to produce a new version of *Didone* at Reggio Emilia, with music by Nicola Porpora.[80] Owen Swiney went to Parma to hear *Camilla* and to negotiate with Faustina concerning her contract with the Royal Academy of Music in London.[81]

During the early eighteenth century opera in Parma had been sporadic, but the production of *Il trionfo di Camilla* ushered in a new period of operatic activity.[82] The drama, the same one that had launched Giovanni Bononcini's career in 1696, was adapted by the newly-appointed court poet Carlo Innocenzio Frugoni. Frugoni was impressed with the production of *Camilla,* and wrote sonnets in praise of both Scalzi and Faustina. The final strophe of his sonnet to Scalzi applies, by extension, to Vinci, the composer of the "amabil canto:"

> Ah! this is song, beloved song! You bear
> Witness to the multitude of praises I have spoken,
> As in harmonious sounds you ascend to the breast of heaven.[83]

The complete score of *Il trionfo di Camilla* has been lost, and only a handful of arias survive in various sources.[84] If there was any special relationship between Vinci and Faustina, artistic or otherwise, it would have ended with *Il trionfo di Camilla* in Parma. A year later she was in London singing for Handel with and against Cuzzoni.

After returning to Naples, Vinci probably spent the summer building up his store of "motivi" to meet the numerous commissions he had obtained for the coming fall/winter season.[85] An oratorio by Vinci was performed for the Confregazione del Rosario at S. Caterina a Formiello to celebrate the Feast of the Rosary on the first Sunday of October 1725:

> In the Royal Convent of S. Caterina a Formiello this
> Sunday...was celebrated the festival of the Virgin of the
> Rosary, with magnificent and lavish display, along with the

---

[80] Libretto in I-Bc, I-MOe, REm; Sartori, *I libretti Italiani*, No. 7755.

[81] Gibson, *The Royal Academy of Music*, 356-57. In light of the subsequent developments in London it seems rather ironic that Swiney predicts that "upon her Engagement depends...the very being, and welfare of the academy for several years."

[82] Libretto in I-Bc; see listing of productions at the court of Parma in: Paulo-Emilio Ferrari, *Spettacoli drammatico-musicali e coreografici in Parma: dall'anno 1628 all'anno 1883* (1884; reprint ed., Bologna: Forni Editore), 30-33.

[83] Carlo Innocenzio Frugoni, *Opere poetiche del signor abate Carlo Innocenzio Frugoni fra gli Arcadi Comante Eginetico* (Parma: Stamperia Reale, 1779), Sonetto CCCVII, 485.

[84] Four arias ("Navicella ch'al mar," "Più non sò finger," "Sembro quell'usignolo," and "Sorge talora") in Bibliothèque du Conservatoire national de musique in Paris (D.14285) and two ("Senza pietà di padre" and "Ti perdono") at the University of California, Berkeley (Slg.10/11).

[85] Marcello describing the modern composer making use of his store of musical themes when composing an opera; *Il teatro alla moda*, 63-64.

usual oratorio performed by the foremost virtuosos of the capital...Music by the renowned...Leonardo Vinci.[86]

Although Strohm has suggested that this may be the première of Vinci's oratorio *Maria Dolorata*, Gaetano Pitaresi has demonstrated that this work follows the tradition of the passion oratorio, as exemplified by the Metastasio *Passione*, making the subject inappropriate outside of Lent.[87] Therefore one is presented with the anomaly that the single surviving complete oratorio by Vinci, *Maria Dolorata*, cannot be traced to any of the contemporary references to Vinci oratorios. *Maria Dolorata* exists in a single posthumous manuscript dated 1734.[88] Hellmuth Hell has suggested 1725 as a "Terminus a quo" because the sinfonia is related to that in *La Rosmira*.[89] However, if *Maria Dolorata* originated during Lent, then it becomes rather difficult to assign a date for the work during these years. In the spring of 1725 Vinci was in Parma with the première of *Il trionfo di Camilla*, while in the spring of 1726 he was on his way back to Naples, having just completed three operas in three cities in three months. One might be closer to the truth by saying that *Maria Dolorata* could have been written during Lent of almost any year of Vinci's career except 1725 and 1726. As for what work would have been performed for the Rosary Festival of 1725, it is possible that it was the untitled oratorio for four voices—Maria, Angelo, Alba, Selim— of which the "Prime Parte" survives in the Conservatory in Naples.[90] The continuous references to garlands of "entwined roses and lilies" and "chains of tears glistening like stars" provide stylized Arcadian descriptions of the rosary. Although Helmut Hell suggests that this *Oratorio à Quattro Voce* dates from 1727 because the opening movement of the sinfonia is similar to that in *Ernelinda*, one is tempted to connect the single surviving part of Vinci's rosary oratorios to this last reference to these works.[91]

---

[86] Thomas Edward Griffin, *Musical References in the 'Gazzetta di Napoli' 1681-1725*, (Berkeley: Fallen Leaf Press, 1993), 122.

[87] Strohm, *Italienische Opernarien* II, 243; Gaetano Pitaresi, "L'oratorio 'Maria dolorata' di Leonardo Vinci e la tradizione della Passione a Napoli," paper presented at the conference *Leonardo Vinci: architetture sonore nella Napoli del viceregno austriaco*, Conservatorio di Musica Francesco Cilea, Reggio Calabria.

[88] *Maria dolorata* is in the process of being prepared in a critical edition by Gaetano Pitaresi and is intended to be one of the first volumes in the projected *Edizione completa delle Opere di Leonardo Vinci*.

[89] Hellmut Hell, *Die Neapolitanische Opernsinfonie in der ersten Hälfte des 18.jahrhunderts* (Tutzing, Schneider, 1971), 538.

[90] Leonardo Vinci, *Oratorio à Quattro Voce*, S-7-5,6.

[91] Hellmut Hell, Op. Cit., 54. The oratorio was revived in Fabriano in 1738. Libretto in I-MAC, Vgc; Sartori, *I libretti italiani* (No. 17162).

## The Court Appointment

On October 22, 1725 Alessandro Scarlatti died and, according to the *Avvisi di Napoli*, was buried a week later amidst the sounds of "choice music a quattro Cori directed by the virtuoso Pietro Auletta."[92] In the subsequent succession at the Real Cappella, Francesco Mancini regained the position of Maestro which had been taken from him in December of 1708 with the return of Scarlatti to Naples and Domenico Sarro regained his position of Vice-Maestro which he had lost in 1707 during the political disturbances caused by the conquest of Naples by the Austrians.[93] With Mancini and Sarro promoted to Maestro and Vice-Maestro, Vinci submitted an application for Sarro's position on October 24:

> Most eminent Signore: Leonardo Vinci submits a petition to Your Eminence, since the position of Maestro of this Real Capella, being vacated by the death of Cavalier Scarlatti, must go to Francesco Mancini, and in his position, Domenico Sarro. Since the position of the said Sarro comes vacant, he humbly begs you to be served, considering the service thus rendered to Conte Emanuel as well as to Monsignore d'Althann; in composing operas and prologues in the Theatres of Naples, Rome and Lombardy, by conferring upon the petitioner the said place and salary enjoyed by Domenico Sarro.[94]

This position was given the rather inelegant title "Pro Vice-Maestro," which Vinci employs in his subsequent operas.[95] The actual title appears to have been a new one, though the position had existed for several years in all but name. In 1707 Sarro had protested his politically-motivated dis-

---

[92] Quoted in Thomas Edward Griffin. Op. cit., 122.

[93] On July 3, 1707 at the oath of allegiance ceremony at Aversa Cathedral in which the new Austrian Viceroy was installed, Mancini and most of the members of the Real Cappella performed a Te Deum by the Maestro Gaetano Veneziano, who was conspicuously absent, having fled Naples with the Spanish Viceroy to the fortress of Gaeta. In the subsequent reorganization of the Real Cappella, those musicians who were absent from the ceremony at Aversa, including both Maestro Veneziano and the Vice-Maestro Sarro, lost their positions, Mancini taking the former position and Giuseppe Porsile taking the latter. (Porsile served Archduke Charles in Barcelona); Ralf Krause, "Das musikalische Panorama am neapolitanischen Hofe: zu Real Cappella di Palazzo im frühen 18. Jahrhundert" *Analecta Musicologica* 30/2: 278-79. The record of the Mancini/Sarro appointments (f. 1707, ex.25-X-1725) is transcribed in Francesco Cotticelli and Paologiovanni Maione, *Le istituzioni musicali a Napoli durante il viceregno austriaco (1707-1734): materiali inediti sulla Real Capella ed il Teatro di San Bartolomeo* (Naples: Luciano Editore, 1993), 84.

[94] Archivio di Stato di Napoli, Italia: Segreteria dei Viceré, fascio 1707, documenti pervenuti il 25/X/1725.

[95] The title appears in different guises, sometimes with the "Vice" and "Maestro" joined as a single word, sometimes without the dash after the "Pro," and sometimes completely lacking the "Pro" designation, which Sarro probably would not have appreciated.

missal and finally, in 1720, succeeded in obtaining a decree directly from the Imperial court reinstating him into the Real Cappella with a salary of twenty-two ducats a month and the promise of succession to his former position as Vice-Maestro.[96] Sarro's unusual arrangement is referred to in a follow-up letter from the Segreteria to the Viceroy:

> inasmuch as Domenico Sarro has had up until now a place in this Reale Cappella, having obtained from his Holy, Imperial and Catholic Majesty the succession and the salary by special dispatch, in the position and salary which he now enjoys ...[he has as well] the promise of Maestro di Cappella.[97]

However, Sarro's "position" was not an official one with the title "Pro-Vice Maestro" but, rather, consisted of "the succession and the salary" that he enjoyed "by special dispatch." Until these appointments following the death of Scarlatti, Sarro, like Vinci employed the generic "maestro di cappella" not as a title connected with a specific appointment but as a synonym for composer, as was the custom at the time.[98]

Vinci's request was granted the next day "Executed the 25 of October" along with the requests of his colleagues:

> His Eminence confirms the position of first Maestro di Cappella to Francesco Mancini and to Domenico Sarro that of Vice-Maestro with the salary of 35 ducats a month conforming to the same already enjoyed by Mancini and the twenty-two and a half ducats enjoyed by Sarro to be divided as follows: to Leonardo Vinci ten ducats, to Leonardo Leo six and a half ducats and to Peppe de Bottis six ducats.[99]

With Sarro finally regaining his former position of Vice-Maestro, his former "posto e soldo" was treated in a rather peculiar manner. It was divided up between three musicians: Leo, Vinci, and the organist, Giuseppe de Bottis. In this division, the lion's share went to Vinci, ten ducats of the "soldo" and first place in "la futtura"— the succession. Along with first place in "la futtura" there came an actual title Pro Vice-Maestro. One gets the impression that the position of Pro Vice-Maestro was designed specifically to get Vinci into the Real Capella succession. This is further suggested by a request made by Vinci for payment of 10 ducats as supernumerary musician the same day appointments were made, a request lacking the usual specification concerning the duration of ser-

---

[96] Krause, Op. cit., 287.

[97] Archivio di Stato di Napoli, Italia: Segretaria dei Viceré, fascio 1707, documenti pervenuti il 27-X-1725.

[98] In the same way that today the term "professor" is used generically to refer to an instructor at University and as the senior level position within the teaching hierarchy.

[99] Archivio di Stato di Napoli, Italia: Segretaria dei Viceré, fascio 1707, documenti pervenuti il 25-X-1725.

vice in this capacity. Three days earlier, the day Scarlatti died, a similar request was made by Giuseppe de Bottis who is described as having served as supernumerary for the past year.[100] De Bottis had entered the Real Cappella the previous year as a *supranumerario*, substituting for Scarlatti who "for his advanced age and for his indisposition can rarely serve," and for his gratis services was admitted to the chapel as *ordinario* in this series of appointments.[101] During the 1720s, when the entrance into the Real Cappella was highly competitive, it was standard to serve for several years as an unpaid *supranumerario* before obtaining a position as *ordinario*.[102] It would seem that for the sake of form, Vinci needed to serve as *supranumerario* if only for a day, and then he not only gained entry as *ordinario*, but moved directly into the Maestro succession behind Sarro—a considerable bending of the rules. This bending of the rules is also apparent in the follow-up letter mentioned above in which the intendant, after speaking about Sarro's succession, mentions the two composers waiting in the wings:

> In case that something should happen to the said Domenico Sarro, if it please Your Eminence, both Leonardo Vinci and Leonardo Leo aspire to the succession and salary. Since they are known to you, I present to Your eminence, that both these are capable and well-known virtuosi. But since Leonardo Leo has had thirteen years in service as organist of the Real Cappella, he aspires to follow the examples of Gaetano Veneziano and Francesco Mancini, who have passed from organist at the Real Cappella to become Maestri di Capella.[103]

In spite of Leo's proven talents and experience and his long association with the Real Cappella, he retains his position as organist while it is Vinci who is given the new position, in the process jumping in front of him in the succession.

It is not known what duties were attached to Vinci's new court appointment. In his application for the post of Vice-Maestro of the Real Cappella in August of 1730, Leonardo Leo complains about the lack of competition during the regime of Cardinal Althan, in particular "the engagement of Bottis, Vinci and the Saxon, who were absent as maestri di Cappella, but still obtained a salary without ever having been part of the

---

[100] Cotticelli and Maione, *Le istituziuoni musicali a Napoli durante il viceregno austriaco*, 80 (f. 1707, ex. 23-X-1725 and ex. 25-X-1725).

[101] Ibid., 79 (f. 1671, ex. 13-IX-1724).

[102] Ibid., 34-35; this is probably one of the reasons for Scarlatti having his son Domenico begin serving as *supranumerario* at the age of sixteen in 1701.

[103] Archivio di Stato di Napoli, Italia: Segreteria dei Viceré, fascio 1707, documenti pervenuti il 27/X/1725.

Real Cappella."[104] The honorific aspect of Vinci's appointment is also suggested in his request for an extended leave of absence from the court in 1729, in which he is described as having "no specific duties there" (see Chapter 9). Therefore, it would appear that Vinci's position at court was primarily honorific, like the court appointments of Rameau and Mozart. While the salary of these honorific appointments was never very substantial (Vinci's ten ducats being at the entry level of an *ordinario*), it was meant to augment the fees that the composer made from theatre commissions and teaching, thereby giving him greater financial stability. This appointment, combined with his regular commissions from the San Bartolomeo and Delle Dame theatres, should have provided Vinci with a certain degree of prosperity.

[104] f. 1910, ex. 18-VIII-1730 quoted in Cotticelli and Maione, Op. cit., 79.

# 5

# FIRST COLLABORATIONS WITH METASTASIO

### Salvi's *Astianatte* and Racine's *Andromaque*

Vinci's new court title appears on the libretto of his next opera, *Astianatte*, as well as in the performance notice in the *Avvisi di Napoli*:

> Sunday evening [was] the première performance of the new *opera in musica* at the Teatro San Bartolomeo, entitled *Astianatte*....The music is by the Provice Maestro of the Royal Chapel Leonardo Vinci.[1]

*Astianatte* was premièred on December 2, 1725 at the Teatro San Bartolomeo. In contrast to Vinci's previous heroic operas, *Astianatte* was not produced for the Emperor's birthday or nameday; in 1725 the honor for the former went to Giovanni Porta's *Amore e fortuna*. Apparently Porta was in Naples for this production and remained there until carnival when his *La Lucinda fedele* was premièred.[2] *Amore e fortuna* was performed along with the intermezzo *Il marito giocatore*. Although this intermezzo has been frequently attributed to Vinci since the mid-eighteenth century, modern scholars have assigned the music to Giuseppe Maria Orlandini.[3]

---

[1] *Avvisi di Napoli*, December 4, 1725 (No. 52).

[2] Although this event seems to indicate that Porta was counterbalancing the trend begun by Vinci in Venice, Porta was actually the last Venetian composer to produce an opera in Naples until Galuppi in 1755. See the list of productions at the Teatro San Bartolomeo in Francesco Florimo, *La scuola musicale di Napoli e suoi conservatori*, IV, 20.

[3] See Giuseppe Maria Orlandini, *Il marito giocatore e la moglie bacchettona (Serpilla e Bacocco)*, [ 68] *Italian Opera 1740-1770*, Preface. Gordana Lazarevich has suggested that the version of the intermezzo in Wolfenbüttel attributed to Vinci (D-W 258) may be an arrangement of Orlandini's score for the 1725 Neapolitan production; Gordana Lazarevich, "The Eighteenth-Century Pasticcio: The Historian's Gordian Knot," *Studien zur italienische-deutschen Musikgeschichte* XI, ed. Friedrich Lippmann, Vol. 17 of *Analecta Musicologica*, 141-42. The question then arises: why didn't Porta make the arrangement since it was his opera that was performed in conjunction with *Il marito giocatore*? According to Strohm this score appears to be a copy of an anonymous manuscript of the same intermezzo in the same collection (D-W 257), both probably originating in Germany c. 1730; Reinhold Strohm, *Italienischer Opernarien*, II, 235.

The cast of *Astianatte* was similar to that of *Eraclea*. Strada and Tesi were the leading ladies, with the alto Tesi receiving the matron role, and Farinello and Vico were the leading men, with the alto Vico performing a trouser role:[4]

    Piro: Diana Vico                  Andromaca: Vittoria Tesi
    Oreste: Carlo Broschi          Ermione: Anna Maria Strada
    Pilade: Francesco Pertici      Urania: Celeste Resse
    Clearte: Agostino Marchetti   Clito: Gioacchino Corrado
        Stage architect: Giovanni Battista Olivero
        Stage painter: Pietro Orta

Johann Joachim Quantz heard this cast earlier that year in Sarro's *Tito Sempronio Gracco* and provided an assessment in his autobiography:

> On January 13 I therefore travelled from Rome to Naples, where I immediately heard an opera composed by Sarri, almost in the style of Vinci. Farinelli, who was then approaching his famous perfection, Strada who later became more famous in England, and Tesi, were brilliant in this opera. The others were only fair.[5]

Although Quantz's reference to Sarro's opera as "almost in the style of Vinci" should be understood from a mid-century perspective when Vinci's music would have been better known than Sarro's, it nonetheless suggests the stylistic kinship between the two composers (proposed in Chapter 3). In his review Quantz singles out Tesi for special mention:

> Tesi was gifted by nature with a masculinely strong contralto voice.... [and] sang on several occasions the kind of arias which are usually composed for bassos. By now she had acquired, in addition to the magnificent serious tone in her singing, a pleasant softness. The range of her voice was extremely wide, neither high nor low notes being difficult for her. A display of virtuosity was not her strong point. She seemed to be born to impress the audience with her acting.[6]

Quantz's unusual statement that Tesi could sing "the kinds of arias which are usually composed for bassos" may be a reference to the raging bass arias, of the type Handel composed for Giuseppe Boschi, with extensive unisons and large leaps. The prominence of unisons and downwards octave leaps in Andromaca's arias suggest that in this role, in contrast to her earlier role of Eraclea, Vinci catered to the "masculine"

---

[4] Libretto in I-Bc, I-Fm, I-Nc, I-Rsc, GB-Lbm, US-NYp; Claudio Sartori, *I libretti italiani*, No. 3273.

[5] Johann Joachim Quantz, "The Life of Herr Johann Joachim Quantz, as Sketched by Himself." Trans. Paul Mueller in *Forgotten Musicians*, ed. Paul Nettl, 302.

[6] Ibid., 302.

character of La Tesi's voice. Most significantly, Vinci created, in Andromaca, a dramatic role to display Tesi's famous acting abilities (see caricature of Tesi, Plate 12 on page 126). Vinci's most celebrated cantata, *Mesta, oh Dio fra queste selve*, was written for La Tesi, either at this time or upon their subsequent collaboration on *Medo* in Parma.[7]

*Astianatte* is Vinci's only setting of a *dramma per musica* by Antonio Salvi, the Florentine court poet whose libretti were frequently set by Handel. *Astianatte* had originally been set to music by Giovanni Antonio Perti for the Pratolino in 1701; it was given a new musical setting for Munich in 1707 by Marco Antonio Bononcini, who is often given credit for the original version;Perti revised his drama in 1716 for a new production in Florence that provided the basis for a flurry of new settings including Gasparini's, composed during his tenure at the Teatro delle dame in 1719 (revived in Milan, 1722) and Giovanni Bononcini's composed in rivalry with Handel at the Royal Academy of Music in London, 1727.[8] The influence of French classical theatre on the *dramma per musica* is exemplified in Salvi's libretti, many of which are based on plays by Thomas and Pierre Corneille, Racine and Molière.[9] Acts I and II of *Astianatte* are based on Racine's tragedy *Andromaque*. The action, set against the defeat of Troy, is based on a fatal love chain: Orestes, son of Agamemnon, is in love with Hermione, daughter of Menalaus, who is in love with her fiancée Pyrrhus, King of Epirus, who is in love with his prisoner Andromaque, who remains faithful to the memory of her husband Hector whom Pyrrhus killed in battle.

> **Synopsis**: Oreste and his faithful friend Pilade come to Epirus to demand the execution of Andromaca's son Astianatte or the return of Ermione to Greece, the Trojan heir being regarded as a threat to the general peace and Ermione's overly-extended

---

[7] Of the many surviving manuscripts of this cantata in both soprano and alto clefs, only the alto version at Montecassino carries the inscription "de S. Vinci per la Sigra. Tesi." Teresa Maria Gialdroni, "Vinci 'operista' autore di cantate," *Studi in onore di Giulio Cattin* (Rome: Edizioni torre d'Orfeo, 1990), 320.

[8] Robert Lamar Weaver and Norma Wright Weaver, *A Chronology of Music in the Florentine Theater 1590-1750: Operas, Prologues, Finales, Intermezzos, and Plays with Incidental Music*, Detroit Studies in Music Bibliography, No. 38 (Detroit: Information Coordinators, 1978), 190-91; and Melania Bucciarelli, "Rhetorical Strategies and Tears in *Astianatte*," *Italian Opera and European Theatre, 1680-1720: Plots, Performers, Dramaturgies*, ed. Albert Dunning (Brepols" Publications of the Pietro Antonio Locatelli Foundation, 2000), 119.

[9] See listing of full-length works based on French sources in Reinhard Strohm, " 'Tragedie' into 'Dramma per musica'" Pt. III *Informazioni e studi vivaldiani: Bolletino annuale dell'istituto italiano Antonio Vivaldi*, Venezia Fondazione Giorgio Cini, II (1990), 13-14. On Salvi's intermezzi based on comedies by Molière, see Chapter 6 below.

**Plate 12.** Caricature of Vittoria Tesi, attributed to Marco Ricci.[10] (Algarotti-Gellman Album, No. 37),

[10] Reproduced from Edward Croft-Murray, *An Album of Eighteenth-Century Venetian Operatic Caricatures*, 67.

Oreste must try to convince Piro to execute Astianatte, his love for Ermione compromises his efforts, hoping secretly that Piro will break off his engagement. Piro at first rejects these demands, in the hope that he can win the affection of Adromaca, but after she rejects his offer of protection, he tells Oreste that he has come to his senses: he will kill the child and marry Ermione. The desparing Oreste decides that with the help of Pilade he will adbuct Ermione and murder Piro.

Caught between her conflicting duties of widow and mother and, after trying every possible means to persuade Piro, Andromaca finally decides to solve the dilemma by marrying Piro to obtain a promise of protection for her son, and then by killing hersef to save her honor. This fateful event is prevented by Oreste's assassination of Piro. Andromaca assumes the role of queen and has Oreste arrested.

Andromaca is touched by Piro having sacrificed himself defending her child, and admits to his minister Clearte that she could have loved him. Clearte informs her that Piro was only wounded by Oreste's attack and Andromaca and Piro are united as lovers. Ermione, now convnced of Piro's treachery and Oreste's fidelity, decides to save the man whom she loved before she was betrothed to Piro. Pilade meanwhile abducts Astianatte vowing to kill the child unless Oreste is released. Piro manages to intercept Pilade in the harbor and is about to attack when Andromaca intercedes, asking Piro to release Oreste as an offering to her love. The opera ends with both couples happily united.

Salvi's libretto is flawed by its forced happy ending. This in itself is not a major problem since this is *settecento* opera; moreover Racine's drama often seems to be on the verge of uniting Andromaque and Pyrrhus and Hermione and Oreste. The real problem is the way in which Salvi spends all of Act III preparing for the happy ending. Salvi would have been better served had he ended his drama as Racine did with the sacrificial scene, allowing for some magnanimous act by Piro to transform tragedy into enlightened vctory. Instead the sacrificial scene comes at the end of Act II, and Act III lapses into cloak-and-dagger escapades.[11] Although

---

[11] Bucciarelli, on the other hand, regards Salvi's rewriting of Racine's tragedy as "perfectly comply[ing] with the demands of classical dramaturgy," even though Salvi diverges considerably from his model. Buccarielli, "Rhetorical Strategies and Tears in *Astianatte*," 124. The same subject was treated by Zeno in his libretto *Andromaca*, originally written for Caldara in 1724. Although both operas are based on Racine's tragedy, Zeno, drawing his material from several sources, introduces the reunion between Ulysses and Telemachus into the tragic love chain of Andromaque, Pyrrhus, Hermione, and Orestes. Apostolo Zeno, *Andromaca*, in *Italian Opera Librettos: 1640-1770*, 52.

Salvi was stil active as a librettist in Venice, there is no evidence that he revised his drama for Vinci, as Stampgilia had done for *Eraclea* and Pasqualigo for *Ifigenia*. The libretto was revised according to current Neapolitan practices by the addition of two comic characters, Clito and Urania, who appear as servants within the drama and perform in the intermezzi at the end of acts.[12] Gioacchino Corrado, who had returned from his engagement in Venice (see Chapter 4) took the role of Clito. His former partner Santa Marchesina, having remained behind in Venice, was replaced by a new comic soprano, Celeste Resse, who took the role of Urania.[13] Unfortunately Vinci's settingn of the intermezzo *Urania/Clito* does not survive.[14]

## *Astianatte*: the Opening Scenes

Francesco Florimo refers to Vinci's *Astianatte* as "one of his most beautiful works."[15] As with his judgment of "his masterpiece," *Ifigenia in Tauride,* this derives directly from Fétis who in turn based his judgment

---

[12] Because *Astianatte* was produced just prior to *Didone* and *Siroe*, Strohm suggests that Metastasio was responsible for revising the libretto for Vinci. (Reinhard Strohm, "Leonardo Vinci's *Didone abbandonata* (Rome 1726)," *Essays on Handel and Italian Opera*, 217-18.) It seems unlikely that Metastasio would have reverted to the role of anonymous adapter after the success of *Didone abbandonata*, especially when the adaptation primarily involved the addition of a comic intermezzo. Metastasio is known to have revised another poet's work on only one occasion: Domenico David's *La forza della virtù*, which, as *Siface re di Numidia* (1723) took on a life of its own as one of Metastasio's dramas.

[13] Santa Marchesina broke out of her comic career, appearing opposite Carestini in Brusa's *L'amor eroico* at the Teatro San Samuele during Ascension 1725. Owen Swiney was impressed by her and recommended her to the Royal Academy of Music. Gibson. *The Royal Academy of Music*, 354-55.

[14] There is a single surviving score of *Astianatto* now located in the Biblioteca del Conservatorio in Naples (Rari 33-6-2). The paper (with the rearing horse watermark) and the scribal style suggest that it is a contemporary manuscript originating in Naples. Giuseppe Sigismondo's signature on the title page indicates that it was one of many scores in his collection. The intermezzo *Urania-Clito* was omitted from this manuscript and cannot be found in any secondary sources. Although the omission of the intermezzo and the lack of any changes or corrections (except for a single obvious copyist error in Act I) seems to indicate that this score was not used in the original production, it was probably copied directly from the production score. The fact that the copyist omitted the intermezzo, simply leaving a blank page before the beginning of the next act, explains the absence of the usual "fine del atto" and "L.D.M.S.V." at the end of Acts I and II. The examples below are taken from this manuscript, which consist of the following musical numbers:

|  |  |
|---|---|
| 26 *da capo* arias | 1 *da capo* duet |
| 1 arietta | 3 accompanied recitatives |
| 2 sinfonias | 1 coro |

totals: 34 set pieces (27 in *da capo* form)

[15] Florimo, *La scuola musicale di Napoli*, III, 186.

on a statement in the *Biografia degli uomini illustri del Regno di Napoli,* which describes how "Naples, the seat of the Muses, heard it with transport."[16] Although Fétis designation of *Astianatte* as "un de ses plus beaux ouvrages" is as artificial and arbitrary as his "chef-d'oeuvre" description of *Ifigenia in Tauride,* one would like to think that the original audiences at the S. Bartolomeo did hear the opera "con trasporto"—in particular the opening scenes, which are indeed impressive.

In the first scene, when Piro reminds Andromaca of her precarious position as slave and prisoner, she replies, in her aria "Misera si, non vile, " that her cruel fate has reduced her to misery, not servitude.[17] The aria is made up of the simplest of materials, a unison descending scale for first theme and a falling octave above a walking bass for second, yet there is a strong gestic quality to this aria, a feature already noted in several of Vinci's comic arias. A skilled actress such as La Teai undoubtedly would have accompanied the descending unison sale and the octave leaps with scornful dismissive gestures:

Example 5.1 "Misera si, non vile" *Astianatte* I/i

[16] François-Joseph Fétis, *Biographie Universelle des musiciens* and *Biografia degli uomini illustri del Regno di Napoli: Ornata de loro rispettivi ritratti,* VI.

[17] The opening scenes of Salvi's opera, whch center on the encounter between Andromaca and Pirro, according to Bucciarelli, represent a dramatization of the expository dialogue between Oreste and Pylade in Racine's *Andromaque.* This serves as a "full exposition of the antecedents," using not only words and music, recitative and aria, but also stage action and stage setting. As an example of the latter, she gives the setting of the opening scenes "Sala con arazzi, dove sono rappresentate l'impresse de Achille e di Pirro nella Guerra di Troia." Thus, while Racine's opening scenes are dominated by references to the Trojan War, the audience of *Astianatte* would have

In the next scene, Oreste as Greek ambassador demands that Piro either execute Andromaca's son Astianatte to appease the fury of the Greeks or return his fiancée Ermione. In "Alma grande nata al soglio," Piro tells Oreste that his noble heart cannot submit to such fear and haughtiness. This aria is written in a similar style to Andromaca's opening aria, but in D major duple rather than C major triple meter with the unison descending scale and walking bass phrases reversed:

Example 5.2 "Alma grande nata al soglio" *Astianatte* I/iii

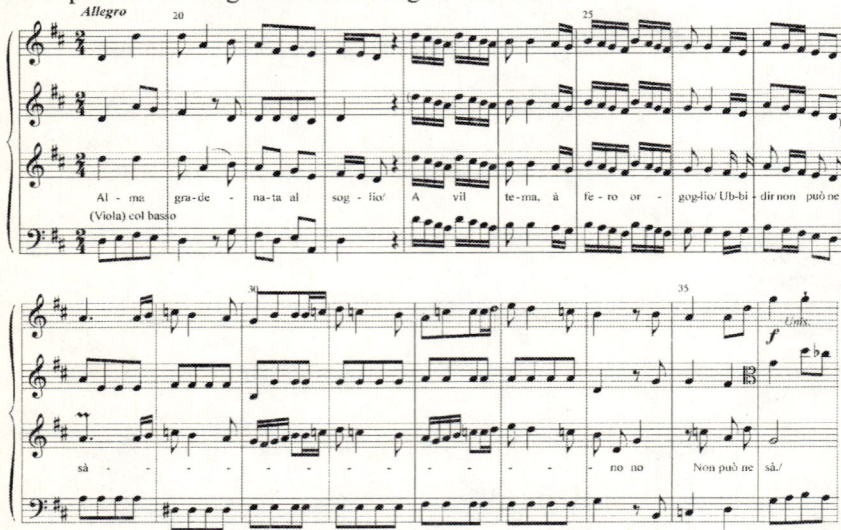

Although both arias capture the royal indignation of the two characters, there is one important difference; the first section in Piro's aria contains a modulation to the subdominant rather than the expected dominant, a surprising effect that suggests all is not right. Although Piro is making a grand gesture of regal defiance, later in the act he will exploit his position as Astianatte's arbiter to compel Andromaca to submit to his desires and when she refuses him, threatens to execute the child. Perhaps Vinci may be foreshadowing this cruel reversal by a modulation to the "weak" subdominant rather than the usual "strong" dominant key (similarly Andromaca's grand oath of fidelity to Hector in Act II which Salvi's heroine will not keep, is accompanied by an elaborated plagal cadence).[18]

---

been continually reminded of the War by the "tapestry, which represents the exploits of Achilles and Pyrhus in the trojan War" decorating the grand hall. (Buccarielli, "Rhetorical Strategies and Tears in *Astianatte*," 125 and 129.

[18] According to the late eighteenth-century theorist Heinrich Christoph Koch, the subdominant was rarely used for caesuras because it was "unable to give a quality of

Another unusual modulation, to the supertonic minor, occurs in the first section of Andromaca's aria "Barbaro prendi, e svena" where it may depict the heroine's internal turmoil as she defiantly tells Piro to kill her son. The modulation to the supertonic minor in major-mode arias was regularly employed by Porpora to create chiaroscuro in arias of intense emotions, as if to temper the new dominance of the major mode. Because Andromaca's aria is addressed to both the tyrant and to her threatened son, Edward Dent draws a parallel between this aria and "Figlio! Tiranno" from Alessandro Scarlatti's *Griselda*.[19] Although the texts and the dramatic situations of these two arias are similar, the music is not. In this instance Scarlatti's is more dramatic and modern (in a Gluckian sense), with its orchestrally-conceived tremolo accompaniment, declamatory vocal line, and daring mixture of affections.[20] Vinci, on the other hand, employs a more static sectionalized approach. Each vocal period begins with the *Presto* unison theme in E-flat major with prominent octave leaps addressed to Piro and leads to a *Lento cantilena* of rather unstable tonality in which she tells her son that he must be sacrificed:

Example 5.3 "Barbaro prendi, e svena" *Astianatte* I/x

---

completeness to the thoughts that end with them." Heinrich Christoph Koch, *Introductory Essay on Composition: the Mechanical Rules of Melody*, Nancy Kovaleff Baker, trans. (New Haven, Conn: Yale University Press).

[19] Edward J. Dent, "Notes on Leonardo Vinci" *The Musical Antiquary*, 198.

[20] Alessandro Scarlatti, *Griselda*, ed. Donald Jay Grout, III: *The Operas of Alessandro Scarlatti*, 121-22. Dent upholds this aria as a model of Scarlatti's skill as a musical dramatist. Edward J. Dent, *Alessandro Scarlatti: his Life and Works*, 164-67.

To emphasize her impetuosity, Vinci has Andromaca begin her aria *subito* without an opening ritornello after the recitative cadence.[21] The sectionalized contrasts within "Barbaro prendi, e svena" not only allowed Tesi to display what Quantz described as her "masculinely strong contralto voice" in singing the unisons and octave leaps typical of "the kinds of arias which are usually composed for bassos," but also her new "pleasant softness" in the passages addressed to Astianatte.

The coordination between music and drama breaks down when Piro tells Oreste that he has regained his reason and will execute Astianatte and marry Ermione. In his aria "Ti calpesto, o crudo amore," Piro boasts of having triumphed over villainous love. This concertante aria for two *corni da caccia* is reminiscent of the music that Vivaldi wrote in hunting scenes (for example "Nella' foresta" from *Catone in Utica),* albeit without the lively harmonies and tuneful melodies. Oreste's reaction to this decision which will deprive him of his beloved Ermione, provides the Act I finale. His soliloquy begins appropriately enough with a tempestuous accompanied recitative, with chromaticism that colors his reference to the blood of the Atreo highlighting Oreste's dark past. The intensity dissipates in his plodding coloratura aria "Per amor se'l cor sospirà." Even Vinci's experiment with incorporating orchestral figuration from the accompanied recitative into the aria does nothing to relieve the repetitive melody and static harmony. When he re-used this aria in *Didone* as Selene's "Se ti lagni sventurato" these flourishes lose their meaning completely, separated from the accompanied recitative.

Andromaca pleads with Piro for the life of her son, but is answered with Piro's stern ultimatum—that she come to the temple either as his bride or as a witness to her son's death. In his aria "Luci spietate," Piro tries to justify his ultimatum by explaining that her cruel eyes have taught him such cruelty. This lilting love song ignores the cruelty of the situation and concentrates only on Piro's infatuation with Andromaca. The thrice-repeated cadential phrases, while appropriate in the busy expansive arias of the mid-century, seem to dwarf the preceding material. Vinci was to find a more appropriate place for this music in "Voi m'insegnate" in *Siroe re di Persia* sung by the love-sick Laodice.

Act II is dominated by Andromaca, torn between maternal love and marital fidelity. In her aria "Con torbido aspetto" she sings that she feels the eyes of Hector upon her, while inside her maternal love calls out for pity. As in Andromaca's previous aria, some type of musical juxtaposition seems to be required but, having already employed this

---

[21] In Leo's *Andromaca* from 1742 this aria begins in the same manner and adopts Vinci's sectionalized structure, intensifying the contrast by a change of meter and recitative-like passages. Leonardo Leo, *Andromaca, Italian Opera 1640-1770*, 39, Act I/ix.

device, Vinci instead writes a routine unison aria, enlivened with some busy arpeggiated figuration in the style of Vivaldi. Oreste resolves that he must murder Piro in order to prevent the marriage to Ermione but, in his aria "Temi di vendicarti," questions his mad desire for blood. Vinci, ignoring this inner conflict, writes an heroic march, without a hint of the frenzied Oreste. This fine aria is a parody of Selene's "Ardi per me fedele" from *Didone*, where it originated in an amorous situation.[22]

In the next scene Andromaca swears eternal fidelity to the memory of her husband in an extended accompanied recitative. The orchestral accompaniment continues even after Clearte enters leading Astianatte to execution. Clearte's simple recitative serves as a foil for Andromaca's accompanied outbursts which culminate in an F-minor arioso as she says farewell to her child. Overcome with emotion, she faints in the middle of the arioso, leaving it incomplete. As Clearte leads the child out to execution, he tells him that he must die because of his barbarous parents. This is accomplished incongruously by a pretty minuet aria *senza basso*, with only the unexpected modulation to the supertonic minor contributing some sense of chiaroscuro. As in Andromaca's "Barbaro prendi, e svena" in Act I, this unexpected modulation coincides with another unfulfilled threat; in fact Clearte will be wounded in Act III defending this child whom he now leads to execution.

When Andromaca realizes what is about to happen she panics and, seeing a vision of her husband condemning her for her too-strict virtue, resolves to save the child by marrying Piro and then save her honor by committing suicide. This critical monologue is set as an accompanied recitative, thereby creating two extended scenes in which simple recitative has been replaced by accompanied recitative. The intensified declamation of the accompanied recitative made it one of the most important vehicles for acting in the *dramma per musica* and, as such, its extensive use in the role of Andromaca was one means of displaying Tesi's acting abilities.[23] Such an extended use of the accompanied recitative, almost a

---

[22] See Reinhard Strohm for a comparison of Vinci's and Sarro's setting of "Ardi per mei" accompanied by a transcription of the former and a facsimile of the latter in *Italienische Opernarien*, I, 45-47 and Vol.II, 83-91. In his analysis of Vinci's setting Strohm praises the depiction of the character and situation of Didone's sister Selene, contrasting it with the awkward setting in the parody "Temi di vendicarti." He draws attention to the slow text declamation (quarter notes in common rather than *alla breve* meter) that produces the effect of a "Melancholischer Marsch wie zuversicht-liche Elegie."

[23] Burney reported that Senesino "gained so much reputaton as an actor" in the accompanied recitatives of Handel's *Giulio Cesare*. Charles Burney, *A General History of Music*, II, 728. Bucciarelli draws attention to the importance of the mute character for whom the opera was named (Astianatte, son of Andromaca and Ettore), in achieving one of the goals in these central scenes for both Salvi and Racine: "of moving their audiences to tears." (Bucciarelli, "Rhetorical Strategies and Tears in *Astianatte*," 139.

hundred measures in total, already anticipated in Tamiri's *scena* in Act II of *Farnace*, in turn anticipates the extended series of accompanied recitatives in *Didone abbandonata* which Vinci may already have begun to compose (see below).[24] Andromaca's accompanied recitatives not only greatly enhance the drama, but create a sense of expectation for her aria—one expects a great lyrical release after this extended and intensified declamatory preparation. Expectation is somewhat disappointed by "Son qual legno in grembo." In this crucial scene, the heart of the drama where Andromaca makes her fatal decision before the funeral urn of Hector, both theater poet and composer have purposely contrived to produce a detached and objective interlude rather than the musical/dramatic climax a modern audience would expect. This is achieved poetically by the use of a conventional and contrived simile replacing Salvi's original dramatic text and musically by the use of the pseudo-academic *alla breve* style. The imagery of being lost at sea in a boat without oars or sails makes nonsense of the decision that Andromaca has just made with fatalistic conviction, while the music in B-flat major is of such a neutral cast that it could have originated as a Kyrie:[25]

Example 5.4 "Son qual legno in grembo" *Astianatte* II/viii

[24] Porpora's *Siface*, which was at that time being rehearsed for its double première in Milan and Venice, similarly contains two consecutive scenes with accompanied recitates for the heroine in Act III and at some point during the run, the interruption was omtted to create a single extended scene of accompanied recitative.

[25] This type of fugal aria can also be found in Porpora's operas, for example "Punirò quel cor" in *Didone abbandonata,* which is a full-fledged fugue.

The objective quality of the music is such that Handel borrowed the second vocal phrase, both the descending scale and arpeggio accompaniment, in the "Envy Chorus" from *Saul*, transforming this neutral material into a perfect reincarnation of the classical Greek chorus.

Before the temple, Ermione tries to dissuade Oreste from his rash plans, flattering his love with vague hope. In the aria "Io non vi credo" he replies that he does not trust her beloved eyes. This lovely pastorale seems rather too pretty for the impetuous Oreste on the verge of regicide —the most serious of crimes during the age of absolutism:

Example 5.5 "Io non vi credo" *Astianatte* II/ix

Although a setting of an original Salvi text, the pastoral lyricism of "Io non vi credo" appears to have been adapted to music that had already been written for Selene's "L'augelletto, in lacci stretto" from *Didone*. [26]

*Astianatte* was revived during Carnival of 1728 at the Teatro Pergola in Florence as the pasticcio *Andromaca*. Although based on Vinci's *Astianatte*, several of the surviving arias were taken from subsequent works by Vinci (*Siroe* and *Gismondo*) and other composers (Porpora and Gasparini).[27] Salvi's libretto was given a new setting by Leonardo Leo for Naples in 1742 with the title *Andromaca*. Leo's libretto refers to Vinci's earlier setting "that at another time, with the title of *Astianatte*, was seen on stage in this city, now returns gloriously in your Royal Theatre to celebrate the day of your immortal and feared Royal Name."[28] Although the "gloriosa" return refers to the new gala production at the Teatro San Carlo, the superlative is also appropriate to Leo's music, which matches the violent intensity of the drama much better than Vinci's.[29]

---

[26] Strohm, "Leonardo Vinci's *Didone abbandonata*," 218.

[27] Strohm, "Pasticci" in *Italienische Opernarien* II, 267. A libretto for this production can be found in US-Wc (Schatz No. 11305). The score for Acts II and III has survived and is now in the Conservatoire in Brussels (2365).

[28] Leonardo Leo, *Andromaca*, Dedication, 52 of *Italian Opera Librettos 1640-1770*.

[29] The Abbé de Saint Non draws attention to Leo's development of the *Arie d'Ostinazione* to depict affects of "la suprize & l'effroi:" Saint Non, *Voyage Pittoresque ou description des Royaumes de Naples et de Sicile*, I, 169. However, Helmuth Christian Wolff is surely overstating the issue when he declares Leo's *Andromaca* "perhaps one of the

Vinci's muse is better suited to heroic romance than classical tragedy, and therefore most of his subsequent operas are heroic melodramas. When tragedy is involved, as in the finales in *Didone* and *Catone*, the arias are dispensed with completely, and the accompanied recitative dominates.

## Vinci and Metastasio's Roman Triumph

Vinci would undoubtedly have departed from Naples immediately after the première of *Astianatte* to begin preparations for his next opera. His *Didone abbandonata* was premièred in Rome on January 14, 1726 at the Teatro Alibert, now stylishly renamed the delle dame "with a beautiful new appearance, the stage having enlarged more than forty *palmi*."[30] According to the *Diario di Roma* of Francesco Valesio, the owner of the theatre, Count Antonio Alibert, had become "alienated by his debts."[31] This situation was probably exacerbated by the theater sitting empty throughout the Holy Year of 1725 because of the ban on theatrical entertainments. In April 1725 it was put up for public auction by a decree of the Governor of Rome and sold to an aristocratic consortium consisting of twelve "proprietari di palchetti."[32] Assailed by debts and apoplexy, Count Alibert retired to the Monastery of S. Antonio alli Monti.[33]

Several of the proprietory owners were Florentine, including Paulo Maria Maccarani, who took the role of impresario. Maccarani was from an old Florentine family with close connections to the theatre, his father having served as impresario at the Teatro Pergola.[34] It is therefore not surprising that the new theatre was organized administratively along the same lines as the Pergola. In a letter from March 1726, Maccarani explained that "he and his partners had bought the Theatre previously known as the Teatro Alibert in order to assure its noble patrons that operatic performances of the first rank should continue in the city."[35] Maccarani,

---

finest achievements in eighteenth-century Italian opera:" Wolff, "Italian Opera 1700-1750" in *Opera and Church Music: 1630-1750*, ed. Anthony Lewis and Nigel Fortune, New Oxford History of Music, V (London: Oxford University Press, 1975), 111.

[30] Francesco Valesio, *Diario di Roma: Libro settima e libro ottavo* [Vol. IV: 1708-1728] ed. Gaetana Scano and Giuseppe Graglia (Longanesi, 1979), 627. The *palmo* was the old linear measurement known as the "handbreath," equivalent to approximately four inches (i.e. an enlargement of about thirteen feet).

[31] Ibid., 637.

[32] Elisabetta Mori, "I Maccarani dal teatro di corte al teatro Alibert," *La musica a Roma attraverso le fonti d'archivio: atti del Convegno internazionale, 4-7 giugno Roma, 1992*, ed. Bianca Maria Antolini, Arnaldo Morelli, and Vera Vita Spagnuolo (Libraria Musicale Italiana, 1994), 187.

[33] Valesio, Op. cit., 637.

[34] Mori, Op. cit., 188.

[35] William C. Holmes, *Opera Observed*, 121.

along with Antonio Viani and his brother-in-law Alessandro Minucci, not only contributed the required three-hundred scudi, but kicked in another thousand for the renovation of the theatre, thereby gaining ascendency over the other members of the consortium.[36]

The modest cast of *Didone abbandonata* may reflect the theater's delicate financial condition:[37]

    Didone: Giacinto Fontana    Jarba: Gaetano Berenstadt
    Selene: Filippo Finazzi      Araspe: Domenico Gizzi
    Enea: Antonio Barbieri     Osmida: Angelo Franchi
        Stage painter and engineer: Alessandro Mauri
          Battle director: Giuseppe Franceschini
            Choreographer: Antonio Saro.

The *primo uomo,* Domenico Gizzi, and the "*seconda donna,*" Filippo Finazzi, had already appeared in similar roles in *Farnace,* while the tenor, Antonio Barbieri, had appeared the previous year as Armindo in *La Rosmira* (and was depicted in caricature as a Roman conqueror which would have been appropriate for this role as well; see Plate 8 on p. 106). The role of Jarba was the first that Vinci created for Gaetano Berenstadt, the Florentine alto castrato of German background who was admired not only for his voice but also for his intellect. According to the artist Pierleone Ghezzi, "this musician was versed in literature and the discourse of doctors."[38] Berenstadt was undoubtedly enthusiastic about taking the role; he had encountered Metastasio's drama the previous winter when Sarro's setting was revived in Florence, describing it as "un libro divino."[39] The title role was taken by Giacinto Fontana, a soprano castrato from Perugia who had taken the *prima donna* role previously at the rival Teatro Capranica in several important productions, including Scarlatti's *Griselda* and Vivaldi's *Giustino*.[40] Fontana specialized in female roles and earned the nickname "Farfallino" because of his graceful appear-

---

[36] Ibid., 189-90. Because of the Vaini's connection with the Knights of Malta, the theater eventually came into the hands of that order, who retained control of it until the mid-nineteenth century. Alberto De Angeles, *Il teatro Alibert o delle Dame,* 55-57.

[37] Libretto in I-BC, I-Fm, I-Nc, I-Rsc, GB-Lbm, US-NYP; Sartori, *I libretti italiani* (No. 7758). Facsimile of libretto in *Italian Opera Librettos: 1640-1770,* 54.

[38] Pierluigi Petrobelli, "Il musicista di teatro settecentesco nelle caricature di Pierleone Ghezzi," *Antonio Vivaldi: Teatro musicale cultura e società,* ed. Lorenzo Bianconi and Giovanni Morelli, Studi di musica Veneta quaderni Vivaldiani 2 (Florence: Leo S. Olschki, 1982), 420. From the discovery of a vast collection of letters by and to Beren-stadt, Lowell Lindgren has written a biography of the singer that details his various activities in music and the arts;" Lowell Lindgren, "La Carriera di Gaetano Berenstadt," *Revista italiana di Musicologia* 18-19 (1983/84), 36-99.

[39] Lindgren, Op.cit., 74.

[40] Although in his study of Vivaldi's Roman singers, Dale Monson describes Fontana as a singer of the old school because of his relatively narrow range (usually an eleventh) and the consistent brilliant treatment of the voice throughout the range, this is

ance (see Plate 13). Along with this remarkable stage grace, Farfallino must have had a violent temperament; during a performance of *Didone* he almost fought a duel with another musician behind the scenes.[41]

Metastasio's *Didone abbandonata* had originally been produced at the Teatro San Bartolomeo in Naples during the carnival season of 1724 with music by Domenico Sarro.[42] Metastasio based his opera, or as he designated it "Dramma da rappresentarsi in musica" on Book IV of Virgil's *Aeneid*. This version of the story is longer and more complex than the familiar one by Tate and Purcell and, as in Berlioz's *Les Troyens*, includes more elements from Virgil, such as the Moorish King Jarba and his amorous and political designs on Didone and her lands. Metastasio's drama begins as Enea resolves to abandon Didone and it develops from two connected chains of unrequited love: Jarba, King of the Moors, loves Didone who loves Enea; and Jarba's confidant Araspe loves Didone's sister, Selene, who loves Enea, who in turn loves only his destiny.[43]

> **Synopsis**: Enea tells Didone's minister Osmida and her sister Selene that the fates have decreed he must leave Carthage to found the new Troy. Didone enters and when she questions him on his coldness towards her, he responds falteringly and rushes out. Selene explains to Didone that Enea is torn between love and duty. When Didone asks Selene to intercede with Enea on her behalf, she reluctantly consents since she is secretly in love with Enea. Didone's overlord, King Jarba, accompanied by his minister Araspe, delivers Didone an ultimatum: either she marry Jarba and hand over Enea for execution or risk the consequences of open war. Didone replies that she will rule over both her heart and her kingdom. Anticipating the outcome, Osmida makes a secret deal with Jarba to help him apprehend Enea in exchange for the governorship of Carthage. They plan to ambush Enea when he meets Didone at the Neptune fountain. Jarba's assassination is foiled by Araspe. Didone condemns Jarba for his attempt

---

contradicted by the type of music Vinci wrote for him, representing the composer at his most innovative and modern. Dale E. Monson, "The Trail of Vivaldi's Singers: Vivaldi in Rome," *Nuovi studi vivaldiani: Edizione e cronologia critica delle opere,* ed. Antonio Fanna and Giovanni Morelli, Venezia Fondazione Georgio Cini, I (1988), 568.

[41] Valesio, *Diario di Roma: Libro settimo e libro ottavo*, 632.

[42] Libretto in F-Pn and US-Wc; Sartori, *I libretti italiani* (No. 7753).

[43] This type of fatal love has already been encountered in *Astianatte* based on Racine's *L'Andromaque*. Metastasio was familiar with Racine's great tragedy and it exerted an influence on his first drama. See Ettore Paratore "*L'Andromaque* e la *Didone abbandonata*" *Scritti in onore di Luigi di Ronga* (Milan: Riccardo Ricciardi, 1973). The connection wth *Andromaque* was undoubtedly a factor in the decision to produce Vinci's *Astianatte* as a follow-up to Sarro's *Didone abbandonata* at the Teatro S. Bartolomeo.

**Plate 13.** *Caricature of Giacinto Fontana "Farfallino" by Pier Leone Ghezzi, Rome, July 1728.* © Biblioteca Apostolica Vaticana (Vatican)[44]

---

[44] Pier Leone Ghezzi, *Il Nuovo Mondo,* III, f. 113; unpublished manuscript in the Biblioteca Apostolica Vaticana, Ottob.lat. 3114 with the following inscription: "Farfallino Perugino, bravissimo soprano, who sang in the opera of the Red Priest at the Teatro di Aliberti in the year 1723, made by me Cavalier Ghezzi on the 20th day of January of this year."

to murder Enea. Left alone, Enea tells Didone that he must abandon her to found a second Troy. Didone responds by accusing him of treachery.

Jarba reprimands Araspe on his presumptuous deed. Araspe has meanwhile fallen in love with Selene. When he declares his love, she tells him that she loves another and they are both condemned to unrequited love. Enea comes to Didone to plead for the life of Jarba. Although she hands him the death sentence, Didone is incensed that he appears untroubled by the end their relationship. When Jarba threatens Enea, the Trojan tears up his death warrant in his face, demonstrating his superior virtue. Didone tries to make Enea jealous by accepting Jarba's proposal of marriage, but to her frustration he blesses the union and departs with haste. Deserted by Enea, Didone tells Jarba her acquiescence was simply a ruse to win back Enea. Enraged and humiliated, Jarba calls for revenge.

Jarba challenges Enea to a duel and is defeated. Though magnanimously spared by the victor, the humiliated Jarba swears that Carthage shall be destroyed. When Osmida comes to Jarba to seek his reward, the infuriated Moor orders his men to execute him. Osmida is spared only by the return of Enea. Enea bids farewell to Selene who pleads with him to stay for Didone's love and her own. Enea replies abruptly that he wants to hear no more about her love or Dido's. Osmida comes before Didone to ask for forgiveness for his treachery, followed by Selene who confesses her secret passion for Enea, followed by Araspe who tells her that Jarba has set fire to the city. Believing herself betrayed by lover, sister and friend, she resolves to die. She curses the gods and hurls herself into the flames of the burning city.

The spectacular tragic finale has precedents in a number of works from the early eighteenth century, among them Piovene's *Tamerlano* and Salvi's *Amore e maestà*.[45] The latter, based on Thomas Corneille's *Le Comte d'Essex*, was produced in Naples in 1718 as *Arsace*, with La Romanina and Nicolino in the lead roles and music by Sarro. As such it served as the model for the original Neapolitan *Didone abbandonata*.[46]

The Roman revival of *Didone abbandonata* was an important event because it was the first work of Metastasio to be produced in his native city. Moreover it also represents Vinci's first collaboration with the great

---

[45] See list of *tragedie per musica* from the early eighteenth century with the *funesta fine* in Reinhard Strohm, "*Tragédie* into *Dramma per musica*" Part III, *Informazioni e studi vivaldiani: Bollettino annuale dell'istituto italiano Antonio Vivaldi* 11 (1990), 15.

[46] For the numerous connections between *Amore e Maestà* and *Didone abbandonata* see Op. cit, Part III, 15-23.

poet who was to become the ultimate librettist of the *dramma per musica*. Metastasio, though a Roman by birth, had spent the past six years in Naples. His first dramas were produced inNaples in collaboration with his former music teacher Nicola Porpora, who had recently composed a new setting of *Didone* for the Modonese court in Reggio Emilia. It is indicative of the eighteenth-century love of novelty that the Roman production featured a new musical setting by Vinci rather than a revival of the recent setting by Porpora or the original setting by Sarro, in spite of the presence of Sarro in Rome for the production of his *Il Valdemaro*, which would conclude the 1726 season at the Teatro delle dame.[47] The other Leonardo, Leonardo Leo was also in Rome during Carnival 1726 for the première of his *Trionfo di Camilla* at the Teatro Capranica. Leo was caricatured by Ghezzi during his stay in Rome along with two of the singers from the production of *Camilla* (see Plate 14 on page 142). According to the note by Ghezzi, Leo's opera was "a miracle and totally good" but the singing of the tenors, Valletta "in the throat" and Rainino "in li ttle voice"" that led to its poor reception.[47] *Camilla* was not the only offailure during this season. According to Valesio, the Chinese locale of the original libretto to *Il Valdemaro*, Zeno's *Tenzone, imperatore della cina*, was changed to Scandinavia because of the troubles between the Pope and the Jesuits in China at the time. In spite of the changes, Sarro's opera failed to please and, according to Cavaliere Antonio Fontana, its lack of success, in turn, added to the success of *La Statira*, which concluded the season at the Teatro Capranica.[48] In a similar manner, the lack of success of Leo's *Il Trionfo di Camilla* probably contributed to the success of Vinci's *Didone abbandonata*, while the failure of *Il Valdemaro* may have led to an imromptu revival of Vinci's opera at the end of the season to substitute for Sarro's, in the same way that Farnace had been revived the previous year after the failure of Predieri's *Scipione*.

The libretto to Vinci's *Didone*, like that of *Farnace*, was dedicated to "Giacomo III Rè della Gran Brettagna." The directors obviously intended James Edward Stuart to see himself as Enea, the great hero destined to establish a kingdom for himself and his heirs on a far-off shore. In fact the image fits so nicely that it seems likely that Metastasio had the principal opera patron in his home town in mind when he wrote the drama.

As was the case in *Eraclea* and *Ifigenia in Tauride*, *Didone* was revised for Vinci by the poet. These revisions for the most part are concentrated in the second half of Act II (scenes vii-xviii) where the scene

---

[47] Pier Leone Ghezzi, *Il Nuovo Mondo*, IV, F. 142.
[48] Valesio, *Diario di Roma*, IV, 636 and Holmes, 119.

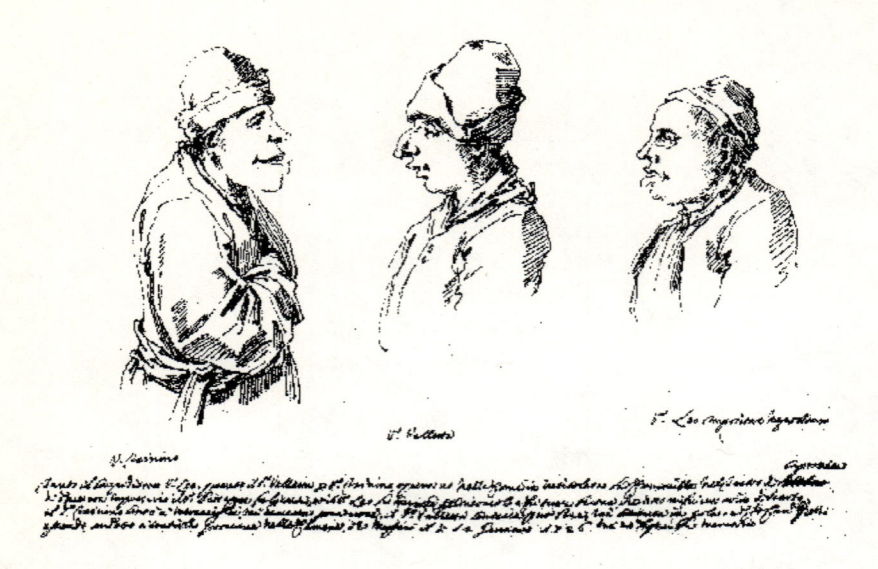

**Plate 14.** *Caricatures of the tenors Giovanni Antonio Reina and Gaetano Valetta with Leonardo Leo by Pier Leone Ghezzi, Rome 1726.* © Biblioteca Apostolica Vaticana (Vatican)[49]

structure and the sequence of events differs from the original version of the drama as set by Sarro. In this section all but two of Metastasio's original aria texts were omitted. Of the five replacement texts two were written specifically to accommodate pre-existing music ("Sono intrepido nell'alma" and "Prende ardire"), while the others were old poems recycled from previous productions.[50] The changes in the remaining parts of the opera were minor, consisting of two arias omitted and two arias replaced.[51] The most obvious result of these changes is that they created a more even balance in the aria distribution. In the original version of *Didone abbandonata* as set by Sarro, the role of Jarba was given greater prominence than the other characters, with eight in-

---

[49] Pier Leone Ghezzi, *Il Nuovo Mondo,* IV, f. 142.

[50] "Amor che nasce" is from *Endimione* and "Se vuoi, ch'io mora" and "Son quest' idoli vani" are from the revised version of *Didone* that Metastasio had made for Albinoni the previous year (libretto in US-Wc [Schatz No. 89]). Although Vinci undoubtedly attended performances of Albinone's *Didone* while he was in Venice the previous Carnival, he probably did not attend the original Sarro production, which was performed in Naples the same time that he was making his Roman debut with *Farnace*.

[51] Although the aria "Grato rende il fiumicello" appears to be another replacement aria, it is actually a rearrangement of "Tu mi scorgi" in which the second strophe is placed first and the first is replaced with a brief new strophe.

stead of six arias. In the revised version that Metastasio concocted for Vinci, all the roles, except the cadet Osmida, are given five arias each (at least before the last-minute revisions).[52]

With *Astianatte* premièred in Naples in December 1725, *Didone abbandonata* in Rome in January 1726, and *Siroe re di Persia* in Venice in February, it was undoubtedly essential that as much of the music as possible for these works was composed before the winter season began.[53] Considering the nature of Metastasio's revisions, confined for the most part to Act II, it is possible that Vinci began the composition of *Didone* some time in the summer after he received the commission, using Sarro's libretto from which he set most of the arias except those in Act II scenes vii-xviii. This would account for two of these arias, "Ardi per me" and "L'augelletto, in lacci stretto," being later parodied for use in *Astianatte* as "Temi di vendicarti" and "Io non vi credo" (see above). An overture was composed that was used for both *Didone* and *Astianatte*, its third movement even being used again in *Siroe*.[54] In such a scenario, the collaboration with Metastasio on the revisions to Act II would have been done when Vinci arrived in Rome some time in December after the première of *Astianatte*. Other adjustments and changes would also have been made to accommodate the singers. One of the changes probably involved replacing Selene's Act III aria "Nel duol, che prova" with a parody text "Si ti lagni sventurato" to accommodate music already written for "Per amor se'l cor" from *Astianatte*. At some time before the libretto went to press, cuts were made via *virgole* to four arias (and the second section to a fifth). Two of these arias were cut from the cadet role, Osmida, who had to be satisfied with a single aria in each act. Perhaps the singer's voice did not meet up to expectations or perhaps when cuts had to be made, the cadet role was a standard place to begin.

---

[51] Lowell Lindgren draws attention to this type of balancing in Gasparini's operaas for the Teatro Alibert, claiming it to be a Roman characteristic; Lindgren, "La Carriera di Gaetano Berenstadt," 51. While four of Vinci's Roman operas support Lindgren's claim, this trend can also be found in two of his Neapolitan operas (*Eraclea* and *La caduta*) and one opf his Venetian oertas (*Siroe*); moreover, the other twoRoman operas (*Farnace* and *Alessandro*) exhibit a hierarchical distribution of arias, with the difference between the two casting approaches usually based on the shifting of one or two arias.

[52] According to Strohm, "Vinci obviously worked, with Metastasio's help, on all three works at more or less the same time" Reinhard Strohm, "Leonardi Vinci's *Didone abbandonata* (Rome 1726)" *Essays on Handel and Italian Opera*, 218. Except on the issue of Metastasio's role in *Astianatte*, the present scenario gives further support to Strohm's speculation

[54] Hellmut Hell, *Die Napolitanische Opernsinfonie in der ersten Halfte des 18. jahrhunderts* (Tutzing, Schneider, 1971), 539-40.

In *Il Teatro alla moda* Marcello satirized the collaboration between composer and poet in the contemporary *dramma per musica*:

> In order not to confuse himself, he [the composer] will take care not to read the entire opera, but rather will compose it verse by verse, immediately informing [the poet] to make further changes in all the arias, to make use of the *motivi* prepared during the year; and if the new words to these arias do not go easily under the notes (which is usually the case) he will torment the poet for new ones until he renders him full satisfaction.[55]

While Marcello's description contains some interesting parallels with the reconstruction of the Vinci/Metastasio collaboration on *Didone*, the differences are more significant. Although Vinci may have composed the majority of the arias during the summer or fall, the original Metastasio texts were available, thereby ensuring that only a handful of aria texts had to be rewritten or replaced when it came to the actual production. Moreover in revising his text, Metastasio restored the recitatives that had been omitted in the Venetian revival of 1726 rather than reducing them, as was often the case when revising a libretto. This reflects not only the prestige Metastasio had gained as a poet, but also Vinci's willingness to include extensive passages of recitative in his opera scores. Finally, when it came to making cuts prior to the première, these were made, with two brief exceptions, in Vinci's arias and not Metastasio's recitative. This accommodation with the poet, which flies in the face of Marcello's satire, could be one of the reasons why Vinci became Metastasio's principal collaborator during his final years in Italy.

A record in the Archives of the Order of Malta states that Metastasio was paid 65 scudi in a watch case with a gold chain.[56] This honorarium would have been not only for his revisions but also for his role as stage director, which was often the role of the stage poet. To judge from Metastasio's advice to the Dresden court poet Pasquini concerning the staging of *Demofoonte* in 1748, stage direction during this period was primarily concerned with the orderly entrance and exit of the characters and their fixed placement on the stage during the scenes.[57] That this formalized placement of the characters on stage had as much to do with class consciousness as drama is exemplified by Metastasio's continued insistence that the most exalted character does not **always** have to be on the right side of the stage.[58]

---

[55] [Benedetto Marcello], *Il teatro alla moda*, 63-64.

[56] De Angelis, *Il teatro Alibert o delle dame*, 145.

[57] Pietro Metastsio, *Tutte le Opere*, III, 337-40 (letter from February 10, 1748).

[58] Ibid., 342-43. This advice occurs both in the letter referred to, and at greater length in a follow-up letter to Pasquini dated February 16, where he makes mention of letters to the Theater Superintendent Baron Dieskau and to Hasse on this same subject.

In spite of the modest cast, Vinci's *Didone abbandonata* was a great success. The Roman newsletter, the *Diario Ordinario d'Ungheria* refers to the "the opera in Musica entitled *La Didone abbandonata* that succeeded with much satisfaction and applause."[59] The Jesuit priest and scholar Giulio Cesare Cordara reported that "every scene produced one continued applause" and "all Rome [was filled] with the fame of this production."[60]

Roman audiences were known for their passionate and capricious reaction to works on the stage. According to a report in Carl Friederich Cramer's *Magazin der Musik* for 1784:

> It is not uncommon that after a perfect opera, [the Romans] remain in the theatre for an hour of more in incessant clapping and rejoicing....Sometimes also the composer of such an Opera is taken [in triumph] in his chair from the orchestra pit.[61]

The report cites Jommelli as the last recipient of this honor. Simlarly Goldoni relates how, while he was in Rome producing his play *La vedova spiritosa*, Giuseppe di Mayo's new opera received a comparable reception at the Teatro delle Dame and "a Part of the pit went out at the close of the entertainment, to conduct the musician home in triumph."[62] One can imagine Vinci and Metastasio receiving a similar ovation at the end of the première of *Didone abbandonata*. Ironically, this enthusiastic approbation of works that pleased the Romans was matched by a vehement disapproval of those that did not do so. Thus while Di Mayo was receiving ovations at the della Dame, Goldoni's *La vedova spiritosa* was being whistled down at the Teatro Tordinona, with calls to bring on Pulcinella.[63] Similarly, the *Magazin der Musik* report on Jommelli's success also describes how, in returning to Rome the following year, "he was compelled by the haughty crowd to leave the theatre, even while conducting the orchestra."[64] Although Vinci enjoyed the enthusiastic approval of the Roman audience with both his *Farnace* and *Didone*, he would also experience its capriciousness in later seasons.

---

[59] *Diario Ordinario d'Ungheria*, T. 53, No. 1319. Quoted in Giuletta Pejrone, "Il teatro attraverso i periodici romani del Settecento," *Il teatro a Roma nel Settecento* (Istituto della Enciclopedia italiana), 603.The *Diario Ordinario d'Ungheria* was founded during the Turkish war to report news from the front and from the Imperial Court, but with the end of the war, the newsletter began to report on events in Rome, taking on the generic title of *Diario Ordinario* (Ibid., 599-601).

[60] Charles Burney, *Memoirs of the Life and Writings of the Abate Metastasio: in which are incorporated Translations of his Principal Letters* (London: Robinson, 1796), I, 36.

[61] Carl Fredrich Cramer, *Magazin der Musik: Zweyter Jahrgung* (Hamburg: Musicalischen Viederlage, 1784), I, 36.

[62] A.M. Nagler, *A Source Book in Theatrical History.0* (New York: Dover), 50-51.

[63] Ibid., 280.

[64] Cramer, Op. cit., 51. There is a problem with chronology in Cramer's anecdote; be-

## *Didone abbandonata*: Dominance of the Title Role

Although Metastasio's revision resulted in an equal redistribution of arias among the cast, Vinci's *Didone abbandonata* is still dominated musically and dramatically by one character. The opera had been originally created by Metastasio as a showpiece for his mentor and mistress Marianna Benti Bulgarelli "La Romanina" (see Plate 15). Acccording to Saverio Mattei La Romanina was involved in the creation of this extraordinary role, particularly singling out her contribution to the final scenes of Act II:

> La Romanina was a great actress, and Metastasio himself learned from her the most admirable theatrical situations, such as that of jealousy in scenes XIV and XV of the second act [of *Didone*], which were entirely the invention of the singer, as the Princess of Belmonte has assured me many times. [65]

Although La Romanina was not allowed to sing her role in Vinci's *Didone* because of the Papal ban, she was probably present at the rehearsals to coach Farfallino, as she did a year later in the role of Emira in Porpora's *Siroe re di Persia*.[66] Moreover, since the sequence of scenes that Metastasio revised for Vinci's *Didone* culminate in these "jealousy" scenes, it is possible that Romanina was involved in the revisions.

Didone's character is established with her first aria, "Son Regina,e sono amante," which is one of the finest examples of Vinci's heroic style.[67] Cordara reports that during the performance at the delle Dame, this scene was particulary applauded:

---

cause of Jomelli's long tenure as *Kapellmeister* in Stuttgart, the last season when these back-to-back productions could have taken place would have been during the early 1750s, when he served as *maestro coadiutore* in the Papal chapel; but these would hardly have been recent in 1784. One could connect this anecdote with the season 1771 after Jommelli's return from Germany, when he presented two works in Rome, the comic opera *L'amante cacciatore* at the Teatro Pallacorda and the heroic opera *Achille in Sciro* at the Teatro delle Dame. However, since Jommelli did not return to Rome, these two contrasting receptions would have occurred during the same season, one of the operas a stunning success, the other a miserable failure.

[65] Saverio Mattei, *Memorie per servire alla vita del Metastasio ed Elogia di N. Jommelli* (Colle: Angiolo M. Martini, 1785; reprint ed. Bologna, Arnaldo Formi, 1987) Biblioteca Musica Bononiensis, III, no. 57, 69.

[66] De Angelis, *Il teatro Alibert o delle Dame*, 146.

[67] In contrast to Vinci's previous operas, *Didone abbandonata* is the first surviving in more than one complete score. The Santini-Sammlung score in Münster originated in Rome, and was initialled and dated September 22, 1730 by the theater copyist Francesco Cantoni (4242 in 3 vols., 17 x 22 cm). Like the score of *Farnace*, which was copied a year earlier, this score may have been produced as part of an attempt to build up the repertoire of the Teatro della Dame. Unlike the score of *Farnace*, which was compiled from pre-existing aria fascicles, this one is through-copied. There is also a score to Acts I and II in the Nationalbibliothek (17710) in Vienna. Another complete score of *Didone abbandonata* is in the Newberry Library in Chicago (VM 1500.V77d). It formerly belonged to the Earl of Aylesford, who inherited it from Charles Jennens.

FIRST COLLABORATIONS WITH METASTASIO 147

*Plate 15.* Caricature of Marianna Benti Bulgarelli "La Romanina" by Pier Leone Ghezzi, Rome, July 1728. © Biblioteca Apostolica Vaticana (Vatican)[68]

Jennens probably bought it from Edward Holdsworth who, in 1732, sent him scores of Vinci's *Artaserse* and Hasse's *Cajo Fabricio* from Rome. Handel, in turn, borrowed this score in 1737 for a pasticcio based on Vinci's *Didone abbandonata*. This beautifully copied score has been published in facsimile in the Garland Italian Opera Series ( 29). The complete score consists of:

| 2 sinfonias | 2 ariosos | 2 ariettas |
| 27 *da capo* arias | | 7 accomapnied recitatives |

Totals: 40 set pieces (27 in *da capo* form)

[68] Pier Leone Ghezzi, *Il Nuovo Mondo*, Vol. V, f. 144, Vaticana Ottob.lat. 3116 with the following inscription: "Marianna Benti detto La Romanina, singer and wife of Bulgarelli, made by me Cavalier Ghezzi on July 14, 1828 on the occasion that a medallion was struck in England where they engrave all the famous musicians and singers. . ."

But who can describe the rapture of the pit, when the queen of Carthage disdainfully rising from the throne, represses the insolent pretensions of the king of Mauritania, with the dignity of an independent princess, by the spirited air, *Son Regina,* &c? The noise [of the applause] seemed to shake the theatre to its foundation.[69]

The opening ritornello contains a subsidiary instrumental figure that reappears in different guises in several of Vinci's later heroic arias, consisting of accelerating repeated notes in the violins with the basses and violas in parallel thirds or sixths (see Example 5.12 on p.164):

Example 5.6 "Son Regina, e sono amante" *Didone abbandonata* I/v

The theme, with its repeated second phrase, is an early example of the ABB format that was to become the standard thematic formula for mid-century composers.[70] The theme also employs the same caesura ornament at the end of its three constituent phrases, which would have been considered wrong by the eighteenth-century theorist Heinrich Christoph Koch because the caesura note "c" remains the same.[71]

---

[69] Quoted in Burney, *Memoirs of the Life and Writings of the Abate Metastasio*, .I, 38-39.
[70] Eric Weimer, *Opera seria and the Evolution of Classical Style: 1755-1772*, Studies in Muscology. No. 78, ed. George Buelow (Ann Arbor, Michigan: UMI Research Press, 1984), 30-32
[71] Heinrich Chrstoph Koch, *Introductory Essay in Composition: the Mechanical Rules of Melody*, Nancy Kovaleff Baker, trans. (New Haven, Conn.: Yale University Press), 92.

That this repetition was not a mistake is proven by the next phrase which takes up this caesura ornament as its basic motive. This repetition contributes to the emphatic character that is such an integral part of this aria. Leonardo Leo, in town for the production of his *Trionfo di Camilla* at the Teatro Capranica, was probably among the people who wildly applauded "Son Regina." Several years later he was to compliment both Vinci and Metastasio in Piro's aria "Son regnante e son guerriero" at the beginning of his *Andromaca*, which refers both in its text and music to this aria.

Didone's "Se vuoi, ch'io mora" in Act II presents the Queen as the lamenting heroine who is so distraught over Enea's indifference to their parting that she asks him to kill her. This pathetic aria in G minor is the only minor-mode aria in the opera. When transposing this aria for Strada in his pasticcio based on Vinci's *Didone*, Handel must have been impressed with the affecting chromaticism of the initial canonic theme. He decided to use it in "Mio dolce amato sposo" at the end of Act III in *Giustino* and then, to cover up the theft, disfigured the aria in the pasticcio by recomposing the opening theme, removing its distinctive chromaticism and canonic imitation:[72]

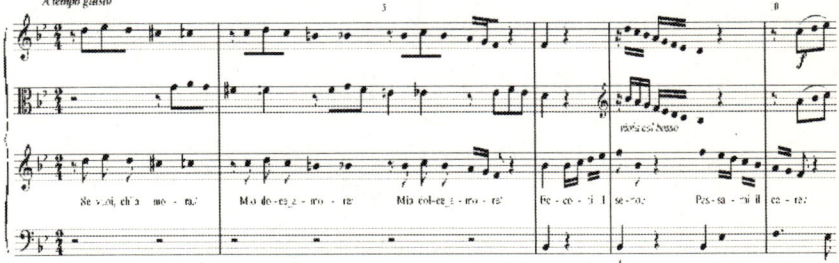

Example 5.7a "Se vuoi, ch'io mora" *Didone abbandonata* II/vii

Example 5.7b "Se vuoi, ch'io mora" Handel's pasticcio *La didone* II/5

Many years later Handel would recall this theme in the sublime duet in Act II of *Theodora*, transposing it down a step to F minor.

---

[72] John H. Roberts, "Handel and Vinci's *Didone Abbandonata*: Revisions and Borrowings" *Music and Letters* 68/2 (1987), 146-48. Handel also borrowed the chromatic melisma on "tormento" in the second section of another aria in *Giustino*, "Zeffiretto, che scorre nel prato" as well as material from Jarba's "Son quell fiume" in "Sollevar il mondo," both arias sung by the hero in Act III.

150                                                                    LEONARDO VINCI

At the end of Act II, the despairing Didone asks the gods to pity her and sings a simile aria about the lost traveller taking consolation in the morning star. According to Strohm, Metastasio wrote the simile text "Prende ardire, e si conforta" to allow Vinci to re-use music he had already composed for "Non vi piacque" from *Siroe*.[73] Vinci must have been very pleased with this aria since it appears in the prime position of Act II finale in both operas. The aria also pleased Handel who borrowed this material in "Fatto scorta al sentier"from *Arminio*.[74]

Example 5.8 "Prende Ardire" *Didone abbandonata* II/xviii

What Handel most appreciated about this aria was not the initial minuet theme, which he later referred to in "O God-like Youth" from *Saul* but, rather, the sequential subsidiary material employed in a similar manner in the ritornello and at strategic points in the rapturous coloratura.[75]

Act III is dominated by Didone, even though she has no arias. Besides her recitative, which exemplifies Vinci's basic compositional technique at its finest, the musical dramatic climax is realized in accompa-

---

[73] Strohm, "Leonardo Vinci's *Didone abbandonata*," 218; that "Prende ardire" is a replacement aria written to accommodate music composed for "Non vi piacque" in *Siroe* is suggested by the fact that the text to the latter becomes the Act II finale in subsequent settings of *Siroe* (such as Sarro's from Naples 1727, Handel's from London 1728, Fiorè's from Torino 1731, and Hasse's from Bologna 1733), as well as the standard text in *Tutte le Opere*, while the text of "Prende ardire"appears in neither the previous settings of *Didone* (such as Sarro's from Naples 1724 and Porpora's from Reggio 1725), nor in subsequent settings (such as Sarro's from Venice 1730 and Hasse's from Dresden 1742), which have the aria "và lusingando amore."

[74] Roberts, Op. cit, 142-45. See *G.F.Händels Werke: Ausgabe der Deutschen Händelgesellschaft*, ed. Friedrich Chrysander (Leipzig: Deutschen Händelgesellschaft), Vol. 89, 84-88.

[75] That the similarity of the theme of "O God-like Youth" is more than coincidental is suggested by the feint into the minor mode prior to the vocal cadence similar to that in the coda of the second vocal period of Vinci's aria.

nied recitative and arioso. In the scenes leading up to the *scena ultima*, Didone is given four accompanied recitatives while the other characters have simple recitative. In the first, "I miei casi infelici," Didone self-consciously muses that her misfortunes will become legendary and appear on the stage. The second, "Sposa d'un tiranno," occurs when she refuses Jarba's final and most threatening proposal, highlighting the words "empio" and "crudel" with tritones. The third, "Solo per vendicarmi," in which she curses Enea, features lively arpeggios, tremolos and scales to depict the verbal images, thunder and lightning, hurricanes and tempests, winds and waves. The fourth, "Ma che feci, empi Numi?" occurs when she questions the cruelty of the gods. In this accompanied recitative Vinci reserved his most intense harmonies for the image of the smoking sacrifices on the altar, which Didone insists she never profaned, while her actual curse of the gods, which signals her downfall, is set as a simple recitative. This rather unusual treatment may have been intended to tone down the flagrant impiety of her curse, emphasizing that, up to this point, Didone had never profaned the gods—impiety towards the gods, however pagan and antiquarian, was considered offensive in *settecento* Italy.

The final scene, Didone's death, is a monologue, consisting of an arioso surrounded by two accompanied recitatives. In the first, Didone's growing fear is depicted by tremolo in the basses with sustained upper strings leading to tremolo throughout the orchestra. The centerpiece of the scene is an arioso, "Vado...ma dove." An agitated declamatory vocal line accompanied by a quasi-ostinato bass is employed as Didone expresses her fear and panic, realizing that she has been abandoned by everyone. Her repeated question "Dunque morir dovrò senza trovar pietà?" is set in a more lyrical style, with chordal accompaniment ending on a phrygian cadence to accompany the question:

Example 5.9 "Vado...ma dove" *Didone abbandonata* III/ultima

In the final accompanied recitative in which she heroically resolves on her death, the descending scale passages in the orchestra depicting the collapse of the burning palace, are immediately taken up by the voice on the phrase "Precitipti Cartago:"

Example 5.10 "E v'è tanta viltà" *Didone abbandonata* III/ultima

These descending scale passages are abandoned at the end of the scene and, surprisingly, Didone's plunge into the flames of Carthage is not accompanied by a flurry of cascading scale passages, as one would find in similar scenes in Handel or Rameau, but simply by a bar-and-a-half flourish of reiterated E-flat harmony. According to Strohm this restraint is due to the great emphasis on poetry in Vinci's opera: "the catastrophe is actually expressed by the extinguishing of the language—which is the life of the whole—by the orchestra, just as Dido's voice is extinguished by the flames."[76] Alessandro Mauri's stage effects, however, may have had more to do with this restraint than Metastasio's poetry. With Didone leaping through flaming backcloths to her doom, Vinci probably felt no need to write cascading scales and diminished harmony.[77]

Although based on the tragic finales in earlier operas such as *Tamerlano* and *Arsace*, Metastasio's finale became famous, particularly in Vinci's setting. The reformer Count Francesco Algarotti singled out the accompanied recitatives in Act III of Vinci's *Didone* as a model for reform-minded composers:

---

[76] Strohm, "Leonardo Vinci's *Didone abbandonata*," 224.

[77] This spectacular finale involved considerable ingenuity to bring off. The backcloths made of canvas were soaked in water, with oil applied on the side facing the audience. This was then set alight while stage hands continued to sprinkle the back with water. (Information supplied by Domenico Pietropaolo of the University of Toronto.)

> What a kindly warmth might be communicated to the recitative, if, where a passion exerts itself, it were to be enforced by the united orchestra! By so doing, the heart and mind at once would be stormed, as it were, by all the powers of music. A more evincing instance of such an effect cannot be quoted, than the greater part of the last act of Didone, set to music by Vinci, which is executed in the taste recommended here: and no doubt but Virgil's self would be pleased to hear a composition so animating and so terrible.[78]

Algarotti's statement must be qualified. The six accompanied recitatives in Act III, extending from between ten and twenty measures, can hardly be considered to represent "the greater part of the last act." The strength and power of the accompanied recitative lies in its infrequent use, generally being reserved for exceptionally intense dramatic situations, of which the finale to *Didone* is a perfect example, or for special scenes such as oaths and incantations. In a letter to Hasse concerning the composition of *Attilio Regolo* in 1749, Metastasio warned the composer "that this ornament should not be rendered too familiar" and requested in the final act of their new opera that "no [accompanied] recitative occurred till the last scene" to ensure the effect of the final accompanied recitatives.[79] Similarly, to compensate for the extravagant use of this ornament in the finale to *Didone*, Vinci refrained from its use throughout the rest of the opera with a single exception in Act I for Enea.

Algarotti's statement must also be qualified for giving the false impression that the accompanied recitative was virtually unheard-of in the early eighteenth century when, on the contrary, most operas contained at least one example. The extended sequences of accompanied recitative in *Didone*, as well as in *Astianatte* and *Farnace*, can be found in contemporary scores such as Handel's *Giulio Cesare, Tamerlano,* and *Rodelinda*. The increase in the length and the frequency of its use in the works of certain enlightened composers during the mid-1720s, such as Porpora, Vinci, and Handel, initiates a trend that would lead to the extensive cultivation of the accompanied recitative in the works of reform composers such as Traetta, Jommelli, and Gluck. This increase in the use of accompanied recitative culminates in Gluck's *Orfeo ed Euridice* where all the recitatives is accompanied by the orchestra. The actual precedents for this bold step, which goes far beyond the extended accompanimied recitatives in reform operas of Jommelli and Traetta (that still contain long stretches of "secco" recitative), may have come, like

---

[78] Francesco Algarotti, conte, *Saggio sopra l'opera in musica*; English ed., 380. Algarotti's opinion was repeated by Stefano Arteaga, *Le rivoluzioni del teatro musicale italiano, dalla sua origine fino al presente* (Venice: C. Palese, 1783).
[79] Burney, *Memoirs of the Life and Writings of the Abate Metastasio*, I, 325.

many of the ideas for *Orfeo ed Euridice*, from the progentior of mid-century opera reform, Francesco Algarotti, from his description of how the "greater part of the last act of Didone" was composed by Vinci in accompanied recitative and how "Virgil's self would be pleased to hear." For Gluck and his reformng collaborators, Calzibigi and Count Durazzo, the only recommendation higher than Algarotti's would be from Virgil himself. Therefore, Gluck's revolutionary exclusion of continuo-accompanied recitative, setting the precedent for nineteenth-century opera, may have orginated from Algarotti's misrepresentaton of Vinci's use of accompanied recitative in Act III of *Didone abbandonata*.

As in Purcell's *Dido and Aeneas*, the other characters in *Didone abbandonata* fade in comparison with the title role. Unfortunately for Vinci's opera, these other characters have considerably more music to sing than Aeneas, Belinda, and the witches, some of it of indifferent quality. Enea's arias rarely attain the heroic grandeur that Metastasio's poetry requires, at least to a modern listener. The closest Enea comes to that grandeur is his opening response to Jarba's threats, "Quando saprai chi sono," which has a definite Handelian flavor with its tirades, dotted rhythms, and pompous gait, replete with "present arms" cadences in the ritornellos.

Much of the music written for Jarba results in an overabundance of unisons, string tremolos and rapid scale passages above static harmony, of the type found too often in *Astianatte*. However, in his final aria "Cadrà fra poco in cenere," a balance of these elements is achieved, producing a fine portrait of this blustering barbarian.[80] Strohm praises how "Vinci isolates a single word—'cadrà' which says all."[81] He0 does not explain why this single word "says all" but it may have something to do with the extended cadential preparation of the preceding ritornello which clearly anticipates that in Handel's coronation anthem *Zadok the Priest* with its celebrated entrance of the chorus (see Example 5.11 on facing page).Originally this was sung at the end of Act III as Jarba orders the destruction of Carthage after his final rejection by Didone, but in Metastasio's Roman revision it was moved to the beginning of the act, perhaps to give Vinci's colleague Gizzi the final aria.[82] In its

---

[80] Lowell Lindgren regards Jarba as one of Berenstadt's finest roles; Lindgren, "La carriera di Gaetano Berenstadt," 76-77.

[81] Strohm, "Leonardo Vinci's *Didone abbandonata*," 222.

[82] In Porpora's setting of *Didone* from the previous spring, "Cadrà frà poco" was moved to this position in revisions to the score prior to the first performance. This was probably due to the revised finale, which replaced the original tragic ending for a more conventional "Armida abandonata" finale—Didone on the beach cursing the departing Enea with storms and tempests. Therefore, in Porpora's finale, with its storm and tempest imagery, Jarba's promise to destroy Carthage is no longer suitable and was moved to a more appropriate place at the beginning of the act, when Jarba's men begin to pillage and burn the city.

Example 5.11 "Cadrà fra poco in cenere" *Didone abbandonata* III/iii

new position, sung after Jarba's defeat by Enea, the aria loses much of its apocalyptic grandeur and appears more as the mean threat of a defeated bully.[83] When Handel arranged the music for his 1737 pasticcio, he returned the aria to its rightful place at the end of the act.

## Handel Caught "Stealing"

*Didone abbandonata* was apparently revived in Vienna later that year, though no libretto survives.[84] If this revival did take place, it would seem that the Emperor was impressed by the drama because four years later Metastasio was appointed as Imperial court poet. *Didone abbandonata* was revived by Handel at Covent Garden in April of 1737 for three performances.[85] A score of this pasticcio revival is preserved in

---

[83] For a different interpretation of this move, see Strohm, "Leonardo Vinci's *Didone abbandonata*," 222-23. According to Strohm, the aria, as sung in this scene, foretells the destruction of Didone's palace and empire. The prophecy, however, is rather immediate at this point as Jarba's troops begin to destroy the city.

[84] Otto Erich Deutsch, "Das Repertoire der Höfischen Opera, der Hof- und der Staatsoper: Chronologischer Teil" *Österriechische Musikzeitschrift* 24/7 (July 1969), 387. Acccording to Strohm, the score of Acts II and III in the Nationalbibliothek in Vienna may have been used for this production (Strohm, *Italienische Opernarien* 2, 229).

[85] Strohm, "Handel's pasticci," *Essays on Handel and Italian Opera*, 197-99.

the British Library. This score, which later belonged to the music publisher Samuel Arnold, contains the following note:

> the recitative in this opera was probably set by Mr. Handel. This copy seems to be written by old Smith [the composer's secretary]: probably the Opera was performed under the Direction of Mr. Handel who may have made some alterations in it....I have a half score in which the notes in the voice part of all the Recitative... are written by Mr. Handel, also the Song "Se vuoi ch'io mora."[86]

As mentioned above, the changes in "Se vuoi ch'io mora" were made to cover up Handel's theft of the material in "Mio dolce amato sposo" in *Giustino*. Because of the usual abbreviation of the recitative, very typical of all English productions, and changes in the cast as well (Enea and Araspe exchange vocal ranges and Selene falls to an alto), Vinci's recitative was substantially revised and re-composed by Handel.[87] In addition, six of Vinci's arias were omitted, six replaced and two new arias added, most of these changes affecting the arias of Enea, Araspe and Selene.[88] The primary effect of these machinations is that Araspe is changed back to a cadet role for the young tenor John Beard and Enea is transformed into a true castrato pasticcio role for Gioacchino Conti, with only two of Vinci's original arias retained. Besides borrowing the passage from "Se Vuoi ch'io mora," Handel helped himself to several other ideas from Vinci at this time. This bit of piracy came to the attention of Charles Jennens who had supplied Handel with certain Vinci scores, including the score of *Didone* from which the pasticcio was arranged.[89] In a letter to Edward Holdsworth from January 1743 Jennens mentions that "Handel has borrow'd a dozen of the Pieces & I dare say I shall catch him stealing from them; as I have formerly, both from Scarlatti & Vinci."[90] This exposure to the music of Vinci and his rivals Porpora, Leo, and Hasse was of great importance to Handel's artistic development and can be regarded as the major factor in the stylistic changes in his music during the decade 1725-1735, changes that would become an essential aspect of his oratorios, allowing for greater lyricism in the arias and, in the process, setting up greater contrasts with the solemn grandeur of the choruses.

---

[86] British Library (Additional 31607).
[87] Ibid., 210-211.
[89] Jennen's score of *Didone*, which is now in the Newberry Library in Chicago (VM1500.V77d) and has been published in facsimile in the Garland Italian Opera Series (Vol.29), contains pencil markings probably in Handel's own hand, intended as transposition instructions for his copyists in preparing the pasticcio.
[90] Roberts, "Handel and Vinci's 'Didone Abbandonata': Revisions and Borrowings," 143.

## Mad Dash to Venice

While Vinci and Metastasio collaborated on the Roman première of *Didone abbandonata*, they were also involved with a new *dramma per musica*, *Siroe re di Persia*, which was premièred during the same season at the Teatro San Giovanni Grisostomo in Venice. The Venetian public had already been introduced to the work of these two masters the previous year: Vinci in *Ifigenia* and *La Rosmira* at the Teatro San Giovanni Grisostomo and Metastasio in Albinoni's setting of *Didone* at the Teatro San Cassiano. The cast of *Siroe re di Persia* consisted of:[91]

    Siroe: Nicola Grimaldi    Emira: Marianna Benti Bulgarelli
    Cosroe: Giovanni Paita    Laodice: Lucia Facchinelli
    Medarse: Giovanni Carestini  Arasse: Pellegrino Tomii
        Choreographer: Gaetano Testagrossa

During the previous season Grimaldi and Bulgarelli had appeared together in Albinoni's *Didone* at the Teatro San Cassiano, while Carestini and Paita had appeared at the Teatro Sant'Angelo. Therefore in *Siroe re di Persia*, the directors at the Teatro San Giovanni brought together the finest talent from the previous season. In contrast to the previous year, Vivaldi spent the Carnival season in Venice, where his new opera *La fede tradita* was produced along with the pasticcio *Cunegonda*. With *La fede tradita* premièred at the end of the season, Vinci and Vivaldi again found themselves in rivalry. In this rivalry, Vinci obviously had the upper hand, setting the latest drama by the new star of *opera seria*, produced at the greatest, most prestigious theatre in Venice. Vivaldi's *La fede tradita*, on the other hand, was a re-setting of an old drama by Francesco Silvani, produced at his usual theatre, the modest Teatro Sant'Angelo.

As in the previous season, the male members of the cast at the San Giovanni were caricatured by Marco Ricci and this time the Persian dress suggests that they were depicted in their roles in *Siroe re di Persia* (see Plates 16-18 on page 158). In addition to this unusual visual record of the performance, Johann Joachim Quantz has provided a review of this cast in his autobiography:

> Cavalier Nicolino, a contralto, Romanina, a low soprano, and the famous tenor Giovanni Paita added lustre to the performance. Nicolino, whose real name was Grimaldi, and Romanina, whose real name was Marianna Benti Bulgarelli, were both only fair singers but excellent actors. Paita had a not very strong, but pleasant, tenor voice which would not have been as beautiful or even by nature if he had not known

---

[91] Libretto in I-Bc -Fm-G, Ivadi -Moe -R, Istit.Germanico -Rsc -Vgc -Vnm, F-pn, US-Lu, SL-Ls; Sartori, *I libretti italiani* (No. 22096).

***Plate 16.*** *Caricature of Nicola Grimaldi in an oriental role, probably in the title role of Vinci's* Siroe, *Venice. 1726 (Algarotti-Gellman Album, No. 32), attributed to Marco Ricci.*[92]

*Plates 17 & 18. Caricatures of Giovanni Paita (left) and Giovanni Carestini (right) in oriental roles, probably as Cosroe and Medarse in Vinci's* Siroe, *Venice, 1726 (Algarotti-Gellman Album, Nos. 28 and 30), attributed to Marco Ricci*[93]

[92] Croft-Murray, *An Album of Eighteenth-Century Venetian Operatic Caricatures*, 62.
[93] Ibid., 58 and 60.

the art of combining the head voice with the chest voice. His way of singing was masterful in an adagio, his delivery moving and ornaments reasonable. He did not sing an allegro with the greatest of fire, but on the other hand, not lifelessly either. He did not use many *passagi*; his acting was fairly good. [94]

In describing the première of the opera that initiated the season, Porpora's *Siface*, Owen Swiney, the Venetian agent for the Royal Academy of Music in London, echoes Quantz's opinions, praising Grimaldi and La Romanina for their acting and Paita for his acting and singing.[95] Metastasio was also impressed by Paita and it would be many years before he would encounter a finer, more "persuasive" tenor.[96] Being an instrumentalist, Quantz mentioned that "the orchestra playing these operas was not bad and was led by the Bolognese Laurenti, a good violinist."[97] Although Quantz could find no fault in the orchestra at the S. Giovanni Grisostomo, he did not praise it as he did Handel's orchestra in London the following year.[98]

According to information derived from Charles Burney, the origins of the new opera would appear to date back to the original production of Metastasio's *Didone abbandonata* in Naples:

> From the great and sudden celebrity of *Didone*, which immediately after its first appearance at Naples, was set by the best composers of the time for the other principal theatres of Italy; the Venetian minister at Rome, where it had been performed to Sarro's music, was instigated to apply to Metastasio to write the opera of *Siroe*, which he sent to Venice, where it met with a success equal to that of Dido, to the great emolument of the author, who was magnificently rewarded for the superior excellence of his poetry. This drama was set by Vinci at Venice, and performed and printed in 1726.[99]

Burney appears to have mixed up the place of commission. Had the commission taken place in Rome, the new production would not have been Sarro's but Vinci's *Didone*, which would have allowed scant turn-around time between the commission and the production of the new opera (a little over a month). Therefore the commission must have taken place in Naples, where a visiting Venetian ambassador to Rome would

---

[94] Quantz, "The Life of Herr Johann Joachim Quantz," trans. Mueller, 305-306 ("Lebensläuffe," 232-33).

[95] Quoted in Elizabeth Gibson, *The Royal Academy of Music 1719-1728: the Institution and its Directors*, 362.

[96] In a letter from 1750 to Farinelli, he described Amorevoli's excellence by comparing him favorably with Paita; *Pietro Metastasio: Tutte le Opere* 3, 549.

[97] Quantz, Op. cit., 306 ("Lebensläuffe," 233).

[98] Ibid, 241-42.

[99] Burney, *Memoirs of the Life and Writings of the Abate Metastasio*, I, 36-37.

have attended the original Sarro premiere during Carnival 1724. Burney's reference to "the opera of *Siroe*, which he sent to Venice" is followed in the next paragraph with: "Metastasio was himself in that city at this time."[100] From this one can infer that Metastasio completed *Siroe re di Persia* before Carnival, sent it to Venice, and only after the première of *Didone* in Rome did he travel to Venice to direct the production of his new drama. Burney's reference to "the opera of *Siroe*" designates the libretto, which would have been sent to the impresario for planning the production and obtaining the approval of the Venetian censors.[101] In being "magnificently rewarded," Metastasio's fee increased from the sixty-five scudi honorarium that he received for his revisions and direction of the Roman *Didone*, to a more lavish 300 scudi for his new drama, the equivalent of what Vinci would have received for his score.[102]

With three premières for the 1725/26 season, Vinci probably began composing some of the arias as soon as or even before the libretto was complete in order to get a head start on a very busy season.[103] If he had begun work on *Siroe* prior to his arrival in Venice, it could well have been the arias for Grimaldi, Bulgarelli, and Paita, the three singers singled out by Quantz. Vinci was familiar with these voices, having worked with Grimaldi and Bulgarelli in *Silla Dittatore* and with Paita recently on *Il Trionfo di Camilla*. Moreover, Bulgarelli and Grimaldi were residents of Naples and it is therefore possible that the collaboration between poet, composer, and principals could have begun during the summer or fall of 1725 in Naples. After supervising the première of *Didone*, Vinci and Metastasio would have travelled post-haste to Venice to initiate rehearsals, at which time Vinci would have prepared the final score. The latter would also coordinate with Burney's statement that "this drama was set by Vinci at Venice," and the fact that all three of the surviving scores are of Venetian origin.[104] When composing the three secondary roles, Vinci

---

[100] Ibid.

[101] Burney, *A General History of Music* 2, 36-37.

[102] Filippo Clementi, *Il carnevale romano nelle cronache con-temporanee: sec. XVIII-XIX*, (Città di Castello: Unione arti grafiche, 1938), II, 35.

[103] Strohm believes that some of the arias in *Siroe re di Persia* were also composed before *Astianatte* went into production. Strohm, "Leonardo Vinci's *Didone abbandonata*," 218.

[104] There are four known manuscript scores of *Siroe re di Persia*, three of which are in England. The score at the Royal Academy of Music (MS 82), from which the examples below are copied, is part of a set that also includes Hasse's *Artaserse* (MS72), Leo's *Catone* (MS75), and Porpora's *Ezio* and *Semiramide* (MS 79 and 81), on the same paper, and are by similar scribes (*Siroe* and *Artaserse* by one copyist and *Catone*, *Semiramide*, and *Ezio* by another). The paper of these manuscripts is the same as that which Vinci used in the autograph of *La Rosmira* the previous year, with triple crescent watermark. This set, which represents the Metastasio productions at the Teatro San Giovanni Grisostomo during the period 1726-1730, was acquired by Sir John Buckworth, an aristocrat who was actively involved in Italian opera in London. Some

# FIRST COLLABORATIONS WITH METASTASIO

reduced the role of Arasse to a single aria from the original three and adapted "Luci spietate" from *Astianatte* for Laodice's "Voi m'insegnate."

*Siroe re di Persia* was a great success. Metastasio wrote to his brother Leopoldo Trapassi in Turin on February 16 shortly after the première: "My *Siroe* is praised to the stars, much more than *Didone* last year."[105] The production of *Didone* to which Metastasio makes his comparison is Albinoni's setting from the previous year rather than the original Sarro from 1724 or Vinci's recent setting. The success of *Siroe* is attested not only by Metastasio, but also by Quantz who heard both Carnival offerings at the Teatro San Giovanni Grisostomo:

> On February 4 I heard an opera at Ferrara, and thereupon went to Venice, via Padua. Here two operas were being performed during the carnival in the theatre which bore the name of St. John Chrysostomus. One was *Siface* by Porpora, the other *Siroe* by Vinci. Both composers were present, but the latter opera was acclaimed more than the former.[106]

Porpora's *Siface* was the second setting of a text that Metastasio had arranged for the composer several years earlier based on an old drama, Domenico David's *La Forza della virtù*.[107] His setting was given simultaneous premières at the S. Giovanni Grisostomo and the Teatro Ducale in Milan. Porpora was just as busy as Vinci during this fecund season. In addition to this simultaneous Milanese/Venetian première, the Teatro

---

of these scores were probably obtained by Sir John in Venice in 1729 when he received the dedication to Porpora's *Semiramide*. The score in the College of Music (1173) is identical in content to the Royal Academy score, including similar title pages for each act edged in gold, but it is written in a large format (19.5 x 31.5 cm.), prob-ably on Venetian paper (with a clover leaf watermark and intials "Vd"). It was part of an original collection of the Concerts of Ancient Music, which was founded in 1776. According to Reinhard Strohm, the score in the Fitzwilliam Museum in Cambridge also originated in Venice (Strohm, *Italienische Opernarien* II, 230). The score (MU.MS.14) was acquired by the famous collector Viscount Fitzwiliam in the late eighteenth century (an inscription on the title page reads "Fitzwilliam 1782"). It differs from the other two only in its three-volume format (18.5 x 25 cm.) and in certain dif-ferences in tempo indications and barring. The fourth manuscript in the Santini-Sammlung in Münster (4246) originated in Rome, and is initialled and dated October 1728 by the Roman theater-copyist Francesco Cantoni. It is one of several Vinci scores that were copied in Rome, though the operas had been originally produced elsewhere. The four manuscript scores contain the following musical numbers:

| 1 sinfonia | 1 coro | 25 *da capo* arias |
| 1 modified *da capo* aria | | 3 accompanied recitatives |

Totals: 31 set pieces (25 in *da capo* form)

[105] Pietro Metastasio, *Tutte le opere*, 45.

[106] Quantz, Op. cit., 305 ("Lebensläuffe, 231).

[107] Although Metastasio states that *Siface* was written for Porpora, the first musical setting was by Francesco Feo in Naples in 1723; see his letter in Pietro Metastasio, *Tutte le Opere*, V, 171.

Ducale saw the première of a second Porpora opera *La verità nell' inganna*. Although Porpora probably supervised both Milanese premières, he was, according to Quantz, back in Venice by the beginning of February. Because of the peculiarly busy schedules of Porpora and Vinci this season, *Siface* had a extended run, its première taking place on December 26, 1725, and was not succeeded by *Siroe* until some time in mid-February, with the season coming to an end on March fifth.

*Siroe re di Persia* is based on the history of Chosroes II who was deposed and killed by his son Kavadh II in 628. Kavadh or Shiruya, in turn, was slain, leading to anarchy within the Kingdom before it was conquered by the Caliphate of Baghdad.[108] According to the preface, both the defeat and death of King Asbite of Cambaja by Cosroe and the internal struggle between Kavadh/Siroe and his younger brother Medarse over the succession to the Persian throne, can be found in "the writers of Byzantine history" but have been "wrapped up" with other "ideas."[109] In the wrapping up or elaboration of this nasty bit of ancient history, Metastasio has exchanged the patricide of Kavadh for the infanticide of Corsroe, in the process creating his hero Siroe:[110]

> **Synopsis**: Cosroe king of Persia asks his sons to swear allegiance to the son that he will choose as successor. The favourite Medarse is quick to swear the oath, while the eldest Siroe refuses, realizing that his father intends by this manoeuvre to deny his birthright. Cosroe explodes in anger, connecting Siroe's refusal with his love for the daughter of his enemy Asbite whose life and kingdom he has taken. Siroe confides in the Minister Idaspe who is none other than his beloved Emira in disguise. She tries to convince Siroe to solve both their woes by killing Cosroe, to which he adamantly refuses. They are interrupted by Cosroe's fiancée Laodice. To punish Siroe, Emira, aware of Laodice's secret passion for Siroe, tells her that Siroe is in love with her, and then leaves. Left alone with an eager Laodice, Siroe tactlessly rejects her, an encounter witnessed by Medarse. To cover her guilt, she agrees to Medarse's suggestion that they tell Cosroe that Siroe made improper advances towards her. Siroe, concerned for his father's safety, writes an anonymous letter

---

[108] Sabine Radermacher, "Pietro Metastasio's *Siroe, Re di Persia* in London," notes to the Capella Coloniensis recording of Handel's *Siroe re di Persia* (Harmonia Mundi HMC 901826.27).

[109] *Siroe Re' di Persia: Drama per Musica di Artino Corasio, Pastore Arcade, da Rappresentarsi nel Famosissimo Teatro Grimani nel Carnevale dell'Anno 1726* (Venice: Apresso MarinoRoselli), Preface.

[110] Sabine Radermacher sees this transformation of Kavadh in Siroe differently, describing it as infusing the hero with the characteristics of the Ancient Persian king Cyrus II, the founder of the Achaemenid dynasty.

warning Cosroe about an assassination plot. Cosroe finds the letter as Laodice is telling him about Siroe's advances. Medarse lays claim to the letter, saying that he did not wish to implicate his brother. In order to protect both Emira and Laodice, Siroe can only reply to these accusations: "defendermi non posso e reo non sono.".

Siroe implicates himself further in Act II during a conversation with Emira which is interrupted by his father just as he offers her his sword, a conventional lovers' ploy which is interpreted by Cosroe as an attempt on the life of his favourite minister Idaspe. He has Siroe arrested. Emira tries to assassinate Cosroe but is prevented by the arrival of Medarse. Cosroe then interrogates Siroe, hoping that promises of clemency will persuade him to reveal the instigator of the plot and accomplices. When Siroe rejects the offer, Cosroe maliciously warns him that this betrayal has made him a tyrant. Amid threats of a rebellion from Siroe's followers, Cosroe orders his general Arasse to execute his son. Emira manages to convince Cosroe to rescind the order, only to have Arasse return with the news of Siroe's death. With the shock of the fatal news, Emira reveals her true identity, telling Cosroe that she was the assassin and Siroe the one who tried to warn him of the plot. Arasse soon reveals to Emira that Siroe was spared, but Medarse enters with news of a rebellion by Siroe's followers, determined to solve the problem by murdering his brother. Emira foils Medarse's plans and rescues Siroe. The grateful Cosroe forgives Emira and abdicates in favor of Siroe. Emira and Siroe are united and both attain their rightful thrones.

The drama *Siroe re di Persia* exemplifies Metastasio's skilful ability to draw upon a variety of sources from contemporary Italian opera and fuse them together into a new creation. As in Stampiglia's *Partenope*, the heroine appears at a foreign court disguised as a man for the purpose of vengeance; her identity is known only by her lover, who is compelled not to reveal it. Her vengeance, however, is not aimed at a wayward lover but, rather, at the man who killed her father and stole her kingdom. This "capa y espada" melodrama is combined with a Persian succession story which serves almost as an object lesson on the evils of tampering with the right of primogeniture.

The drama also shows a kinship with Domenico Lalli's *Tigrane,* which was set by Scarlatti in Naples in 1715: in addition to its Persian background, one can find the disguised princess (Meroe) seeking to avenge her father's death, the virtuous prince (Tigrane) implicated in her attempt on the life of the monarch (Tamiri), and the prince's silence in the face of all accusations in order to avoid revealing the identity of the princess. Even the suggestion of incest between Siroe and Laodice finds its parallel in the relationship between Tamiri and Tigrane.

## *Siroe re di Persia* and the Accolades of Quantz

From a musical/dramatic perspective, the roles Vinci created for Grimaldi as Siroe, Bulgarelli as Emira, and Paita as Cosroe, stand out above the others in the score. This may have been a factor in Quantz singling out these three singers above the rest, making no mention of either Lucia Facchinelli or Carestini who were also of star status.

Siroe's opening aria "Se al ciglio," in which he tactlessly assures Laodice that he does not love her, contains chromatic inflections that give the aria a certain dark unsettled quality, suggesting that Siroe has graver issues of his mind than Laodice:

Example 5.12 "Se al ciglio" *Siroe re di Persia* I/vi

The subsidiary material in this aria uses a formula that Vinci had already employed with success in the ritornello of "Son Regina" from *Didone*, consisting of accelerating repeated notes in the treble, with basses and violas in parallel thirds (compare with Example 5.6 on p. 148). The subsequent arias written for Siroe are characterized by certain formal irregularities and, though these are rather subtle, they are noticeable set amid the strictness of Vinci's five-part *da capo* form. Formal irregularities can also be found in the arias that Porpora composed for Grimaldi in the title role of *Ezio* in the fall of 1728 at the San Giovanni Grisostomo,

FIRST COLLABORATIONS WITH METASTASIO                                    165

suggesting that the idea for these innovations may have originated with Grimaldi, who wished to create opportunities for his celebrated acting skills.[111] In "La sorte mia tiranna" Siroe laments having been implicated in a double conspiracy against his father without the ability to defend himself. Into this declamatory aria Vinci introduces a striking passage of accompanied recitative at the beginning of the second vocal period in which Siroe forcefully reiterates that he stands accused by "brother, enemy, lover, and father." Vinci had previously employed this innovation in one of the serious arias from *La festa di Bacco*, "O chisto, o la morte."

In "Mi credi infedele" another formal irregularity is introduced to enhance the dramatic situation as Siroe is implicated in yet another crime by his father: that of trying to kill his minister Idaspe. Although the aria is marked *da capo* in the sources, this must be a copyist error or a post-compositional concession to convention. Vinci composed the aria as a radically abbreviated *da capo*. The second section ends in the tonic rather than the usual mediant and leads directly to a brief allusion to the first section, followed by a closing ritornello:

Example 5.13 "Mi credi infedele" *Siroe re di Persia* II/iii

The allusion to the first section consists of the first verse set as a *largo* phrygian cadence, giving the impression that Siroe is deliberating whether

---

[111] In Porpora's *Ezio*, all of Grimaldi's arias, with one exception, are conceived in a concise declamatory manner without coloratura or opening ritornellos—quite unexpected for the *primo uomo* role in an *opera seria*.

or not to continue with the expected *da capo* repeat. This is followed by the last verse set to an *allegro* final cadence as if the hero has decided that he is too upset to complete the usual *da capo*.

At the end of Act II, in order to solve his dilemma, Siroe turns the tables on Emira, telling her that under her assumed identity as the royal minister Idaspe, she must be the arbiter of his fate. In "Fra' dubbi affetti miei" Siroe sings of the doubtful feelings that only she can resolve. In the second section of this G-minor aria, *largo* phrygian cadences are introduced as Siroe lists her options. A more subtle irregularity is the omission of the usual subsidiary material in the opening ritornello, which causes it to cadence on the relative major rather than the expected tonic —a rare occurrence. This "missing" material is first introduced in the intermediate ritornello and then ingeniously works its way into the second vocal period, which it gradually comes to dominate:

Example 5.14 "Fra' dubbi affetti miei" *Siroe re di Persia* II/xiii

The gradual introduction of subsidiary material that one expected at the end of the opening ritornello seems to suggest Siroe's "dubbi affetti" which, at first ignored, then acknowledged and finally triumphant, plunges plunges the hero into anguisheed indecisiveness—the latter depicted by the extended Neapolitan harmony (mm. 47-50).

The role of Emira was the last that Metastasio created for La Romanina. Although lacking the tragic grandeur of Didone, the role would have provided her with numerous opportunities for displaying her acting skills (and her legs). Her first aria, "Ancor'io penai d'amore," gives the impression of a lament with its slow tempo, minor mode, expressive downward leaps and rustling triplet thirds (the latter similar to Mozart's "dream style," but used as subsidiary rather than accompanimental material). The downward leaps often resolve onto interrupted cadences which at the end of the ritornello sets in motion a descent in the violins through more than three octaves, pushing the ritornello into the depths before the entrance of the voice with its austere fugue-like theme:

Example 5.15. "Ancor'io penai d'amore" *Siroe re di Persia* I/iv

If one unfamiliar with Italian were following the opera with only a synopsis, one might assume that in this aria Emira laments the death of her father at the hands of Cosroe. Nevertheless, as in "Mi piace m'inamora" from *Farnace*, this lament-like aria is not used in a tragic but in an amorous situation as Emira ironically warns Laodice about the pains of love, a cliché that as always seems to draw the best from Vinci.

In the aria "Vedeste mai sul prato," Emira skilfully evades the questions of Medarse and Laodice on her contractory behavior towards Siroe with a simile abnout the summer rain falling on roses and violets. In Act II, the simile aria is again ingeniously employed to extract Emira from a difficult situation, allowing her to express her true feelings. In this scene her assassination attempt on Cosroe is foiled by the entrance of Medarse and she is compelled to explain her unsheathed sword. In the second section, when the malicious line "I will attack the snake in the nest," allows Emira to express her real intentions obliquely, the music takes off in a Vivaldian flurry of sequential coloratura and tremolo before returning to the neutral material of the first section via the *da capo* repeat. Left on stage at the end of Act II, Emira can finally express her tormented emotions in an accompanied recitative and aria. With the peculiar dynamic of eighteenth-century *dramma per musica*, which sees the first two acts conclude with soliquies, the combination of accompanied recitative and aria is a common method of giving greater weight to the finales of Act I and II. After expressing her hatred for Cosroe and love for Siroe, she sings an aria about how she envies the simple shepherdess whose only care is her flock and swain. As mentioned above, the music of "Non vi piacque" had already appeared in *Didone abbandonata* as "Prende ardire." Because the text of the latter did not appear in the original *Didone*, while this text remained an integral part of *Siroe*, one can assume that "Non vi piacque" is the original, and "Prende ardire" is the parody (see Example 5.8 on p. 150). This supports the assumption that some of the arias from *Siroe* were composed before *Didone*. Emira's final aria, "Facciano il tuo spavento," occurs after the supposed execution of Siroe when she reveals her identity and Siroe's innocence, to the shocked Cosroe. As she is lead away to prison, she sings of the torments Cosroe will experience now that he has been duped into executing his son. In the spite of the thin texture and banal harmony and melody, the aria, if played at a real *Presto*, takes on an almost minimalistic aggressiveness that could make the aria effective in this dramatic situation, rather like Cesare's "Al lamp dell'armi' from Handel's *Giulio Cesare*.

The character of Cosroe is motivated by a psychotic fear that eventually compels him to order his son's execution. His fear is kindled in the opening scene when Siroe refuses to swear allegiance to his younger brother Medarse should Cosroe choose him as heir to the throne. In the opening aria "Se il mio paterno amore," he threatens that henceforth he shall be more of a severe judge than father. Although there is nothing particularly severe or threatening in this fine heroic aria, the overall sonority is appropriate to Cosroe's regal stature:

Example 5.16 "Se il mio paterno amore" *Siroe re di Persia* I/i

As in the opening aria of Vinci's previous Venetian opera, there is a suggestion of Vivaldi in the fanfare ritornello theme with its mix of anapests and dactyls, its cascading scales (mm. 1-3), and the subsidiary syncopated sequences (mm. 4-5), all supported by a walking bass and a viola in repeated sixteenths. Vivaldi's influence is even more apparent in Cosroe's second aria, "Dal torrente, che ruina," with its prominent unison theme followed by sequences and tremolo passages.

The unusual orchestral accompaniment of "Fra sdegno ed amore" is made up of almost gamelan-like rhythmic layers of ornamented Scotch snaps in the first violins, triplet sixteenths in the second violins and reiterated eighths in the basses, the type of texture that Pincherle singled out in certain Vivaldi concertos.[112] It does not appear to have any descriptive intent but provides a neutral backdrop for the powerful declamatory melody in which Cosroe sings of his conflicting emotions of parental love and royal disdain. The latter triumphs and Cosroe orders the execution of Siroe. After Emira casts aside her disguise, telling him that Siroe was innocent and she was behind the conspiracy, the horrified king reacts to this *peripezia* in the aria "Gelido in ogni vena." Reinhard Strohm compares this aria with Vivaldi's setting from the following year.[113] Both arias employ similar phrase structure in the vocal part and a syncopated tremolo accompaniment, suggesting that Vivaldi was familiar with Vinci's setting:

Example 5.17 "Gelido in ogni vena" *Siroe re di Persia* III/v

[112] Marc Pincerle, *Vivaldi: Genius of the Baroque* (New York: Norton, 1957), 100-106.

[113] Strohm, *Italienische Opernarien*, I, 51-55. Both arias are transcribed in II, 93-100.

In such an intense dramatic situation, today's audience would probably prefer Vivaldi's *furioso* F-minor setting of Vinci's heroic B-flat major, especially since Vivaldi's ritornellos are reminiscent of "L'inverno" from *Quatro stagione*. The connection with "L'inverno" comes from the opening line, "Gelido in ogni vena" (I freeze in every vein), the measured tremolo and the grinding seconds depicting the frozen imagery as in the famous concerto. In Vinci the seconds are generated by a lazy bass that often changes a half-beat late, like a *Trommelbass* version of the bass suspension. The measured tremolo occurs in the second violins, as if to suggest trembling and fear from inside, whereas the spiky staccato leap at the end of each trembling group gives the impression of striking the first volins, setting in motion the palpitating syncopations in the voice.[114] Both the Vinci and Vivaldi arias are examples of what the Abbé de Saint-Non referred to as *Arie d'Ostinazione*, a type of aria characterized by its conspicuous independent accompaniments that "maintain a consistent and sustained pace which depicts the subject or movement, of water or some other continuous sound, presented through different modulations;" according to Saint Non, "the goal of the composer is thus to produce surprise and fear," which is certainly accomplished in both arias.[115]

The high quality of music, particularly evident in these three lead roles, makes *Siroe re di Persia* one of Vinci's finest operas, in spite of the fact that it lacks the powerful dramatic scenes that are characeristic of *Astianatte* and *Didone*. In *Siroe*, Vinci achieved a degree of stylistic consistency, a feature that it shares with his later masterpieces such as *Catone in Utica* and Artaserse. Although the arias may not always reflect the dramatic situation perfectly, a consistent heroic style, which admirably suits the refined aristocratic sentiments of Metastasio's poetry, is maintained. Vinci seems to have been primarily concerned with developing a new musical style that would match the heroic libretti he set to music. This new restrined, dignified heroic style attains an idealized classical sonority suitable to the refined, sensitive prince of the Enlightenment, as exemplified by Siroe and other Metastasian heroes.

---

[114] Helga Lühning analyzes Hasse's setting of "Gelido in ogni vena" from his 1733 *Siroe* (Bologna) and his revision of this aria in his 1763 *Siroe* (Dresden), comparing it not only to Vinci's, Vivaldi's, and Handel's settings, but to other pieces she sees as descendants, including the famous chorale from Cantata BWV 147. Lühning, "Cosroes Verzweiflung, Regel und Erfindung in Hasse Seria-Arien," *Colloquium Johann Adolf Hasse und die Musik Seiner Zeit,* ed. Friedrich Lippmann, *Analecta Musicologia*, 25.

[115] Abbé de Saint Non, *Voyage Pittoresque ou description des Royaumes de Naples et de Sicile* (Paris: 1781), I, 169. Because Saint states that he knew of "no other composer who succeeded like Leo" in the *Arie d'Ostinazione*, one might be tempted to regard Vinci's "Gelido in ogni vena." as exemplifying the influence of Leo after confronting *Il Trionfo di Camilla* in Rome. However, Vinci had already composed even finer examples of this type of aria in Eraclea's "Son ombre di Eraclea" where the orchestra depicts the ghostly imagery of the text (see Examples 4.5a and 4.5b on pages 95-96).

## *Miserere* and Farewell to Venice

The *Miserere II* in C minor attributed to Pergolesi may be a work by Vinci. According to a study of the Miserere settings by Magda Marx-Weber, two of the earliest sources for this work in Berlin attribute it to Vinci.[116] She suggests that the organization and scoring of this Miserere link it to Northern Italy. The Venetian origins would also fit in with the fact that the attribution to Vinci on the title page is in the hand of the Venetian copyist Giuseppe Baldan. Since Baldan was responsible for misattributing the oratorios *Il Sacrifizio di Jefte* and *Gionata* to Vinci, Reinhard Strohm has placed the *Miserere* among Vinci's spuriosities.[117] Therefore it is possible that this *Miserere*, like *Jefte* and *Gionata*, could be the work of Galuppi or Pescetti, or some other Venetian under the sway of the new Neapolitan style.[118] The overall style is similar to Vinci's, in particular the regular periodic structure of the solos (i.e. one verse per phrase, each phrase delimited by a caesura and rest, the caesura decorated with standard appoggiaturas or ornaments). Moreover, the powerful choral writing, with some impressive contrapuntal passages, is similar to that in the Vinci *Missa Brevis*. As in the *Missa Brevis* (and also *Li zite 'n galera*), the penultimate aria in the *Miserere* features an oboe obbligato. In addition, the powerful orchestral accompaniment of the opening is similar to that in "Nube di dentro orrore" from Vinci's next opera *Ernelinda*. Although Baldan played fast and easy with Vinci's name with *Jefte* and *Gionata*, it does not necessarily mean that all the works he attributed to Vinci are spurious. It is possible that Baldan may have tried to stretch out a couple of Vinci sacred works by including them in a manuscript collection with lesser-known masters in the same way that Walsh may also have done with the "Twelve Solos For a German Flute"(see Chapter 4). Marx-Weber suggests that this setting of the Miserere could have been written during Vinci's Venetian sojourns of 1725 and 1726, though she expresses some doubts because of the mid-century style. However, one of the great fascinations about Vinci is that he was capable of writing mid-century sounding music in the 1720s.

---

[116] Magda Marx-Weber, "Die G.B.Pergolesi Fälschlich Zugeschriebenen Miserere-Vertonungen" *Florilegium Musicologicum: Hellmut Federhofer zum 75. Geburstag*, ed. Christoph-Hellmut Mahling (Tutzing: Schneider,1988), 214-16. The two manuscripts are in Berlin: one from the Königlichen Bibliothek (Mus.ms.22372), a copy of one in the Amalienbibliothek (AmB259) with the title "Miserere/A quattro Voci/Con Strumenti/del Sig/Leonardo Vinci."

[117] Strohm, *Italienische Opernarien*, II, 244.

[118] The author advances Vinci's claim with caution: a recent study by Hellmut Hell proposed Antono Lotti as a possible composer; see Hell, "Die Betrogene Prinzessin: Zum Schreiber 'L.Vinci I' in Der Amalien-Bibliothek der Staatsbibliothek zu Berlin" *Scrinium Berolinse Tilo Brandis zum 65. Geburstag*, ed. Peter Jörg Becker, Eva Bliembach, Holgert Nickel, Renate Schipke, Giuliano Staccioli (Wiesbaden: Reichert, 2000), II, 631-48.

In spite of the great success of *Siroe re di Persia*, it was Vinci's last Venetian opera. One would think that its success would have led to future commissions for Venice. Porpora may have had something to do with Vinci's comet-like Venetian career. The libretto of the Venetian *Siface* describes Porpora as "Maestro del Pio Ospitale degl' Incurabili."[119] With his appointment at the Ospedale, Porpora was in a better position to obtain commissions from Venetian theatres. Quantz' descriptions of the productions of *Siroe* and *Siface* hints at a rivalry that ties in with Burney's reference to a "quarrel with Porpora" during Vinci's student days at the Conservatorio dei Poveri di Gesù Cristo (see Chapter 1). Burney refers to this again in his chapter on Venetian opera where he introduces Porpora as "Vinci's rival" and goes on to describe him as "a powerful competitor [who] not only stimulates diligence, but by the fermentation of hope, fear, and perhaps vanity, awakens, invigorates, and sublimes genius."[120] This rivalry with Porpora seems to run like a thread throughout Vinci's life, and could very well be one of the main reasons for the rapid development of the new style, with each composer trying to out-do the other in setting the fashion.

**Plate 19** *Engraving of Nicola Porpora by C. Biondi (1819)*[121]

---

[119] *Siface: drama per musica Da Rappresentarsi nel famosissimo Teatro Grimani di S. Gio: Grisostomo nel Carnevale dell'Anno MDCCXXVI* (Venice: Marina Rosetti, 1726), 5.
[120] This rivalry between Vinci and Porpora is described in an 1825 *Dictionary of Musicians*, but the opera names are mixed up as are the places and dates of Vinci's first opera. *A Biographical and Historical Dictionary of Musicians.*
[121] G.B.G. Grossi, "Nicola Porpora: Celebre Maestro di Capella Nato in Napoli nel 1687, Ove mori nel 1767" in *Biografia degli uomini del Regno di Napoli: Ornata de loro rispettivi rostratti.* Vol. VI (Naples: Niccola Gervasi Gigante, 1819).

# 6

# "GOTHICK" HISTORIES, POLITICAL ALLEGORIES AND ASSORTED SCANDALS

## *L'Ernelinda* and *La fede tradita*

After the busy winter of 1725-26, Vinci's next opera was not produced until the following autumn, presumably giving the composer a much-needed respite. While in Venice during the previous Carnival Vinci probably attended performances of Vivaldi's *La fede tradita* at the Teatro Sant' Angelo, which was premièred at the same time as his *Siroe re di Persia*. His next opera, *L'Ernelinda*, is based on the same *dramma per musica* by Francesco Silvani. *L'Ernelinda* was premièred at the Teatro San Bartolomeo on November 4, 1726. Like most of Vinci's Neapolitan operas, this one was performed for an official occasion, Emperor Charles's name-day, and dedicated to the Viceroy, Cardinal Althann. The cast consisted of:[1]

>  Rodoaldo: Filippo Giorgi   Vitige: Carlo Scalzi
>  Ernelinda: Marianna Benti Bulgarelli   Ricimero: Gaetano Berenstadt
>  Éduige: Maddalena Salvai   Edelberto: Antonia Pellizzari
>  Rosmeno: Caterina Politi   Erighetta: Celeste Resse
>  Don Chilone: Gioacchino Corrado
>  Stage design: Pietro Orta "allievo dei signori Bibiena"

La Romanina had created the role of Emira in Vinci's *Siroe* earlier that year. This was her penultimate role prior to her retirement in the spring of 1727, her final role being Emira in Sarro's new setting of *Siroe*. Scalzi had already served as *primo uomo* in *Ifigenia*, *La Rosmira* and *Camilla*, while Berenstadt had played the villain in *Didone*. Gioacchino Corrado took his usual buffo role alongside his new partner Celeste Resse.

The musical scene in Naples had changed since the production of Vinci's *Astianatte* at the Teatro San Bartolomeo the previous year. A new impresario, Angelo Carasale, had taken over the management. In engaging a new cast, Carasale contracted with two sopranos, Maddalena Salvai and Margherita Gualandi "La Campioli."[2] Under the impression that she was the *prima donna*, La Campioli was furious to learn, upon

---

[1] Libretto in I-Nc, US-NYp; Claudio Sartori, *I libretti italiani* (No.9166)
[2] William C. Holmes, *Opera Observed*. See Chapter 6, "Margherita Gualandi and the Scandal in Naples (1726)."

arriving in Naples, that she would be sharing the honors with Salvai as Cuzzoni and Faustina were doing in London that season. La Campioli was unhappy with her role in the first opera *Sesostrate* by Hasse, even after the composer replaced three of her arias. A few days before the première she fled Naples, causing a considerable scandal. The première went ahead on May 13 as planned, with some abrupt changes in the cast—according to one Filippo Nozzoli: "Salvai had to sing Gualandi's part, Pellizzari took over Salvai's part, and a local woman had to sing Pellizzari's role with the score in her hands."[3] In spite of, or perhaps because of, the compromised première, *Sesostrate* was given a gala revival for the Empress's birthday in August and the composer obtained a commission for a second opera in December, *Astarto*. The young composer making his Neapolitan debut was Johann Adolph Hasse and the revival and second commission suggest that he made a favorable impression. The première of *L'Ernelinda*, therefore, was sandwiched between the gala revival of Hasse's first Neapolitan opera and the appearance of his second. In the Metastasio *Memoirs* Burney describes Vinci as "the competitor of Porpora and Hasse."[4] Thus, in addition to Porpora, Vinci had a new and formidable rival in Hasse and during the years 1727-29 each of them produced an opera at the Teatro San Bartolomeo.

Vinci's *Ernelinda* is based on Francesco Silvani's *La fede tradita e vendicata*, originally set to music by Francesco Gasparini for the Teatro San Cassiano during Carnival 1704.[5] This *dramma per musica* may have been intended as a sequel to Silvani's *La Costanza in trionfo*, written for Pietro Antonio Ziani in 1696. Both are set in medieval Norway and include a usurper to the Norwegian throne as the principal character (Rodoaldo/Gustavo), in whose custody are two princesses, his daughter (Ernelinda/Marianne) and the daughter of the murdered king (Eduige/Leonilde). Although in other respects the cast and plot are quite different, in Act III, the hero (Vitige/Sveno) is thrown into prison and his beloved is compelled to take part in his execution, an execution that is prevented in the eleventh hour by a coup d'etat:[6]

> **Synopsis**: Rodoaldo usurper of the Norwegian throne has been deposed by Ricimero King of the Goths with his allies Prince Vitige of Denmark and Prince Edelberto of Bohemia in order to restore the rightful heir, Eduige, daughter of the

---

[3] Quoted in Ibid., 111.
[4] Charles Burney, *Memoirs of the Life and Writings of the Abate Metastasio*, I, 72.
[5] Strohm, *Italienische Opernarien*, II, 230. Libretto to *La fede tradita* in US-Wc (Schatz no. 3566).
[6] In 1721 *La Costanza in trionfe* served as the basis for Paolo Rolli's *Floridante*, Handel's second Royal Academy opera. See Winton Dean and John Merrill Knapp, *Handel's Operas 1704-1726* (Oxford, Clarendon Press, 1876), 385-390.

late king. Although Ricimero intends to marry Eduige, thereby uniting the Kingdoms of Norway and Sweden, when he sees Rodoaldo's daughter Ernelinda, he falls in love with her, forgetting his promise to Eduige. As conqueror, he decides he can marry Ernelinda and still unite the two kingdoms. Ricimero's designs on Ernelinda conflict with that of his ally Vitige, who is also in love with her. Ernelinda returns his love but must display anger towards him because of his participation in the defeat of her father. When Ricimero tries to bribe Rodoaldo by granting him freedom in exchange for the hand of his daughter, Rodoaldo haughtily rejects the offer. Infuriated at his impudence, Ricimero orders his death, and when Vitige tries to intervene, condemns his ally for treason. By this deadly act of defiance Vitige finally placates the anger of both Ernelinda and Rodoaldo over his alliance with Ricimero.

The rejected Eduige warns Ricimero that there is no lack of champions to take up her cause after such scandalous treatment. Ernelinda comes to Ricimero to plead for the lives of Rodoaldo and Vitige. The sadistic Goth replies that her tears have softened his heart; only one need to be sacrificed for his offended majesty, but she must decide which one is to be sacrificed. After much agonizing between love and duty, she curses Ricimero and signs the death warrant for her lover Vitige. Informed of Ernelinda's decision, Ricimero gives Vitige the option of returning to Denmark in exchange for renouncing any claims on the princess. Vitige rejects the bribe and prepares to meet his fate. Ernelinda goes mad with remorse. Meanwhile, Eduige sets up a conspiracy against Ricimero, enlisting the aid of Edelberto who is in love with her. Eduige warns Ricimero to revoke the death warrant and return to his original promise. When he rejects her warning, the conspirators, led by Edelberto and the liberated Rodoaldo and Vitige, burst into the throne-room and arrest Ricimero. Rodoaldo is returned to his throne and Ernelinda and Vitige are united thereby joining the crowns of Denmark and Norway. Eduige gives up her claims to the crown of Norway to become Queen of Bohemia as the wife of Edelberto.

Although *L'Ernelinda* is set in medieval Norway, the action undoubtedly would have been interpreted in a contemporary light against the background of the War of Spanish Succession. Silvani probably intended the defeated Rodoaldo to represent his patron Ferdinando Carlo, the exiled Duke of Mantua, and the conquering Ricimero to represent Prince Eugene, the Imperial commander in Italy. The vacillating Vitige, on the other hand, may have been intended to represent Venice, which was torn between both factions.[7] In its original form the opera contained a subtle political message for the audience—namely that the Venetians should support the Duke of Mantua in his attempt to drive the foreign conquerors from Italy in the same way that Vitige supported Rodoaldo to drive out Ricimero.[8]

*La Fede tradita* was one of the more popular libretti of the eighteenth century, frequently appearing under the title *Ricimero*.[9] The reason for this popularity may be found in the complex and ambivalent relationships that mirror a variety of political situations, thereby providing an idealized enactment of political reality. After the defeat of the Spanish regime by the Austrians in the summer of 1707, the first opera to be performed at the Teatro San Bartolomeo was *La fede tradita*, adapted for the Neapolitan stage by the poet Carlo de Petris and the composer Giuseppe Vignola.[10] The revised libretto was dedicated to the Imperial General. The new production of *La fede tradita* appears to have been intended as a subtle warning to the new Habsburg overlords that they should avoid the tyranny of their predecessors lest they, like Ricimero, be overthrown. Such a political interpretation seems more appropriate to Verdi's *risorgimento* Italy than Vinci's Naples. Nevertheless, that this drama was produced three times during the brief Habsburg regime—the third time disguised by changing the names under the new title of *Il prigionier superbo* with music by Pergolesi[11]— suggests that the work

---

[7] John Julius Norwich, *A History of Venice* (Harmonsworth, Middlesex: Penguin Books, 1983), 575-82. At the beginning of the war, Venice had allowed Prince Eugene's troops to cross through its territory taking the French army by surprise, hence Vitige's original alliance with Ricimero. One of Prince Eugene's first actions was to occupy the Duchy of Mantua between December 1701 and July 1792, which compelled the Duke of Mantua to flee to Monferrato; Ursula Kirkendale, "The War of the Spanish Succession Reflected in the Works of Antonio Caldara," *Acta Musicologica* 36 (1964), 221-33.

[8] Agostino Piovene's *Tamerlano* (1711), which was also first set to music by Gasparini for the Teatro San Cassiano, contains numerous similarities with *La Fede tradita*. Though less obvious than those in *La Costanza in trionfo*, these similarities are more profound and far-reaching. Both libretti are based on medieval history, and include a defeated monarch (Rodoaldo/Bajazet), his devoted daughter (Ernelinda/Asteria), a barbaric eastern conqueror in love with the daughter (Ricimero/Tamerlano), his jilted, long-suffering fiancée (Eduige/Irene), and a genteel prince with loyalties to both the conqueror ansd the conquered (Vitige/Andronico). As in *La Fede tradita*, the drama seems to contain a political allegory centered on Ferdinando Carlo, Duke of Mantua, but now representing the strange turn of events since 1704. See the author's entry on *Tamerlano* in the *New Grove Dictionary of Opera*.

[9] John A. Rice, "Pergolesi's *Ricimero* Reconsidered" in *Studi Pergolesiani* I, ed. Francesco Degrada (Florence: Scandicci, 1986), 80-82.

[10] In contrast to most other Italian courts, opera at Naples was regularly produced throughout the war years. De Petris and Vignola were employed at the San Bartolomeo during 1707-1708 in similar revivals. Libretto in US-Wc (Schatz No. 3567).

[11] Mario Armellini looks at these changes as a standard aspect of revising a *dramma per musica* during the first half of the eighteenth century. He quotes from a letter to the Viceré from the Intendant of theaters, informing him of the delay in the première

had some special significance. At this time many Neapolitan noblemen, among them Vinci's former pupil Prince Sansevero, began to look towards the young Don Carlo de Borbone of Spain as the savior of Naples.[12] A year later, this thrice-stated warning, whether intentional or not, became a reality and, like Ricimero, the Habsburg viceroys were overthrown in the most successful coup d'etat of the century, which established a new Neapolitan dynasty.

Vinci's version of Silvani's libretto was adapted by Carlo De Palma who, like De Petris two decades before, was employed by the Teatro San Bartolomeo to adapt old libretti. The original De Petris intermezzo, *Lesbina e Milo,* was omitted and De Palma adapted another intermezzo, *Erighetta e Don Chilone.* This substitution must have been a later development. In the score of *L'Ernelinda* the opening scene still contains the entrance of Milo who brings Rodoaldo news of the defeat of his forces; although Milo is omitted from subsequent scenes, no attempt has been made to introduce either Don Chilone or Erighetta into the drama proper. Another change by De Palma is the addition of a new character, Prince Rosmeno, who serves as a second suitor for Eduige and an additional conspirator in the coup d'etat. This superfluous addition was probably made to accommodate an extra singer in the cast, Caterina Politi.[13] Being once removed from the original, the use of replacement aria texts in *L'Ernelinda* is taken to a much further degree than in the 1707 setting of *La fede tradita.* While the De Petris/Vignola libretto contained nine replacement arias, by the time De Palma finished his revision only six of Silvani's original texts were set by Vinci. Although it seems likely that Vivaldi's *La fede tradita* provided the inspiration for Vinci's *Ernelinda*, Vivaldi's version of the libretto did not serve as the model for Vinci's— the two libretti contain only a single aria text in common.[14]

---

of the work, warning the Viceré that he may be displeased because "la conversazione dei cantanti assai debole." However, it is possible that his real concern about the dramatic dialogue is not its weakness but rather its political overtones. The Intendant goes as far as suggesting the Viceré may prefer to attend a concert of aria excerpts instead of the complete opera. Mario Armellini, "Il prigionier superbo di Pergolesi e le sue fonti librettistiche" in *Studi Pergolesiani/Pergolesi Studies*, ed. Francesco Degrada (Jesi: Fondazione G.B.Pergolesi-G. Spontini, 2000) 258-59.

[12] *Biographie universale: ancienne et moderne*, ed. Joseph François Michaud (Paris: Michaud, 1811-62), "Sansevero, Raimondo."

[13] One wonders whether the unnamed woman who sang Pelisari's role from score during the première of Hasse's *Sesostri* was Caterina Politti, whose eleventh hour substitution was rewarded with a contract for the 1726 season. Her career, with the exception of an appearance in Messina in 1724, seems to have been confined to Naples during the 1725-26 seasons (Sartori, *I libretti italiani*, appendix). The original *La fede tradita* did contain an additional character, Ricimero's jilted fiancée, Princess Gildippe of Sarmatia, who had been omitted in the DePetris/Vignola version of the opera.

[14] Libretto in US-Wc (Schatz No. 10676).

## Ernelinda's Maddening Dilemma

Typical of Vinci's operas from the years 1724/25, some of the music in *L'Ernelinda*,[15] exhibits Vivaldian characteristics. In *L'Ernelinda* Vinci appears to have reserved the Vivaldian style for expressions of bellicose anger and revenge. In "L'impero ha nel mio petto" the haughty Rodoaldo has the audacity to curse Ricimero after he has released him from prison. This aria demonstrates how Vinci could, on occasion, successfully adapt this style, combining a concise, balanced theme (m.8-10), a unison transition (m.11-13), and sequential instrumentally-conceived coloratura, enveloped by percussive string fanfares (m.5-7):

Example 6.1 "L'impero ha nel mio petto" *L'Ernelinda* I/xiii

[15] There are two scores of *L'Ernelinda* that survived from the eighteenth century. A complete score containing both the drama and intermezzo, now in the Biblioteca dell' Abbazia at Montecassino (126 E22, 1 vol. 20 x28 cm.), was formerly part of the collection of the Neapolitan aristocrat, Don Vincenzo Bovio. This Neapolitan manuscript is similar in format to the Montecassino score of *Eraclea* except that it is bound in a single volume and contains neither corrections nor alternative performance materials. According to Reinhard Strohm, the score of *L'Ernelinda* in the Biblioteca del Conservatorio in Naples (Rari 32-2-39) is a copy of the Montecassino score from the early nineteenth century by Giuseppe Sigismondo (*Italienische Opernarien* II, 230). The score at the Royal College of Music (633; 1 vol. 19 x 23 cm.), from which the examples below are taken, is also of Neapolitan origin. It belonged to the Concerts of Ancient Music and was listed as part of their original catalogue of 1827. This score contains the same mix of paper with rearing horse and fleur de lys watermarks that is found in the autograph score of Vinci's *Li zite 'ngalera*. Like the sole surviving

The isolated *largo* phrase on the initial word "L'impero" seems to call for some type of defiant gesture, while its downward octave leap dominates the subsequent material, giving full expression to the implications of this initial motto. The motive of the coloratura sequence, which outlines the octave, is repeated five times. This type of sequential abundance, though rather uncharacteristic of Vinci, can be encountered in other Vivaldi-inspired arias such as "In vanno s'affanna" from *Eraclea/ La Rosmira* (see Example 4.7 on page 109). Not all the Vivaldian pieces are as skilful, and the first dramatic climax of the opera is unhappily saddled by one of Vinci's more inept imitations of Vivaldi's style. When Vitige comes to the aid of Rodoaldo in the face of Ricimero's threats, the latter explodes in anger and condemns them both to death. This stern sentence is reiterated in his aria "Si sveni si s'uccida," a plodding concertante aria for horns similar musically and dramatically to Piro's anti-climatic concertante arias in *Astianatte*.

After being compelled to make a choice between father and lover, Ernelinda reluctantly signs Vitige's death warrant.[16] She then sings the

---

manuscript of *Astianatte*, it lacks the intermezzi, though the format suggests that it was copied as if the intermezzi did not yet exist. The penultimate scenes in Acts I and II (i.e. the scenes that precede the intermezzi) are followed by the designations "Fine dell Atto" and the salutations "L.D.M.S.V." and scenes iv and vi in Act III (i.e. the scenes that frame the final intermezzo) follow directly upon each other on the same page. The complete score of *L'Ernelinda* at Montecassino consists of the following set pieces:

**The drama:**

| | |
|---|---|
| 3 *del segno* arias | 4 ariettas |
| 25 *da capo* arias | 4 accompanied recitatives |
| 1 *da capo* duet | 1 coro |

Sinfonia

**The intermezzo:**

| | |
|---|---|
| 3 *da capo* arias | 3 *da capo* duets |

Totals: 45 set pieces (35 in *da capo/del segno* forms)

[16] According to Mario Armellini, this scene is central to the drama because the heroine is forced to choose between "amor congiugale e amor filiale" as the tyrant forces her

aria "Empia mano tu scrivesti" as she curses her hand for sealing the fate of her lover. The angular melody and dotted rhythms of the independently conceived accompaniment for unison orchestra may well have provided a talented actress such as La Romanina with a good opportunity for some su itably violent and remorseful gestures with the hands:

Example 6.2 "Empia mano tu scrivesti" *L'Ernelinda* II/xiii

[musical example]

The use of a declamatory arioso-style melody in a concise *da capo* form is rather surprising, particularly since it is in the crucial position of Act II finale where one would expect a grand bravura or cantabile aria.

Act III begins with a lament in which Vitige expresses the horrors of his imprisonment. In keeping with the galant fear-of-the-minor-mode-and-slow-tempo, "Se barbara catena" is limited to an arietta. Even here the minor mode is no sooner established than the tonality shifts into the relative major with the second phrase (see Example 6.3 on facing page). After Vitige rejects Ricimero's ultimatum, accepting the sentence signed by the beloved hand, he sings in a full *da capo* aria of his unshakeable loyalty to Ernelinda's beautiful eyes. In spite of Vitige's desperate situation, the optimism of the text allows Vinci to abandon the pathetic style and write an F-major minuet decorated with extended coloratura passages, lombard rhythms, and appoggiaturas. This type of scene structure anticipates the cavatina/cabaletta of the late eighteenth and early nineteenth centuries, except that the interruption takes place in simple recitative .

---

to sign the death warrant of either her father or her lover (Armellini, Op. cit., 254). This "maddening dilemma" would have had much greater impact in an age of arranged marriages when sons or daughters were routinely compelled to ignore their own desires for "amor congiugale" in order to follow the dictates of "amore filiale" for the sake of family interests.

Example 6.3 "Se barbara catena" *L'Ernelinda* III/i

The minuet rhythm returns in the next aria "Non avvilisca il pianto" in which the stoic Rodoaldo bids farewell to Ernelinda and commands her not to weep because it is a sign of weakness. The ingenious manner in which the descending unison scale (m.5) is balanced by a rising sequence that is notched up a step each time by an ascending *tirade* (m.7-12), gives the opening ritornello a dynamic Haydnesque quality:

Example 6.4 "Non avvilisca il pianto" *L'Ernelinda* III/iii

A contrived scene follows in which Ernelinda tries to kill herself in order to express her remorse for having signed Vitige's death warrant. Only after she has proven her remorse and has been safely disarmed can the lovers take their leave in a farewell duet. Like the duet in *Silla*, "Dimmi una volta addio/Non posso dirti addio" employs a double exposition, following upon the parallel structure of the verse. The first vocal paragraph consists of a five-bar period for Vitige, which in turn is repeated by Ernelinda, and a five-bar duet passage that concludes with a dominant cadence (Example 6.5 below begins with Ernelinda's repetition of Vitige's initial melody). Unlike the duet in Silla, this one is written in the latest style. The slow harmonic rhythm is emphasized by the extended dominant pedals prior to the cadences. The first dominant pedal supports a syncopated melisma on the phrase "il mio dolor" (mm. 14-

Example 6.5 "Dimmi una volta addio/Non posso dirti" *L'Ernelinda* III/v

16) which, in turn, resolves onto a new cadential formula associated with the later eighteenth century, with its characteristic leap of a fifth from the dominant to supertonic, the latter undoubtedly decorated with a trill. A later composer such as Jommelli or Mozart would have introduced the cadence sooner or would have added more dissonance or figuration to avoid the somewhat static effect just prior to the cadence. The static effect, however, is alleviated by the subsequent introduction of diminished and major seventh harmonies. The subsidiary instrumental theme in the ritornello (mm. 21-22) is similar to that in the previous aria with its sequential motive above a pedal embellished with *tirades* (see Example 6.4 on p. 181) except contracting downward rather than expanding upward. The type of echo, either thematic or technical, can be encountered on occasion in Vinci's works.

In the next scene Ernelinda goes mad from grief and imagines herself imprisoned in an underwater kingdom. As with Sandrina in *La finta Giardiniera* (as well as Tom Rakewell in *The Rake's Progress*), Ernelinda's madness in depicted by her distorted references to classical mythology. Silvani's original mad scene has been substantially shortened; two dialogue airs have been omitted and Ernelinda's final aria has been replaced by a repeat of her opening arietta, "Tuo mal grado o nume." This arietta, the only aria text that Vinci's and Vivaldi's settings have in common, is dominated by flying figuration in the violins and voice on the repetitions of "fugirò." Although the repeat of the arietta is introduced by an accompanied recitative, the rest of the scene is set as simple recitative for Ernelinda and the other characters; in this instance, Vinci for some unknown reason purposely avoided the extended accompanied recitatives that he had recently employed in *Didone* and *Astianatte*. At the center is a mid-scene *da capo* aria, created from one of Silvani's ariettas in which Ernelinda sings about the lovesick Neptune in his watery kingdom. The basic materials of this aria are derived directly from the imagery of the text, a favorite technique of Porpora, with the *Trommelbass* depicting the "freddi soggiorni," the downward octave leaps depicting the "acque profonde" and the unison coloratura depicting the "onde:"

Example 6.6 "Nei freddi soggiorni" *L'Ernelinda* III/vi

Aside from these pictorial elements, however, the diatonic harmony and overall heroic style make the aria appear somewhat neutral for this frenetic situation, particularly with the absence of the accompanied recitative.

The next three scenes depict the conspiracy against Ricimero engineered by his jilted fiancée Eduige. In parallel scenes Eduige manages to secure from Ricimero's allies, Edelberto and Rosmeno, commitments to redress her dishonor, promising her hand to the one who serves her best. The first of these scenes, for Eduige and Edelberto, originated as an extended interpolation in Ernelinda's *scena*, which Carlo De Palma, Vinci's collaborator, detached to form a separate scene. When Eduige has obtained commitments from both Edelberto and Rosmeno, she exits with a cantabile aria that has a strong flavor of the soubrette, and if sung in a light-hearted manner, would be worthy of Serpina at her most charming. The *mezzo carattere* playing off of one suitor against another for political reasons, may have been Vinci's idea, derived from the Selinda/Gilade/Aquilio triangle in *Farnace*.

## The Molière Intermezzo

As with *La fede tradita*, the intermezzo *Erighetta e Don Chilone* was originally set to music by Francesco Gasparini for the Teatro San Cassiano in Venice, programmed between the acts of his heroic opera *Anfitrione* from 1707.[17] Typical of the French influence on Italian opera during the early eighteenth century, the libretto is loosely based on a French play, Molière's *Le malade imaginaire,* which provides the work with an actual title, *L'ammalato immaginario.* This work was the second of four intermezzi based on Molière comedies that were produced at the San Bartolomeo, the others being *L'avaro* in Porta's *La Lucinda fedele* from Carnival 1726, *L'artigiano gentiluomo* in Hasse's *L'Astarto* from December, and *Porsugnacco e Grilletta* in Hasse's *Gerone* from November 1727.[18]

---

[17] Charles E. Troy, *The Comic Intermezzo,* 149.
[18] Reinhard Strohm, "Comic Tradition in Handel's Orlando," *Essays on Handel and Italian Opera,* 254-55. An earlier intermezzo, *Madame Dulcinea ed il cuoco,* based on

After its first setting in 1707 *L'ammalato immaginario* appears to have lain dormant for over a decade until revived as an independent intermezzo at the Teatro Pergola in Florence in 1718 by the famous comic duo Rosa Ungarelli and Antonio Ristorini.[19] Because all four of the Molière intermezzi were part of the Ungarelli/Ristorini repertoire, it seems likely that Corrado and Resse intended to imitate this highly successful comic duo by adopting their repertoire—including their most famous intermezzo, Salvi and Orlandini's *Il marito Giocatore*. The idea for this appropriation may have come from the beautiful and ambitious Celeste Resse who had recently replaced Corrado's former partner, Santa Marchesina.[20]

*L'ammalato immaginario* subsequently attained a certain popularity being produced in Vienna in 1725, Mannheim in 1726, Brussels in 1728 and St. Petersburg in 1734.[21] Except for the Viennese production, which featured a new setting by Francesco Conti, the composers of the other productions are unknown though these probably were based on either Conti and/or Vinci's music.

In contrast to the score of *Ernelinda*, the music of *L'ammalato immaginario* does not look that promising on paper. However, the tuneful melodies and the overall gestic quality of the music provide numerous opportunities for a skilful group of musicians to bring the work to life.[22] The first part of the intermezzo begins with a mock lament in which Erighetta complains of being a poor widow in black garments, having spent the past year in mourning. The lilting *minore* melody allows Erighetta to swan around the stage in her elegant widow's weeds, indulging in her grief in a subtle mix of touching sentiment and cynical detachment. At the end of the aria, she resolves that she has had enough and is ready to marry the first man who comes along. When Don Chilone

---

Molière's *Les précieuses ridicules* was performed at the San Bartolomeo in 1715; Gordana Lazarevich, "Humor in Music: Literary Features of Early Eighteenth-Century Musical Theatre," *International Musicological Society: Report of the Eleventh Congress, Copenhagen, 1972*, ed. Henrick Glahn, Sören Sörenson, and Peter Ryom (Copenhagen: Wilhelm Hansen), I, 534.

[19] Troy, Op. cit., 143.

[20] For additional information on this fascinating singer, who may have have been the original model for Serpina in *La Serva Padrona*, see Strohm, "Comic tradition in Handel's *Orlando*."

[21] Troy, Op. cit., 143.

[22] This was proven in a recent production of the work at the Festival dell'Aurora in Crotone by Antonio Florio and the Cappella della Pietà dei Turchini with Maria Ercolano as Erighetta and Giuseppe Naviglio as Don Chilone. The producton was part of a concert devoted to the music of Vinci that concluded a mini-conference on Vinci in Strongoli, organized by Sergio Iritale, Dinko Fabiris, and Gian Francesco Russo.

enters, she decides that this rich hypochondriac, who spends most of his time confined to his bed, will be easy to manage. She insinuates herself into his confidence by pitying him and then tells him that she knows of an excellent physician who performs wonderful cures, declaring that had she known him during her husband's illness, she would not be a widow. He agrees to see this miraculous physician. In the concluding duet, they arrange this appointment in a lively dialogue wherein Don Chilone's enthusiasm is contrasted with Erighetta's cynical asides as she boasts that she now has her gullible prey within her grasp.

In the second part of the intermezzo, which occurs at the end of Act II, Erighetta disguises herself as the doctor and comes to visit the bedridden Don Chilone. After the usual doctor/patient dialogue of questions and complaints, "il dottore" tells Chilone that the only cure for his ills is marriage and then proceeds to dictate a matrimonial prescription in the form of an aria. The aria is dominated by teasing word repetitions on "guarirà" and "subito" to highlight this recipe for an instant cure. Don Chilone responds to this convincing recipe with an enthusiastic aria, "Lo provar," highlighted by sustained high notes and more word repetition. The exit of "il dottore" is followed by the return of Erighetta who asks Chilone the outcome of their meeting. When he describes the physician's strange prescription that cannot be purchased at the pharmacy, Erighetta tells him she can fulfill it by providing "the hand of a certain young lady." After a playful interrogation about who the bride should be, Chilone suggests Erighetta and promises her complete control of his entire household. The final duet of Act II juxtaposes jaunty two-part note-against note dueting, in which they celebrate this sure recipe for curing hypochondria, with recitative passages in which Erighetta incredulously asks "Tell me truthfully, have your ailments gone?" to which Don Chilone tentatively replies "Quasi, quasi." This duet is one of the few set pieces by Vinci scored only for *basso continuo*. Perhaps the composer adopted this archaic means of accompaniment to better integrate the recitative passages, allowing the singers greater flexibility in their stage action.

The third part of the intermezzo does not occur in its usual place prior to the *scena ultima* of the opera, but rather in the middle of Act III, providing a useful break between Ernelinda and Vitige's farewell duet, and the heroine's mad scene which sets up the resolution of the drama and leads directly to the finale. In this third section of the intermezzo, Erighetta complains that marriage may have solved all of Don Chilone's problems, but she now misses her freedom, and in the final duet, she tells him that she is going to leave. It seems rather anti-climactic to spend two extended intermezzi, consisting of four recitatives, three *da capo* arias and two duets, to arrange this marriage, only to have it broken in a single recitative and a modest *Presto* duet.[23]

The plot of this intermezzo is similar to *Pimpinone,* produced a year after the original *L'ammalato immaginario*. In this popular intermezzo by Pietro Pariati, the courtship, marriage and separation of Pimpinone and Vespetta is evenly distributed among the three intermezzi. The author of the text of *L'ammalato immaginario* is unknown. Strohm assumed the author was Antonio Salvi, since two of the other Molière-inspired intermezzi, *L'avaro* and *L'artigiano gentiluomo*, are by Salvi.[24] Considering the numerous similarities between *L'ammalato immaginario* and Pariati's *Pimpinone,* as well as the fact that both had their premières alongside dramas by Zeno and Pariati, Pariati is undoubtedly the author of both intermezzi, coming up with a more balanced plot in the later work.

When he returned to Florence at the end of the season, the castrato Gaetano Berenstadt raved about his Neapolitan experience, describing "the air, the climate, the situation of the city, the life of the cultured people is all an excellent thing."[25] One of the things that impressed Berenstadt was the music of Vinci. He was probably involved in the revivals of *Astianatte* and *Ernelinda* at the Teatro Pergola during Carnival 1728, joining Salvai in the cast.[26] In *Ernelinda* he took his original role and Salvai was promoted to the title role.[27] This Florentine revival spawned two further productions, one at neighbouring Livorno and the other in Brussels later that year.[28] During the fall of 1727, Berenstadt acquired a position at the Real Capella, receiving a stipend of nine ducats a month, and after the Florentine Carnival he and his sister moved to Naples.[29]

---

[23] In the Crotone revival, Antonio Florio omitted the third part, providing a satisfying and rather intriguing ending. No one in the audience was aware of the omission except for the handful of Vinci scholars at this important concert of Vinci's music.

[24] Strohm, "Comic tradition in Handel's *Orlando*," 254-55.

[25] Lindgren, "La carriera di Gaetano Berenstadt," 79.

[26] Ibid., 80.

[27] Libretto to the Florentine *Ernelinda* in I-Bc -Fc -Fm - Fn -Rn; Sartori, *Il libretti italiani* (No, 917).

[28] Libretto for the Livorno production in I-Vgc (Sartori [No. 9168]) and for the Brussels production in B-Bc (not in Sartori but listed by Strohm, *Italienische Opernarien* II, 230). According to Strohm the pasticci scores of Act II of *Ernelinda* and Acts II and III of *Astianatte* now in the Bibliothèque du Conservatoire of Brussels (2364 & 2365) originated from the Vinci pasticci productions during the winter of 1727/28 in Florence (Ibid., 229-30). One could speculate that these scores, produced in Florence as a set with the same format, on the same flimsy paper and by the same copyists, were then sent to Brussels for planned productions of *Astianatte* and *L'Ernelinda,* of which only the latter seems to have taken place.

[29] Lindgren, Op.cit., 80.

## A "Polish" Opera for a Runaway Polish Princess

After the first three performances of *Ernelinda*, which Vinci was required to conduct by contract, he undoubtedly left for Rome to begin preparations for his next opera. His *Gismondo re di Polonia* was premièred on January 11, 1727 at the Teatro delle Dame in Rome and remained on stage until it was succeeded by Porpora's *Siroe re di Persia* on the ninth of February.[30] The Roman *Siroe*, like the Roman *Didone* the previous year, received a new musical setting, in spite of the fact that in each case the composer of the original setting, Sarro for *Didone* and Vinci for *Siroe*, was not only in town but employed by the same theatre to produce a new opera. This creative extravagance, that today appears illogical and uneconomical, is proof of the fetish for new music in eighteenth-century Italy.

Porpora's opera was a great success. The dress rehearsal was made a gala occasion by coordinating it with the wedding of Prince Ruspoli's daughter. The diarist Francesco Valesio attended the première and was impressed by the staging, "particularly the final scene which represented a grand colonnade."[31] *Siroe*'s reputation even spread to the monastery of the Campo Marzio where permission was obtained from the Vicar General for musicians from the delle Dame to visit the monastery and perform "some of the *ariette*"[32] If Burney was correct in his account of the youthful rivalry between Porpora and Vinci, a rivalry that would have been renewed during the previous season in Venice, then this rivalry would have continued in Rome. The directors of the delle Dame appear to have based their season on the 1726 season at the S. Giovanni Grisostomo except with Porpora rather than Vinci setting the new Metastasio drama. Therefore this rivalry may well have been part of the design.

It is not known how Vinci's opera fared. The only reference relating to *Gismondo* in Valesio's *Diario* is to a performance on January 28 at which the Princess Borghese lost a diamond cross when leaving the theater.[33] The cast of *Gismondo re di Polonia* consisted of:[34]

---

[30] Francesco Valesio, *Diario di Roma: Libro settimo e libro ottavo*, [ IV: 1708-1728], 765 & 775.

[31] Ibid., 775-76.

[32] Ibid., 779. This performance was part of a mini-revolt by several Roman monasteries in an attempt to relax the restrictions on their routine and included the performance of a comedy, *Matilde,* at S. Silvestro and some comic intermezzos at S. Ambrogio della Massima. In spite of its success in Rome and its subsequent revivals in Perugia in 1733 and Faenza in 1738, no score of Porpora's *Siroe re di Persia* has survived, and only a handful of arias preserved in various collections.

[33] Ibid., 771.

[34] Libretto in I- Bc -MAC -Mb -Nn(Lucchesi Pal.) -PAc -Rsc -Vgc; B-bc; C-Tu (Th. Fischer), F-Pc, PL-Kc.,US-BE -Wc (Schatz 10747); Sartori, *I libretti italiani* (No. 12080).

Gismondo: Giovanni Battista Minelli   Otone: Filippo Balatri
Cunegonda: Giacinto Fontana   Primislao: Antonio Barbieri
Giuditta: Giovanni Maria Morosi   Ernesto: Giovanni Ossi
Ermano: Giovanni Tassi
    Stage painter and engineer: Pietro Baistrocchi
    Choreographer: Domenico Dalmas

The casting at the delle Dame this season was rather haphazard because the tenor Giovanni Battista Pinacci had broken his contract with the theatre late in the negotiations and signed with the rival Teatro Capranica.[35] Although this caused a great scandal that eventually involved the Governor General of Rome, Antonio Banchieri, Cardinal Ottoboni, and James III, the eventual resolution was simple and straightforward; Pinacci agreed to sing at the delle Dame the following year and the directors managed to re-hire the tenor from the previous season, Antonio Barbieri. The scandal, however, scared off their main quarry, Farinelli, who broke off negotiations with the delle Dame and signed with the Capranica. Therefore, not only did the delle Dame have to find a *primo uomo* and tenor late in the season, but whoever they managed to find would have to compete against two of the finest in the business. The touch-and-go situation is described in a letter by one Cavaliere Antonio Fontana, dated May 21, 1726:

> The directors of the Teatro delle Dame are at the moment all dispersed on their holidays. Marchese Maccarani and Abbé Placidi are in Venice, from where they will both visit Modena and Parma, in order to see if they can find a capable singer. They hope to be able to sign Balatri who is in Venice, as a soprano in place of Farinelli who they have already lost, as I am afraid will also happen with Pinacci... They are forced to file a civil suit against Pinacci and the impresario of the Capranica.[36]

They managed to sign Filippo Balatri, though he sang only in *Gismondo* being replaced by the tenor Gaetano Valletto in Porpora's *Siroe* (see Plate 14 on page 142). Balatri was a novelty on the Italian stage, having made a career for himself as a chamber singer at the courts of Northern Europe. Although he has the distinction of being the only castrato to have written an autobiography, he unfortunately makes no mention of *Gismondo*, in spite of the fact that it was one of his rare stage appearances.[37] Although Balatri was already in his fifties when he appeared in

---

[35] William C. Holmes, *Opera Observed, Views of a Florentine Impresario*, Chapter 6: "Margherita Gualandi and the Scandal in Naples (1726)."
[36] Quoted in Ibid., 125.
[37] See Filippo Balatri, *Frutti del Mondo*, ed. Karl Vossler (Milan: Remo Sandron, 1924), Chapter 27. This omission could be due to the picaresque nature of the autobiography or to his lack of success in Rome (he was replaced in mid-season) and preferred not to mention the event. One of his other rare appearances was as Rodoaldo in an English production of the original *Ernelinda* from 1713.

*Gismondo*, he was given the role of the lover Otone, which is probably a good indication of the durability of his voice.[38] Farfallino took the lead female role in both *Gismondo* and *Siroe* and in the latter as Emira he was coached by La Romanina, for whom Metastasio originally created the role.[39]

The libretto of Vinci's *Gismondo re di Polonia* is an anonymous revision of Francesco Briani's *Il vincitor generoso* first set to music by Antonio Lotti in 1708 for the Teatro San Giovanni Grisostomo in Venice.[40] *Gismondo* is the only Roman opera by Vinci in which the composer did not collaborate with the original poet. In this respect it resembles his Neapolitan operas which, for the most part, are adaptations of Venetian works from the turn of the century.[41] As in *L'Ernelinda* from two months previous, the plot of *Gismondo* is northern and feudal rather than Mediterranean and antique.[42] The historical background of *Gismondo* is Renaissance Poland, an unlikely setting for a *dramma per musica*. Besides their common Venetian origin and northern feudal background, both operas feature a heroine who, caught in the midst of a feudal struggle, chooses to support her father against her lover, and a lover who is forced to fight and defeat the father of his beloved. The plot of *Gismondo re di Polonia* appears to be based on the negotiations between King Zygmunt August II and the Estates of Lithuania that resulted in the Union of Lublin in 1569 whereby Poland and Lithuania became a commonwealth or *respublica* unified by a common parliament and an elected monarch[43] Both the Union of Lublin from the end of the King's reign and his love affair with Barbara Radziwell from the early part of his reign are represented in the opera by moving the Diet of Lublin back in time to the reign of his father Zygmunt August I.[44] In the union of Poland and Lithuania in *Gismondo*, as in the uniting of Denmark and Norway in *Ernelinda*, the librettist is reinforcing the pragmatic union of two nations, part of a generalized trend towards maintaining the political status

---

[38] According to one contemporary, he could still sing when he was in his seventies; Angus Heriot, *The Castrati in Opera* (London: Secker & Warburg, 1856), 229.

[39] Alberto De Angelis, *I teatro Alibert o delle dame: 1717-1863*, 146.

[40] Strohm, *Italienische Opernarien* I, 230; libretto to *I vincitor generoso* in US-Wc (Schatz 5726).

[41] In his study of *La fede tradita*, Mario Armellini concludes that the reason for all these adapted libretti is that there was a scarcity of good opera libretti available during the 1720s (Armellini, "Il prigioner superbo di Pergolesi...," 254-55).

[42] Briani's *Isacco tiranno* provided the source for Handel's *Riccardo primo*, one of his few Medieval "historical" plots.

[43] Daniel Stone, *The Polish-Lithuanian State, 1386-1795*, History of East Central Europe (Seattle: University of Washington Press, 2001),IV, 36-66.

[44] Briani's ingenious interweaving of events from Polish-Lithuanian history are the subject of the author's paper "A Polish Opera for a Runaway Polish Princess" presented at the 12th Biennial International Conference on Baroque Music in Warsaw, July 26-30, 2006.

quo. This is something that was dear to the politicans in the Post-Spanish Succession era, as exemplified by the Emperor's "Pragmatic Sanction."[45]

> **Synopsis**: the drama centers around the act of homage that Primislao as Duke of Lithuania owes to Gismondo King of Poland. The haughty Primislao, believing that he has just as much right to the Polish throne as Gismondo, wages war against his sovereign. The opera begins as Primislao has been convinced by his peers to give up his rebellion and negotiate a peace treaty. To seal the peace, Primislao's daughter Cunegonda and Gismondo's son Otone will be married, thereby uniting the two nations. Because of their love for each other, Cunegonda and Otone look forward to the peace with great anticipation. The cynical Primislao makes Cunegonda swear that in the event of further conflict, her role as daughter will take precedence over that of lover. The subplot consists of the rivalry between Prince Ermano of Moravia and Prince Ernesto of Livonia for the hand of Gismondo's daughter Giuditta. Although Giuditta flatters both suitors, she is secretly in love with her father's rival Primislao.
>
> Primislao reluctantly comes to sign the peace treaty and pay the homage he owes Gismondo. During the ceremony the pavilion collapses. Primislao interprets this incident as a betrayal by Gismondo and declares for war. The incident was intentional but was engineered by Ermano as a means of avenging the death of his brother by Primislao. Cunegonda proves herself true to her word by immediately denouncing Otone who in turn laments that she could suspect he was involved in such a cowardly act. Gismondo, infuriated at his son's sympathy for the enemy, orders Otone to lead his troops against Primislao and to return victorious or die in the attempt.
>
> Primislao and Cunegonda lead their troops into battle. The Lithuanians are defeated, Primislao is wounded and Cunegonda is captured by Otone. Ermano is about to kill the wounded Primislao, but is prevented by Giuditta who then tends to his wounds. At the palace Otone despairingly presents Gismondo with his prisoner, who in turn furiously demands the body of her father. Giuditta tells Gismondo that Primislao is alive. Gismondo orders Primislao to be brought in to the lamenting Cunegonda. Father and daughter are united. Ermano's guard delivers his master's suicide note in which

---

[45] The "Pragmatic Sanction" was the Emperor's continued attempt to secure the Imperial succession for his daughter Maria Theresa that became the cornerstone of Imperial foreign policy throughout this period. Penfield Roberts, *The Quest for Security: 1715-1740*, ed. William L. Langer, The Rise of Modern Europe Series (New York: Harper & Row, 1947).

the prince takes full responsibility for the pavilion incident that set off the war. Assured of Gismondo's innocence, Primislao asks for forgiveness for his rebellion and at the same time for the hand of his daughter Giuditta. Both of these requests are granted by "Il vincitor generoso." Otone and Cunegonda are united and the opera ends as Primislao pays homage to Gismondo re di Polonia.

Although Vinci's libretto often follows the Briani original quite closely, there are several major changes in addition to the usual replacement of aria texts. Primislao has been transformed into the hero by adding the role of lover to that of rebel and father. In Briani's original subplot Ernesto triumphs over Ermano in his courtship of Giuditta. Through revisions, both suitors lose out to Primislao, who becomes the object of Giuditta's passion. This change renders Ernesto, the original *secondo uomo*, superfluous; in the revision, three of his arias have been transferred to Gismondo, whose role in the original is surprisingly modest.

This new relationship involved the addition of several scenes which stand out from the norm of the *dramma per musica*. For example, in the scene appended to Act II in which Giuditta tells Otone about her secret passion for her father's enemy, she recounts how she fell in love with him at a court ballet playing Minerva to Primislao's Mars. The interpolated scenes in Act III feature Giuditta frantically searching the battlefield for her beloved Primislao whom she later saves from the murderous hands of Ermano. In this type of plot, the daughter should not be in love with her father's enemy but rather with the son of her father's enemy.[46] The new relationship between Primislao and Giuditta may be based on that between Silla and Valeria in Vinci's second *dramma per musica, Silla Dittatore*. This suggests that Vinci may have been involved in the initial revision of the libretto. There is an additional detail that supports this supposition. Giuditta's aria "Tu sarai il mio diletto," in which she flatters Ermano and Ernesto with hope, contains stage directions in the score indicating which phrases are addressed to Ermano, to Ernesto, and to herself. These stage directions can be found only in the original *Il vincitor generoso*, not in Vinci's libretto, suggesting that the composer may have been familiar with the original libretto and thus involved in *Gismondo re di Polonia* from the outset.

These changes were probably made in consideration of the patron to whom the opera was dedicated, "Giacomo III Re della Gran Brettagna." The haughty and rebellious Primislao, like his equally indefatigable coun-

---

[46] When Metastasio utilized a similar relationship the following year in *Catone in Utica*, the enemy Cesare was intended to be younger than the father Catone, the age difference being an important aspect of their conflict. (See Chapter 7).

terpart Farnace, was undoubtedly intended to represent James Edward Stuart, the Old Pretender. The alteration to *Il vincitor generoso* which unites Primislao with Giuditta "principessa di Polonia" can be seen as a reference to James Edward's Polish princess, his wife Maria Clementina Sobieska. In addition, the alteration of the villain's fate, whereby Ermano's final repentance leads to a disgraceful suicide rather than the magnanimous pardon he receives from Primislao in the Briani original, may refer to certain conspirators within the Stuart camp.[47]

While the king may have appreciated these correspondences in the libretto, he did not have the opportunity to appreciate them on stage; the libretto dedication mentions the absence of "the luminous honor of your royal presence."[48] During Carnival 1727 James and the princes were in Bologna where they were treated to a series of banquets and balls in their honor.[49] James had retired to Bologna in the fall of 1726 as a means of escaping the high cost of living in Rome and also the gossip and rumors. In November of 1725, Clementine had fled to the convent of Santa Cecilia in the Trastavere because of James's supposed affair with the Duchess of Inverness. This separation, which was to last until 1728, was one of the more celebrated scandals of the period.[50] While Primislao and Giuditta may have presented an idealized portrait of James and Clementina during the early years of marriage, the audience may well have perceived a more realistic portrait of the couple in the explosive relationship between Cunegonda and Otone, who are in conflict for the better part of the opera. Whether or not this allegorical richness was intentional or purely accidental, it may have provided the audience with a topic for conversation after the theatre.

## *Gismondo re di Polonia*: the Lead Roles

In contrast to *Didone abbandonata* and Vinci's subsequent Roman operas, the distribution of arias in *Gismondo* is hierarchical rather than balanced, favoring the *primo uomo /prima donna* roles of Ottone and Cunegonda. This bias is also reflected in the music of these roles.[51] The role of Cunegonda featured the star performer from the previous season,

---

[47] For example, John Erskin, Earl of Mar secretly negotiated with the Hanoverians in 1721 and in 1724 had to leave the service of the Stuarts in disgrace. (Martin Haile, *James Frances Edward: The Old Chevalier* (London: J.M.Dent, 1907), 302-305.

[48] *Gismondo re di Polonia: dramma per musica da rappresentarsi Nel Teatro detto Dame nel Carnevale dell'anno 1727* (Rome: Bernabò, 1727.)

[49] Peggy Miller, *James* (London: George Allen & Unwin, 1971), 281.

[50] Haile, Op. cit., 313.

[51] There are two surviving scores of *Gismondo re di Polonia*. The one in the Santini-Sammlung in Münster (4233, 3 vols. 16 x 22 cm.) has been signed and dated at the

Giacinto Fontana "Farfallino." The role of Otone was conceived for the aging chamber singer Filippo Balatri, who was something of a makeshift in the casting. To judge from the music written for him, however, Vinci appears to have been inspired by the voice and the role. In spite of his age, Balatri's opening aria "Vado à i rai" has all the hallmarks of the modern style, with its lilting syncopated triadic theme above a descending repeated-note bass:

Example 6.7 "Vado à i rai" *Gismondo re di Polonia* I/I

end of Act III: "Fine nel Drama/25 8bre 1729./G.F.Cantoni" Like the Santini *Farnace*, this score is not through-copied but consists of a series of seventeen separate aria fascicles on different paper, each individually titled "Gismondo del Vinci/1727." These fascicles have been connected by the recitative and the other twelve arias that have been through-copied by Cantoni on the standard paper (with fleur de lys watermark) found in Vinci's other Roman manuscripts. Therefore the through-copied parts of this score date from October 1729, while the aria fascicles date from the 1727 production, copied originally as souvenirs for connoisseurs in the audience. The inelegant appearance of the patchwork *Farnace* and *Gismondo* scores, with their inclusion of additional performance material, suggests that they were intended for theater use rather than the library of some aristocratic patron. The score of *Gismondo*, like the Cantoni scores of *Farnace*, *Didone*, and *Siroe*, which were copied during the same period, represents a concerted effort, probably on the part of the Teatro delle Dame, to collect the works of Vinci. These scores are responsible for the fact that all of Vinci's Roman operas have survived complete, whereas those of his rivals at the Teatro Alibert/delle Dame during the period 1718-1730 have been lost, with the exception of Porpora's. This preferential treatment, indicative of Vinci's position as virtual house composer at the delle Dame, was consolidated in 1729 when he became one of the impressarios (see below). Particularly suggestive of this preferential treatment is the fact that the collection of Cantoni's scores contains Vinci's Venetian *Siroe*, while Porpora's Roman *Siroe* has been lost. An additional score of *Gismondo*, which Strohm considers to be of Roman origin, now survives in two different libraries: Act I in the Staats-und Universitätsbibliothek in Hamburg (M A/677) and Acts II and III at the Conservatoire Royal de Musique in Brussels (2366); Strohm, *Italienische Opernarien,* II, 230. The Santini score of *Gismondo*, from which the examples below are taken, consists of the following musical numbers:

| | | |
|---|---|---|
| 1 sinfonia | 1 march | 27 *da capo* arias |
| 2 *da capo* ensembles | 2 additional *da capo* arias | 1 interrupted duet |
| 4 accompanied recitatives | 1 coro | 1 interrupted arietta |

Total: 40 set pieces (31 in *da capo* form)

In this cantabile aria Otone expresses his joy over the prospect of marriage to Cunegonda. The subsidiary material, which consists of a static treble above a melody in the bass and violas, is similar to that which Vinci had employed with success in two other opening arias, "Son regina" from *Didone* and "Se al Ciglio" from *Siroe* (Examples 5.6 on page 147 and 5.12 on page 163). Similar subsidiary material is employed again in Cunegonda's "Son figlia è vero," enlivened with syncopation:

Example 6.8 "Son figlia è vero" *Gismondo re di Polonia* I/iv

Although Cunegonda reassures her father that the duties of daughter take precedence over those of lover, the phrygian cadences in the second section (mm.51-52) indicate the princess's doubts about her loyalties.

Otone and Cunegonda pledge their love for each other in a miniature continuo duet which is interrupted by the entrance of Primislao who warns them about the possibility of war. Cunegonda's subsequent aria,

"Sentirsi il petto accendere" is almost identical to Ernelinda's aria of the same title. Ernelinda's version of the aria seems to be the original because its text is more closely connected to the drama; she complains of the feelings of love that arise in her breast— which she must hide with cruelty because of Vitige's betrayal— whereas Cunegonda expresses in a more generalized manner her hopes and fears amid the tenuous peace. This expansive cantabile aria exemplifies Vinci's mature style at its finest. Because Cunegonda's version of this aria is not in the prime position of the Act I finale, Vinci shortened the opening ritornello by thirteen measures via a *del segno* repeat. Otone concludes Act I with a simile aria about the lovesick nightingale. "Quell' usignuolo" is the only aria in all of Vinci's operas after *Farnace* that requires flutes and the only aria in all Vinci's surviving operas wherein flutes are combined with horns.

After the pavilion incident, Cunegonda expresses her outrage to Otone in "Tu mi traditi ingrato." Phrygian cadences, already employed in "Son figlia è vero," appear in the first section of this aria to accompany her ironic questions "quest'è la fede, questo è l'amore?"(a line that Metastasio was to borrow in the duet in *Alessandro nell'Indie*):

Example 6.9 "Tu mi traditi ingrato' *Gismondo re di Polonia* II/iii

The phrygian cadences tend to slow down the *Andante* tempo further, making this F-minor aria appear more expressive of sorrow or melancholy than anger. Several of the arias in *Gismondo* exhibit certain archaic features. In this aria the usual bipartite organization of the first section is abandoned, leaving a single continuous period without a modulation to a secondary key (in the Example above the intermediate ritornello should occur at the end of m.8). The modulatory second section, on the other hand, contains two settings of the second strophe, giving it almost the same dimensions as the first section (as in the turn-of-the-century *da capo*). In Otone's subsequent aria, "Vuoi ch'io moro?" the first section contains two text settings, but there is no intermediate ritornello and the modulation is to the supertonic minor rather that the expected dominant, the latter perhaps to depict the phrase "io moro." The infrequency of slow tempos in Vinci's mature *da capo* arias makes the *Lento* tempo somewhat conspicuous. Perhaps Balatri's old-school training compelled him to insist that he sing at least one example of what Francesco Tosi described as the "so-much-longed-for *Adagio*." "Vuoi ch'io moro?" is also notable for its obbligato bassoons, one of only two arias in Vinci's surviving operas that specifically request the bassoon. In this aria these instruments are written on two staves in a high register in the bass clef with the designation "fagottino"— a small bassoon pitched an octave higher than the standard *fagotto*.[52]

Otone resolves to seek out Cunegonda in the enemy camp in "Assalirò quel core," an heroic aria accompanied by strings and horns. The subsequent encounter leads to the lovers' duet "Dimmi una volta addio" which is identical to the one in *L'Ernelinda* (see Example 6.5 on page 182). Although this duet occurs in neither Silvani's nor Briani's original drama, the imagery of the text appears to be more concrete when placed within its context in previous work.[53] In order to insert this duet at the end of Act II of *Gismondo*, the original drama had to be altered to allow for a temporary reconciliation between the lovers. In the original *Il Vincitore generoso* Cunegonda breaks off her engagement with Otone immediately after the pavilion incident and the lovers remain unreconciled until the *scena ultima*.

In Act III, after the captured Cunegonda has been informed of her father's death, she curses her captor, Otone. In an interpolated mid-scene accompanied recitative, Cunegonda envisions the ghost of her father declaring that his deadly wounds are "the sweet fruits of your dear love." The condemning utterance is accompanied by sustained seventh and diminished harmonies above a gradually descending chromatic bass in trembling repeated notes to complete the *ombre* vision:

Example 6.10 "Misera! Ah si ti veggo" *Gismondo re di Polonia* III/ii.

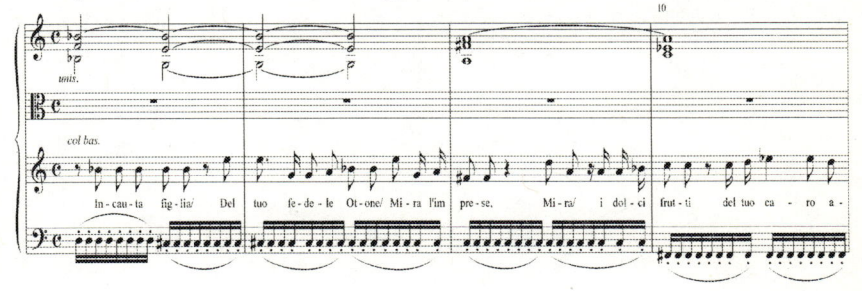

---
[52] *The New Grove Dictionary of Music and Musicians*, "Bassoon" by William Waterhouse.
[53] Vitige's phrase "I pardon the rigor of my cruel fate" probably refers to his death warrant signed by Ernelinda, while Ernelinda's phrase "my sorrow turns me to ice" anticipates her mad scene.

[Musical notation: continuation of previous example with text "mor-e, Da te tra-di-to io fui, da te sven-a-to, *al'Otone* Uc - ci - di - mi uc-ci-di-mi spie-ta-to,"]

For the final condemning utterance, the orchestra plays agitated unison figures. Otone tries to placate Cunegonda, but she replies in "Ama chi t'odia ingrato" that she will never be placated. Vinci brings the aria to a forceful conclusion by emphasizing the key phrase "mai di placarmi" in the second vocal period, first with an abrupt shift to unison writing in a descending scale that comes to rest on the dominant and then a cadential phrase in a rising see-saw sequence, generating distorted speech rhythms:

Example 6.11 "Ama chi t'odia ingrato" *Gismondo re di Polonia* III/ii

[Musical notation: Presto, 3/8, with text "sol per tuo tor - men - to, Bar - ba - ro, nè spe - rar Ma-i di pla - car - mi,"]

[viola] *col basso*

[Musical notation continuing with text "Nè spe - rar mai di pla - car - mi, Ne spe - rar mai di pla - rar - mi, Bar - ba - ro,"]

The *Presto* tempo and continuous semi-quavers of the second violins would give this D-minor aria a shimmering accompaniment. With its minor mode, fast-tempo, driving rhythms, and syllabic setting, this is one of the earliest examples of the *aria parlante* or *agitata*, a type of art that was to become a standard feature of the mid-century *dramma per musica*, replacing the old Baroque lament.

At the royal palace, Gismondo and Otone attempt to comfort their prisoner, offering to take the place of father and husband respectively.

Cunegonda fiercely rejects these untimely offers. There follows a trio in which Gismondo and Otone try to convince Cunegonda to accept their offers while she rejects them with scorn. Incensed by her rejection, they rather surprisingly accuse her of being cruel and tyrannical. This trio, which replaces an aria for Cunegonde in the original, does not suit the dramatic situation and like the duet may have been added to accommodate the composer's penchant for ensemble writing. The pairing of Gismondo and Otone against Cunegonda results in a double exposition wherein Gismondo's plea is first stated and rejected by Cunegonda and then Otone's plea is stated and, in turn, rejected, creating two repeated melodic periods. Only in the cadential phrase are the three voices are finally brought together. Although there is a more extended trio section in the second vocal paragraph, the cadential phrase is set as a solo for Cunegonda who is given the last word.

In the *scena ultima* Cunegonda enters full of fury to ask for the body of her father so that she may wash his wounds with her tears. She reiterates her request in the aria "Dì, rispondi ò traditor," one of only two arias that have retained the original text by Briani. This aria balances Primislao's "Vendetta, ò Ciel" at the beginning of the act; both are miniature *da capo* arias without the expected exit, addressed to characters on the stage. Vinci reserved the key of E$^b$ major for intense emotional situations such as "Son qual legno" in *Astianatte*, "Non ha ragione" in *Didone* and "La sorte mia tiranna" in *Siroe*. In "Di rispondi ò traditor" the simple syllabic melody is augmented by a continuous syncopated accompaniment, creating an effect similar to that in "Gelido in ogni vena" in *Siroe*, another tragic aria in the related key of B$^b$ (see Example 5.17 on p. 169). In this instance, however, the repeated cadences seem to anticipate Pergolesi's comic style, creating somewhat of an ambivalent effect for the modern ear.

Example 6.12 "Dì, rispondi ò traditor" *Gismondo re di Polonia* III/xi

Conegonda/Farfallino and Otone/Balatri each have an area *aria agiunta* appended at the end of Act III in the Santini score. Both arias were borrowed directly from *L'Ernelinda*: Cunegonda's "Nube di denso orrore," a *da capo* version of Vitige's *del segno* simile aria on the same text and Otone's "Se al mio doglioso," a parody of Vitige's "Se quel vezzo pianto."

Besides these *arie agiunta*, Cunegonda's "Sentirsi il petto accendere" and the lover's duet, there are two additional borrowings from *L'Ernelinda*, the overture and Gismondo's "Se soffio irato." In the overture, the orchestration has been expanded to include an additional trumpet, two horns and two oboes, the orchestra at the delle Dame being one of the first to employ players for both trumpets and horns. In "Se soffio irato" the subject of the "tempesta" simile text has been changed from a "navecella" to a "tortorella."[54] These borrowings, like those in *Astianatte*, *Didone*, and *Siroe*, suggest a close relationship between *L'Ernelinda* and *Gismondo*, albeit a simple direct one in which the earlier work was composed first and then pillaged for material in the later work.[55] Moreover, the relationship between *Gismondo* and *L'Ernelinda* is further strengthened by their common Venetian origins and northern feudal background.

---

[54] One can assume that Ricimero's is the original—in the eighteenth-century opera, boats are usually caught in storms while doves usually languish for their absent mates. Moreover, the second theme is similar to the second phrase in "Son qual legno in grembo" from *Astianatte* (see Example 5.4 on page 135), which is also a simile text about a boat caught in a tempest. In the original, Vinci employed a lengthy twenty-measure ritornello that included extended subsidiary mateiral to depict the storm at sea. When the aria was re-used in *Gismondo*, this material was omitted.

[55] Their relationship is similar to that between Pergolesi's Neapolitan *Adriano in Siria* and Roman *L'Olimpiade*, both of which are on Metastasio texts, the latter borrowing music from the former.

# 7

# STAMPIGLIA, METASTASIO, AND THE ROMAN REPUBLIC

## A Scantily Revised *La caduta de' Decemviri*

Vinci returned to Naples in the spring of 1727, at which time he produced *Stratonica* at the Teatro San Bartolomeo, the second of only two known pasticci by the composer. The libretto, arranged by Carlo de Palma, is based on *Antioco* by Zeno and Pariati and first set to music by Gasparini for Venice in 1705.[1] The preface to the libretto states that "to better accommodate the actors, the arrangement of the arias is left at liberty to their satisfaction."[2] Therefore, in *Stratonica* the singers had an important role in the creation of the work, selecting arias by Vivaldi, Porta, Orlandini, Porpora, and Hasse.[3] Vinci was responsible for arranging the music and composing the recitative, the intermezzo, and several new arias. Although the score of *Stratonica* has been lost, two of Vinci's arias have survived.[4]

Vinci returned to the dramas of Stampiglia for his next Neapolitan opera, *La caduta de'Decemviri*, premièred on October 1, 1727 at the Teatro San Bartolomeo in celebration of the Emperor Charles' birthday, with the dedication to the Viceroy, Cardinal Althann.[5] The cast of *La caduta*, which was almost identical to *Stratonica*, consisted of:

    Appio: Carlo Scalzi            Valeria: Anna Bagnolesi
    Lucio: Antonio Barbieri       Claudia: Giustina Turcotti
    Icilio: Antonia Colasanti      Virginia: Barbara Stabile
    Flacco: Gioacchino Corrado  Servilia: Celeste Resse
        Stage design: Francesco Saracino
        Gladiatorial games: Nicola Gigli

---

[1] Reinhard Strohm, *Italienische Opernarien*, II, 230. Citation to Gasparini's opera in Taddeo Wiel, *I teatri musicali veneziani del Settencento*, 8.

[2] *Stratonica: drama per musica da rappresentarsi nel Teatro di San Bartolomeo nella primavera del corrente anno 1727* (Naples: Angelo Vocolo).

[3] Strohm, Op. cit. II, 283.

[4] Ibid. "D'un cor che adoro" can be found in the Bibliothèque nationale in Paris and "Se a danni miei" in the Biblioteca Casanatense in Rome.

[5] Libretto in I-Bc -Nc -PLcom, B-Bc, US-NYp - Wc; Sartori, Op. cit. (No. 4341).

Vinci had collaborated with Scalzi and Barbieri, during his first trip to Venice, in *Ifigenia*, *La Rosmira* and *Camilla* and, more recently, with Scalzi in *L'Ernelinda* and with Barbieri in *Gismondo*. Scalzi had already sung the role of Appio in 1724, in Porta's setting of *La caduta* for Milan.[6] With Corrado and La Celestina in their usual comic roles, the cast was rounded out with a trio of Florentine ladies who appeared at the San Bartolomeo during the years 1727/28. While Anna Bagnolesi and Barbara Stabile had only recently begun their careers, Giustina Turcotti was a well-established singer who had been performing since 1717. She was still singing in 1740, when the Florentine impresario Luca Casimiro degli Albizzi ranked her above both Cuzzoni and Faustini, though he complains that she had become "monstrously fat."[7] One peculiarity in the casting of *La caduta de' Decemviri* is that the roles of the heroine and hero of the drama are taken by relatively unknown singers, Stabile and Colasanti. Perhaps Virginia and Icilio's low social status, among the few non-aristocratic principals in the genre, may have made these roles unsatisfactory to the class-conscious singers of the eighteenth century.[8] Antonia Colasanti, in the role of Icilio, was the only member of the cast who did not sing in *Stratonica*. Colasanti was borrowed from the Teatro Fiorentino, where she frequently took trouser roles in the *commedia per musica*.[9]

Silvio Stampiglia's *La caduta de' Decemviri* had originally been set to music by Alessandro Scarlatti in 1697, the first of a series of collaborations that would include *Eraclea* and *Turno Aricino*.[10] In contrast to the libretto of Vinci's *Eraclea*, which was modified by Stampiglia to accommodate the formalism of the 1720s, *La caduta* was produced after the poet's death in 1725. Although it is not known who arranged the libretto for Vinci, a likely candidate would be Carlo De Palma, who collaborated with the composer on *L'Ernelinda* and *Stratonica,* or perhaps it was Stampiglia's son who had adapted his father's *Turno Aricino* for the Vinci pasticcio of 1724. Vinci's collaborator treated Stampiglia's libretto with more respect than the poet himself, to judge from his revisions of *Eraclea* for Vinci in 1724. Of all the old libretti that Vinci set,

---

[6] Libretto in US-Wc (Schatz No. 8389).
[7] Quoted in William C. Holmes, *Opera Observed,* 103.
[8] The Chevalier Nicolini, however, did not take exception to the role of Icilio in the original version by Scarlatti.
[9] See cast lists at the Teatro Fiorentini in Francesco Florimo, *La scuola musicale di Napoli,* IV, 44-47. Icilio was also a trouser role in the Milanese production of *La caduta* in which Scalzi participated.
[10] See Alessandro Scarlatti, *La caduta de' decemviri,* ed. Hermine Weigel Williams, IV of *The Operas of Alessandro Scarlatti* (Cambridge, Mass: Harvard University Press, 1980).

not only is this the oldest but it is also the one that comes closest to resembling the original. Except for the comic scenes, the scene structure and most of the dialogue has remained intact and half of the arias and ensembles are settings of original Stampiglia texts. Moreover, several of the new arias and ensembles are clever composites of texts in the original (see below). This deference to the original libretto contrasts with the more cavalier treatment in the revisions to *L'Ernelinda* and *Gismondo,* which retained only a few of the original aria texts.

*La caduta de'Decemviri* is based directly on an episode from Livy's *History of Rome* that relates the story of Verginia, a young plebeian woman murdered by her father Lucius Verginius to prevent her from being abducted by the Decemvir Appius Claudius. This atrocity set off a revolt by the Plebians, led by Verginius and Verginia's fiancée Icilius, resulting in the downfall of the Decimvirs.[11] Although Stampiglia follows the outlines of Livy's story closely, even deriving the comic couple Flacco and Servilia from Appius's henchman Claudius and Verginia's nursemaid, the obligatory *lieto fine* compelled Stampiglia to have Virginia survive her wounds, allowing her to be united with Icilio in the end:

> **Synopsis**: At the games of Consus, Decemvir Appio, the host of the games, falls in love with Virginia, the daughter of the plebeian officer Lucio. Appio's attraction is the cause of some concern for both his fiancée Valeria and Virginia's fiancée Icilio. Lucio enters to inform Appio of the difficult situation with the Volsci and Aequi. Appio orders the people to prepare for war. Later Appio confesses his love for Virginia and tries to purchase her love through gifts. Virginia rejects the gifts but, realizing her vulnerability, flatters his love with hope. Appio gets into a dispute with Icilio, claiming that Virginia has promised him love. When the two confront Virginia, she denies having affection for either.
>
> In parallel scenes Virginia explains to Icilio that she denied her love to protect him from Appio's rage and to Appio that she denied her "love" to conceal her "infidelity" to Icilio. When confronted by Valeria about his infatuation for Virginia, Appio merely reminds her of how she rejected him in the past. The Decemvir then tells his servant Flacco to accuse Virginia of being his runaway slave. Since Appio is judge for Rome, he will decide in favor of Flacco, who then will deliver Virginia to his master. Things do not go according to

---

[11] *The History of Rome by Titus Livius,* I (London: J.M.Dent, 1926), 188-97. From the outset Livy describes The Story of Virginia as a cautionary tale on the dangers of tyranny: "the result of brutal lust, which occurred in the City and led to consequences no less tragic than the outrage and death of Lucretia, which had brought about the expulsion of the royal family." Ibid., 188.

plan and Appio is compelled to defer the sentence a day so that her father can be brought back from the front to testify to her paternity.

Lucio returns to Rome, calling for the downfall of the traitorous Decemvir. When in judgment Appio decides in favor of Flacco, Lucio tries to kill his daughter to prevent her from falling into the lustful hands of Flacco and Appio. This sacrifice sparks off an uprising. Appio and Flacco attempt to escape Rome in disguise but are apprehended. Appio is spared execution only by the intervention of Valeria, who forgives him and takes him back as her lover. Moreover, Virginia's wounds are not fatal, and she is united with Icilio.

There are two subplots: a slapstick *buffo* subplot between Flacco and Servilia and a sentimental *mezzo carattere* one between Lucio and Appio's sister Claudia (who is not in Livy). These subplots are realized in self-contained scenes interpolated into the story. The combination of main plot and subplots results in the union of four couples at the end of the opera.

The tragic, maudlin central episode clashes with Stampiglia's witty style and light-hearted subplots. Although in the original this problem was partially alleviated by avoiding any type of clowning during the climactic judgment episodes which straddle Acts II and III, in Vinci's version this central tragic sequence was broken by the interpolation of the second part of the comic intermezzo at the end of Act II. Moreover, not only does Virginia survive her murder, but she appears in the next scene in convalescence speaking to a much-relieved Icilio. Miraculously, at the end of the scene she gets up from her bed and sings a full-scale *da capo* aria complete with obligatory exit.

As in *L'Eraclea* and *Partenope*, Stampiglia's *La caduta de' Decemviri* contains an elaborate allegory, though not concerned with power politics prior to the War of Spanish Succession but rather, with domestic events at the Viceregal court in Naples. The story of Decemvir Appio's destructive passion for the plebian Virginia must have been intended to parallel the love affair between Viceroy Don Luigi de la Cerda, Duke of Medinaceli and the singer "la Giorgina," Angela Voglia. This affair, which began in Rome when Medinaceli was Spanish ambassador, continued when he was appointed as Viceroy in Naples in 1696; he brought not only "La Giorgina" to Naples as *prima dama* to his wife, but also La Georgina's sister Barbara and her adopted father Carlo Giorgini.[12] The

---

[12] Benedetto Croce, *I teatri di Napoli secolo XV-XVIII*, 201-22. Lucio's paternity, the vague relationship between "La Giorgina" and her adopted father, and the derivation of the daughter's first name from the surname of her father (Lucio Virginio-Virginia and Carlo Giorgio - "La Giorgina") are parallels/coincidences that may have inspired the choice of this cautionary tale on tyranny and lust as the subject for an opera.

original libretto was dedicated to the Duchess of Medinaceli who may have commissioned it as an object lesson for her wayward husband. The Duchess of Medinaceli probably intended herself to be represented by Appio's fiancée Valeria who, although a superficial addition to Livy's story, has the largest musical role in Scarlatti's score. Instead of heeding the Duchess' message, the Viceroy took over the direction of the theater, thereby ensuring that he would have complete control over future productions.[13] Vinci's *La caduta de' Decemviri* may have been intended as a subtle criticism of the current Viceroy; the warning concerning the abuse of power is essentially the same as in *L'Ernelinda*. According to Benedikt, Cardinal Althann was sent to Naples to reform the Kingdom's corrupt administration but, after making a valiant attempt, soon succumbed to the corruption.[14]

## *La caduta de' Decemviri*: a Study in Contrasts

Although the libretto to Vinci's *La caduta de' Decemviri* may closely resemble Stampiglia's original, there is absolutely no resemblance between Vinci's score and the original setting by Scarlatti.[15] As with *Eraclea*, Vinci composed *La caduta* as if Scarlatti's opera had never existed. For example, while Edward Dent could single out Scarlatti's original setting

---

[13] Ibid., 212.

[14] Heinrich Benedikt, *Das Königreich Neapel unter Kaiser Karl VI*, 262-63.

[15] The principal source for Vinci's *La caduta de' Decemviri* is the manuscript in the Biblioteca dell'Abbazia in Montecassino (6-B-20/2 formerly 126 E23, 1 vol., 21 x 28 cm.). Like the other Vinci scores at Montecassino, it was formerly part of the collection of the Neapolitan patrician Vincenzo Bovio. The score is of Neapolitan origin and the interpolation of an alternative aria indicates connections with the original production. According to Strohm, the score of *La caduta* in the Biblioteca del Conservatorio in Naples (32-4-10), like the *L'Ernelinda* in the Conservatorio, is an early nineteenth-century copy of the Montecassino score by Giuseppe Sigismondo. However in checking the examples below taken from the Montecassino manuscript against the Naples manuscript, the author found a number of discrepancies, suggesting that the latter may derive from another source (the examples are thus based on both sources). Besides this copy, the Conservatorio also possesses a collection of arias, also of Neapolitan origin (34-5-26). A contemporary score of Act III of *La caduta* can be found in the British Museum (14240, 1 vol. 20.5 x 27 cm.). This score has been initalled F.T.F. by an un-known copyist whom Strohm considers to have been Neapolitan (Strohm, *Italienische Opernarien* II, 231). The Montecassino score consists of:

*La caduta de' Decemviri:*

| 18 *da capo* arias | 9 *dal segno* arias | 1 alternate *da capo* aria |
| --- | --- | --- |
| 3* *da capo* ensembles | 2* interrupted ariettas | 3 accompanied recitatives |
| 1 binary aria à 3 | 1 coro | 1 sinfonia |

*Servilla e Flacco*

| 3 *da capo* arias | 2 *da capo* ensembles |
| --- | --- |
| 2 accompanied recitatives | 1 binary duet |

Totals: 47 set pieces (36 *da capo/dal segno* forms)
*the repeated ensembles and arietta are counted as single items.

for its abundance of "cloying airs in 12/8 time, all charming and all exactly alike," Vinci's setting does not contain a single aria in compound meter.[16] The radical changes that had taken place in Italian opera since 1697 would have made Scarlatti's score appear almost as obsolete as one by Monteverdi or Cavalli. Nevertheless, *La caduta* retains a certain formal flexibility that gives it more of a kinship with Vinci's earlier Stampiglia operas, setting it apart from his recent works.

Like *La Rosmira*, *La caduta* begins with a tableau which employs non-exit forms. The tableau in *La caduta* represents the games of Consus which would have been depicted by Nicola Gigli's "giochi gladitori."[17] Besides these gladiatorial games, the tableau employs two interrupted ariettas: the first is sung by Appio as he makes his entrance, and the second by Valeria and repeated by Icilio as they react to Appio's infatuation with Virginia. Only after the crowd exits amid the sounds of trumpets (represented in the score by a blank page) comes the first *da capo* aria. Later in the act occurs one of the few extended through-composed pieces in Vinci's operas. Virginia comes upon Valeria and Claudia, the former furious because of Appio's new infatuation, the latter sympathetic because of her love for Lucio. After a verbal standoff, Virginia finally asks her social superiors if she should stay or go. This is accomplished in Virginia's full-scale bipartite aria, with Valeria and Claudia giving their answers as cadential echoes—their occasional single-syllable affirmations insufficient to consider this simple minuet aria an actual trio.

Although these scenes are interesting from a formal perspective, some of the finest music within the opera can be found at the end of Act I and the beginning of Act II. It is characteristic of Vinci that this sequence occurs between the expository scenes at the beginning and the courtroom scenes at the climax of the opera, and are concerned primarily with amorous intrigue rather than dramatic action. After an unsuccessful attempt to buy Virginia's love with a diamond necklace, Appio sings of how he has been ravished by her eyes. In this type of situation, after a declaration of love, Vinci was likely to employ a minuet aria either in a minor key or in a major key with feints into the minor mode.[18] Instead, Vinci writes an heroic coloratura aria which may reflect the

---

[16] Edward J. Dent, *Alessandro Scarlatti: his Life and Works* (London: Edward Arnold, 1905) reprint ed. with preface and notes by Frank Walker (Scholarly Press, 1976), 65.

[17] If the "giochi gladitori" were accomplished by music, as in a ballet, this was probably provided by Nicola Gigli, since no music survives. This is the type of scene that would have given a French composer the perfect opportunity for a danced divertissement (for example, the Isthmian games in Rameau's *Naïs*).

[18] For example, Ernesto's "D'adorarvi begl'occhi" from *Gismondo* and Iliso's "Aprir ti il seno" from *Eraclea* in the minor mode and Araspe's "Amor che nasce" from *Didone* and Acquilio's "Talor due pupile" from *Farnace* in the major mode.

sentiments of the previous recitative in which Appio vows to compensate for Virginia's humble birth. The heroic opening theme, which is similar to Selene's "Ardi per me fedele," is compromised, like Appio's own motives, by a buffo-like second theme with its twice-stated scale cadence, each launched by highly accented repeated notes:

Example 7.1a & 1b "Con forza ascosa' *La caduta de' Decemviri* I/xii

[musical notation: a. with text "Con for-za a sco-sa ne' rag-gi su-i/ La mi-a vez-zo-sa ra-pim-mi in se"; b. with text "La mia vez-zo sa ra-pim-mi in se con for-za asc-co-sa ra-pim-mi in se la mia vez zo-sa ra-pim-mi in se/"]

At the end of the act, Appio and Icilio ask Virginia to decide which of them is her beloved. Much to their chagrin, she tells them that she made promises to neither. In a trio the two rivals accuse her of infidelity while she replies that she was only teasing them. The trio combines the sentiments of two separate pieces from Stampiglia's original libretto, a vengeance duet for for Appio and Icilio and a mocking aria for Virginia. The "a chi" retorts of Virginia, in turn, are derived from the buffo duet that originally preceded this scene which, in the process of revision, was moved to the end of the act (see below). This trio, like so many other ensembles in Vinci's operas, appears to have been added to the libretto specifically for the composer. The parallel accusations are presented consecutively in unison, but instead of straight repetition, Vinci gives Appio's accusation more intensity by extending the initial note of each phrase and following it with a string of sixteenth notes (see Example 7.2 on page 208). The trio is essentially an aria à 3, since the melodies of the three characters can, for the most part, be written as a single shared melody.

In Act II Icilio replies to Virginia's explanation for her apparent infidelity in his aria "S'io non t'amasi tanto," saying that he would not be so fearful if he did not love her so much. Although the aria begins as a rather modest gavotte, the extended coloratura passages, with prominent syncopations and trills and subtle major-mode chromaticism, give the aria a mid-century flavor. In a parallel scene, Appio responds to her

Example 7.2 "Giurasti fedi/A' chi" *La caduta de' Decemviri* I/xiv

alternate explanation by praising her discretion. Virginia assures Appio of her love in the aria "Sei tu solo" which is punctuated by asides in which she negates her promises. Instead of the expected soubrette dance-air, Vinci writes a plodding *cacciatore* piece, with static pedals and fanfares for *trombe de caccia,* of the type he usually reserved for infuriated tyrants such as Piro and Ricimero. After unsuccessfully trying to embrace her, Appio then tries to assure himself of Virginia's love by repeating her words. Unfortunately this results in a complete repetition of the previous aria, with Virginia again providing the negative asides. This type of Stampiglian repetition can be very witty, as for example in "Io le diró"/ "Tu le dirai" from Handel's setting of Stampiglia's *Serse*, where the catchy melody and miniature form benefit from the repetition. In this aria, however, the four-fold repetition of the plodding A section unnecessarily multiplies the tedium.

After Virginia leaves, Valeria, who has overheard the preceding exchange, rushes on to accuse Appio of infidelity. Appio denies the charge and their accusations and denials erupt into a brief arioso duet, courtesy of Stampiglia. Valeria's anger finally explodes in her vengeance aria "Se tu sei crudo." The lean declamatory vocal melody of this minor-mode *aria parlante* is enriched by the suspensions of the orchestral writing, which may account for the moderate tempo rather than the *Allegro* or *Presto* that one would expect in this type of dramatic aria:

Example 7.3 "Se tu sei crudo" *La caduta de' Decemviri* II/iv

The restatement of the first theme to emphasize the new key (compare mm. 27-30 with mm. 36-39) is a relatively rare procedure that Vinci had virtually abandoned after *Silla Dittatore*.

While accusing Appio, Valeria says she just heard Virginia making fun of him (the theatrical convention is such that Valeria, in the wings, could hear Virginia's asides but Appio could not). When Flacco enters and asks what's the matter, Appio begins to rave about revenge against Virginia. He orders Flacco to accuse Virginia of being a run-away slave and bring her before him as judge. In his aria "Sento amor che piange," Appio sings of how his love weeps while his heart calls for vengeance. These two contrasting affects are depicted in the first section of this *da capo* aria by two contrasting sub-sections: a quadruple-meter *affetuoso cantilena* with prominent dotted rhythms to depict "amor che piange," and a triple-meter *allegro* with rumbling octave pedal to depict "mio core vendetta farà:"[19]

---

[19] He may have picked up the unusual octave pedal from the Porta operas of the previous year. An good example of this device can be found in "Memoria del rio" from *Numitore*.

Example 7.4. "Sento amor che piange" *La caduta de' Decemviri* II/v

While this type of sectionalization as a means of highlighting contrasting affects is not uncommon between sections of the *da capo* aria, it is rare within a section.[20]

    The sectionalized contrasts in Appio's aria, which had already been employed in Valeria's "Spietati gelosia" in Act I, would appear three more times before the end of the act: in Luccio's "Onor mi chiama," in Valeria's "T'apri o Ciel," and in the comic duet in the second intermezzo. None of these sectionalized da capos are set to original Stampiglia texts, but, rather, to new texts that have been added to the libretto, presumably to accommodate the wishes of the composer. This rather striking experiment with *da capo* form is accomplished in close proximity in a single opera, and is then virtually abandoned. Such an inconsistent approach to formal innovation can be encountered from time to time in Vinci's music, suggesting that within the composer's artistic make-up, a romantic desire for change would occasionally disrupt the predominant need for symmetry and order. These sectionalized structures undoubtedly had an impact on his pupil at the time, Pergolesi, who would employ them with great effect in certain comic scenes, notably Serpina's triumph over Umberto, "A Serpina penserete" from *La serva padrona*.

---

See Giovanni Porta, *Numitore* in 4 of *Handel Sources: Materials for the Study of Handel's Borrowing*, ed. John H. Roberts (New York: Garland Publishing, 1986).
[20] Dean pays particular attenton to this type of sectionalization in "Deggio dunque" from *Radamisto*. Winton Dean, *Handel and the Opera Seria*, 166-67.

## *Flacco e Servilia*: Comic Scenes and Intermezzo

The intermezzo in *La caduta de' Decemviri* is a partial transformation of Stampiglia's original *seicento* comic scenes into a *settecento* intermezzo. Of its three constituent parts, the first is a composite of the two original comic scenes in Act I. The intermezzo begins with an *accompagnato buffo* in which Flacco reads a love poem to Servilia. Servilia's cynical original aria has been replaced by a second accompanied recitative wherein she returns Flacco's poetic compliment in ceremonial "ottava rime;" Vinci had previously used accompanied recitative for "ottava rime" in Bellucia's reading of Tasso in *Li zite 'ngalera* (Example 2.7). The scene ends with the duet "Io da te bramo," the text of which was salvaged from the discarded comic scene at the beginning of the act. In this duet Flacco vows to serve his beloved, while Servilia makes him promise that should he ever break faith, he will never look at her again. "Io da te bramo" is a minuet in which the simple melody is continually interrupted by Servilia's repeated questions "e chi?" and "e tu?" These interruptions, which provided the idea for Virginia's questions in the trio, are now heard as a comic echo of the serious ensemble.

In Act II the characters not only appear as servants in the drama, but are important in the plot development. In the central courtroom sequences in Acts II and III, Flacco and Servilia play the role of prosecution and defence respectively. Therefore the stock servant roles expand as Flacco becomes Appio's villainous accomplice and Servilia becomes Virginia's protector. It has been already been mentioned that Stampiglia avoided comedy during the serious events following Flacco's abduction of Virginia, not only to prevent a jarring juxtaposition of comedy and tragedy but also to ensure that Flacco and Servilia's new roles will be taken seriously. Vinci's collaborator, however, interpolated an intermezzo in the midst of these serious events, upsetting the balance between comic and tragic. This new intermezzo relates directly to the previous scene. Outside the Judgment Hall, Servilia, furious with Flacco for his base betrayal of Virginia, is determined to knock some sense into him. Servilia's righteous indignation is portrayed in an heroic coloratura aria in B-flat major [21] (see Example 7.5 on page 212). Because of the consistent avoidance of coloratura in the comic arias of Vinci's heroic operas, its singular use in "Nobil destrier feroce" in combination with the heroic style would seem to represent a conscious effort on the part of the composer to ennoble Servilia, in the same way as he had done with Capitano Mariano in *Li zite 'ngalera*. In the final duet, wherein

---

[21] "Nobil destrier feroce" is included on a disc devoted to Vinci arias by Maria Angeles Peters: *Leonardo Vinci Arie d'opera* (Nuova Era 6997).

Example 7.5 "Nobil destrier feroce" *La caduta de 'Decemviri* II/xvi

the conflict between Servilia and Flacco comes to a climax, the sectionalized structures employed earlier in the act return, providing a comical echo of the previous heroic arias. The duet, however, is not in *da capo* form, but, rather, consists of an alternation of *Largo* 3/8 and *Presto* 2/4 sections, organized into a large-scale binary form, with the sectionalization continuing throughout. As in the second duet from *Erighetta e Don Chilone*, this one is also written for basso continuo accompaniment only—one of the few extended pieces in Vinci's surviving operas that is not accompanied by the string orchestra. The use of only *basso continuo* accompaniment at this time, like the flexible scenic structure, is another example of the strong ties of the intermezzo to the traditions of the seventeenth century.

In Act III Stampiglia's comic scenes have been retained and have not been transformed into a detachable intermezzo. After Virginia's miraculous recovery from her wounds, Servilia ironically sums up the situation in the same way that her tenor predecessors had done during the previous century, contrasting Lucio's fanatical stoicism with the easy life of unscrupulous men. Turning away from her flirtation with the heroic style, Servilia returns to the comic style with the teasing internal repetitions of her melody that create an almost dizzying effect. Sectionalized structure is employed yet again, but this time in the second section of the *da capo* form. This extended second strophe, which is considerably longer than the first, is set to alternating *Largo* and *Allegro* phrases, each separated by brief ritornellos, creating an expansive second section in nine subsections (76 measures long).

The final comic scene presents a humorous parody of the previous scene wherein Appio attempts to escape Rome in disguise during the uprising. The difference between the two scenes is that Flacco is disguised as an old woman and, instead of being haunted by guilty spectres, complains of being tormented by a lack of sleep because of his excessive fear. Flacco sings a peculiar unison aria, "Mistiro sbadiglio," based on a repeated three-note motive derived directly from the three-syllable phrases of the original Stampiglia text. The fleeting three-note phrases of the vocal part are linked with similar fragments in the syncopated bass, creating rhythmic enchainments. Vinci was to employ similar enchainments in a tragic situation for his next opera, *Catone in Utica*, in the process creating a new aria type (see Example 7.11 on page 228). When Servilia captures Flacco, he stubbornly denies his identity, all the while stuttering to disguise his voice. Their accusations and denials continue in their duet, which exploits the stuttering for its slapstick humor.

## An Opera for Giovanni Battista Pinacci

In January of 1727, La Romanina made her farewell stage appearance in Sarro's setting of *Siroe re di Persia* in Naples. For this important production, Metastasio again modified the text he wrote for Vinci and revised for Porpora and it is this version that became the standard text for this drama.[22] After her retirement, she and her husband Domenico Bulgarelli moved to Rome. Along with them came their guest and protegé Metastasio and, according to Burney, "from the time of his arrival in that city, till his departure for Germany, they all lived under the same roof, and constituted one family."[23] With La Romanina's retirement and the end of her considerable performance fees, there is a marked change in Metastasio's creative output. In contrast to the years 1720-27, when works appear sporadically as if the product of a dilettante, Metastasio's last years in Italy see a change to a more professional approach, with a more regular production of major works.

Vinci and Metastasio's *Catone in Utica* was premièred at the Teatro delle Dame in Rome on January 19, 1728, with a cast consisting of:[24]

[22] Pietro Metastasio, *Tutte le Opere*, I, 70-123.

[23] Charles Burney, *Memoirs of the Life and Writings of the Abate Metastasio*, 39-40.

[24] Although the date is given as January 13 in several sources, including *Opere*, Valesio's entry for the première in his *Diario* is for January 19. Francesco Valesio, *Diario di Roma; Libro settimo e libro ottavo*, 897: "Monday 19 Rain. This evening the drama entitled *Catone in Utica* by Pietro Metastasio went on stage at the Teatro Ali- bert or delle Dame." The January 13 date may be that of the dress rehearsal which, according to Friedrich Marpurg, was as important as the première (see Chapter 9). Libretto for *Catone* in I-Bc -Fm -Mb -M(Gentili Tedeschi) -MOe -Rsc -Vge -Vnm, B-Bc, US-AUS -BE -Wc (Schatz No. 10746); Sartori, *I libretti italiani* (No. 5232).

Catone: Giovanni Battista Pinacci    Arbace: Giovanni Battista Minelli
Cesare: Giovanni Carestini                   Marzia: Giacinto Fontana
Fulvio: Filipo Giorgi                              Emilia: Giovanni Ossi
              Stage painter and architect: Alessandro Mauri
              Choreographer: Monsù Sarò

This was first *primo uomo* role Vinci created for Carestini, who had previously sung the role of the scoundrel Medarse in *Siroe*. Minelli, Fontana, and Ossi had appeared previously in *Gismondo*. According to Giambattista Mancini, Minelli sang "in a levelled style, with a noble *portamento di voce* and with reason has acquired the name of a sage artist."[25] Pinacci, however, was the tenor who had caused a scandal in 1726 by breaking his contract with the Teatro delle dame and going over to the rival Capranica (see Chapter 6). In resolving the incident, it was agreed that Pinacci would sing at the delle Dame for the 1728 season. Although this was the first time Vinci had worked with him, the tenor had sung the title role in the Florentine *Farnace* in 1726 (Plates 20 and 21 reproduce caricatures of Pinacci and Minelli, suggesting the two may have been somewhat of a mismatch on stage).[26]

It is possible that *Catone in Utica* had originally been commissioned by the Teatro delle Dame after the success of Vinci's *Didone abbandonata* for Carnival 1727, but with the disaffection of Farinello and Pinacci, the singers for whom the principal roles were probably intended, to the Capranica (see Chapter 6), *Catone* was postponed, replaced by *Gismondo*. The scenario may account for the fact that the subsequent published editions of the drama were dated 1727 and had to be corrected by "a chronological note affixed to each drama by the same author."[27] It would also account for the differences between *Gismondo* and Vinci's other Roman operas. Although one might assume that Vinci composed the music to *Catone in Utica* directly after the première of *La caduta de' Decemviri* in October of 1727, the libretto had probably been in existence for some time, and thus he may have begun it earlier, perhaps during the summer in Naples. Regardless of exactly when and where the score was composed, Vinci would have left for Rome at the beginning of December, which can be inferred from a request to the Viceroy from the following year.[28]

---

[25] Giambattista Mancini, *Riflessioni pratiche sul canto figurato*, 3rd ed. (Milan, 1777),

[26] In his study of Vivaldi in Rome, Dale Monson provides sketches of the vocal style of Minelli, Ossi, and Pinacci (as well as the one for Farfallino described above in conjunction with *Didone*) based on roles created for these artists in operas by Vivaldi, Vinci, Scarlatti, and Sarro. Dale E. Monson, "The Trail of Vivaldi's Singers: Vivaldi in Rome," *Nuovi studi vivaldiani: Edizione e cronologia critica delle opere*, ed. Antonio Fanna and Giovanni Morelli, Venezia Fondazione Giorgio Cini, I (1988), 574-86.

[27] Pietro Metastasio, *Tutte le Opere*, I, 1398.

[28] In the request, Vinci says that he "needs to extend by another four months the leave already granted"— the extended leave beginning four months before April 2, i.e. December 1, 1727; Archivio di Stato di Napoli, Italia: Segretaria dei Viceré, fascio 1795.

Giovanni Battista Pinacci     Giovanni Battista Minelli

***Plates 20 & 21.*** *Caricatures of Giovanni Battista Pinacci and Govanni Battista Minelli, the latter in the role of a Roman General; attributed to Marco Ricci.* [29] *(Algarotti-Gellman Album, Nos. 27 & 5)*

The season was rather sombre because a dispute between the Pope and the King of Portugal over the appointment of Cardinals caused the Pope to prohibit the *festini* (i.e. balls, banquets and parties) that were an essential part of the Carnival; an exception to this ban was made for the visit to Rome of Violante di Baviera, Grand Duchess of Tuscany, and her nephew the Elector of Cologne.[30] The libretto of *Catone in Utica* was dedicated to Princess Violante; James III and Clementina, the usual dedicatees of Vinci's Roman operas, were still separated, making the

---

[29] Edward Croft-Murray, *An Album of Eighteenth Century Venetian Operatic Caricatures: formerly in the Collection of Count Algarotti*, 57 & 35.

[30] Filippo Clementi, *Il Carnevale Roman: nelle cronache contemporanee* (Città di Castello: Unione arti grafiche, 1938), II, 39. At a rehearsal of a cantata in honor of the foreign guests, Metastasio was requested by the Grand Duchess to make a "spiritosa composizione," undoubtedly a poetic improvisation, which was a specialty of the young poet; Valesio, *Diario di Roma*, IV, 890. In Valesio's entry Metastasio is still described as "allievo del Gravina."

first tentative maneuvers towards a fragile marital reconciliation.[31] To counter the delle Dame première of Metastasio's long-awaited new drama, the Teatro Capranica featured the return of Farinelli, who may have been enticed away for the production of his brother Riccardo Broschi's *Isola d'Alcina*. The Grand Duchess, the Elector and "tutta la nobiltà" attended the premières of both *Isola d'Alcina* at the Capranica and the delle Dame's initial offering, *Ipermesta* by Francesco Feo. The latter was judged to be a "a rather melancholic achievement,"[32] thereby putting more pressure on Metastasio and Vinci to succeed. Vinci's score would have been more or less complete by December 29 when, according to Valesio's *Diario*, "the Elector of Cologne was presented with some arias from the opera set to music by Vinci;" since he had to leave Rome prior to the première, the Archbishop/Elector rewarded the composer with "a golden case filled with ducats" for this private preview of the new production.[33] According to Cametti, the Grand Duchess, to whom the opera was dedicated, assisted with the production until she departed from Rome; according to Valesio, on January 24 prior to her departure from Rome, she left the theatre after the second act, taking with her "numerous ladies invited to a *festino* that she gave with copious refreshments."[34] Considering the interest she took in the production, it is possible that this *festino* was a cast party rather than a sign of disapproval.

## And He Chose a Subject "to Please the Romans"

*Catone in Utica* was the first drama Metastasio wrote specifically for Rome and, according to Burney, the poet "chose the subject purposely to please the Romans, supposing that he should gain both applause and gratitude by displaying the virtue of one of their own heroes."[35] Metastasio based his new drama on an episode from the civil wars of Caesar and Pompey, the defeat of the Republican forces of Marcus Porcius Cato the Younger by Julius Caesar in 46 BC:

> **Synopsis**: Catone, besieged by Cesare in Utica, awaits the arrival of his enemy. He believes himself to be the last champion of ancient Roman liberty, struggling against the dictatorial tyranny of the usurper. To consolidate his precarious position, Catone intends to marry his daughter Marzia to his ally King Arbace of Numidia. Marzia protests

---

[31] Haile, *The Old Chevalier,* 323-24 & Miller, *James,* 281-83.
[32] *Diario di Roma,* IV, 891.
[33] Ibid., 892.
[34] Cametti, "Leonardo Vinci e i suoi drammi in musica al Teatro delle Dame," 298; Valesio, *Diario di Roma,* IV, 898.
[35] Burney, *Memoirs of the Life and Writings of the Abate Metastasio,* I, 40.

against this political marriage all the while concealing her love for Cesare. Marzia convinces Arbace to delay the marriage a day, hoping that in the interim she can reconcile father and lover, thereby making marriage to Cesare a possibility. The first meeting between Cesare and Catone is interrupted by Emilia, the widow of Pompeo, who storms in demanding vengeance for the death of her husband by the orders of Cesare. In the subplot, Emilia enlists the aid of Cesare's general Fulvio, who is in love with her. While Emilia exploits Fulvio's infatuation as a means to avenge the death of her husband, Fulvio in turn exploits Emilia's confidence as a means to infiltrate the enemy camp.

After stalling and posturing on both sides, a second meeting between Cesare and Catone takes place. The haughty Catone demands that Cesare abandon his title of Emperor and give himself up as a traitor to Rome. Ignoring these preposterous demands, Cesare offers to divide up his empire with Catone in return for the hand of his daughter. Catone dismisses the former as a bribe and the latter as an insult to his family. The two declare war. Catone orders Marzia and Emilia to leave the city by an underground aqueduct. Under pressure from Catone to seal the alliance, Arbace comes to claim his prize. To prevent the marriage, Marzia finally admits her love for Cesare. Catone explodes in anger and disowns his daughter.

The frantic Marzia says farewell to Cesare, asking him to spare her father in battle. She tries to escape the city by the underground aqueduct. In this same passage, Emilia has laid an ambush for Cesare, which is ironically foiled by the entrance of Catone in search of the lovers. Catone is about to have Cesare arrested when Fulvio arrives with news that Utica has capitulated to the Romans. Within the city, Arbace is about to lead a counterattack against the Imperial troops when he is informed of Catone's suicide. Marzia tries to comfort and placate the dying Catone. He demands that she marry Arbace and swear eternal hatred to Cesare as the price of his forgiveness. Marzia submissively agrees. Cesare enters and is first cursed by Catone and then rejected by Marzia. Cesare throws his victory laurel to the ground and curses his victory.

Although the historical outlines of the drama can be found in Plutarch, much of the action is fanciful elaboration, with only slight connection to the facts; for example replacing Cato's sons with a daughter and Pompey's father-in-law Scipio with Pompey's widow Cornelia (albeit with her name changed to Emilia) to provide the love interest; and transforming Cato's correspondence with Octavius and Lucius Caesar into the fateful meeting with Julius Caesar. Both the appearance of Caesar in Utica and the love between Cato's daughter and Caesar can be found in *Catone Uticense* by Matteo Noris, a *dramma per musica* produced in 1701 in Venice.[36]

Much of Metastasio's *tragedia per musica* is derived neither from Noris' libretto nor Plutarch's history but, rather, from Joseph Addison's tragedy *Cato*. Although Metastasio could not read English, an Italian translation of *Cato* was performed in Livorno in 1715 and published the same year in Florence.[37] From Addison Metastasio borrowed both the characterization of Cato as the final bastion of the virtues of the Ancient Roman Republic, and of Juba, the genteel Nubian prince in love with his daughter Marcia. Metastasio changed the name of Juba to the more fashionable Arbace, but he retained the daughter's name (in Noris she is called Flamina). Moreover, significant portions of the dialogue are based directly upon Addison: most notably, the dialogue between Cato and the Imperial emissary in Act II of the play provides the foundation for the central dialogue between Catone and Cesare in Act II of the opera; and the impassioned exchange between Marcia, Juba and the dying Cato in the final scene of the play is the inspiration for the tragic finale of the opera. Thus, Metastasio's *Catone in Utica* is one of the first examples of what was to become a trend in the late eighteenth and early nineteenth centuries: Italian opera libretti based on English rather than French literary sources.

According to Burney, Metastasio's efforts to please the Romans backfired and *Catone in Utica* "was instantly attacked by the satirical genius of the Romans."[38] Act III in particular seems to have offended Roman pride and sensibility. Metastasio and Mauri's novel setting, in an underground aqueduct, departed from the standard palatial and pastoral settings of the *dramma per musica*, anticipating the *capricci* of Piranesi.[39] One critic tacked a note to the balustrade of the orchestra pit complaining "Cruel Metastasio, you have here reduced all the heros of the Tiber into a drainpipe."[40] In addition, the innovative tragic ending, based on the successful finale in *Didone abbandonata*, was considered

---

[36] The love interest is taken a step further in Noris' drama by having Cato's son in love with Caesar's sister Sabina. Libretto in Us-Wc (Schatz No. 8276). Besides the Noris *Catone Uticense*, the preface to the *Opere* edition mentions several French sources: *Caton D'Utique* by Deschamps and two tragedies by Corneille, *La morte de Pompée* and *Sentorius*. However, the two Corneille plays have little connection with Metastasio's drama other than the presence of Pompée's wife, Cornelia.

[37] *Il Catone, Tragedia: Tradotta dall Originale Inglese* (Florence: Stamperia di S.A.R., 1715).

[38] Burney, *Memoirs of the Life and Writings of the Abate Metastasio*, I, 41.

[39] Piranesi began his career in Rome in the 1740s. Julius S. Held and Donald Posner, *17th and 18th Century Art: Baroque Painting, Sculpture, Architecture* (Englewood Cliffs, N.J.: Prentice Hall), 352.

[40] Quoted in Alberto Cametti, "Leonardo Vinci," 298.

offensive because the dying Catone comes on stage having just stabbed himself (that Didone's suicide was not considered offensive is probably related to its brevity—she simply leaps into the flames of Carthage at the final curtain). A *pasquinata* was circulated which invited "the Company of the Dead to come in mercy to the Teatro delle Dame to bury the remains of Catone."[41] In response to his critics Metastasio wrote a polemic in which he complained about "the envious mob" who "accuse my Catone of too much realism and arrogance," insisting that "he should make Catone speak like a French cavalier to a beautiful lady."[42]

The tragic finale, the Roman subject and the North African setting suggest that *Catone* was planned as a sequel to *Didone*. There are some striking similarities between *Catone in Utica* and another Vinci opera, *Silla Dittatore*, enough to suggest that Vinci may have had some input in the initial creation of the drama. Both *Silla* and *Catone* have as their central theme the struggle between old Republican Rome, as personified by Domizio and Catone, and new Imperial Rome, as personified by Silla and Cesare (Sulla's dictatorship being the historical precursor of Julius Caesar's). This monumental struggle is complicated by the love of the daughter of the Republican champion (Valeria and Marzia) for her father's Imperial adversary.

From a political allegorical perspective, one could interpret the old Roman Republicanism of Catone as representative of Italy of the city states and duchies (Venice, Genoa, Parma, Modena) and the new Roman Imperialism of Cesare as representative of Habsburg Imperial Italy (Naples, Milan, Mantua). Marzia, who continually tries to reconcile Cesare with Catone, could in turn represent the Papacy trying to mediate between these warring factions. Perhaps Emilia, who continually seeks revenge against Cesare, represents Spain under Elizabeth Farnese conspiring to regain the lost Spanish possessions in Italy. The poltical allegory is supported by the fact that it is based on the three major additions to the

---

[41] Ibid. *Pasquini* or Pasqinades were originally satiric poems that were posted on an ancient statue group (Meneleus supporting Patroclus) in a small piazza just off the south end of the Piazza Navona. The statue was nicknamed Pasqino after a local tailor renowned for his wit, who was given credit for initiating the tradition of posting satiric notes on the statue. Although the posting of these notes, which were often critical of the government, was considered a crime punishable by death, the law was never enforced, providing an unusual venue for political dissent in *settencento* Rome. Sometimes the notes were addressed to one of the other "talking statues" in the city, most notably Marforio, a statue of an ancent river god that used to be located at the bottom of the Capitoline Hill but is now in the entrance of the Capitoline Museum; Information derived from the *Michelin Tourist Guide: Rome* and the Blue Guide: Rome and Environs.

[42] Metastasio, *Tutte le Opere,* I, 1408-09; Apparently the production at the Capranica ran into problems later in the season when Farinelli, having lost at gambling, refused to sing, causing the cancellation of a performance for which the impressario Faliconti was placed under arrest by the Governor of Rome. Clementi, *I carnevale romano*, II, 38.

historical account in Plutarch (i.e. the symbolic meetings between Cesare and Catone and the addition of the characters Marcia and Emilia). If this interpretation of the political allegory of *Catone in Utica* is correct, then one must admire Metastasio's skilful diplomacy which cleverly portrayed both Catone and Cesare in a favorable light. Catone was sypathetic enough for the Venetians on one hand, while Cesare was heroic enough for Emperor Charles on the other.[43]

## *Catone in Utica*: the Tragic Hero and his Daughter

As in *Didone abbandonata*, *Catone in Utica* is dominated by the title role, in this case conceived for the troublesome tenor Giovanni Battista Pinacci.[44] Catone's music is characterized by its overall forceful and energetic quality, and by the presence of certain archaic elements—the former in keeping with Catone's position as rebel against the dictatorship of Cesare and the latter perhaps alluding to his position as guardian of the ancient ideals of the Roman Republic. In Catone's first aria, "Con sì bel nome," he tells Arbace that only by fighting as a Roman will he be recognized as his son. With Vinci reserving the trumpets for Cesare's

---

[43] Catone's personification of the Roman Republic even made the work appealing during the revolutonary period, when productions were mounted in Naples and Rome "per lo spirito della libertà;" Metastasio, *Tutte le Opere*, 1398.

[44] There are several manuscript scores of *Catone in Utica*. The score in the Santini-Sammlung in Münster (4241, 3 vol. 17 x 22 cm.) was initialled and dated by the Roman theater copyist F. C. Cantoni in 1728. Although dating from the same year as the original production, the inclusion of the sinfonia and ten arias from *Medo* at the end of Acts II and III, which are included in Cantoni's table of contents, suggests that the complete opera score dates from some time after the première of *Medo* in May. This is further suggested by the patchwork structure of the score. Like the Cantoni scores of *Farnace* and *Gismondo*, this one is made up of eighteen pre-existing aria fascicles in a neat spacious style, each designated by the title "Catone" beginning on the recto page. These independent fascicles, originating from the production, have been connected by through-copied recitative and ten remaining arias, which can begin on either recto or verso and are not quite as neat or as spacious. This manuscript included additional performance material: an "aria trasportata" at the end of Act I and an "aria nove in ciambio"—the latter appearing directly after Fulvio's "Piangendo ancora" as a replacement. A sonnet in praise of Metastasio that contains references to *Artaserse* and *Temistocle* presumably was added when the score received its present binding in the 1730s. The score in the Staatsbibliothek in Berlin (22376), that formerly belonged to the composer Johann Friedrich Reichardt, is identical to the Cantoni score in its content, including the additional performance material, but it is decidedly different in ts layout, suggesting that it is either copied and adapted from the Cantoni score or that both works derive from the same source.. The manuscript in the Biblioteca del Conservatorio in Naples (Rari 7-3-15) differs from the contemporary scores of Vinci's Neapolitan operas in its large format (23 x 36 cm.) and its heavy paper with fleur de lys watermark, thereby suggesting a mid-century origin. The incomplete score in the Royal College of Music in London (631 in 3 vols., a third of which is lost) is part of a large set belonging to the Concerts of Ancient Music that also included *Artaserse*,

battle aria, "Se in campo armato," Catone's heroic stature is depicted by an heroic D-major march in triple meter with triadic fanfares and punctuating repeated eighths scored for oboes and strings.[45] According to Strohm, Vinci borrowed the opening theme of this aria from "Impara da quest'alma" from Giovanni Maria Capelli's *Venceslao* (Parma, 1724), reorganising Capelli's material to fit Metastasio's text as if it were newly composed.[46] The energetic coloratura passages, with large leaps, dotted rhythms and trills, were probably intended to suggest strength and power through their virtuosity. In his second aria, "Si sgomenti alle sue pene," in which he tells Emilia to restrain her emotions so as not to shame the memory of Pompeo, a more old-fashioned sort of florid writing is employed, with rapid sequential coloratura passages in a narrow range. The aria is based on a theme rather similar to that in "Dopo notte" from Handel's *Ariodante* and is complemented by a vigorous walking bass and lively orchestral figuration.

In "Và, ritorna al tuo Tiranno" in Act II, Catone tells Fulvio that he has no intention of talking peace to Cesare. It is written in the learned style of the *alla breve* aria. Although counterpoint in the *alla breve* aria is usually limited to a fugue-like theme and bits of imitation, this aria is a fugue in *da capo* form, the opening ritornello containing a complete fugal exposition with countersubject and codetta, the only irregularity being in the second answer's appearance (m. 10) in the first violins rather than in the violas where it might be expected:

---

*Semiramide*, and *Alessandro* as well as operas by other contemprary composers. They have been copied by the same group of scribes on the same thick, coarse paper, in the same three-volume format, with green covers and leather spines engraved with golden initials C. A. M. (Concerts of Ancient Music) and volume numbers. Their modest format, their uniformity, and their scope (*Catone in Utica* is Vol. 18 while Giay's *Eumene* is Vol. 36) suggests that they were part of a large retrospective collection of Italian opera. The paper and repertoire indicates a contemporary Italian origin. The set did not make its way into the collection of the Concerts of Ancient Music until the second quarter of the nineteenth century since they were not included in the organization's original catalogue from 1827. The excerpts below are taken from the Santini score of *Catone in Utica,* which consists of the following:

| | |
|---|---|
| 23 *da capo* arias* | 1 *da capo* quartet |
| 3 *del segno* arias | 7 accompanied recitatives |
| 1 replacement *da capo* aria | 1 sinfonia |

Totals: 36 set pieces (28 in *da capo* form)

* includes one aria in two different versions

[45] This formula, with the addition of the trumpet, is common in the *aria di bataglia*; for example "The trumpet shall sound" from *Messiah*, "Sound an Alarm" from *Judas Maccabeus*, "The trumpets loud clangor" from *Ode to St. Cecilia's Day*, and "Se in campo armato" from Vivaldi's setting of *Catone in Utica*.

[46] Strohm, *Italienische Opernarien*, I, 55-59. All of Vinci's aria is reproduced in facsimile, as well as part of Capelli's aria in transcription in II, 101-108.

Example 7.6 "Và, ritorna al tuo Tiranno" *Catone in Utica* II/ii

Subsequent fugal statements are presented at the beginning of the vocal periods and are connected by developmental episodes, the first employing canon at the fifth, the last repeated prior to the closing ritornello. This adaptation of the Baroque fugue, which can also be found in certain arias by Porpora (for example "Punirò quel cor" from *Didone abbandonata*), clearly anticipates the finale to Mozart's Jupiter symphony which probably owes more to the *alla breve* aria than the fugues of Bach usually cited as the source of inspiration.

When Marzia tells Catone of her love for Cesare, Catone raises his hand to strike her, an action prevented by Arbace and by eighteenth-century stage etiquette.[47] He expresses outrage and shock in his G-minor aria, "Dovea svenarti allora." Vinci's fascination with sectionalized *da capo* arias in *La caduta* was short-lived. This aria, in which Catone alternately expresses his outrage to Marzia and his bewilderment to Emilia and Arbace, would have been an ideal opportunity for this type of sectionalized structure; instead Vinci wrote a continuous monothematic aria; so continuous that the standardized binary form of the first section is avoided, as if to suggest that Catone's rage exceeds all bounds. In the first vocal period Catone rushes through the expected relative major before coming to cadence in the darkened region of the subdominant minor (m.27):

---

[47] Catone's violent rejection of his daughter seems to be derived from an argument with his son, whose servant hid his father's sword to prevent him from committing suicide. In his anger, Cato struck the servant so hard that he hurt his hand and botched his suicide, hence his long agonizing death. Plutarch, *The Lives of the Noble Grecians and Romans*, trans. John Dryden, rev. Arthur Hugh Clough (New York: The Modern Library, 1912).

Example 7.7. "Dovea svenarti allora" *Catone in Utica* II/xiii

The short fragmented phrases begin or end with downward leaps, suggesting some type of dramatic gesture on the part of Catone. The overall style of this G-minor *Presto* clearly anticipates the so-called *Sturm und Drang* style of the later eighteenth century, which undoubtedly has its roots in the agitated *aria parlante* of the *dramma per musica*.

Count Algarotti may have had the coloratura arias of Act I in mind when he made the sarcastic remark: "Recently Vinci in his softness, obliged Porzio Catone to warble away his death with long trills and florid cadenzas."[48] This criticism certainly does not apply to "Dovea svenarti allora" or Catone's death scenes in Act III. As in the title role in *Didone abbandonata*, which Algarotti so admired, Catone has no arias in Act III and therefore no trills or coloratura of any kind, all of his music being set as recitative. This includes three accompanied recitatives, the first of which is a rare example of an accompanied recitative for two persons. Usually when the accompanied recitative is employed in a dialogue, the orchestral accompaniment is reserved for one of the characters, the others being accompanied by basso continuo as in Act III of *Didone abbandonata* and Act II of *Astianatte*.[49] This accompanied recitative dialogue is begun by Marzia, who tries to comfort and placate her dying father, but it is completed by Catone who replies that only in accepting

---

[48] Francesco Algarotti, *Epistola a Fillide* in *Opere* (Venice: Palese, 1791), I, 19. Quoted in Metastasio, *Tutte le opere*, II, 1399.

[49] A similar accompanied recitative dialogue can be found in Porpora's *Orti esperidi* from 1721 and Vivaldi's *Giustino* from 1724; Vinci would have been familiar with both.

Arbace as husband and swearing eternal hatred to Cesare can she hope to placate his ghost. This statement and response is highlighted by sustained accompaniment for Marzia and tremolo accompaniment for Catone, the latter to depict Catone's failing strength and the "ombra" imagery of the text. The next accompanied recitative occurs after Marzia has reluctantly given in to her father's request and Catone embraces her for the last time. Strangely enough the orchestral accompaniment is abandoned after only six measures, with the remainder of this emotionally intense scene set as simple recitative (a similar anomaly takes place in Didone's *scena*, see Chapter 5).

The finale, dominated by Catone's death, is an extended accompanied recitative for Catone, with the comments of the others set as simple recitative. The accompaniment consists primarily of punctuated chords and arpeggio flourishes, with sustained accompaniment for two climactic passages of diminished harmony: when Catone defies the power of Imperial Rome, and when his strength fails him. In deference to eighteenth-century stage etiquette, he asks to be led off to die away from the eyes of Cesare:

Example 7. 8 "Stelle ove son!" *Catone in Utica* III/ultima

As in the death scene in Ippolito Zanelli's revision of Agostino Piovene's *Tamerlano*, which probably served as the model for this scene, Metastasio has attempted to suggest Catone's failing strength by inserting pauses between the words. However, Vinci avoids the realistic chokes and gasps of Handel's setting of Bajazet's suicide, and produces a restrained, literal realization of the pauses in Metastasio's text (compare with text setting in Example 7.8):[50]

> *Cat.* Ecco ... al mio ciglio ...
>    Già langue ... il dì .
> *Ces.* Roma chi perdi !
> *Cat.* Altrove ...
>    Portatemi ... a morir .
> *Mar.* Vieni .
> *Emi. & Arb.* Che affanno !
> *Cat.* Nò , .. non vedrai ... tiranno ..
>    Nella ... morte .. . vicina ...
>    Spirar ... con me ... la libertà ... Latina .
>       *Catone sostenuto da Marzia, e da Arbace*
>          *entra morendo.*
> *Ces.* Ah se costar mi deve
>    I giorni di Catone il serto , il trono ,
>    Ripigliatevi o Numi il vostro dono .
>          *getta il lauro.*

The final accompanied recitative, in which the remorseful Cesare throws his laurel to the ground and curses his victory, should be regarded as an extension of Catone's *scena*; it follows directly after the two-measure ritornello, makes use of the same punctuated chordal accompaniment and arpeggio flourishes, and ends with a similar two-measure orchestral ritornello.

The character of Cesare provides more of a foil rather than a true counterpart to Catone. In Act I Cesare spends more time in confrontation with Emilia and Marzia than Catone, while in Act II he does every rejects his second and third offers, in the process calling into question his courage and honor, Cesare declares his readiness for battle in the aria "Se in campo armato." Although the coloratura and full orchestration complement his heroic pose, these additions do not fully compensate for the decline in musical inspiration. Vinci's Cesare is at his best as a languishing lover, in his arias "Chi un dolce amor condanna" in Act I and "Quell'amor che poco accende" in Act III, which have a rapturous, one might say narcissistic beauty, almost as if Carestini were meditating upon his own voice.[51] In Vivaldi's setting of *Catone*, Cesare's amorous

---

[50] [Pietro Metastasio], *Catone in Utica: tragedia per musica di Artino Corasio, pastore arcade* (Rome: Stamperia del Bernabò, 1728). 84.

[51] Both "Chi un dolce amor condanna" and "Quell'amor che poco accende" are on a disc

aria "Se mai senti spirarti" partakes of a similar lyricism, but is balanced by his call to arms, "Se in campo armato," in Vivaldi's finest heroic style and one of the highlights of the opera.[52]

In many ways the dramatic and musical counterpart of Vinci's Catone is his daughter Marzia. Although she never goes as far as Valeria in openly rebelling against her father in favor of her lover, she is not afraid to use manipulation and intimidation in her attempts to reconcile father and lover and avoid a political marriage. In the opening scene Marzia asks Arbace to postpone the marriage until the next day as proof of his love. In her aria "Non ti minaccio sdegno," Marzia says that, though she requires this proof, she will neither threaten nor promise him anything in return. The music of this pointed *aria parlante* seems to negate the meaning of the text, particularly the opening line; dispensing with the opening ritornello, the voice, reinforced by unison violins, hammers on the tonic, ending the phrase with an octave leap on the dominant on the word "sdegno" as the rest of the orchestra enters in imitation:

Example 7.9. "Non ti minaccio sdegno" *Catone in Utica* I/ii

Although Marzia says she is not threatening Arbace, the music suggests otherwise. This type of dramatic irony, while rare in Vinci, has already been observed in Silla's "Vedrò se gli occhi" and several arias in *Astianatte*. At the end of Act I Marzia realizes she has unwittingly revealed her secret love for Cesare to the vengeful Emilia. In her aria "E'folia se nascondete" Marzia sings of the folly of lovers who try to conceal their true emotions. Because she is referring to her love for Cesare, it is perhaps not a coincidence that this aria refers back to his opening aria with regards to its key, meter, thematic contours, and dance rhythms (a minuet and passepied respectively).

---

of Vinci arias by Maria Angeles Peters: *Leonardo Vinci Arie d'opera* (Nuova Era 6997); the recording of these arias was preceded by a staged production of Vinci's *Catone in Utica* in December, 1997 in Lugo featuring Maria Angeles Peters as Marzia and directed by Rinaldo Alessandrini conducting the Orchestra Sinfonia dell'Emilia-Romagna.

[52] The surviving Acts II and III have been recorded by Claudio Scimone and I Solisti Veneti, with Cecilia Gasdia in the role of Cesare (Erato ECD 88142).

Marzia's next aria, "In che ti'offende," is a slow minuet with a suggestion of sarabande. In this scene, which continues the confrontation between the ladies, Emilia openly accuses Marzia of being in love with Cesare. Marzia obliquely replies in her aria by asking Emilia why she scorns her love, why she despises her dream. Marzia's rhetorical questions are set to phrygian cadences followed by grand pauses; even the opening ritornello ends with a phrygian cadence—one of the few preludes in Vinci's arias that do not close in the tonic:

Example 7.10 "In che ti'offende" *Catone in Utica* II/vi

The theme is a major-mode equivalent of Fulvio's "Piagendo ancora" from Act I. It is possible that Marzia is making an ironic reference to Emilia's attachment to Fulvio (whose aria refers, via a simile, to the grieving Emilia).

Marzia's sprightly B-flat major aria "Sò, che godendo vai" with its busy violin obbligato, coming after her admission of love for Cesare and her father's violent reaction, creates something of an anticlimax to Act II. Metastasio does not help matters by having Marzia blame the whole violent incident on Emilia and Arbace.[53] Perhaps the reason for this restraint is that Vinci has reserved Marzia's violent outburst for Act III when she makes her frenetic farewell to Cesare. Her aria "Confusa, smarrita spiegarti vorrei" is an agitated F-minor *aria parlante*, the counterpart of Catone's "Dovea svenarti."[54] The first three lines of the *scenario* aria text are treated as *ternario* couplets and set as short fragments of three quavers each, which are in turn enchained onto the syncopated accompaniment of the bass, giving the aria a surging breathless quality:

---

[53] This annoying tendency of many of Metastasio's characters to shirk responsibility in difficult situations can be regarded as one of the poet's major flaws as a dramatist. Both "So che godendo vai" and "In che t'offende" are included on the Vinci disc by Maria Angeles Peters (See fn. 50).

[54] In Leo's setting of *Catone in Utica*, not only does he employ the *aria agitata* for "Dovera svenarti allora" and "Confusa smarita,' but uses it as well for Marzia's aria at the end of Act II, resulting in three agitated fast-tempo/quadruple-meter/minor mode arias in close proximity.

Example 7.11 "Confusa, smarrita" *Catone in Utica* III/ii

[Musical example with text: Con-fu-sa, smar-ri-ta! Spie-gar-ti vor-re-i! Che fos-ti... che se-i...! In-ten-di-mi oh Di-o!/ Oh Di-o!/ Par-lar non pos-s'i-o!/ Oh Di-o!/ Mi sen-to mo-rir!/ Oh Di — o!/ Mi sen-to mo-rir!/ Mi se-to mo-rir!/]

This effect is enhanced by the lack of opening ritornello and the confused interruptions in Marzia's speech, indicated in the libretto by ellipses and realized in the music by grand pauses and the frenzied repetitions of "oh Dio"—a phrase that had greater impact then than now, hence the need for the "avvisi" at the beginning of most Italian libretti. In the second vocal period, when more extended phrases are formed (beginning at the end of Example 7.11), the melody tends to hang upon a single note and its octave creating a frozen, almost zombie-like effect. Although Vinci had recently employed these breathless minor-mode enchainments in a comic context, in Flacco's "Mistiro sbadiglio" from *La caduta* (see above), beginning with "Confusa, smarrita" they would become a standard formula for distressed heroes and heroines in the *aria agitata* of mid-century *opera seria*.

The frenetic declamation of "Confusa, smarrita" is continued and intensified in "Pur veggo alfine un raggio." This extended accompanied recitative takes place in the infamous subterranean aqueduct and, like Andromaca's monologue in *Astianatte*, dominates the entire scene. Marzia tries to make her escape through the aqueduct to the harbor where she will meet up with her brother, the admiral of the Republican fleet.[55]

---

[55] Marzia's escape from Utica probably derives from the escape of the Roman senators by ship in Plutarch; Catone's subsequent pursuit of Marzia, to ensure she has not remained behind with Caesar, derives from Cato's trip to the harbor to ensure the safe passage of the senators. Plutarch, *The Lives*, 955.

The initial sustained accompaniment, in which Marzia describes the darkness and gloom, changes to tremolo as she expresses her fear—the repeated monotone appropriately introducing the phrase "aere ristretto." Marzia arrives at the end of the passage only to find the exit blocked; her fear is depicted by the diminished sevenths, while the blocked exit is depicted by reiterated staccato arpeggios. When she hears the footsteps and voices of people echoing through the passage, the strings play lively figuration reinforced by the addition of horns. The use of wind instruments in Italian recitative is rare before the later eighteenth century.[56] As the sounds advance towards her, the frightened Marzia hides, and the accompanied recitative concludes in E-flat major, the key with which it began, as Emilia and her henchmen enter to set an ambush for Cesare.

While Emilia's attempt to murder Cesare is prevented by the arrival of Catone, whose attempt to arrest Cesare is, in turn, prevented by the arrival of Fulvio with news that Utica has capitulated to the Romans. Catone and Emilia throw down their swords in defeat thereby setting up the dramatic situation for the quartet. In the quartet, Cesare and Marzia try to placate Emilia and Catone who reply they only want vengeance and death. This quartet is similar to the one in *Farnace* and the trios in *La Rosmira* and *Gismondo*; like them it coincides with the dramatic climax prior to the dénouement. Because of Vinci's penchant for writing ensembles, combined with the omission of the quartet in Metastasio's subsequent revision of the libretto, one can assume that the idea for the ensemble came from the composer and not the poet. Although musically a fine piece, this ensemble is not quite as successful as some of Vinci's others; the dramatic situation, with the victor placating the vanquished, is contrived and musical contrast between the characters largely ignored. The absence of an opening ritornello and the late introduction of the "corni di caccia e trombini" playing fanfare material during the subsequent ritornellos may have been intended to represent the battle taking place in the city. Although the contrived manner in which Metastasio stuffs all his characters into the "condotto" makes one sympathize with Metastasio's critics, the novel effects of this scene —the Piranesian aqueduct, with Marzia groping her way through the darkness, the subterranean rumblings from the battle above and the climactic ensemble—compensate for the awkwardness with which they are initiated.

*Catone in Utica* can be regarded as one of Vinci's finest achievements. A high level of inspiration is maintained throughout most of the score in both the arias and the recitatives; the latter, both simple and

---

[56] By way of contrast, J. S. Bach frequently added oboes, flutes, and even trumpets and drums to certain cantata recitatives.

accompanied, are particularly impressive. The few flaws that do arise, most notably in Act II, are mitigated by the role of Catone, which is one of the finest in all of Vinci's operas.

## *Catone* Revisions and Revivals

In response to the criticisms of the Roman public, Metastasio rewrote much of Act III, and this revised version was used the next year in Florence and Venice.[57] The aqueduct scene was considerably shortened, taking place in front rather than inside the offending structure, and Catone's suicide was completely removed from the stage, being merely reported by Marzia in a brief recitative. That he had not renounced his original ending is proven by Metastasio's insistence that both versions be published when Bettinelli brought out his edition of the *Opere* in 1733.[58]

The Florentine production was a revival of Vinci's opera with Metastasio's revised finale and several new arias which appear to be parodies of arias from other works by Vinci.[59] Although Vinci and Metastasio were at the time busy in Rome with the première of *Semiramide riconosciuta*, these revisions suggest that both may have been involved in the Florentine production, perhaps with their colleague, the Florentine castrato Gaetano Berenstadt, serving as intermediary.[60] As with the Florentine *L'Ernelinda*, this revival of *Catone* was produced a year later at neighboring Livorno.[61]

The production of *Catone* at the Teatro San Giovanni Grisostomo in Venice was the première of a new setting by Leonardo Leo.[62] If one compares Leo's and Vinci's settings of *Catone in Utica,* one notices many correspondences, too many in fact to dismiss them as coincidence

---

[57] Clementi assumed that Metastasio made the changes during the Roman production in order to "assicurato un piano successo" (Clementi, *Il Carnevale Romano*, II, 4), but this seems rather unlikely since such an extensive revison should have produced a revised version of the libretto and a revised setting of the finale to be included with the alternate arias. Thus it would seem that the revison was done by Metastasio for either the Venetian or Florentine productions or for both.

[58] *Pietro Metastasio, Tutte le Opere*, II, 1399.

[59] Strohm, *Italienische Opernarien*, II, 231; libretto in I-Bc -Fc -Mc -Rb; Sartori, *I libretti italiani* (No. 5233).

[60] That very season Berenstadt was singing for Vinci in the première of *Semiramide* in Rome and his favored position with the composer and poet is manifest in the expansive role of his character, Jarba, which was then cut back substantially in the Venetian production and in Metastasio's later revision of the libretto.

[61] Libretto in I-Bc; Sartori *I libretti italiani* (N. 5236). According to Strohm, *Catone* was also produced at Brescia during Carnival 1731 and perhaps at Genoa as well; Strohm, *Italienische Opernarien*, II, 231.

[62] Leonardo Leo, Op. cit.

or part of a common style.[63] Some of these same parallels would later turn up again in Vivaldi's setting of the libretto for Verona in 1737, thereby linking it with Vinci's via Leo's setting. With the continued resetting of Metastasian dramas, musical parallels in settings of the same text become something of a tradition.[64]

The Neapolitan production of Vinci's *Catone in Utica* from November of 1732 retained the original ending, but added an intermezzo.[65] A complete score from this production is found in the Biblioteca dell'Abbazia in Montecassino; although some arias have been omitted and others replaced, most of the new pieces are parodies of arias from other Vinci operas.[66] Subsequent revivals may also have taken place in Perugia the following year and in Bologna the year after that.[67] When Vinci's *Catone in Utica* was produced in Venice at the Teatro San Cassiano in 1747, it was augmented with arias by Jommelli.[68]

---

[63] For example, as in Vinci's opera, in Leo's: 1."Non ti minaccio" begins without opening ritornello with voice and volins in unison; 2. "O nel sen di qualche stelle" is set in D major with triadic themes and busy figuration; 3. "Se in campo armato" is set in D-major duple meter for trumpets and oboes with initial colartura flourishes on "armato;" 4. "Dovea svenarti" is conceived as an *arie parlante* in minor-mode duple meter; 5. "Confusa, smarrita" is set in F-minor duple meter with chromaticism and the same interlocking three-note rhythmic patterns between voice and bass.

[64] See the parallel comparisons in Hellmuth Christian Wolff, "Italian Opera 1700-1750" in *Opera and Church Music: 1630-1750*, V.

[65] Libretto in I-NC, CS-Pu, US-Nyp; Sartori, *I libretti italiani* (No. 5238).

[66] 126 E20, 3 vols. bound as one (20 X 27cm.), lacking the opening sinfonio and title page. Strohm, *Italienische Opernarien*, II, 231.

[67] According to Strohm, the Bolognese production from Carnival 1734 (I-Bc) was based on Vinci's score with added arias by other composers, while Sartori lists the music as "di diversi." On the other hand, one of the libretti for a production in Perugia in 1733 (I-Fc) attributes the music to Vinci. Sartori, *I libretti italiani* (Nos. 5240 and 5241).

[68] Libretto in I-Rsc -Vgc, US-Au -Wc (Schatz 10754); Sartori, *I libretti italiani* (No. 5259).

# 8

# THE WEDDING AT PARMA

## *Fratello* Leonardo

Vinci cut short his stay in Rome during Carnival 1728 and returned to Naples. His original leave of absence would have been for four months and yet he returned after only two (see below). According to the records at S. Caterina a Formiello, Vinci became a member of the Congregazione del Rosario on the first of February:

> Leonardo Vinci, Maestro della Regal Cappella, has been received as a brother in our congregation on February 1, 1728 with the entrance fee of six ducats which he promises to pay at the time of his death and the usual monthly fee from this day henceforth.[1]

Although Villarosa attributes Vinci's membership in the Neapolitan confraternity to his "pio e religioso" character,[2] Florimo provides the following anecdote:

> Having conceived a serious passion for a Roman Lady from a class much different from his, to forget her, he went to take the habit of a monk in 1728 in the Congregation of the Rosary located in the cloister of the monastery of S. Caterina a Formiello.[3]

While there is a possibility that Vinci was motivated by a love affair with a Roman Lady (see Chapter 10), Di Giacomo accuses Florimo of creating the false impression that Vinci had actually taken holy orders, explaining that the composer's membership in the Congregazione was not that of "frate" or monk but rather of "confrate" or lay

---

[1] *Libro maggiore ove stanno ascritti li Fratelli della Venerabile Congregazione del SS. Rosario construtta dentro il chiostro della Real Chiesa di S. Caterina a Formello, Anno 1725*; quoted in Salvatore Di Giacomo, *I quattro antichi conservatorii di musica di Napoli*, II, 84. These records are no longer at S. Caterina a Formiello, nor can they be found at the other depositories for this type of material in Naples, the Archivio Storico Diocesano and the Archivio di Stato.
[2] Marchese di Villarosa, *Memorie dei compositori di musica del Regno di Napoli*, 223.
[3] Francesco Florimo, *La scuola musicale di Napoli e i suoi conservatori*, II, 187.

brother.[4] Fétis, for his part, saw no contradiction between piety and romance: "following the morals of the time, Vinci's pious devotion, would not have prevented him from loving the ladies."[5]

## Congregazione del Rosario

The Congregation of the Rosary was not a monastic order but, rather, a series of fraternities under the direction of the Dominican order made up of both *spirituale de fratelli* and *temporale de fratelli,* with a specific set of rules for each class of brethren.[6] The goal of the Congregazione del Santissimo Rosario in the cloister of the Royal Convent of S. Catterina a Formello, according to its statutes from 1744, was to fight against "our enemies, the world, the devil, and the flesh" through "the assistance of Maria *Sempre Virgine*," who has rewarded us with "her Holy Rosary."[7] Besides the principles of humility, charity, and obedience which are an essential part of becoming a "true son of Maria," the *fratello* is obliged "to practice works of mercy, to avoid strife and dissension, to always maintain a peace with all, and to set an example to others."[8] The *fratello* is advised to be "frequent in the sacraments, thereby making their devotions every Sunday."[9] The devotions of the Brethren are described in some detail:

> Upon entering the Congregation, the Fratello takes holy water and crosses himself and very modestly and with composure, kneels and salutes the Virgin with three Ave Marias. . . Having made the reverence to the Altar, in turn, reverences the Prior in his place and the others on the bench and to the other Brethren. . . and then goes and sits down in his place where he remains quiet and modest in everything during his time in the Congregation. When they say the Litany and recite the Rosary, and likewise when they celebrate the Holy Mass, he will be on his knees in complete devotion.[10]

---

[4] Di Giacomo, *I quattro antichi conservatorii*, II, 84.

[5] François-Josef Fétis, *Biographie Universelle*, 357.

[6] *Regole e Constituzioni della Unbile Congreg.ne del SS.mo Rosario, eretta dentro il Chiostro del Real Convento di S.ta Catt.a à Formello, 1744.* These statutes can now be found in manuscript in the Archivio di Stato in Naples, in the collection Cappellano Maggiore Statuti e Congregazione, B. 118/32.

[7] Ibid.

[8] Ibid.

[9] Ibid.

[10] Ibid.

This, then, is how Leonardo Vinci was supposed to spend his Sundays when he was in Naples. Although the *spirituale de Fratelli* participated directly in the devotions, prayed for the souls of the departed brethren, and took part in processions in honor of the Virgin Mary, this was hardly an ascetic order. The observances of the lay brethren, or *temporale de fratelli,* were in the spirit of the eighteenth century, in the tradition of the *honnete homme* who is modest and composed in all things, including his devotions— hence the importance of the word "modesto" in the description above. The pragmatic aspects of the lay practice come out very clearly in the admonishments to attend Mass every Sunday and not to talk or show off in church and to maintain a spirit of harmony within the ranks, suggesting that this was not always the case within the congregations. There was undoubtedly a social aspect to the Congregation common to most fraternities and this had to be balanced with the pious foundations of the order.

The other important aspect of the Congregation, which it shared with most other lay fraternities and sororities, was its connection to the *culto dei morti*. Not only was the Congregazione concerned for the spiritual and physical welfare of its members in this life (including free though limited access to the Congregation's "medico"), but also with the passing into the next. The Statutes are dominated by issues concerning the burial of its members and the praying for their souls in Purgatory. In fact the initial description of the burial services has a definite flavor of a funeral home advertisement:

> When it comes to the death of a Fratello, the funeral will be executed only by the Brethren, as is practised by the most conspicuous congregations of this City, who in habit of the Confraternity come to take the body from its home and take it to the church. Before the Church door, the Most Reverend Fathers will receive it, and they will sing the "Libera" with candles in hand according to the usual practice. They will celebrate for the soul of each deceased Fratello, a sung mass over the body if it is in the morning, as is the practice and a *Messe cento lette*.[11]

In the description of the funeral practice, there is an emphasis on the importance of the gathering of the Fratelli around the body of the deceased, for moral support, spiritual power and personal prestige. All of the Fratelli were obliged to take part in the proceedings regardless of their station:

---

[11] Ibid.

> When the death of some Fratello of the Congregazione occured, or Sorella if she is a wife or family member of the Fratello, all the Brethren must gather around the body, dressed as confrati and take part in that which is established....[12]

Therein lay the power of the proceedings of the Congregazione, wherein each Fratello was guaranteed a solemn and prestigious funeral attended by the entire congregation. With the death of a Fratello or Sorella, each member "must pay ten granna...or if he has the authority deputed, he must say a Mass for the soul of the Departed or say the Rosary *di 15 poste* or an office."[13] Therefore all of the benefits of the Congregazione came at a price. While the *spirituale de Fratelli* provided most of these services, the *temporale de fratelli* paid various fees. Besides the death fee and the entrance fee, there was a regular monthly *mesate* of fifteen grana. To ensure that these fees were paid, there were specific punishments for falling behind in the payments (see Chapter 10).

Considering how popular and fashionable these confraternities were in eighteenth-century Naples, there was undoubtedly a certain prestige in joining them—something of the modern "you have arrived" ploy used in marketing luxury products. On the other hand, considering the prominent aspect of the *culto dei morti,* joining these institutions undoubtedly came along with a certain realization on the part of the initiate that life does not last forever. Taken from the perspective of the composer's career, both aspects were probably significant when Leonardo Vinci joined the Congregazione dell' Santissimo Rosario in February of 1728.

While one would assume that his membership in the Congregation of the Rosary would have encouraged Vinci to compose more oratorios and sacred music, this was apparently not the case. After 1725 one cannot identify any sacred music or references to sacred music by Vinci, unless the *Maria Dolorata* dates from this period.[14] The other peculiarity about Vinci's entry in the Congregazione del SS. Rosario is the deferring of the entrance fee, which suggests that the composer was short of cash, this in spite of the fact that he had

---

[12] Ibid.

[13] Ibid.

[14] Perhaps the sacred parodies of several Vinci cantatas originated at this time; these sacred parodies are the subject of a study by Teresa Maria Gialdroni, "Leonardo Vinci e la cantata spirituale a Napoli nella prima metà del settecento," *Musica senza aggettivi: studi per Fedele d'Amico*, ed. Agostino Zino (Florence: Leo S. Olschki, 1991), 123-34.

just completed two major opera commissions in Naples and Rome and should have been solvent. An additional entry for Vinci in the *Libro maggiore* of the Congregazione del Santissimo Rosario states simply "Salda maggio 1728."[15] This would suggest that Vinci had settled something—perhaps he had paid the entrance fee or, at least, made arrangements for it to be paid upon his death.

## Frugoni's Wedding Opera

Vinci spent the late spring and early summer of 1728 in Parma where he provided music for celebrations connected with the marriage of Antonio Farnese Duke of Parma to Enrichetta d'Este of Modena. Vinci's request for a leave of absence from the Neapolitan court, dated April 2, 1728, indicates that it was conceived as an extension of the leave already obtained for the production of *Catone in Utica* in Rome during the recent Carnival:

> Leonardo Vinci Vice maestro of the Real Cappella, requesting specifically from Your Eminence in order to conclude some of his business affairs, needs to extend by another four months the leave already granted by Your Eminence and should the supplicant be worthy to be favoured with another four months, he will have eight in all....[16]

The original leave of absence, probably beginning December 1, 1727, would have been extended to August 1, 1728. It is not known why the request was made as an extension, since Vinci had cut short his stay in Rome by two months and had been in Naples since February. In contrast to Vinci's other applications, which clearly indicate the operatic nature of the leave, the unspecified "affari" of this leave may be due to the delicate political situation in Parma at this time (see below).

As part of the celebrations connected with the marriage of Antonio Farnese Duke of Parma to Enrichetta d'Este of Modena, Vinci, in conjunction with the court poet Carlo Innocenzio Frugoni, produced the opera *Medo* and the equestrian ballet *Le nozze di Nettuno L'equestre con Anfitrite*.[17] The ducal wedding had actually taken place

---

[15] Quoted in Di Giacomo, *I quattro antichi conservatorii*, II, 84.
[16] Archivio di Stato di Napoli: Segreteria dei Viceré, fascio 1795, documenti pervenuti 2-IV-1728.
[17] Frugoni also edited a large anthology of poetry in celebration of the wedding, consisting of more than six hundred pages of poems and sonnets in Italian and

in February of 1728 in Modena, the couple returning to Parma without ceremony a few days later.[18] While *Le nozze di Nettuno* was premièred on July 22 for the official entry of the Duke and his new bride into Parma, *Medo*, produced earlier in May, can be regarded as the climax of the unofficial, albeit actual marriage celebrations. The libretto of *Medo*, rather than being designated in celebration of the marriage, is simply dedicated to the new bride Enrichetta d'Este who is already described as "Duchessa Regnante di Parma."[19] Because of the gala occasion, a new set of elaborate scenes were created by Pietro Righini accompanied by detailed stage descriptions.[20] The complete set of stage designs were engraved and published by Martin Engelbrecht in 1735 (see Plates 22-29 on pages 238-41).

*Medo* was premièred in May of 1728 in the Teatro Ducale, the same theatre where three years earlier Vinci's *Il trionfo di Camilla* had been produced. It featured an outstanding cast:

Medo: Antonio Bernacchi  Asteria: Costanza Posterla
Giasone: Carlo Broschi   Medea: Vittoria Tesi
Perse: Giovanni Paita    Artace: Dorotea Lolli
    Stage design: Pietro Righini
    Choreography: Francesco Massimiliano Pagnini
    Costumes: Natale Canziani

The last time Vinci had worked with Farinello was in *Eraclea*, when he appeared with Tesi. La Tesi, who more recently had portrayed Andromaca for Vinci, held the title of "Virtuosa" in the service of the Dukes of Parma. Vinci was also familiar with the tenor Paita, who had appeared in *Camilla* and *Siroe*. Both Bernacchi and Posterla were

---

Latin in honor of the bridal couple. Most of the writers are obscure, except for Frugoni and Vinci's countryman, Giambattista Vico; Carlo Innocenzio Frugoni *Poesie per le acclamatissime nozze delle Altezze Serenissime. . .Antonio Farnese duca di Parma...Colla...Principessa Enrichetta d'Este* (Parma, 1728).

[18] Alan Yorke-Long, *Music at Court: Four Eighteenth Century Studies*, preface by Patrick Trevor-Roper and introduction by Edward Dent (London: Weidenfeld and Nicolson, 1954), 15.

[19] Libretto in I-Bc -Mb -Moe -PAc -Rsc -Vgc, F-Pn, US-Wc (Schatz No. 10748); Sartori, *I libretti italiani* (No. 15327).

[20] If all eight of Rhigini's scenes were completely new creations in wood and canvas, this would have been an extraordinary event. According to William C. Holmes, one criterion by which to judge an opera impressario, was the number of new sets that his productions generated. Luca Casimirio degli Albizzi, the foremost impressario in Florence during this period, was praised by contemporaries for having produced "a total of nine new stage settings" during his career; quoted in William C. Holmes, "Righini in Florence: an Artistic Conflict" *Early Music* (November 1989).

***Plate 22.*** *Pietro Righini, Stage Design for* Medo, *Act I/i: "Lavish arch near the palace consecrated to the Sun and to Diana, flanked by a ancient grove of laurels with a distant view of a vast arid countryside, with flocks, herds, and shepherds. On the right of the arch rises the statue of the Sun and on the left that of Diana."*[21]

***Plate 23.*** *Pietro Righini, Stage Design for* Medo, *Act I/ix: "Attrium in the palace with a ground-level loggia bathed by the Fasi River, beyond which is seen the ruins of a demolished suburb."*[22]

---

[21] [Frugoni], *Medo: dramma per musica*, p.12. Reproduced from Martin Engelbrecht, *Theatralische Veränderungen vorgestellt in eine zu Mayland gehaltenen Opera inventiert von Pietro Righini* (Augsburg: Kupferstecher, und Kunst-Verleger, c. 1735), pl. 6. Because the scene descriptions are more detailed in the libretto, the plate citations have been taken from the libretto (either within the act or from the "Mutazioni di scene" on 12-13), hence the quotations marks and composite citations.

[22] Frugoni, 12; Engelbrecht/Righini, pl.3.

**Plate 24.** Pietro Righini, Stage Design for Medo, Act II/i: "Small gallery adjoining the apartments of Enotea all ornamented in marble and precious stones, with niches and statues representing the legend of Perse, and amid these is the statue of Medea with a golden veil on a spear" [on the far left].[23]

**Plate 25.** Pietro Righini, Stage Design for Medo, Act II/ix: "Royal baths and in the middle a grand fount ornamented with groups of Tritons and Nereids."[24]

---

[23] Frugoni, 39; Engelbrecht/Righini, pl. 2.
[24] Frugoni, 12; Engelbrecht/Righini, pl. 5.

**Plate 26.** Pietro Righini, Stage Design for Medo, Act III/i: "Place remote from the palace shaded by dense cypresses with a large magic grotto formed of rough tuffa rock, among which is seen dark images and frightful serpents. From the one side is seen the instruments of the divinatory art and on the other those for necromancy and in the circle laden with bundles of poison and other herbs and poisonous roots, the skulls of dogs and wolves etc."[25]

**Plate 27.** Pietro Righini, Stage Design for Medo, Act III/v: "Courtyard in the quarters of the Royal Guard with a view of the cell of Artace at an angle."[26]

[25] Frugoni, 59; Engelbrecht/Righini, pl. 8.
[26] Frugoni, 64; Engelbrecht/ Righini, pl. 4.

# THE WEDDING AT PARMA

***Plate 28.*** *Pietro Righini, Stage Design for* Medo, *Act III/xi: "Horrid menagerie for beasts where the death of Antinoo is to be carried out."*[27]

***Plate 29.*** *Pietro Righini, Stage Design for* Medo, *Act III/scena ultima: "The scene is transformed and appears as a magnificent palace with grand staircase in view, from which Asteria descends attended by Artace with guards and followed by ladies and knights of the court and rejoicing people. On the floor of the Palace one can see in the niches, two regal thrones."*[28]

[27] Frugoni, 71; Engelbrecht/Righini, pl. 7.
[28] Frugoni, 79; Engelbrecht/Righini, pl. 1.

new singers for Vinci. Bernacchi had appeared with Farinello in Bologna the previous year in Orlandini's *La fedeltà coronata*, a production in which the Bolognese Bernacchi actually attracted greater applause than his more celebrated rival.[29] The idea for pairing Bernacchi and Farinello in *Medo* undoubtedly originated from this production.

The libretto to *Medo* is by Carlo Innocenzio Frugoni, the court poet at Parma, who had previously revised *Il trionfo di Camlla* for Vinci in 1724. Frugoni's drama is based on the legend of Medus, son of Medea and her second husband Aegeus. Medus, with the help of his mother, regains the throne of his grandfather Aeetes, which had been lost in a struggle with Perse, a fraternal struggle between two sons of the ancient sun god Helius or Sol.[30]

> **Synopsis**: Perse, King of Colco, lives in perpetual fear because an oracle predicted that he would be killed by a descendent of his brother Aeta, whose kingdom he has usurped. Perse's other problem is that in punishment for this usurpation, the goddess Diana caused the kingdom to be afflicted by drought. In the opening scene. Perse comes to the Temple of the Sun and Diana to ask his father to intercede for him. During this ceremony, the disguised Medea arrives on her dragon chariot and introduces herself as Enotea, priestess of Diana, come to set things right for Perse. Besides trying to appease Diana and protect hIMself from the offspring of Aeta, Perse also seeks to win the heart of his captive Asteria not only to satisfy his amorous desires, but also to legitimize his conquest of her father's kingdom of Iberia. Asteria, however, is in love with Antonoo of Corinth who is actually Medo disguised as a Greek prince in search of Medea. Medo's purpose is twofold: to punish Medea for her crimes and to avenge himself against Perse for the usurpation of his grandfather's throne. A subplot is created when Medea's husband Giasone arrives on the island disguised as Climaco. Medea instantly recognizes Giasone. She becomes doubly infuriated when he betrays her again by falling in love with her own transformation of Enotea.

---

[29] Giovenale Sacchi, *Vita del cavaliere Don Carlo Broschi detto il Farinello*, ed. Alessandro Abbate with a preface by Vittorio Paliotto (Naples: Flavio Pagano, 1994; originally pubished in Venice, 1784), 38.

[30] Edward Trip, *Crowell's Handbook of Classical Mythology* (New York: Thomas Y. Crowell, 1970) 362-63. Helius was identified with Pheobus Apollo and several of his stories became part of the Apollo myth, most notably that of Phaeton (Ibid, 267-69, & 65).

Medea tells Perse to sacrifice all the Greeks on the Island in order to appease Diana's anger. By this advice she hopes to kill her son Medo who intends to punish her for trying to poison his half-brother Teseo and plotting against himself and his father, Egeo. On Asteria's urging, Medo goes into hiding but is captured. Asteria helps Medo escape, but both are caught and imprisoned. Although Perse offers to pardon Asteria, she stubbornly refuses. To punish Giasone, Medea has him give Perse a poisoned talisman which drives the king mad. Perse commits suicide and Medea implicates Giasone in the crime. In the sacrificial scene Medea, with axe in hand, is about to execute both Giasone and the disguised Medo, but when she comes face to face with her son, she cannot bring herself to do the deed. Her maternal love even compels her to forgive Giasone. With Perse's suicide, Asteria and Medo can be united as King and Queen of Colco and Iberia and Medea and Giasone, now reconciled, can return to Thessalia.[31]

This is, without doubt, the most contrived and complicated libretto that Vinci set to music. Three of the six characters are in disguise until the end of the drama. Although the disguises of Medo and Medea are an essential part of the original legend, the superficial addition of a third disguised character pushes credibility to the brink; to confuse things further, these characters go by their assumed names throughout the opera, being designated by their real names only in the cast list. Athough no mention is made of the infanticide from the Jason and Medea tragedy, Frugoni emphasizes the attempted infanticide of

---

[31] Although there is considerable variation in the legend, Frugoni departs from it in several significant ways. In the original legend both Medea and Medus were banished from Athens by Aegeus after Medea tried to poison Theseus, Aegeus' son from another marriage, in order to secure the succession to the Athenian throne for her son. Medea sends Medus back to her homelnd of Colchis, hoping that together they can reclaim the throne of her father Aetees. Upon arriving in Colchis, Medus introduces himself as Hipotes, son of KinG Creon of Corinth come to seek revenge on Medea for kiling his father and sister—Creon having convinced Jason to divorce Medea and marry his daughter. Perses suspects that this Hipotes is one of the dreaded descendants of Aetees and has him arrested. Diana causes the drought after the arrest of Medus, which, in turn, brings the disguised Medea to Colchis as a priestess of Diana. Having heard that the son of Creon is in Colchis searching for revenge, she convinces Perses to deliver Hipotes to her as a sacrifice to Diana, hoping to rid herself of an old enemy. It is only in the temple scene when she realizes that Hipotes is none other than her son Medus, that she promptly hands him her sword and he slays Perses, thereby fulfilling the prophacy of the Oracle. (*Crowell's Handbook of Classical Mythology*, 362-63.)

the Medus legend (see footnote 31) by removing the accidental element, having Medea actually intent on sacrificing her son. This change, however, weakens the sacrificial scene, where the focus should be on Medea's recognition of her son, the pivotal event of the drama that instantly transforms her from executioner to king-maker. In Frugoni's libretto, Medea has known all along that the Prince of Corinth is Medo and it is only the actual sight of her son that compels her to forgive both him and Giasone.

Frugoni was aware of at least some of the faults of his first drama. In the *Argomento* he self-consciously explains:

> that the many licences taken without sufficient support in this drama, will be excused as trifles by discrete and clever judges...invented solely to serve the genius of the music, the beauty of the scene, and the delectation of the audience.[32]

Frugoni requests that the drama not be judged prejudicially by placing it in "the rank of grave and judicious tragedies," a request he repeats in one of his letters:

> Do not imagine to see a work that exhibits rules from Aristotle and the best tragedies. In the story I must have recourse to satisfy the primary intentions of those who command me. I am finished; but what have I accomplished? For my part I do not know.[33]

Although the plot is overly complex and many of the situations contrived, there are also certain romantic elements to the libretto, such as the enigmatic figure of Medea, the madness of Perse, the spiritual intensity of Asteria, and the violence of the sacrificial scene which anticipate Frugoni's later reforms in collaboration with Tomaso Traetta.

The superficial addition of Giasone to the Medus legend may be motivated by a topical reference. Duke Antonio Farnese inherited the title from his older brother Francesco, who died childless in 1727. Being the last of the male line of the Farnese, Don Antonio's first concern upon inheriting the title was to marry and produce an heir, the next in the line of succession being Don Carlos, the son of Elizabeth Farnese and Philip V of Spain. In order to produce this much-desired

---

[32] [Carlo Innocenzio Frugoni], *Medo: dramma per musica di Comante Eginetico, pastore arcade* (Parma: Eredi di Paolo Monti, 1728), 11.

[33] Extract from a letter to Atelmo Leucasiano, quoted in the preface to Frugoni's *Opere poetiche del signor abate Carlo Innocenzio Fugoni fra gli Arcadi Comante Eginetico*, I, xiv.

heir, Duke Antonio had to abandon his mistress, the Countess Borri.[34] The character of Giasone continually caught between two loves ,"l'antico e il nuovo," could represent Duke Antonio caught between his mistress Countess Borri and his bride Enrichetta d'Este, his eventual forgiveness representing some type of resolution of this love triangle.

Surprisingly, when set against this political background one could develop a subversive allegory. If one interprets Duke Antonio as Perse rather than Giasone, then Medea, who helps her son Medo regain the throne of Aeta, would represent Elizabeth Farnese and her attempts to gain a crown for "baby Carlos." Moreover, the background of the drought, as well as the references to "pertinace sterilezza" and "deplorabile sterilità" in the Argomento, could be oblique references to the Duke's inability to sire an heir. Like Medea, Elizabeth Farnese triumphed in the end. In January 1731 Duke Antonio died. Two days after the entry of Don Carlos into Parma in October of 1732, Frugoni's equestrian ballet *Ascanio venuto in Italia* was performed before the new Duke. Therefore it is possible that Frugoni incorporated this hidden allegory, realizing which way the succession winds were blowing.[35]

## *Medo*: Baggage Arias, Entrance Arias, and Righini's Sets

The official interpretation of Giasone as Duke Antonio could also account for the anomaly that this superficial addition to the drama is sung by the *primo uomo* extraordinaire, Farinello. Of the three roles Vinci created for Farinello, this is the finest, his six arias representing the composer at his most stylish.[36] While the production of Vinci's *Il trionfo di Camilla* produced sonnets in praise of Faustina and Scalzi from the pen of Frugoni (see Chapter 4), Farinello's two appearances

---

[34] Yorke-Long, *Music at Court*, 15.

[35] Frugoni probably depicted himsel in the character of Artace, who, in the cadet role as Perse's henchman, gets a considerable portion of text (including three arias), to describe his predicament, having sympathetic feelings for Asteria, yet loyally serving his master. This ambivalence allows him to suavely transfer his services to Asteria after the death of Perse and then in the coronation-like *scena ultima*, lead her entourage.

[36] There are two surviving complete manuscripts of *Medo*. The one in Brussels (2196, 3 Vols. 27 x 20 cm.) is signed by the copyist Francesco Faelli and, according to Strohm, originated in Parma (*Italienische Opernarien* II, 232).The manuscript is missing a title page and the final aria in Act II, "Navigante ch non spera," is in a different hand and on different paper (with triple crescents of the type used for Vinci's Venetian operas). With the exception of this aria, the manuscript is very neat and may have been executed for the court. The score in the Biblothèque du conservatoire national de musique in Paris (D. 11899) is described by Strohm as of

in Parma, in Capelli's *I fratelli riconosciuti* and Vinci's *Medo*, generated four sonnets in praise of the great castrato, plus an additional sonnet on his appearance in Bologna in 1727.[37]

By delaying the entrance of the star until the end of Act I, Frugoni intended to create a sense of expectancy in his audience. Farinello's entrance is given greater impact by his opening aria "Scherzo dell'onda instabile," which is not the usual miniature arietta but a full-scale *da capo* aria. At this point Climaco appears on a shipwrecked boat, singing a storm-at-sea simile as he rides in on the current (see Righini's stage design, complete with the little boat, in Plate 23, page 238). It is hard to believe that the audience would have taken this seriously, but according to Addison the London audience did so when Nicolino made a similar entrance in Handel's *Rinaldo* "exposed to a Tempest in Robes of Ermine, and sailing in an open Boat upon a Sea of Paste-board."[38] The opening theme is rather static, with all the phrases ending with the same caesura, as in 'Son Regina' from *Didone* but without the dramatic justification. This static theme gives way, however, to more lively passage work, particularly the triplet against duplet eighths, leading to the climactic syncopations and scale cadence:

Example 8.1 "Scherzo dell'onda instabile" *Medo*, Act I/xi

Roman origin. Both the Brussels and Paris scores have been incorrectly ascribed to a later hand, the former to Leo and the latter to Alessandro Scarlatti. There are also two aria collections that survive, both in the Santini-Sammlung in Münster (4262 and 4241). One of these collections is contained within appendices at the end of Acts II and III of the Roman manuscript of *Catone* (see chapter 7). The score in Brussels, from which the subsequent examples are taken, consists of the following musical numbers:

| | |
|---|---|
| 30 *da capo* arias | 2 ariettas |
| 1 *del segno* aria | 5 accompanied recitatives |
| 1 *da capo* ensemble | 1 arietta with Chorus |
| 2 sinfonias | 1 coro |

Totals: 43 set pieces (32 in *da capo* form)

[37] Frugoni, *Opere poetiche*, II, CCCIX-CCCXIII, 487-91.

[38] [Joseph Addison], *The Spectator* No. 5., Tuesday, March 6, 1711.

[musical notation: Las-ci-a che tor-ni à res-pi-rar — à res-pi-rar]

The actual storm at sea is relegated to the second section where it is depicted by the tremolo chordal accompaniment of the strings. Because "Scherzo dell'onda" is an entrance aria, Giasone/Climaco remains on stage and two scenes later sings a *da capo* aria. The delayed entrance, therefore, allows Farinello to have two *da capo* arias in close succession, giving his calculated late entrance great impact. This second aria, "Cervo in bosco," is also a simile aria. This simile about the wounded stag seems rather unusual following Giasone's reminiscence of his courtship of Medea. The aria is based on a strong heroic theme, of the type Pergolesi was to use in the "Sancta Mater istud agas" from his *Stabat Mater*, and features brilliant coloratura, particularly the difficult consecutive trills prior to the final ritornello and rapid passage work in the first violins.[39] As in the previous aria, the second section is highlighted by musical contrasts, this time a minuet in the parallel minor.

In "Sento due fiamme in petto," sung after Medea/Enotea accuses him of having betrayed Medea, Giasone describes himself caught between two loves, one new and one old. This concertante aria for oboe and strings is probably the aria that Frugoni celebrates in his Sonnet CCCXIII "Per l'incomparabile oboista il signor Alessandro Besozzi e il preddetto Signor Broschi." In his poem Frugoni praises these two soloists "who, with equal honor, performed a paragon in an aria," singling out in particular the way "the song and the sound compete and imitate one another" so that in the end the two soloists "together contesting with equal valor, share the gifts of Nature and Art."[40] To judge from the music as written, there was more imitation than competition, with the two parts conceived as a sonorous duet:

---

[39] "Cervo in bosco" was also performed in the production of Leo's *Catone* in Venice and subsequently included in the manuscript published in facsimile; see Leonardo Leo, *Catone in Utica*, 70 of *Italian Opera 1640-1770*, 155-160.

[40] Frugoni, *Opere poetiche*, Sonetto, CCCXIII.

Example 8.2 "Sento due fiamme in petto" *Medo*, Act II/iv

The competition undoubtedly came to the fore in the cadenzas, perhaps attaining something of the intensity of the celebrated duel between Farinello and the trumpeter in Rome. At the end of Act II, after Medea/ Enotea tempts Giasone with false hope, he decides that Enotea rather than Media is his best choice. In another simile aria, "Navigante, che non spera," he sings about navigating the waves to seek comfort on an alluring new beach. The bird-in-the-hand justification and the beach simile produce an effect that suggests the librettist may again be making sport of his patron through the character of Climaco/ Giasone. The aria is based on a descending arpeggio theme, with echo-like imitations in the upper strings. In the ritornello, the wide-ranging triplet arpeggios in the violins represent the waves, while the unusual parallel thirds in thirty-second notes seem to be related to the beach—their single appearance with the voice occurring in the second vocal period on the phrase "spiaggia lusinghiera." Like Farinello's opening aria, the melody and harmony are rather bland, but the special effects, the virtuoso vocal coloratura, and violin passage work, if performed skillfully, could bring the aria to life.[41]

[41] The *Largo* tempo seems rather out of place in this storm-at-sea aria and perhaps

In Act III Enotea/Medea tells Giasone to give Perse a talisman when he announces the news of Antinoo/Medo's capture, a talisman that she has poisoned. The obliging Giasone sings further of his amorous torments in "Innamorata dolce mia fiamma." This spirited heroic aria had been composed originally for Scalzi as "Con forza ascosa" in Act I of *La caduta de' Decemviri* (see Example 7.1 on page 207).[42] Later in the Act Giasone tells Medea that he has delivered the talisman, to which Enotea/Medea ironically replies that he will soon receive his just rewards for his passion. In a melancholic C-minor *Andante,* Giasone sings of how her promises console and flatter him. Although one could interpret this as musical irony suggesting the tragic overtones of Medea's promise, more likely it is another example of Vinci's penchant for employing the minor mode and moderate triple meter in amorous situations as a means of suggesting sexual passion.

Giasone was one of Farinello's favorite roles. Of the small number of "baggage arias" he recycled in other operas, three are from *Medo*.[43] During the next Carnival in Venice, Farinello introduced "Cervo in bosco" and "Scherzo dell'onda" into Leo's setting of *Catone in Utica*. "Cervo in bosco" was so successful that it was also introduced into the final opera of that same season, Pollarolo's *L'abbandono di Armida*.[44] Farinello included "Navigante che non spera" in Araja's *Demetrio* for Vincenza in 1734, one of his final appearances on the Italian stage.

Although the roles directly connected with the main plot are not as impressive, they contain some dramatically effective pieces. Perse makes his entrance in the introductory air and chorus "O'del giorno," in which he addresses a prayer to the Sun; his prayer is taken up in turn by Asteria, Medo, and Artace. Medo's imprisonment and escape in Act II produce two fine arias for Bernacchi. In "Vengo a voi, funesti orrori," Medo defies death now that he is inspired by Asteria's "presagio fortunato." This heroic coloratura aria

---

should be interpreted literally as "broadly" to allow for the correct execution of the special effects, rather than "slowly," which would place too much emphasis on the overly-diatonic harmony and melody.

[42] The overture to *Medo* was also borrowed from the same source; Hellmut Hell, *Die Neapolitanishe Opernsinfonie in der ersten Hälfte des 18.jahrhunderts*, 543.

[43] See list of Farinello's baggage arias in Robert Freeman, "Farinello and his Repertory" *Studies in Renaissance and Baroque Music in Honor of Arthur Mendel* ed. Robert L. Marshall (Kassel: Bärenreiter, 1974), 316.

[44] In "Farinello and his Repertory," Freeman implies that the aria was first performed in *Armida* before turning up in *Catone*, which is unlikely since the former is designated as "ultima sera di carnevale;" Sartori, *I libretti italiani* (No. 12).

in C major is characterized by extended passages of stubbornly-reiterated dominant four-two harmony, probably intended to accompany some type of defiant gesture. In a similar manner in "Incerto...dubbioso," Vinci uses expressive leaps of a major seventh generating jarring appoggiaturas and diminished harmony to highlight Medo's curse of the gods and perhaps to suggest a hero on the verge of madness:

Example 8.3 "Incerto...dubbioso" *Medo*, Act II/xii

Sung as Medo bids farewell to Asteria after escaping from prison, this agitated *aria parlante* in C minor is similar in both its dramatic situation and musical style to Marzia's "Confusa smarrita" from *Catone* (see Example 7.11 on page 228), employing an enchainment between melody and accompaniment to create a breathless effect. As in Marzia's "Confusa, smarrita," the connection is generated by the *senario* text which is broken into *ternario* couplets. The latter are emphasized by ellipses which are incorporated into Vinci's setting, falling between the three-note fragments of the melodic pattern.

In the simile aria "Se dal feroce nemico artiglio" at the end of Act II, Asteria compares Medo's escape from Perse's prison to the dove avoiding the enemy's talons. The syncopated subsidiary material of this heroic coloratura aria in F major represents the evasive flight of the dove. In Act III "Fra le catene" is sung as both Asteria and Medo are led off in chains to prison (see Righini's stage design, Plate 27 on page 240). This is another concerted aria, for solo violin and continuo. The violin solo, with its wide-ranging arpeggios and multiple stops, is distinguished by its rhythmic variety. The free mixture of dotted rhythms, lombards, triplets, and thirty-seconds creates a lively if somewhat diffuse effect more characteristic of the mid-century (see Example 8.4). Constanza Posterla, the singer who created the role of Asteria, was married

THE WEDDING AT PARMA                                              *251*

to the violin virtuoso Giovanni Piantanida and, since husband and wife often travelled together, one could assume that the solo was intended for her husband.[45]

Example 8.4  "Fra le catene" *Medo*, Act III/v

The sorceress Medea was conceived for the powerful alto voice and celebrated acting talents of Vittoria Tesi. Like Farinello, La Tesi is given an entrance *da capo* aria, sung after Medea descends in her magic chariot (see Righini's stage design Plate 22 on page 238). "Terra amica" provides for an appropriate introduction for the murderous sorceress as she addresses prayers to the Earth in the first section and to Diana in the second of the da capo aria. With its pounding dotted rhythms and disjunct declamatory melody, Medea's aria creates the effect of an incantation scene (see Example 8.5 on page 252). At the beginning of Act II, Medea has an extended monologue consisting of two accompanied recitatives enveloping an arietta. The monologue ties in closely with Pietro Righni's stage designs, a gallery "with niches and statues representing the family of Perse, and amid these is the

---

[45] Piantanida and Posteria appeared together in Russia, Holland, and England during the 1730s. *The New Grove*, "Piantanida, Giovanni" by Guido Salvetti.

Example 8.5 "Terra amica" *Medo*, Act I/iii

statue Medea with a golden veil on a spear (see Righini's stage design Plate 24 on p. 239). The initial accompanied recitative is addressed to the statues of her ancestors and contains a particularly striking passage when she sees the statue of her brother Absirto whom she murdered and dismembered when aiding Giasone's escape from Colco; the mysterious violin figuration depicting the ghost of Absirto changes to tremolo diminished harmony as she is overcome with guilt:

Example 8.6 "O Sole, o Padre" *Medo*, Act II/ii

The dotted rhythms of her initial aria return in the arietta "Quasi furia d'Acheronte" as Medea expresses her desire to avenge her betrayal by Giasone. The arietta passes into accompanied recitative as she resolves to murder both Giasone and Antinoo/Medo to satisfy this desire.

As the poisoned talisman drives him inexorably into madness, Perse has an extended monologue consisting of an accompanied recitative and *da capo* aria. While the accompanied recitative is as impressive as Medea's, the aria, "Sento l'ombra del mesto Germano," is somewhat flawed by its overabundance of diatonic harmony — the continual rattling away on the tonic and dominant of F major not being particularly suggestive of madness (though Vinci thought highly enough of the aria to reuse it later that year in *Il Farnace*).

The drama is resolved in the sacrificial scene as Medea abandons her plans for revenge, the resolution culminating in a trio for Medea, Medo, and Giasone. Like many of Vinci's ensembles, this one contains a double vocal exposition, accommodating the parallel statements of Medo and Giasone, and Medea's responses to each. Because of the pairing of Medo and Giasone against Medea, the trio passages are constructed as chamber duets with interpolations. The grouping of two voices against one is not for the purpose of conflict, the drama at this point having already reached a happy conclusion, but to distinguish two different reactions to the happy turn of events. As in many similar circumstances, the ensemble appears to have been an addition to the drama intended to satisfy the composer's penchant for writing vocal ensembles.

Instead of withdrawing, Medea says that the gloomy surroundings do not reflect her joy and she then transforms the scene into "a magnificent palace with grand staircase in view, from which Asteria descends attended by Artace with guards and followed by ladies and knights of the court and rejoicing people" (see Righini's stage design, Plate 29 on page 241). This transformation coincides with the traditional scene change for the *scena ultima*, demonstrating the restraint with which the supernatural is treated in the Arcadian *dramma per musica*. It is unfortunate that accompanied recitative was reserved for this superfluous transformation, while it is completely absent from the crucial sacrificial scene where it could have been used to much greater effect (as in Mozart's *Idomeneo*). The final miniature *coro* consists of only eight measures without repeats but was intended to be performed in conjunction with Massimiliano Pagnani's ballets, which provided "regular and pretty interruptions for the *coro*" thereby extending the finale to a more reasonable length.[46] In its elaborate set design and ballet, with the ornate staircase and throne and dancing courtiers, the finale to *Medo* resembles that to Handel's *Ariodante*. The latter, however, employed a musicians' gallery with wind band that played trio passages in the extended *ballo/coro* and rondeau. Righini had a reputaton for his "proud and uncivil manner" but to judge from the ingenious coordination between the staging and the drama and music, one would conclude that Vinci and Frugoni were able to work creatively with the difficult artist.[47]

*Medo* was revived in December 1735 as *Medea riconosciuta* at the Imperial Court at Vienna.[48] The score for this pasticcio revival survives in Vienna and features a new sinfonia, intermezzo, ballets, and ten replacement arias by other composers.[49]

## The Gala Equestrian Ballet

As already mentioned, the equestrian ballet *Le nozze di Nettuno L'equestre con Anfitrite* was the official entertainment "on the occasion celebrating the wedding of his most serene highness Antonio Farnese Duke of Parma and Enrichetta Princess of Este."[50] In this entertainment, Vinci and Frugoni collaborated with the aristocratic pupils of the Ducal Collegio de' Nobili in Parma. *Le nozze di Nettuno* was not premièred in the Teatro Ducale where *Medo* and *Camilla* had been presented, but in the old Teatro Farnese, one of the last and most famous of Renaissance theatres. The Teatro Farnese had not been used since the lavish wedding festivities of Duke Antonio's half-brother Odoardo and Princess Dorothea Sophia of Neuberg in 1690.[51] The extended delay between the actual marriage and the official celebrations in Parma may have been due to the renovations that were necessary for the old theatre. Equestrian ballet must have been something of a speciality of Parma; Monteverdi's *torneo Mercurio e Marte*

---

[46] Frugoni, *Medo: dramma per musica*, 80.
[47] Quoted in Holmes, "Rigini in Florence," 546.
[48] Libretto in A-Wn, D-Dl, Bfb, and US-Wc (Schatz No. 15311); Claudio Sartori, *I libretti italiani* (No. 16744).
[49] Ms. 12945 in the Österreichische Nationalbibliothek; Strohm, "Pasticci" in *Italienische Opernarien*, II, 277.
[50] Libretto in I-Bc -Bu -Mb -Tn -Vgc, GB-Lbm, US-U; Sartori, Op. cit, No. 16744. The title reads somewhat differently in the version of the libretto published in Frugoni, *Opere poetiche*, 7, 452-59.
[51] Yorke-Lang, *Music at Court*, 11-12.

contained an equestrian ballet and was produced at the same theatre by the pupils of the same College of Nobles in 1628.

Like Monteverdi's *Mercurio e Marte*, the music for Vinci's *Le nozze di Nettuno* has been lost. Both Frugoni's text and Righini's stage designs survive, providing an idea of what this unusual production was like.[52] The subject of *Le nozze di Nettuno* is the marriage of Neptune with Anfitrite. Although Neptune was originally a minor Roman marine deity, he gradually took on the attributes and mythology of the Greek god of the sea, Poseidon. Poseidon was also the god of horses, and for this reason he is most often depicted coursing through the waves in his horse-drawn chariot, trident in hand,[53] as best exemplified in the contemporary Fontana di Treve. In spite of this obvious horsy connection, Frugoni spends a goodly number of lines in both the poem and the scenario justifying the equestrian ballet. Nettuno and Anfitrite are obviously allegorical representations of Duke Antonio and Princess Enrichetta, their wedding celebrations becoming those of the ducal couple. The set represents the vestibule of Nettuno's palace, where the God of the Sea dresses his horses.

*Le nozze di Nettuno* consisted of an *Introduzione* sung by Nettuno, Anfitrite, and Proteo and an equestrian ballet danced by the pupils of the Noble College and their horses.[54] The *Introduzione* is divided into three scenes that frame the equestrian ballet in two parts. The opening scenes introduce the three protagonists: first Proteo in a recitative and arietta, and then Anfitrite and Nettuno in a recitative dialogue with *da capo* arias for both bride and groom. Following an ancient tradition, Proteo and the bridal pair make their entrance in elaborately decorated chariots accompanied by an entourage of marine divinities. These colorful entrances were accompanied by sinfonias; the bridal carriage, for example, was accompanied by "a vivacious sinfonia of wind instruments at a distance."[55]

---

[52] Pietro Righini's stage design for *Le nozze di Nettuno* is in the Bibliothèque de l'Arsenal in Paris and is reproduced in Irene Mamczarz, *Le Théatre Farèse de Parme et le drama musical italien (1618-1732)*, Teatro studi e testi, 5 (Leo S. Olschki Editore, 1988), Figures 73-75.

[53] *Crowell's Handbook of Classical Mythology*, 395 & 490-95.

[54] Proteus was an ancient marine deity, who over time was demoted to Neptune/Poseidon's seal-herd but retained his gift of prophesy, as well as a talent for transforming himself into anything he wished; *Crowell's Handbook of Classical Mythology*, 502.

[55] Frugoni, *Opere*, 440; similar entertainments involving elaborately decorated chariots accompanied by wind instruments sometimes appeared on the Corso as part of the celebrations of the Roman Carnival.

Nettuno's *da capo* aria introduces the first half of the equestrian ballet, danced by sixteen riders on the floor of the theater.[56] In the second scene of the introduction, Proteo falls into a prophetic trance predicting a bright future for the houses of Farnese and D'Este. The trance ends with a *da capo* aria for the prophet ushering in the second half of the ballet. The final scene consists of celebratory remarks by the three protagonists and a concluding chorus for the entourage of marine divinities. Vinci wrote music for the recitative and arias of the *Introduzione*. The choreographer Francesco Massimiliano Pagnini may have provided the music for the ballet as he did in *Medo*. However, considering the importance of the occasion and the presence of the ballet at the center of the entertainment rather than as a self-contained entr'acte, it is possible that Vinci wrote the ballet music in *Le nozze di Nettuno*, or at least for sketched out the music as he did in *Eraclea*.[57]

## An Opera for the New Viceroy

According to Prota-Giurleo, during the summer of 1728 Vinci was appointed interim Maestro at the Conservatorio dei Poveri di Gesù Cristo, succeeding his alleged teacher Gaetano Greco who died earlier that year. In October, when Francesco Durante was appointed as maestro, the following payment is supposed to have been made: "to Maestro di Cappella Leonardo Vinci for assistance over several months and for some books of music, 44 ducats."[58] As has been the case with Prota-Giurleo's other records concerning Vinci, this one cannot be found,[59] the reason being that there is no 1728 volume of the *Libro di tutte le Spese* in the Archives of the Conservatorio dei Poveri di Gesù Cristo in the Diocesiano in Naples, something that was noted by Di Giacomo back in the 1920s.[60] Thus it would seem Prota-Giurleo's

---

[56] A print from the production of *La venuta d'Ascanio*, the equestrian ballet from 1732 modelled on *Le nozze de Nettuno*, gives an idea of how the ballet would have been executed in the Teatro Farnese; reproduced in Mamczarz, Op. cit, Figure 76.

[57] Perhaps some of the music of this ballet survives in various minuets and airs attributed to Vinci published in several collections, such as Boivin and LeClerc (Paris, 1737) and J. Simpson (London, 1750); Strohm, *Italienische Opernarien*, II, 245.

[58] Quoted in Ulisse Prota-Giurleo, "Leonardo Vinci" *Convegno musicale* II (1965), 8.

[59] This was first pointed out to me by Rosa Cafiero in a di scussion following her paper "Il 'venerabile conservatorio di S. Maria della Colonna, detto de' Poveri di Gesù Cristo' negli anni di Leonardo Vinci" presented at the conference *Leonardo Vinci: Architetture sonore...*, Reggio Calabria, 10-12 June 2002.

[60] Salvatore Di Giacomo, *I quattro antichi conservatorii di musica di Napoli*, 109; this may have something to do with the student riots during that year (see Ibid., 111-114).

record is an historical reconstruction based on two facts: the interregnum between the tenures of Greco and Durante and the presence of Pergolesi at the Conservatorio at this time. These are combined with a reference in Burney describing how, when Pergolesi "quitted the conservatorio, he totally changed his style, and adopted that of Vinci, of whom he received lessons in vocal composition."[61] Prota-Giurleo's record has the format of many of the records under *Spese diverse* from the 1726/27 and 1729 volumes that the author looked through on the off-chance that they might contain this phantom record. Thus it would seem that a record was created in order to present as fact Prota-Giurleo's speculation concerning the most likely time that Vinci would have provided vocal instruction to Pergolesi, i.e. the interregnum between Greco and Durante in mid-1728. However, if Vinci actually did serve as interim teacher at the Poveri di Gesù Cristo, one might question why did he not apply for this post himself, like so many other Neapolitan composers, such as his colleagues Leo and Porpora. A possible answer would be that, in conrast to Leo and Porpora, everything in his life and music indicate that Vinci specialized as an opera composer, in the same way that Durante specialized as a teacher.

Vinci's supposed interregnum at the Conservatorio dei Poveri di Gesù Cristo coincided with an actual interregnum at the court. On July 31 Cardinal Althann left Naples, worn out by administrative corruption and by the continuous intrigue of his enemies.[62] Until his replacement arrived in the fall, the administration was taken over by the Marques de Almenara, the Imperial Viceroy for Sicily. There is a *Cantata à 6,* attributed to Vinci in the Deutsche Staatsbibliothek in Berlin celebrating the homecoming of a clerical dignitary, which has been identified by Strohm with Cardinal Althann's return to Austria.[63] However a recent study by Nicolò Maccavino and Tonio Battista has demonstrated that this is actually the serenata for five voices *Il Ritratto dell'Eroe* by Giovanni Porta and Domenico Lalli, produced in the fall of 1726 in celebration of the return of Cardinal Pietro Ottoboni to Venice.[64] The visit represented a reconcilliation after an extended

---

[61] Charles Burney, *A General History of Music,* II, 920.
[62] Heinrich Benedikt, *Das Königreich Neapel unter Kaiser Karl VI*, 373-74.
[63] Staatsbibliothek. Ms. L.280a; Strohm, *Italienische Opernarien*, II, 238.
[64] Tonio Battista & Nicolò Maccavino *"Il Ritratto dell'Eroe* (Venice, 1726) Una serenata di Giovanni Porta dedicata al cardinale Pietro Ottobone, falsamente attribuita a Leonardo Vinci" in *Leonardo Vinci e il Suo Tempo: Atti dei Convegni internazionali di studi, Reggio Calabria, 10-12 giugno 2002: 4-5 giugno 2004*

diplomatic row between the Ottoboni family and the Republic over Cardinal Ottoboni's controversial appointment as Protector of the Affairs of France at the Vatican in 1709.[65] This return not only produced considerable political negotiation between Venice, Rome, and France, but some impressive music as well, including the gala revival of Porpora's setting of Stampiglia's *Imeneo in Atene* (the same drama Handel set as his penultimate opera).

In October and November Vinci was busy with a new opera, *Flavio Anicio Olibrio,* and its accompanying intermezzo, *Il corteggiano affettato,* which were premièred at the Teatro San Bartolomeo on December 11, 1728. As with the production of *Le ddoie lettere* in 1719, that of *Flavio Anicio Olibrio* was a gala occasion, coinciding with the inauguration of a new Viceroy, Graf Alois Thomas Harrach, who took over the government on December 9 from the Marques de Almenara.[66] In one of his letters to the Emperor, the new Viceroy mentions the success of Vinci's première: "most of the nobility showed up so that they were almost standing upon one another, in spite of the large theatre."[67] The Viceroy attributed the success of the opera to "the outstanding music by Your Regal Majesty's local Vice Maestro di Cappella Vinci."[68] This season in Naples featured the castrati Carestini and Bernacchi, the latter perhaps recruited by Vinci in Parma. Viceroy Harrach mentions in this same letter to the Emperor that a rivalry developed between Bernacchi and Carestini that resembled the rivalry between Cuzzoni and Faustina in London the previous year: "the local women cannot agree in their patronage and taste, while some declare themselves for Bernacchi, others for Carestini; these both are true arch-enemies."[69] For his part, the vice-

---

(Reggio Calabria: Iiriti editore, 2005) 339-406. Porta's autograph in Stockholm and the libretto inVenice indicate that singers of both the choruses and arias were from the Pietà where Porta served as *maestro di capppella*; Faun Taunenbaum Tiedge & Michael Talbot "The Berkeley Castle Manuscript: Arias and Cantatas by Vivaldi and his Italian Contemporaries, *Studi Vivaldiani*, 2003, III, 33-86.

[65] Michael Talbot, *Tomaso Albinoni: the Venetian Composer and his World* (Oxford: Clarendon Press, 1990), 32-34.

[66] Benedikt, Op. cit., 374. En route to Naples, the new Viceroy had been fêted in Venice with the première of Porpora's *Ezio*. In the dedication, the impressario Lalli refers to "The impatience in which the beautiful Partenope [i.e. Naples] lives, to enjoy the sweetness and justice of your command" Pietro Metastasio, *Ezio: Dramma per Musica di Artino Corasino* (Venice: Carlo Buonario, 1728), 2.

[67] Quoted in Ibid., 655.

[68] Quoted in Ibid., 655-56.

[69] Quoted in Ibid., 655.

roy considered "the buffo part in the intermezzi the best," perhaps intrigued by the beauty and wit of the *buffa* Celeste Resse.[70]

*Flavio Anicio Olibrio* was Vinci's only setting of a libretto by Zeno and Pariati, unless one includes the pasticcio *Stratonica*. The drama had originally been written for Francesco Gasparini in 1707 for the Teatro San Cassiano. It may have had Porpora associations, having served the composer as his second opera for Naples in 1711 and his second opera for Rome in 1722. The score of Vinci's *Flavio Anicio Olibrio* is lost, though arias survive in several collections, including five arias in the Santini-Sammlung in Münster and an aria and a trio in the British Museum, the latter a contrafactum of the trio in *Medo*. The aria "Per l'africane arene" was sung by Annibali in a revival of Handel's *Poro* in 1736, one of the few baggage arias that Handel allowed in his operas and it was subsequently published as such in the Appendix of Chrysander's edition.[71]

## Metastasio's Roman/Venetian Premières

In spite of the problems with *Catone in Utica* from the previous year, Vinci and Metastasio collaborated again on a new opera for the Carnival of 1729. Arriving in Rome some time after the production of *Flavio Anicio Olibrio* in December of 1728, Vinci would have spent all of January completing the score of his new opera. According to De Angelis, Vinci received three-hundred scudi for the score, presumably the going rate.[72] The new opera *Semiramide riconosciuta* was premièred on February 6th at the Teatro delle Dame, with a cast consisting of:[73]

    Semiramide: Giacinto Fontana    Scitalce: Antonio Barbieri
    Tamiri:  Pietro Morici            Mirteo: Carlo Scalzi
    Sibari:   Giovanni Ossi        Ircano: Gaetano Berenstadt
          Stage design:  Pompeo Aldobrandini
          Choreography:  Pietro Gugliantini
          Costumes:  Antonio Banci
          Battle direction:  Decio Berrettini

---

[70] Quoted in Ibid., 656.

[71] George Frideric Handel, *Poro*, 79 of *G.F.Händels Werke: Ausgabe der Deutschen Händelesellschaft,* ed. Friedirch Chrysander (Leipzig: Deutschen Händelgesellscaft, 1880), 111-114. Chrysander has included, at the end of the aria, a second cemblo part, which illustrates how the additional keyboard instrument would have been employed in performance (i.e. only in the orchestral ritornelli).

[72] Alberto De Angelis, *Il teatro Alibert o delle dame, 1717-1863,* 149.

[73] Albert Cametti, "Leonardo Vinci: e suoi drammi in musica al Teatro della Dame (1724-30)" *Musica d'oggi,* 6 (1924), 298.

With regards to the singers and their roles, the cast is typical of Vinci's Roman productions: Fontana as *"prima donna,"* Scalzi as *primo uomo*, Barbieri as heroic tenor, Berenstadt as blustering villain, and Ossi as the cadet.

*Semiramide riconosciuta* was the second Metastasio drama to be produced that season at the Teatro delle Dame, the other being Pietro Auletta's setting of *Ezio,* which opened the season on January 2nd.[74] The relatively unknown Auletta was probably chosen as a substitute for Vinci, who was busy with the gala première of *Flavio Anicio Olibrio* in Naples. The choice of Auletta may have originated with Cardinal Coscia, the Pope's favorite, whom Valesio refers to as Auletta's "protettore."According to Valesio, Auletta was not a good choice: "the music of the *maestro di cappella* Napoletano, did not please."[75]

Both *Ezio* and *Semiramide* were new dramas. Arrangements were made so that both Metastasio dramas were also premièred during the same season at the Teatro San Giovanni Grisostomo in Venice. For the Venetian premières, Metastasio's texts were revised by Domenico Lalli, the impresario and poet for the San Giovanni Grisostomo, and set to music by Porpora. Strohm speculates that this double première was accomplished "with Lalli's help, and possibly with a large thank-offering to the new star librettist."[76] These dual premières may have been motivated by Metastasio's need for cash in the wake of his move to Rome. Although the Roman première was the official one because of the presence of the poet, in the case of *Ezio,* the Venetian première preceded the Roman by a month, being dedicated to the new Imperial Viceroy as he passed through Venice on his way to Naples. These facts, combined with Lalli's restrained editing of the text, suggest that Metastasio intended *Ezio* for Venice, for his former maestro Porpora rather than the novice Auletta, just as he intended *Semiramide* for Rome, for his current musical collaborator Vinci.

---

[74] Strohm gives the date, December 26, 1728 (Strohm, *Italienische Opernarien,* Vol. II, 315) but Valesio states that the première took place on January 2, 1729 (Francesco Valesio, *Diario di Roma: Libro nono e libro decimo* [Vol.V: 1729-36], 3).

[75] Valesio, Op. cit., 3 and 8. Later that month, Cardinal Coscia, bedridden with gout, arranged to have private performances of the operas at both the Capranica and delle Dame theaters at his palace. While the musicians performing Costanzi's *Rosmene* were rewarded with refreshment and a "ragalo" of twenty scudi, those performing *Ezio* had to be content with refreshments, only. Valesio adds that Auletta would have to be satisfied with "la protezione" of the Cardinal.

[76] Reinhard Strohm, "The Neapolitans in Venice" *Studies in Italian Opera, Song, and Dance, 1580-1740,* ed. Iain Fenlon and Tim Carter (Oxford: Clarendon Press, 1995), 269.

The Old Pretender, James Edward Stuart, attended the first performance of Vinci's *Semiramide*, having arrived the same day from Bologna.[77] James had made a similar trip to Venice earlier that season–his operatic excursions justified, according to the Bishop of Rochester, as a means of making his comings and goings less predictable "so that when opportunity arrived for a longer one [i.e. the much-planned invasion of England], it might be the less noticed."[78] Surprisingly, the libretto was not dedicated to James or any other regal patron but to the Ladies: "in the theatre called 'the ladies' dedicated to the same." Amid the flowery rhetoric of the dedication the management tried to bolster attendance by appealing to the ladies, pointing out they had an obligation to attend the theatre named in their honor:

> There is no one who does not know that this theatre is yours by right: hence in presenting *Semiramide riconosciuta* to you, we do not require the merit of a new donation. We would like on the contrary to remind you in this manner, that when you deigned to allow this theatre to be adorned with your name, you were silently obliged to support with your favor all that on its stage in the future must be displayed to the judgment of the public: and it is up to you, since you rendered it the most glorious, so you [can] render it the most fortunate; you are obliged to do so.[79]

From this dedication, one could infer that subscriber attendance had fallen off—perhaps due to the failure of Auletta's *Ezio*, the antagonistic reception of *Catone in Utica,* and the indifferent reaction to Feo's *Ipermestra* the previous year. The management apparently thought that convincing the ladies to return to their *palchi* would boost the attendance at the theatre (a strategy now regularly used in the clubs).

The other cause for concern was the new competition. This season the Teatro della Pace re-opened after five years of closure, with Costanzi's *Rosmene* and Leo's *Arianna e Teseo*.[80] The Capranica,

---

[77] Alberto Cametti, Op. cit., 298. Valesio described the unexpected arrival of James but does not mention his attendance at the opera (Valesio, Op. cit., 26).
[78] Martin Haile, *James Francis Edward: The Old Chevalier*, 331.
[79] *Semiramide riconosciuta Drama per Musica di Pietro Metastasio. . .Da rappresentarsi nel Carnevale dell'anno 1729, Nel Teatro detto delle Dame, Dedicato alle medesime* (Rome: Zemple and Meij, 1729). Copies of the libretto in A-Wn, C-Tu, Th.Fisher, CS-Pu, F-Pn, GB-Lbm, I-Bc -Fm -FE, Walker -Mb -MOe -R, Istit. Germanico -Rsc -Vgc, US-AUS -NYp -Wc; Sartori, *I libretti italiani* (No.1534).
[80] This small opera theater off the Piazza Navona ran intermittently between the years 1717-29 only to close down at the end of this season, remaining closed until mid-century. Arnaldo Rava, *I teatri di Roma* (Rome: Fratelli Palombi, 1953), 114-15.

on the other hand, brought in Vinci's former collaborator at the Teatro Fiorentini, Bernardo Saddumene, along with Giovanni Battista Fischetti who together produced a pair of comic operas, *La Costanza* and *La Somiglianza*.[81] Although intermezzi were encountered from time to time during the 1720s in Rome, either between the acts of serious operas (as in Filippo Falconi's *Burlotto/Brunetta* in his *Ginevra* from 1724) or on their own (as in Feo's *Don Chischiotte della Mancia* from 1726), this was the first full season of comic opera in Rome.[82] These were full-length *commedie per musica* along the Neapolitan model, sung half "in lingua toscana" and half "in lingua napolitana," with regulars from the Teatro Fiorentini, Simone di Falco and Giovanni Rommanelli, singing the latter. There may have been some type of collusion between the Pace and the Capranica theatres this season. The new owner of the Pace, Giuseppe Polvini Faliconti was, or had been, the impresario at the Capranica, his position there having been taken over by Antonio Mango on the first of February.[83] Mango, who is described as "Napoletano," may have been essential in organizing this Neapolitan comic season at the Capranica, taking over mid-season from Faliconti who, in turn, was busy at the Pace (see caricature of Faliconti in Plate 34 on page 335). Collusion or no, the repertoires of the two theatre complimented each other and together would have offered considerable competition to the Teatro delle Dame.

The libretto to one of the comic operas, *La Costanza,* is apparently a re-working of *Li zite 'ngalera* and has been regarded by Strohm and Romana Veneziano as a revival of Vinci's opera.[84] This seems unlikely. Surely if this was an actual revival, the composer's reputa-

---

[81] Sartori, *I libretti italiani* (Nos. 6767 and 22285).

[82] This comic season had been prefigured the previous year with a season of comic opera at the Teatro de' Granari. These full-length comic operas, designated as *dramma giocoso*, featured the *commedia dell'arte* character Pulcinella and were performed by puppets "rappresentarsi con figurine." The Pulcinella cycle had begun the previous year with *Pulcinella marchese di Girapetra*, the libretto of which makes no mention of the puppets but mentions the author, Tomaso Mariani, a Roman who had written several *commedie* for Naples. Thus it would seem that comic opera in Rome was established by Tomaso Mariani during the 1727 and 1728 seasons with a series of puppet operas based on the character of Pulcinella—*dramme giocosa* for puppets. See Sartori, *Il libretti italiani*(Nos. 19316-19318).

[83] Maria Grazia Pastura Ruggiero, "Fonti per la storia del teatro romano nel Settecento conservate nell'Archivio di Stato di Roma" *Il teatro a Roma nel Settecento,* ed. Gianni Eugenio Viola (Rome: Istituto della Enciclopedia Italiana, 1989), 527 & 540.

[84] Reinhard Strohm, *Die italienische Oper im 18. Jarhhundert*. Taschenbücher zur Musikwissenschaft 25 (Wilhelmshaven: Heinrichshafens Verlag, 1979) and Giulia Anna Romana Veneziano, "La maestria nel comico: *Li zite 'ngalera*," article accompanying the libretto for the production of *Li zite 'ngalera* in Bari, 1999.

tion in Rome at this time was such that the opera would have been acknowledged as his in the libretto and the little-known Fischetti, to whom the music is attributed, would have been relegated to the role of adapter (as Giuseppe Sellito was with the Neapolitan revival of *La Mogliere fedele* in 1731).[85]

After the controversial Roman subject of *Catone*, Metastasio returned to the exotic Persian background of *Siroe* in his new drama. *Semiramide riconosciuta* is based on the history of Semiramis the legendary queen of Assyria who, after the death of her husband Ninus, ruled the kingdom for forty years; during her reign great cities, temples, monuments and roads were built and the kingdom enjoyed great prosperity. Semiramis had already been featured as the heroine in several operas. Giovanni Andrea Moniglia's *La Semiramide* from 1671, is concerned with the change of identities between Semiramis and her son Ninus, and is set amid a revolt in Babylon. Francesco Silvani's *Semiramide* from 1714 is set during the siege of Battra and relates how she became queen of Assyria. Although Metastasio did not set his drama against one of the supposed historical events of her reign, he makes allusion to the legendary sexual promiscuity of Semiramis through Scitalce's stubborn belief in her infidelity. The extensive background to Metastasio's drama consists of an elaboration of the flight of Semiramis from Egypt and her ascent to the Assyrian throne.

> **Synopsis**: During her youth the Egyptian Princess Semiramide eloped with the Indian Prince Scitalce. Scitalce's confidante Sibari, secretly in love with Semiramide, convinced him that she had been unfaithful. In a jealous rage Scitalce stabbed Semiramide. The wound was not fatal and Semiramide escaped to Assyria where she eventually married the king. Upon his death, she took over the monarchy disguised as her son Nino who was retired to the seraglio. Princess Tamiri of Battri comes to her court to choose a husband. There are three suitors: Prince Ircano of Scythia, Prince Mirteo of Egypt who is the brother of Semiramide, and Prince Scitalce of India, Semiramide's former lover, accompanied by Sibari.
>
> The drama opens as Semiramide is recognized by Sibari who promises to keep her secret. The three princes each present their suit: the boastful Ircano, the genteel Mirteo,

---

[85] Unless the Capranica was reviving *Li zite 'ngalera* under a new guise as a means rivalling Vinci with his own music; in the same way that Handel was rivalled by revivals of his Chandos masques *Esther* and *Acis and Galatea* during the 1732 season in London—the event that would launch Handel's oratorio career.

and Scitalce. The latter recognizes Semiramide but manages to conceal his surprise, intending to continue his suit of Tamiri. The Princess is about to choose him when Semiramide interrupts the ceremony, saying that Tamiri needs time to think over this decision. When Semiramide and Scitalce finally speak to each other, they both dissemble. Scitalce asks Semiramide to intercede on his behalf with Tamiri. Infuriated, Semiramide warns Tamiri that Scitalce is false and also warns the other suitors that Scitalce is favored and they need to plead their cause to Tamiri more strongly. Ircano resolves to kill his rival.

Sibari convinces Ircano not to slay Scitalce but to allow the cup with which he will toast Tamiri at the engagement ceremony to be poisoned. At the ceremony Tamiri chooses Scitalce, but when Scitalce is about to make the toast, he withdraws his offer of marriage. When Ircano insists that he drink the toast, Scitalce offers it to Ircano who refuses on the grounds that he was not chosen first. Tamiri, disgraced by the action, calls for vengeance, but when Ircano and Mirteo rush to her defence, Semiramide has Scitalce arrested. Sibari convinces Ircano that he should abduct Tamiri. Left alone with Scitalce, Semiramide reveals her identity, but is cruelly rejected as a traitress.

Ircano's abduction plot is discovered and Mirteo and the Assyrians arrive, putting the Scythians to flight, defeating Ircano. Sibari tells Mirteo that Scitalce was the man who murdered his sister, hoping in this way to rid himself of an old rival—the only one who can implicate him as the instigator of Scitalce's crime. Mirteo comes before Semiramide to ask for revenge but she sends him away with a promise, hoping to use the situation to her advantage. Semiramide offers to save Scitalce, but he again rejects her. She swears that now she will live only for his punishment. Scitalce storms off and asks Tamiri to marry him; she accepts just as Mirteo rushes in to challenge him to a duel. In the royal amphitheatre filled with spectators, Mirteo explains the reason for his challenge. To defend his crime, Scitalce blames Semiramide's infidelity, producing Sibari's letter of denunciation as proof. Sibari, realizing he has been caught in his own snare, is about to reveal the Queen's true identity, when she reveals her own deception. After the people have heard her story, they acclaim her as their rightful queen. Semiramide and Scitalce are reunited and Tamiri makes a better second choice with Mirteo. Sibari is forgiven and Ircano returns to the Caucasus.

Of all the Metastasio libretti that Vinci set, this is the most complicated and the most closely connected to the seventeenth century. As in *Siroe re di Persia*, another drama with a strong *seicento* bias, *Semiramide riconosciuta* has a Middle Eastern setting and features a heroine disguised as a man throughout the opera. There are even more parallels with another libretto set by Vinci with a similarly disguised heroine, Stampiglia's *Partenope*. Tamiri's three suitors, Scitalce, Mirteo, and Ircano, and their respective personalities are derived from Partenope's three suitors: the traitorous Arsace, the genteel Armindo, and the barbaric Emilio. Both Scitalce and his counterpart Arsace are aware of the former lover's disguise but refuse to reveal her identity, albeit for different reasons. The main difference between *Partenope* and *Semiramide* is that Metastasio has reversed the roles of his heroines: in *Semiramide* the disguised heroine who strives to retrieve her wayward lover is the queen rather than the foreign princess and the heroine courted by the suitors is the foreign princess rather than the queen. This complex *seicento* quality in *Semiramide* may be one of the reasons for Metastasio's massive revision and abbreviation of the libretto in 1752.[86] After completing the revision, he wrote to Farinello in Madrid that "this work, with which I was not fully satisfied, has now become my dearest."[87] Therefore Metastasio had reservations about the libretto he wrote for Vinci and only after extensive revisions was he convinced of its sterling qualities.

## *Semiramide riconosciuta*: Act II Confrontation and Aftermath

After a cursory glance at the score of Vinci's *Semiramide riconosciuta*, the piece that immediately stands out is the chorus "Il piacer, la gioja scende," which is sung during the engagement ceremony at the beginning of Act II.[88] It is one of the rare examples of an extended chorus in the *dramma per musica* of the first half of the eighteenth century. Like similar choruses in Handel's *Ariodante* and *Alcina*, "Il piacer, la gioja scende" was accompanied by dancing; unlike Handel's choruses, which were sung by an actual choir, Vinci's

---

[86] This revised and abbreviated version is the one printed in *Opere*, with the cuts from the original Vinci version gathered into the appendix; Pietro Metastasio, *Tutte le Opere*, I, 1412-42.

[87] Metastasio, Op. cit., I, 768.

[88] There are three manuscript scores of *Semiramide riconosciuta*. The score in the Santini-Sammlung in Münster (4245) is probably of Roman origin, employing the same format and similar paper as the other Vinci scores in this collection (3 vols.,

was sung by soloists, their names appearing beside the parts as in the usual *coro* finale. This chorus, as sung by the soloists, would have substituted for the absence of an extended ensemble, which is a standard feature of most Vinci operas.

As in *L'Ernelinda*, much of the music in Acts I and II is rather undistinguished. Both music and drama come to life at the end of Act II, when Semiramide reveals her identity to Scitalce only to have him cruelly reject her as an adulteress, without any remorse for his crime. After Semiramide's "Tradita, sprezzata," she offers him a knife to finish the deed he began many years ago. This C-minor aria is a fine example of the agitated *aria parlante* with its syllabic text setting, fast tempo, and minor mode. As Strohm has pointed out, this is the type of aria that Anna Giro requested in Goldoni's oft-quoted anecdote about his collaboration with Vivaldi.[89] In their first meeting, Vivaldi is reported to have told him:

---

20 x 27 cm., with fleur de lys watermark). Unlike the other Santini scores, this manuscript was not copied by Francesco Cantone, but by two anonymous scribes. The manuscript is lacking both the overture and a title page and is in poor condition, with much paper discoloration and what looks like termite damage. The score in Naples (32-4-11, 1 vol. 20 x 28 cm.) provides the missing overture but is lacking the final two scenes of Act II (the manuscript, having been rebound, shows no sign of the omission). According to both Hell and Strohm, this score is also of Roman origin (Hell, *Die Neapolitanische Opernsinfonie*, 533 and Strohm, *Italienische Opernarien*, II, 232). The paper, with fleur de lys in double circle, appears to be Roman from the first half of the eighteenth century (similar to Heawood No. 1592: Rome, n.d.; Heawood, *Watermarks: Mainly of the 17th and 18th Centuries*). Unlike the Cantone manuscripts of *Farnace* and *Catone in Utica*, this one is through-composed in a very neat hand with ornate capitals for each act, though orchestration is provided only for arias with additional winds. Given the omissions in these two Roman scores, the only complete manuscript is in the Biblioteca dell' Abbazia at Montecassino (6-C-1; formerly 126 E 21). Like the scores of *Eraclea*, *L'Ernelinda*, and *La caduta*, this manuscript was formerly part of the collection of Don Vincenzo Bovio and is in a similar format (3 vols. bound as one, 20 x 27 cm.). The thick heavy paper, with fleur de lys watermark within a single circle, suggests mid-century Naples (similar to Heawood No. 1573; D.G.M. Pancrazi, *Antichità Siciliane spiegata*, Naples, 1752). A score of Act I that survives in the Royal College of Music (634) is part of the large set of Italian operas that formerly belonged to the Concerts of Ancient Music. There also exists a score to Acts II and III in the Staats- und Universitätsbibliothek in Hamburg (A/680) that, according to Strohm, may have originated in Dresden (Strohm, *Italienische Opernarien*, II, 232). The excerpts below are taken from the complete score in Montecassino, comprising the following musical numbers:

| | | |
|---|---|---|
| 29 *da capo* arias | | 2 ariettas |
| 4 accompanied recitatives | 2 Sinfonias | 2 choruses |

Totals: 37 musical numbers (29 in *da capo* form)

[89] Strohm, *Italienische Opernarien*, I, 63.

Mlle. Giraud is not fond of languishing songs; she wishes something expressive and full of agitation, an expression of the passions by different means, by words interrupted, for example, by sighs, with action and motion.[90]

In "Tradita, sprezzata," as in similar arias by Marzia and Medo (see Example 7.11 on page 228), this agitation derives from the *senario* verses that are treated as *ternario* couplets; the enchainments between melody and bass in this aria are less apparent because the three-note segments are not separated by rests. Instead the melody is occasionally interrupted by dramatic pauses which would have been accompanied by some equally dramatic gestures rather than a cadenza:[91]

Example 8.7 "Tradita, sprezzata" *Semiramide riconosciuta* II/xii

These gestic interruptions are probably what Vivaldi had in mind when he specified "words interrupted, for example, by sighs, with action and motion." By the second quarter of the eighteenth century, the agitated *aria parlante* had come to rival the pathetic lament as one of the principal highlights of the *dramma per musica*—hence Anna Giro's request to replace the "languishing songs" in Vivaldi's *Griselda*.

In an accompanied recitative Scitalce complains that her lament has left him trembling with rage and sighing with pity. In his aria

---

[90] Carlo Goldoni, *Memoirs of Carlo Goldoni: Written by Himself*, 162-63.
[91] For a detailed analysis of this aria, see Strohm, Op. cit., I, 63-65. The complete aria is transcribed in II, 115-119.

"Passaggier, che su la sponda" he compares himself to a passenger of a shipwrecked vessel who does not know whether to stay on the wreck or throw himself into the sea. After a rather neutral opening theme, the music comes to life in an agitated transition depicting the "teme il mar" with measured tremolo and rapid ascending/descending scales:

Example 8.8 "Passaggier, che su la sponda" *Semiramide riconosciuta* II/xiii

The period is extended by a deceptive cadence and coloratura passages (mm.24-26), creating one of Vinci's most expansive opening periods. This final sequence to Act II of *Semiramide* is similar to that in Act I of *Didone*, consisting of a climactic dialogue between the lovers leading to an aria for the distraught heroine, followed by an accompanied recitative and aria for the cruelly resolute hero. While these two scenes are among the most disappointing in Vinci's *Didone*, the succession of Semiramide's agitated *aria parlante* and Scitalce's accompanied recitative and bravura aria can be regarded as the musical/dramatic climax of the opera. Although there are no correspondences between Vinci and Porpora's settings of Metastasio's drama, the two operas having been composed at the same time, Porpora's setting of "Passaggier, che su la sponda" is modelled on Vinci's "Son Regina" from *Didone*, from which it draws its theme and overall style. Moreover the ABB form of this famous aria inspired Porpora to adopt this melodic formula with greater frequency in *Semiramide* than in his earlier work.

In Act III Sibari informs Mirteo that Scitalce murdered his sister. Mirteo resolves to ask the king for justice. In his aria "In braccio a mille furie" he describes how the furies rage within him because of this horrible crime. This rage is depicted by an extended coloratura on the word "freme" that straddles the first two phrases, with disjunct unisons at the end of the initial thematic phrase (m.16) resolving onto the rising extended trills of the second coloratura phrase (m.17):

Example 8.9 "In braccio a mille furie" *Semiramide riconosciuta* III/iv

The descending motion of the first phrase is nicely balanced by the ascending motion of the second, the latter accomplished in two waves, in extended trills, and in a whirlwind of coloratura, all above a tonic pedal. When the harmony finally begins to move in the transition, the effect of movement seems much greater than it actually is, owing to the previous static harmony.[86]

In the next scene Sibari anticipates that Mirteo's vengeance will remove his rival and clear a path to the throne via Semiramide. In "Quando un fallo" he muses in Machiavellian fashion that crimes committed on the "strada al Regno" are transfigured by the splendor of the throne. This *alla breve* aria makes use of a distinctive counter motive that appears in the bass at strategic points in the aria (mm. 29 and 38):

Example 8.10 "Quando un fallo è strada" *Semiramide riconosciuta* III/v

Semiramide tries to stall Mirteo's vendetta, hoping to use his threat of vengeance to bring about a reconciliation with her beloved. When

---

[86] In June of 2003, this aria was given a stunning performance by Maria Grazia Schiavo at the Festival dell'Aurora in a concert dedicated to the music of Vinci. The power of her coloratura and the animated fluidity of her phrasing combined the with beauty of her voice and stage presence, recreated for the author something of the excitement and awe that must have been responsible for the eighteenth-century fasciation with coloratura.

she tells Scitalce that the only way to save himself from Mirteo's fury is to marry her, he cruelly rejects her a second time. In her aria "Fuggi dagl'occhi miei" she tells him to leave, threatening that henceforth she will seek only his punishment. The main theme of this aria is based on a technique Vinci often employs for instrumental subsidiary themes, consisting of a static declamatory melody above a bass and middle voice moving in parallels:

Example 8.11 "Fuggi dagl'occhi miei" *Semiramide riconosciuta* III/vii

Although the crossing of the melody and middle voice results in some unexpected dissonance, the even-flowing movement of this aria gives it more of a brooding than a vengeful affect. The repeated phrase "ingannator" with its pungent diminished harmony is reminiscent of Pergolesi.

Scitalce storms off and asks Tamiri to marry him. Just as she consents, Mirteo rushes in to challenge him to a duel. He accepts, but heaps scorn on the pomposity of the challenge in "Odi quel fasto?"—a miniature heroic aria similar to those Vinci wrote for Enea during his encounters with Jarba. When Mirteo asks why Tamiri betrayed him, she replies in her air "D'un genio, che m'accende" that "love has no reasons." This coloratura aria is somewhat *mezzo carattere* in style, suggestive of the Pergolesian comic soubrette; the phrases call out for a witty parlando interpretation with light coloratura and a hint of *rubato* (see Ex. 8.12 on page 272). The gestic pauses of "Tradita, Sprezzata" reappear in coquettish guise, separating her reiterated question "Tu vuoi ragion da me?." Alone, Mirteo complains of his betrayal in the aria "Sentirsi dire dal caro bene," the aria text quoting from Tamiri's previous speech in which she admits to being "bound by other chains." This heroic *alla breve* aria is somewhat marred by the continuous *Trommelbass* accompanying main, transition, and closing phrases without a break.

Example 8.12 "D'un genio, che m'accende" *Semiramide riconosciuta* III/x

    Semiramide and Ircano are each given ariettas in the amphitheatre scene prior to the duel. Although Ircano's is a crude reworking of "Nei freddi soggiorni" from *L'Ernelinda*, Semiramide's "Fra tanti affanni miei" is a lovely period that moves from solemn declamation to florid lyricism. Semiramide reveals her identity to her subjects in an extended accompanied recitative that ends with a brief choral passage as the people acclaim her queen. This finale formula, consisting of a climactic revelation in accompanied recitative followed an enthusiastic choral acclamation by the crowd, was employed again by Metastasio in two of his later dramas, *L'Olimpiade* from 1733 and *Attilio Regolo* from 1740.

    *Semiramide riconosciuta* was revived as a pasticcio by Handel for the Haymarket Theatre in London (October, 1733), receiving four performances. The score for this pasticcio survives in Hamburg, and indicates that only a dozen of Vinci's arias were retained, the rest omitted or replaced by arias by other composers, most notably Hasse.[87]

    With settings of *Semiramide riconosciuta* by both Porpora and Vinci appearing during the same season, the rivalry from the previous year continued, albeit at a distance and in a more subtle man-

---

[87] Mss. A/1051; Reinhard Strohm, "Handel's pasticci," *Essays on Handel and Italian Opera*, 206-207.

ner.[88] Porpora's setting is at least as fine as Vinci's, his best arias often coming where Vinci is at his weakest, for example in the initial interview between Semiramide and Scitalce. A pasticcio of the two works could produce a very fine opera. This may well have been what happened in several subsequent productions of *Semiramide riconosciuta*, none of which list a composer: Pistoia from summer 1733, Brescia and Perugia from Carnival 1735, Genoa from autumn 1737, and Florence from Carnival 1740.[89]

## New Impressarios at the delle Dame

From the plea contained within the dedication to *Semiramide*, one could infer that the attendance at the delle Dame had fallen off. This declining interest in opera parallels that in Handel's London that lead to the failure of the Royal Academy of Music the previous year. In Rome as in London, the directors had to deal with the rising costs of production, in particular the salaries of the star singers. While in London this situation was exacerbated by a certain antagonism towards the language of this exotic foreign entertainment, especially with the sudden popularity of ballad operas in the vernacular, in Rome opera was hidebound by its all-male casts and its single short season. The latter meant it was necessary to fill the theatres to capacity during Carnival, hence the reason for the large Roman theatres.[90] Even before the end of the season, Valesio relates that:

> Creditors of Count Alibert, who until now had produced the dramas in the theatre at their expense with little profit, have leased it for nine years at 780 scudi per annum and the new impresarios are Milesi the Venetian Courrier, Porzio Cavanna and Vinci.[91]

---

[88] Scores of Porpora's *Semiramide riconosciuta* survive at the Royal Academy of Music in London (ms. 81), in the same series as the Academy score of Vinci's *Siroe*, and in the Biblioteca dell'Abbazia in Montecassino (126 A25). The facsimile score published in the Garland series is Porpora's revised version of this opera, produced in Naples in 1739; see Nicolà Antonio Porpora, *Semiramide Riconosciuta*, Vol. [30] of *Italian Opera 1640-1770*. In contrast to Leo's settings of *Astianatte* and *Catone*, this later revision shows no influence of Vinci's setting, though, as already mentioned, the original exhibits certain specific Vinci characteristics.

[89] Libretto for Pistoia in I-Bc -FE, Walker; for Brescia in I-Palazzola, Civica; for Perugia in I-Vgc; for Genoa in GB-Lbm; and for Florence in I-Bc; Sartori, *I libretti italiani* (Nos. 21541, 21542, 31543, 21544, 21546).

[90] To alleviate this problem a second season for Ascension was instituted in 1731, but political problems scuttled it after only two seasons.

[91] Valesio, *Diario di Roma*, V, 14.

Therefore as in London, after the dismantling of the Royal Academy of Music, the aristocratic directors leased the King's Theatre to Handel and Heidegger, in Rome the aristocratic owners/directors leased the Teatro delle Dame to Vinci, Francesco Cavanna, and the Venetian Courrier.[92] Considering that Vinci did not have the six ducats required for entrance in the Congregazione del Rosario the previous year, it seems likely that Cavanna and Milesi were responsible for paying the 780 *scudi* for the lease on the delle Dame, as well as any down payment. Vinci would undoubtedly provide his share of the investment in the forthcoming season in kind (see Chapter 9). It probably attests to Vinci's reputation at this time that he is designated only by his last name, whereas the other two partners are further identified.

This declining interest in opera collided with Metastasio's attempt to establish himself as a free-lance poet. The impact of this collision undoubtedly provides the background for Charles Burney's description of Metastasio's "narrow circumstances [which] threw him into so profound a fit of melancholy."[93] By the end of the summer, however, Metastasio was roused from his melancholy by a letter from Prince Pio di Savoia, Inspector of the Imperial Theatres in Vienna informing him that: "his Imperial Majesty...is desirous to engage you in his service, on such conditions, as shall seem most worthy of your acceptance."[94]

## A Second *Farnace*

On August 28 1729 *Il Farnace* was premièred in celebration of birthday of Empress Elizabeth at the Teatro San Bartolomeo, with a cast that included Tesi, Barbieri, and Minelli in the lead roles.[95] Although considered a revival of the original Roman *Farnace*, a comparison of the libretto and surviving arias with the libretto and score of the 1724 *Farnace* indicates that this was a new opera and not a revival. For this second *Farnace* Lucchini's drama was considerably revised and shortened.[96] In deference to Neapolitan tradition, an intermezzo,

---

[92] In the diplomatic world of Rome, the Courrier had a prestigious position at this time, serving as the vital link between the embassy and the court that they served. Their comings and goings were of considerable interest and were frequently noted by Valesio in his *Diario*.

[93] Burney, *Memoirs of the Life and Writings of the Abate Metastasio*, I, 43.

[94] Ibid., I, 44. The negotiations on these conditions continued into the fall, with Metastasio almost overstepping himself by asking for the same salary as his predecessor Apostelo Zeno.

[95] Libretto in US-NYp.

[96] In the new *Il Farnace* the character of Pompeo has been idealized while the

*L'amante Geloso*, was inserted between the acts for Corrado and Resse. To accommodate the addition of an intermezzo, the number of arias has been reduced from thirty-nine to twenty-four. Of the remaining twenty-four arias, only four are original Lucchini texts.

In composing the new *Farnace*, it is unlikely that Vinci reused the music from the original. Half of the arias from the new *Farnace* survive in two collections and none of these show any trace of music from 1724, including two of the four on original Lucchini texts.[97] Surprisingly the only borrowing that can be identified is Farnace's "Del mio figlio odo l'ombra" which is a parody of Perse's "Sento l'ombra del mesto germano" from *Medo*. The absence of contrafacta from *Farnace* and the resetting of at least two of the four original aria texts strongly suggests that the remaining arias ignore the music of the Roman original. The reuse of recitative is also highly unlikely. Although the outline of the plot remains the same, scenes have been cut, modified, and shifted. These changes, combined with the fact that the Neapolitan cast involved new registers for half the characters, would have made the re-use of recitative from the 1724 score next to impossible.[98] Vinci's apparent reluctance to reuse the music from the original 1724 *Farnace* in the 1729 production contrasts with the successful revival of Handel's operas in London and Rameau's in Paris decades after their original productions without complete re-composition. This phenomenal rate of obsolescence is indicative, not only of the fetish for new music in *settecento* Italy, but also of the innumerable stylistic changes that had taken place in Vinci's musical style between the years 1724 and 1729—changes that would have made the music of the Roman *Farnace* almost as archaic as that of the elder Scarlatti.

---

character of Farnace made even more ferocious, setting up a polarity between the civilized "virtù" of the Latin conqueror and the barbaric ferocity of the oriental despot. The amusing rivalry between Acquilio and Gilade for the affection of the flirtatious Selinda has been omitted by cutting the character of Acquilio and transforming Gilade and Selinda into a more respectable second couple. La Pace has been cut out, thereby simplifying the denouement.

[97] There are eight arias each in collections in the Biblioteca dell'Abbazia in Montecassino (126 E 18) and Biblioteca del Conservatorio di Musica S. Pietro Majella in Naples (34-5-24).

[98] The only possible places where music from the original *Farnace* could have been employed is the quartet, Tamari's accompanied recitative "Figlio o troppo tardi," and Pompeo's entrance aria "Senza rugiade." All three would have involved substantial changes because of the new registers for Tamari, Farnace, and Pompeo in the quartet, the recitative interruptions in "Senza rugiade," and the textual changes in the first two sections of the soliloquy.

Although the new *Farnace* was commissioned for the celebration of the Empress's birthday, it was dedicated to Ernestina Margarita Contessa di Harrach, wife of the new Viceroy. This was actually Ernestina Margarita's second term as viceregent, since she was also the widow of Graf Gallas, her first entry to Naples as consort of Graf Gallas, honored with the production of Vinci's *Le ddoie lettre* (see Chapter 2). *Il Farnace* was preceded by an elaborate *cuccagna* designed by the artist Domenico Antonio Vaccaro based on the myth of the Golden Fleece.[99] Vaccaro came up with the idea of concealing fireworks in the heads of two bulls guarding the golden fleece that were to go off during the plundering of the carriage. This supposedly comic addition to the ritualistic plundering of the *cuccagna* did not go according to plans. The carriage caught fire during the pyrotechnics and a major tragedy was averted only because the absence of winds allowed the blaze to subside after a half on hour.[100]

At this time Vinci also provided music for Annibale Marchese's *Massimiano*, one of a set of ten *Tragedie cristiane* that was published in 1729 by Felice Mosca.[101] These tragedies, based on the biblical dramas of Racine, were highly regarded. Marchese includes on his title page a flattering endorsement by the Neapolitan philosopher Giambattista Vico:

> he is worthy of universal applause for his noble birth as well as for the singular virtue of his soul, from whence...that sublime naturalness derives, which is necessary in the highest degree to make a species of great poetry.[102]

Each tragedy contains a set of *cori* to be inserted between acts like the *intermedi* of old. Typical of the contemporary bias towards the solo voice, these *cori* are actually monodies for soprano and basso continuo. The term *cori* is an anachronism that provided Marchese with an antique, and therefore theoretically sanctioned, synonym for the aria. Metastasio was to employ the term in a similar manner in his *Estratto*

---

[99] Benedikt, *Das Königreich Neapol unter Kaiser Karl VI*, 619-20.

[100] Ibid. Although the court chronicler mentions one death in his report to the emperor, the Viceroy covered up the incident by saying that the fire did not break out until after the plundering.

[101] *Tragedie christiane del duca Annibale Marchese, dedicate all'imperador de' christiani Carlo VI, il Grande...* (Naples; Stamperia di F. Mosca, 1729); Mosca had recently married one of Porpora's sisters, the Porpora family having close connections to the publishing industry.

[102] Ibid. Quoted in Andrea della Corte, "Cori monodici di dieci musicisti per le 'Tragedie cristiane' di Annibale Marchese" *Rivista italiana di musicologia*, I (1966), 192.

*dell'Arte Poetica* as a means of legitimizing the regular introduction of arias into his dramas.[103] Each set of *cori* is by a different composer: Hasse, Prince D'Ardore, Leo, Vinci, Porpora, Durante, Sarro, Fago, Mancini, and Carapella.[104] With the exception of Carapella— an elderly organist and choirmaster for several Neapolitan churches— the list of contributors reads like a who's who of Neapolitan composers.[105] Such an impressive list suggests that either Marchese payed well or it was considered an honour to be included among the contributors. The *cori* were contained within a forty-page appendix at the end of the volume which allowed the composers to display their talents alongside their colleagues in a work dedicated to Emperor Charles.

---

[103] Pietro Metastaio, "Estratto dell'Arte Poetica" in *Tutte le Opere*, II, 970.

[104] Corte, "Cori monodici per le 'Tragedie cristiane' di A. Marchese," 196-200.

[105] Durante's aristocratic pupil Giacomo Francesco Milano Principe d'Ardore has become the subject of a conference and subsequently a large published study: *Giacomo Francesco Milano e il ruolo dell'aristocrazia nel patrocinio delle attività musicale nel secolo XVIII*, atti del Convegno Internazionale di Studi, Polistena - San Giorgio Morgeto, 12-14 ottobre 1999, ed. Gaetano Pitarresi (Reggio Calabria: Laruffa Editore, 2001).

# 9

# THE TRIPLE COLLABORATION WITH METASTASIO

### The Dauphin's Birthday Cantata

*Il Farnace* is Vinci's only Neapolitan *dramma per musica* that was not written for the fall season. This change in the composer's routine was certainly propitious and undoubtedly intentional. Vinci spent the fall in Rome where he collaborated with Metastasio on *La contesa de' numi*. This *componimento drammatico,* or serenata, was commissioned by the French ambassador in Rome, Cardinal de Polignac, to celebrate the birth of the Dauphin, a momentous event that finally secured the Bourbon succession in France after the long minority of Louis XV.[1]

Although the Cardinal was informed of the birth in mid-September of 1729, the official celebrations did not take place until late November. According to the *Mercure de France* the Cardinal delayed the celebrations "until after S. Martin's Day, when the Cardinals, Prelates and Nobility would be returning from the country."[2] The delay was due not only to the returning clergy and nobility and the elaborate preparations, but also to the casting of the opera, which was almost identical to that of the Teatro delle Dame for the 1730 Carnival season. This suggests that the cantata was produced in conjunction with the Teatro delle Dame, with plans that may well have originated with those for the season as a whole. Vinci was the composer for *La contesa de' numi* and the two Carnival operas and, as one of the new impresarios at the della Dame, he would have been involved in planning the 1730 season and its connection to the celebrations of Cardinal Polignac. In order to be in Rome for the celebrations, Vinci altered his usual commission at the S. Bartolomeo from fall to summer and requested permission to leave Naples on October 3, hence the summer production of *Il Farnace*, with the fall commission going to Hasse whose *Il Tigrane* was produced in November.

---

[1] The last time the French court celebrated the birth of the Dauphin was in 1661 (i.e. the son of Louis XIV and the grandfather of Louis XV).

[2] *Mercure de France*, Decembre 1729, (Geneva: Slatkine Reprints, 1968), XVII, July-Dec. 1729, 3125.

Instead of the usual four-month leave of absence, his request states that "Leonardo Vinci, supernumerary *maestro* of the *Capella Reale* wants to leave Naples for a year."[3] Despite the extended nature of the leave, Viceroy Harrach was "pleased to concede this since the supplicant owes nothing to the chapel and has no specific duties there"—the rationale clearly indicative of the honorary nature of Vinci's court appointment (see Chapter 5). Apparently confident of obtaining his leave, Vinci submitted a request concerning his transportation on September 30, several days before the leave was granted:

> Leonardo Vinci humbly presents to Your Excellency, that he must travel to Rome on horse *per il suo proprio servizio*, and consequently requests Your Excellency to deign to command that he be permitted the extraction of this horse [from the Viceregal Stables], without paying anyone directly, and for this you will receive grace *ut Deus*.[4]

While it is known that in their journeys J.S. Bach walked and Handel travelled by coach, Leonardo Vinci rode a horse, at least on this important journey to Rome.[5] Typical of Vinci, the supplicant is short of cash and rather audaciously asks the Viceroy to be excused from paying for the horse. While the extended leave was in part due to his early departure from Naples to collaborate with Metastasio on *La contesa de' numi*, it would seem that Vinci had plans that went beyond the Carnival season in Rome, perhaps to accompany Metastasio on his journey to Vienna.

The formal celebrations for the Dauphin included several illuminations, a solemn mass with Te Deum at S. Luigi Francesi, horse races on the Corso, an elaborate fireworks display in the Piazza Navona and gala performances of *La contesa de' numi* in the courtyard of the Palazzo Altemps just north of the Piazza Navona. The solemn Te Deum with illumination and fireworks was a standard means of celebrating special events in Rome, while the horse races on the Corso were a regular feature of Carnival.[6] The horse races, which took place on the day of the

---

[3] Archivio di Stato di Napoli, Italia: Segreteria dei Viceré, fascio 1870, documenti pervenuti il 3-X-1729.

[4] Archivio di Stato di Napoli, Italia: fascio 1869, documenti pervenuti il 30-IX-1729. Although the phrase "il suo proprio servizio" could be translated as "in your service"—referring to the Imperial service in which both Vinci and the Viceroy were employed—the nature of the request as a favor suggests that it is "in his own ser-vice" or interest that the trip is taken (i.e. to produce opera).

[5] Upon discovering the record, the romantic imagery of Farinelli galloping between the courts of Europe on horseback from Gérard Cordiau's 1994 film *Farinelli Il Castrato* came to mind.

[6] The latest Te Deum with illuminations and fireworks had been produced for the Spanish ambassador, Cardinal Bentivoglio, in honor of the double wedding between the Spanish and Portugese royal families in 1728, the marriage that would bring Domenico Scarlatti to Spain; Francesco Valesio, *Diario di Roma: Libro settimo e libro*

second performance of the cantata and on the day of the fireworks display, were the *corsi dei barberi*, the racing of wild riderless horses down the Corso. It was not only the combination of these events but also their scale and lavishness that gave this celebration its special significance.[7] The fireworks lasted an hour and a quarter according to the entry in Valesio's diary, rather extended by modern standards; moreover, solemn Te Deums, with their associated illuminations and fireworks, were sung at Trinità de' Monti and S. Giovanni Laterano during the following weeks.[8] The elaborateness of these festivities, besides celebrating the glory of the French crown, may also have been intended as retaliation for the papal snub that caused the Cardinal to abandon his box at the Teatro delle Dame during Carnival 1726 in protest of the Imperial Ambassador's two *palchetti*.[9]

There were three performances of *La contesa de' numi*, a dress rehearsal on November 18, followed by two performances on November 25 and 26. In an article entitled "Rejouissances faites à Rome, par le Cardinal de Polignac" the *Mercure de France* provided a detailed account of production:

> The entire city proceeded to the palace of his eminence where the exterior illumination made for an admirable effect, the windows being lighted by white wax candles and the cornices lined with lamps. ...
>
> The court, which is admirable for its architecture and symmetry, resembled a magnificent theatre, as much by the number of chandeliers that illuminated it as by the richness and good taste of its ornaments. The ground floor was garnished with high-warp tapestries, with a number of mirror plaques, each of which carried several candles. All the windows of the first floor, to the right and to the left, were ornamented by crimson damask in festoons, above which they

---

*ottavo*, [IV: 1708-1728], ed. Gaetana Scano and Giseppe Graglia (Milan: Longanesi, 1979), 964-65.

[7] In a booklet published in conjunction with the celebrations, it is stated emphatically on the title page that these celebrations were intended to revive the antique grandeur of the "circo agonale di Roma;" facsimile of the title page in Francesco Valesio, *Diario di Roma: Libro nono e libro decimo*, [V: 1729-1736], 145-46.

[8] Ibid., 147-51; although the second Te Deum, at Trinità de' Monti did without the illuminations and fireworks, it featured the singing of the castrato Peppino.

[9] This was the opening salvo of the "Palchetti War," which is the backdrop for the author's paper: "The Eventual Premiere of *Issipile*: Porpora and the Palchetti War," presented at the conference *Music in Eighteenth-Century Italy*, Cardiff, June, 1998. It is not known what arrangements the Cardinal made for the Pope and the Imperial Ambassador, whether they were invited and, if so, whether they attended and, if they did attend, whether they were accommodated in one box or two, since the Cardinal specifically arranged his palace as a theatre with boxes.

placed the coat of arms of the King, of the Queen and Monseigneur the Dauphin. Each crest was surmounted by a pavilion in the form of a crown, with curtains being sustained by two gilded cupids. Each pilaster was garnished by a fabric painted in *Lapis Lazuli*, encrusted with golden Fleur de Lys and Dolphins, and illuminated by a chandelier of twelve candles.... The principal façade of the courtyard was occupied by a stage supported by some nude figures, where the 130 players of all sorts of instruments were arranged, and dressed as genii, with laurel crowns on their heads and with black belts and sashes garnished with jewels. The six singers representing Giove, Apollo, Marte, Astrea, Pace, and Fortuna, were seated on clouds, each dressed as these divinities are usually represented, with their [appropriate] attributes. The five arcades formed five charming perspectives...at the end of which one could see at a distance golden statues of the five greatest Kings of France from whom the Dauphin descends in direct lineage, Hugh Capet, Philippe Auguste, St. Louis, Henry IV, and Louis the Great. Above the Theatre there was the Coat of Arms of the Dauphin, covered with a great crown in a Baldachin, with curtains representing a silver cloak sprinkled with gold fleur de lys and azure Dolphins, sustained by two gilded cupids. Above the roof, which was hidden by some clouds, one saw the rising sun [Apollo] who conducted his chariot, drawn by four horses and surrounded by rays, that gave off a very great light. ...

In the middle of each arcade hung a chandelier of 24 candles, besides those that were in front of the pilaster; the spell of this grand light, combined with the quantity of jewellery which adorned all the princesses and ladies who occupied the windows of the upper and lower apartments, created a surprising brilliance. ...

When all the audience was seated, they then drew up the curtain which hid the decoration; everyone applauded for such a beautiful spectacle. The sinfonia began and the cantata was executed admirably. Between the first and second Parts, they distributed a prodigious amount of refreshments to all the spectators....Thus finished this day without any accident or disorder, in spite of the quantity of people who attended this Fête, the parterre and vestibule alone contained about 3000 persons; they also secured the avenues around the Palace with several detachments of soldiers who made the carriages file one after the other. The great houses of the city and many lesser ones were also illuminated for a good part of the night.[10]

---

[10] *Mercure de France*, Decembre 1729, 3125-26.

As in many descriptions of operatic productions from the seventeenth- and eighteenth-centuries, this one concentrates on the spectacle. When the author finally turns to *La contesa de' numi*, the poetry that gains the attention:

> The Italian cantata, which is mentioned in this report, is a very beautiful piece of poetry, which could carry another title, because of the new form that the author has decided to give to it; it is in the dramatic genre...that is to say that it is not the author who speaks, but the characters who act.[11]

The distinctions the writer in the *Mercure de France* makes concerning *La contesa de' numi* are rather naive, since a dialogue between allegorical characters is a standard feature of the serenata or *componimento drammatico*: the comparison to a type of cantata in which "the author...speaks" is rather puzzling, unless he is here referring to the usual pastorale soliloquy that provides the *soggetto* to most Italian cantatas. No mention is made of either the composer or poet. Valesio's account of the première of *La contesa de' numi*, which he describes as 'the rather esteemed composition of Pietro Metastasio,' closely matches that in the *Mercure* but it is more concise, less detailed.[12]

Within Vinci's works, *La contesa de' numi* stands out for its orchestration. In contrast to the infrequent use of wind instruments in Vinci's operas, in this work more than half the pieces employ wind instruments, and in three of the twelve arias, as well as in the opening sinfonias and closing choruses, the full orchestra of strings, oboes, trumpets and horns are employed. The increased use of wind instruments was probably conditioned by the outdoor performance, in the same manner that they are exploited by Handel in his two orchestral suites. Fortuna's "Se vorria fidarsi" is particularly notable for its orchestral coloring, employing pizzicato and arco strings, pairs of transverse flutes and horns, and obbligato "saltiero" or psaltery.[13] To judge from the number of manuscript scores that survive from the eighteenth century, the work must have attained considerable success.[14]

---

[11] Ibid., 3137 (reprint: XVII, 437).

[12] Valesio, *Diario di Roma*, V, 142; so closely do they match that it is likely that they both relied on the official booklet "Circo Agonale di Roma resitituito all'antica form con illuminazione, e machine artificiali dall' eminentiss. e Reverendiss. Sig. Cardinale," the title page and verso of which is included in Valesio's *Diario* (145-46).

[13] There must have been a psaltery virtuoso in Rome, as there had been during the 1724 season when both Vinci and Vivaldi composed obbligato arias in their carnival operas and again in 1732 when Porpora included it in the sinfonia to his Christmas Cantata.

[14] Manuscripts can be found in Montecassino, Naples, London, Vienna, Paris, and Münster—in fact more scores of *La contesa de' numi* survive than any other work by Vinci except *Artaserse*. According to Laura Pietrantoni, these various scores differ only in notational details. The modern première of *La contesa de'numi* took place in 1999 at the Palazzo Altemps, performed by the Concerto Italiano under the direction

A magnificent painting by Vinci's contemporary Gian Paolo Pannini in the Louvre, entitled *Concert, donné à Rome le 26 novembre 1729, à l'occasion de la naissance du Dauphin, fils de Louis XV*, depicts a lavish performance of a serenata in celebration of the Dauphin.[15] It differs from the detailed description of the performance in that: it takes place in a theatre rather than in a courtyard; is sung by four soloists rather than six; and is attended by an audience in mid-century fashions. These differences are due to the title of the painting which is incorrect and dates back to its purchase in 1832; the original title is:

> *Fête musicale donnée sur les ordres du cardinal de la Rochfoucauld au théatre Argentina de Rome le 15 Julliet 1747 à l'occasion du second mariage de Louis, Dauphin de France et fils de Louis XV, avec Marie-Josèphe de Saxe.*[16]

This painting is now identified with another *componimento drammatico* by Francesco Scarselli and Nicolò Jommelli produced for these wedding celebrations in 1747.[17] There are, however, enough similarities between the Pannini painting and the description of *La contesa* in the *Mercure* to understand why the painting was mistakenly linked to the 1730 celebrations, particularly since its companion piece in Louvre, *Prépararifs du feu d'artifice sur la place Navone*, represents the preparations in the Piazza Navona for the fireworks display in 1729. It would seem, therefore, that the French embassy based the celebration of the Dauphin's wedding on that of his birth in 1730, with the elaborate fireworks in the Piazza Navona and the lavish production of an allegorical *componimento drammatico*. With the latter, the similarities extend to the staging, suggesting that perhaps some of the decorations, sets and

---

of Rinaldo Alessandrini in the very same courtyard where it was first performed 270 years earlier; a critical edition based on this production is to be published by the Accademia Nazionale di Santa Cecilia, Serie II Musica Palatina: *La Contesa de 'Numi di Pietro Metastasio e Leonardo Vinci: Una cantata a Palazzo Altemps per la nascita del Delfino di Francia*, ed. Rinaldo Alessandrini, with essays by Laura Pietrantoni and Amilcare Gaviglia.

[15] The painting is frequently reproduced in accounts of eighteenth-century music, for example, *The Larouse Encyclopedia of Music* (London: Hamlyn, 1971) and H. C. Robbins Landon's *Handel and his World* (London: Weidefeld and Nicolson, 1984).

[16] Letter from Jacques Foucart, Conservateaur Général du Patrimonie, Chef du Service d'Etude et de Documentation du Département des Peintures, Musée du Louvre; for a detailed discussion of the painting and its mate, *Prépararifs du feu d'artifice sur la place Navone*, see Michael Kiene, *Pannini*, Les dossiers du musée du Louvre, département des Peintures, 41 (Paris: Editions de la Réunion des musées nationaux, 1992), 33-61.

[17] The painting is identified with the Scarselli/Jommelli *componimento drammatico* in the entries on "Rome" in the *Enciclopedia dello spettacolo* and in *The New Grove Dictionary of Music and Musicians*.

**Plate 30.** Salvatore Colonnelli: *Courtyard of the Palazzo Altemps decorated for the production of* La contesa de'numi *in November 1729.*[18]

---

[18] Salvatore Colonnelli: "Cortile de Palazzo Altemps abitato dall'Em:mo e R:mo Sig.e Cardinal MELCHIOR DI POLIGNAC Ministro della Maestà Cristianissima in Roma, Magnificamente ornato col Disegno del eruditissimo Cavalier Pietro Leone Ghezzi ...destinato per sei scelti Musici, e per Cento cinquanta sonatori; vestiti alla Teatrale che doverano operare nella Cantata composta in versi dal Sig.e Pietro Metastasio, e in Musica dal Sig.e Leonardo Vinci fattavi fare dal medessimo Sig.e Cardinale in occasione della nascita DEL REAL DELFINO DI FRANCIA il di 26 Novembre 1729;" Museo di Roma (n. 255).

costumes may have been recycled.[19] Pannini undoubtedly attended the première of Vinci's *componimento drammatico* soince he was a protégé of Cardinal Polignac at the time. Had Pannini painted the 1729 production of Vinci's serenata, it would have looked like the print of the actual performance by Salvatore Colonelli, engraved by Filippo Vasconi (see Plate 30 on facing page).[20] Colonelli depicted both the production of the Vinci/Metastasio *La contesa* and the elaborate architecture for the fireworks display. This architecture, which is also the subject of Pannini's *Prépararifs du feu d'artifice sur la place Navone*, was the work of another of Cardinal Polignac's protégés, Pier Leone Ghezzi, who designed the elaborate stage set for *La contesa de' numi*.[21]

Ghezzi had drawn caricatures of Vinci in 1722 and 1724. There is an additional undated one entitled simply "Vinci Napoletano, very famous composer of music, drawn by me, Cavalier Ghezzi" (see Plate 31 on page 286). Although the side-profile of the face is based directly on the first sketch Ghezzi did of Vinci in 1722, this second full-length caricature seems to date from the late 1720s; it appears in the fifth Volume of Ghezzi's *Il Nuovo Mondo* caricatures which almost exclusively drawn during the years 1728-1731.[22] When compared with the 1724 caricature, this one shows a somewhat more rotund composer, in a less elegant coat and lacy shirt, without sword and hat. Instead of striking a gentlemanly pose, he is depicted in one of the early representations of conducting in the modern fashion, before a lectern rather than from the harpsichord beating time with what was to become the standard baton for the eighteenth century, a rolled up piece of manuscript paper. Because the

---

[19] For example: 1. the large orchestra with musicians wearing laurel wreaths and bejewelled black sashes; 2. singers dressed as their respective deities seated upon clouds; 3. the stage supported by large nudes; 4. high warp tapestries (on the floor rather than on the walls); 5. the stage architecture consisting of five arches with perspectives illuminated by chandeliers; 6. the painting of Apollo and his chariot drawn by four horses surmounted by illumination; 7. coats of arms of the King, Queen and Dauphin surmounted by crowns and draped with crimson festoons supported by cupids.

[20] Carla Benocci, "Francesco Nicoletti e Paolo Anesi a Villa Doria Pamphilj (1748-1758)" in *Carlo Marchionni: achitettura, decorazione e scenografia contemporanea*, ed. Elisa Debenedetti (Rome: Multigrafica Editrice, 1988), 209-210.The inspiration for this production probably came from the famous engraving of the première of Lully's *Alceste* (1674) in the Marble Courtyard at Versailles.

[21] *Mercure de France*, December 1729, 3133.

[22] Pier Leone Ghezzi, *Il Nuovo Mondo*, V, f. 13; unpublished manuscript in the Biblioteca Apostolica Vaticana, Ottob.lat 3116. According to Rostirolla, the caricature depicts a man of about forty-five rather than twenty-five.; he then goes on to suggest that Vinci's birthdate be moved back. (*Il "Mondo Novo" musical di Pier Leone Ghezzi*, 303) It makes more sense to move the date of the caricature ahead to 1729, like the others in the volume, making Vinci about forty years old, which coordinates with the Sigismondo/Villarosa c. 1690 birthdate.

**Plate 31.** *Caricature of Leonardo Vinci by Pier Leone Ghezzi, Rome, c.1730.*[23]
© Biblioteca Apostolica Vaticana (Vatican)

[23] Pier Leone Ghezzi, *Op. cit.*; the inscription by Ghezzi reads: "Vinci Napoletano, famocissimo Comp. re di Musica fatto da mei Cav. Ghezzi"

lectern stands on a table, it gives the impression that Vinci is conducting a concert or rehearsal in a private home rather than a performance in a theatre, perhaps a rehearsal of *La contesa de' numi* at the palace of Cardinal Polignac or a concert at one of Ghezzi's Wednesday evening concerts at his home in the Via Giulia.[24]

## Two Operas for the Price of One

In the fall of 1729, Metastasio was appointed Imperial court poet for Emperor Charles in Vienna. In officially accepting his position on November 3, 1729, Metastasio arranged a delay in taking up his duties until after Carnival 1730 because of "some engagements to fulfil with the managers of the Roman theatre, to whom I had promised two new dramas."[25] Vinci set both these dramas. The reason for this exception to the composer's usual practice of one opera per city per season was, according to Charles Burney, "that Vinci set both operas for half price to gratify his enmity to Porpora who was his rival in that city."[26] Although to Burney it may have appeared that Vinci's actions were motivated purely by enmity, this two-for-one arrangement was probably due to Vinci's new position as one of the impresarios at the Teatro delle Dame (see Chapter 8). The fee of three-hundred scudi that he denied himself for one of the operas might well have been his contribution to the partnership with Cavanna and Milesi, who undoubtedly had paid for all or most of the 780 scudi for the Theatre lease. This two-for-one deal, which allowed a single composer to provide both Carnival operas, in turn, allowed the rival Teatro Capranica to do likewise and Porpora was called from Venice (perhaps purposely to exploit an old rivalry) to première his *Mitridate* and revive his *Siface*.[27] Besides the Capranica, a new theatre was inaugurated, the Nuovo Teatro Valle, which presented two new operas: *Eupatra* by Cardinal Ottoboni's protégé Giovanni Battista Costanzi and *Andromaca* by Francesco Feo.[28]

---

[24] Lucia Guerrini, *Marmi antichi nei disegni di Pier Leone Ghezzi*, Biblioteca Vaticana documenti e riproduzione 1 (Vatican: Biblioteca apostolica, 1971), 9.

[25] Charles Burney, *Memoirs of the Life and Writings of the Abate Metastasio,* I, 51.

[26] Charles Burney, *A General History of Music*, II, 916.

[27] A similar arrangement had occurred during the 1719 and 1720 seasons when Gasparini provided both Carnival operas for the Teatro Alibert; this was countered in 1719 by the directors of the Teatro Pace who brought in Bononcini for two operas and by the directors of the Capranica in 1720 who brought in Alessandro Scarlatti for two.

[28] Villarosa describes Feo as a friend of Vinci (Villarosa, *Memorie dei compositori di musica del Regno di Napoli,* 225). His *Andromaca* is published in the Garland Series (Francesco Feo, *Andromaca* [31]) of *Italian Opera 1640-1770*. With the simultaneous operation of three opera theatres, the directors of the Teatro della Pace decided to

In his *Kritische Briefe über die Tonkunst* from 1760 Friedrich Marpurg provides a colorful portrait of the animated controversy that was generated by the back-to-back productions of Vinci and Porpora:

> At one time Leonardo Vinci and Nicolo Porpora, well-known composers in their day, each produced two new operas in Rome during Carnival. Each of them had his own theatre; each had his own society of good singers; each had also followers; each was jealous of the other; each had his own coffeehouse, where he came together with his friends, and from time to time gave vent to his bitterness towards the other.[29]

The flavor of this passage with its boisterous coffeehouse backdrops reminds one of the Handel and Bononcini controversy in London during the mid-1720s and the rivalry between Porpora himself and Handel during the mid 1730s. In contrast to the London rivalries, where there does not appear to have been any personal animosity between Handel and his Italian rivals, with this controversy, there was apparently no love lost between Vinci and Porpora.

The first of Vinci's pair, *Alessandro nell'Indie*, initiated the carnival season at the Teatro delle Dame a little over a month after the première of the *La contesa de'numi*.[30] The cast of *Alessandro*, which was almost identical to that of the serenata, consisted of:

> Alessandro: Raffaele Signorini   Cleofide: Giacinto Fontana
> Poro: Giovanni Carestini         Erissena: Giuseppe Appiani
> Gandarte: Francesco Tolve        Timagene: Andrea Tassi
>    set designer: Giovanni Battista Olivieri
>    choreographer: Pietro Gugliantini
>    battle director: Decio Berrettini

Carestini took the *primo uomo* role, as he had done in *Catone* in 1728, while Fontana was in his usual "*prima donna*" role. Vinci had not worked with the other singers before, though the Neapolitan Tolve had appeared the previous year at the Capranica in the Saddumene/Fischetti comic operas. Giuseppe Appiani was a Milanese pupil of Porpora. Rather

---

produce spoken comedy, but then ran into trouble with the censors (Valesio, *Diario di Roma*, V, 162).

[29] [Friedrich Wilhelm Marpurg], *Kritische Briefe über die Tonkunst: mit kleinen Clavierstüken und Singoden begleitet* (Berlin: Friedrich Wilhelm Birnstiel, 1760 reprint ed., Hildesheim: Gorg Olms Verlag, 1974) Vol. I, 225.

[30] Although Cametti gives the date of the première as December 26, 1729, Valesio describes the première in his diary as taking place on January 2, 1730 (Cametti, "Leonardo Vinci", 298 and Valesio *Diario di Roma*, Vol. 5, 129), the difference may be due to the similarity in function of dress rehearsal and première (see below). Libretto to *Alessandro nell'Indie* in I-Bc -Fc -Fm -MAC -P,Museo civico -Vgc, B-Bc, C-Tu, Th. Fisher, F-Pn, GB-Lbn, US-AUS; Claudio Sartori, *I libretti italiani*, No. 2930.

surprisingly, he was not making his stage debut in an opera by his maestro but in one by his maestro's rival, in the transvestite role of Erissena.[31]

Metastasio's *dramma per musica* is based on the conquest of India by Alexander the Great in 326 BC. Although Alexander defeated King Porus at the battle of Hydaspes, he not only spared his life but restored him to the throne as vassal king. As stated in the *Argomento*, this celebrated act of magnanimity, rather than the actual conquest, is the subject of drama.

> **Synopsis**: After being defeated at the battle Idaspe, Poro is prevented from committing suicide by his general Gandarte, who convinces him to live for his beloved Cleofide and to exchange the royal crown for his helmet to deceive the approaching enemy. Under the assumed identity of Asbite, Poro is captured by Alessandro who, impressed by the nobility of his prisoner, sets him free to deliver his proposal of peace to the Indian King. Alessandro also releases Poro's sister Erissena. The Greek general Timagene has fallen in love with her and is jealous of her infatuation with the conqueror. He gives vent to his hatred for the man responsible for his father's death, resolving to conspire with Poro. At the palace of Cleofide Poro accuses the Queen of infidelity in love and war by negotiating with Alessandro. Cleofide replies that by appeasing Alessandro she tried to save her kingdom from destruction. Poro promises not to doubt Cleofide's faith, but his suspicions are revived when Erissena arrives singing Alessandro's praises. Cleofide decides to seek out Alessandro, assuring Poro that she will always be faithful. Gandarte tells Poro that Timagene will assist them in their struggle against Alessandro. Ignoring Gandarte, Poro resolves to follow Cleofide in disguise to Alessandro's camp. As Cleofide manages to pacify Alessandro's anger for aiding the rebellious Poro, the disguised Poro rushes in, warning Alessandro not to trust her. Cleofide, angered by Poro's broken oath, declares that she is in love with Alessandro, who, concealing his infatuation for Cleofide, makes a hasty exit, leaving the lovers alone to accuse each other of breaking their promises.
>
> Gandarte tells Poro of the trap he has set for Alessandro at the bridge over the River Idaspe. Cleofide goes out to meet Alessandro, but as he crosses the bridge he is attacked by Gandarte and his troops. Fleeing from the battle Cleofide meets Poro. After threatening to drown herself, the lovers are reconciled as the Greek army approaches. To prevent their capture, they resolve on suicide, but are foiled by

---

[31] *Enciclopedia dello spettacolo*, "Appiani, Giuseppe" by Emilia Zanetti.

Alessandro. Timagene tells Alessandro that the army wants revenge upon Cleofide who they believe responsible for the ambush on the bridge. Alessandro has Cleofide placed under arrest and the disguised Poro placed in Timagene's custody. To protect Cleofide from the fury of his troops, Alessandro tells her the only way to save herself is to marry him. Gandarte enters disguised as Poro claiming full responsibility for the ambush. This sacrificial act so impresses Alessandro that he pardons him and cedes his claim over Cleofide. When Alessandro goes out to release his other prisoner, Erissena rushes in to tell Cleofide and Gandarte that Popo has commmitted suicide, instantly transforming the joyous scene into tragedy.

Poro appears to Erissena, asking her not tell Cleofide that he is alive because of the assassination that is planned. To reassure her doubts about Timagene, Poro gives her a letter outlining the details of the plot. Alessandro enters angered by the opposition of the Greeks to his marriage to Cleofide. Believing that he has discovered the plot and fearing she will be implicated, Errisena hands him Timagene's letter. When Timagene returns to tell Alessandro that he has quelled the opposition of his troops to the marriage, he is presented with his letter. The dumbfounded Timagene is doubly surprised when Alessandro forgives him, telling him that his shame will be sufficient punishment. When Poro comes to arrange the assassination, Timagene tears up the letter in disgust. Erissena rushes in to tell them that Cleofide has agreed to marry Alessandro. At the temple of Bacchus, Alessandro is about to offer his hand to Cleofide when she pushes him away and rushes towards the funeral pyre burning for the supposedly deceased Poro. When Alessandro tries to stop her, she tells him of the Indian funeral custom. As she is about to leap upon the funeral pyre, Poro, convinced of her fidelity, comes out of hiding, asks for forgiveness from Cleofide and surrenders to Alessandro. In a grand act a magnanimity Alessandro restores to him both Cleofide and Kingdom.

The unusually concise *Argomento* does not mention the sources Metastasio employed for his drama. The *Historiarum Alexandri Magni* of Quintus Curtius Rufus provides the basic historical background of Alesander's defeat of Porus at the River Hydaspes and the conqueror's magnanimous restoration of his throne.[32] The most important source is Racine's tragedy *Alexandre le Grand* (1666), which is based on the same

---

[32] *Quintus Curtius: with an English Translation by John C. Rolfe* (Cambridge, Mass.: Harvard University Press, 1946), II, 336-359.

historical incident. The elaboration of the character of Poro also comes from Racine who was accused of having made Porus too great, hence Metastasio's Poro is the *primo uomo,* not Alessandro. The character of Cleofide is actually a composite of two characters in *Alexandre le Grand*— Poro's wife Axiane and Alexandre's mistress Cleofide—resulting in her complex and contradictory character, appearing for much of the opera as flirtatious and opportunistic but in the end emerging a paragon of virtue. The drama of jealousy between Poro and Cleofide and Gandarte and Erissena derives from two other sources, Claude Boyer's tragicomedy *Porus, ou la générosité d'Alexandre* (1648) and Domenico David's libretto *L'amante eroe* (1693).[33]

*Alessandro nell' Indie* is a drama of repetitions and symmetries which at times are pushed to extremes. Because the subject of the drama is "la nota generosità...da Alessandro il Grande," the opera is full of examples of the hero's magnanimity. Alessandro is continually vanquishing his enemy only to forgive them and set them free. The grand magnanimous gesture, which provides the conclusion to most Metastasian dramas, occurs twice in *Alessandro,* in the middle of Act II and at the end of Act III. In both instances Alessandro forgives Poro, Cleofide and Gandarte, unites Poro and Cleofide in marriage, and restores their kingdoms. The only difference in the two situations is that in the former, Poro and Gandarte have exchanged their true identities and their deception necessitates that this action be repeated at the end of the opera with their identities restored.[34] The abundance of magnanimous gestures is matched by an abundance of attempted suicides. Poro, Cleofide and Gandarte each attempt suicide twice, as well as Poro and Cleofide's attempted double suicide, while Poro's additional faked suicide provides the entire raison d'être of Act III. It seems that every time these characters have an important point to make, they have to threaten to kill themselves in order to convey the message. Metastasio must have become aware of this overuse and in his revision from 1753/54 removed two of the attempted suicides, Cleofide's first and Gandarte's second.[35]

---

[33] For a detailed analysis of how Metastasio wove together his drama from these three sources, see Reinhard Strohm, "Metastasio's *Alessandro nell'Indie* and its earliest settings," *Essays on Handel and Italian Opera,* 232-248.

[34] The idea for this changing of identities comes from Quintus Curtius (343) who describes how Alexander and his general Atalus exchanged helmets and cloaks as part of the Macedonian battle plan.

[35] The revised version is the one published in Pietro Metastasio, *Tutte le Opere,* I, with the cuttings from Vinci's original appearing in the Appendix, 1442-74. On the revisions that Metastasio made to four of his *drammi* for Farinello during the years 1750-54, see Reinhard Weisend, "Le revisioni di Metastasio di alcuni suoi dramma e la situazione della musica per melodrama negli anni'50 del settecento" in *Metastasio e il mondo musicale,* ed. Maria Teresa Muraro (Florence: Leo S. Olschki, 1986): 171-97.

These repetitions and symmetries also provide the drama with its strengths. Poro and Gandarte's change of identity at the beginning of the drama seems to involve more than mere identity. Throughout most of the opera Gandarte maintains a certain regal majesty that befits his assumed kingship, while Poro exhibits all the impetuosity of an amorous youth. The drama of jealousy that is enacted between Cleofide and Poro is balanced by a similar drama between Erissena and Gandarte, with numerous parallels. The flirtatious and high-spirited characters of Cleofide and Erissena and the impetuous and sulky characters of Poro and Gandarte makes them among Metastasio's most endearing, at times reminiscent of the two couples in *Cosi fan tutti*. This drama of jealousy, true to its tragicomic sources, often verges on the realm of the comic, which, in turn, contributes a distinctive dynamic to the drama. Metastasio evidently became aware of this and in his subsequent revisions treated these scenes with greater reserve.[36]

Vinci's partner Francesco Cavanna dedicated the libretto to James III, pretender to the British throne. In spite of Cavanna's fawning comparisons between James Edward and Alexander the Great, Metastasio undoubtedly intended the character of the indefatigable Poro to represent the Stuart pretender.[37] In his political allegory, Metastasio was probably influenced by Lucchini's *Farnace*, also dedicated to James III, which featured an equally determined hero who continually tries to overthrow a foreign conqueror. Other parallels with *Farnace* include the hero as Eastern potentate who goes underground to continue his struggle against the foreign conqueror, his captive wife who captivates the conqueror, and his captive sister who seduces the conqueror's general, convincing him to switch sides. Considering the number of ingredients in Metastasio's libretti that can be found in previous Vinci operas (*Partenope* in *Siroe* and *Semiramide*, *Silla* in *Catone*, and *Farnace* in *Alessandro*) one gets the impression that the composer had an important influence on the poet in his early dramas. There are also certain anti-imperialist statements which appear rather surprising considering Metastasio's recent appointment in Vienna. For example, Poro's pointed question: "What reason brings Alessandro to the realm of Aurora to disturb her peace? Are the sons of Giove therefore so inhuman?"[38]

---

[36] Helga Lühning, "Alexanders Grosmut und Poros' Eifersuch," article accompanying the recording: Johann Adolf Hasse, *Cleofide*, William Christie, dir. (Capriccio 10193/96, 1987).

[37] The equally flattering portrait of his rival, King George as Alessandro may be the reason for the prompt English premiere a year later by Handel.

[38] *Alessandro nell'Indie: Drama per musica di Pietro Metastasio...da rappresentarsi Nel Teatro detto delle Dame nel Carnevale dell'Anno 1730* (Rome: Zemple & De Mey, 1730) Act I/ii.

Whether or not they represent Metastasio's personal feelings or were intended to appeal to the latent national sentiments of his audience, they were omitted from his subsequent revision, undoubtedly in deference to his Imperial patron.[39]

According to Marpurg "the first opera of each [Vinci's *Alessandro* and Porpora's *Mitridate*] attained success."[40] In his *Diario* Francesco Valesio refers to the "gran concorso" that surrounded the première of *Alessandro nell'Indie* and in a performance on January 11 mentions that someone was arrested for encoring arias—a practice that had recently been banned.[41] However, when he attended a performance on January 15, he complained that "so little in esteem is the drama at the Teatro Alibert [delle dame] that this evening in the pit there were not a hundred persons there.[42] From Valesio's account, it would seem that the ladies ignored the plea the directors addressed to them the previous season in the dedication of *Semiramide* and were not in regular attendance in their stalls.

## Alessandro and the Quarrelling Lovers

By virtue of its music and drama, Act I of *Alessandro nell'Indie* can be regarded as one of the most attractive in Vinci's operas.[43] The initial aria, "E' prezzo leggiero," is sung by Gandarte after he exchanges iden-

---

[39] The entire passage is included among the cuttings from the original *Alessandro nell'Indie* in the Appendix to Metastasio, *Tutte le Opere*, I, 1445.

[40] Marpurg, *Kritische Briefe über die Tonkunst*, I, 225.

[41] Valesio, *Diario di Roma*, V, 159 and 162.

[42] Ibid., 163. The poor turnout on January 11 could be due to the "influenza de'raffredori" which, according to the *Diario Ordinario*, was responsible for the restrained Carnival season of 1730; *Chracas Diario Ordinario (di Roma): Sunto di notizie e indici, I (1718-1739)*, ed. Associazione Culurale (Rome: Alma Roma, 1997), 76.

[43] There are two principal manuscript sources for *Alessandro nell'Indie*. The one in the Biblioteca dell'Abbazia in Montecassino (E 126 E19) is in large-scale format (23 x 36 cm.) with an ornate title page. According to Strohm the score in the Conservatory in Naples copied by Giuseppe Sigismondo, dated August 1811, is a copy of this manuscript (*Italienische Opernarien* II, 233). The other principal manuscript is in the King's Music Library in the British Museum (R.M.23.c.8-10). Like the Montecassino score, it employs a large format (22 x 33 cm., 3 vols.) and a similar watermark, a *fleur de lys* in double circle with initial "V," similar to R. Venuti, Antiqua Numismata, Rome, 1732 (Edward Heawood, *Watermarks: Mainly of the 17th and 18th Centuries* I, No. 1592), the latter giving support to Strohm's claim that both principal manuscripts originated in Rome. The King's score differs from the Montecassino in that it omits the opening aria "E prezzo leggiero" without a break in the manuscript to indicate the omission. Six arias and the sinfonia from this manuscript are reproduced in the Appendix to the Garland facsimile edition of the 1735 production of *Alessandro* in Munich (see below). The King's manuscript was produced as a set with the manuscript of *Artaserse* in the same collection; both are by the same copyist and bound in three volumes in fine white leather. Like the Montecassino score, the *Alessandro* in Brussels (2367) is in a large-scale format with fancy title page; like the King's score it is paired with a score of

tities with Poro, explaining that his life is slight payment for the safety of his sovereign. The sextuplet garlands in the violins (usually associated by Vinci with flight and flightiness) probably depict the "prezzo leggiero/slight price," while the coloratura extension on the words "Re" and "impero" may suggest the continuity of king and empire. The next aria, "Vedrai con tuo periglio" is sung by the disguised Poro when he is set free by Alessandro to serve as peace emissary to the Indian King. To demonstrate his goodwill, Alessandro gives him the sword of Dario. Asbite/Poro replies in his aria that Alessandro will regret his gift when this sword flashes above his head in battle. An ornamental mordent, apparently one of Vinci's latest discoveries, is used in rapid octave displacements to depict the sword flashing above the donor's head—a figuration requiring speed and agility from the violinists at *Allegro* tempo:

Example 9.1 "Vedrai con tuo periglio" *Alessandro nell' Indie* I/ii

*Artaserse* in this same collection. This eighteenth-century manuscript, which Strohm believes originated in Brussels, is incomplete, missing the first act (*Italienische Opernarien* II, p. 233). The copy of Act I in the Royal College of Music is not the missing act to the Brussels score, but part of the large series of Italian operas that formerly belonged to the Concerts of Ancient Music. There is also a manscript copy of the King's score from the 1900s in the Library of Congress in Washington. None of these scores have any connection to the first production and conversely give the impression they were intended for libraries. The excerpts below are taken from the manuscript in the British Library. The complete manuscript of *Alessandro nell' Indie* in Montecassino contains the following musical numbers:

    24 *da capo* arias    2 ariettas    3 *del segno* arias
    1 duettino    1 *da capo* ensemble    1 accompanied recitative
    2 sinfonias    2 choruses
    Totals: 36 set pieces (28 in *da capo* form)

This chirping mordent is augmented by a sextuplet cadential figure and descending tirades in the violins which probably depict the cut and thrust of the sword. The next prisoner that the magnanimous Alessandro frees is Poro's sister Erissena. In his "Vil trofeo d'un alma imbelle," Alessandro proudly proclaims that he has not come to India to conquer distressed damsels. Although the words are not as war-like as the previous text, Vinci introduces pairs of trumpets and oboes to give Alessandro's first aria a martial character.[44] These additional instruments are confined to the ritornello, allowing this heroic triple-meter aria to generate a more lyrical quality than usual in Vinci's martial arias.

Alessandro's general Timagene falls in love with Erissena but his advances are cruelly rebuffed. When he accuses her of being in love with Alessandro, she replies in her aria "Chi vive amante" that she cannot be in love because she does not languish and lament the way modern lovers do. Vinci set this tongue-in-cheek satire of contemporary love as a tuneful *alla breve*, the only hint of irony being the slight overemphasis of the words "lagno/complain" with syncopated coloratura and "sempre sospira/ever sighing" with a tritone and hiccup. The opening sequence of scenes ends with a soliloquy for Timagene who sets the plot in motion by resolving to conspire with Poro against Alessandro in order to seek revenge for the death of his father.[45] In the simile aria "O su gli estivi ardori" he compares himself to a snake in the flowers stalking the unsuspecting shepherds. The unusual second theme seems to be programmatically inspired: the repeated semi-quavers depict the stalking snake and the cadential leaps and trill depict the snake striking its victims:

Example 9.2 "O su gli estivi ardori" *Alessandro nell'Indie* I/v

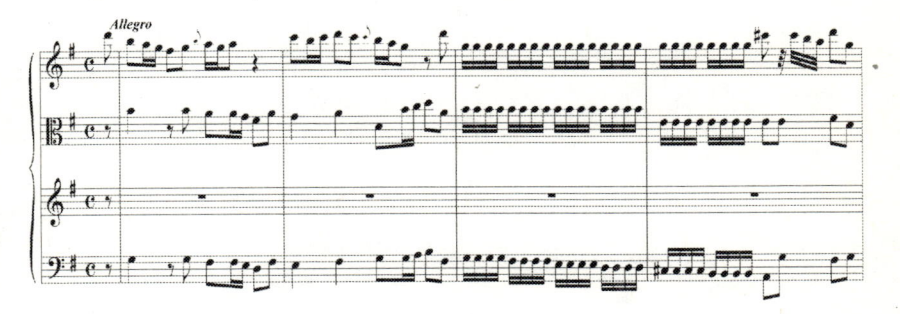

---

[44] On the relationship between music and the Metastasian conception of monarchical power and responsibility, see Reinhard Strohm, "Rulers and states in Hasse's *drammi per musica,* in *Dramma per per Musica: Italian Opera Seria of the Eighteenth Century* (New Haven: Yale Univesity Press, 1988), 270-93.

[45] In Metastasio's revision, this reference is removed to purge the character of the Emperor from any crime, another change made with his new patron in mind; see Metastasio, *Tutte le Opere,* I, 316.

The first theme, with its imitative accompanimental figure, is similar to that in the aria "D'amor nei primi istanti" from Handel's *Imeneo*.

Just as Frugoni had delayed the Farinello's appearancein *Medo*, Metastasio delayed the Farfallino's appearance in *Alessandro* until the middle of Act I.[46] At Cleofide's palace, Poro hurls accusations concerning her fidelity, while she counters by explaining that all her actions were motivated by her concern for his welfare. With his jealously finally assuaged, Poro, in the arietta "Se mai più sarò geloso," swears he will never again be jealous. Unlike most of Vinci's melodies, this lovely melody must have been conceived independently of the words, since it ignores the verse structure completely.[47] In the first vocal period, the first and second verse endings are ignored (mm.10 and 12), with the only *caesura* occurring in the middle of the third verse, prior to the cadence:

Example 9.3 "Se mai più sarò geloso" *Alessandro nell' Indie* I/vi

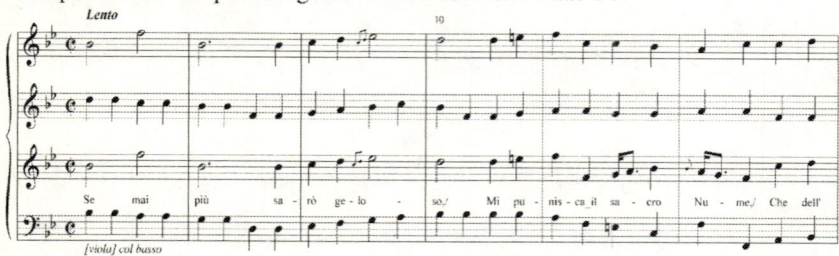

---

[46] This dynamic was ruined in Hasse's setting, *Cleofide* which gave his wife Faustina Bordoni-Hasse the opening aria; see the recording Johann Adolf Hasse, *Cleofide*, dir. William Christie (Capriccio 10193/96, 1987), which reproduces the original libretto.

[47] On the system behind Vinci's periodic melody, see the author's article: "Burney's Assessment of Leonardo Vinci," *Acta Musicolgica*, 68/2 (1995), 142-63.

Since the arietta does not require an exit, Poro remains on stage only to be plunged into another fit of jealousy as Cleofide abruptly decides to visit Alessandro at his camp after hearing from Erissena of the conqueror's generosity. When Poro tries to prevent her from leaving, she reminds him of his promise by making a parody of it for her own promise of fidelity. The parody relationship between the aria texts is reflected musically by making Cleofide's aria a parody of Poro's arietta. Although Cleofide's aria is a full-fledged *da capo*, the first section is basically the same as Poro's arietta except that the second vocal period is expanded by a coda and a more expansive final ritornello. Having been tantalized by this lovely *cantabile* melody, one is pleased to hear it again developed to its full potential in a *da capo* aria.[48]

Upon Cleofide's exit, the distraught Poro expresses his doubts about her intentions to his sister Erissena who is anything but sympathetic. When Poro resolves to follow Cleofide in disguise to Alessandro's camp, his friend Gandarte tries to convince him otherwise. Poro can now finally react to these unexpected events in a full-fledged *da capo* aria. In "Se possono tanto" he complains to Gandarte of the torments he suffers because of the power of Cleofide's "due luci vezzose/two beautiful eyes" This A-major aria is written in the diffuse rapturous style that Vinci had employed for Carestini in "Chi un dolce amor condanna" and "Quell'amor che poco accende" from *Catone in Utica*. Although the lightly syncopated lyrical melody and the garlands of sextuplets gives the impression that the composer is concentrating on the beautiful eyes of the beloved, the lover's torment is suggested by the subtle chromaticism which gradually comes to dominate the second vocal period, with the chromatics often appearing in the slow moving bass. In a parallel scene Erissena arouses Gandarte's jealousy by continually speaking of Alessandro. When he tries to assert his prerogative as her fiancée, she decrees that, as a true lover, he must indulge her flirtations and faithfully serve her. In her aria "Compagni nell'amore" Erissena warns that if the lover does not know how to suffer, he will never find a heart that will shine for him. This amorous apostrophe is realized in an unusual G-minor aria reminiscent of a *corrente* with teasing hemiola and two-part counterpoint. The short vocal phrases are linked by a peculiar unison motive in the orchestra that recurs throughout the aria, almost like an *idée fixe*, emphasized by *forte* dynamics to the usual piano accompaniment:

---

[48] In Hasse's setting, *Cleofide* from 1731, the heroine's aria is an expanded variant of the hero's arietta, while in Handel's setting, *Poro* from 1731, the aria is set to music in a contrasting style. For a detailed comparison of Vinci's, Hasse's and Handel's settings of this scene and their implications in the Act I duet, see Graham Cummings, "Reminiscence and Recall in Three Early Settings of Metastasio's *Alessandro nell' Indie*" Proceedings of the Royal Musical Association 109 (1982-83):80-104.

Example 9.4 "Compagni nell'amore" *Alessandro nell'Indie* I/x

The modulation to the relative major and shimmering syncopations (mm. 15-16) admirably depicts the verse "Che avvampi mai per te/ that ever shines for you" and culminates in an octave displacement to the upper register for the elegant repeated scale cadence. After this ray of light, the restatement of the G-minor theme in the tonic after the intermediate ritornello creates a rather melancholic effect. This is emphasized by the fact that the rest of the section remains in the tonic minor and then turns to the dominant minor in the second section. Moreover the repeated unison motive that linked the short vocal phrases of the theme returns with a vengeance in the coda. The distinctive character of this aria gives the impression the composer is suggesting that the pleasures of love are outweighed by the suffering (for the aptness of this message, see Chapter 10). Left alone, Gandarte complains about the plight of the modern man, wishing for a return to the age of male dominance. Vinci ignores the irony in Gandarte's "Voi che adorate" by writing a rather neutral C-major *allegro*.

After Poro interrupts Cleofide's negotiations with Alessandro, she spitefully declares that she is in love with the conqueror. The shocked Alessandro replies in his aria "Se amore a questo petto" that if love was not an emotion foreign to his warlike temperament, he would certainly return her love. The pompous gait of this heroic aria is enlivened by mixing lombards with the dotted rhythms.[49] The subsidiary material of

---

[49] In Metastasio's revision Cleofide's abrupt declaration of love and Alessandro's conceited refusal were omitted to simplify this scene and the subsequent encounters between these two characters; see Metastasio, *Tutte le Opere*, I, 325-26.

the ritornello, based on Vinci's chirping mordent set in rising sequences, returns in the vocal periods with the phrase "m'accendere" to depict the flames of love that Alessandro admits he could feel for Cleofide. The act ends with a duet in B-flat major for Poro and Cleofide as each quotes the other's promise, resulting in two further statements of the "Se mai" melody (Example 9.3) arranged as the double exposition of a typical Vinci duet.[50] These ironic quotations lead to a quarrel between the two lovers as they accuse each other of breaking their promise and apostrophize on their harsh fate in shared asides. Although this could have been set as a duet of opposition, as Hasse was to do in his *Cleofide* the following year, Vinci sets each accusation separately in declamatory recitative style. The voices then come together in the shared aside beginning imitatively but soon falling into neat parallel harmonies. Thus, the expansive first vocal period contains two distinct segments:

Example 9.5 "Se mai turbo/Se mai più" *Alessandro nell' Indie* I/xvi

[50] In comparing Galuppi's setting of the revised text from 1754 with Vinci's setting of the original from 1730, Reinhard Weisend concentrates on the music of Act I, where he detects a general increase in the duration of the arias, with Vinci's arias accounting for about an hour of music and Galuppi's about ninety minutes (using approximate timings). In the settings of certain arias, such as "Vedrai con tuo periglio" and the *da capo* and duet versions of "Se mai turbo," this increase would result in more than double the length in Galuppi's new settings. This increase in the length of the arias is, in turn, partially offset by a decrease in the amount of recitative due to the substantial cuts that Metastasio made to his text in the 1754 revision; Wiesend, "Le revisioni di Metastasio di alcuni suoi drammi," 181-83.

the quotations that cadence on the dominant of F and the accusations and asides that come to a close on the unexpected subdominant of E♭ major (the latter appearing at the beginning of Example 9). The second vocal period fuses the two segments of the first by juxtaposing the initial fragment of each accusation (mm.38-39 and 43-44) with the opening phrase of each quotation (mm. 40-43 and 45-48) arranged again as a double exposition. After a further exchange of accusations (mm. 48-52), the section and duet conclude with the sonorous parallel harmonies of the shared aside. The melodic repetitions generated by the "Se mai" arietta, aria, and the duet can be found in most settings of Metastasio's drama, giving a certain unity to the Act, which is rare in this modular genre.[51] The idea for these quotations may derive from another drama based on this subject — Ortensio Mauro's *La superbia d'Alessandro* that was arranged and published by Paolo Rolli as *Alessandro* and set to music by Handel in 1726. In Rolli's *Alessandro* the hero pays court to both heroines, Rossane and Lisaura, in two ariettas; in both instances Alessandro is unaware that the other is listening and is later humiliated when each quotes the arietta he had previously sung to her rival.

Although the music of Act II is not as attractive as Act I, the initial demonstration of magnanimity produces some of the finest music in the opera. When Alessandro unites Cleofide with the man whom he thinks is Poro, he tells him to honor the giver by honoring the gift since Cleofide is indeed worthy of love. This duple-meter cantabile aria, with its lilting syncopated rhythms and regular periodicity, seems to match perfectly Metastasio's galant magnanimity. The opera could very well end at this point with the reunion of the lovers, but as Cleofide awaits to be re-united

---

[51] Although in Handel's *Poro* the contrasting music of the arietta and aria ignore the parody, it highlights the ironic quotation of oaths at the beginning of the duet; George Frideric Handel, *Poro* Vol. 79 of *G. F. Händels Werke: Ausgabe der Deutschen Händelgesellschaft*, ed. Friedrich Chrysander; for Graham Cummings, Handel "emphasized the individual characters of Poro and Cleofide in their arias...so that their diverse musical elements could be brought together and integrated in the duet," Cummings, "Reminiscence and Recall," 99.

with the real Poro, Erissena rushes in with the news of Poro's supposed suicide. This artificial manipulation, which catapults the drama back into action for yet another act, generates one of Vinci's finest tragic arias. In "Se il ciel mi divide" Cleofide questions why the gods have separated her from Poro. This F-minor *Presto* is an example of the agitated *aria parlante*, with its syllabic setting, fast tempo, and minor mode. As in "Tradita, sprezzata" from *Semiramide* (Example 8.11), the *senario* verse is set to short repeated rhythmic patterns, creating the effect of *ternario* couplets, enchained to the offbeat arpeggios of the accompaniment:

Example 9.6 "Se il ciel mi divide" *Alessandro nell'Indie* II/xiv

An ornamented falling third, perhaps related to one of Vinci's chirping figures, punctuated by rests and enhanced by diminished harmony and *forte-piano* contrasts, creates the effect of pathetic sobs at the end of the ritornellos (mm. 6-9) and second vocal period.

Edward J. Dent dismissed Vinci's *Alessandro nell'Indie* as 'a commonplace and mediocre work, still retaining traces of Scarlatti's influence," preferring *Semiramide riconosciuta*, "which belongs quite definitely to the later generation."[52] While the influence of Scarlatti is negligible in *Alessandro*, as in most of Vinci's mature works (a notable exception being Example 9.13 below), from the perspective of style, both definitely belong "to the later generation." Moreover, it must be admitted that both operas contain their share of "commonplace and mediocre" material, particularly Act I in *Semiramide* and Act III in *Alessandro*.

[52] Edward J. Dent, "Notes on Leonardo Vinci" *The Musical Antiquary* IV (1912/13), 199.

Were the palm to be given to one of these two operas, *Alessandro nell' Indie* would be a better choice because the sentimental grace and noble heroism of Vinci's melodies match the characters in this delightful drama that often verges on the *mezzo carattere*.

Vinci's *Alessandro nell'Indie* was revived in Livorno for Carnival 1731 and a year later in Florence and Reggio Emilia.[53] Costanza Posterla sang Cleofide in Livorno and Florence (in the former with Berenstadt in the title role), while in Reggio Emilia, Andrea Tassi returned as Timagene. The libretto of *Alessandro* in Urbino during Carnival 1734 is almost identical to the Roman one, suggesting that this was a true revival without the usual revisions.[54] The one produced in Munich during Carnival 1735, however, approaches pasticcio. Here, the sinfonia and six of Vinci's arias were replaced, while three arias and a march have been added to the score.[55] *Alessandro* was also revived in Parma in 1736 and perhaps at neighbouring Prato.[56]

## Berenstadt's Snuff Caper

The second of the two operas by Vinci and Metastasio to appear at the Teatro delle Dame during Carnival 1730 was *Artaserse*. The double Roman/Venetian premières of the previous year continued with this drama, but with Porpora in Rome, the S. Giovanni Grisotomo featured Vinci's other rival, Hasse. That *Alessandro nell'Indie* did not receive a double première is probably due to Porpora taking up the double bill at the Capranica. As with *Ezio* from the previous year, the Venetian première of *Alessandro nell'Indie* would have been originally intended for Porpora.

---

[53] Libretto for the Livorno production in I-Fm, for the Florentine in I-N (Lucchesi-Palli), and for the Reggio in I-REm; Sartori, *I libretti Italiani*, Nos. 715, 717 and 719.

[54] Libretto in C-Tu(Th.Fisher); Sartori, *I libretti Italiani*, No. 724; Strohm (*Italienische Opernarien*, II, p. 233) lists revivals in Genoa and Brescia in 1732 and 1733, but the former cannot be substantiated by either a libretto or a score and the latter is probably a revival of the 1732 Venetian setting by Pescetti. The libretto for the Brescian production (I-Mb) does not mention a composer, but the libretto is dedicated by *primo uomo* Francesco Finazzi, who had sung the same role in Pescetti's setting in Venice in 1732.

[55] This manuscript has been published in facsimile: Leonardo Vinci, *Alessandro nell' Indie*, arr., Giovanni Battista Ferrandini, *Italian Opera 1640-1770*, Vol. [72]. Several of the new arias have been identified: from Hasse's *Euristeo* (1732), Sarro's *Tito Sempronio Gracco* (1725) and Schiassi's *Alessandro* (1734); some of the others are probably by Giovanni Battista Ferrandini, Vice-Maestro di Cappella at Munich who is thought to be responsible for this production; Reinhard Wiesend, "Zur Physiognomie einer Oper im Spannungsfeld zwischen Werk und Aufführung: Der Münchner *Alessandro nell'Indie* von 1735," *Von Isaac bis Bach: Festschrift Martin Just zum 60.Geburtstag*, ed. Frank Heidlberger, Wolfgang Osthoff, and Reinhard Wiesend (Kassel: Bärenreiter, 1991), 229-39.

[56] Libretto for Parma in I-Mb and for Prato in I-Fm; Sartori, *I libretti italiani*, Nos. 729 and 730; the latter without composer designation, could have been based on Hasse's setting or a pasticcio of the two.

However, in taking up the double bill at the Capranica, he could hardly produce a second setting of the same drama that Vinci was about to produce at the delle Dame and so he may have used his claim to the second setting of *Alessandro nell'Indie* as a bargaining chip in re-organizing an extremely busy Carnival season. In its stead Riccardo Broschi's *Idaspe* and Giovanni Maria Giai's *Mitridate* were produced.[57] In coming up with two new operas for Rome, Porpora decided to revive *Siface* from 1726 and to compose his own setting of Filippo Vanstryp's *Mitridate*, the one to be set by Giai, in the process creating another double première of a new drama in Rome and Venice, albeit not a Metastasian one. Porpora's subsequent setting of *Alessandro nell'Indie* would be premièred the following year, not in Venice but in Turin under the alternate title of *Poro*, in a gala performance at the Regio Teatro "in the presence of Their Royal Majesties, the Kind and Queen of Sardinia."[58]

Although the Vinci and Hasse settings of *Artaserse* appeared at the same time, at the end of the Carnival season, as was the case with *Semiramide* the previous year, Vinci's opera was the official première, with Metastasio's libretto revised for the Venetian producion by the theatre poet, who at this time was Giovanni Boldini.[59] Vinci's cast, which was almost the same as that for *Alessandro nell'Indie*, consisted of:

    Arbace: Giovanni Carestini    Mandane: Giacinto Fontana
    Artaserse: Raffaele Signorini    Semira: Giuseppe Appiani
    Artabano: Francesco Tolve    Megabise: Giovanni Ossi
        stage design: Giovanni Battista Olivieri and Pietro Orte
        choreography: Pietro Gugliantini

The only difference between the casts of *Alessandro* and *Artaserse* was that Giovanni Ossi replaced Andrea Tassi in the cadet role and Decio Berrettini, the battle director at the della Dame, was replaced by a sec-

---

[57] Weil, *I Teatri Musicali Veneziani*, 98-99.

[58] According to Strohm, Hasse's eventual setting of *Alessandro nell'Indie* as *Cleofide*, to inaugurate the Hasse/Bordoni regime at the Saxon court, may have been part of the negotiated contract with that court, "a precondition for appointment" like tying his appointment to that of his new bride Faustina; Reinhard Strohm, "Hasse's Opera 'Cleofide' and Its Background," article accompanying the recording: Johann Adolf Hasse, *Cleofide*, William Christie, dir. (Capriccio 10193/96, 1987).

[59] In tracing the complex background to Hasse's appointment to the Saxon court, Daniel Heartz is incorrect in stating that Metastasio was in Venice during Carnival 1730 for the production of Hasse's *Artaserse*. If he had been, there would have been no need for Boldini to revise the text for Hasse. Moreover, the possibility that Metastasio saw one of the later performances of Hasse's *Artaserse* on his way to Vienna is also ruled out by the fact that he did not arrive in Vienna until July of 1730, suggesting that Metastasio used the period after the première of Vinci's *Artaserse* to prepare for his life-changing journey. Daniel Heartz, "Hasse at the Crossroads: *Artaserse* (Venice 1730), Dresden and Vienna" *The Opera Quarterly* 16.1 (Winter 2000): 24-33.

ond stage designer—*Artaserse* being Vinci's only Roman opera without a battle scene. Although the singer Gioacchino Conti "Gizziello" is reputed to have made his debut in Vinci's *Artaserse*,[60] the cast list in the libretto clearly shows that this was not the case.[61] In his book on the castrati, Angus Heriot combines Conti's supposed debut in *Artaserse* with an anecdote which relates how Caffarelli rode post-haste to Rome, between his own performances in Naples, to hear him sing in *Artaserse*.[62] While this makes for a good story, it is not only contradicted by the cast list of *Artaserse*, but also by the fact that Caffarelli was in Rome during the Carnival of 1730 singing with Porpora at the Teatro Capranica.[63]

Another anecdote of greater substance is told by Friedrich Marpurg in his *Kritische Briefe über die Tonkunst*; he describes how the rivalry between Vinci and Porpora came to a ludicrous climax prior to the *Artaserse* première. This lengthy anecdote is presented in its entirety because it is the only extended one connected with Vinci (the beginning, relating to the production of *Alessandro*, having already been quoted above):

> The second [opera] of Porpora [*Siface*] was to be produced one day sooner than the second of Vinci [*Artaserse*]. The followers of Porpora went to considerable lengths to trumpet abroad the merits of his second [opera] over the first which had already excited great expectations among music lovers. Now Vinci feared to be defeated with his new opera, especially since it must make its appearance a few days later. He imagined that his rival's work would in advance capture all the success from his work. Advice from his friends was of no avail. [However] he discovered a means to hinder the progress of the other. Immediately he would buy 150 entrance tickets to Porpora's theatre, and distribute these to his friends who then at the dress rehearsal would whistle and make noise; only he did not have enough money. Yet another plot occurred to him which was no less ingenious. Please remember that in Rome, the good or bad success of the opera dress rehearsal, which was heard and examined with greatest attention, very

---

[60] "Conti, Gioacchino" in Carlo Schmidl, *Dizionario universale dei musicisti* (Milan: Casa Editrice Sonzogno, 1937). This information is repeated in the entries on Conti in both the *Enciclopedia dello spettacolo* and *The New Grove*.

[61] Except on the off-chance that the young Conti was called in at the last moment as a substitute, in the same way that he was called upon to replace Nicolini in 1732 in Pergolesi's *Salustia*.

[62] Angus Heriot, *The Castrati in Opera* (London: Secker & Warburg, 1956), 115-116.

[63] According to Monaldi, this anecdote took place several years later when Conti was singing in *Didone* at the Teatro Argentina; Gino Mondali, *Cantanti evirati celebri: secolo xvii-xviii* (Rome: Società editrice, 192), 74.

often decided the fate of the entire opera. Therefore what was to be done? The good Vinci was desperate, and awaited the fate of his new opera with fear, certain that it would bite the dust.

There happened to be a singer under Vinci, a castrato named Gaetano Berenstadt, who had not yet sung in many works, but on the other hand was very advanced in his [scholarly] studies (a rare occurrence among singers) and as a result gained access to many aristocratic homes. Generally he satisfied himself with performing the cadet roles. To his misfortune, Porpora by chance one time had spoken badly about him. This situation presented Berenstadt with an easy opportunity to revenge himself upon Porpora and to help Vinci in his need. Therefore he spoke to Vinci with encouragement and requested that he leave everything to him. He then took a few pounds of the driest and finest Spanish snuff that he could obtain, and filled up many small paper cylinders, each with a small opening above and below. Armed with these, he went incognito to the theatre where Porpora's opera must be rehearsed for the last time. In the upper circle, he rented a single box and kept himself hidden as much as possible. As now before a very numerous assembly the rehearsal began and the ever-present friends of Porpora began to express their approval and admiration, Berenstadt also began to blow out as strongly as he could the tobacco from the cylinders. The tobacco spread itself out at once above the parterre and fell little by little on the listeners standing below. They soon became aware of the source of this unusual rain from above. However no sooner had the falling tobacco got into their raised noses than they began to sneeze. Berenstadt, not bounded by this, continued to fire from his tobacco cartridges. The more they looked up, the more universal was the sneezing, and the noise from this strange incident. The cries of the women with their clothes and lace despoiled, began to drown out the voices of the singers; and finally everyone tried to get out of the theatre, so that by the end of the first act, no listeners could be seen. Because there had been no chance to hear or scrutinize the rehearsal, the opera of poor Porpora thus received a powerful blow, as is often the case in Rome; and in exchange Vinci's second opera [*Artaserse*] attained even greater success. A very wicked prank by a joking singer. [64]

The anecdote certainly is bizarre, though not much more so than Cuzzoni and Faustina coming to blows on the stage of the King's Theatre in the

---

[64] F. W. Marpurg, *Kritische Briefe über die Tonkunst: mit kleinen Clavierstüken und Singoden begleitet* (Berlin: Friedrich Wilhelm Birnstiel, 1760; reprint ed., Hildesheim: Georg Olms Verlag, 1974), I, 225-27.

Haymarket. Tobacco, then as now, was a controversial commodity and government attempts to control it produced a flourishing black market, the fine Spanish snuff being particularly prized. A few days prior to the *Artaserse* première, Valesio describes a botched sting operation by Count Giraud, the controller of tobacco, with the smugglers managing to escape with their jars of fine Spanish snuff and sacks of cut tobacco.[65]

The anecdote does, however, have its problems. Gaetano Berenstadt himself was busy during this season, starring in the title role in Porta's *Il gran Tamerlano* in Florence, premièred on 25 January.[66] This does not rule out the possibility of Berenstadt travelling to Rome between performances in Florence, as Caffarelli was supposed to have done from Naples to hear Conti, or as the Old Pretender did from Bologna during the previous season to hear *Semiramide*. Berenstadt, as we have seen, was one of Vinci's regular singers. Mention has already been made of his reputation as a scholar, collector, and connoisseur, to which the anecdote makes reference; to reconcile these facts to this nasty bit of artistic espionage seems rather difficult. However, one can find a similar anomaly in his friendship with the physician Antonio Cocchi, which came to an abrupt end in November of 1734 after he caught Berenstadt spreading gossip and rumors about him, wilfully continuing even after he was confronted on the issue.[67]

Another problem with the anecdote is that Valesio makes no mention of the incident in his *Diario* and he was just as prone to report on incidents in the theatre as on the actual performance; for example, he makes no mention of the première of *Artaserse* but describes in some detail an incident between a member of Prince Ruspoli's regiment and a servant of the nephew of General Stanhope that took place in front of the theatre during one of the subsequent performances.[68] When Valesio does refer to Porpora's *Siface*, it is to report only that it received "poco sodisfazione" and that the directors of the Capranica "have had the first [i.e. *Mitridate*] put back on stage."[69] The most important issue with which to take exception is the motivation for Vinci's fear. Why should

---

[65] Valesio, *Diario di Roma*, V, 170-171.

[66] Because of this Lowell Lindgren tries to connect the anecdote to the 1732 season when Berenstadt was singing at the Teatro delle Dame in the pasticcio *Didone abbandonata* and Giai's *Demetrio*, while Porpora's *Germanico in Germania* was performed at the Capranica. However, the anecdote relates directly with the 1730 season when both Vinci and Porpora produced a pair of operas; Lowell Lindgren, "La Carriera di Gaetano Berenstadt" *Revista italiana di musicologia*, XIII-IXX (1983/84), 86.

[67] Lindgren, Lowell. Ibid., 95-97.

[68] Valesio, *Diario di Roma*, V, 173.

[69] Ibid., 174. For that matter neither does Valesio mention the stormy première of Pergolesi's *L'Olympiade* at the Teatro Tordinona during the spring of 1735 when the composer was supposedly hit in the head with an orange; Ibid., 797.

he have had anything to fear from a revival of Porpora's *Siface*? He had already come up against the original *Siface* with his *Siroe Re de Persia* in Venice in 1726 and, according to Quantz, he came out the winner. As in Venice, Vinci had the novelty card, with the première of a new drama (actually two new dramas) from the new literary star, and by this time, word would have probably gotten around that this was to be his final work before leaving for the Emperor's court. And yet, in spite of all its problems, the manner in which Marpurg's story coordinates with other information concerning the season and its participants—the old rivalry with Porpora, the Vinci and Porpora double bills at the delle Dame and Capranica theatres, Vinci's chronic insolvency, Berenstadt's irascible and contradictory character, the failure of Porpora's *Siface* and the eventual success of Vinci's *Artaserse*, even the abundance of fine Spanish snuff in Rome—places it within the realm of belief and strongly suggests that at least, it originated in Rome at this time. Regardless of whether or not the anecdote is true, it is plausible; it provides a picaresque vignette of the Vinci/Porpora rivalry and brings to life an opera season that would otherwise be reported, like countless others in *settecento* Italy, as just another set of titles, theatres, dates, and names.

Perhaps it was poetic justice that Vinci's *Artaserse* had its own fateful interruption. During the final performance on February 21, "scarcely at the end of the First Act, orders came to cease, following upon the death of the Pope."[70] Pope Benedict XIII had been stricken with fever on February 19 and died two days later, causing the immediate closure of all the theatres. The Pope's death amid the boisterous revelry of *martedì grasso* gives this momentous season a final bizarre twist.[71]

*Artaserse*, like *Siroe re di Persia*, is a dynastic melodrama set in Ancient Persia. As stated in the *Argomento*, the drama centers on the murder of King Xerxes the Great in 465 BC by his vizier Artabanus who then conspires to have Xerxes' eldest son Darius murdered and his youngest son Artaxerxes I placed on the throne as his creature. When Artabanus begins to plot against the young king, Artaxerxes, informed about his crimes, kills him to avenge the deaths of his father and brother. Although the outlines of the plot are based on historical events related by Marcus Junianus Justinus in his sumary of the *Historiae Philippicae*, these events for the most part are confined to the opening scenes, with the majority of the drama consisting of romantic elaboration.

---

[70] Valesio, *Diario di Roma*, V, 179.
[71] The irreverences continued the following *Ceneri* when an angry crowd gathered in the Borgo shouting "Fuori gli beneventani," calling for the downfall of the Pope's favorites from Benevento, in particular, the corrupt Cardinal Coscia; Ibid., 180.

**Synopsis**: After Arbace is banished from the palace by King Serse because of his love for his daughter Mandane, Arbace's father, the royal counselor Artabano, murders Serse. Although his real motive for killing the king is to place his son on the Persian throne, he tells Arbace that he has murdered Serse to avenge his banishment. He gives him the bloody sword and tells him to flee the palace. Artabano then sets up the execution of Serse's son Dario by implicating him in the murder to his brother Artaserse. His plans, however, are upset by the capture of Arbace with the murder weapon. This is doubly tragic for the new king Artaserse; not only is he torn by remorse for his over-hasty execution of his innocent half-brother, he is faced with concrete evidence that his best friend was his father's murderer. Although Arbace insists upon his innocence, he refuses to reveal the murderer. So as not to raise any suspicions, Artabano disowns his son as a traitor. The forlorn Arbace is then rejected both by his sister Semira and his beloved Mandane.

Allowed to visit Arbace in prison, Artabano tells him of a secret passage where his troops await, pledged to overthrow Artaserse and place him on the throne. Arbace indignantly refuses and calls for the guards. Artabano informs his confederate Megabise that their plans to murder Artaserse must be postponed. To fortify their alliance, Artabano gives Megabise consent to marry his daughter Semira who in turn protests because of her love for Artaserse. The distraught Semira meets Mandane who wants revenge, believing that it was Arbace's love that compelled him to murder her father. Entering the Royal Council wherein Artaserse meets with the Grandees of the realm, Mandane calls for revenge and Semira for mercy. Arbace is brought before Artaserse. Reluctant to believe his best friend capable of such a crime, Artaserse appoints Artabano to judge, anticipating paternal clemency. Artabano, not wanting his conspiracy to be discovered, condemns his son to death, a sentence which the obedient Arbace willingly accepts. Mandane accuses Artabano of inhumanity, saying that it was her duty to avenge the death of her father just as it was his duty to save his son. Semira, believing that her father's judgment was subservient to the law, condemns Artaserse, the only one capable of subverting the law to save Arbace.

Artaserse, unwilling to accept the judgement, enters the prison and sets Arbace free. Later when Artabano and the conspirators enter the prison to rescue Arbace, the empty cell is interpreted as a sign that the Arbace has been executed. Megabise convinces Artabano to continue with the revolt.

When Semira and Mandane are informed about Arbace's disappearance, Semira blames Mandane. Alone, the grieving Mandane is surprised by the appearance of Arbace. She calls him a traitor but tells him to flee the palace. At his coronation Artaserse takes his vows and is about to drink from the sacred cup which Artabano has poisoned, when Semira rushes in to tell him the palace is besieged by the rebels. As Artaserse begins to suspect that Arbace has betrayed him, Mandane enters with news that Arbace has slain Megabise and convinced the conspirators to lay down their arms. Arbace enters victorious. Artaserse accepts his silence asking only that he swear his innocence by drinking from the sacred cup. Frantically warning Arbace not to drink the cup, Artabano is forced to admit not only his plot to overthrow Artaserse but also his murder of Serse. Artabano tries to kill the King but Arbace threatens to drink the cup if he does not lay down his weapon. Artabano surrenders and Arbace convinces Artaserse to punish his father with exile rather than death. Arbace and Mandane and Semira and Artaserse are united in marriage.

While Metastasio based his drama on the historian Justian, there are other, more contemporaneous, sources which Charles de Brosses easily recognized: "it is...one of the best pieces of Metastasio, who has taken as much from *Stilicon* of Thomas Corneille as from *Xerxès* by Crébillon."[72] Crébillon stays much closer to the historical events, concentrating on the murder of Xerxes and the conspiracy against Darius, which in *Artaserse* takes place in the opening scenes. The love interest between Artaxerxes and the daughter of Artabanus provides the source for the romance between Artaserse and Semira. Although Thomas Corneille's *Stilicon* has nothing to do with the Artaxerxes story, the tragic hero Eucherius provides the model for the *primo uomo* Arbace.[73] Eucherius is in love with the sister of Emperor Honorius but is implicated in a plot against the Emperor engineered by his father Stilicon. Rather than reveal his father's guilt, he is banished from Rome, but then vindicates himself by dying in battle against the rebels. Metastasio had already employed a variant of the *Stilicon* plot the previous year in *Ezio*; in this drama, the hero is implicated in a conspiracy against the Emperor that is instigated by the father of his beloved Fulvia whom he refuses to betray. The reason for this second *Stilicon* remake, is probably due to the failure of *Ezio*, which, according to Valesio, was due to Auletta's music;

---

[72] Charles De Brosses, *Lettres familières écrites d'italie a quelques amis en 1739 et 1740* (Paris: Poulet-Malassis et de Broise, 1858), 256.

[73] For a detailed discussion of these sources, see Robert Burns Meikle, "Leonardo Vinci's *Artaserse*: An Edition, with an Editorial and Critical Commentary," Ph.D. Thesis, Cornell University, 1970 (Ann Arbor, Michigan: UMI, 1971), 319-34.

presumably the drama was received favorably and Metastasio decided to treat the subject again, but this time with his regular collaborator, Vinci. The wayward poisoned toast, which provides for the resolution of the drama in *Artaserse*, also appeared the previous year in the engagement scene in Act II of *Semiramide*.

Metastasio's libretto has no connection with Zeno and Pariati's *Artaserse*, originally produced in Venice in 1705, nor with the *Artaserse* that was produced at the Teatro Alibert during the Carnival of 1721, based on Francesco Silvani's *Il tradimento traditor di se stesso* from 1711.[74] Both the Zeno/Pariati and the Silvani libretti are concerned with Artaxerxes II (404-359 BC) and the conflict between his sons for the Persian succession.

### *Artaserse*: Grétry's Critique Expanded

André Grétry's *Essais sur la Musique* contains an analysis of two arias from the end of Act I of *Artaserse* that provides an interesting late-eighteenth-century perspective on Vinci. Grétry first presents two short excerpts from Semira's aria "Torna innocente" in which she tells her brother Artaserse that she cannot pity him until he has proven he is innocent of Serse's murder. Grétry must be quoting the tune from memory since neither excerpt is correct; for example his first excerpt represents a telescoping of the first vocal period, containing the opening and closing phrases with a made-up connecting phrase to replace two internal ones:

Example 9.7a "Torna innocente" as quoted by André Grétry:[75]

Example 9.7b "Torna innocente" *Artaserse* I/xiii

---

[74] Libretti in US-Wc (Schatz Nos. 1706, 5710 and 5712); Library of Congress, *Catalogue of Opera Librettos Printed before 1800*, ed. O. G. T. Sonneck (Washington: Government Printing Office, 1914).

[75] Quoted from André Ernest Modeste Grétry, *Mémoires, ou Essais sur la Musique* (Paris: 1797; reprint, Bruxelles: Oscar Lamberty, Editeur, 1924) I, 257.

Grétry takes exception to the way in which Vinci repeats the word "torna" in the coda of the second vocal period (not shown in Example 9.7), detaching it from the following word and tacking it on to the word "t'ascolterò."[76] Metastasio himself allowed for this type of repetition as

---

[76] Because of the posthumous success of *Artaserse*, there are numerous manuscript scores, in fact more than for all the other Vinci operas combined. Although the majority of these manuscripts, at least sixteen, correspond with Vinci's original version of the opera, only one can be connected with the original production. The following discussion is based on the author's survey of these manuscripts and on the two previous surveys, by Robert Meikle in his dissertation "Leonardo Vinci's *"Artaserse"* I, 8-16 and by Reinhard Strohm in the *Italienische Opernarien des frühen Settecento*, II, 233-35. References to watermarks are in Heawood, *Watermarks: Mainly of the 17th and 18th Centuries*:

    1. The score in the British Museum (Additional 22106) is a complete collection of aria fascicles from the original production, like those incorporated into the Santini scores of *Farnace* and *Gismondo*. Each of these aria fascicles begins on the recto, hence the frequent verso blanks, with the title "Alle Dame/1730/L'Artaserse/Del Sig.Leonardo/Vinci." The arias are by two different hands on two different types of paper, which further highlight its origins as a collection. The manuscript was acquired in 1857 by Charles Hamilton who presumably added the note based on De Rochement "Leonardo da Vinci's opera of 'Artaserse' his Chef-d'Oeuvre, and amongst the first productions of the Italian Theatre."

    2 & 3. The King's Collection of the British Library possesses two complete scores of *Artaserse*: one (R.M.23.c.2-4) intended as a mate to the *Alessandro* in this same collection; the other (R.M.23.c.5-7) apparently having never been used, with the blotting sand still in abundance between the pages. Both contain similar watermarks, fleur de lys in a double circle, suggesting a Roman origin; the former similar to R. Venuti, Antiqua Numismata, Rome 1732 and the latter similar to A. A. Georgi, Alaphabeticum Tibetanum, Rome, 1762 (Heawood, Nos. 1592 and 1599).

    4 & 5. The *Artaserse* in the Conservatoire Royale de Musique in Brussels (2368) was produced as a pair with the *Alessandro* in the same collection. This score, as well as one in the Lord Exeter's Library at Burghly House in Lincolnshire, contains a different setting of Semira's aria "Non è ver," suggesting a connection between the two (Meikle I, 15; the aria is included in the appendix of Vol. II, 269). The possibility that this *siciliano* aria is an alternate aria from Vinci's original production is diminished by the awkward word setting and the virtual absence of 12/8 meter in Vinci's operas, suggesting that the text was adapted to pre-existing music by a non-Italian.

    6. The score of *Artaserse* in the Royal College of Music (630) is Volume 14 of the large collection of Italian operas that formerly belonged to the Concerts of Ancient Music. Because the title page refers to "nel Teatro delle Dame/L'anno 1730 e 1731," Strohm connected it with the 1731 revival but the incipts match the original libretto from 1730.

    7. Unlike the *Artaserse* scores in the Conservatoire Royale and the Kings Music Library, the one in the Biblioteca dell'Abbazia in Montecassino (E26-29) is not a paired companion of the *Alessandro* in this same collection. Although both scores were part of the collection of Vincenzo Bovio, the *Artaserse* is in different format (20 x 27 cm., 3 vols.) and on different paper, suggesting a late-eighteenth-century Neapolitan origin; the *fleur de lys* watermark in a double circle is similar to "Terremoto" Naples, 1784 (Heawood, No. 1589).

    8. The *Artaserse* in the Conservatorio di Musica S. Pietro e Maiella in Naples (3-1-8) is a composite manuscript, Acts I and III probably originating in Rome in the 1730s. According to Meikle the score was used as a source for the Neapolitan production of 1738; faint pencil markings in the recitatives correspond with the beginning of eleven of the thirteen recitative cuts in Acts I and III (Meikle I, 296). Act II is by a different hand and on

long as the text had been reproduced complete thereby "concluding the sentiment,which is the case in this aria by measure 8.[77] Quibbling over word repetitions, combined with blatant carelessness in quoting Vinci's melody, does not inspire confidence in Grétry's critique. He then, however, singles out a problem that is not so easily dismissed:

> In the mouth of the princess, the sister of Arbace, this gigue air should be what we call an *air de fureur*. A noble anger can interest us even when it is unjust; but an anger that is not ennobled is always distasteful. The most trivial contradiction would be to compose a gay dance air to express fury; it is, if you like, the anger of Pulcinella.[78]

Although Grétry's references to a gigue and Pulcinella push the point too far—the aria is closer to a forlana and a more appropriate character from the *commedia delle arte* would be Isabella—one cannot deny that the lack of coordination between music and drama in this aria is noticeable, not only at the turn of the millennium, but in the late-eighteenth century as well. This problem has already been encountered on several

---

different paper; apparently the original Act II went missing in the later eighteenth century and a replacement was made by Giuseppe Sigismondo to complete the score.

9. The manuscript in the Biblioteca Nazionale Marciana originated in Venice during the 1730s (Strohm, II, 233).

10 & 11. Vienna possesses two scores in the Nationalbibliothek. According to Strohm, the *Artaserse* in the Fonds Kiesewetter (SA 68.c.24) originated in Rome. It is possible that this could have been used as the source for the Vienna production of 1730 (see below), perhaps brought to Vienna by Metastasio, hence the title "L'Artaserse/ Drama per Musica/ Del Sig. Pietro Metastasio/ Romano." The other manuscript (19120), which Strohm believes originated in Italy during the mid-eighteenth, includes a complete set of string parts for first and second violin, viola and cello, the only surviving set of parts from a Vinci opera (Strohm, II, 233 and Meikle I , 15).

12 & 13. There are two late eighteenth-century scores of Italian origin in Berlin, both with erroneous title pages: the score in the Amalienbibliothek (263) gives the wrong theatre and city, "Rappresentato nel teatro di San Giov: Grisostomo," while the score in the Nationalbibliothek (22/25) gives the right city but the wrong date, "Composta in Roma, 1731." The latter not only omits the recitative, with the single exception of the *accompagnato* prior to "Vò solcando," but also the arias in scenes ii-vii of Act III (Strohm, II, 233 and Meikle I ,10 and 15).

14, 15 & 16. Strohm lists several scores of *Artaserse* that he considers to date from the nineteenth century: (GB-Lgc, F-Pc.D.14258, and D-B 22375), the manuscripts in Berlin and Paris being of German origin (Strohm II, 233). These nineteenth-century sources suggest that this classical masterpiece had not been totally forgotten during the age of Romanticism.

Finally *Artaserse* is the only opera by Vinci that exists in a modern edition. The score is contained in Volume II of Robert Burns Meikle's Ph.D. Thesis from Cornell University (1971). Unfortunately the score is much reduced and is often difficult to read. Meikle based his edition on fifteen scores and has provided copious editorial notes, cataloguing every variant in his desire to arrive at a definitive text. Some of his editorial changes seem rather questionable at a distance of thirty years. The above listed scores of the original *Artaserse*, including R.M.23.c.2-4 in the Kings's Collection from which the excerpts below are taken, consist of the following musical numbers:

| 27 *Da capo* arias | 1 Arietta | 1 *Del segno* duet |
| 4 Accompanied recitatives | 1 Ternary aria | 1 Sinfonia |
| 1 Coro | Totals: 36 set pieces (28 in *da capo* form) | |

[77] Saverio Mattei, *Memorie per servire alla vita del Metastasio ed Elogio di N. Jommelli* (Colle: Angiolo M. Martini, 1785; reprint ed. Bologna, Arnaldo Forni, 1987; Bibliotheca Musica Bononiensis, III no. 57), 79.

[78] Grétry, *Mémoires,* I, 257.

occasions, particularly with Vinci's works from the mid-1720s. If one regards this as Vinci's major flaw as an opera composer, it is one that he shares with many of his predecessors and contemporaries, including Scarlatti, Vivaldi, and Hasse. One must, however, strongly disagree with Grétry's subsequent statement that "Torna innocente" demonstrates that Vinci:

> had not yet perceived that melody had as much power, or more, as harmony..., that it can descend into the depths of the heart, in order... to express all the moral sentiments in following the infinite nuances of declamation.[79]

Vinci's melody was generally regarded as his most progressive aspect, precisely because it followed "the infinite nuances of declamation," as Burney had pointed out a decade before Grétry's critique; conversely, Vinci's harmony, is sometimes one of his weaker elements, at least to a modern ear used to the harmonic riches of J.S. Bach.

Grétry then turns his attention to Arbace's storm-at-sea simile aria "Vò solcando un mar crudele," one of the most popular arias of the eighteenth century:

> How distant is this aria from *Vò solcando* by the same composer? In the latter, the melody and above all the accompaniment absolutely match the words; it is the first [truly dramatic] scene that was made in music; it is the first ray of light towards the truth. The Romans experienced an inexpressible delight when they heard for the first time, this sublime union of music with the just expression of the words.

> Vinci was the first inspired [composer], so say the old teachers in Rome, and, as founder, he merits the statue that they erected of him in the Pantheon.[80]

Grétry's description of the reaction of the Roman audience was perhaps derived from his teacher Giovanni Casali, one of "the old teachers in Rome" during his student years there in the 1760s. When Grétry describes how "the melody and above all the accompaniment absolutely

---

[79] Ibid., 258.
[80] Ibid., 257-58. I am flattered that the section on Vinci in Daniel Heartz's *Music in European Capitals: The Galant Style, 1720-80* (New York, W. W. Norton, 2003) derives from my dissertation. In a footnote to the analysis of "Torna innocente" and "Vo solcando," Heartz states that my translation of Grétry ( or rather the final phrase in the passage above) is too literal, that the composer was here referring to the abstract "Pantheon of the Arts;" however, the reference to the Pantheon comes within a specific context: Vinci's reputation among "the old teachers in Rome," which, in turn, suggests something more specific, namely, the Pantheon in Rome. (For a possible explanation see fn. 63 in Chapter 10.) In the same footnote, Heartz mentions that these pieces have been mistakenly assigned to *Semiramide* in my entry on Vinci in *The New Grove Dictionary of Opera*. I have no idea how the mix-up occurred. I certainly did not write it that way.

match the words" he probably had in mind details such as the melody on the phrase "Freme l'onde" (roaring waves), which represents a crashing wave, accompanied by a disjunct syncopated figure in the violins on "freme" and arpeggiated triplets in the violins against static duplets in the horns on "l'onde;" or the billowing coloratura on "vento" (wind) accompanied by reiterated chords with an implied upper pedal and crescendo:

Example 9.8 "Vò solcando un mar crudele" *Artaserse* I/xv

Of the hundreds of storm-at-sea simile arias that were written during the eighteenth century, this is one of the finest. Coming after Arbace had been accused of regicide by his best friend, disowned by his father (who committed the crime), and rejected by both his sister and beloved, this standardized simile matches the intensity of the situation through the strength of Metastasio's poetry and Vinci's music, giving the aria a significance similar to the climactic storming of the elements in a Javanese shadow play. For Grétry, "Vò solcando un mar crudele" supported his assumption that Vinci was the first composer to depict in musical sounds "the agitation of a heart that compares its diverse movements to those of a vessel tormented by the tempest."[81] Grétry's admiration for the aria was such that he used it as one of the models for the expansive Italian ariette "Frà l'orror della tempesta" that dominates the divertissement to Act II of his *opéra-ballet La Caravane du Caire*.[82]

---

[81] Ibid., 258.
[82] Albeit the inflence was defused through Pergolesi's setting of this same text interpolated into his comic opera *Lo frate 'nnamorato* that contained an obbligato for solo flute, also found in Grétry's aria.

Grétry could have continued with similar juxtapositions between arias judged as dramatically appropriate and inappropriate within the drama. For example Mandane's "Dimmi, che un' empio sei"—the aria that separates the two discussed by Grétry—is a furious E-minor *presto* that conveys the heroine's rage as she condemns Arbace for murdering her father. This is one of the few full-length arias in Vinci's operas that is not in *da capo* form, its singularity exemplifing the dominance of the *da capo* in Metastasia *opera seria*. The reason for this exception is that the aria text is not in the usual double-strophe format, but in three strophes, the third a composite of the first and second. Vinci responds by composing a tripartite aria, wherein the third section is a combination of both the *furioso* concerted passages for voice and violins from the first section (addressed to Arbace) and cadential passages that resemble material from the second section (addressed to herself):

Example 9.9 "Dimmi, che un' empio sei" *Artaserse* I/xiv

The aria that began this sequence, Artaserse's "Deh respirar lasciatemi," is just as dramatically effective. After Arbace is captured with the murder weapon, Artaserse thinks over the tragic events that have compelled him to play the roles of lover, friend, criminal, judge and king in succession. The melody is based on a motive that was a favourite of Porpora's, a falling fifth onto a reiterated tonic, that in this case is supported by a descending detaché walking bass suggestive of the passacaglia (see Example 9.10 on page 316). The aria has a dark brooding quality that admirably depicts Artaserse's sorrow and anxiety. This is due not only to the minor mode, moderate tempo and soupçon of passacaglia, but also to a certain gestic quality: the reiterated tonic note and prominent suspensions of the me-

Example 9.10 "Deh respirar lasciatemi" *Artaserse* I/xi

lody evocative of a pensive nodding of the head and inquiring gestures with the hands; the tentative walking bass suggestive of nervous pacing.

On the other hand, the beginning of the act, which is based on historical events, contains arias wherein the musical setting ignores or even contradicts the dramatic situation. "Su le sponde del torbido Lete" is sung by Artabano after he has murdered Serse and is about to convince Artaserse to execute Dario for the crime. To drive home his argument Artabano sings about the ghost of Serse calling for revenge. In this aria Vinci completely ignores the basic affect of vengeance, the "ombre" imagery, and Artabano's evil character, and instead writes a neutral *alla breve* aria in C major, with a pompous fugue-subject theme that is never fugally realized. The subsequent scene between Artaserse and Semira presents a somewhat different problem. Artaserse's aria "Per pietà, bell' idol mio" is a gentle syncopated G-major *Andante* similar to the "Inflamatus est" from Pergolesi's *Stabat Mater:*

Example 9.11 "Per pietà, bell'idol mio" from *Artaserse* I/v

Although Artaserse is trying to hide the tragic events from Semira, one would have liked some suggestion of the seriousness of the situation— an underlining tremolo, the continued repetition of a motive, a sudden modulation to the minor mode on the words "infelice, e sventurato"— Artaserse has just been informed of his father's murder and is contemplating the execution of his brother.

In the second act one can make similar juxtapositions. In "Se d'un'amor tiranno" Mandane sings of overthrowing the tyrant Amore after Semira has reminded her of the love she shared with Arbace. Mandane's defiance of Semira and Amore, as well as her internal conflict between love and vengeance, are ignored in this ingenious two-part invention, adorned with fashionable ornaments, lombards, and sextuplet cadences. Vinci, however, rises to the occasion two scenes later in Arbace's "Per quel paterno amplesso" that provides an admirable counterpart to "Vò solcando" that would achieve considerable popularity (the two arias often found together in aria collections).[83] Arbace sings this aria after he has been condemned to death by his father, kissing the hand that signed the death warrant. In the aria he bids farewell to his father asking him to comfort Mandane and to defend the new king. In this situation Vinci's usual restraint is most effective because Arbace is trying to contain his emotions in a tragic situation. The intensity breaks through the serenity of this lyrical G-major aria in the codetta of the first section where the descending lombard pairs on "difendimi" and the fragmented repetition of the word "addio" suggests holding back the tears (see Example 9.12 on p. 318). The manner in which Vinci detaches the final word from the second verse "Questo estremo addio," tacking it on to the final verse (thereby changing the noun into a farewell), is the same treatment that infuriated Grétry in "Torna innocente."[84]

Besides "Vò solcando" and "Per quel paterno amplesso," the other piece that achieved considerable celebrity during the eighteenth century was the duet "Tu vuoi, ch'io vivi, o cara." Ernst Ludwig Gerber, writing at the turn of the nineteenth century, stated that Vinci's "opera *Artaserse*

---

[83] Daniel Heartz, "Metastasio, 'Maestro dei maestri di cappella drammatici'" in *Metastasio e il mondo musicale*, 315-38, contains an extended analysis of Arbace's Act III aria "L'onda dal mar divisa," wherein particular attention is paid to the subtle interaction between the text and the music and musical structure. The aria is then compared with Hasse's setting of the same text from 1760 (the text not having been used in Boldini's version of the drama set by Hasse for Venice in 1730.

[84] This peccadillo is further emphasized in the Dresden/Washington and Rochester scores of *Artaserse* by having the "addio" addressed to Mandane; this is adopted in Meikle's edition with an editorial *sotto voce* direction; Meikle, "Leonardo Vinci's *Artaserse*," 185.

Example 9.12 "Per quel paterno amplesso" *Artaserse* II/xi

achieved immortality for him; one must especially admire the duet *Tu vuoi ch'io viva, o cara* and the aria *Vo solcando un mar crudele*, both of which are exemplary models of their type."[85] After Arbace's enforced escape from prison, he goes to say farewell to Mandane. To persuade her of his innocence, he resorts to the stratagem that was so overused in *Alessandro nell' Indie*—he offers to kill himself. When Mandane tries to stop him, Arbace asks if she still loves him—a question that she cannot answer. This stand-off is sustained in the duet, with Arbace's opening line simply continuing his interrogation. There are some rather distinctive reminiscences of Scarlatti in this duet, which are rather surprising for a composer who appears to have virtually shunned the influence of the elder Scarlatti in his mature operas. This Scarlattian influence is apparent in both its main theme and its nervous obbligato for violins, that bring to mind the ensembles in *La Griselda*. After the usual double exposition, made more touching by Mandane's entrance on the tonic minor to highlight her distress, the voices participate in a lively dialogue which is soon joined by the first and second violins:

---

[85] Ernst Ludwig Gerber, *Neues Historisch-Biographisches Lexikon der Tonkünstler (1812-14)*, III, c. 452. Gerber's assessment is based on that of the Abbé de Saint Non in his *Voyage Pittoresque ou description des Royaumes de Naples et de Sicile* (Paris: 1781), I.

Example 9.13 "Tu vuoi, ch'io vivi, o cara" *Artaserse* III/vii

This dialogue is developed at greater length in the second vocal period where the interaction between Arbace's pleas and Mandane's rejections suggests stage action. The climax is reached on the phrase "la vostra crudeltà." The violins drop their *obbligato* for tremolo chords and the voices sustain a major third on the word "crudeltà"—as if Vinci were using the old madrigalian symbol for harshness— which then expands to a tritone. Typical of many of Vinci's arias, this climactic phrase is repeated in the codetta.

Grétry's critique (and the expansion of it), while in keeping with later opera aesthetics, would not have been valid for contemporary Italian audiences. Vinci was merely satisfying contemporary expectation. Martello's *Della tragedia antica e moderna* from 1715 contains advice on aria construction that, though intended for librettists, also applies to composers:

> Keep in mind that in the aria, the more general the propositions, the more they will please the people....Avoid generalities [only] in the *arie di azione* ...that are in spirit adapted to one action and no other.... [Therefore] do yourself honor in the recitative, and in one or two arias in each act. [86]

Similarly, the co-ordination of music and drama in Vinci's arias is generally relegated to one or two arias per act, often *arie di azione*. The

---

[86] Pier Jacopo Martello, *Della tragedia antica e moderna: dialogo* (Rome: Francesco Gonzaga, 1715).

remainder of the arias tend to be more generalized, usually tuneful and dance-like or simple and declamatory. These, however, can be very attractive, such as "Torna innocente," "Per pietà, bell'idol mio," and "Se d'un amor tiranno" and undoubtedly accomplished what they were intended to do, namely to "please the people"—a quality that most of Vinci's arias undoubtedly still possess.

## The *Artaserse* Revivals

*Artaserse* was produced in Vienna on August 28, 1730 in celebration of the Empress's birthday.[87] Although no copies of the libretto have survived, several scores of the opera are preserved in Vienna, as well as a production score wherein Vinci's music was augmented by the intermezzo *Pancrazio/Fiammetta* and additional arias, including "Lusinghe cara" from Handel's *Alessandro*.[88] This was perhaps intended as a tribute to the new court poet, who arrived in Vienna the previous month; his involvement in the production, however, seems rather unlikely because of the inclusion of certain non-Metastasian texts, such as "Lusinghe cara."

According to the Archives of the Academia Infuocati, an *Artaserse* featuring Caffarelli was also produced at the Teatro Cocomero in Florence in October of 1730. Weaver and Weaver draw attention to one Gaetano Bracci who received a payment "per *L'Artaserse*," suggesting that he was the composer.[89] However the catalogue of the Libreria dello Studente in Florence contains a citation to a missing libretto, a Florentine *Artaserse* from 1730 with music by Vinci, while Strohm draws attention to copies of Arbace's arias "Mi scacci sdegnato" and "Vò solcando" designated as having been sung by Caffarelli in 1730 in Florence.[90] Considering the interest shown by the Florentines in the works of the composer, it seems likely that Gaetano Bracci was responsible for arranging Vinci's score for Florence. The subsequent production of Vinci's *Artaserse* at the Cocomero in 1740 would in turn be a revival of this 1730 revival.[91] The *Artaserse* that appeared in Milan during Carnival 1731, although it was anonymous, featured Carestini in his original role

---

[87] Otto Erich Deutsch, "Das Repertoire der Höfischen Oper, der Hof- und der Staatsoper: Chronologischer Teil" *Österreichische Musikzeitschrift*, 24/7 (July 1969), 388.

[88] Manuscript Q2100; Strohm, *Italienische Opernarien*, "Werkverzeichnisse", II, 233.

[89] Robert Lamar Weaver & Norma Wright Weaver, *A Chronology of Music in the Florentine Theater, 1590-1750: Operas, Prologues, Finales, Intermezzos and Plays with Incidental Music*, Detroit Studies in Music Bibliography, No. 38 (Detroit: Information Coordinators, 1978), 257.

[90] Sartori, *I libretti italiani*, No. 2928 and Strohm, *Italienische Opernarien*, Vol. II, 234; arias in F-Pc L.5331 & B-Bc 4956.

[91] Libretto in I-Fm, Sartori, *I libretti italiani*, No. 2964.

and Caffarelli as Artaserse; there is no doubt that it contained some of Vinci's music.[92]

*Artaserse* was popular in many of the smaller cities in central Italy. A year after its Roman première, it was produced in Livorno on the West coast and Fano and Pesaro on the East coast.[93] The Livorno *Artaserse* was produced along side its sister-work *Alessandro* with Berenstadt in the cast; presumably a success, it was revived there in 1738 with Francesca Cuzzoni as leading lady.[94] The Fano *Artaserse*, for which a score survives, featured Farfallino in his original role as Mandane.[95] *Artaserse* was revived in the autumn of 1731 in Ferrara with a strong cast that included Vittoria Tesi and Farinello.[96] Subsequent productions of Vinci's *Artaserse* appeared in Perugia for Carnival 1732 and a year later in Camerino.[97] When the Perugian *Artaserse* was revived for Carnival 1734, Farfallino, a native of Perugia, again appeared in his original role.[98] The production in Macerata in 1740 is related to the one in Fano in that it featured the same *primo uomo*, Castoro Castorini, and was arranged and conducted by the same maestro, Antonio Gaetano Pampino.[99]

These provincial revivals pale in comparison with the Roman revival, which took place on June 19, 1731, coinciding with the expansion of the Roman opera season into the spring. Again the libretto does not survive but there are several important contemporary references. The cast would have been the same as that of Araja's *Cleomene* which initiated this first Ascension season in Rome, featuring Carlo Scalzi, Farfallino, and Giovanni Battista Pinacci.[100] The final performance on July 18 was so successful that it was given two additional performances on July 21/22 "ad istanza universale."[101] The success of this revival is the subject of one of Metastasio's letters to La Romanina, dated July 7, 1731:

---

[92] Libretto in I-Lurago, Sormani -Ma; Ibid. No. 2937.
[93] Libretto for Livorno in I-Fm, for Fano in I-FAN -MAC, and for Pesaro in I-PESo; Ibid., Nos. 2936, 2934 and 2938.
[94] Libretto for the 1738 Livornese revival in I-Bc; Ibid, No. 2953.
[95] The score of the Fano production is located in Biblioteca Comunale Federiciana in Fano; Strohm, *Italienische Opernarien*, II, 234.
[96] Libretto in I-Bc -MOe,US-AUS; Sartori, *I libretti italiani*, No. 2935.
[97] Libretto for Perugia in I-PEc and Camerino in I-Fm; Ibid., Nos. 2939 and 2941.
[98] Libretto in I-Vgc; Ibid. No. 2945; Farfallino retired from the stage in 1735 and returned to Perugia a wealthy landowner; with the money he made, presumably from his more than twenty years on stage, he purchased a house in the city and several farming estates in the suburbs; Biancamaria Brumana, "Il cantante Giacinto Fontana detto Farfallino e la sua carriera nei teatri di Roma" *Roma moderna e contemporanea: rivista interdisciplare di storia*, IV/1 (1996), 75-112.
[99] Libretto I-MAC -Rsc -Vgc; Sartori, *I libretti italiani*, No. 2966.
[100] Ibid., No. 5831.
[101] Cametti, "Leonardo Vinci: e suoi drammi in musica al Teatro delle Dame," 299.

> I was in the utmost anxiety for the fate of *Artaserse*, not having found a syllable about it in your letter by the last post. But to-day I hear of its success, not only from yourself, but Bulga, Leopold and Peroni. And am extremely happy, well knowing the pleasure it will afford you all, on my account. You can answer for the patriotic gratitude which I must feel to a city like Rome, when it thus deigns to interest itself in my labors. May my productions, some time or other, justify, in the opinion of the world, its partiality!
>
> I am assured from all quarters of the zeal and accuracy of the performers. I beg you will thank them in my name, particularly the incomparable *Scalzi*, and *Farfallino*, whom I salute and embrace.[102]

Metastasio's reference to being "in the utmost anxiety for the fate of *Artaserse*," caused Edward Dent to come to the conclusion that the *Artaserse* of 1730 was "not produced with Vinci's music" and that this was the real première of Vinci's opera.[103] While there are several reasons why Metastasio could have been anxious for the fate of *Artaserse* in 1731—the new cast, the absence of Carestini, and, most probably, the fact that this was the first Roman production that he did not personally direct—it was most certainly not because Vinci's music was being performed for the first time as Dent suggests. There is a collection of arias in the Royal College of Music that derives from this revival, consisting of individual aria fascicules of eighteen of the twenty-eight arias in *Artaserse*, many with the heading "Nell Artaserse 1731."[104]

Although Burney knew that the première of *Artaserse* took place in Rome during Carnival 1730, Gerber and Villarosa did not, the former stating that it took place in Rome in 1731, the latter that it took place in Naples in 1732 at the Teatro San Bartolomeo.[105] While Gerber, like Dent,

---

[102] Burney, *Memoirs of the Life and Writings of the Abate Metastasio*, 72. Original in Pietro Metastasio, *Tutte le Opere*, III, 57

[103] Edward J. Dent, "Notes on Leonardo Vinci" *The Musical Antiquary*, IV (1912/13), 199-200. Dent's conclusion is refuted by Sonneck in his entry for the original 1730 libretto; Library of Congress, *Catalogue of Opera Librettos Printed before 1800*, I, 168.

[104] Royal College of Music (ms. 629),without the libretto one cannot be certain if these arias, in a variety of hands and a variety of papers, are simply a collection of miscellaneous arias c. 1731 dominated by the season's "hit," *Artaserse*, with a few arias from the work that opened the season, Araja's *Cleomene* thrown in. However, the arrangement of the arias—the Vinci arias in their proper order with Hasse's setting of the opening aria "Conservati fedele" following immediately upon Vinci's as if an alternate and another nine arias coming at the end of the volume, two each by Vinci, Porpora, and Araja and one each by Feo, Porta, and Pollarolo as if replacements of the ten missing arias—does suggest that this may be an approximation of the 1731 revival.

[105] Ernst Ludwig Gerber, *Historisch-Biographisches Lexikon der Tonkünstler (1790-*

mistook the Roman revival for the actual première, Villarosa, following Sigismondo (see below), mistook the Neapolitan revival for the première. The first production of Vinci's *Artaserse* in Naples took place during the early 1730s but, as with the Roman revival, it cannot be substantiated by a libretto or score and has been the subject of some speculation.[106] Sigismondo describes this production, which he thought was the première, assigning the generic date of 1730 and providing a list of the principals: Elizabetta Uttini, Francesca Cuzzoni, Carlo Scalzi, and Francesco Tolve.[107] This is the same cast as that for Hasse's *Ezio*, the libretto of which gives a generic 1730 date. Since it is not known which two operas were produced at the San Bartolomeo at the end of 1730, the records being scanty during these years, it would appear that one was Hasse's *Ezio* and the other this revival of Vinci's *Artaserse*.[108] Prota-Giurleo mentions another revival of *Artaserse* for Carnival 1733, this one with Faustina, Gizziello, and Tolve.[109] While such a production was planned, it did not take place because earthquakes in November and December of 1732 caused the closure of the theatres for the following carnival as a sign of public penance.[110]

---

*1792)* I, c. 731; Marchese di Villarosa, *Memorie dei compositori di musica del Regno di Napoli* (Naples: Stamperia Reale, 1840), 225; Florimo repeats Villarosa's information, adding only that the opera was written in Rome; Francesco Florimo, *La scuola musicale di Napoli e suoi conservatori*, II, 187.

[106] Lowenberg and Hucke state that this revival took place in October of 1730: Alfred Loewenberg, *Annals of Opera, 1597-1940: Compiled from Original Sources*, 2nd ed. (Geneva: Societas Bibliographica, 1955), c. 164 and Helmut Hucke, "Vinci, Leonardo" in *Die Musik in Geschichte und Gegenwart: Allgemeine Enzyklopädie der Musik*. Prota-Giurleo states that it took place in the fall of 1731, quoting from what appears to be a review of the performance but without providing a source ("Leonardo Vinci," 8); however the issues of the *Avvisi di Napoli* for the period 1726-33 are missing and the text is almost identical to an assessment of the 1738 revival quoted by Croce, making the Prota-Giurleo quote highly suspect.

[107] Giuseppe Sigismondo, *Apoteosi dell'Arte Musicale*, (Naples, 1820; unpublished manuscript in Berlin catalogued as "Materialien zu einer Geshichte der Musik der Neapolitaner Schule"), III, 109.

[108] Because the sequence of operas at the S. Bartolomeo from the early years of the 1730s is somewhat faulty in Strohm and incomprehensible in Florimo, it can be reconstructed from the citations in Sartori as follows:

**1730** Leo's *Semiramide* (Carnival), Riccardo Broschi's *Idaspe* (Aug. 28), Hasse's *Ezio* and Vinci's *Artaserse* (fall and winter)
**1731** Sarro's *Artemisia* (Carnival), Leo's *Argene* (summer), Araja's *Semiramide riconosciuta* (Oct. 1), Pergolesi's *La Salustia* (winter)
**1732** Mancini's *Alessandro nell'Indie* (Carnival), Leo's *Il Demetrio* (summer), Hasse's *L'Issipile* (Oct. 1), Vinci's *Catone in Utica* (Nov. 19)
**1733** Vinci's *Artaserse* (Carnival, cancelled due to earthquake), Pergolesi's *Il prigionier superbo* (Aug. 28), Leo's *Nitocri regina d'Egitto* (Nov. 4), Hasse's *Cajo Fabricio* (winter).

[109] Prota-Giurleo "Leonardo Vinci, 11; following Prota-Giurleo, Strohm includes revivals of *Artaserse* at the Teatro San Bartolomeo for the fall of 1731 and Carnival 1733 in his "Repertoireübersicht" in *Opernarien*, II, 318 and 320.

[110] Benedetto Croce, *I teatri di Napoli: secolo XV-XVIII*, 298.

*Artaserse* was revived in January of 1738 during the opening season of the new Teatro San Carlo in a gala production conducted by Leonardo Leo in celebration of King Carlo's birthday; it included "some arias by other authors" and a Prologue by Leo to celebrate the engagement of the new King.[111] Strohm equates the score of *Artaserse* in the Biblioteca Oratorio dei Filippini in Naples with this performance because of the designation "Musica del quondam Leonardo Vinci et alcune arie del sig. Leonardo Leo."[112] Porpora was supposed to have provided the opera for this celebration, but was unable to send the score in time and Vinci's *Artaserse* was substituted, which proved propitious; according to the Prince of Campoflorido the music "was, with great pleasure, appreciated by all, as it was seven years ago" (i.e. the original Neapolitan revival from late 1730).[113] In 1743 *Artaserse* was revived again in Naples, with Caffarelli as Arbace and Vinci's music "accomodato" by Genarro Manna and also at the Teatro S. Cecilia in Palermo, the only Vinci opera to appear on the island half of the Kingdom Naples.[114]

Handel produced *Artaserse* in January of 1734 under the title *Arbace*, featuring Carestini in his original role and Scalzi as Artaserse. As in the Viennese, Roman, Florentine and Neapolitan revivals from the early 1730s, no libretto survives, but Handel's conducting score is preserved in the Staats- und Universitätsbibliothek in Hamburg. In contrast to most of Handel's pasticci, this one stays fairly close to its model, with only six new arias.[115] *Artaserse* was produced along with pasticci of Vinci's *Semiramide* and Hasse's *Cajo Fabricio* to counter the opening season of the Opera of the Nobility under Porpora.[116] The Handel/Vinci *Artaserse* was moderately successful, receiving eight performances, and the firm of Walsh published a volume of *Favorite songs from Arbace*.[117]

---

[111] Libretto in I-Mb; Sartori *I libretti italiani*, No.2954; the text of the prologue is included in an Appendix in Meikle, "Leonardo Vinci's *Artaserse*," 572-580.

[112] Strohm, *Italienische Opernarien*, "Werkverzeichnisse," II, 234.

[113] Croce, *I teatri di Napoli*, p. 338-39.

[114] Libretto for Naples in I-Bc and for Palermo in I-Pl,Pagana; Sartori, *I libretti italiani*, Nos. 2976 & 2977; Strohm, *Italienische Opernarien*, "Werkverzeichnisse," II, 234.

[115] Manuscript M A/1004; Reinhard Strohm, "Handel's pasticci," *Essays on Handel and Italian Opera*, 209.

[116] During the initial season this rivalry between Handel and Porpora produced complementary works, the most notable being the rival *Arianna*s of the first season. The appearance of the pasticcio *Artaserse* at the beginning of the next season with music by Porpora, Hasse, and Riccardo Broschi, may also be part of this game. Libretto in GB-Lbm; Sartori, *I libretti italiani*, No. 2947.

[117] Strohm, "Handel's pasticci," *Essays...*,183; this publication is not listed in William C. Smith and Charles Humphries, *A Bibliography of the Musical Works Published by the Firm of John Walsh: During the Years 1721-1766* (London: The Bibliographical Society, 1968), 335-36.

*Artaserse* was also revived during the opening season of the Nuovo Real Teatro in Dresden during the summer of 1746 by the company of Pietro Mingotti.[118] Although Robert Meikle tries to connect this production with the score that was formerly in Dresden, he admits that there are too few correspondences.[119] In this score, eight arias are transposed, four arias omitted and three arias replaced.[120] Meikle fails to notice that two of the replacement arias are by Handel: "Lusinghe cara" from *Alessandro* and "Da tempesta" from *Giulio Cesare*, the latter with a parody text. The presence of Handel's "Lusinghe cara" may suggest a connection with the Viennese production from 1730 which also included this aria.

Vinci's *Artaserse* became a repertory piece, a relatively rare phenomenon in the style-conscious world of eighteenth-century Italian opera. Charles de Brosses, familiar with the classical tradition of Lully, was amazed by the Italians' fetish for novelty: "They do not want to see again neither an opera, nor a ballet, nor a stage set, nor a singer that they have already seen another year, unless it be some excellent opera by Vinci or some very famous voice."[121] De Brosses' comment should be qualified. While most Italian operas were produced for a single season and forgotten, outstanding works had always became repertory pieces (Cesti's *Orontea* and Bononcini's *Camilla* being early examples). The life of these repertory pieces, however, was certainly not as extended as the classics of the French theatre, such as the century life-span of Lully's *Armide*. By mid-century new settings by composers such as Jommelli and Galuppi and later Piccinni, Paisiello, and Cimarosa soon crowded out the original *Artaserse*. The last known productions of Vinci's *Artaserse* took place around mid-century in central Italy: in Pistoia (1749), and Parma (1754), the latter apparently the last performance of a Vinci opera until the Florentine revival of *Li zite 'ngalera* in 1979.[122] By mid-century, however, *Artaserse* had achieved the status of a classic and could thereafter be referred to as "amongst the first productions of the Italian theatre."[123]

---

[118] Libretto in D-Dl -Mbs, US-Wc; Sartori, *I libretti italiani*, No. 2983.

[119] Meikle, "Leonardo Vinci's *Artaserse*," 298; this manuscript was destroyed during the war but survives in a copy score in the Library of Congress (M 1500 V64 A6).

[120] Because of the correspondences between the libretto for this production and Hasse's libretti from 1730 and 1740, Meikle suggests that Hasse's recitative was employed rather than Vinci's. The three replacement arias are included in the appendix of the Meikle edition; Ibid., 13-14; (Ibid., 299).

[121] Charles De Brosses, *Lettres familièrs écrites d'italie*, 237.

[122] Libretto for Pistoia in I-PS and for Parma in B-Bc; Sartori, *I libretti italiani*, Nos. 2988 & 3021. The production of *Artaserse* at the Teatri Bonacossi in Ferrara in 1745 was a composite: "Musica di Leonardo Vinci e di Adolfo Asse, detto l Sassone" (libretto in I-Bc, Sartori, No. 2982).

[123] Note by Charles Hamilton on a manuscript of *Artaserse* in the British Museum, Additional 22106.

# 10

# DEATH AND POSTHUMOUS FAME

### Vinci, Hasse, and Metastasio

All the revivals of *Artaserse*, beginning with the Viennese production in August 1730, were posthumous. The performance notice in the *Diario ordinario* for the Roman revival of 1731 describes *Artaserse* as "composed by Signor Abate Pietro Metastasio, and set to Music by the late Signore Maestro di Cappella Leonardo Vinci."[1] Metastasio's enthusiastic reception of the news of the great success of this revival was tinged with regret over the death of his collaborator:

> Poor Vinci! Now that merit will be known, which during his life, was blasted by his enemies. What a miserable being is man! He thinks fame the only good that can render him happy; but alas! He must die ere he is allowed to enjoy it.[2]

Metastasio's words provide a poetic epitaph for the composer and a glimpse of a man much concerned with worldly success who, during the course of a brief career, strove for a fame that continually eluded him.

Although the theatre directors were ultimately responsible for their collaboration, Metastasio admired and respected Vinci as a man and an artist, in contrast to his stormy relationship with his former teacher Porpora and his indifference towards his Viennese collaborators, Caldara, Conti, and Reutter, with whom he was artistically at odds.[3] Not until his collaboration with Hasse, beginning with *Ipermestra* in 1744, would Metastasio find a composer who was personable and shared his artistic

---

[1] *Diario ordinario*, No. 2169, June 16; quoted in Francesco Piovano, "A propos d'une récente biographie de Léonard Leo," *Sammelbände der Internationalen Musik-Gesellschaft*, 8 (1906-1907), 75-76.

[2] Letter dated July 7, 1731, Vienna quoted in Charles Burney, *Memoirs of the Life and Writings of the Abate Metastasio*, I, 72-73; Pietro Metastasio, *Tutte le Opere*, III, 57.

[3] The complex relationship between Porpora and Metastasio is addressed in the author's conference paper "The Eventual Première of *Issiple*; Porpora and the Dueling Ambassadors," *Music in Eighteenth-Century Italy*, July 12-15, 1998, University of Wales, Cardiff.

ideals.[4] According to Burney, Metastasio preferred Hasse to Vinci as a collaborator:

> the operas of Metastasio, which he set for Rome and Venice after the decease of Vinci, were not only more applauded by the public, but more consonant to the ideas of the poet himself, as I discovered in conversing with him on the subject, at Vienna, in 1773.[5]

Burney's statement is somewhat problematic since Hasse set only two Metastasio texts for these cities during the decade after Vinci's death: *Demetrio* in 1732 and *Viriate/Siface* in 1739 of which only the former was produced in Metastasio's Vienna. This judgment was probably colored by the fact that Hasse was his principal collaborator during the later part of his career. Regardless of whether or not Metastasio actually preferred Hasse over Vinci, he must have regarded the music of both composers as an ideal realization of his dramas—hence his negative opinion concerning music during his later years.[6] Significantly he compared the composer of the next generation that most impressed him to both Hasse and Vinci in a letter to Farinello from November of 1749:

> You know that a Neapolitan *maestro di cappella* named Niccolò Jomelli has composed here two of my works, a man about thirty-five years old, with a rotund figure, peaceful temperament, charming countenance, excellent style and the most amiable manner. He has surprised me. I found in him all the harmony of the Saxon, all the grace, all the expression and all the fecundity of Vinci.[7]

For Metastasio "armonia" probably had more to do with the harmonious sound of Hasse's music than the more specific modern notion of rich harmony. "Fecondità" could refer both to Vinci's prolific creativity (i.e. three operas in a single season) and "invention" as Burney translates the term, with an abundance of interesting themes and figurations. In the latter sense "fecondità" could include the many stylistic innovations established by Vinci that had become the foundations of the Classical style of Burney's day.

---

[4] See Metastasio's correspondence with Hasse concerning the production of *Attilio Regolo* in Burney, *Memoirs of the Life and Writings of the Abate Metastasio*, I, 315-30.
[5] Charles Burney, *A General History of Music*, II, 918.
[6] For example in a letter to Farinelli from August of 1750 Metastasio complains that "in Italy at present there reigns a taste for extravagance, of the *sinfonia con la voce* in which one sometimes find a great violin or an excellent oboe [solo], but one never finds a man who can really sing; hence music no longer moves any other affect than that of wonder. Things have reached such an excess that henceforth, either they must change or we will become, with reason, the buffoons of all the nations;" Pietro Metastasio, *Tutte le Opere* III, 555.
[7] Pietro Metastasio, *Tutte le Opere* III, 444.

## Sorting Through the Death Records

The date of Leonardo Vinci's death has been the subject of conjecture since the eighteenth century. Although Sigismondo gives the year 1730, most sources adopt 1732 as given by the Abbé de Saint Non and repeated in Gerber's *Neues Historisch-Biographisches Lexikon*.[8] These include Villarosa who in other respects follows, and in some instances copies, Sigismondo.[9] Francesco Piovano, who at the turn of the twentieth century found the performance notice of the Roman revival of *Artaserse* that refers to the death of Vinci, was the first since Sigismondo to put forward the year 1730.[10]

In 1928 Salvatore Di Giacomo discovered the burial record from S. Caterina a Formiello in the *Libro maggiore* of the Congregation of the Rosary:

> The said brother has passed on to a better life in June 1730, and since he was found contumacious, he was not given funeral rites: but because he has served the Congregation many times in his position as *Maestro di cappella*, he was given burial only, and at the expense of his heirs was given the rites.[11]

A reading of the *Regole e Constituzioni della Umbile Congregazione del SS. Rosario* provides a specific context for this strange judgment of contumaciousness. The fees of the Congregation of the Rosary were light—the *mesate* or monthly of twenty grana, for example, could buy a chicken and three carafes of wine.[12] However, the Congregazione depended upon their regular collection and thus graduated penalties for not paying the fees were clearly spelled out in the *Regole e Constituzioni*:

> Coming to death, some Fratello, who is found contumacious for not having paid the Monthly for the space of three months, remains in judgement of the Fratello Superiore, and from the Board will receive burial and the association of the Brethren only.[13]

---

[8] Abbé de Saint Non, *Voyage Pittoresque ou description des Royaumes de Naples et de Sicile* (Paris: 1781), I, 168; Ernst Ludwig Gerber, *Neue Historisch-Biographisches Lexikon der Tonkünstler*, III, c. 452; the earlier edition from 1790-1792 gives the year 1733.

[9] Marchese di Villarosa, *Memorie dei compositori di musica del Regno di Napoli* (Naples: Stamperia Reale, 1840), 223.

[10] Piovano, "A propos d'une récente biographie de Léonard Leo," 74-76.

[11] *Libro maggiore ove stanno ascritti li Fratelli della Venerabile Congregazione del SS. Rosario*, quoted in Salvatore Di Giacomo, *I quattro antichi conservatorii di musica di Napoli*, II, 84. As previously mentioned, these records are no longer at S. Caterina a Formiello, nor can they be found at the other depositories for this type of material in Naples, such as the Archivio Storico Diocesano and the Achivio di Stato.

[12] *The Historical Archive of Banco di Napoli* (Naples: Banco di Napoli, 1988), 32.

[13] *Regole e Constituzioni della Umbile Congreg.ne del SS.mo Rosario, eretta dentro il Chiostro del Real Convento di S.ta Catt.a à Formello, 1744*, unpublished manuscript in the Archivio di Stato in Naples, in the collection Cappellano Maggiore Statuti e Congregazione, B 118/32.

Once the Fratello has been judged contumacious, it was not a simple matter of paying the fees; "the said Fratello must come in person in the Congregation to pay the said Monthly."[14] If the Fratello deferred this penitential settling of accounts,

> paying for the contumaciousness and all that which remains owing at the time of death, [then] all the other expenses that occur in candles, palls, decorated coffin and any other debt, will be charged to the house of the deceased Fratello, and the Congregazione will not have to be wholly present at the house.[15]

Leonardo Vinci's situation was apparently more serious because at the time of his death there was neither time nor money to "purge" away the contumaciousness. For this reason his "casa" or "eredi" had to pay for all the funeral rites and no mention is made of any gathering of the Brethren. Moreover, there may have been an additional complicating factor in his contumaciousness, had Vinci's sudden death and insolvency also prevented him from paying the entrance fee that he had promised to pay "at the time of his death" as agreed to in his entrance record.[16]

The reference to "eredi" suggests that Vinci had some family in Naples. Although there are no other references to Vinci's family, there is an entry in the *Libro dell' defonti* of S. Giovanni Maggiore to one Aniello Vinci son of Giuseppe Vinci and Agata Tramonti, resident of Ilolo who died in 1744 at the age twenty-one.[17] Because the name Vinci is not a common one in Southern Italy, this could be a reference to a cousin and uncle or even a brother and father. There is also a painting from 1776 in the Civico Museo Bibliografico Musicale in Bologna of one Francesco Vici *maestro di cappella* in Fano (see Plate 32 on page 331).[18] The aged features of Francesco resembling those of Vinci, could make him a *nipote* (in the real or Papal sense of the term).[19]

---

[14] Ibid.

[15] Ibid.

[16] Unless the "salda" addendum to his entrance record signified that he changed his mind and paid this fee in May of 1728. (See Chapter 8.)

[17] *Libro dell' defonti di S. Giovanni Maggiore*: Adi 17d. 1744: "Entry 17 1744: Aniello son of Giuseppe Vinci and Agata Tramotana, twenty years of age, resident of Ilolo Piccolo received the Holy Sacrament and was buried at Paulo Salvo."

[18] This painting was brought to my attention by Dinko Fabris in his paper "La fortuna europea di Vinci nel Settecento" presented at the conference *Leonardo Vinci: architetture sonore nella Napoli del viceregno austriaco: convegno internazionale di studi*, Conservatorio di Musica Francesco Cilea, Reggio Calabria, June 10-12, 2002.

[19] Francesco Vici was ordained in 1747, which suggests a birthdate somewhere in the 1720s. Vici served as *pro-maetro della cappella* at the cathedral in Fano until his death in 1782. Although he had something to do with opera productions in Fano he would have been too young to have been involved in the production of Vinci's *Artaserse* in 1731. He was friends with Padre Martini in Bologna and four of his letters to Martini survive, providing most of what is known about this obscure provincial musi-

Prota-Giurleo's discovery of the original death record did not clear up the matter.[20] The discovery of this record must have been a difficult task considering the number of churches in Naples and the fact that there appears to be no earlier reference as to where Vinci lived in the city. The record comes from the parish church of S. Maria della Neve and indicates that Vinci was a resident of the Chiaia—his residency there perhaps dating back to his association with the Pignatelli family, who still have their palace on the Chiaia. At that time the Chiaia was a fashionable suburb straddling the Bay of Naples north towards Posilippo (see Plate 33 on page 332). However, not content with having found this important record, Prota-Giurleo appears to have invented yet another record of death. Following upon the fact that in the fifteenth century the parish of S. Giovanni Maggiore was sub-divided into five filial parishes, one of which was S. Maria della Neve, with separate records made at both the filial parish and at S. Giovanni, Prota-Giurleo appears to have used this as the precedent to construct his second record, which improves upon the first. This record, like those in the *Libro dell' defonti* of S. Giovanni Maggiore, provides date of death and age, place of residence, place of burial, name of parents and type of last rites:

> Entry 29 May 1730. Leonardo Vinci, about 34 years old, son of Giuseppe and Antonia Vinci, resident of the Chiaia, received the Holy Sacrament, [and was] buried at S. Maria al formelli.[21]

The place of residence and the place of burial for this record come from the S. Maria della Neve record. The names of the parents appear to derive from the death record for Aniello Vinci mentioned above, except replacing Agate Tramonti with one Antonia Vinci, undoubtedly to avoid the suggestion that the composer was born out of wedlock. The date of May 29 connects with the May 27 in S. Maria della Neve and the unspecified June date of the record in S. Caterina a Formiello. The change of age from forty to thirty-four would seem to coordinate with Edward J. Dent's suggestion that the 1790 date of birth is too early for Vinci's subsequent career (see Chapter 1). The change of the circumstances of the death also seems to involve a certain enhancement of the facts, from simply making the sign of the cross to receiving the Holy Sacrament, as if to improve Vinci's chances in the next life. Using a strategy similar to Artusi in his famous critique of Monteverdi, Prota-Giurleo then weighs

---

cian. Unfortunately, there is no mention in the letters of any connection to Leonardo Vinci; Anne Schnobelen, *Padre Martini's Collection of Letters in the Civico Museo Biblografico Musicale in Bologna: An Annotated Index* (New York, Pendragon Press, 1979), 653, letters 5585-88.

[20] Ulisse Prota-Giurleo, "Leonardo Vinci" *Convegno musicale* II (1965), 10.

[21] Quoted in Ibid; compare with the record for Aniello Vinci in Footnote 17.

**Plate 32.** *Portrait of Don Francesco Vici* maestro di cappella *in Fano by Carlo Magini, dated 1776.*[22]

the pros and cons of the two death records before coming down on the side of the "second." Because this very brief record is so informative, it has been used by several subsequent writers as the foundation for entries on Vinci, including the present author in the *New Grove Dictionary of Opera* and the revised *New Grove Dictionary of Music and Musicians*. Unfortunately this record is not in the *Libro dell'defonti* at S. Giovanni Maggiore and, according to the director of the Curia Archives at the Cathedral of Naples, does not exist and cannot have existed because by the eighteenth century S. Maria della Neve was an independent parish church, the principal parish in the Chiaia without any association

---

[22] Civico Museo Bibliografico Musicale in Bologna: portrait of "D. Francesco Vici M.ro di Cappella di Fano" by Carlo Magini "pittore in Fano 1776."

**Plate 33.** *View of the city of Naples, taken from the suburb of the Chiaia by Berteaux after a painting by Vernet, engraved by Nicollet.*[23]

with S. Giovanni Maggiore. However, just to make things more complicated, the eighteenth-century records of several churches in the Chiaia are now kept at S. Giuseppe a Chiaia, where the authentic record of death can be found today in the *Libro dell defonti della. . .Chiesa di S. Maria della Neve di Chiaia*:

> Vinci: on the 27 of May, after giving the sign of the cross, died Signore Lonardo Vinci, forty years old, Bachelor, and was buried at the church of S. Caterina a Formiello.[24]

This entry, like the payment records for Vinci with the Banco dello Spirito Sancto, uses the Neapolitan form of his name.

A fourth account of Vinci's death exists in a note appended to the 1724 caricature of Vinci by Pier Leone Ghezzi, who often filled in obituary notices for the subjects of his caricatures (see Plate 6, page 81):[25]

---

[23] [Jean Claude Richard] Abbé de Saint Non, *Voyage Pittoresque ou description des Royaumes de Naples et de Sicile* (Paris: 1781), I, Plate 16, opposite 64.

[24] *Libro dell defonti della. . .Chiesa di S. Maria della Neve di Chiaia*, Iniziando della 1728, 9. The author would like to thank the director at the Curia Arcivescovile di Napoli Don Antonio Illibato and the Vice-Parroco of S. Giuseppe a Chiaja for their assistance in finding this important document.

[25] That Ghezzi did not append this information to his more recent caricature of Vinci was due to the fact that in his first caricature of Vinci from 1724, he left room under the title specifically for this obituary information as was his usual practice, whereas in his recent caricature, with its more realistic setting, the title is placed at the very bottom of the page.

> He died in Naples on 28 May 1730 on Sunday at the 17th hour; he died from a colic pain in an instant without even being able to confess, and if not for the intercession of the sister of his Eminence [Cardinal] Ruffo he could not even have been buried, because they found on him less than three paoli [a Papal coin of small denomination].[26]

Ghezzi's note is the most specific and, although written in Rome some time after Vinci's death, was penned by someone who knew the composer personally. This account corroborates the two authentic records at S. Maria delle Neve and S. Caterina a Formiello. As in the S. Caterina account, there was no money for a funeral. The intervention of Cardinal Ruffo's sister was necessary to arrange for a simple burial, with the fees for funeral rites, performed after the burial paid by his family. Therefore, the discrepancy in the dates of the three records (May 27, 28, and June 1730) may be due to the negotiations that went on between his death and the simple burial through the intervention of the Cardinal's sister (May 27/28), and the performance of the funeral rites after the payment of fees by the family (some time in June). The intercession of the sister of Cardinal Ruffo bespeaks good connections; the Cardinal was one of the most "papabile" in the recent conclave, losing out only in the end to Cardinal Corsini who became Clement XII.[27] Most intriguing of all, considering the rumors that circulated after his death, is the fact that both the Ghezzi and the S. Maria delle Neve accounts indicate that Vinci's death came suddenly. According to Ghezzi "he died from a colic pain in an instant without even being able to confess" or, perhaps just enough time to make a desperate "sign of the cross" as stated in the official death record at S. Maria delle Neve. The other curious aspect concerning Vinci's death is that it took place in Naples. Six months previously he had requested a year's leave of absence from the court (see Chapter 9) and, with such a request, one would have thought he had plans to travel abroad after the productions of *Alessandro* and *Artaserse* in Rome— perhaps, considering Metastasio's recent appointment to the Imperial court to accompany the new poet laureate on his journey to Vienna.

### Vinci "Il Giocatore"

In the brief annotation on his caricature, Ghezzi provides some precious information on the composer's personality:

> he was a man who would have gambled his eyes [away]; he was a "valentuomo" in music who composed with much spirit,

---
[26] Pier Leone Ghezzi, *Il Nuovo Mondo*, IV, f. 135; unpublished manuscript in the Biblioteca Apostolica Vaticana, Ottob.lat 3115.
[27] Francesco Valesio, *Diario di Roma: Libro nono e libro decimo*, [V: 1729-1736], ed. Gaetana Scano & Giuseppe Graglia (Longanesi, 1979), 218-219.

but his behavior was diverse from the talent that he had. May God give him paradise for his talent.[28]

According to Ghezzi, Leonardo Vinci was a gambler and for this reason died penniless. This addiction to gambling undoubtedly accounts for the chronic lack of cash that runs like a thread throughout his short life, perhaps going right back to Lonardo Vencia being expelled from the Conservatorio for late payment of his fees. It would also account for Vinci being unable to pay his entrance fee of six ducats when he joined the Congregation of the Rosary in February of 1728 and then at some point falling behind in his monthly fees; for having to ask the Viceroy for one of his horses "without paying for it" in September of 1729; for composing two operas for the price of one during Carnival 1730, presumably to cover his share as impresario at the Teatro della Dame, (perhaps even for being unable to buy up a block of tickets for the opening night of Porpora's *Siface* in Marpurg's anecdote); and ultimately for dying penniless, leaving his family to pay for the funeral. Ironically in most of these instances Vinci should have been solvent, having just completed important opera commissions, but presumably the gambling was devouring the money faster than he could make it.

Gambling was very popular during the eighteenth century, with fortunes won and lost on a single card or toss of the dice. Gambling gained aristocratic respectability at the court of Louis XIV where it served, like the opera and ballet, as a diversion to amuse a troublesome aristocracy. In Venice the famous *ridotti* were just as much an attraction as the opera houses and brothels. Vinci's sojourns in that city may well have been spent earning money at the Teatro San Giovanni Grisostomo and losing it at the nearby Ridotto of S. Moisé, the most celebrated of the Venetian gambling casinos. Gambling also went on in the theatres, not only in the boxes but even in the orchestra pit where orchestral musicians gambled between the arias. Gambling was so common in the opera theatres that they sometimes doubled as gambling casinos, with tables set up in the foyers—this was the principal reason why Rossini and his impresario Domenico Barbaia became so wealthy in the 1820s.

The superficial glamour and elegance of gambling by the aristocracy is perfectly captured by Alexander Pope in *Rape of the Lock*. The cruder, more violent plebian manifestations are depicted in two contemporary Italian sources. The first is a caricature by Ghezzi drawn this same year in Rome, depicting the impresario Giuseppe Polvini Faliconti playing cards with the publisher Filippo de' Rossi—one can imagine the disembodied hand in the far left, representing an unknown third party, belonging to a caricature of Vinci (see Plate 34 on facing page). The

---

[28] Pier Leone Ghezzi, *Il Nuovo Mondo*, IV, f. 135.

**Plate 34.** *The impressario Giuseppe Polvini Faliconti playing cards with the publisher Filippo de' Rossi, by Pier Leone Ghezzi, Rome, 1730.*[29] ©Biblioteca Apostolica Vaticana (Vatican)

[29] Pier Leone Ghezzi, *Il Nuovo Mondo*, V, f. 2; unpublished manuscript in the Biblioteca Apostolica Vaticana, Ottob.lat 3116.

other depiction of gambling is in an opera, Salvi and Orlandini's *Il marito giocatore*.[30] This popular intermezzo is particularly appropriate to Vinci, having been incorrectly attributed to him since the mid-eighteenth century.[31] One can imagine Vinci, like Bacocco in the opening scene, returning to his room in the early hours of the morning, cursing his bad luck, after:

> a badly spent night without supper, without sleep, besides money, ring and watch, I have lost, my sword, hat and cloak.[32]

The subsequent events of the intermezzo illustrate in a humorous but realistic manner the evil consequences of Bacocco's addiction to gambling: infidelity, divorce, robbery, and murder, the latter prevented only by the conventional "lieto fine." Unfortunately Leonardo Vinci's story did not have a mandatory happy ending.

## A Love Vendetta

Not only did Vinci die penniless but rumors began to circulate shortly after his death that he was the victim of foul play. Baron de Pollnitz, in a letter from Rome dated March 10, 1731, mentions that the Romans have just lost one of the ablest Men of that Class; viz. Leonardo Vinci, who, they say, was poisoned at Naples."[33] Several years later in Naples, Charles De Brosses provides more details, giving greater substance to the rumor: "they say that he was insolent and that having been punished more than once for a gallantry he conducted too openly with a Lady, he died by being poisoned."[34] If the details of De Brosses' account are true, one of the punishments for Vinci's "galanterie" may have occurred during the production of *Catone in Utica* in January 1728, hence his early return to Naples that year. This in turn would tie in with Florimo's anecdote, which connects Vinci's subsequent enrolment in the Congregation of the Rosary to a love affair with a Roman Lady (see Chapter 8).

The description of Vinci in the Abbé de Saint Non's *Voyage Pittoresque ou description des Royaumes de Naples et de Sicile* from 1781, provides more details:

---

[30] Scores of the Verona production of 1715 and the Venetian production of 1719 are reproduced in [68] of *Italian Opera 1640-1770*.
[31] This misattribution can be found in Robert Eitner, *Biographisch-Bibliographisches Quellen-Lexikon: der Musiker und Musikgelehrten* as well as in a more recent source: *The Mellen Opera Reference Index: Opera Composers and their Works*, ed. Charles H. Parsons (Lewiston, New York: Edwin Mellen Press, 1986).
[32] [Antonio Salvi], *Il marito giogatore, e la moglie bacchettona: intermezzi per musica* (Venice: Marino Rossetti, 1719), 3; facsimile in XV of *Italian Opera Librettos: 1640-1770*.
[33] *The Memoirs of Charles-Lewis, Baron de Pollnitz* (London: D. Browne, 1737), 66.
[34] Charles De Brosses, *Lettres familièrs écrites d'italie à quelques amis en 1739 et 1740*, I, 255.

> This great and celebrated musician died in 1732 at the age of forty-two. He was poisoned, so they say, with a cup of chocolate; they claim that Vinci had publicly boasted during his stay in Rome of having the favors of a Lady of the highest rank; a relative of this Lady found himself in Naples and was instructed to avenge the musician's indiscretion by having him poisoned.[35]

While the Abbé gives the wrong death date, his description of the composer's age ties in with the death record at S. Maria delle Neve, and, in turn, with the date of birth in Sigismondo. The presence of the "relative of this Lady" who "found himself in Naples" and was responsible for the deed, takes on a certain realism, set against the expulsion of the "Benevantani" from Rome after the death of Pope Benedict XIII.[36] Gerber's *Historisch-Biographisches Lexikon* from 1790/92, gives a new twist to the story: "in Naples he was, through the envy and jealousy of other composers, executed with poison."[37] Published the year after Mozart's death, this account of Vinci's murder by his colleagues may have been influenced by the rumors concerning Mozart and Salieri, or it may have originated in Naples; the manner in which Vinci ousted Leonardo Leo from positions of privilege and then in turn was replaced by him upon his death, may well have been sufficient to start the rumor mill—it certainly catches the attention when comparing their employment records. In the expanded entry on Vinci in the revised edition of the Lexikon, however, Gerber provides an almost verbatim translation of the account of the Abbé de Saint Non, bringing in the composer conspiracy at the end, without explaining the relationship between the two: "Therefore impudence on his part, and not without the jealousy of other composers, was the cause of his death."[38]

In the accounts of De Brosses and Saint Non, Vinci's crime was not so much his illicit affair but, rather, his indiscretion in conducting this affair. In contrast to the princely courts throughout Europe where the position of mistress had been institutionalized, Rome had its own distinctive sexual tradition, that of the *cicisbei*, the young lovers of married women. This relationship was generally carried on with the knowledge of the husband; it was said sarcastically that Roman marriage contracts of the time contained a clause specifying that "the husband will

---

[35] Abbé de Saint Non, *Voyage Pittoresque*...I, 168.

[36] The Roman underworld had flourished during the reign of Pope Benedict XIII, who allowed the city to be run by the "unscrupulous scoundrel" Cardinal Nicolà Coscia (J. N. D. Kelly, *The Oxford Dictionary of Popes*). The corruption was so rampant that with the election of the new Pope, Clement XII, the "Beneventani" were driven from the city and probably a number of them ended up in Naples rather than returning to nearby Benevento.

[37] Gerber, *Historisch-Biographisches Lexikon der Tonkünstler* (1790-1792), I, c. 731.

[38] Gerber, *Neues Historisch-Biographisches Lexikon*... (1812-14), II, c. 452.

never accompany his wife outside the house on walks, to the theatre and on visits; she will always be accompanied by her *cavalier servente*."[39] A celebrated example of this tolerance is the relationship between Metastasio and La Romanina and her husband Domenico Bulgarelli; when the soprano returned to Rome after her retirement from the stage in 1727, she was accompanied by both husband and lover and together "they all lived under the same roof, and constituted one family."[40] The one caveat to this sexual freedom was that women should not be openly promiscuous and flaunt their *cicisbei*.[41] For example "La Romanina" was officially Metastasio's mentor and friend and even years after her death Burney still referred to her discreetly as "his generous friend" and "his amiable friend."[42] According to the accounts of De Brosses and Saint Non, Vinci was not discreet but was insolent, openly boasting of his conquest and as a consequence paid the price. In spite of the easy-going life of eighteenth-century Rome, there was a dark undercurrent of violence:

> The Romans remained a fiercely contentious people, quick to flare up in anger and slow to forgive. Murders were frequent, both crimes of passion and premeditated killings carried out in pursuit of revenge.[43]

According to the accounts of De Brosses and Saint Non, Vinci was a victim of the latter.

### Vinci's "*Grosso Frego*" and the Siren's Sword-wielding "*Protettore*"

The account of Saint Non also appears in Sigismondo's entry on Vinci in the "Apoteosi dell' Arte Musicale."[44] After expressing a certain cynicism over the Abbé's account, Sigismondo then goes on to provide his own contribution to the story:

> I do not know how much faith one should attribute to the assertion of this traveller, but I do know, through the report of my maternal uncle Sig. Francesco Pagano, a great dilettante of music, a scholar of Leo, and a *confratello* at the very same congregation, that Vinci, whom he knew and had dealings

---

[39] Quoted in Filippo Clementi, *Il carnevale romano nelle cronache contemporanee: sec. XVIII-XIX* (Città di Castello: Unione arti grafiche, 1938), II, 55-56.
[40] Burney, *Memoirs of the Life and Writings of the Abate Metastasio*, I, 40.
[41] Christopher Hibbert, *Rome: the Biography of a City* (Harmondsworth, Middlesex: Penguin Books, 1985), 219.
[42] Burney, *Memoirs of the Life and Writings of the Abate Metastasio*, I, 42.
[43] Hibbert, *Rome: the Biography of a City*, 213.
[44] Saint Non's account of the love vendetta turns up again in the entry on Vinci in: François-Joseph Fétis, *Biographie Universelle des musiciens, et bibliographie générale de la musique*, 2nd ed., III, 357.

> with, carried a large mark on his face which he used to hide with the big wig of the day known as the *Delfina*—a mark inflicted on him by a swordsman protector of a opera singer: something moreover not difficult to happen, to a musician who is obliged to have dealings with similar sirens, in jealousy or in revenge of the same.[45]

With Sigismondo's account in mind, one cannot help but notice the presence of this "grosso frego" in the shadows of the painted portrait of Leonardo Vinci at the Conservatorio di San Pietro a Majella (see the reproduction on the book cover). The painting appears to be part of a series from the eighteenth and early nineteenth centuries depicting Neapolitan composers and includes portraits of Alessandro Scarlatti, Pergolesi, Feo, Durante, Jommelli, Cimarosa, and others. Representing the new historical consciousness of the late eighteenth century, the series serves as a visual counterpart of the emerging concept of the "Neapolitan School" extending from Alessandro Scarlatti to Cimarosa, dominating the music of eighteenth-century Italy. The paintings may have been brought together as a series by Giuseppe Sigismondo as an adjunct to his monumental study of Neapolitan composers, the "Apoteosi dell'Arte Musicale," providing the Conservatory with a virtual alumnus portrait gallery. Because of the distinctiveness of each of these portraits, they appear to be based on previous paintings and engravings, many of which have been subsequently lost. Thus, the portrait could be based on an original painting from Vinci's last years, depicting the composer as an abbé, which was very fashionable in Rome at this time[46] (for another interpretation on the origins of this painting, see fn. 51). The intense realism of the face, with features that bear a rather striking resemblance to those in the Ghezzi caricatures (the pursed lips, highly arched eyebrows, and beaked nose), is accentuated by the depiction of this nasty gash on the left side of his face. This gash, which gives visual evidence of the account in Sigismondo, is also apparent in several engravings of the composer from the early nineteenth century (see Plate 35 on page 340).[47] In these engravings the features are more idealized, with the composer sporting a late-eghteenth-century powdered wig with tail, of the type worn by Mozart and Haydn, which was just starting to come

---

[45] Giuseppe Sigismondo, *Apoteosi dell'Arte Musicale*, (Naples, 1820; unpublished manuscript in Berlin catalogued as"Materialien zu einer Geschichte der Musik der Neapolitaner Schule"), III, 106-107.

[46] Hibbert, *Rome: the Biography of a City*, 202; according to Casanova, "Everyone in Rome...was either a priest or trying to look like one."

[47] G.B.G. Grossi, "Leonardo Vinci: Celebre Maestro di Cappella, Nacque in Napoli nel 1690, Ove morì nel 1732" in *Biografia degli uomini illustri del Regno di Napoli: Ornata de loro rispettivi ritratti*, ed. Martuscelli, Vol.VI (Naples, Niccola Gervasi Gigante 1819) & *Iconografia italiana degli uomini e delle donne celebri, dall' epoca del Risorgimento delle scienze e belle arti fino ai nostri giorni* (Milan: A Locatelli, 1837).

**Plate 35.** *Engraving of Leonardo Vinci by C. Biondi in* Biografia degli uomini illustri del Regno di Napoli *from 1819.*[48]

into fashion during the late 1720s (see, for example, the caricature of Farfallino, Plate 13 on page 139). In addition, the gash appears on the other side of the face, suggesting that somewhere along the line something got reversed. Without refuting or confirming the poisoning story, Sigismondo seems to be suggesting another "conspiracy theory," to use modern parlance, concerning the sudden death of Leonardo Vinci: rather, with a singer that brought about his demise at the hands of her the usual "protettore." The *protettore* of Sigismond's story would not have been

---

[48] G.B.G. Grossi, "Leonardo Vinci: Celebre Maestro di Cappella," in *Biografia degli uomini illustri del Regno di Napoli: Ornata de loro rispettivi ritratti.*

the usual impresario-type, as satirized by Marcello, eager to advance the interests of his protégé and maximize his cut, but an aristocratic lover. Singers often became the mistresses of great princes, La Georgina and Viceroy Medinaceli for example. In an age of arranged marriages among the aristocracy,"messing around" with a nobleman's mistress was just as dangerous as "messing around" with his wife, as Stradella found out in his love affair with the mistress of Alvise Contarini.[49] As in the De Brosses/Saint Non accounts, Sigismondo describes a love vendetta, but the Lady is a colleague, while the *protettore* is presumably of the "highest rank" asserting his privilege in order to crush a rival. In both stories Vinci would have fallen victim to the revenge of an aristocratic *protettore* over an illicit love affair that he stubbornly pursued even after having been violently punished on a previous occasion.

Although this scenario, derived from Sigismondo's anecdote, ties in with De Brosses's description of Vinci "having been punished more than once" before being poisoned, the story of the "opera singer" and "siren" runs counter to the Roman backdrop of Saint Non's account. Sigismondo's incident would more likely have taken place in either Venice or Naples where female singers were abundant, as opposed to Rome where their roles were taken by castrati due to the old Papal prohibition. This anomaly seems to suggest that either Saint Non got the place wrong or Sigismondo's anecdote is a separate incident, in the same way that Stradella's love affair with the mistress of Alvise Contarini in Venice had nothing to do with his eventual murder in Genoa, presumably carried out by the Lomellini family over another love affair.[50]

That this is probably a separate incident is suggested by some subtle visual evidence. Again with Sigismondo's anecdote in mind, if one looks carefully at Ghezzi's second caricature, one can see this "grosso frego" beginning under his eye and extending around his prominent cheekbone (Plate 31 on page 286). This gives the immediate impression that the gash can be traced directly to the caricature of Vinci by Ghezzi, a caricature drawn from life during the composer's last years. Moreover the positioning of the gash is almost identical to that in the painted portrait of Vinci.[51] This scar, though not as prominent, can be seen in the sketch

---

[49] See Carolyn Gianturco, *Alessandro Stradella: 1639-1682: His Life and Music* (Oxford:Clarendon Press, 1994), 33-45.

[50] Ibid., 56-60.

[51] The similarity between the painting of Vinci in Naples and the painting of Don Francesco Vici in Bologna has been noted by Dinko Fabris in "La fortuna europea di Vinci nel Settecento" presented at the Vinci Conference in Reggio Calabria in June 2002 (compare reproduction on the front cover with Plate 32 on page 331). Not only are the pictures similar in subject matter—a portrait in *mezzo figura* of an abate composer holding a symbol of his profession in a musical manuscript—but they are also

of the face used in this caricature, which is dated February 1722, suggesting that Vinci may have carried this distinguishing feature throughout most of his career. This seems to indicate that Sigismondo's incident would have taken place before 1722, relegating the event to Naples and the "siren" to one of the comic singers at the Teatro Fiorentine. Although the outlines of this gash are only barely visible in the other caricature from 1724 (Plate 6 on page 81) and its sketch, the gash appears to be more in evidence in the darkened spot on the side of the nose of the unidentified gentleman in the Faustina caricature (See Plate 7 on page 100)—the tip of the "grosso frego" allowing one to more securely identify this figure as Vinci. Therefore, the outcome of these various rumors and clues suggests that Vinci was involved in a violent incident over a liaison with an opera singer in Naples during the early 1720s, which left him with a disfiguring scar on his face and that he died amidst gossip that he had been poisoned over another love affair he had conducted too openly in Rome with "a lady of highest rank," a relationship he stubbornly refused to give up, even after being previously punished .

## Poison

At a time when the study of medicine was still in its infancy and post-mortems were far from universal, poison was one of the most common forms of murder. The extent of this practice was revealed by the infamous "Affaire des Poisons," which scandalized France during the late 1670s and early 1680s.[52] A similar poison scandal occurred in Palermo earlier in the century known as the "Grand stagione" and later Giulia Tofana, who operated out of Naples and Rome, invented the infamous "Acqua Tofana," which was the standard poison of the eighteenth century, the same that Mozart was convinced he had been given.[53] The

---

similar in appearance, with the large pointed nose, the cupids-bow lips, arched eyebrows, etc. Although one could dismiss the similarity as a manifestation of the stylized nature of eighteenth-century portraiture, the similarity of appearance, name, and profession of the subjects could suggest some sort of familial relationship. The other way to explain the similarity would be to develop a scenario of a relationship between the paintings; that the Conservatory portrait of Leonardo Vinci dates from the late eighteenth/ early nineteenth century and is based on the portrait of Francesco Vici dated 1776, except that the facial features, including the gash, are derived from Ghezzi's second caricature, as is the distinctive hand clutching the rolled-up manuscript paper (compare the portrait on the cover with Plate 31 on page 286); the objection to this is that the artist who painted the Vinci would have to have had access to both the Vici portrait in Bologna and the second Ghezzi caricature in Rome, neither of which was published.

[52] See Jean-Christian Petitfils, *L'Affaire des Poisons: Alchimistes et sorciers sous Louis XIV* (Paris: Albin Michel, 1977).

[53] John Walton, Paul Beeson, and Ronald Bodley Scott, *The Oxford Companion to Medicine* (Oxford: Oxford University Press, 1986), II, 1113; Maynard Solomon, *Mozart: a Life* (Harper Collins, 1995), 489.

Affair of the Poisons involved great aristocrats, including the King's mistress Madame de Montespan. Besides the spectacular, diabolically-driven poisonings of "L'Affaire," there were the mundane domestic poisonings:

> the immediately fatal and vulgar poisons, the criminal dose in the domestic soup, in the sauce, in the gravy, in the cream [or cup of chocolate]; rat poison promoted to a liberating function, in the asphyxiation of husband or wife, in the impossible love affair; in the possible but tardy inheritance....And generally administered by the hand of a meticulous woman, adulterating the gastronomic attention in the preferred plate of the victims.[54]

Poison in eighteenth-century Italy was the scoundrel's "quick fix." For example, during his early years in Italy, Ranieri de' Calzabigi was accused of attempting to poison his brother-in-law, having obtained a vial of "acquetta" from a friend in Naples, in order to get out of paying a posthumous dowry after the death his sister.[55]

There are several reasons why one should give more credence to this story than to the other tales of poisoned eighteenth-century composers. First, it is the earliest and may have provided the basis for the similar stories about Pergolesi and Mozart. Second, it is not compromised by reports of death by natural causes: tuberculosis for Pergolesi and rheumatic inflammatory fever for Mozart. Third, it contains a viable reason for murder, a love vendetta being the most common motive (as in the quote above). As for the composer conspiracy introduced in Gerber, this is probably as apocryphal as it is in similar accounts of the deaths of Mozart and Pergolesi—as well as Terradellas, who was supposedly stabbed by Jommelli and thrown into the Tiber. That contemporaries could imagine composers killing each other in jealousy is indicative of the competition that existed between composers of the eighteenth century when there was an imbalance between talented artists and career opportunities.

Finally, the poison story ties in with the death reports. Both the Ghezzi and the S. Maria delle Neve accounts indicate that Vinci's death came suddenly; according to Ghezzi "he died from a colic pain in an instant without even being able to confess." Vinci's death could have been from natural causes, such as acute appendicitis, or from unnatural

---

[54] Rosario La Duca, *I veleni di Palermo*, Introduction by Leonardo Sciacia, (Palermo: Sellerio, 1988), 9.

[55] Enrico Masini, "La famiglia Calzabigi: in documenti inediti livornesi" *La figura e l'opera di de Ranieri de' Calzabigi: Atti del convegno di studi*, Livorno, 1987, Federico Marri, ed. (Florence: Leo S. Olschki, 1989), 178-79; although this purported poisoning supposedly took place in Naples c.1750 resulting in Calzabigi's departure for Paris, recent research suggests that it took place in Livorno in the late 1730s.

causes, such as poison. Although the story of Vinci's poisoning cannot be proven, it cannot be disproved, as is the case of similar stories connected with the deaths of Pergolesi and Mozart. Because we have this story from several reliable authorities without any obvious contradictions, one must let the story stand as is, within the realm of possibility.

## Vinci *in Memoria*

Sigismondo describes an elaborate memorial service for Vinci at S. Caterina a Formiello arranged by Franceso Feo and performed by the musicians of Naples:

> Maestro Francesco Feo, his friend and contemporary, collaborated with all the *professori di musica* in our city, taking care to make for him a sumptuous mausoleum with solemn funereal adornment; two grandiose orchestras wherein all the musicians of the city took part in the expiation of the Office, that of the Mass for the Dead. In this gesture is seen the estimation in which our friend Vinci was held and the concord there was among the musicians, who at their own expense, honored the memory of their compatriot, colleague, and friend.[56]

The emphatic nature of this statement suggests that Sigismondo may have included it to counter the rumors connecting the untimely death of Vinci with the envy of his Neapolitan colleagues and rivals, hence the repeated reference to "all the *professori*" and "all the musicians." Moreover, to guarantee the truth of his report he even states his sources, namely "the books of my Confraternity" and the report of "Giacobbe Calandra, a fine violinist...and friend of Vinci at the Conservatory" and probably a performer in one of the orchestras.[57] This elaborate service at S. Caterina a Formiello was undoubtedly intended and regarded as a replacement and compensation for Vinci's very compromised burial and funeral rites due to the charge of contumaciousness within the Congregazione del SS. Rosario. Although Sigismondo does not specify what music was performed at Vinci's service, one might assume that the centerpiece would have been a Requiem for double choir and orchestra by Feo, who was celebrated in his day for his church music and is known to have written at least one requiem mass.[58] The Requiem was perhaps augmented with music by the deceased, as it was at the funeral of Rameau, where the *Requiem de Giles* was augmented with excerpts from the composer's

---

[56] *Apoteosi dell'Arte Musicale* III, 103-104.

[57] Ibid., 104-105. Calandra entered the Conservatory as *convittore* the year after Vinci.

[58] Feo's *Missa defunctorum* in D minor from 1718; "Feo, Francesco" by Hanns-Bertold Dietz in *The New Grove Dictionary of Music and Musicians*.

eras, adapted to sacred texts.[59] Vinci's memorial service, which involved "all the musicians of the city" and undoubtedly a sizeable audience, anticipates the large public funerals of composers such as Handel and Rameau.

The death and the memorial service were undoubtedly factors in the revival of several Vinci operas at the Teatro San Bartolomeo and the Teatro Nuovo during the early 1730s, which can be regarded almost as a retrospective in honor of the composer's memory.

> *Artaserse* (winter 1730)
> *La mogliere fedele* (autumn 1731)
> *Lo castiello saccheato* (*Carnival* 1732)
> *Catone in Utica* (autumn 1732)
> *La festa de bacco* (autumn 1732)
> *Artaserse* (Carnival 1733, cancelled due to earthquake but performed again in 1738)

For the revival of *La Mogliere fedele*, the libretto states that, though the recitative had been recomposed by Giuseppe Sellito, "the rest is for the good memory of Lonardo Vinci."[60] These revivals would have contributed to establishing Vinci's style as a model for the next generation of composers, especially Pergolesi and Jommelli.

Another tribute came with Filippo Juvarra's *Memorie sepolcrali dell'homini più insigne di questo secolo conosciuti da Me*, a set of engravings of imaginary funeral monuments that included many of the major Italian artists of the early eighteenth century.[61] Besides fellow artists such as Carlo Fontana, Giovanni Battista Gaulli, Carlo Maratta, and Pietro Le Gros, the great architect also included five composers: Andrea Fioré Arcangelo Corelli, Carlo Francesco Pollarolo, Francesco Gasparini, and Leonaardo Vinci. Fioré, the former *maestro di capella* at the Savoyard court, had been Juvarra's colleague in Turin, while Corelli, Gasparini, and Pollarolo would have been acquaintances from his early career (1708-14) as stage designer for Cardinal Ottolboni's private theatre at the Palazzo Cancelleria. Juvarra probably met Vinci during his visit to Rome in 1724, when he, like Vinci, was caricatured by Ghezzi.[62] The design for this monument consists of a large funerary urn with the inscription

---

[59] Cuthbert Girdlestone, *Jean-Philippe Rameau: His Life and Works*. 2nd ed. (New York: Dover, 1969), 513.
[60] *La mogliere fedele: commeddea pe mmusica, da rappresentarese a lo Teeatro Nuovo ncoppa Monte Cravaneo nchist' autummo dell'anno corrente 1731* (Naples, 1731).
[61] Oscar Mischiati, "Una memoria sepolcrale di Filippo Juvarra per Arcangelo Corelli," *Nuovi studi corelliani: atti del secondo congresso internazonale*, Fusignano, Sept. 1974, ed. Giulia Giachin (Florence: Leo S. Olschki, 1978), 105-112.
[62] M. Viale Ferrera, *Filippo Juvarra: scenografo e architetto teatrale* (Turin: Fratelli Pozzo), 67-68. Ghezzi's caricature of Juvarra dated October 1724 is reproduced opposite the book's title page.

*Plate 36.* Filippo Juvarra "Monumento a L. Vinci" *in* Memorie sepolcrale.[63]

[63] Filppo Juvarra, "Monumento a L. Vinci," no. 5 in *Memorie sepolcrale dell homini più insigne di q.o. secolo conosciuti da me* (Turin, 1735).

"Vinci insigne maestro di musica per teatri morì in Napoli 1729" upon a pedestal surrounded by several manuscripts, a laurel crown, and a lyre (see Plate 36 on facing page). It stands in front of a monument that features a bust of the composer within a laurel wreath.[64] Although the facial features are stylized and rather difficult to make out, there are the faint outlines of a scar, again on the opposite side of the face and flipping up rather than down. Because Juvarra was probably drawing from memory, the contradictions of right or left side, curving up or down, are less important than the fact that what Juvarra remembered about Leonardo Vinci was the "grosso frego" on the side of his face and the Dauphin wig.

That Juvarra considered Vinci one of "the most famous men of this century" was primarily due to his dominance of the musical scene in Rome during the 1720s and the posthumous success of *Artaserse*, the latter perhaps enhanced by his early death amid rumors of foul play. Vinci attained additional celebrity in France during the *Querelle des Bouffons*, being regarded by adherents on both sides as one of the foremost exponents of the Italian style alongside Pergolesi. Although De Rochement in his *Réflexions sur l'Opera* from 1755 supported the cause of French opera, he singles out Vinci's *Artaserse* and Lully's *Armide* as the masterpieces of Italian and French musical theatre: "*Artaserse* of Vinci passes for the most beautiful opera of Italy, in the same way as *Armide* is the masterpiece of French composition."[65] The *bouffonistes* were more lavish in their praise. Rousseau, in his *Lettre sur la Musique Françoise* from 1753, could emphatically state that "Corelli, Bononcini, Vinci, and Pergolesi are the first who have made music" as opposed to simply "harmony and sounds."[66] One can find other similar lists of great composers from this period and, though the names will vary, Pergolesi and Vinci are often the common denominators.[67]

---

[64] Grétry's reference to Vinci meriting "the statue that they erected of him in the Pantheon" (see Chapter 9) is rather puzzling since the composer was buried at S. Caterina al Formiello in Naples and there is no reference to any such monument in the other sources. When Burney visited the Pantheon in 1770 he referred to "Corelli's and Raphael's monuments" but makes no mention of any monument to Vinci (*Music, Men, and Manners in France and Italy: 1770*, 152). Perhaps Grétry, familiar with Juvarra's engravings, assumed that Vinci's was matched up with an actual monument in the Pantheon, as was the case with Corelli's.

[65] [De Rochemint], "Réflexions d'un patriote sur l'opera françois, et sur l'opera italien," *La querelle des Bouffons: texte des pamphlets*, LIX, 2057.

[66] Jean-Jacques Rousseau, "Lettre sur la musique françoise," *La querelle des Bouffons: texte des pamphlets*, Vol. XXXIII, 717.

[67] The author has investigated the complex and fascinating background of this posthumous celebrity of Vinci and Pergolesi in the paper "Music Criticism in Italy during the Second Half of the Eighteenth Century: Too Many Ornaments, Too Many Instruments, and Too Many Notes," paper presented at the American Musicological Society, Chapter Meeting, St. Louis, March 22-23, 2003.

Michael F. Robinson in *Naples and Neapolitan Opera* relates the diffusion of the Neapolitan style to the rise of the new sensibility, as exemplified by the philosophy of Rousseau, the sentimental novel, domestic genre painting, English gardens, the *Emfindsamer Stil*, etc.[68] The figure of Pergolesi contributed greatly in forging this link between music and sensibility. His early tragic death captured the imagination of those influenced by the new sensibility who heard "the sublime" in the sweet sentimental lyricism of his music. Robinson speculates that Vinci could have "been built up as the sentimental hero" had not Pergolesi surpassed him in writing sweet sentimental melodies and in dying young.[69] Just as Vinci was overshadowed by Pergolesi during the later eighteenth century, so was Pergolesi in turn overshadowed by a "new sentimentalized hero" who died tragically young at the end of the eighteenth century, one whose music and life would coordinate with the emergence of romanticism and Germanic musical hegemony.

[68] Michael F. Robinson, *Naples and Neapolitan Opera*, 29-30.
[69] Ibid., 30.

# SELECTED BIBLIOGRAPHY

## Eighteenth-Century Sources

**Algarotti, Francesco, conte**. *Saggio sopra l'opera in musica*. (Livorno: Colltellini, 1763; English ed., *An Essay on the Opera*, [Glasgow: R. Urie, 1768]).

**Arteaga, Stefano**. *Le rivoluzioni del teatro musicale italiano dalla sua origine fino al presente*. (Venice: C. Palese, 1785).

**Bach, Carl Philipp Emanuel**. *Essay on the True Art of Playing Keyboard Instruments*. Tr. by William J. Mitchell. (New York: W.W. Norton, 1949; originally published as *Versuch über die wahre Art das Clavier zu spielen*, [Berlin: George Ludewig Winter, 1759]).

**Balatri, Filippo**. *Frutti del Mondo: autobiografia di Filippo Balatri da Pisa (1676-1756) edita per la prima volta*. Ed. by Karl Vossler. (Milan: Remo Sandron, 1924).

**Bonlini, Carlo**. *Le glorie della poesia, e della musica contenute nell' esatta notitiz de' teatri della città di Venezia*. (Venice: C. Bonarigo, 1730; reprint ed.,[Bologna: Arnaldo Forni Editore, 1979]).

**Brown, John**. *Letters upon the Poetry and Music of the Italian Opera; addressed to a Friend*. (Edinburgh: Bell and Bradfute, 1789).

**Burney, Charles**. *A General History of Music: from the Earliest Ages to the Present period (1789)*. Critical and historical notes by Frank Mercer. (New York: Dover, 1957;[originally published in London, 1776-89]).

_____. *Memoirs of the Life and Writings of the Abate Metastasio in which are incorporated his Principal Letters*. (London: C.G. & J. Robinson, 1796; reprinted [New York: Da Capo, 1971]

_____. *Music, Men, and Manners in France and Italy: 1770*. Ed. by H. Edmund Poole. London: Folio Society, 1969.

_____. *The Present State of Music in France and Italy*, 2nd. ed. (London: T. Becket, 1773; reprint ed., Monuments of Music and Music Literature in Facsimile 70, [New York: Broude Brothers, 1969]).

*Chracas Diario Ordinario (di Roma): Sunto di notizie e indici*, I (1718-1739). Edited by Associazione Culturale, Alma Roma, 1997.

**Cramer, Carl Friedrich**. *Magazin der Musik: Zweyter Jahrgang*. (Hamburg: Musicalischen Niederlage, 1784); reprint ed., [Hildesheim: George Olms, 1971]).

**De Brosses, Charles**. *Lettres familièrs écrites d'Italie a quelques amis en 1739 et 1740*. (Paris: Poulet-Malassis et de Broise, 1858).

**De Chastellux, François-Joseph**. *Essai sur l'union de la poésie et de la musique*. (Paris: La Haye, 1765; reprint ed., [Geneva: Slatkine Reprints, 1970)].

[**De Rochemont, Charles Pictet?**]. "Réflexions d'un patriote sur l'opera françois, et sur l'opera italien." In *La querelle des Bouffons: texte des pamphlets*, No. 59. (Paris: La Hayne, 1752-54; reprint ed., with Introduction and notes by Denise Launay, [Geneva: Minkoff, 1973]).

**Dumont, Gabriel Pierre Martin**. *Parallele de Plans des plus Belles Salles de Spectacles d'Italie et de France avec des détails de Machines Théatrales*. (Paris: Mia au Tour, c.1774; reprint ed., [New York: Benjamin Blom, 1968]).

**Fenaroli, Fedele**. *Regole musicali per i principianti di cembalo*. (Naples, Vincenzo Mazzola-Vocola, 1775; reprint ed., [Bologna: Forni, 1975]. From Website *Saggi Musicali Italiani*: agigerl@Isu.edu

**Frugoni, Carlo Innocenzio**. *Opere poetiche del signor abate Carlo Innocenzio Frugoni fra gli Arcadi Comante Eginetico*. (Parma: Stamperia Reale, 1779).

**Gasparini, Francesco**. *The Practical Harmonist at the Harpsichord*. Tr. by Frank S. Stillings and ed. by David L Burrows. (New Haven, Conn.: Yale University Press, 1968; originally published as *L'armonico pratico al cimbalo*, [Venice: Antonio Bartoli, 1708]).

**Gerber, Ernst Ludwig**. *Historisch-Biographisches Lexikon der Tonkünstler (1790-1792)*. Ed. by Othmar Wessely (Leipzig: J.G.I. Breitkopf, 1790; reprint ed., [Graz: Akademische Druck-u.Verlagsanstalt, 1977]).

**Ghezzi, Pier Leone**. *Il Nuovo Mondo*, II, IV & V. Unpublished manuscripts in the Biblioteca Apostolica Vaticana, Ottob.lat 3113, 3115 & 3116.

**Goldoni, Carlo**. *Memoirs of Carlo Goldoni: Written by Himself*. Tr. by John Black, ed. by William A. Drake. (London: Alfred A Knopf, 1926; originally published as *Mémoires*, [Paris: Veuve Duchesne,1787]).

**Grétry, André Ernest Modeste**. *Mémoires, ou Essais sur la Musique*. (Paris: 1797; reprint ed., [Bruxelles: Oscar Lamberty Editeur, 1924]).

"**Josse de Villeneuves** Brief über den Mechanismus der italienischen Oper von 1756." Tr. by Robert Hass. *Zeitschrift für Musikwissenschaft* 7/2 (Dec., 1924): 129-163; originally published as *Lettre sur le mechanisme de l'opera italien*, (Naples [Paris], Duchesne & Lambert, 1756).

**Koch, Heinrich Christoph**. *Introductory Essay on Composition: the Mechanical Rules of Melody*. Tr. by Nancy Kovaleff Baker. (New Haven, Connecticut: Yale University Press; a translation of Sections 3 & 4 of *Versuch einer Anleitung zur Composition*, 2. Abtheilung, [Leipzig: Adam F. Böhme, 1787 & 1793]).

_____. *Versuch einer Anleitung zur Composition*, 2. Abtheilung. (Leipzig: Adam Friedrich Böhme, 1787 & 1793; reprint ed., [Hildesheim: Georg Olms, 1969]).

**Kollmann, Augustus Frederic Christopher**. *An Essay on Practical Musical Composition: According to the Nature of That Science and the Principles of the Greatest Musical Authors*. (London: 1799; reprint ed., with a new Introduction by Imogene Horsley, [New York: Da Capo, 1973]).

**Mancini, Giambattista**. *Riflessioni pratiche sul canto figurato*, 3rd ed. (Milan, 1777).

**Manfredini, Vincenzo**. *Difesa della musica moderna e de'suoi celebri esecutori*. (Bologna, 1788; reprint ed., [Bologna: Forni, 1972; Biblioteca musica Bononiensis. Sezione 2, no. 73]).

[**Marcello, Benedetto**]. *Il teatro alla moda: osia metodo sicuro, e facile per ben comporre, & esequire l'Opere Italiane in Musica all' uso moderno*. (Venice: "Aldaviva Licante," c.1720; reprint ed., [Venice: Tipografia dell'Ancora, 1887]).

**Marpurg, Friedrich**. W. *Kritische Briefe über die Tonkunst: mit kleinen Clavierstüken und Singodenbegleitet*. (Berlin: Friedrich Wilhelm Birnstiel, 1760; reprinted., [Hildesheim: Georg Olms Verlag, 1974]).

[**Marmontel, Jean François**]. "Essai sur les révolutions de la musique en France." In *Querelle des Gluckistes et des Piccinnistes: texte des pamphlets*, I, 153-93. Introduction, Commentary and Index by François Lesure. (Paris: Journal de Paris, 1771; reprint ed.,[Geneva: Minkoff, 1984]).

**Martello, Pier Jacopo.** *Della tragedia antica e moderna: dialogo.* (Rome: Francesco Gonzaga, 1715).

**Martignoni, Ignazio.** "Saggio sulla musica" in *Operette varie* (Como: Ostinelli, 1783):59-92. From Website *Saggi Musicali Italiani*: agigerl@Isu.edu

**Mattei, Saverio.** *Memorie per servire alla vita del Metastasio ed Elogio di N. Jommelli.* (Colle: Angiolo M. Martini, 1785; reprint ed., Bibliotheca Musica Bononiensis III/57 [(Bologna: Arnaldo Forni, 1987]).

**Mattheson, Johann.** *Der vollkommene Capellmeister.* A Revised Translation with Critical Commentary by Ernest C. Harriss. (Ann Arbor, UMI Research, 1981; originally published, [Hamburg: Christian Herold, 1739]).

**Metastasio, Pietro.** *Tutte le Opere.* Ed. Bruno Brunelli. (Milan: Arnoldo Mondadori, 1953).

**Milizia, Francesco.** *Del teatro.* (Venice: Presso Giambatista Pasquali, 1773).

_____. *Trattato completo, formale e materiale del teatro.* (Venice, 1794; reprint ed., Biblioteca musica Bononiensis. Sezione 2, no. 64 [Bologna: Arnoldo Forni, 1969]).

**Napoli-Signorelli, Pietro.** *Storia critica de' teatri antichi e moderni,* VII. (Naples: Vincenzo Orsino, 1790).

**Oliva, Francesco.** *Opere Napoletane.* Ed. Carla Chiara Petrone. (Rome: Bulzoni Editore, 1977).

**Planelli, Antonio.** *Dell' opera in musica: Trattato.* (Naples: Stamperia di Donato Campo, 1772; modern ed. by Francesco Degrada, [Friesole: Discanto, 1981]).

**Pollnitz, Karl-Ludwig, Baron de.** *The Memoirs of Charles-Lewis, Baron de Pollnitz.* (London: D. Browne, 1737).

**Quantz, Johann Joachim.** "Lebenslauffe." In Friedrich Wilhelm Marpurg's *Historisch-kritische Beyträge zur Aufnahme der Musik.* (Berlin: Verlag Joh. Jacob Schüzens, 1754; reprint ed., [Hildesheim: Georg Olms, 1970]).

_____. "The Life of Herr Johann Joachim Quantz, as Sketched by Himself." In *Forgotten Musicians*, 280-319. Ed. by Paul Nettle. (New York, 1951; originally published as Quantz's "Lebenslauffe" in Friedrich Wilhelm Marpurg's *Historisch-kritische Beyträge zur Aufnahme der Musik*, [Berlin, 1754]).

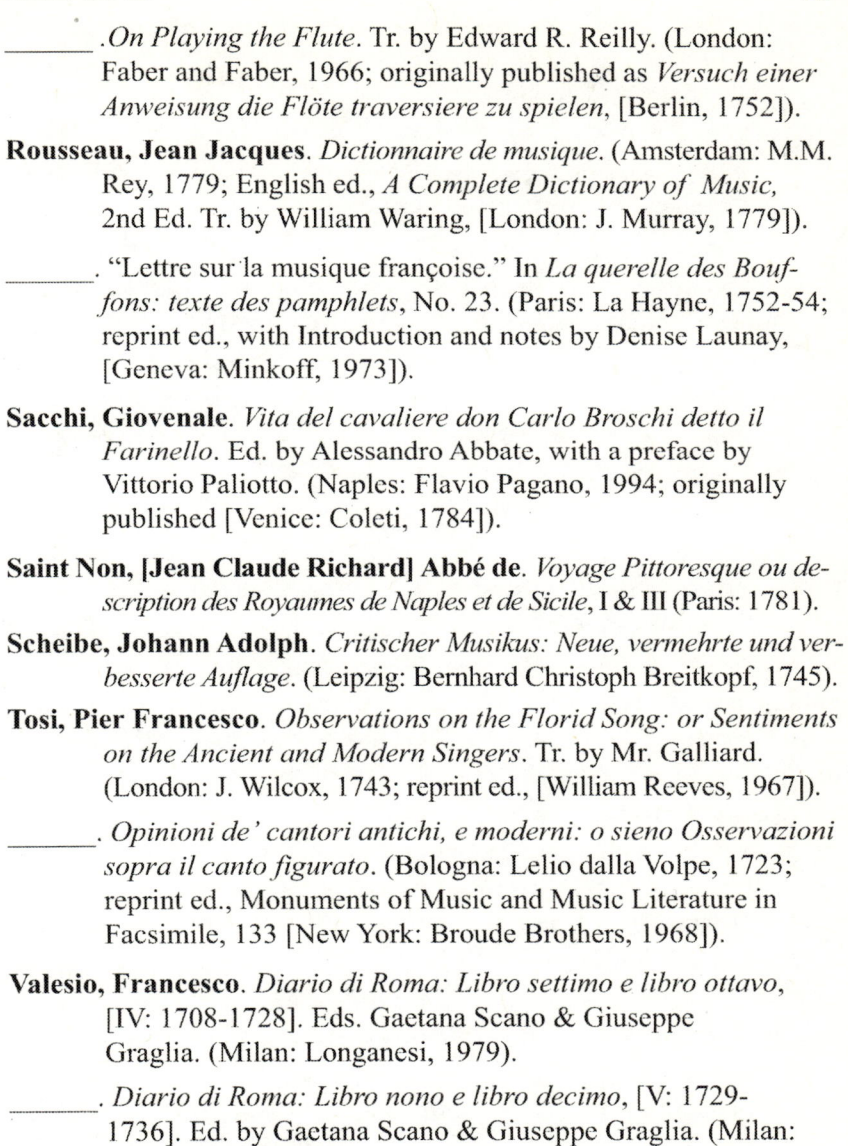

_____.*On Playing the Flute*. Tr. by Edward R. Reilly. (London: Faber and Faber, 1966; originally published as *Versuch einer Anweisung die Flöte traversiere zu spielen*, [Berlin, 1752]).

**Rousseau, Jean Jacques**. *Dictionnaire de musique*. (Amsterdam: M.M. Rey, 1779; English ed., *A Complete Dictionary of Music*, 2nd Ed. Tr. by William Waring, [London: J. Murray, 1779]).

_____. "Lettre sur la musique françoise." In *La querelle des Bouffons: texte des pamphlets*, No. 23. (Paris: La Hayne, 1752-54; reprint ed., with Introduction and notes by Denise Launay, [Geneva: Minkoff, 1973]).

**Sacchi, Giovenale**. *Vita del cavaliere don Carlo Broschi detto il Farinello*. Ed. by Alessandro Abbate, with a preface by Vittorio Paliotto. (Naples: Flavio Pagano, 1994; originally published [Venice: Coleti, 1784]).

**Saint Non, [Jean Claude Richard] Abbé de**. *Voyage Pittoresque ou description des Royaumes de Naples et de Sicile*, I & III (Paris: 1781).

**Scheibe, Johann Adolph**. *Critischer Musikus: Neue, vermehrte und verbesserte Auflage*. (Leipzig: Bernhard Christoph Breitkopf, 1745).

**Tosi, Pier Francesco**. *Observations on the Florid Song: or Sentiments on the Ancient and Modern Singers*. Tr. by Mr. Galliard. (London: J. Wilcox, 1743; reprint ed., [William Reeves, 1967]).

_____. *Opinioni de' cantori antichi, e moderni: o sieno Osservazioni sopra il canto figurato*. (Bologna: Lelio dalla Volpe, 1723; reprint ed., Monuments of Music and Music Literature in Facsimile, 133 [New York: Broude Brothers, 1968]).

**Valesio, Francesco**. *Diario di Roma: Libro settimo e libro ottavo*, [IV: 1708-1728]. Eds. Gaetana Scano & Giuseppe Graglia. (Milan: Longanesi, 1979).

_____. *Diario di Roma: Libro nono e libro decimo*, [V: 1729-1736]. Ed. by Gaetana Scano & Giuseppe Graglia. (Milan: Longanesi, 1979).

## Nineteenth-Century Sources

**Ademollo, Alessandro**. *Il carnevale di Roma: nei secoli XVII e XVIII*. (Rome: A. Sommaruga, 1883).

**Bertini, Giuseppe**. *Dizionario storico-critica degli scrittori di musica*. (Palermo: Tipographia Reale di guerra, 1814-15).

*Biografia degli italiani illustri nelle scienze, lettere ed arte del secolo XVIII, e de'contemporanei*, VII. Ed. Emilio de Tipaldo, (Venice: Alvisopoli, 1840).

*Biografia degli uomini illustri del Regno di Napoli: Ornata de loro rispettivi ritratti*.... Ed. B. Martuscelli. (Naples: Nicola Gervasi Gigante, 1819).

*A Biographical and Historical Dictionary of Musicians, from the Earliest Ages to the Present Time*. (London: Sainsbury, 1825).

**Choron, Alexandre Étienne & François Joseph Fayolle.** *Dictionnaire historique des musiciens: artistes et amateurs, morts ou vivans.* (Paris: Valade, 1811).

**Croce, Benedetto.** *I teatri di Napoli: secolo XV-XVIII.* (Naples: Luigi Pierro, 1891).

**D'Arienzo, Nicola.** "Origini dell'Opera comica." *Revista Musicale Italiano* 4 (1897):421-59 & 6 (1899):473-95.

**Ferrari, Paolo-Emilio.** *Spettacoli drammatico-musicali e coreografici in Parma: dall'anno 1628 all'anno 1883.* (Parma: 1884; reprint ed., [Bologna: Forni Editore]).

**Fétis, François-Joseph.** *Biographie Universelle des musiciens: et bibliographie générale de la musique*, 2nd ed. (Paris: Firmin-Didot, 1884).

**Florimo, Francesco.** *La scuola musicale di Napoli e i suoi conservatori*, 4 vols. (Naples: V. Morano, 1880-82; reprint.ed., [Bologna: Forni, 1969]).

**Gerber, Ernst Ludwig.** *Neues Historisch-Biographisches Lexikon der Tonkünstler (1812-14).* Ed. Othmar Wessely. (Leipzig: A. Kühnel,1812; reprint ed., [Graz: Akademische Druck- u.Verlagsanstalt, 1966]).

**Grossi, G.B.G.** "Leonardo Vinci: Celebre Maestro di Cappella, Nacque in Napoli nel 1690, Ove mori nel 1732." In *Biografia degli uomini illustri del Regno di Napoli: Ornata de loro rispettivi ritratti*. Ed. Martuscelli, Volume VI. (Naples, Niccola Gervasi Gigante 1819).

**Scoppa, Antonio.** *Traite de la poésie italienne, rapportée a la poésie française.* (Versailles: L'imprimerie de Jacob, 1803).

**Sigismondo, Giuseppe.** *Apoteosi dell'Arte Musicale*, III. (Naples, 1820) unpublished manuscript in Berlin catalogued as "Materialien zu einer Geschichte der Musik der Neapolitaner Schule."

**Villarosa, Marchese di.** *Memorie dei compositori di musica del Regno di Napoli.* (Naples: Stamperia Reale, 1840).

**Wiel, Taddeo.** *I teatri musicali veneziani del settecento: catalogo delle opere in musica rappresentate nel secolo XVIII in Venezia.* (Venice: Fratelli Visentini, 1897).

## Twentieth-Century Sources

**Acton, Harold.** *The Bourbons of Naples: 1734-1825.* (London: Methuen, 1974).

**Antolini, Bianca Maria & Wolfgang Witzenmann,** eds. *Napoli e il teatro musicale in Europa tra sette e ottocento: studi in onore di Friedrich Lippman.* (Florence: Leo S. Olschki, 1993).

**Armellini, Mario.** "*Il prigionier superbo* di Pergolesi e le sue fonti librettistiche." In *Studi Pergolesiani/Pergolesi Studies* IV (Jesi: Fondazione G.B. Pergolesi - G. Spontini, 2000), 253-72.

_____. "'... Meco sola è l'innocenza / che mi porta a naufragar:' Tradimento, abbandono e deriva degli affetti nell' *Artaserse* di Metastasio e Vinci." Paper presented at the conference *Leonardo Vinci: architetture sonore nella Napoli del viceregno austriaco: convegno internazionale di studi*, Conservatorio di Musica Francesco Cilea, Reggio Calabria, 10-12 June 2002.

**Arnold, Denis, Anthony Newcombe, Thomas Walker, Michael Talbot, Donald J. Grout, and Joel Sheveloff.** *The New Grove Italian Baroque Masters.* (New York: W.W. Norton, 1984).

**Barbier, Patrick.** *Farinelli: Le castrat des Lumières.* (Paris: Bernard Grasset, 1994).

**Battista, Tonino & Nicolò Maccavino.** "*Col bel lume*: una serenata di Leonardo Vinci per il cardinale Althann?" Paper presented at the conference *Leonardo Vinci: architetture sonore nella Napoli del viceregno austriaco: convegno internazionale di studi*, Conservatorio di Musica Francesco Cilea, Reggio Calabria, 10-12 June 2002.

**Bauman, Thomas & Marita Petzoldt McClymonds,** eds. *Opera and the Enlightenment* (Cambridge: Cambridge University Press, 1995).

**Beckwith, Hubert E.** "Text and Harmony in Pergolesi's Recitatives for Stage and Chamber." In *Studi Pergolesiani I: Proceedings of the International Symposium, Jesi, 1983*, 116-23. Ed. Francesco Degrada. (Stuyvesant, New York: Pendragon Press, 1986.)

**Bédarida, Henri**. "L'opéra Italien jugé par un amateur Français en 1756." *Mélanges de Musicologie: offerts a M. Lionel de la Laurencie*, 185-200. (Paris: Société Française de Musicologie, 1933).

**Bellina, Anna Laura, Bruno Brizi, & Maria Grazia Pensa**. *I libretti Vivaldiani: Recensione e collazione dei testimoni a stampa.* (Florence: Leo S. Olschki, 1982).

**Benedikt, Heinrich**. *Das Königreich Neapel unter Kaiser Karl VI: Eine Darstellung auf Grund bisher unbekannter Dokumente aus den österreichischen Archiven*. (Vienna: Manz Verlag, 1927).

**Blichmann, Diana**. "La *Semiramide riconosciuta* tra Roma e Venezia: annotazioni drammaturgico-musicali sulle intonazioni di Leonardo Vinci e Nicola Porpora." Paper presented at the conference *Leonardo Vinci: architetture sonore nella Napoli del viceregno austriaco: convegno internazionale di studi*, Conservatorio di Musica Francesco Cilea, Reggio Calabria, 10-12 June 2002.

**Bossa, Renato**. "Vinci, Leonardo." In *Dizionario enciclopedico universale della musica e dei musicisti*. Ed. Alberto Basso. (Turin: Unione Tipografico, 1988).

**Boyd, Malcolm**. "Rome: the Power of Patronage." In *The Late Baroque Era: From the 1680s to 1740*, 39-63. Ed. George J. Buelow. (Englewood Cliffs, N.J.: Prentice Hall, 1994).

**Bucciarelli, Melania**. *Italian Opera and European Theatre, 1680-1720: Plots, Performers, Dramaturgies*. Speculum Musicae, VII. Ed. Albert Dunning. (Brepols: Publications of the Pietro Antonio Locatelli Foundation, 2000).

_____. "Rhetorical Strategies and Tears in *Astianatte*" In *Italian Opera and European Theatre,1680- 1720*...119-171.

**Buelow, George J.**, ed. *The Late Baroque Era: From the 1680s to 1740* (Englewood Cliffs, N.J.: Prentice Hall, 1994).

**Bukofzer, Manfred F**. *Music in the Baroque Era: From Monteverdi to Bach*. (New York, W.W. Norton, 1947).

**Brumana, Biancamaria**. "Il Cantante Giacinto Fontana Detto Farfallino e la sua carriera nei teatri di Roma." *Roma moderna e contemporanea: revista interdisciplinare di storia*, IV/1 (1996):75-112.

**Cafiero, Rosa**. "Il' venerabile conservatorio di S. Maria della Colonna, detto de' Poveri di Gesù Cristo' negli anni di Leonardo Vinci." Paper presented at the conference *Leonardo Vinci: architetture* *sonore nella Napoli del viceregno austriaco: convegno internazionale di studi*, Conservatorio di Musica Francesco Cilea, Reggio Calabria, 10-12 June 2002.

**Cagli, Bruno**, ed. *Le muse galanti: La musica a Roma nel settecento.* (Rome: Enciclopedia italiana, 1985).

**Cametti, Alberto**. "Leonardo Vinci: e suoi drammi in musica al Teatro delle Dame (1724-30)." *Musica d'oggi* 6 (1924), 297-98.

**Cappellieri, Alba**. "Il teatro di San Bartolomeo da Scarlatti a Pergolesi." In *Studi Pergolesiani/Pergolesi Studies* IV Ed. Francesco Degrada. (Jesi: Fondazione G.B. Pergolesi-G. Spontini, 2000), 253-72.

**Cavallini, Ivano**. "'Musica sentimental' e 'teatro della commozione:' la poetica del melodramma nelle *Osservazioni sulla musica* di Gianrinaldo Carli." *Recercare* 2 (1990), 5-34.

**Celani, Enrico**. "Musica e Musicisti in Roma: 1750-1850." *Rivista musicale Italiana* 18 (1911),1-63.

**Celletti, Rodolfo**. "I cantanti a Roma nel XVIII secolo." In *Le muse galanti: La musica a Roma nel settecento*, Ed. Bruno Cagli. (Rome: Enciclopedia italiana, 1985), 101-107.

**Clementi, Filippo**. *Il carnevale romano nelle cronache contemporanee: sec. XVIII-XIX*, II. (Città di Castello: Unione arti grafiche, 1938).

**Collins, Michael & Elise K. Kirk**. *Opera & Vivaldi*. (Austin: University of Texas Press, 1984).

**Costantini, Danilo & Ausilia Maguadda**. "Attività musicali promosse dalle confraternite laiche nel Regno di Napoli (1677-1763)." In *Fonti d'archivio per la storia della musica e dello spettacolo a Napoli tra XVI e XVIII secolo.* Ed. Paologiovanni Maione. (Naples: Editoriale Scientifica, 2001), 79-204.

**Cotticelli, Francesco**. "L'approdo alla scena: Ancora sulla nascita dell' opera comica." Paper presented at the conference *Leonardo Vinci: architetture sonore nella Napoli del viceregno austriaco: convegno internazionale di studi*, Conservatorio di Musica Francesco Cilea, Reggio Calabria, 10-12 June 2002.

**Cotticelli, Francesco & Paologiovanni Maione**. *Le istituzioni musicali a Napoli durante il viceregno austriaco (1707-1734): materiali inediti sulla Real Capella ed il Teatro di San Bartolomeo.* (Naples: Luciano Editore, 1993).

**Croce, Benedetto.** *History of the Kingdom of Naples.* Translated by Frances Frenaye and edited with an Introduction by H. Stuart Hughes. (Chicago: University of Chicago Press, 1970).

**Croft-Murray, Edward.** *An Album of Eighteenth Century Venetian Operatic Caricatures: formerly in the Collection of Count Algarotti.* (Toronto: Art Gallery of Ontario, 1990).

**Cross, Eric.** *The Late Operas of Antonio Vivaldi: 1727-1738.* Studies in British Musicology. (Ann Arbor, Michigan: UMI Research Press, 1981).

**Cummings, Graham.** "Reminiscence and Recall in Three Early Settings of Metastasio's *Alessandro nell'Indie*." *Proceedings of the Royal Musical Association* 109 (1982-83):80-104.

**Dean, Winton.** "A French Traveller's View of Handel's Operas." *Music and Letters* 55 (1974):172-78.

_____. *Handel and the Opera Seria.* (Berkeley: University of California Press, 1969).

_____."The Performance of Recitative in Late Baroque Opera." *Music and Letters* 58 (1977):389-402.

**Dean, Winton & John Merrill Knapp.** *Handel's Operas 1704-1726.* (Oxford: Clarendon Press, 1987).

**De Angelis, Alberto.** *Il teatro Alibert o delle dame: 1717-1863.* (Tivoli: Arti Grafiche A. Chicca, 1951).

**De Siena, Francesco.** *Leonardo Vinci: vita ed opera del compositore calabrese detto "Lo Strongoli."* Opera Patrocinata dall' Amministrazione Comunale di Strongoli. (Crotone: Futura, 1997)

**Della Corte, Andrea.** "Cori monodici di dieci musicisti per le 'Tragedie cristiane' di Annibale Marchese." *Revista italiana di musicologia* 1 (1966):190-202.

_____. *Piccinni: Settecento italiano.* (Bari: G. Laterza, 1928).

**Della Seta, Fabrizio & Franco Piperno**, eds. *Francesco Gasparini 1661-1727: Atti del primo convegno internazionale, Camaiore, 1978.* (Florence: Leo S. Olschki, 1981).

**Dent, Edward J.** "Notes on Leonardo Vinci." *The Musical Antiquary* 4 (1912/13):193-201.

_____. *Alessandro Scarlatti: his Life and Works.* Preface and additional notes by Frank Walker. (London: Edward Arnold, 1905; reprint ed. [St. Clair Shores, Michigan: Scholarly Press, 1976]).

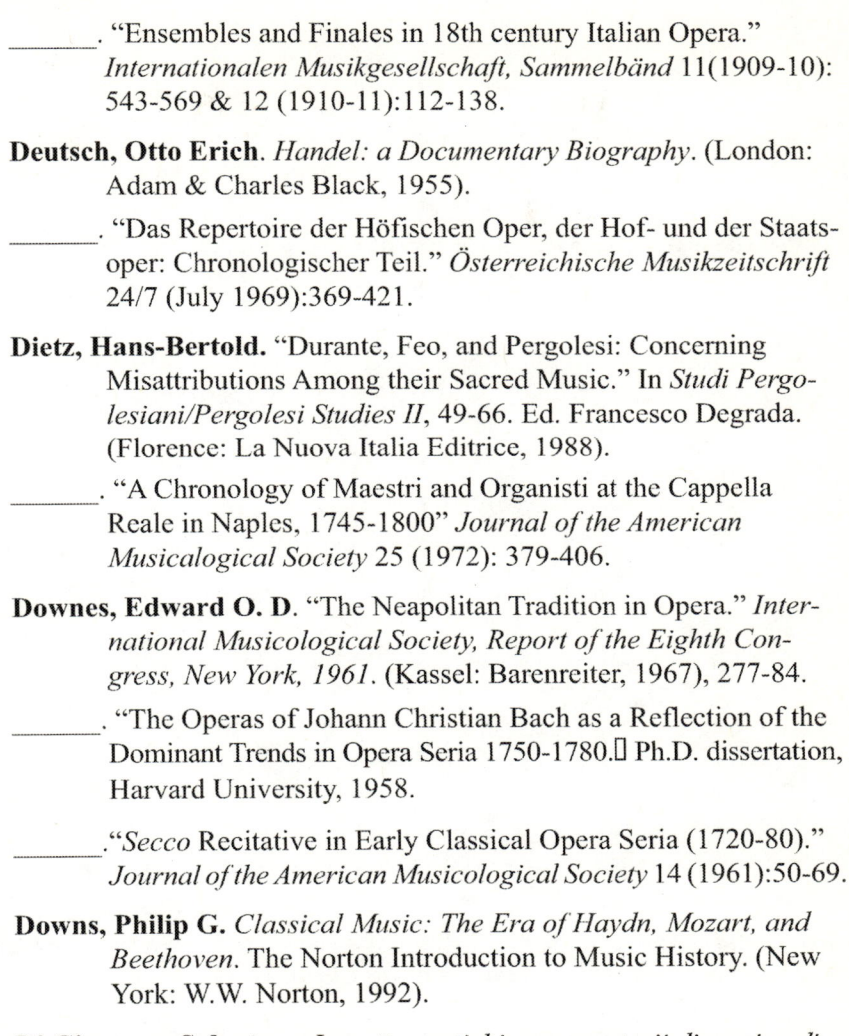

_____. "Ensembles and Finales in 18th century Italian Opera." *Internationalen Musikgesellschaft, Sammelbänd* 11(1909-10): 543-569 & 12 (1910-11):112-138.

**Deutsch, Otto Erich**. *Handel: a Documentary Biography*. (London: Adam & Charles Black, 1955).

_____. "Das Repertoire der Höfischen Oper, der Hof- und der Staatsoper: Chronologischer Teil." *Österreichische Musikzeitschrift* 24/7 (July 1969):369-421.

**Dietz, Hans-Bertold**. "Durante, Feo, and Pergolesi: Concerning Misattributions Among their Sacred Music." In *Studi Pergolesiani/Pergolesi Studies II*, 49-66. Ed. Francesco Degrada. (Florence: La Nuova Italia Editrice, 1988).

_____. "A Chronology of Maestri and Organisti at the Cappella Reale in Naples, 1745-1800" *Journal of the American Musicological Society* 25 (1972): 379-406.

**Downes, Edward O. D.** "The Neapolitan Tradition in Opera." *International Musicological Society, Report of the Eighth Congress, New York, 1961*. (Kassel: Barenreiter, 1967), 277-84.

_____. "The Operas of Johann Christian Bach as a Reflection of the Dominant Trends in Opera Seria 1750-1780." Ph.D. dissertation, Harvard University, 1958.

_____."*Secco* Recitative in Early Classical Opera Seria (1720-80)." *Journal of the American Musicological Society* 14 (1961):50-69.

**Downs, Philip G.** *Classical Music: The Era of Haydn, Mozart, and Beethoven*. The Norton Introduction to Music History. (New York: W.W. Norton, 1992).

**Di Giacomo, Salvatore**. *I quattro antichi conservatorii di musica di Napoli*. (Milan: Remo Sandron, 1928).

**Fabris, Dinko**. "La fortuna europea di Vinci nel Settecento." Paper presented at the conference *Leonardo Vinci: architetture sonore nella Napoli del viceregno austriaco: convegno internazionale di studi*, Conservatorio di Musica Francesco Cilea, Reggio Calabria, 10-12 June 2002.

**Feldman, Martha**. "Magic Mirrors and the *Seria* Stage: Thoughts toward a Ritual View." *Journal of the American Musicological Society* 48/3 (Fall 1995):423-84.

**Ferraro, Giuseppe.** "Appunti Biobibliografici su Leonardo Vinci." In *Miscellanea musicologica calabrese*. Ed. Felicia di Salvo & Francescantonio Pollice. (Lamezia Terme, 1994),67-83.

**Freeman, Robert.** "Farinello and his Repertory." In *Studies in Renaissance and Baroque Music in Honour of Arthur Mendel*. Ed. Robert L. Marshall. (Kassel: Bärenreiter, 1974), 301-323.

_____. *Opera without Drama: Currents of Change in Italian Opera, 1675-1725*. Studies in Musicology. Ed. George Buelow. (Ann Arbor, Michigan: UMI Research Press, 1981).

_____. "The Travels of Partenope." In *Studies in Music History: Essays for Oliver Strunk*. Ed. Harold Powers. (Princeton, New Jersey: Princeton University Press, 1968), 356-85.

**Fubini, Enrico.** *Music and Culture in Eighteenth-Century Europe: A Source Book*. Eds. Wolfgang Freis, Lisa Gasbarrone & Michael Louis Leone. Translation ed. by Bonnie J. Blackburn. (Chicago: University of Chicago Press, 1994).

**Gallo, Salvatore.** *Vecchio Campanile: La Chiesa di Strongoli nella storia della città dall'alto medio evo alla soppressione del Vescovato*. (Cosenza: Fasano Editore, n.d.).

**Gerber, Rudolf.** *Der Operntypus Johann Adolf Hasses und seine textlichen Grundlagen*. Berliner Beiträge zur Musikwissenschaft, II. ( Leipzig: Fr. Kistner & C.F.W. Siegel, 1925).

**Gialdroni, Teresa Maria.** "Arie operistiche di Leonardo Vinci nelle biblioteche romane." Paper presented at the conference *Leonardo Vinci: architetture sonore nella Napoli del viceregno austriaco: convegno internazionale di studi*, Conservatorio di Musica Francesco Cilea, Reggio Calabria, 10-12 June 2002.

_____. "Leonardo Vinci e la cantata spirituale a Napoli nella prima metà del settecento." In *Musica senza aggettivi: studi per Fedele d'Amico*. (Florence: Leo S. Olschki, 1991), 123-43.

_____. "Vinci 'operista' autore di cantate." In *Studi in onore di Giulio Cattin*. (Rome: Edizioni Torre d'Orfeo, 1990), 307-29.

**Gianturco, Carolyn.** *Alessandro Stradella: 1639-1682: His Life and Music*. (Oxford: Clarendon Press, 1994).

_____. "Naples: A City of Entertainment." In *The Late Baroque Era: From the 1680s to 1740*. Ed. George J. Buelow (Englewood Cliffs, N.J.: Prentice Hall, 1994), 94-128.

**Gibson, Elizabeth.** *The Royal Academy of Music 1719-1728: the Institution and its Directors.* (New York: Garland Publishing, 1989).

**Geiringer, Karl.** "Eine Geburtstagskantate von Pietro Metastasio und Leonardo Vinci." *Zeitschrift für Musikwissenschaft* 9 (1926-27):270-83.

**Griffin, Thomas Edward.** *Musical References in the 'Gazzetta di Napoli' 1681-1725.* (Berkeley: Fallen Leaf Press, 1993).

**Grout, Donald Jay.** *Alessandro Scarlatti: An Introduction to his Operas.* (Berkeley: University of California Press, 1779).

_____. *A Short History of Opera*, 2nd ed. (New York: Columbia University Press, 1965).

**Guerrini, Lucia.** *Marmi antichi nei disegni di Pier Leone Ghezzi.* Biblioteca Vaticana documenti e riproduzione 1. (Vatican: Biblioteca apostolica, 1971).

**Hansell, Sven Hostrup.** "The Cadence in 18th-Century Recitative." *Musical Quarterly* 54 (1968): 228-48.

**Haile, Martin.** *James Francis Edward: The Old Chevalier.* (London: J.M. Dent, 1907).

**Hardie, Graham Hood.** "Leonardo Leo (1694-1744) and his Comic Operas *Amor vuol sofferenze* and *Alidoro*." Ph.D. dissertation, Cornell Univerity, 1973.

**Heartz, Daniel.** "Critical Years in European Musical History: 1740- 1760," [First paper].*In International Musicological Society, Report of the Tenth Congress, Ljubljana, 1970.* (Ljublana: University of Ljublana, 1970), 159-68.

_____. "Hasse at the Crossroads: *Artaserse* (Venice, 1730), Dresden and Vienna" *The Opera Quarterly* 16:1 (Winter 2000): 24-33.

_____. *Haydn, Mozart, and the Viennese School, 1740-1780.* (New York: W. W. Norton, 1995).

_____. "Metastasio, 'Maestro dei maestri di cappella drammatici'." In *Metastasio e il mondo musicale*, 315-38. Ed. Maria Teresa Muraro. (Florence: Leo S. Olschki, 1986).

_____. *Mozart's Operas.* Ed., with contributing essays, by Thomas Bauman. ( Berkeley: University of California Press, 1990).

_____. *Music in European Capitals: The Galant Style, 1720-80.* (New York: W. W. Norton, 2003).

**Heawood, Edward**. *Watermarks: Mainly of the 17th and 18th Centuries*. I of *Monumenta Chartae Papyraceae Historian Illustrantia*. (Hilversum, Netherlands: The Paper Publications Society, 1950).

**Hell, Hellmut**. "Die Betrogene Prinzessin: Zum Schreiber 'L.Vinci I'"in Der Amalien-Bibliothek der Staatsbibliothek zu Berlin, in *Scrinium Berolinense, Tilo Brandos zum 65. Geburtstage*. II: Peter Jörg Becker, Eva Bliembach, Holgar Nickel, Renate Schipke, Giuliano Staccioli, eds. 2 vols.(Wiebaden: Reichert, 2000) 631-48.

_____. Die Neapolitanische Opernsinfonie in der ersten Hälfte des 18.jahrhunderts. (Tutzing: Schneider, 1971).

**Heriot, Angus**. *The Castrati in Opera*. (London: Secker & Warburg, 1956).

**Hibbert, Christopher**. *Rome: the Biography of a City*. (Harmondsworth, Middlesex: Penguin Books, 1985).

**Holmes, William C**. *Opera Observed: Views of a Florentine Impresario in the Early Eighteenth Century*. (Chicago: University of Chicago Press, 1993).

_____. "Righini in Florence: an Artistic Conflict." *Early Music* (November 1989): 539-50.

**Hucke, Helmut**. "Die beiden Fassungen der Oper 'Didone abbandonata' von Domenico Sarri." *Gesellschaft für Musikforschung, Bericht über den Internationalen Musikwissenschaftlichen Kongress, Hamburg, 1956*, 113-117. ( Kassel: Bärenreiter, 1961).

_____."Die Neapolitanische Tradition in der Oper." In *International Musicological Society, Report of the Eighth Congress, New York, 1961*, 253-77. (Kassel: Barenreiter, 1967).

_____."Pergolesi in der Musik geschichte oder: Wie gross was Pergolesi." In *Studi Pergolesiani/Pergolesi Studies II*, 7-19. Ed. Francesco Degrada. (Florence: La Nuova Italia Editrice, 1988).

_____. "Verfassung und Entwicklung der alten neapolitanischen Konservatorien." *Festschrift Helmuth Osthoff sum 65. Gerburtstage*. (Tutzing: Hans Schneider, 1961).

_____. s.v. "Vinci, Leonardo." In *Die Musik in Geschichte und Gegenwart: Allgemeine Enzyklopädie der Musik*. Ed. Friedrich Blume. (Kassel: Bärenreiter-Verlag, 1949-51).

_____. s.v. "Vinci, Leonardo." Enciclopedia dello spettacolo. (Rome: Le Maschere, 1954-62).

**Kelly, J. N. D.** *The Oxford Dictionary of Popes*. (Oxford: Oxford University Press, 1986).

**Kirkendale, Ursula.** "The Ruspoli Documents on Handel." *Journal of the American Musicological Society* 20 (1967):222-272.

_____. "The War of the Spanish Succession Reflected in the Works of Antonio Caldara." *Acta Musicologia* 36 (1964):221-33.

**Krause, Ralf.** "Das musikalische Panorama am neapolitanischen Hofe: zu Real Cappella di Palazzo im frühen 18. Jahrhundert." *Analecta Musicologica* 30/2 (Laaber: Laaber-Verlag, 1998): 271-295.

**LaRue, Jan.** "Watermarks and Musicology." *Acta Musicologia* 32 (1961):120-46.

**Lazarevich, Gordana.** "Eighteenth-Century Pasticcio: The Historian's Gordian Knot." *Analecta Musicologica* 17 (Cologne: Arno Volk, 1976).

_____. "Hasse as a Comic Dramatist: the Neapolitan Intermezzi." In *Colloquium Johann Adolf Hasse und die Musik seiner Zeit, Siena, 1983*. Ed. Friedrich Lippmann. *Analecta Musicologica* 25 (Laaber: Laaber-Verlag, 1987), 287-303.

_____. "The Neapolitan Intermezzo and its Influence on the Symphonic Idiom." *Musical Quarterly* 57 (1971):294-313.

_____. "Pergolesi and the *Guerre des Bouffons*." In *Studi Pergolesiani/Pergolesi Studies II*. Ed. Francesco Degrada. (Florence: La Nuova Italia Editrice, 1988), 49-66.

**Lester, Joel.** *Compositional Theory in the Eighteenth Century*. (Cambridge: Harvard University Press, 1992).

**Libby, Dennis.** "Italy: Two Opera Centers." In *The Classical Era: From the 1740s to the End of the 18th Century*. Ed. Neal Zaslaw. (Basingstoke, Hampshire: Macmillan, 1989), 15-60.

_____. "Giuseppe Sigismondo, an Eighteenth-Century Amateur, Musician, and Historian." In *Studi Pergolesiani/Pergolesi Studies II*. Ed. Francesco Degrada. (Florence: La Nuova Italia Editrice, 1988), 49-66.

**Lindgren, Lowell.** "A Bibliographic Scrutiny of Dramatic Works Set by Giovanni and his Brother Antonio Maria Bononcini." Ph.D. dissertation, Harvard University Press, 1972.

_____. "Il dramma musicale a Roma durante la carriera di Alessandro Scarlatti (1660-1725)." In *Il teatro a Roma nel Settecento,* Ed. Gianni Eugenio Viola. (Rome: Istituto della Enciclopedia italiana, 1989), 35-57.

_____. "La Carriera di Gaetano Berenstadt." *Revista italiana di musicologia* 18/19 (1983/84): 36-99.

**Library of Congress.** *Catalogue of Opera Librettos Printed before 1800.* Ed. Oscar George Theodore Sonneck. (Washington: Government Printing Office, 1914).

**Lippmann, Friedrich.** "Sulle composizioni per cembalo di Gaetano Greco." In *La Musica a Napoli durante il seicento: atti del Convegno internazionale di studi Napoli, 1985.* Ed. Domenico Antonio D'Alessandro & Agostino Ziino. (Rome: Edizione Torre d'Orfeo, 1987), 285-306.

**Loewenberg, Alfred.** *Annals of Opera, 1597-1940: Compiled from Original Sources,* 2nd ed. (Geneva: Societas Bibliographica, 1955).

**Lühning, Helga.** "Cosroes Verzweiflung, Regel und Erfindung in Hasses Seria-Arien." In *Colloquium Johann Adolf Hasse und die Musik seiner Zeit, Siena, 1983.* Ed. Friedrich Lippmann. *Analecta Musicologica* 25. (Laaber: Laaber-Verlag, 1987),79-130.

_____. "Alexanders Grosmut und Poros' Eifersuch." Article accompanying William Christie's recording of Johann Adolf Hasse's *Cleofide.* Capriccio 10193/96, 1987.

**McClymonds, Marita P.** *Niccolò Jommelli: the Last Years 1769-1774.* Studies in Musicology, No. 23. Ed. George Buelow. (Ann Arbor Michigan: UMI Research Press, 1980).

**Magaudda, Ausilia & Danilo Constantini.** "Le corrispondenze dall'Abruzzo nella Gazzetta di Napoli: un contributo per la ricostruzione dei rapporti musicali fra la capitale e le province." In *Archivo Storico per la Province Napoletane,* (Naples: Società Napoletana di Storia Patria, 2000), 365-443.

_____. "Una sconosciuta rappresentazione di un' opera comica di Leonardo Vinci a Vasto come esempio della circolazione tra la capitale e le province." Paper presented at the conference *Leonardo Vinci: architetture sonore nella Napoli del viceregno austriaco: convegno internazionale di studi,* Conservatorio di Musica Francesco Cilea, Reggio Calabria, 10-12 June 2002.

**Maione, Paologiovanni**. "'Tanti diversi umori a contentar si suda': il dibattito sulla 'commedeja' nel primo Settecento." Paper presented at the conference *Leonardo Vinci: architetture sonore nella Napoli del viceregno austriaco: convegno internazionale di studi*, Conservatorio di Musica Francesco Cilea, Reggio Calabria, 10-12 June 2002.

_____. "Le carte degli antichi banchi e il panorama musicale e teatrale della Napoli di primo Settecento." In *Studi Pergolesiani/ Pergolesi Studies* IV. Ed. Francesco Degrada. (Jesi: Fondazione G.B. Pergolesi - G. Spontini, 2000), 253-72.

**Mamczarz, Irene**. *Le Théatre Farnèse de Parme et le drame musical italien (1618-1732)*. Teatro studi e testi, 5. (Florence: Leo S. Olschki, 1988).

**Manferrari, Umberto**. *Dizionario universale delle opere melodrammatiche*. (Florence: Sansoni Antiquariato, 1955).

**Mangini, Nicola**. *I teatri di Venezia*. (Milan: U. Mursia Editore, 1974).

**Manno, Giovanni**. "Leonardo Vinci e l'opera in musica." *Rassegna Musicale Curci* 40 (1987):15-19.

**Markstrom, Kurt**. s.v. "Artaserse" "Didone abbandonata" & "zite 'ngalera, Li." In *The New Grove Dictionary of Opera*, Stanley Sadie, ed. (London: Macmillan, 1993).

_____. "Burney's Assessment of Leonardo Vinci." *Acta Musicologica*, 68/2 (1995):142-63.

_____. "The Eventual Premiere of *Issipile*: Porpora and the Palchetti War." Paper at the conference *Music in Eighteenth-Century Italy*, Cardiff, June, 1998.

_____. "Metastasio's Delay in Reaching Vienna." *Studies in Music at the University of Western Ontario* 16 (1997):1-25.

_____. s.v. "Vinci, Leonardo." In *The New Grove Dictionary of Opera*, Stanley Sadie, ed. (London: Macmillan, 1993).

_____. s.v. "Vinci, Leonardo." *The New Grove Dictionary of Music and Musicians* (London: Macmillan, 2001).

_____. "Una stagione calamitosa per Leonardo Vinci a Roma: il *Catone in Utica* al Teatro delle Dame." Paper presented at the conference: *Leonardo Vinci: architetture sonore nella Napoli del viceregno austriaco: convegno internazionale di studi*, Conservatorio di Musica Francesco Cilea, Reggio Calabria, June 10-12 June 2002.

**Markstrom, Kurt & Michael F. Robinson,** s.v. "Porpora, Nicola Antonio." *The New Grove Dictionary of Music and Musicians* (London: Macmillan, 2001).

**Marx-Weber, Magda.** "Die G. B. Pergolesi Fälschlich Zugeschriebenen Miserere-Vertonungen." In *Florilegium Musicologicum: Helmut Federhofer zum 75.Geburtstag.* Ed. Christoph-Hellmut Mahling. (Tutzing: Hans Schneider, 1988), 209-218.

**Mazzaeo, Antonio.** *Opere rappresentate in Siena nel sec. XVIII al teatro dell'Accademia degli Intronati.* (Siena: Cantagalli, 1994)

**Meikle, Robert Burns.** "Leonardo Vinci's *Artaserse*: An Edition, with an Editorial and Critical Commentary." Ph.D. Thesis, Cornell University, 1970. (Ann Arbor, Michigan: UMI, 1971).

──────. s.v. "Vinci, Leonardo." In *The New Grove Dictionary of Music and Musicians.* (London: Macmillan, 1980).

*The Mellen Opera Reference Index: Opera Composers and their Works.* Ed. Charles H. Parsons. (Lewiston, New York: Edwin Mellen Press, 1986).

**Melisi, Francesco, ed.** *Catalogo dei libretti d'opera in musica dei secoli XVII e XVIII.* (Naples: Conservatorio di Musica S. Pietro a Majella di Napoli, Biblioteca, 1985).

**Miller, Peggy.** *James.* (London: George Allen & Unwin, 1971).

**Millner, Fredrick L.** *The Operas of Johann Adolf Hasse.* Studies in Musicology, 2. (Ann Arbor: UMI Research Press, 1979).

**Mischiati, Oscar.** "Una memoria sepolcrale di Filippo Juvarra per Arcangelo Corelli." In *Nuovi studi corelliani: atti del secondo congresso internazionale, Fusignano, 1974.* Ed. Giulia Giachin. (Florence: Leo S. Olschki, 1978), 105-110.

**Monaldi, Gino.** *Cantanti evirati celebri: secoli xvii-xviii.* (Rome: Società editrice, 1920).

**Monelle, Raymond.** "Recitative and Dramaturgy in the *Dramma per Musica.*" *Music and Letters* 69/3 (July 1978): 245-67.

**Monson, Dale E.** "Evidence for Pergolesi's compositional method for the stage: the *Flamino* autograph." In *Studi Pergolesiani/ Pergolesi Studies II.* Ed. Francesco Degrada. (Florence: La Nuova Italia Editrice, 1988), 49-66.

──────. "The Last Word: the Cadence in *recitativo semplice* of Italian Opera seria." In *Studi Pergolesiani I: Proceedings of the*

*International Symposium, Jesi, 1983*. Ed. Francesco Degrada. (Stuyvesant, New York: Pendragon Press, 1986), 89-105.

_____. "*Recitativo Semplice* in the *Opere Serie* of G.B. Pergolesi and his his Contemporaries." Ph.D. dissertation, Columbia University, 1983.

_____. "*Semplice o secco*: Continuo Declamation in Early 18th- century Italian Recitative." *Studi Pergolesiani I: Proceedings of the International Symposium, Jesi, 1983*. Ed. Francesco Degrada. (Stuvesant, New York: Pendragon Press, 1986), 107-15.

_____."The Trail of Vivaldi's Singers: Vivaldi in Rome." In *Nuovi studi vivaldiani: Edizione e cronologia critica delle opere*. Ed. Antonio Fanna & Giovanni Morelli. (Venezia Fondazione Giorgio Cini, 1988), 563-89.

**Morey, Carl**. "The Late Operas of Alessandro Scarlatti." Ph.D. dissertation, Indiana University, 1965.

**Mori, Elisabetta**. "I Maccarani dal teatro di corte al teatro Alibert." In *La musica a Roma attraverso le fonti d'archivio: atti del convegno internazionale*, Rome, June 4-7, 1992. Ed. Bianca Maria Antolini, Arnaldo Morelli & Vera Vita Spagnuolo. (Lucca: Libraria Musicale Italiana, 1994).

**Muraro, Maria Teresa**, ed. *Metastasio e il mondo musicale*. (Florence: Leo S. Olschki, 1986)

**Nagler, A. M**. *A Source Book in Theatrical History: Sources of Theatrical History*. (New York: Dover. n.d.).

**Paratore, Ettore**. "*L'Andromaque* e la *Didone abbandonata*" In *Scritti in onore di Luigi di Ronga*. (Milan: Riccardo Ricciardi, 1973), 515-47.

**Pastura Ruggiero, Maria Grazia**. "Fonti per la storia del teatro romano nel Settecento conservate nell' Archivio di Stato di Roma." In *Il teatro a Roma nel Settecento*. Ed. Gianni Eugenio Viola. (Rome: Istituto della Enciclopedia Italiana, 1989), 505-555.

**Pauly, Reinhard G**. "Benedetto Marcello's Satire on Early 18th Century Opera." *Musical Quarterly* 34 (1948):222-233

**Paymer, Marvin E**. "The Pergolesi Autographs: Chronology, Style, and Notation." In *Studi Pergolesiani I: Proceedings of the International Symposium, Jesi, 1983*. Ed. Francesco Degrada. (Stuyvesant, New York: Pendragon Press, 1986), 11-23.

**Pejrone, Giulietta**."Il teatro attraverso i periodici romani del Settecento." In *Il teatro a Roma nel Settecento*. Ed. Gianni Eugenio Viola. (Rome: Istituto della Enciclopedia Italiana, 1989), 599-615.

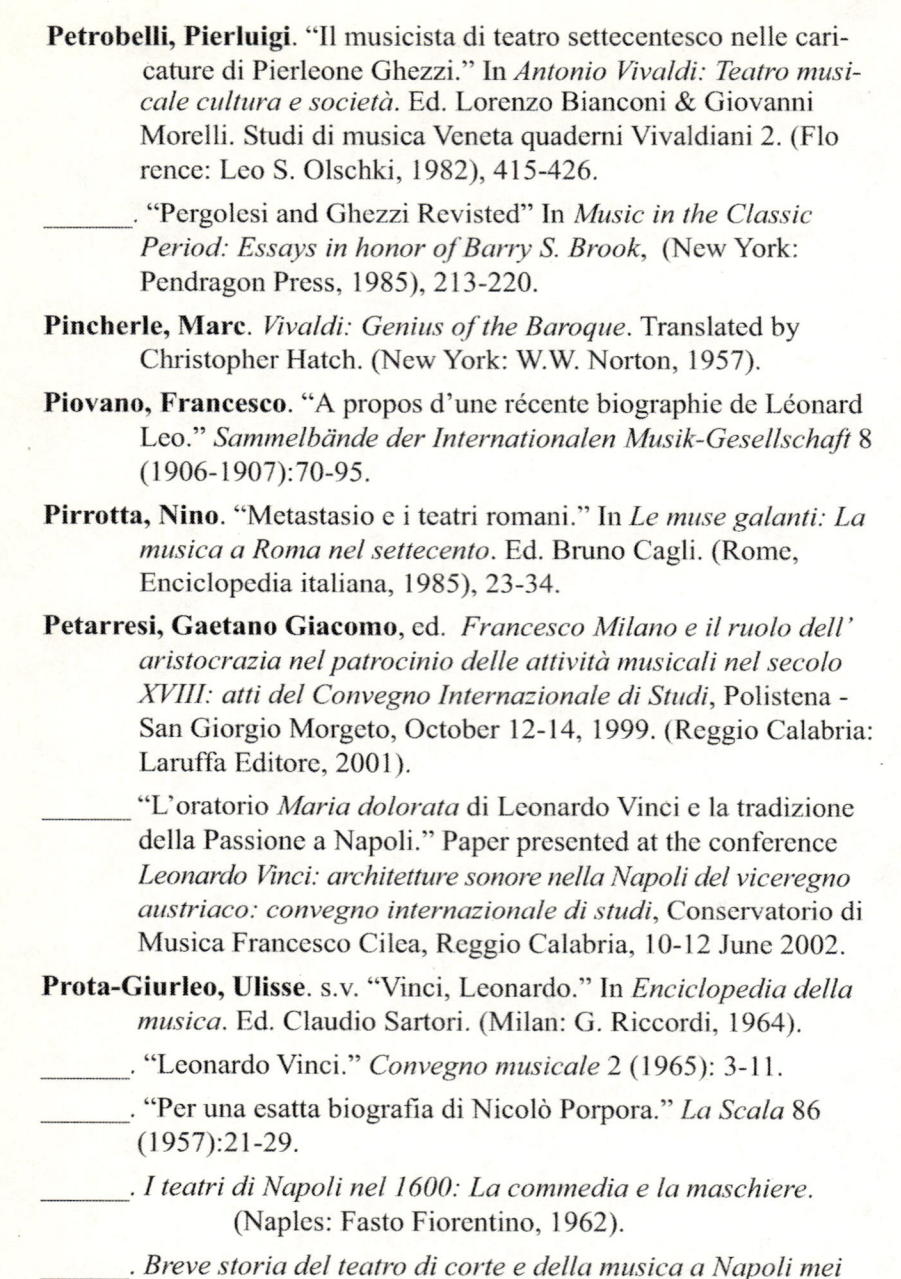

**Petrobelli, Pierluigi**. "Il musicista di teatro settecentesco nelle caricature di Pierleone Ghezzi." In *Antonio Vivaldi: Teatro musicale cultura e società*. Ed. Lorenzo Bianconi & Giovanni Morelli. Studi di musica Veneta quaderni Vivaldiani 2. (Florence: Leo S. Olschki, 1982), 415-426.

_____. "Pergolesi and Ghezzi Revisted" In *Music in the Classic Period: Essays in honor of Barry S. Brook*, (New York: Pendragon Press, 1985), 213-220.

**Pincherle, Marc**. *Vivaldi: Genius of the Baroque*. Translated by Christopher Hatch. (New York: W.W. Norton, 1957).

**Piovano, Francesco**. "A propos d'une récente biographie de Léonard Leo." *Sammelbände der Internationalen Musik-Gesellschaft* 8 (1906-1907):70-95.

**Pirrotta, Nino**. "Metastasio e i teatri romani." In *Le muse galanti: La musica a Roma nel settecento*. Ed. Bruno Cagli. (Rome, Enciclopedia italiana, 1985), 23-34.

**Petarresi, Gaetano Giacomo**, ed. *Francesco Milano e il ruolo dell' aristocrazia nel patrocinio delle attività musicali nel secolo XVIII: atti del Convegno Internazionale di Studi*, Polistena - San Giorgio Morgeto, October 12-14, 1999. (Reggio Calabria: Laruffa Editore, 2001).

_____ "L'oratorio *Maria dolorata* di Leonardo Vinci e la tradizione della Passione a Napoli." Paper presented at the conference *Leonardo Vinci: architetture sonore nella Napoli del viceregno austriaco: convegno internazionale di studi*, Conservatorio di Musica Francesco Cilea, Reggio Calabria, 10-12 June 2002.

**Prota-Giurleo, Ulisse**. s.v. "Vinci, Leonardo." In *Enciclopedia della musica*. Ed. Claudio Sartori. (Milan: G. Riccordi, 1964).

_____. "Leonardo Vinci." *Convegno musicale* 2 (1965): 3-11.

_____. "Per una esatta biografia di Nicolò Porpora." *La Scala* 86 (1957):21-29.

_____. *I teatri di Napoli nel 1600: La commedia e la maschiere*. (Naples: Fasto Fiorentino, 1962).

_____. *Breve storia del teatro di corte e della musica a Napoli mei secoli xvii-xviii*. (Naples, L'Arte tipografica, 1952).

**Ratner, Leonard G**. *Classic Music: Expression, Form, and Style*. (New York: Schirmer Books, 1980).

———. "Eighteenth-Century Theories of Musical Period Structure." *Musical Quarterly* 42/4 (October 1956):439-54.

**Rava, Arnaldo**. *I teatri di Roma*. (Rome: Fratelli Palombi, 1953).

**Rice, John A**. "Pergolesi's *Ricimero Reconsidered*." In *Studi Pergolesiani I: Proceedings of the International Symposium, Jesi, 1983*. Ed. Francesco Degrada. (Stuyvesant, New York: Pendragon Press, 1986), 80-88.

**Roberts, John H**. "Handel and Vinci's *Didone Abbandonata*: Revisions and Borrowings."*Music and Letters* 68/2(1987):146-48.

**Roberts, Penfield**. *The Quest for Security: 1715-1740*. The Rise of Modern Europe Series. (New York: Harper & Row, 1947).

**Robinson, Michael F**. *Naples and Neapolitan Opera*. (Oxford: Clarendon Press, 1972).

———. "The Da Capo Aria as Symbol of Rationality." In *La musica come linguaggio universale: genesi e storia di un' idea*. Ed. Raffaele Pozzi. (Florence: Leo S. Olschki, 1990), 51-63.

**Romana Veneziano, Giulia Anna**. "Dal 'tono humano' al 'divino': cantate di Vinci in Spagna." Paper presented at the conference *Leonardo Vinci: architetture sonore nella Napoli del viceregno austriaco: convegno internazionale di studi*, Conservatorio di Musica Francesco Cilea, Reggio Calabria, 10-12 June 2002.

———. "La cantata da camera tra Napoli e Spagna nel primo Settecento: Vinci e Porpora." Paper presented at the *X Congreso Bienal de Musica Barroca*, Universidad de La Rioja, 17-21 July, 2002.

———. "Un *Corpus* de cantatas Napolitanas del siglo XVIII en Zaragoza: Problemas de difusión del repertorio italiano en España." *Artigrama: Revista del Departamento de Historia del arte* 12 (1996-97):277-91.

———. "La maestria nel comico: *Li Zite 'n Galera*." Article accompanying the libretto for the production of *Li Zite 'n Galera* in Bari, 1999.

**Rosselli, John**. *Singers of Italian Opera: the History of a Profession*. (Cambridge: Cambridge University Press, 1992).

———. *The Opera Industry in Italy from Cimarosa to Verdi: The Role of the Impresario*. (Cambridge: Cambridge University Press, 1984).

**Rostirolla, Giancarlo**. *Il "Mondo Novo" musicale di Pier Leone Ghezzi*. With essays by Stefano La Via & Anna Lo Bianco. (Rome: Accademia Nazionale di Santa Cecilia & Milan: Skira, 2001).

———. "Nuovi documenti sulla presenza di Leonardo Vinci a Roma." Paper presented at the conference: *Leonardo Vinci:architetture sonore nella Napoli del viceregno austriaco: convegno internazionale di studi*, Conservatorio di Musica Francesco Cilea, Reggio Calabria, 10-12 June 2002.

**Rushton, Julian**. *Classical Music: a Concise history from Gluck to Beethoven*. (London: Thames and Hudson, c.1986).

**Sartori, Claudio**. *I libretti italiani a stampata dalle origini al 1800: catalogo analitico con 16 Indici*. (Cuneo: Bertola e Locatelli Editori, 1990).

**Scherillo, Michele**. *L'opera buffa napoletana durante il settecento: storia letteraria*, 2nd ed. (Milan: R. Sandron, 1917).

**Selfridge-Field, Eleanor**. *Pallade Veneta: Writings on Music in Venetian Society, 1650-1750*. (Venice: Edizione Fondazione Levi, 1985).

**Shearon, Stephen**. "Musical Activity in Early Eighteenth-Century Naples: the Memoirs of Bonifacio Pecorone." Paper given at the Conference: *Music in Eighteenth-Century Italy*, Cardiff University, 12-15 July 1998.

**Sheldon, David A**. "The Galant Style Revisited and Re-evaluated." *Acta Musicologica* 47 (1975):240-70.

**Silva, Giuseppe Silvestri**. *Illustri musicisti calabresi: Leonardo Vinci*. (Genoa: Tipografia Nazionale, 1934).

**Smith, William C. & Charles Humphries**. *A Bibliography of the Musical Works Published by the Firm of John Walsh: During the Years 1721-1766*. (London: The Bibliographical Society, 1968).

**Strohm, Reinhard**. "Alessandro Scarlatti and the Eighteenth Century." In *Essays on Handel and the Italian Opera*, (Cambridge: Cambridge University Press, 1985)15-33.

———. "Comic Tradition in Handel's *Orlando*." In *Essays on Handel and the Italian Opera*. (Cambridge: Cambridge University Press, 1985), 249-267.

———. "A Context for *Griselda*: the Teatro Capranica in Rome, 1711-1724." In *Dramma per Musica: Italian Opera Seria of the Eighteenth Century*. (New Haven, Conn.: Yale University Press, 1988), 33-60.

———. "The Critical Edition of Vivaldi's *Giustino* (1724)." In *Nuovi studi vivaldiani: edizione e cronologia critica...*, Eds. Antonio Fanna & Giovanni Morelli. Studi di musica Veneta quaderni Vivaldiani 2. (Florence: Leo S. Olschki, 1988), 299-415.

_____. *Dramma per Musica: Italian Opera Seria of the Eighteenth Century*. (New Haven, Conn.: Yale University Press, 1998).

_____. "Francesco Gasparini's Later Operas and Handel." In *Essays on Handel and the Italian Opera*. (Cambridge: Cambridge University Press, 1985), 80-92.

_____. "Handel's *Ezio*." In *Essays on Handel and the Italian Opera*. (Cambridge: Cambridge University Press, 1985), 225-31.

_____. "Handel and his Italian Opera Texts." In *Essays on Handel and the Italian Opera*, 34-79.

_____. "Handel's pasticci." In *Essays on Handel and the Italian Opera*. (Cambridge: Cambridge University Press, 1985), 164-211.

_____. "Introduction: the *dramma per musica* in the eighteenth century." In *Dramma per Musica: Italian Opera Seria of the Eighteenth Century*. (New Haven, Conn.: Yale University Press, 1988), 1-29.

_____. *Italienische Opernarien des frühen Settecento (1720-1730)*, 16/I & II of *Analecta Musicologica*. (Cologne: Arno Volk, 1976).

_____. *Die italienische Oper im 18.Jahrhundert*. Taschenbücher zur Musikwissenschaft 25. (Wilhelmshaven: Heinrichshafens Verlag, 1979).

_____. "Leonardo Vinci's *Didone abbandonata* (Rome 1726)." In *Essays on Handel and the Italian Opera*. (Cambridge: Cambridge University Press, 1985), 213-24.

_____. "Metatstasio's *Alessandro nell'Indie* and its earliest settings." *Essays on Handel and the Italian Opera*. (Cambridge: Cambridge University Press, 1985), 232-48.

_____. "The Neapolitans in Venice." In *Con che soavità: Studies in Italian Opera, Song, and Dance, 1580-1740*. Ed. Iain Fenlon & Tim Carter. (Oxford: Clarendon Press, Oxford, 1995), 249-74.

_____. "Rulers and states in Hasses's *drammi per musica*." In *Dramma per Musica: Italian Opera Seria of the Eighteenth Century*. (New Haven, Conn.: Yale University Press, 1988), 270-93.

_____. "Sinfonia and drama in *opera seria*." In *Dramma per Musica: Italian Opera Seria of the Eighteenth Century*. (New Haven, Conn.: Yale University Press, 1988), 237-51.

_____. "Towards an Understanding of the *opera seria*." In *Essays on Handel and the Italian Opera*. (Cambridge: Cambridge University Press, 1985), 93-105.

———. "*Tragédie* into *Dramma per musica*," Parts I-III. *Informazioni e studi vivaldiani: bollettino annuale dell'istituto italiano Antonio Vivaldi* 9 (1988):14-24, 10 (1989):57-101 & 11 (1990):11-25.

———. "Vivaldi's Career as an Opera Producer." *Essays on Handel and the Italian Opera*. (Cambridge: Cambridge University Press, 1985), 122-163.

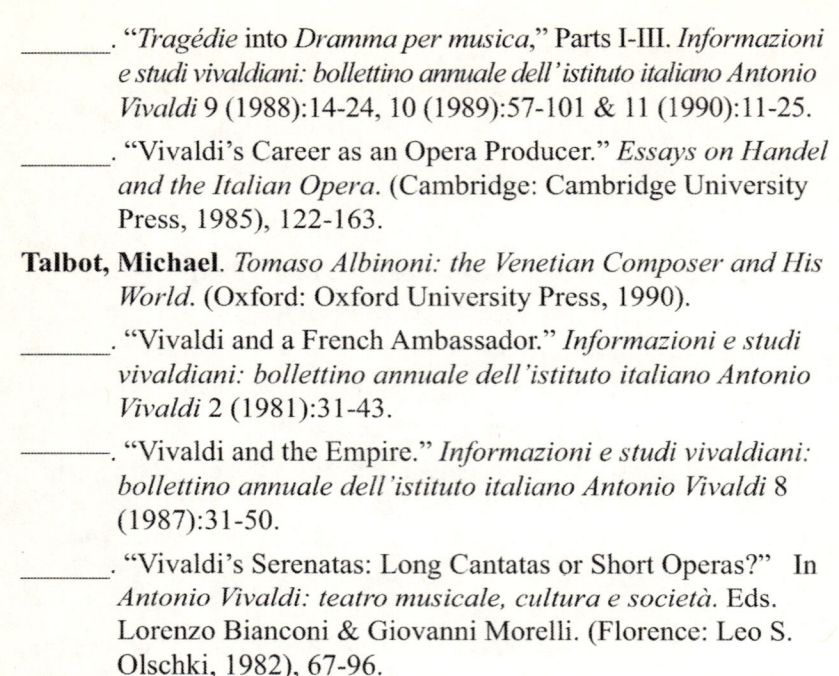

Talbot, Michael. *Tomaso Albinoni: the Venetian Composer and His World*. (Oxford: Oxford University Press, 1990).

———. "Vivaldi and a French Ambassador." *Informazioni e studi vivaldiani: bollettino annuale dell'istituto italiano Antonio Vivaldi* 2 (1981):31-43.

———. "Vivaldi and the Empire." *Informazioni e studi vivaldiani: bollettino annuale dell'istituto italiano Antonio Vivaldi* 8 (1987):31-50.

———. "Vivaldi's Serenatas: Long Cantatas or Short Operas?" In *Antonio Vivaldi: teatro musicale, cultura e società*. Eds. Lorenzo Bianconi & Giovanni Morelli. (Florence: Leo S. Olschki, 1982), 67-96.

Termini, Olga. "Carlo Francesco Pollarolo: Follower or Leader in Venetian Opera?" *Studi Musicali* 7 (1979):223-271.

Treadwell, Nina. "Female Operatic Cross-Dressing: Bernardo Saddumene's Libretto for Leonardo Vinci's '*Li Zite'n Galera*' (1722)." *Cambridge Opera Journal* (July 1998): 131-56.

Troy, Charles E. *The Comic Intermezzo*. (Ann Arbor: UMI Research Press, 1979).

Venturi, Franco. *Italy and the Englightenment: Studies in a Cosmopolitan Century*. Tr. Susan Corsi. (London: Longman, 1972).

Viviani, Vittorio. *Storia del teatro Napoletano*. (Naples: Guida Editori, 1969).

Walker, Frank. "A Chronology of the Life and Works of Nicola Porpora." *Italian Studies* 4 (1951):29-62.

Weaver, William. "Florence [review of the production of *Li Zite 'ngalera* at the 42nd Maggio Musicale Fiorentino]." *Opera News* 44/5 (Nov. 1979):56-57.

Weaver, Robert Lamar. "Florentine Comic Operas of the Seventeenth Century." Ph.D. dissertation, University of North Carolina, Chapel Hill, 1959.

**Weaver, Robert Lamar & Norma Wright Weaver**. *A Chronology of Music in the Florentine Theater, 1590-1750: Operas, Prologues, Finales, Intermezzos and Plays with Incidental Music*. Detroit Studies in Music Bibliography, 38. (Detroit: Information Coordinators, 1978).

**Weigel Williams, Hermine**. *Francesco Bartolomeo Conti: His Life and Music*. (Aldershot, Hants: Ashgate, 1999).

**Weiss, Piero**. "Metastasio, Aristotle, and the *Opera Seria*." *Journal of Musicology* 1 (1982):385-394.

_____. "Ancora sulle origini dell'opera comica: il linguaggio." In *Studi Pergolesiana I: Proceedings of the International Symposium, Jesi, 1983*, 124-47. Ed. Francesco Degrada. (Stuyvesant, N.Y.: Pendragon Press, 1986).

**Weimar, Eric**. *Opera seria and the Evolution of Classical Style:1755-1772*. Studies in Musicology, No. 78. Ed. George Buelow. (Ann Arbor, Michigan: UMI Research Press, 1984).

**Wiesend, Reinhard**. "Le revisioni di Metastasio di alcuni suoi drammi e la situazione della musica per melodrama negli anni '50 del settecento." In *Metastasio e il mondo musicale*. Ed. Maria Teresa Muraro. (Florence: Leo S. Olschki, 1986), 171-97.

_____."Zur Physiognomie einer Oper im Spannungsfeld zwischen Werk und Aufführung: Der Münchner *Alessandro nell'Indie* von 1735." In *Von Isaac bis Bach: Studien zur älteren deutschen Musikgeschichte: Festschrift Martin Just zum 60.Geburtstag*. Eds. Frank Heidlberger, Wolfgang Osthoff & Reinhard Wiesend. (Kassel: Bärenreiter, 1991).

**Wittkower, Rudolf**. *Art and Architecture in Italy 1600-1750*, 3rd ed. The Pelican History of Art. Eds. Nikolaus Pevsner & Judy Nairn. (Harmondsworth, Middlesex: Penguin Books, 1973).

**Wolff, Hellmuth Christian**. "The Fairy-tale of the Neapolitan Opera." In *Studies in Eighteenth-Century Music: Essays for Oliver Strunk*. Ed. Harold Powers. (Princeton, New Jersey: Princeton University Press, 1968), 401-405.

_____. "Italian Opera 1700-1750." In *Opera and Church Music: 1630-1750*. Eds. Anthony Lewis & Nigel Fortune. New Oxford History of Music, V. (London: Oxford University Press,1975), 1-168.

_____. "Leonardo Leo's Oper *L'Andromaca* (1742)." *Studi Musicali* 1 (1972):285-315.

**Worsthorne, Simon Towneley**. *Venetian Opera in the Seventeenth Century*. (Oxford: Clarendon Press, 1954; reprint London: Oxford University Press, 1968).

**Wotquenne, Alfred**. *Alphabetisches Verzeichnis der Stücke in Versen aus den dramatischen Werken von Zeno Metastasio und Goldoni*. (Leipzig: Breitkopf & Härtel, 1905).

**Yorke-Long, Alan**. *Music at Court: Four Eighteenth Century Studies*, with Preface by Patrick Trevor-Roper & Introduction by Edward Dent. (London: Weidenfeld and Nicolson, 1954).

**Zanetti, Emilia**. "La presenza di Francesco Gasparini in Roma gli ultimi anni 1716-27: cronologia e documenti." In *Francesco Gasparini: 1661-1727: Atti del primo convegno internazionale, Camaiore, 1978*. Eds. Fabrizio Dell Seta & Franco Piperno. (Florence: Leo S. Olschki, 1981), 259-319.

**Zanetti, Roberto**. *La musica italiana nel settecento*. (Milan: Bramante Editrice, 1978).

**Zaslaw, Neal, ed**. *The Classical Era: from the 1740s to the end of the 18th Century*. (Englewood Cliffs, N. J.: Prentice Hall, 1989).

# INDEX

ABB themes in da capo aria, 148, 269
Addison, Joseph, (1672-1719, writer), *Cato*, 218
"L'affaire des Poisons," 342
Albinoni, Tomaso (1671-1751, composer), *Didone abbandonata*, 66-67, 97, 99, 142, 157; *Il tiranno eroe*, 51
Aldobrandini, Pompeo (stage designer), 259
Algarotti, Francesco (1712-1764, opera reformer), 67; on accompanied recitative in Act III of Vinci's *Didone*, 152-54; on coloratura in the role of Catone, 223
Alibert, Count Antonio (1670-1731, theatre owner), 136
Almenara, Marques de (interim Viceroy for Naples), 257
Althann, Count Carl Emanuel (1702-56, nephew of the Viceroy of Naples), 83, 119
Althann, Cardinal Michael Friedrich, Bishop of Waitzen (1680-1734, Viceroy of Naples), 39, 50, 119, 173, 201, 257-58
Appiani, Giuseppe (1712-42, castrato), 288-89, 304
Aquilante, Francesco (fl.1719-42, ballet master), 103
Araja, Francesco (1709-?1770, composer), *Cleomene*, 321-22; *Demetrio*, "Navigante che non spera" from *Medo* as baggage aria, 249
Auletta, Pietro (c.1698-1771, composer), *Ezio*, 260-61; music for the funeral of Alessandro Scarlatti, 118
Austrian Regime in Naples, 17, 21, 28, 37, 39, 46, 52, 119, 176-77
*Avvisi di Napoli* (court newsletter), 15, 19, 21, 22-24, 28, 39, 47, 49-50, 60-61, 77, 82-84, 97-99, 117-18, 123
Aylesford, Earl of, 147

Bach, Johann Sebastian, (1685-1750), harmony compared with Vinci's, 313
Bagnolesi, Anna (soprano), 201-202
Baistrocchi, Pietro (stage painter and engineer), 189
Balatri, Filippo (castrato), 189-90, 193
Baldan, Giuseppe (2$^{nd}$ half of 18$^{th}$ century, Venetian copyist), misattributing sacred music to Vinci, 171
Baldi, Raffaeli (castrato), 64
Ballad operas, 273
Ballet, Algarotti's view of Italian ballet, 67; in *dramma per musica*, 66-68; Vinci and Scio integrating the *ballo* into opera, 89-90; in Vinci's comic operas, 23
Banchieri, Antonio, (Governor General of Rome), 189
Banci, Antonio (costume designer), 259
Banco di Napoli, Vinci's payment records, 37-42
Barbaia, Domenico (?1778-1841, impresario), 334
Barbieri, Antonio (tenor; fl. 1720-43), 103-105, 137, 189, 201-202, 259, 274; caricature, 105
Beard, John (tenor; c1717-1791), 156
Benedict XIII Orsini (1649-1730, Pope), 83, 206, 215, 307, 337; death, 307; dispute with the King of Portugal, 215; expulsion of the "Benevantani," 337
Benti, Bulgarelli, Marianna "La Romanina" (?1684-1734, soprano), 51, 85, 97, 146-47, 157, 159-60, 173; role in the creation of Didone, 146; caricature by Ghezzi, 147; Metastasio's letter, 321-22
Berenstadt, Gaetano, (1687-1734, castrato) 137, 154, 173, 187, 230, 259; Marpurg's anecdote, 303-307
Berlioz, Hector (1803-1869, composer), *Les Troyens*, 138
Bernacchi, Antonio (1685-1756, castrato), 237, 242; rivalry with Carestini, 258

*375*

Bernardi, Carlo (castrato) 103-104; caricature, 105
Bernardi, Francesco "Senesino" (d.1759, castrato), 104
Berrettini, Decio (battle director), 259, 288
Besozzi, Alessandro (1702-1793, oboist), praised by Frugoni, 247
*Biografia degli uomini illustri del Regno di Napoli*, judgments on Vinci's works, 102, 128-29
Birini, Agniolo (librettist), *Le ddoie lettere*, 20-21
Boldini, Giovanni (theatre poet), 303
Bononcini, Giovanni, (1670-1747, composer), assessment by Rousseau, 347; *Astianatte*, 125; *Camilla*, 71, 325
Bononcini, Marco Antonio (1677-1726, composer), *Astianatte*, 125
Bordoni, Faustina, (1697-1781, soprano) 47, 49, 98-100, 103, 106-107, 117, 173, 323; caricature, 99-100; at the Royal Academy, 117; in Venice, 98-99, 106-107; Frugoni's praiseful sonnets, 117; rivalry with Cuzzoni, 258, 306; relationship with Vinci, 99-100; "La partenza del Faustina", 49, 99
Borghese, Marc' Antonio, Prince of Sulmona (Viceroy of Naples), 28, 37
Boschi, Giuseppe (bass), 124
Bottone, Berardino (librettist/impresario), 22-23; librettist to *Lo scagno & Lo scassone*, 22; payments to Vinci, 38-42; plea to Cardinal Schratenbach, 22; taken to court by Vinci, 40-42
Boyer, Claude (1618-1688, dramatist), *Porus, ou la générosité d'Alexandre*, 291
Bracci, Gaetano (composer/arranger), revising *Artaserse* for Florence, 320
Briani, Francesco (fl.1709-10, librettist), *Il vincitor generoso/Gismondo re di Pologna*, 190-92
Broschi, Carlo "Farinello" (1705-1782, castrato), 64-65, 84-85, 124-25, 189, 237, 242, 265, 291, 321, 327; caricature, 65; baggage arias in *Medo*, 247; duel with Roman trumpeter, 95, 247; Frugoni's praiseful sonnets, 245-47; Metastasio's letters, 327
Broschi, Riccardo (c.1698-1756, composer), *Idaspe*, 303; *Isola d'Alcina*, 216

Brusa, Francesco, (1700-1768, composer), *Il Trionfo della virtù*, 115
Bulgarelli, Domenico (husband of "La Romanina"), 213, 337
Burney, Charles (1726-1814, music historian), 213; on Hasse's use of accompanied recitative, 153; on Metastasio's "narrow circumstances" 274; on Metastasio's evaluation of Vinci and Hasse, 327; on Neapolitan Conservatories, 9-10; on performance standards at the Conservatories, 10; on the declamatory inspiration of Vinci's melody, 313; on the origins of *Siroe re di Persia*, 159-60; on the success of *Farnace*, 78; on the success of Vinci's *Didone*, 145-46, 148; on Vinci's influence on Pergolesi, 257; on Vinci's rivalry with Hasse, 174; on Vinci's rivalry with Porpora, 12, 172; on Vinci's Venetian debut, 98, 101; speculation on Vinci's birth, 1

Caffarelli, see Majorano, Gaetano
Cafiero, Rosa (musicologist), 7
Calantro, Filippo (comic falsetist/castrato), 29-30
Calantro/Calandra, Giacobbe (violinist), 29; at Vinci's funeral service, 344
Calzabigi, Ranieri de' (1714-1795, librettist), 343
cantatas, as princely entertainment, 16; cantatas vs. serenatas, 282
Cantone, Francesco (Roman copyist), 70, 146, 194, 220
Canziani, Natale, (costume designer), 237
Cappelli, Giovanni Maria (1648-1726), arias in Vinci pasticcio *Turno Aricino*, 97; *I fratelli riconosciuti*, 246; *Venceslao*, "Impara da quest'alma," 221
Carasale, Angelo (impresario), 173
Carestini, Giovanni (c1704-c1760, castrato), 157-59, 214, 288, 304, 320; caricature, 158; rivalry with Bernacchi, 258
Cassiano, Vicenzo (librettist), *Il tiranno eroe / Silla Dittatore*, 51
Castorini, Castoro (c1700-after1740, castrato), 321
Cavanna, Porzio (impresario), 273-74, 292
Cerillo, Rosa (comic soprano), 22, 29

Cesti, Pietro Antonio, (1623-1669, composer), *Orontea*, 31, 325

Ceva, Nicola, (*maestro*), as Vinci's teacher, 13

Charles III, Bourbon (1716-1788, King of Spain, King of Naples), 88; succession to the Duchy of Parma, 244-45; conquest of Naples, 177; revival of *Artaserse*, 323-324

Charles VI, Habsburg (1685-1740, Holy Roman Emperor), 21, 46, 48-49, 84, 123, 155, 173, 190, 201, 220, 258, 277

Chiaia, suburb in Naples, 5, 330-32

Chiusano, Prince (patron), 24

Christina Vasa (1626-1689, Queen of Sweden), 64

Cimarosa, Domenico (1749-1801, composer), 339; *Artaserse*, 299

Ciocchetti, Giuseppe (battle director), 64

Clement XII, Corsini (Pope; 1652-1740), election, 333; driving the "Beneventani" from Rome, 337

Cocchi, Antonio (physician), 306

Colasanti, Antonia (soprano), 201-202

Cologne, Elector of, 215-16

Colonelli, Salavtore (artist/engraver), 283-85; engraving of the première of *La contesa de' numi*, 284

*Commedia de capa y espada*, influence of Spanish comedy on the *commedia per musica*, 27

*Commedia dell'arte*, 26

*Commedia per Musica*: "second generation" comedies, 29; audience, 83; Bernardo Saddumene's description, 26-27; casting, 30; comic finale & the *imbroglio*, 35-37; first Neapolitan *commedia per musica*, *La Cilla*, 24; first surviving *commedia per musica*, *Li Zite*, 27; influence of Neapolitan folk music, 31; influence of Spanish *commedia de capa y espada*, 27; links with 17th century Venetian opera, 27, 30-31; Neapolitan dialect, 24; origins and the Teatro Fiorentino, 24-25; precedents in 17th opera, 25-26; style of language, 30; transvestite roles, 30; Tuscanization experiment, 26

Conducting, in the modern style, 285-87

Congregation of the Rosary, 45-46, 60, 82, 117, 232-36; devotions, 233-34; *culto dei morti*, 234-35, 328-29; fees, 235, 328; Vinci judged contumacious, 328-29, 344; memorial service for Vinci, 344

Conservatories of Naples, deployment of staff, 9; financial Administration, 6; fees, 6, 14; origins, 6; life of the students, 9-10; studies in composition, 13; exams, 13; participation in Music and Processions, 9-10, 18; *flotte* (liturgical procession), 10-11; moving through the ranks: *paranza*, 11-12; *capoparana*, 11-12; *maestrocello*, 14

Conservatorio dei Poveri di Gesù Cristo, origins, 6; chapel, S. Maria della Colonna, 6; financial administration, 6; records in the Archivio storico diocesano in Naples, 7, 256; student boarders or *convittori*, 7-8; participation in the Music and Processions, 9-10, 18; *flotte* (principal liturgical procession), 10-11; Vinci as a student, 7-8; Vinci as interim maestro, 256-57

Conservatorio S. Maria di Loreto, board of Governors, 9; humanities courses, 9; student boarders or *educandi*, 7; *flotte* (principal liturgical procession), 11

Conti, Francesco (1681/2-1732, composer), *Erighetta e Don Chilone: L'ammalato immaginario*, 185

Conti, Gioacchino "Gizzziello" (1714-1761, castrato), 156, 304, 306

Cordara, Giulio Cesare (Jesuit priest), on the success of Vinci's *Didone*, 145-46, 148

Corelli, Arcangelo (1653-1713, composer) assessment by Rousseau, 347; funeral monument in Juvarra's *Memorie sepolcrali*, 345; funeral monument in the Pantheon, 347

Corneille, Thomas (1625-1709, playwright), *Le Comte d'Essex*, 140; *Stilicon*, 309-310

Corrado, Gioacchino (fl. 1705-44, comic basso), 49, 51, 97, 124, 128, 173, 185, 201-202

Corvo, Nicola (librettist), *La mogliere fedele*, 84

Coscia, Nicolò (Cardinal), corruption during the reign of Benedict XIII, 307, 337; "protettore" of Pietro Auletta, 206
Costa, Ippolita (comic soprano), 22, 29
Costanzi, Giovanni Battista (1704-1778, composer), *Eupatra*, 287; *Rosmene*, 261
Cotticelli, Francesco (musicologist), 119
Cramer, Carl Friederich, (1752-1807, writer on music), 145
Crébillon, Prosper Jolyot (1674-1762, playwright) *Xerxès*, 309
Croce, Benedetto (1866-1952, historian), 22
*Cuccagna* (Neapolitan festivity), connection with opera, 47, 276
Cuzzoni, Francesca (soprano; 1696-1778), 174, 321, 323; rivalry with Faustina in London, 258, 306

Dalmas, Domenico (ballet master/choreographer), 189
Daun, Wirich, Marshal (1669-1741), Viceroy of Naples, 21
David, Domenico (d.1698, librettist), *L'amante eroe*, 291
De Bottis, Giuseppe (organist at the Real Cappella), 120-21
De Brosses, Charles (1709-1777, travelogue writer), on *Artaserse*, 325; on the dominance of the major mode, 75; on the sources of Metastasio's *Artaserse*, 309; rumors concerning Vinci's death, 336-38, 341
De Falco, Michele (?1688-1732), collaborates with Vinci on *Lo castiello saccheato*, 23, 40
De Falco, Simone (comic tenor), 29-30, 262
De Palma, Carlo (theatre poet), adapts *La fede tradita* for Vinci, 177, 202; *Lesbina e Milo* replaced by *Erighetta e Don Chilone*, 177
De Petris, Carlo (theatre poet), adapts *La fede tradita* for Carlo Vignola, 176; addition of intermezzo *Lesbina e Milo*, 177; *La Spellecchia*, 25
De Sanctis, Francesco (1693-1740, architect), Spanish Steps/Piazza di Spagna, 64
De Siena, Francesco (local historian), 5

De Simone, Roberto, (b. 1933, opera producer), modern revival of *Li zite 'ngalera*, 28
Degli Albizzi, Luca Casimiro (Florentine impresario), 202
Del Po, Aurelio (impresario), at the Teatro S. Bartolomeo, 48
Dent, Edward (1876-1957, musicologist), birthdate for Vinci, 2, 330; description of *Silla Dittatore*, 52-53; on the Roman revival of *Artaserse*, 322; assessment of Vinci's operas: *Alessandro & Semiramide*, 302; *Silla dittatore*, 52-53
Di Giacomo, Salvatore (1860-1934, music historian), 232
Di Mayo, Giuseppe (1697-1771, composer), reception in Rome, 145
Dietrichstein, Ernestina Margarita, Countess of Harrach (1688-1745), 21, 276
*Dramma per musica* (opera seria), ABB themes in *da capo* aria, 148; accompanied recitative, 153; alternate five-act format, 101; aria distribution, 142; ballet, 66-68; magic transformations in *opera seria*, 253; production, 61-62
Dresden, revival of *Artaserse* for the inauguration of the Teatro Nuovo, 324
Durante, Francesco (1684-1755, composer/teacher), 256-57; portrait at the Conservatory in Naples, 339

Elizabeth, Empress of Austria (wife of Charles VI), 274, 320
*Emfindsamer* style, 111, 348
Engelbrecht, Martin (publisher), Righini's stage designs for *Medo*, 238-41
Erbestein, Countess Barbara (wife of Marshall Daun), 21
d'Este, Enrichetta, (Duchess of Parma), 236-37, 254-56
d'Este, Rinaldo (Duke of Modena), 116
Euripides (Dramatist; c.485 BCE- c406 BCE), 101

Facchinelli, Lucia (fl 1724-39 soprano), 157
Faggioli, Michel'Agnolo, (1666-1733, composer), *La Cilla*, 24
Falconi, Filippo, (d.1738, composer), *Ginevra*, with intermezzo *Burlotto/Brunetta*, 262

INDEX

Faliconti, Giuseppe Polvini (Roman impresario), 262
Farfallino, see Fontana, Giacinto
Farinelli/Farinello, see: Broschi, Carlo "Farinello"
Farnese, Antonio, (1679-1731, Duke of Parma), marriage to Enrichetta d'Este of Modena, 236-37, 254-56; love affair with Countess Borri, 245
Farnese, Elizabeth (1692-1766, Queen of Spain/ wife of Phillip IV), 245
Farnese, Francesco, (1678-1727, Duke of Parma), 116
Faustina, see: Bordoni, Faustina,
Federici, Domenico (castrato), 64
Felli Guiliano, (castrato), 64
Feo, Francesco, (1691-1761, composer) individual works: *Andromaca*, 287; *Don Chischiotte della Mancia*, 262; *La Forza della virtù*, 26; *Ipermesta*, 216, 261; Requiem in D minor, 344; *Siface*, 161; portrait at the Conservatory in Naples, 339; conducts the Requeim service for Vinci, 344
Ferrandini, Giovanni Battista (c1710-1791, composer), arranges *Alessandro nell' Indie* for Munich, 302
Ferraro, Giacomina (comic soprano), 22, 29
Festival dell'Aurora (Crotone), revival of Vinci's operas, 88, 108, 185, 187, 270
Fétis, François-Joseph (1784-1871, music historian) on Vinci in *Biographie universelle...*, 2, 338; on Vinci, religion and women, 233
Finazzi, Filippo (?1706-1776, castrato), 64, 137
Fioré, Andrea (1686-1732, composer), monument in Juvarra's *Memorie sepolcrali*, 345
Fischetti, Giovanni Battista (1692-1743, composer), *La Somiglianza*, 262; *La Costanza*, revision/resetting of *Li zite 'ngalera*, 262-63
Florence, productions of Vinci operas, 187, 230, 302, 321; role of Berenstadt, 321; connection with Brussels, 187
Florimo, Francesco, (1800-1888, music historian), *Ifigenia in Tauride* as Vinci's "masterpiece" 102; on *Astianatte*, 128-29; on Vinci and the Congregazione del Rosario, 232
Florio Antonio, (conductor of the Cappella de'Turchini), recording of *Li zite 'ngalera*, 28; revival of *Partenope* at the Festival dell' Aurora, 108
Fontana, Antonio (aristrocrat), 189
Fontana, Carlo (1634/38-1714, architect), 345
Fontana, Giacinto "Farfallino" (fl. 1712-35, castrato), 137-39, 189, 193, 214, 259, 288, 296, 304, 321, 341; caricature, 139; retirement, 321
Franceschini, Giuseppe (stage fights director), 137
Franchi, Angelo (castrato), 137
Freeman, Robert, (b. 1935, musicologist), Vinci's debt to Sarro's *Partenope*, 107-108
Frugoni, Carlo Innocenzio (1692-1768, librettist), adapted Stampiglia's *Il trionfo di Camilla* for Vinci, 117; *Ascanio venuto in Italia*, 245; *Ifigenia in Tauride*; 102; *Le nozze di Nettuno L'equestre con Anfitrite*, 254-56; *Medo*, 236-37, 242-45; double political allegory, 244-45; depicts himself as the character Artace, 245; synopsis, 242-43; self assessment, 244; sonnets in praise of singers, 117, 245-47

Galland, Christophe (opera producer), modern revival of *Li Zite 'ngalera*, 28
Gallas, Graf Johann Wenzel, Duca di Lucera (1669-1719, Imperial diplomat), 21
Galli-Bibiena, Francesco (1659-1739, stage designer/architect), 69
Gallupi, Baldasare (1706-85), *Alessandro nell'Indie*, 299; *Artaserse*, 299
gambling, 333-36; in the 18th century, 334; connection between gambling and opera, 334; Salvi and Orlandini's *Il marito giocatore*, 334, 336;Ghezzi's caricature of the impresario Polvini Faliconti gambling, 334
Gasparini, Francesco (1661-1727; composer), 66; individual works: *Anfitrione*, 184; *Erighetta e Don Chilone*, 184-85; *Flavio Anicio Olibrio*, 259; *Tigrena*, 66; monument in Juvarra's *Memorie sepolcrali*, 345 Roman operas, 66, 70

Gaulli, Giovanni Battista (1639-1709, painter), 345
Gaultieri, Nicolo (impresario), at the Teatro S. Bartolomeo, 48
Gender/Sexual ambiguity, 30, 87, 104
Gerber, Ernst Ludwig, (1746-1819, music historian), date and place of Vinci's birth, 1; *Ifigenia in Tauride* as Vinci's "first opera" 102; the Roman revival of *Artaserse*, 322; Vinci's death, 337
Ghezzi, Pier Leone, (1674-1755, artist), caricatures in *Il Nuovo Mondo*, 37, 65, 79-81, 99-100, 139, 142, 285-87, 345; reproductions: "Farinello" Carlo Broschi, 65; first of Vinci, 81; second of Vinci, 285-87, 339, 341; Faustina and Vinci, 100; "Farfallino" Giacinto Fontana, 139; Leonardo Leo, with Giovanni Antonio Reina & Gaetano Valetta, 142; Impresario Giuseppe Polvini Faliconti and publisher Filippo de' Rossi, 334; designer of stage archticture, 285; Vinci obituary notice, 332-33; Wednesday evening concerts, 79, 287
Giai, Giovanni Antonio (1690-1764, composer), *Mitridate*, 303; *Demetrio*, 306
Gigli, Nicola (choreographer), 201
Gilles, Jean (1668-1705, composer), *Requiem*, 344
Giorgi, Filippo (tenor), 173, 214
Giucciardi, Francesco (tenor), 84
Gizzi, Domenico (c1680-1758, castrato), 64, 66, 97, 137, caricature, 67
Gluck, Christoph, Willibald (1714-1787, composer), *Orfeo ed Euridice*, use of accompanied recitative, 153
Goldoni, Carlo (comic playwright; 1707-1793); *La vedova spiritosa*, reaction of Roman audience, 145; description of Vivaldi's request for *agitata* arias, 267
Gonzaga, Ferdinando Carlo (Duke of Mantua), 175-76
*Grand stagione*, poisonings in Palermo, 342
Greco, Gaetano (c.1657-1728, maestro), Vinci's teacher, 6, 13; departure from Naples, 13; return to Naples, 13; succeeded by Durante, 256-57

Grétry, André Ernest Modeste, (1741-1813, composer), 310-15; Grétry's teacher in Rome, Giovanni Casali, 313-314; *La Caravane du Caire*, ariette "Frà l'orror della tempesta," 315; mistaken notion of a monument to Vinci in the Pantheon, 313, 347
Grimaldi, Nicola "Nicolino" (1673-1732, castrato), 51, 85, 157-60; caricature, 158; formal innovation in the *da capo* aria, 164-66
Gualandi, Margherita "La Campioli," (?1680s-d. after 1738), 173-74
Gugliantini, Pietro (ballet master/choreographer), 259, 288, 304
Guglielmini, Anna (soprano), 84

Handel, George Frideric (1685-1759), *Alcina*, 90, 266; *Alessandro*, 300; "Lusinghe cara," 320, 325; *Amadigi*, 85; *Ariodante*, "Cieca notte," 113; "Dopo notte" 221; use of ballet and chorus, 90, 254, 266; Concertos for Organ, Op. 4, no. 2, 20; *Giulio Cesare*, "Tutto può donna" 20; "V'adoro pupile", 92; Cesare's accompanied recitatives, 133, 153, "Al lampo dell' armi," 168;"Da tempesta," 325; *Giustino*, "Mio dolce amato sposo" & "Zeffiretto, che scorre nel prato," 149; *Imeneo*: "D'amor nei primi istanti," 296; *Jephtha*, "Deeper and Deeper Still," 20; *Messiah*, "How beautiful are the feet," 20; *Partenope*, 103, 109, 114; "Care mura" 109; "Un core infedele." 113; Pasticcio *Arbace* (Vinci's *Artaserse*), 324; Pasticcio *Cajo Fabricio* (after Hasse), 324; Pasticcio *Didone Abbandonata* (after Vinci), 155-56; theft of "Se vuoi, ch'io mora" 149; Pasticcio *Elpidia* (after Vinci), 113-116, the role of Owen Swiney, 114-116; Pasticcio *Semiramide* (after Vinci), 324; *Poro*, 258; "Per l'africane arene," 258; "Se mai" arietta, aria, & duet, 296, 300; *Radamisto*, "Qual nave smarrito," 90; "Deggio dunque," 210; *Saul*, "Envy Chorus," 135; *Serse*, "Io le diró/Tu le dirai," 208; *Tamerlano*: "Bajazet's death scene," 225;

*Theodora*, Act II duet, 149; *Zadok the Priest*, 154; influence of Vinci/borrowings, 20, 77, 92, 113-16, 135, 155-56; possible influence on Vinci, 53-54; revival of operas, 275; rivalries with Bononcini and Porpora, 288

Harrach, Graf Alois Thomas (1669-1742, Viceroy in Naples), 258, 278-79

Hasse, Johann Adolf (1699-1783, composer), arias in Vinci pasticci: *Turno Aricino*, 97; *Stratonica*, 201; beginnings of career, 24; Burney/Metastasio's comparison of Vinci and Hasse, 326-27; individual works: *Artaserse*, 303; *Astarto*, 174; intermezzo, *L'artigiano gentiluomo*, 184; *Attilio Regolo*, use of accompanied recitative, 153; Handel's Pasticcio based on *Cajo Fabricio*, 324; *Cleofide*, 296, 299, 303; *Demetrio*, 327; *Ezio*, 323; *Ipermestra*, 326; *Porsugnacco e Grilletta*, 184; *Sesostrate*, 174; *Il Tigrane*, 278; *Viriate/Siface*, 327; position in the Real Cappella, 121; rivalry with Vinci, 174, 303

Heartz, Daniel (b. 1928; musicologist), on Vinci, 313

Holy Year 1725, the closing of the theatres in Rome, 88, 136

Innocent XII, Pignatelli (1615-1700, Pope), 5

Innocent XIII, Dei Conti (1655-1724, Pope), 82

Intermezzo, 24, 49

Italian verse structure, 94

James Edward Stuart, (1688-1766, "the Old Pretender/Giacomo III"), 64, 70, 141, 189; separation from his wife Clementina, 192-93, 215-16; as a subject of operas, 70, 192 292; attendance at performance of Vinci's *Semiramide*, 260-61, 306

Jennens, Charles, (1700-1773, librettist), 147; on Handel's borrowing from Vinci, 156

Jommelli, Nicola, (1714-1774, composer), collaboration with Noverre, 90; compared to Hasse and Vinci, 327;

individual works: *Artaserse*, 325; *componimento drammatico*, 283; portrait at the Conservatory in Naples, 339; reception in Rome, 145; revising Vinci's *Catone in Utica*, 153

Justinus, Marcus Junianus (Ancient Historian; fl. 3rd c. AD), *Historiae Philippicae*, 308

Juvarra, Filippo, (1676-1736 architect), Vinci's monument in *Memorie sepolcrali*, 345-47, 346

Knights of the Order of Malta, 137, 144

Koch, Heinrich Christoph (1749-1816, music theorist), classical caesura ornaments in the *Versuch*, 148

Lalli, Domenico (1679-1741, librettist) revisions to Metastasio's *Ezio* and *Semiramide riconosciuta*, 260; *Il Ritratto dell'Eroe*, 257-58; *Tigrane*, 59, 71, 163

Le Gros, Pietro (1666-1719, sculptor), 345

Leo, Leonardo (1694-1744, composer), *arie d'Ostinazione*, 135; beginnings of career, 24, 44; Ghezzi's caricature, 142; individual works: *Arianna e Teseo*, 261; *Andromaca*, 135; "Son regnante e son guerriero," 149; Prologue to revival of Vinci's *Artaserse*, 323; *Catone in Utica*: 230-31; "Cervo in bosco" & "Scherzo dell'onda" from *Medo*, 246, 249; *Timocrate*, 97; *Trionfo di Camilla*, Ghezzi's description of production, 141, 149; *Turno Aricino*, pasticcio by Vinci and Leo, 97; "trading places" with Vinci, 44; succession at the Real Cappella in Naples, 120-21

Levi, Caterina (alto), 51, 84-85

Librettists: see individual writers, Metastasio, Stampiglia, etc.

Livorno, Vinci productions from Florence, 230, 302, 321

Livy, or Titus Livius (59/64 BC – 17 AD), *The War with Hannibal*, 85-86; *The History of Rome*, 203-204

Lolli, Dorotea (alto), 237

Lombard Rhythms, 78-79, 181, 250-51, 299, 317

Lotti, Antonio, (1666-1740), composer of the Vinci/Pergolesi Miserere, 171; arias in Vinci pasticcio: *Turno Aricino*, 97; *Il vincitor generoso*, 190
Louis XIV (1638-1715, King of France), 278, 281, 342
Louis XV (1710-1774, King of France), 278
Louis, Dauphin of France (1729-65), 278-87
Lucchini, Antonio Maria (fl.1716-30, librettist), *Farnace*, 68-70
Lully, Jean-Baptiste (1632-1687, composer), *Armide*, 325

Maccarani, Paulo Maria (impresario), 136-37, 189
Magda Marx-Weber (musicologist), on the Miserere II attributed to Pergolesi and Vinci, 170-71
Maione, Paologiovanni (musicologist), 119
Majorano, Gaetano "Caffarelli" (1710-1783, castrato), 304, 306, 320, 324
Major mode and the classic style, 111-112
Mancia, Luigi (?1665- after 1708, dilettante composer), *Partenope*, 104
Mancini, Francesco (1672-1737, composer), 13, 53; appointment as *maestro* at the Real Cappella, 118-21
Mancini, Giambattista, (1714-1800, writer), *Riflessioni pratiche sul canto figurato*, 214
Mango, Antonio (impresario), 262
Manna, Genarro (1715-1779, composer) revises/conducts Vinci's *Artaserse*, 324
Maratta, Carlo (1625-1713, painter), 345
Marcello, Benedetto, (1686-1739, dilettante composer), on sopranos and Neapolitan cantatas, 98; on the *Trommelbass*, 111; on the use of sextuplet coloratura, 112; on composers building up"motivi," 117; on the soprano's "protettore," 340
Marchese, Annibale (b.1686, writer), *Tragedie cristiane*, 276-77; Vinci's "cori" for *Massimiano*, 276; use of "coro" as anachronism for aria, 276-77
Marchetti, Agostino (castrato), 124
Maresca, Nicola (playwright), *La deana o lo lavenaro*, 26

Mariani, Tomasi (fl. 1728-39, comic writer/composer), 262
Marpurg, Friedrich (1718-1795, music theorist), anecdote on the Vinci/Porpora rivalry in, 287-88, 293, 303-307
Martello, Pier Jacopo (1665-1727, writer/dramatist), advise on composing arias, 319; *L'Ifigenia in Tauris* (play), 101
Martini, Giovanni Battista, Padre (1706-84, music theorist/teacher), Francesco Vici's letters to , 329
Mattei, Saverio, (1742-1795, writer), *Memorie per servire alla vita del Metastasio*, 146
Mauri, Alessandro (stage painter and engineer), 137, 152, 214; stage set for *Catone in Utica*, 218
Mauro, Tomaso de (fl.1701-09, composer), *La Spellecchia*, 25
Medinaceli, Don Luigi de la Cerda, Duke of (Viceroy of Naples), affair with the singer Angela Voglia "la Giorgina," 204-205, 341
Meikle, Robert Burns (musicologist), edition of Vinci's *Artaserse*, 311-312
Melani, Jacopo, (1623-1676, composer), originator of the Florentine *commedia per musica*, 25
Mengoni, Luca (castrato), 64
Mereghi, Antonia (alto), 47, 50, 103-104
Metastasio, Pietro (1698-1782 librettist/poet), staging of *Demofoonte*, 144; appointment to the Imperial court, 274, 287; character's shirking of responsibility, 227; double premières in Rome/Venice, 260, 303; epitaph for Vinci, 326; *Estratto dell'Arte Poetica*, 276-77; *Impresario delle isole Canarie*, 85, 97; individual dramas: *Alessandro nell'Indie*, 287-92; synopsis, 289-90; appointment to the Imperial court, 287; comic elements, 292; drama of repetitions and symmetries, 291; influence of *Farnace*, 292; influence of Racine's *Alexandre*, 290-91; mixed response, 292; *Artaserse*, 305-26; synopsis, 308-309;breaking with the *da capo* norm, 315; Charles de Brosses identifies the sources, 309-310; con-

# INDEX 383

nections with *Ezio* and *Semiramide*, 310; death of the Pope, 307; revival in Vienna, 320; revival in Rome and the death of Vinci, 321-22, 326; *Catone in Utica*, 216-20, 227; synopsis, 216-17; adverse reaction, 218-19; influence of Addison's *Cato*, 218; political allegory, 219-20; *La contesa de' numi*, 278-87; the birth of the Dauphin, 278-80; the report in the *Mercure*, 280-82; *Didone abbandonata*, 85, 97, 99, 101, 138-44; synopsis, 138-39; collaboration with "La Romanina", 146; collaboration with Vinci, 141-44; tragic ending, 140, 152, 154; *Ezio*, 258, 260-61, 310; *Semiramide riconosciuta*, 259-65; synopsis, 264-65; competition intensified, 261-62; dedication to the Ladies, 261; Domenico Lalli as Venetian reviser, 260; double première with *Ezio* in Rome & Venice, 260; dramatic precedents, 263; relationship to *Siroe re di Persia* & *Partenope*, 265; revision for Farinello, 265; *Siface*, 134, 161-62; Porpora's double première, 161-62; *Siroe re di Persia*, 159-63; synopsis, 162-63; match of poetry and music, 170; origins of the drama and collaboration with Vinci, 159-60; Porpora's setting, 188-90; Sarro's setting and La Romanina's retirement, 213; similarities with Stampiglia's *Partenope* & Lalli's *Tigrane*, 163; influence of *commedia per musica*, 30; move to Rome, 213; opinion of mid-century music, 327; opinion of Vinci and Hasse, 326-27; poetic improvisations, 215; "profound fit of melancholy," 274; relationship with "La Romanina," 337

Milano, Giacomo Francesco, Principe D'Ardore (1699-1780, dilettante composer), 277

Minelli, Giovanni Battista (b?1687-d. after 1735, castrato), 189, 214-15, 274; caricature, 215

Minucci, Alessandro, 136-37

Modulations in first section of the *da capo* aria, affective/supertonic, 131; strong/dominant and weak/subdominant, 130

Molière, Jean Baptiste Poquelin: (1622-1673, playwright), 184

Moniglia, Giovanni Maria, (1624-1700, librettist), originator of the Florentine *commedia per musica*, 25

Montespan, Madame de (1641-1707, mistress of Louis XIV), 342

Monteverdi, Claudio, (1567-1643, composer), *Mercurio e Marte: Torneo*, 255; Artusi Controversy, 330

Morici, Pietro (castrato), 259

Morosi, Giovanni Maria (castrato), 189

Mosca, Felice (Neapolitan publisher), 276

Mozart, Wolfgang Amadeus, (1756-1791), as Germanic sentimental hero displacing Vinci/ Pergolesi, 347; court appointment, 122; individual works: *La finta Giardiniera*, "Mad Scene," 183; *Lucio Silla*, 51; *Idomeneo*, "Sacrificial scene, 253; Symphony No. 41 in C, K. 551 "Jupiter" fugue finale, 222; rumors surrounding his death, 337, 343-44

Naples: Archivio Storico Diocesano, 7, 256, 332; Austrian Regime, 17, 21, 28, 37, 39, 46, 52, 176-77; Chiaia, 330, engraving after Vernet, 331; chronology of operas from the early 1730s, 323; churches: S. Caterina a Formiello, 45-46, 60, 82, 117, 332; S. Giovanni Maggiore, 330, 332; S. Giuseppe a Chiaia, 332; S. Maria della Neve, 330, 332; congregations/ confraternities, 44-45; conservatories, 6-16; *cuccagna* and opera, 47, 276; earthquakes of 1733, 323; lawyers and court cases, 41; music in churches, chapels and convents, 10-11; Neapolitan dialect in *commedia per musica*, 24-27; problems for non-Neapolitan singers, 25, 27; Neapolitan school, 339; Neapolitan viceroys: Althann, Cardinal Michael Friedrich, Bishop of Waitzen, 39, 50, 119, 173, 201, 257-58; Borghese, Marc' Antonio, Prince of Sulmona, 28, 37; Daun, Wirich, Marshal, 21; Gallas, Graf Johann Wenzel, Duca di Lucera, 21; Harrach, Graf Alois Thomas, 258, 278-79;

Schrattenbach, Cardinal Wolfgang, Bishop of Olmutz, 21, 24; Real Cappella, succession after Scarlatti's death, 119-21; Real Palazzo, 44; engraving of the Piazza and Palazzo Real, 48; S. Carlo Theatre, inauguration, 323

Nicolini/Nicolino, see: Grimaldi, Nicola

Noris, Matteo, (d.1714, librettist) *Catone Uticense*, 218

Noverre, Georges (1727-1810, choreographer), collaboration with Jommelli, 90

Oliva, Francesco (?1671-1736?, writer), author of satire *La Violejeda*, 22; librettist to *Lo castiello saccheato*, 22-23

Olivieri, Giovanni Battista (stage designer), 85, 124, 288, 304

opera production, carnival season scenario, 61-62

Orefice, Antonio, (fl.1708-34, composer), early Neapolitan comic opera, 23, 25; individual works: *Il Gemino amore*, 26; *Patrò Calienno de la Costa*, 25

Orlandini, Giuseppe Maria (1676-1760, composer), arias in Vinci pasticci, *Stratonica*, 201, *Turno Aricino*, 97, individual works: *Berenice*, 101-105, 114-115; *La fedeltà coronata*, 237; *Ifigenia in Tauride*, 101; *Il marito giocatore*, intermezzo attributed to Vinci, 123, 185, 334-36

Orta/Orte, Pietro (Stage designer/painter), 124, 173, 304

Ossi, Giovanni (fl. 1716-34, castrato), 103-105, 189, 214, 259, 304; caricature, 105

Ottoboni, Pietro, Cardinal, (1667-1740, patron/diplomat) 189, 257-58, 345; *Il Ritratto dell'Eroe*, serenata in honor of his homecoming to Venice, 257-58

Ovid (43 BCE-17 CE, ancient poet), 101

Pacini, Battista (castrato), 47

Pagnini, Francesco Massimiliano (ballet master/choreographer), 237, 256

Paita, Giovanni (fl. 1708-29, tenor), 157-60, 237; caricature, 158; skill in combining head and chest voice, 157

Pampino, Gaetano (c1705-1775, conductor), the revivals of *Artaserse* in Fano and Macerata, 321

Pannini, Gian Paolo (1691-1765, painter), paintings in honor of the French monarchy in Rome, 283-85

Papal conclaves, 28, 83, 333

Pariati, Pietro (librettist; 1665-1733): individual dramas: *Antioco* (with Zeno), 201; *Artaserse* 310; *Flavio Anicio Olibrio* (with Zeno), 258; *Pimpinone*, 187; probable author of *L'ammalato immaginario*, 187

Parma, 299; Vinci's side trip, a Venetian spin-off, 116-17; Vinci and the Ducal wedding, 236-5

Pasqualigo, Benedetto (librettist; fl.1706-34), *Berenice*, 101, *Ifigenia in Tauride*, 101-102

*Pasquinata* (satiric tradition in Rome), 219

Pellizzari, Antonia (fl. 1710-27, soprano), 173-74

Percorone, Bonifacio (bass), chamber musician for Prince Sanseverini, 16

Pergolesi, Giovanni Battista (1710-1736, composer), as a capoparanze at the Conservatory, 12; assessment by Rousseau, 347; individual works: *Il Flamino* "Mentre l'erbetta," 32; *Lo frate 'nnamorato*: "Passo ninno da ccà," 32; "Vò solcando un mar crudele," 315; *Missa Romana*, 60; *Il prigionier superbo*, political content, 176-77; *Adriano in Siria*, 200; *L'Olimpiade*, 200; *La serva padrona*, "A Serpina penserete," 210; *Stabat Mater:* "Fac, ut partem Christe mortem," 95; "Sancta Mater istud agas," 247; "Inflamatus est," 316; influence of Vinci, 95, 210, 247, 316, 345; studied with Vinci, 257; nicknamed "Jesi," 12; portrait at the Conservatory in Naples, 339; rumors concerning poison, 343-44

Peri, Jacopo (1561-1633, composer), comparison to Vinci, 34, 210

Perti, Giovanni Antonio (1661-1756, composer), *Astianatte*, 125

Pertici, Francesco (tenor), 124

Perugia, revival of *Artaserse* with Farfallino, 321

# INDEX

Piantanida, Giovanni (1706-1773, violinist), husband of Costanza Posterla, 250
Piasiello, Giovanni, (1740-1816, composer) *Artaserse*, 299
Piccinni, Niccolò (1728-1800, composer): *Artaserse*, 299; debut at the Teatro Fiorentine, 24; deployment of Conservatory staff, 9; description of the conservatories in Naples, 9
Pignatelli family, 4-5; devotion to the Rosary, 46; palace in the Chiaia, 5
Pignatelli, Francesco, Archbishop of Naples, 5-6
Pignatelli, Girolamo, Prince of Strongoli, 4-6; connections to Vinci, 4-6; move to Naples, 5-6
Pinacci, Giovanni Battista (1694/5-1750, tenor), 189, 214-15, 220, 321; scandal in Rome, 189, 214; caricature, 215
Pio Fabri, Annibale (1697-1760, tenor), 47, 51
Piovene, Agostino (1671- died after 1721, librettist); *Publio Cornelio Scipione*, 48; *Tamerlano/Bajazete*, tragic ending, 140, 225
Piranesi, early influences, 218
Piscopo, Aniello (comic librettist), *Lo cecato fauzo: commedia per musica*, 19, 26; subject of satire *La Violejeda*, 22
Pistoia, revival of *Artaserse*, 324
Plutarch, (fl. c50-c120 CE) *The Lives of the Noble Grecians and Romans*, 217-20, 222
Po, Aurelio del (impresario), at the Teatro S. Bartolomeo, 48
poison, 342-344; scandals of the 17th century, 342-43; rumors concerning Vinci's death, 336-38; stories of other poisoned composers, 343-44
Polignac, Melchiorre de, Cardinal, (1661-1742, diplomat), celebrating the birth of the Dauphin, 278-80; initiating the Palchetti War in Rome, 280
Politi, Caterina (alto) 173, 177
political allegory in *opera seria*: in *Silla Dittatore*, 52; in *Farnace*, 70; in *Partenope* and *Eraclea*, 106; in *Gismondo re di Polonia*, 192-93; in *Medo*, 244-45

Pollarolo, Carlo Francesco (c.1653-1723, Venetian Composer), individual works: *Publio Cornelio Scipione*, 48; *Cosroe*, 66; *L'abbandono di Armida*, "Cervo in bosco" from *Medo*, 249 monument in Juvarra's *Memorie sepolcrali*, 345
Pollnitz, Charles Lewis, Baron de (writer), opera in Rome, 62, 64, 67; the death of Vinci, 336
Pope, Alexander, (1688-1744, poet), *Rape of the Lock*, 334 to), 173, 177
Porpora, Nicolo Antonio (1686-1768, composer), appointment to Ospedale degl'Incurabili, 172; arias in Vinci pasticci: *Turno Aricino*, 97; *Stratonica*, 201; beginning of career, 24, 66; opera debut in Naples, 12; continued association with the Conservatory, 12; debuts of students, 66, 85, 288; descriptive derivation of thematic material, 183; engraving, 172; extended accompanied recitatives, 77, 134; favorite theme, 315; influence of Vinci, 269; individual works: *Adelaide*, 66; *Angelica*, 77; *Didone abbandonata*, 141; "Punirò quel cor," 134, 222; "Cadrà fra poco in cenere," 154; *Ezio*, 258, 260, innovative role for Grimaldi, 164-65; *Flavio Anicio Olibrio*, Neapolitan and Roman settings, 259; *Gli orti esperidi*, 77; "Se fedel, cor mio" borrowings by Vinci and Handel, 91; *Germanico in Germania*, 306; *Mitridate*, 287, 303, 307; *Poro*, gala première in Torino, 303; *Semiramide riconosciuta*, 260, "Passaggier, che su la sponda," 269; pasticcio of Vinci and Porpora's settings, 272-73; *Siface*, consecutive scenes of *accompagnato*, 134; double première, 161-62; 1730 revival, 187, 287, 303, 304-307; *Siroe re di Persia*, 146, 188, 194; *La verità nell'inganna*, 161; Opera of the Nobility in London, 324; rivalry with Vinci, 12, 171-72, 188; at the Conservatory, 12, 172; in Venice, 161-62; Vinci's brief Venetian career, 171; in Rome, 188, 287-88, 293, 303-307

Porsile, Giuseppe (1680-1750, composer), appointment to the Real Cappella in Naples, 119

Porta, Giovanni (c1675-1755, composer), arias in Vinci pasticci: *Turno Aricino*, 97; *Stratonica*, 201; individual works: *Agide*, 99-100; *Amore e fortuna*, 123; *La caduta de' Decemviri*, 202; *La Lucinda fedele*, 123; inter mezzo, *L'avaro*, 184; *Il gran Tamerlano*, 306; *Numitore*, "Mormorio del rio," 209; *Il Ritratto dell'Eroe*, serenata formerly attributed to Vinci, 257-58

Posterla, Costanza (soprano), 237, 250-51, 302

Predieri, Luccio Antonio, (1688-?1767, composer), *Scipione*, 77, 141

Prota-Giurleo, Ulisse, (1886-1966, music historian), Vinci's death record, 330; the "second" death record, 2, 330, 332 Vinci's phantom records at the Conservatory, 7, 13, 256-57

Purcell, Henry (1658/9-1695), *Dido and Aeneas*, 138, 154

Quantz, Johann Joachim (1697-1773, composer), the Lombard style in Rome, 78-79; review of casts: Vinci's *Astianatte*, 124-25; Vinci's *Siroe*, 157-61; Scarlatti's Sinfonias for flute, 116

*Querelle des Bouffons*, 347

Racine, Jean, (1639-1699, playwright), *Andromaque* as source for *Astianatte*, 125, 127, 133; *Alexandre le Grand* as source for *Alessantro nell'Indie*, 290-91; biblical dramas, 276

Rameau, Jean Philippe (1683-1764, composer), court appointment, 122; *Naïs*, Isthmian games, 206; revival of his operas, 275; Rameau's funeral, 344-45

Real Palazzo (Naples), 44, 48

Reciting formulas, influence, 34

Reina, Antonio (tenor), 141 caricature, 142

Resse, Celeste (fl. 1725-34, comic soprano), 124, 128, 173, 185, 201, 258

Ricci, Marco, (1676-1730, artist), opera caricatures, 104-105,157-58; Vittoria Tesi, 125-126; G.B. Pinacci and G.B. Minelli, 214-15

Righini, Pietro (1683- 1742, stage designer), 237-41, 246, 250-53; stage designs for *Medo*, 238-41; stage sets in musical context, 246, 250-53

Ristorini, Antonio (comic bass), 185

Roberti, Frigimelica (1653-1732, librettist), *Il Mitridate Eupatore*, 101

Roberts, John (librarian/musicologist), Handel's borrowings from Vinci's *Didone*, 149-50

Robinson, Michael F. (b. 1933, musicologist), 347

Romana Veneziano, Giulia Anna (musicologist), Vinci's villanciccos, 17

Romanielli, Giovanni (comic bass), 22, 29, 262

Romanticism and Germanic musical hegemony, 348

Rome: Carnival, 60-62, 255; churches: SS. Trinità de' Pellegrini, 64; S. Trinità de' Monti, 280; S. Giovanni Laterano, 280; Corso, horseraces *(corsi dei barberi)*, 279-80; Fontana de Treve, 255; Monastery of the Campo Marzio, concert, 188; Monastery Santa Cecilia in the Trastavere, 193; opera: ban of women on stage, 64, 273, 341; introduction of comic opera, 262; restricted to Carnival, 273; attempt to expand opera into spring season, 321; Palazzzo Altemps, première of *La contesa de' numi*, 279-82; Palazzo Colonna, Faust ina's Roman debut, 99-100; Pantheon, 313, 347; Piazza di Spagna, 64; Piazza Navona, 279-80, 283; saltiero/psaltery virtuoso, 282; tradition of the *cicisbeo*, 337-38; violence in Roman society, 338

Rossini, Gioachino, (1792-1868), 334

Rostirolla, Giancarlo, (b. 1941, musicologist), discovery of 1722 Vinci caricature, 37

Rousseau, Jean-Jacques, (1712-1778), *Lettre sur la Musique Françoise*, 347; mid-century sentimentalism, 348

Royal Academy of Opera, London, production of Vinci pasticcio *Elpidia*, 114-115; Swiney's signing of Faustina, 117; collapse and continuation by Handel and Heidigger, 273

# INDEX

Ruffo, Cardinal, runner-up in the 1730 Papal Conclave, 333
Rumi, Domenico (castrato), 64
Ruspoli, Francesco Maria, Prince (1672-1731), composition of Handel's cantatas, 16; daughter's wedding, 188

Saddumene, Bernardo (fl. 1721-34, librettist), explanation of the Neapolitan *commedia per musica*, 26; individual works: *Albino e Plautilla*, intermezzo to *Silla Dittatore*, 58; *Don Ciccio*, 23; *Lo Labborinto*, 40; *Publio Cornelio Scipione*, arranger of Piovene's drama, 48; *Ermosilla/Bacocco*, 48; *Silla Dittatore*, arranger of Cassiano's drama, 58; *Li Zite 'ngalera*, 29-31; introduces Neapolitan *commedia per musica* to Rome, 262
Saint Non, Abbé (writer), description of Strongoli, 3-4; rumors concerning Vinci's death, 336-38; on "Vò solcando" & "Tu vuoi, ch'io vivi" from *Artaserse*, 318
Sallé, Marie (?1707-1756, dancer), collaboration with Handel, 90
saltiero/psaltery virtuoso in Rome, 72, 282
Salvai, Maddalena (fl. 1716-31,soprano), 173-74, 187
Salvi, Antonio (1664-1724, librettist), individual works: *Amore e maestà*, 140; *Astianatte* 125-128, 133; *Il marito Giocatore*, 185, 334-36
Sanseverini, Prince Carlo (patron), biweekly cantata performances, 16
Sansevero, Don Paulo di Sangro Prince (patron), Vinci's first position as *maestro di cappella*, 15-16, 19; music teacher to the heir/nephew Raimondo, 15-16; composition of cantatas, 16
Sansevero, Don Raimondo di Sangro, Prince (1710-71), 15-16; support for Don Carlo di Borbone, 177
Santa Marchesina (soprano), 49, 51, 97, 185
Santo Lapis (composer), Sonate da Camera a due, Op. 1, 116
Saracino, Francesco (stage designer), 201
Saro, Antonio (ballet master/choreographer), 137, 214

Sarro, Domenico (1679-1744, composer) reinstated to the Real Cappella, 119; individual works: *Arsace*, dance-inspired arias, 53, 90, 140; *Partenope*, 49, 103, 106-108; *Didone abbandonata*, 85, 133, 138, prominence of the role of Jarba, 142-43, showcase the acting ability of "La Romanina", 146; *Siroe re di Persia*, La Romanina's final role, 213; *Impresario delle isole Canarie*, 85; *Tito Sempronio Gracco*, 124; *Il Valdemaro*, 141; influence on Vinci, 53-54, 106-108; succession at the Real Cappella in Naples, 118-122;
Scalzi, Carlo (fl. 1718-38, castrato;), 103, 173, 201-202, 259, 321-22, 323; caricature, 105; Frugoni's praises, 117
Scarlatti, Alessandro (1660-1725, composer), arias in Vinci pasticcio: *Turno Aricino*, 97; departure and return to Naples during the War, 13; death and the succession at court, 118-19; final operas at the Teatro Capranica, 66; influence on Vinci, 49-54, 302, 318; compared with Vinci, 19, 50, 59, 71; individual works: *La caduta de' Decemviri*, 202-206; *Eraclea*, 85, 88; septet "Che maestà," 89; *La Griselda*, 66, 71, 131, 137, 318, "Figlio! Tiranno" 131; *Il Mitridate Eupatore*, 101; *Tigrane*, 59, 71, 163; *Il Trionfo dell'onore*, 26; *Turno Aricino*, 202; Sinfonias for flute, 116; portrait at the Conservatory in Naples, 339
Schrattenbach, Cardinal Wolfgang, Bishop of Olmutz (Viceroy of Naples), 21, 22, 23, 24
Scio, Sebastiano (ballet master), 64-65, 84, 88-90; replaces intermezzo in *Eraclea*, 87-88
Sellito, Giuseppe (composer; 1700-1777), revival of Vinci's *La Mogliere fedele*, 345
Sexual mores in 18th century Italy, 337-38, 340
Sigismondo, Giuseppe, (1739-1826) *Apoteosi dell'Arte Musicale*, 2, 339; concept of the Neapolitan School, 339; date and place of birth for Vinci, 2; mistakes the Neapolitan revival of

*Artaserse* as première, 322; scores in his collection, 128, 178; Vinci's "grosso frego," 338-42; alternate death scenario, 339-41
Silvanni, Francesco (librettist; c1660-d.1728-44), individual works: *La fede tradita*, 157, 174-77; *Il tradimento traditor di se stesso* (also known as *Artaserse*), 310
Sixtus V (1520-1590, Pope), banned women from the stage, 64
Sobieska/Stuart, Maria Clementina (1702-35, wife of James III), 192-93
Sophocles (c.496 BC- 406 BC, dramatist), 101
Sorosini, Benedetta (fl. 1722-32, soprano), 51
Spanish Succession War, 48, 106, 175-76; conquest of Naples by the Austrians, 119, 176
Spinola, Maria Livia (wife of Viceroy Marc'Antonio Borghese), 28
Stabile, Barbara (soprano), 201-202
Stampiglia, Marco (son of librettist), adapted *Turno Aricino* pasticcio for Vinci and Leo, 97, 202
Stampiglia, Silvio (1664-1725, librettist), individual works: *La caduta de' Decemviri*, 201-205, 207-208, 210-213; *Eraclea*, 85-88, 96; *Partenope (La Rosmira)*, 104-107 163; *Turno Aricino*, 97, 202
Strada, Anna (fl. 1719-40, soprano), 48, 84-85, 124
Stradella, Alessandro (1639-82, composer), affair with the mistress of Alvise Contarini, 341; death in Genoa, 341
Stravinsky, Igor, (1882-1971), *The Rake's Progress*, "Bedlam scene," 183
Strohm, Reinhard (b. 1942, musicologist), Sarro and Vinci's settings of "Al mio tesoro" compared, 108; survey of the manuscript sources of Vinci's *Artaserse*, 311-312; Vinci's sacred music in Berlin dismissed, 83, 171; Vivaldi and Vinci's settings of "Gelido in ogni vena" compared, 169-70
Strongoli (city in Calabria), 3-4
*Sturm und Drang*, relationship with the aria agitato, 223

Swiney, Owen (1676-1754, associate of the Royal Academy), 103-104; cast of Vinci's *Siroe* reviewed, 159; description of the cast of *La Rosmira*, 103-104; role in the creation of the pasticcio *Vinceslao*, 115; role in the creation of the Vinci pasticcio *Elpidia*, 114-16; trip to Parma to engage Faustina, 116

Tasi, Giovanni (castrato), 189
Tassi, Andrea, (castrato), 288, 302
Tasso, Torquato, (1544-1595, poet) *Gerusalemme liberata*, quotation, 34
Tesi, Vittoria (1700-1775, alto;), 84-85, 124-25, 237, 251, 274, 321; caricature, 126; "masculine" quality of her voice, 124-25, 132; reviewed by Quantz, 124
Testagrossa, Gaetano (c.1700-?1774, ballet master/choreographer), 157
Theatres:
  Alibert/delle Dame (Rome), 37, 50, 60-64, 136-37, 145, 188-89, 213-14, 259-60, 273-74, 278, 287; change of owners/ change of name, 136-37; compared with the Royal Academy of Music in London, 273; description by Baron de Pollnitz, 62; expanding opera into a spring Season, 321; floor plan by Gabriel Dumont, 63; James Edward Stuart, "the Old Pretender/ Giacomo III" patron, 64; Pinacci scandal, 188, 212-14; renovations by Galli Bibiena, 50; rivalry with the Capranica, 189, 287, 393, 303-307; Vinci and Cavanna as impresarri, 273-74, 278, 287; Capranica (Rome), 66, 68, 102, 137, 188-89, 215, 393, 303-307; rivalry with the delle Dame, 189, 287, 393, 303-307; Scarlatti's final operas, 66; season of Neapolitan *commedia per musica*, 261-62; Vivaldi's Roman operas, 66, 68, 102;
  Cocomero (Florence), 320;
  Covent Garden (London), 155;
  de' Granari (Rome), 262;
  Della Pace (Naples), 29; inauguration with Vinci's *La mogliere fedele*, 83;
  Della Pace (Rome), 261-62;
  Ducale (Milan), 161

# INDEX

Farnese (Parma), 254-55
Fiorentini (Naples), 19-29, 38-42, 44, 49, 262; Bottone, Berardino, impresario, 22, 38-42; introduction of ballet, 23; lending a singer to the S. Bartolomeo, 202; orchestra, 25; origins of the Neapolitan comic opera, 24-25; phasing out the *dramma per musica*, 25; Vinci as "house composer", 24, 40, 42; Vinci's affair with one of the singers, 341
Haymarket Theatre (London), 306; leased to Handel and Heidigger, 274
Pergola (Florence), 25, 79, 135; origins of the Florentine *commedia per musica*, 25; theatrical organization copied by Teatro delle Dame
Sant'Angelo (Venice), Vivaldi's theatre, 68, 157, 173
S. Bartolomeo (Naples), 24, 44, 46, 47, 50, 58, 84, 87, 123, 201-202, 274; rivalry with the Teatro Fiorentini, 25; renovations, 50, 84; rivalry between Vinci and Hasse, 174; borrowing a singer from the Teatro Fiorentini
San Carlo (Naples), inauguration, 323; Leo's *Andromaca*, 135
San Cassiano (Venice), 174, 184, 231
S. Cecilia (Palermo), 324;
San Gio vanni Grisostomo (Venice), 97-98, 103, 114-115, 157, 161-62, 188, 190, 230, 334; as venue for Neapolitan opera, 97-98; coordinating the 1726 season, 157, 161-62; description by Bonlini, 98;
Tordinona (Rome), 145
Tobacco smuggling, 306
Toffana, Giulia, inventer of Acqua Tofana, 342
Tolve, Francesco (tenor), 288, 304, 323
Tomii, Pellegrino (tenor), 157
Tosi, Francesco, (1654-1732, singing teacher/writer) *Opinioni de'cantori antichi e moderni*, 73, 196
Traetta, Tomaso (1727-1779, composer), use of accompanied recitative, 153; collaboration with Frugoni, 244
Tramonti, Agata (mother/stepmother or aunt of Vinci), 329, 330
Transvestite roles, 30, 85, 104

*Trommelbass* and the classic style, 111
Tullio, Francesco Antonio (1660-1737, librettist), first Neapolitan comic opera, 24; Tuscan experiment, 26
Turcotti, Giustina (soprano; c1700-d. after 1763), 201-202

Ungarelli, Rosa (fl. 1709-32, comic soprano), 185
Uttini, Elizabetta (soprano), 323

Vaccaro, Domenico Antonio (1681-1750, painter/artist), 276
Valeriani, Domenico (c.1708-c.1770, stage designer), 103
Valeriani, Gioseppe (c.1708-1762, stage designer), 103
Valesio, Francesco (diarist), *Diario di Roma*, 136, 188, 216, 257, 260, 282, 293, 306-307, 373-74
Valetta, Gaetano (tenor), 141, 189; caricature, 142,
Vanstryp, Filippo (librettist), *Mitridate*, 303
Veneziano, Gaetano (1665-1716, composer), position at the Real Cappella in Naples, 119, 122
Venice: Neapolitan dominance of Venetian opera, 97-98; Ospedale degl'Incurabili, 171; Ospedale della Pietà, 171, 258; ridotto di S. Moisé, 334; Metastasio premières in Venice and Rome, 260, 303
Viani, Antonio (share holder of the Teatro delle Dame), 136-37
Vici, Francesco (*maestro di cappella* in Fano), 329, 341-42; portrait in Bologna, 331
Vico, Diana (fl. 1707-26, alto), 84-85, 124
Vico, Giambattista (1668-1744, philosopher), 237, 276
Vienna: Metastasio appointed to the Imperial court, 287; Vinci plans to travel to Vienna with Metastasio, 279, 333; production of *Didone*, 155
Villancicco, Vinci's Villanciccos and relationship to Italian cantata, 17
Vignola, Giuseppe, (1662-1712, composer), *La fede tradita*, 176

Vinci, Aniello (brother or cousin of Leonardo?), 329, 330
Vinci, Giuseppe (father or uncle of Leonardo?), 329, 330
Vinci, Leonardo (c.1690-1730) (*see* Vinci Index, p.392)
Violante di Baviera, Grand Duchess of Tuscany, 215-216
Virgil (70 BCE - 19 BCE, ancient Roman poet), 138
Vivaldi, Antonio (1678-1741), arias in Vinci pasticci: *Turno Aricino*, 97; *Stratonica*, 201; influence of Vinci and the Neapolitans, 72, 75-76; influence on Vinci, 72, 102, 108-110, 178-79; individual works: *Il Catone in Utica*: "Nella foresta", 132; *Catone*, "Se mai senti spirarti," 226; "Se in campo armato," 226, parallels with Vinci via Leo, 231; *Dixit Dominus* (RV 594), 60; *La fede tradita*, 157, 173, 177, 183; *Giustino*, 68, 72, 75-76, 78-79, 102, 137, 139; *Griselda*, 267; *L'Incoronazione di Dario*: "Lo spietato, e crudo amore," 109; *Ottone in Villa*, use of *Trommelbass*, 111; pasticcio: *Cunegonda*, 157; *Quattro stagione*/Four Seasons, "Inverno/Winter," Quantz's description of Vivaldi creating the Lombard style, 78- 79
Voglia, Angela "la Giorgina," affair with Viceroy Medinaceli, 204-205, 341

Walsh, John the Elder (1665-1736), publishing firm: editions of arias from the pasticcio *Elpidia*, 115; Sonatas for flute by "Vinci and other Italian Authors" 116, 171; *Favorite Songs from Arbace*, 324

Zanelli, Ippolito (theatre poet) revision of Piovene's *Tamerlano/Bajazete*, 225
Zaragoza Cathedral, 17
Zeno, Apostelo (1668-1750, librettist) individual works: *Andromaca*, 127; *Antioco* (with Pariati), 201; *Artaserse*, 310; *Flavio Anicio Olibrio* (with Pariati), 258; *I rivali generosi*, 115; *Scipione nelle Spagne*, 77
Ziani, Pietro Antonio (c.1616-1684, composer), *La Costanza in trionfo*, 174

# INDEX OF VINCI'S WORKS

**Sacred Music**:
*Gionata* (oratorio misattributed to Vinci), 171
*Il Sacrifizio di Jefte* (oratorio misattributed to Vinci), 171
*Le Gloria del S.S. Rosario/La Protezione del Rosario*, 45-46
*Maria Dolorata*, oratorio, 118
*Maria, Angelo, Alba, Selim* (untitled oratorio) "prime Parte," 117-18
Miserere II in c (attributed to Pergolesi and Vinci), 170-72
*Missa Brevis*, 60, 82
sacred music "a più cori" (ascribed), 60
Te Deum (misattributed to Vinci), 82-83
villanciccos, 17

**Cantatas, miscellaneous works for the stage & instrumental Music**:
*Cantata à 6* misattributed to Vinci, 257-58
Chamber Cantatas, 17
　*Parto ma non qual core* "La partenza dell Faustina" 49, 99
　*Mesta, oh Dio fra queste selve*, 125
　*La contesa de' numi* (birthday cantata for Dauphin), 278-87
*Massimiano (cori* for the *tragedia cristiane)*, 276-77
*Le nozze di Nettuno L'equestre con Anfitrite* (equestrian ballet), 254-56
Sonatas for flute (published by J. Walsh), 116, 171

**Comic Operas**:
*Albino e Plautilla* (Intermezzo to *Silla Dittatore*), 57-60; aria "A E I O U bella cosa" with example, 58-59;
duet "Mia sposa/Mio Sposo" with example, 59-60
*Lo barone de Trocchia*, 23
*Lo castiello saccheato*, 22-23, 40, 42, 345
*Lo cecato fauzo*, 19-20; arias: "Sò le ssorva" with example, 20; "Che bella nzalatella," 20; "Cechimma fauza mo crepa" with example, 20
*Il corteggiano affettato* ( intermezzo to *Flavio Anicio Olibrio*), 258-59
*Le ddoie lettere*, 20-21, 276
*Don Ciccio*, 23-24
*Ermosilla/Bacocco* ( intermezzo to *Publio Cornelio Scipione*), 49
*La festa di Bacco*, 39-43, 345; arias: "Voglio vedere mprimmo" with example, 42-43; "Sento nò speretillo" with example, 42-43; "O chisto, o la morte," 44
*Lo Labborinto*, 40-43, 49; aria "Comm' à cerva feruta" with example, 42-43
*Il marito giocatore*; intermezzo by Orlandini misattributed to Vinci, 185, 334-36
*La mogliere fedele*, 83-84, 263, 345
*Lo scassone*, 22, 31-32
*Lo scagno*, 22
*Urania-Clito* ( intermezzo to *Astianatte*), 128
*Li zite 'ngalera*, 27-37; arias: "Vorria reventare sorecillo" with example, 31; "Come quanno è notte scura" with example, 32; "Mme senta allegrolillo" with example, 32; "Và dille, che'è no sgrato" with example, 33; accompanied recitative: "Qual doppo lunga" with example, 35; duet: "Core, mio carillo" 32-33; quartet: "Vi che masto" with example, 36

**Heroic Opera**:
*Alessandro nell'Indie*, 287-302; libretto, 289-292, 318; synopsis, 289-90; arias: "E' prezzo leggiero," 293-94; "Vedrai con tuo periglio" with example, 294-95; "Vil trofeo d'un alma imbelle," 295; "Chi vive amante," 295; "O su gli estivi ardori" with example, 295-96; "Se mai più sarò geloso" with example, 296-97; "Se mai turbo," 297; "Se possono tanto," 297; "Se è ver, che t'accendi," 301, "Se il ciel mi divide" with example, 301; duet "Se mai turbo/Se mai più" with example, 299-301

*Artaserse*, 305-326; libretto, 307-310; synopsis, 308-309; arias: "Torna innocente" with examples, 310-313, 317, 319; "Vò solcando un mar crudele" with example, 313-15, 317-18, 320; "Dimmi, che un'empio sei" with example, 315; "Deh respirar lasciatemi" with example, 315-16; "Per pietà, bell'idol mio" with example, 316-17, 319; "Se d'un'amor tiranno," 317, 319; "Per quel paterno amplesso" with example, 317-18; duet: "Tu vuoi, ch'io vivi, o cara" with example, 318-319

*Astianatte*, 123-36; libretto, 125, 126-27; synopsis, 125, 127; arias: "Misera si, non vile" with example, 129; "Alma grande nata al soglio" with example 130; "Barbaro prendi, e svena" with example, 131-132; "Ti calpesto, o crudo amore", 132; "Per amor se'l cor sospirà" 132; "Luci spietate", 132, 161; "Con torbido aspetto," 131-33; "Temi di vendicarti," 133; "Son qual legno in grembo" with example, 134-35; "Io non vi credo" with example; accompanied recitatives, 133-34

*La caduta de' Decemviri*, 201-13; libretto: 201-205, 207-208, 210-213; synopsis: 203-204; arias: "Con forza ascosa" with example, 206-207, 249; "S'io non t'amasi tanto," 207; "Sei tu solo," 208; "Se tu sei crudo" with example 208-209; "Sento amor che piange" with example 209-210; "Mistiro sbadiglio" with example, 213; "Nobil destrier feroce" with example, 211-12

*Catone in Utica*, 213-31, 259; libretto, 216-20; synopsis, 216-17; arias: "Con sì bel nome," 220-21; "Si sgomenti alle sue pene," 221; "Và, ritorna al tuo Tiranno" with example, 221-22; "Dovea svenarti allora" with example, 222-23; "Se in campo armato," 221, 226; "Chi un dolce amor condanna," 226, 297; "Quell'amor che poco accende," 226, 297; "Non ti minaccio sdegno" with example, 226; "E'folia se nascondete," 227; "In che ti'offende" with example, 227; "Sò, che godendo vai," 227; "Confusa, smarrita spiegarti vorrei" with example, 227-28, 250; "Compagni nell'amore," 298; "Voi che adorate," 298; "Se amore a questo petto," 299; quartet: "Deh in vita ti serba," 229; accompanied recitatives: for Catone and Marzia in Act III, 223-25; "Stelle ove son!" with example, 224-25; "Pur veggo alfine un raggio," 228-29

*Didone abbandonata*, 136-56; libretto, 136-44; synopsis, 138, 140; accompanied recitatives: "Ma che feci, empi Numi?" 151; "Vado...ma dove" with example, 151; "E v'è tanta viltà" with example, 152; arias: "Se ti lagni sventurato," 132; "Ardi per me fedele," 133; "Son Regina, e sono amante" with example, 146-148, 269; "Se vuoi, ch'io mora" with example, 149; "Prende ardire" with example. 150, 167-68; "Quando saprai chi sono," 154; "Cadrà fra poco in cenere" with example, 154

*Elpidia* (pasticcio based on Vinci), 113-116

*Eraclea*, 84-96, 202-203; libretto, 85-88; synopsis, 86-87; arias: "M'accese vibrato" with example 90-91; "Sento già che và nascendo" with example,

# INDEX

91-92; "Non scherzi con amor" with example, 92; "Non sà che sia" with example, 92; "L'ape ingegnosa" with example, 92-93; "Il ruscelletto amante dell'erbe" with example, 93-94; "Son tormentato di una tiranna" with example, 94-95; "Son l'ombre d'Eraclea" with examples, 95-96; "Stando Amore," 95

*Erighetta e Don Chilone: L'ammalato immaginario*, 184-87

*Ernelinda*, 173-87, 202-203; libretto, 174-77: synopsis, 174-75; arias: "Nube di dentro orrore," 171; "L'impero ha nel mio petto" with example, 178-79; "Empia mano tu scrivesti" with example, 179-80; "Se barbara catena" with example, 180-81; "Non avvilisca il pianto" with example, 181-82; duet: "Dimmi una volta addio/Non posso dirti" with example, 182, 197; "Tuo mal grado o nume," 183; "Nei freddi soggiorni" with example, 183-84, 272

*Farnace*, 60-81; libretto, 68-70; synopsis, 69; accompanied recitative: "O Figlio, o troppo tardi" with example, 76-77; arias: "Bei labri io penserò" with example, 71; "Un caro e dolce sguardo" with example, 71-72; "Lascierò d'esser spietato" with example, 72; "Mi piace m'inamora" with example, 73; "Da quel ferro" with example, 74; "Sbigottisce il pastorello" with example, 74-75; "Non trova mai riposo" with example, 75

*Il Farnace*; second setting of Lucchini's libretto, 274-76, 278:

*Flavio Anicio Olibrio*, 258-59

*Gismondo re di Polonia*, 188-200; libretto, 190-93, 197; synopsis, 191; arias: "Tu sarai il mio diletto," 192; "Vado à i rai" with example, 193-95; "Son figlia è vero" with example, 195; "Sentirsi il petto accendere," 195; "Tu mi traditti ingrato" with example, 196; duet "Dimmi una volta addio/Non posso dirti" with example, 182, 197; "Ama chi t'odia ingrato" with example, 198; "Dì, rispondi ò traditor" with example, 199; "Se soffia irato," 199-200; accompanied recitative "Misera! Ah sì ti veggo" with example, 197-98

*Medo*, 220, 236-54, 296; libretto, 242-45; synopsis, 242-43; accompanied recitative: "O Sole, o Padre" with example, 251-53; arias: "Scherzo dell'onda instabile" with example, 246-47; "Cervo in bosco," 246; "Sento due fiamme in petto" with example, 247-48; "Navigante, che non spera," 248; "Innamorata dolce mia fiamma," 249; "O' del giorno," 249; "Vengo a voi, funesti orrori," 249; "Incerto...dubbioso" with example, 250; "Se dal feroce nemico artiglio" with example, 250-51; "Terra amica" with example, 251-52; "Sento l'ombra del mesto germano," 253, 276; trio: "Ti rendo il primo/Sento scherzar/Sento tornar, 253-54;

*Publio Cornelio Scipione*, 46-49, 98, 103; intermezzo, *Ermosilla/Bacocco*, 49

*La Rosmira fedele* (*Partenope*), 103-108; libretto, 104-107; synopsis 104-106; arias: "Al mio tesoro," 108; "Spiegati, e di che l'ami" with example, 108; "In vano s'affanna" with example, 109-110; "Sento che và comprendo" with example, 110-111; "Tormentosa crudel gelosia" with example, 111; "Amante che incostante" with example, 112; "Barbara mi schernisci" with example, 112-113; "Un core infedele" with example, 113-114

*Semiramide riconosciuta*, 259-73; libretto, 263-65; synopsis, 264-65; arias: "Tradita, sprezzata" with example, 266-267, 271, 301; "Passaggier, che su la sponda" with example, 268-269; "In braccio a mille furie" with example, 269; "Quando un fallo è strada" with example, 270; "Fuggi dagl'occhi miei" with example, 271; "Odi quel fasto?" 271; "D'un genio, che m'accende" with example, 271-72; "Sentirsi dire dal caro bene," 271; "Fra tanti affanni miei," 272; chorus: "Il piacer, la gioja scende," 265-66

*Silla Dittatore*, 49-60, 71, 75, 84; libretto, 51-52; synopsis, 51-52; arias: "Non pensi quel Altera" with example, 54-55; "Del tuo più bel sembiante" with example, 55; "Vedrai negl'occhi" with example, 55-56; "No hà quell'augelleto" with example, 56-57; "Quel traditore tiranno amore" with example, 57

*Siroe re di Persia*, 156-72, 307; libretto, 162-63; synopsis, 162-63; arias: "Voi m'insegnate," 132; "Non vi piacque" with example, 150, 167-68; "Se al ciglio" with example, 164; "La sorte mia tiranna," 165; "Mi credi infedele" with example, 165-66; "Fra' dubbi affetti miei" with example, 166; "Ancor'io penai d'amore" with example, 166-67; "Facciano il tuo spavento," 168; "Se il mio paterno amore" with example, 168-69; "Fra sdegno ed amore," 168-69; "Gelido in ogni vena" with example, 169-70

*Stratonica* (pasticcio), 201, 258

*Il trionfo di Camilla*, 116-17, 160, 237

*Turno Aricino*, pasticcio arranged by Vinci and Leo, 97